A War of Logistics

FOREIGN MILITARY STUDIES

History is replete with examples of notable military campaigns and exceptional
military leaders and theorists. Military professionals and students of the art and
science of war cannot afford to ignore these sources of knowledge or limit their
studies to the history of the U.S. armed forces. This series features original works,
translations, and reprints of classics outside the American canon that promote a
deeper understanding of international military theory and practice.

SERIES EDITOR: Roger Cirillo

An AUSA Book

A WAR OF LOGISTICS

Parachutes and Porters in Indochina, 1945–1954

CHARLES R. SHRADER

UNIVERSITY PRESS OF KENTUCKY

Copyright © 2015 by The University Press of Kentucky

Scholarly publisher for the Commonwealth,
serving Bellarmine University, Berea College, Centre College of Kentucky,
Eastern Kentucky University, The Filson Historical Society, Georgetown College,
Kentucky Historical Society, Kentucky State University, Morehead State
University, Murray State University, Northern Kentucky University, Transylvania
University, University of Kentucky, University of Louisville, and Western
Kentucky University.
All rights reserved.

Editorial and Sales Offices: The University Press of Kentucky
663 South Limestone Street, Lexington, Kentucky 40508-4008
www.kentuckypress.com

Cataloging-in-Publication data is available from the Library of Congress.

ISBN 978-0-8131-6575-2 (hardcover : alk. paper)
ISBN 978-0-8131-6577-6 (epub)
ISBN 978-0-8131-6576-9 (pdf)

Member of the Association of
American University Presses

Tân công trên troi! [Here come the air porters!]

—Viet Minh exclamation on seeing
French C-47s over Dien Bien Phu

Contents

Photographs follow page 248

Maps, Tables, and Figures

Maps

Tables

Figures

Table of Equivalencies

1 meter = 39.37 inches	1 barrel = 42 U.S. gallons
1 kilometer = 0.6214 miles	1 cubic meter (m^3) = 35.3 cubic feet (ft^3) = 201.987 U.S. gallons = 4.81 barrels
1 sq meter (m^2) = 1.196 sq yards	1 kilogram = 2.2046 pounds
1 sq kilometer (km^2) = 0.39 sq miles	1 short ton = 2,000 pounds = 907.2 kilograms
1 hectare = 2.471 acres	1 long ton = 2,240 pounds
1 liter = 0.2641 U.S. gallons	1 metric ton (tonne) = 2,204.62 pounds = 0.98 long ton = 1.1 short ton

Note on Translation, Acronyms, and Measurements

The following procedures have been adopted in this volume in an attempt to simplify the process of identifying political (territorial) entities and military organizations. Most French and Vietnamese words and terms are shown in italics. Upon first mention in each chapter, French Union and Viet Minh political entities and military organizations are identified in full by an English translation of the original French or Vietnamese designation, which follows immediately in parentheses along with the corresponding French or Vietnamese abbreviation. Thus, one finds the French General Headquarters in Indochina (*État-Major Interarmées et des Forces Terrestres*, EMIFT), the 6th Colonial Parachute Battalion (*6e Bataillon de Parachutistes Coloniaux*, 6e BPC), Interzone V (*Lien Kieu V*, LK V), and the 302nd Viet Minh Division (*Dai-Doan 302*, DD 302). For subsequent references one or another of the three forms may be used, usually the French acronym. The most frequently used French and Vietnamese acronyms and their English equivalents are listed in the glossary, as are other terms and abbreviations. Indochinese place and proper names generally follow contemporary French usage, except that place names are given in the presumably more correct divided form. For example, one will find Na San rather than Nasan and Hoa Binh rather than Hoabinh.

In most cases, distances are given in miles, temperatures in the Fahrenheit system, and volume in gallons or barrels. However, measurements taken directly from French sources, particularly in the tables, are given in the metric system, and unless otherwise noted the word ton refers to the metric ton (tonne) of 2,204.62 pounds. For more on measurements, please see the table of equivalencies above.

Preface

Logistical considerations permeated every aspect of the First Indochina War of 1945–1954, dictating the selection of objectives, the organization of forces, the timing and duration of operations, and even the eventual outcome of the conflict. Accordingly, this study focuses on the organization and capabilities of both French Union and Viet Minh logistical units and on the logistical aspects of ground operations during the period of active conventional warfare in Indochina between October 1950 and May 1954. The key questions that this study seeks to answer are: How were the French and Viet Minh logistical systems organized and operated? Which of the two systems was better adapted to the existing physical and operational environment? To what degree were operational decisions based on logistical considerations? To what extent did logistical factors influence the outcome of combat operations? How effective were the logistical systems of the French Union and Viet Minh forces? The emphasis is thus on military logistics as traditionally defined—that is, on the procurement, storage, issue, and maintenance of food, clothing, weapons, vehicles, ammunition, petroleum products, and other military equipment and the distribution of such materiel by land, water, and air transport. The discussion of medical support is generally excluded, and only a limited discussion of engineer operations and of the logistical support of air and naval forces is provided. Special attention is given to transportation operations, particularly the French use of air transport and aerial resupply techniques and the Viet Minh utilization of large numbers of porters. The external logistical support provided to the French Union forces by the United States and to the Viet Minh forces by Communist China are also covered in some detail.

This study is based primarily on declassified contemporary French official documents and U.S. intelligence materials. The reports and memoirs of French participants and contemporary Western observers have also been used, and a wide range of secondary studies of the First Indochina War, the French and Viet Minh armed forces, and the involvement of Communist China and the United States have been consulted. Viet Minh sources are limited largely to contemporary documents captured by the French, French intelligence reports and prisoner of war interrogations, and the writings of the Viet Minh leaders Ho Chi Minh and Vo Nguyen Giap.

I am particularly indebted to the late Sterling Hart for his assistance in the preparation of the original version of this study. His keen editorial eye and sound advice are sorely missed. I am grateful also to the staff of the *Service Historique de l'Armée de Terre* in the Château de Vincennes for their patience and aid to a

novice *client.* As always, the staff of the U.S. Army Military History Institute at
Carlisle Barracks, Pennsylvania, particularly John Slonaker, Dennis Vetock, and
Louise Arnold-Friend, were most helpful in pointing out and locating interesting
and pertinent materials. I also gratefully acknowledge the patience and love of my
wife, Carole, who cheerfully supported an often reclusive and grouchy writer over
an extended period of time. Of course, such sins of commission or omission as the
reader may find are mine alone.

1

A War of Logistics

The First Indochina War ran from 1945 to 1954 and has been described as "a war in which logistics decided the outcome."[1] Indeed, every aspect of the struggle between the French Union forces and the Viet Minh for the control of Indochina was permeated by logistical considerations, and the way in which the French and their Viet Minh opponents organized and employed their logistical resources to meet the physical and operational challenges of the war determined in large part the outcome of not only the battles and campaigns, but the overall conflict. For both sides the objectives, scope, timing, duration, and general nature of all major operations were determined in large measure by logistical constraints, particularly the means of transporting men and materiel to the area of operations. Every campaign constituted a test of the efficiency and effectiveness of the logistical systems of the opposing forces upon which rested victory or defeat.

The efforts of the French and the Viet Minh to develop efficient and effective logistical systems in Indochina were shaped by both the physical environment and their respective internal political, social, and economic situations. The difficult terrain, harsh climate, great distances, and limited transportation infrastructure of Indochina had a profound impact, as did the commitment of each side to the struggle, the national resources of money, men, expertise, and materiel that they could bring to bear, and outside support. To a very great degree their respective national goals, level of technological sophistication, and very different military philosophies also shaped not only their strategy, tactics, and organization of combat forces, but their respective logistical doctrines and organizations as well.

In addition to the common challenges faced by both opponents, each of them also faced a number of more specific challenges that particularly influenced the evolution of their respective logistical systems. For the French Union forces, the specific factors that shaped their supply and transportation systems included the magnitude and diversity of the forces supported, the necessity of converting what was essentially a static support system into one capable of supporting mobile forces in extended operations over a wide area, and the restrictions on air and ground transport imposed by the physical environment and enemy action. For the Viet Minh, the unique challenges that shaped their logistical support system included an initial lack of logistical experience and technical expertise, the vulnerability of their logistical facilities and lines of communication to French airpower, and a comparatively low level of military technology.

The Physical Environment

Perhaps no single factor had a greater impact on the organization and employment of both French Union and Viet Minh forces than did the physical environment of Indochina. The terrain and climate of Indochina are generally unfavorable for large-scale conventional military operations.[2] The steep mountains, dense forests and jungle, abundant waterways, swamps, and intensely cultivated rice paddies with their dikes and drainage ditches restrict cross-country mobility even on foot during the dry season and make large areas virtually impassable during the rainy season. The difficult topography and limited transportation infrastructure (see map 1.1) combine to impede motorized transport and to limit vehicular traffic to a few constricted routes. Armor operations, while not impossible, are severely restricted. The dense vegetation that covers most of Indochina also limits mobility while providing excellent concealment and ambush sites. As one French staff officer noted, "Although the terrain is never absolutely impenetrable, its nature is such as to confer upon it a coefficient of penetrability which exerts a direct and profound influence upon the nature and the rhythm of the operations."[3] A French correspondent, Lucien Bodard, described the situation even more succinctly, "From mountain peak to mountain peak, it was a Fenimore Cooper kind of war."[4]

The monsoon climate of Indochina as well as the consistently high humidity and temperature also affect military operations to an important degree. Rain and fog restrict visibility both on the ground and from the air and limit flying operations during the rainy season. The floods, swollen streams, washouts, landslides, and mud that accompany the rainy season further restrict ground mobility. The timing and tempo of combat operations are thus largely determined by the prevailing climatic conditions. Accordingly, most major combat operations during the First Indochina War took place during the dry season from October to May. Of the twenty-six offensives launched by the Viet Minh against the French between September 1952 and July 1954, nineteen were initiated during the relatively dry "winter–spring" season, and of the other seven, four were continuations of attacks begun during the preceding dry season.[5]

To the hazards of terrain, vegetation, and climate must be added the impact on personnel of a generally unhealthy climate, disease, and dangerous fauna. The heat and high humidity prevalent throughout most of Indochina as well as torrential rain during the rainy season can take a high toll on the soldier. Serious diseases, including malaria, dengue fever, cholera, hepatitis, typhoid, and tropical ulcers, are common. For example, between 1950 and 1954 about one-fourth of all French Union troops were infected by schistosomiasis and leptospirosis.[6] Most of Indochina is also infested with leeches, a variety of biting insects, crocodiles, and poisonous snakes, including the cobra, krait, eyelash viper, and sea snake.[7] Attacks

Map 1.1. Geography of Indochina.

by tigers, wild elephants, and wild pigs are not unknown. "And," as one historian has written, "there were rats, big and savage, that could find their way even into a jungle fort's bunkhouse to bite through a sleeping soldier's boot into his foot."[8]

The military problems posed by the inhospitable environment of Indochina were compounded by the lack of a well-developed transportation system.[9] Trans-oceanic and coastal water transport were important links in the military supply system of the French—and to a lesser degree of the Viet Minh. However, the limited development of Indochinese ports restricted major military cargo importation to only a few major ports, principally Saigon and Haiphong, both of which were perpetually clogged. Natural conditions limited the military use of inland waterways, few of which were improved sufficiently to support heavy, sustained military personnel and cargo movements. The limited rail network, its capacity degraded by the poor condition of the existing right-of-way, was also inadequate to support major military movements. Moreover, the many culverts, bridges, and tunnels made the Indochinese rail system extremely vulnerable to sabotage and ambush. Similarly, the highway network of Indochina was not well-suited to support military operations in the more remote regions, particularly northwestern Tonkin, Upper Laos, and the Central Highlands. The lack of routes into the remote areas, inadequate road construction and maintenance, and the vulnerability of bridges, culverts, ferries, and other facilities to the effects of both climate and enemy action restricted the military use of the Indochinese highway network for both the French and the Viet Minh, although the impact was greater on the more motorized French Union forces, which consequently relied increasingly on air transport for the rapid movement of personnel and supplies. Even so, the few all-weather airfields available in Indochina were inadequate and poorly positioned to support sustained airlift operations, and the construction of new airfields was both expensive and technically challenging.[10]

One additional geographical factor that has been little recognized but which made military operations in Indochina more difficult for both the French and the Viet Minh was the lack of accurate maps. Much of Indochina was uncharted by the French, and the maps that did exist were frequently inaccurate. The lack of adequate maps and accurate survey data adversely affected the plotting of artillery fires and air strikes, the location of airdrop and paradrop zones, route reconnaissance, and aerial observation as well as general operational planning. In the more remote regions, such as Upper Laos, it was even difficult to obtain native guides, since the inhabitants were so isolated that they frequently were unfamiliar with the terrain outside their home valley. The deficiencies of their maps were never fully corrected by the French, as became readily apparent to U.S. military personnel in the early 1960s. U.S. forces subsequently resurveyed almost the entire region using aerial photography.

The impact of terrain and climate on logistical operations was particularly profound. The difficult terrain forced both sides to decentralize their logistical operations and to reduce as much as possible the logistical burden on combat units. The prevailing conditions also limited motor transport operations, for which the French substituted air movement and the Viet Minh substituted manpower. Food and equipment deteriorated rapidly in the hot and humid climate of Indochina, and the corrosive effects on weapons, vehicles, and aircraft of salty coastal air and dust during the dry season were significant.

The prevailing environmental conditions and poor transportation infrastructure affected both sides, but tended to favor the more lightly equipped Viet Minh and the guerrilla tactics that they employed throughout most of the war. In general, the Viet Minh proved more adaptable to the physical environment in which the war was conducted. They became very adept at conducting relatively large-scale movements on foot over the difficult terrain and at utilizing the dense vegetation for concealing such movements from French aerial observation. They also made excellent use of heavily forested areas for concealing their supply installations and for preparing ambushes against the usually road-bound French Union forces.

Despite the considerable resources at their command, the French proved relatively inflexible and unable to adapt to the hostile physical environment. The highly mechanized French Union forces were frequently thwarted by the lack of adequate roads, obstacles to cross-country mobility, and poor trafficability, particularly in the rainy season. The one significant French advantage, airpower, was largely negated by frequently poor flying conditions and the hazards of flying in the largely uncharted mountainous regions. In sum, as contemporary U.S. intelligence officers noted, "In a country where mountains, forests, swamps, waterways, and rice fields make movement off the road virtually impossible for vehicles other than amphibians or tanks, the guerrilla-like Viet Minh have a great advantage of tactical mobility over the French ground forces."[11] Indeed, the physical environment of Indochina offered opportunities as well as challenges for the antagonist who was prepared to seize them.

The Operational Environment

The changing operational environment also had a profound impact on the development of the logistical systems of both sides. Operationally, the First Indochina War can be divided into two main periods set apart by the beginning in 1949–1950 of large-scale logistical support of the Viet Minh by Communist China and of the French Union forces by the United States.[12] Before 1950, the war in Indochina was largely confined to small-scale guerrilla and counterguerrilla operations that did not seriously strain the logistical structure or the logistical resources of either side. With the increased resources available to both sides after 1950, the tempo and scope of the war increased and it became, at least in Tonkin (the key theater of operations), a conventional war involving large, well-armed forces engaged in extended, complex offensive operations covering wide areas. Such operations imposed additional support requirements that in turn required substantial changes in the logistical organizations and methods of both sides.

The two logistical systems that evolved between 1945 and 1954 differed significantly in size, structure, technological level, doctrine, and methods, but it was their relative efficiency and effectiveness in overcoming the various environmental and operational challenges that they faced that in the end determined the outcome of the First Indochina War. Although size and technological sophistication seemed to give the French an overwhelming initial advantage, they in fact imposed tremendous logistical burdens with which the French were unable to cope.[13] Commenting on that fact, American historian Ronald H. Spector wrote: "Observers also tended to err in assessing the French supply and transport system as superior to that of the Viet Minh. In fact, the reverse was true, for the road-bound French supply convoys, with hundreds of trucks constantly exposed to ambush, were far more vulnerable and less flexible than the primitive Viet Minh supply services."[14] Ultimately, it was the simpler and less technologically advanced Viet Minh system that proved better adapted to the existing physical and operational environment and thus more effective.

The degree to which logistical considerations influenced the nature and outcome of the war differed for each of the two opponents. Although both the French and the Viet Minh faced many of the same logistical challenges imposed by the physical and operational environment, their reactions were quite different, and in effect there were two wars fought simultaneously in Indochina between 1945 and 1954.[15] The French war against the Viet Minh was essentially a limited struggle to regain and maintain control over a hostile (or at best indifferent) population, a war with a very definite air and water dimension especially in the logistical arena, and largely a war of position and a contest for control of the few available lines of ground communication. The Viet Minh war against the French was a total war for national liberation, almost exclusively a ground war, and very much a war of mobility. Furthermore, for the Viet Minh the main battlefield was largely confined to the Red River delta and the hills and mountains of Tonkin and Upper Laos, while for the French the entire length and breadth of Indochina had to be considered. The difference in the war from the Viet Minh and French perspectives was clearly understood by Ho Chi Minh and Vo Nguyen Giap, the leaders of the Viet Minh, but it seems to have largely escaped the notice of the higher level commanders and staff officers of the French Union forces despite the fact that the warning—"REMEMBER—THE ENEMY IS *NOT* FIGHTING THIS WAR AS *PER* FRENCH ARMY REGULATIONS"—was prominently posted in the French guerrilla warfare school in Tonkin and appeared on the masthead of the school's monthly magazine.[16]

The very different nature of the two "wars" that comprised the conflict in Indochina can best be seen by studying the three main campaigns into which the operational logistics history of the war can be divided. These three logistical campaigns overlapped each other and extended over the entire course of the war, but each dominated a particular temporal period to which they gave a particular character.

From the logistical point of view, the first campaign of the Indochina war was fought in the period between the return of French forces to Indochina in August 1945 and December 1950. This was the period in which both sides built up their forces, worked out their strategy, and developed their logistical doctrine and organization while conducting mainly small-scale guerrilla and counterguerrilla operations that did not seriously strain their logistical resources. The initial phase, in which both sides sought a political accommodation, ended with the Viet Minh uprising in the Haiphong-Hanoi area in December 1946. Unsuccessful in their first attempt at a conventional victory, the Viet Minh retreated to their protected base areas north and south of the Red River delta and subsequently concentrated on building a main battle force capable of defeating the French Union forces in large-scale conventional operations. Harassed by sabotage, ambushes, and local guerrilla attacks on isolated outposts, the French worked to develop their forces and a strategy that would facilitate their efforts to regain control of the people and territory that had fallen under Viet Minh domination and to eliminate the Viet Minh menace. Meanwhile they contented themselves with limited clearance operations and small-scale raids into the Viet Minh base areas. In October 1947, the French unveiled a more aggressive military posture in Operation LEA, the first of a series of major operations against the Viet Minh bases in northern Tonkin.

Beginning in 1948, the French refocused their efforts on pacification of the territory already under their control, particularly the vital Red River delta in Tonkin, while the Viet Minh progressively increased the scope and scale of their military activities in the direction of more conventional operations. Despite a number of serious setbacks, the Viet Minh, beginning to receive significant support from the Chinese Communists, concluded the period with the first major test of their newly formed regular units, a large-scale attack on the French outposts on the Chinese border in the fall of 1950 that resulted in a crushing defeat for the French Union forces in northern Tonkin by cutting their supply lines while at the same time gaining free access for the Viet Minh to their major supplier of war materiel, Communist China.

The second logistical campaign involved a struggle for control of the base areas held by the two sides and reached its greatest intensity between December 1950 and July 1953. At the end of 1950, the newly formed regular divisions of the Viet Minh were committed in a sustained campaign to gain control over the resources of the Red River delta. Those extended conventional operations revealed the limitations of the still immature Viet Minh logistical system, and in a series of hard-fought battles at Vinh Yen, Mao Khe, and the Day River between January and June 1951 the French successfully defended the loyal population and rice production of the Red River delta. However, the French were unable to deliver a knockout blow against the Viet Minh, who retired to their protected bases and reverted temporarily to guerrilla warfare. Meanwhile, the French initiated their own series of operations designed to seize the Viet Minh strongholds in the Viet Bac and elsewhere. These efforts ranged in scope from commando raids, such as the very successful Operation MARS (March 1951), to full-scale coordinated offensives by French Union airborne, waterborne, and ground elements, such as the battle of Hoa Binh (November 1951–February 1952), Operation LORRAINE (October 1952), and Operation HIRONDELLE (July 1953).

The third logistical campaign of the war was the struggle for control of the lines of communication that extended over the entire course of the war but reached its peak between late 1952 and May 1954. Having corrected many of the faults found during the battles for the base areas, the Viet Minh sought to seize the initiative with a series of offensive operations beginning in the fall of 1952. Viet Minh offensives in the T'ai country of northwest Tonkin (October–December 1952) and in Upper Laos (April–May 1953) exposed their forces to the strains of campaigning far from their sources of supply and support. Accordingly, in mid-1953 the French abandoned their primarily defensive strategy and launched a series of vigorous offensive operations designed to isolate the main Viet Minh combat elements and force upon them a decisive battle under unfavorable logistical conditions. The French strategy achieved some minor successes in south and central Viet Nam but led eventually to Operation CASTOR, the establishment of a fortified advance base at Dien Bien Phu beginning in November 1953.

The extended long-range operations in 1952–1953 increased the operational importance of interdicting the enemy's lines of communication. The interdiction of French ground and water communication had always been a major component of the Viet Minh strategy for winning the war. Similarly, the French had always placed a high priority on the air interdiction of the Viet Minh lines of supply. Such interdiction operations became even more important in 1953–1954 as Chinese Communist aid to the Viet Minh increased in scale and the principal locus of the struggle shifted to remote regions far from the base areas of either side. The size and effectiveness of the Viet Minh logistical system increased enormously during this period, evolving in the direction of greater motorization of their transport system, which increased its vulnerability and made the lines of communication between southern China and the Viet Minh base areas in northern Tonkin a major focal point of French air interdiction efforts. At the same time, the French were increasingly forced to rely on air transport and aerial resupply as the principal means of supporting their forces in the field.

Foreshadowed by the establishment, defense, and eventual evacuation of the

French entrenched camp at Na San in 1953, and interrupted by diversions that dissipated logistical support (Operation ATLANTE by the French in Annam and the third invasion of Laos by the Viet Minh), the siege of Dien Bien Phu (November 1953–May 1954) reflected aspects of all three logistical campaigns. The objectives, forces committed, timing, and duration of the battle were all clearly dictated by logistical considerations, and Dien Bien Phu became the ultimate test of the efficiency and effectiveness of the logistical systems devised by the French and the Viet Minh during the preceding eight years of war.

2

French Union Combat Forces

From 1945 to 1954, French leaders in Indochina were faced with reestablishing French civil administration and suppressing various criminal and dissident elements as well as combating their strongest adversary, the Viet Minh, but the military forces available to accomplish all of these tasks were inadequate. At first, the French Union combat forces were sufficiently large and well-equipped to offer the tantalizing prospect of victory over the weaker Viet Minh, but they never became strong enough to overwhelm the nationalists outright nor to overawe them and disabuse them of the notion that they might indeed be able to throw the French into the South China Sea. Not only were the French Union forces insufficient in numbers, they also proved inadequate in terms of their adaptation to the physical and operational environment despite their clear advantages in the air and on the water and their constant attempts to tailor the ground combat and support forces to the situation.

The Reoccupation of Indochina

The first major French unit to return to Indochina after World War II and the Japanese occupation was the so-called Light Intervention Corps (*Corps Léger d'Intervention*, CLI), which was later redesignated the 5th Colonial Infantry Regiment. Raised in North Africa and transported to Indochina by the British, the CLI arrived in Saigon in late October 1945. The vanguard of the larger French Far East Expeditionary Corps (*Corps Expéditionnaire Français d'Extrême-Orient*, CEFEO) led by General Philippe Leclerc, which would arrive along with air and naval contingents by the end of 1945, the CLI was organized with two parachute infantry companies, two light commando units, and a Special Air Service battalion (known as the *Commando Ponchardier*) composed of naval infantrymen who had undergone parachute and commando training.[1]

The CEFEO, which numbered over 46,500 men in December 1945, was a mobile organization designed for conventional battle against Japanese forces, either in Indochina or as part of the Allied invasion of the Japanese home islands.[2] It consisted of the 3rd and 9th Colonial Infantry Divisions, the 2nd Armored Division, a Far East Brigade composed of colonial troops formerly stationed in Madagascar, and a Far East Marine Brigade composed of two infantry battalions, an armored battalion, and an artillery battalion. The Far East Marine Brigade was intended as the amphibious assault element of the corps. The CEFEO, which was organized and equipped similarly to American battle corps of the time, would eventually be transformed into a territorial organization but remained the core of French ground combat power in Indochina.

Higher Command and Territorial Organization

The principal French civilian official in Indochina was known as the governor-general until the end of World War II, when the title was changed to high commissioner. On April 27, 1953, the title changed again, to commissioner-general. The successive high commissioners/commissioners-general who served from September 23, 1945, to July 21, 1956, are shown in table 2.1.

At the end of October 1945, Vice Admiral Georges Thierry d'Argenlieu was named high commissioner and commander of all French forces in the Far East and was given the mission of reestablishing French sovereignty in Indochina. As high commissioner, Vice Admiral Thierry d'Argenlieu exercised civil power as governor-general of Indochina through a civil cabinet, a number of directories (police and security, telecommunications, etc.), technical counselors (diplomatic, judicial, economic, etc.), and commissioners in the various territorial divisions.[3] In November 1945, he created a Military Committee to assist him in carrying out his military functions. The senior French ground forces commander served as vice

Table 2.1. French High Commissioners/Commissioners-General in Indochina, 1945–1956

Incumbent	Term
Jean Marie Arsène Cédile (acting)	September 23–October 5, 1945
Philippe François Marie de Hauteclocque (*dit* Leclerc)	October 5–31, 1945
Georges Louis Marie Thierry d'Argenlieu	October 31, 1945–April 1, 1947
Émile Bollaert	April 1, 1947–October 20, 1948
Léon Marie Adolphe Pascal Pignon	October 20, 1948–December 17, 1950
Gen. Jean Joseph Marie Gabriel de Lattre de Tassigny	December 17, 1950–January 11, 1952
Lt. Gen. Raoul Albin Louis Salan (acting)	January 11, 1952–April 1, 1952
Jean Letourneau[a]	April 1, 1952–August 17, 1953
Maurice Dejean	August 17, 1953–April 10, 1954
Gen. Paul Henri Romuald Ély	April 10, 1954–June 2, 1955
Henri Hoppenot	June 2, 1955–July 21, 1956

[a] Commissioner-general from April 27, 1953
Source: "List of Governors-General of French Indochina," http://en.wikipedia.org/wikiList_of_Governors-General_of_French_Indochina (accessed March 25, 2014).

president of the committee, which also included as members the commanders of the French naval, marine, and air forces in Indochina.

In 1954, the U.S. Military Assistance Advisory Group–Indochina (MAAG-Indochina) reported that the organization of the higher political and military echelons of French power in Indochina had been reorganized as follows:

> In concert with the Prime Ministers of the Associated States, the Commissioner General [M. Dejean, the representative of M. Marc Jacquet, French minister of state for the Associated States] and the military commander in chief, Lt General Henri Navarre, prescribe the conduct of the war and the necessary local support measures therefor. . . . Political decisions affecting military operations are reached in sessions of the High Committee by representatives of the States, France, and the Commander in Chief. Essentially military problems are resolved in a Permanent Military Committee in which the military chiefs of the Associated States together with the Commanding General of Headquarters, Joint and Ground Forces, Far East (EMIFT), participate.[4]

The actual command of the French Union military forces in Indochina was vested in a senior commander (*commandant supérieur*) of troops in Indochina, who was charged with carrying out, under the high commissioner, such military measures as were necessary to accomplish the stated political objectives. The first *commandant supérieur* was General Philippe François Marie de Hauteclocque (*dit* Leclerc), who arrived in Saigon on October 5, 1945. He was replaced on July 18, 1946, by Lieutenant General Jean-Étienne Valluy. On June 15, 1948, the senior French military commander in Indochina was designated the commander in chief (*commandant en chef*). The general officers who held the position of *commandant supérieur/commandant en chef* from October 1945 to April 1956 are shown in table 2.2.[5]

To assist him in the performance of his duties, the *commandant en chef* had a joint General Staff, originally called the General Staff of the Senior Commander of French Troops in the Far East, organized with five principal bureaus (General Staff sections): *1e Bureau* (Organization and Personnel), *2e Bureau* (Intelligence), *3e Bureau* (Operations and Plans), *4e Bureau* (Logistics), and *5e Bureau* (Propaganda and Civil Affairs).[6] The joint General Staff was reorganized on September 6, 1949, and renamed the Armed Forces General Staff-Far East, at which time a Bureau of National Defense (for studies of economics, mobilization, finance, and American aid) and a Bureau of Organization (for general organizational matters, personnel, and Muslim affairs) were added, as were two senior deputies: one to oversee intelligence and operations and the other to oversee administration and logistics. The staff was again reorganized on December 29, 1950, and renamed the

Table 2.2. Senior French Commanders in Indochina, October 1945–April 1956

Incumbent	Term
Gen. Philippe François Marie Jacques de Hauteclocque (*dit* Leclerc)	October 1945–July 1946
Lt. Gen. Jean Étienne Valluy	July 1946–February 1948
Lt. Gen. Raoul Albin Louis Salan (acting)	February 1948–June 1948
Lt. Gen. Roger Charles André Henri Blaizot	June 1948–September 1949
Gen. Marcel Maurice Carpentier	September 1949–December 1950
Gen. Jean Joseph Marie Gabriel de Lattre de Tassigny	December 1950–January 1952
Lt. Gen. Raoul Albin Louis Salan (acting)	January 1952–April 1952
Lt. Gen. Raoul Albin Louis Salan	April 1952–May 1953
Lt. Gen. Henri Eugène Navarre	May 1953–June 1954
Gen. Paul Henri Romuald Ely	June 1954–June 1955
Gen. Pierre Elie Jacquot	June 1955–April 1956

Source: Compiled by the author.

Joint and Ground Forces General Staff (*État-Major Interarmées et des Forces Ter-restres,* EMIFT).[7] A Bureau of General Studies and Plans was added in 1953 for the planning of operations and infrastructure development, and on December 10, 1954, the EMIFT was renamed the General Staff of the General Commander in Chief (*État-Major du Général Commandant en Chef,* EMCEC) and continued to exist until April 28, 1956. Although minor changes were frequent, the French high command in Indochina during most of the period from 1945 to 1954 was organized as shown in figure 2.1.

The *commandant en chef,* acting through the EMIFT, controlled all French Union military forces in Indochina, both territorial and mobile. Although his control of ground forces was complete, the *commandant en chef* exercised only operational control over French naval and air forces in Indochina; the French naval and air force commanders had their own staffs and reported administratively to their respective ministries in Paris.[8]

The *commandant en chef* also exercised operational control over the small but gradually growing forces of the Associated States (Viet Nam, Cambodia, and Laos). Each of the Associated States had its own armed forces chief of staff and a General Staff that was concerned primarily with recruitment, training, personnel management, and limited logistical activities.[9] In his May 1954 debriefing, Major General Thomas J. H. Trapnell, the former chief of MAAG-Indochina, noted: "Although a quadruplication of facilities exist in the form of several national general staffs and territorial organizations, actually a reasonably efficient channel of command is maintained by the French. Diplomatic liaison with the States coun-

```
                    ┌─────────────────────┐
                    │        High         │
                    │    Commissioner     │────────────┐
                    │  Commander in Chief │      ┌──────────────┐
                    └─────────────────────┘      │    Civil     │
                              │                   │  Functions   │
                    ┌──────────────────┐          └──────────────┘
                    │     Military     │
                    │    Committee     │
                    └──────────────────┘
                    ┌──────────────────┐
                    │     Joint &      │
                    │  Ground Forces   │
                    │  General Staff   │
                    └──────────────────┘
```

(Operational Control Only)

French Air Forces	French Naval Forces	French Ground Forces		Vietnamese National Army

		Territorial Commands	Mobile Forces	Royal Cambodian Army

| | | | | Laotian National Army |

North Viet Nam	South Viet Nam	Central Viet Nam	Central Highland	Cambod-ia	Laos

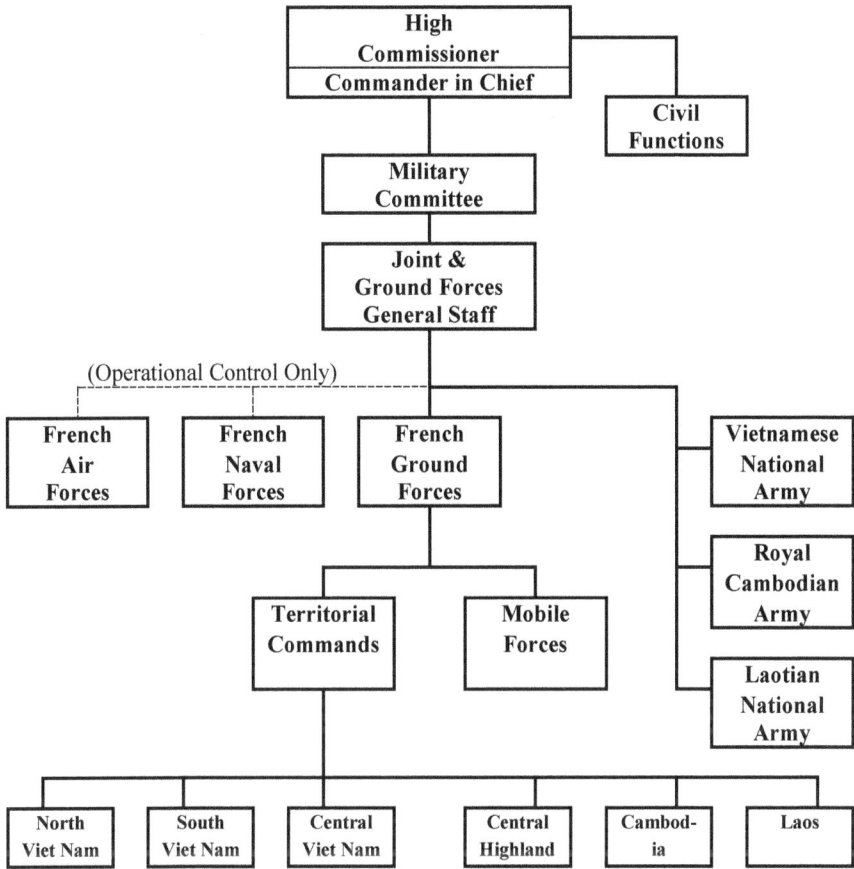

Figure 2.1. French High Command in Indochina, 1952. (Based on "Organigramme de la Logistique," item 9 in folder "1e Section, 4e Bureau, EMCEC, Archives 1952 (decembre)— Directives Logistique," box 10 H 1536, Fonds Indochine, SHAT.)

terpart organizations is exercised wherever coordination is required. This highly complex arrangement of joint and combined staffs and pooling of national forces may be likened to a miniature NATO at war, except that by necessity, the senior and more professionally qualified partner, France, exercises the dominant role."[10]

The basic organization of ground forces for most of the period between 1945 and 1954 was territorial, although mobile offensive forces became more prominent after 1950. During the colonial era, Indochina had been divided for administrative purposes into six main areas: Tonkin, Annam, Cochinchina, Cambodia, Laos, and the Central Highlands (*Plateaux des Montagnards*). Each of the major divisions was further subdivided into provinces, districts, and villages based on natural terrain features. In 1946, Indochina was divided for military purposes into a number of territories, zones, sectors, and subsectors roughly corresponding to preexisting political subdivisions. The component elements of the CEFEO, originally designed as parts of a mobile battle corps, were broken up in December 1946 to form the Ground Forces, Far East (*Forces Terrestres d'Extrême-Orient*, FTEO), the territorial command for Indochina.[11] The three division headquarters of the CEFEO became the principal territorial headquarters for Tonkin, Annam, and Cochinchina, and other elements of the CEFEO were used to form the territorial headquarters at the various lower levels (zone, sector, and subsector). In general, the territories (Tonkin, Annam, and Cochinchina) were commanded by general officers, zones by lieutenant colonels, and sectors by majors. The French military officers assigned to command each area exercised civil as well as military functions.

The French high command progressively broke up the available ground forces of the CEFEO and "implanted" most of the troops as static defense forces in the various geographical areas. Initially they retained a central reserve, and later created mobile forces to conduct offensive operations, while the units assigned to the various territorial subdivisions performed principally static defense duties. Because the military subdivisions did not always coincide precisely with the political and administrative subdivisions, some problems were encountered when military operations were conducted in an area that took in two or more political subdivisions. As noted by Peter D. Jackson, under the territorial arrangement the *commandant en chef* could shift combat battalions, the principal maneuver unit, from one area to another to meet security and operational requirements.[12] As the French Union forces in Indochina expanded during the war, the CEFEO grew from corps to field army size and the territorial divisions to corps size, with corresponding increases at lower levels.

French Naval Forces

In April 1950, French naval strength in Indochina included some five hundred officers and eight thousand men, of whom about twenty-eight hundred were marines serving in five marine commando units.[13] The French naval vessels present in Indochinese waters at that time numbered some 229 ships and small craft, including one aircraft carrier, one old light cruiser, twenty-four minesweepers, two seaplane tenders, one transport, three LSTs (Landing Ship, Tank), two tankers, three submarine chasers, fourteen harbor defense craft, 161 landing craft of various types, and a variety of other types of vessels.[14] French naval air assets included eight PBY5A Catalinas, nine Sea Otters, one Loire 130, one C-47, and four Morane 500s, a total of twenty-three aircraft.[15] By May 1953, the French naval forces in Indochina included one light aircraft carrier (CVL), two gunboats (PG), eight escorts (PCE), sixteen submarine chasers (PC and SC), six motor mine-sweepers (AMS), four Landing Ships, Tank (LST), thirteen Landing Ships, Infantry, Large (LSIL), six Landing Ships, Support, Large (LSSL), nineteen Landing Craft, Utility (LCU), 211 miscellaneous small landing craft, and sixty-two auxiliary and service vessels, plus twenty-two F6F-5 and twelve SB2C-5 carrier-based combat aircraft, eight PB4Y-2 long-range patrol planes, eleven JRF-5 Grumman Goose seaplanes, two S-51 helicopters, six Morane 500 Criquet liaison planes, and one C-47A Dakota transport.[16]

After 1947, the French had one or two aircraft carriers on station off Indochina at any given time.[17] The escort carrier *Dixmude* first took station in 1947 and was also used to ferry aircraft from the United States. The light carrier *Arromanches,* with thirty to forty-four aircraft, first took station in November 1948. The light carriers *La Fayette* and *Bois Belleau,* both on loan from the United States and each with twenty-six aircraft, took station in 1951 and April 1954, respectively. Various types of carrier-based aircraft were embarked, including Douglas SBD-6 Dauntlesses and Curtiss SB2C Helldiver dive-bombers, Grumman F6F Hellcat and F8F Bearcat fighters, and Chance Vought F4U Corsair fighter-bombers.

The French Navy was hard put to maintain the necessary personnel in Indochina. The situation was particularly critical in Tonkin, where by 1954 about three-quarters of all naval operations were taking place. Less than half the French naval personnel in Indochina were stationed in Tonkin, the staff and administrative billets in Saigon being more comfortable.[18] The number of French naval personnel in Indochina in 1952 totaled 11,166, including 715 officers (including one Vietnamese) and 10,451 enlisted personnel (including 435 Vietnamese), or about 18 percent of all French naval personnel.[19] The French naval commander in the Far East also controlled the training and operations of the Vietnamese national navy, which by 1954 included twenty-two officers, eighty-four noncommissioned officers (NCOs), and 750 sailors as well as 183 French cadres (twenty officers and 163 NCOs and enlisted specialists).[20]

French Air Forces

Like French naval forces, the French air forces in Indochina were under the operational control of the *commandant en chef,* but the senior air force officer (*Commandant de l'Air en Extrême-Orient,* CAEO) also reported directly to the air minister in Paris. Relations between the *commandant en chef,* always a ground officer, and the CAEO were usually poor, in part because of very different concepts of how airpower should be employed.[21] French airmen, like those in the United States, were focused on the doctrines of strategic bombardment and air superiority, while ground commanders generally favored the use of airpower for close air support and interdiction tasks. The situation improved somewhat after May 1953 when Lieutenant General Henri Charles Lauzin replaced Lieutenant General Lionel Max Chassin as CAEO, and Lieutenant General Henri Navarre replaced Lieutenant General Raoul Salan as *commandant en chef.*

Paralleling the territorial structure of the French ground forces in Indochina, the French air forces were organized into five tactical air groups (*Groupement Aérien Tactique d'Attaque et de Choc,* GATAC) covering Tonkin, central Viet Nam and the Highlands, South Viet Nam, Cambodia, and Laos. Light observation aircraft were assigned to the Aerial Artillery Observation Group (*Groupe aérien d'observation d'artillerie,* GAOA). Majors or lieutenant colonels initially commanded the GATACs, but later brigadier generals commanded them so that they would be "competitive" with the territorial commanders.[22]

French commitments at home, in Africa, and (after 1949) to NATO limited the resources of the French Air Force committed in Indochina. At the end of 1948, 30 percent of the effectives of the French Army were in Indochina, but only 8.4 percent of the French Air Force strength was so committed.[23] Although by the time of the cease-fire in 1954 over ten thousand officers and men and some 388 aircraft (about 20 percent of the total number of aircraft in the French Air Force) were stationed in Indochina, the growth in French airpower there was uneven, and even at its peak there were significant shortfalls in operable aircraft of suitable types, in pilots, and in qualified maintenance personnel.[24]

The original assignment of units to Indochina in 1946 included three squadrons (one transport and two fighter) plus a pickup squadron of World War II-era German Junkers Ju 52 Toucan transports. Budget constraints at home, commitments elsewhere, and a lack of interest in the close air support and interdiction missions required in Indochina served to restrict increases in French airpower in Indochina, as did the unwillingness (until 1949) of the United States to provide additional and more modern aircraft.[25] As late as April 1950, the French Air Force in Indochina, organized into three fighter squadrons and three transport squadrons, was equipped with only eighty-six tactical aircraft (twenty-three old British-made Spitfires and sixty-three U.S.-made P-63 Kingcobras), all of which were in very poor condition, less than 40 percent being operational at any one time.[26]

In December 1951, General Jean de Lattre de Tassigny assumed the post of *commandant en chef* in Indochina and planned to increase his air forces to four bomber squadrons, four fighter squadrons, and three transport squadrons equipped with U.S.-supplied aircraft.[27] De Lattre's plan was subsequently implemented but was not completed before the end of the war. In November 1953, on the eve of the decisive battle for Dien Bien Phu, French Air Force strength in Indochina included over 365 aircraft and 10,508 personnel, including 363 pilots, 375 other flying personnel, and 2,833 technicians.[28] On April 10, 1954, just before the battle for Dien Bien Phu reached its climax, the French Air Force in Indochina had four squadrons of Bearcat fighter-bombers (ninety-eight aircraft), one flight of eighteen Bearcat photo reconnaissance aircraft, three squadrons of B-26 light bombers (eighty-four aircraft), one light tactical reconnaissance flight of modified B-26s, four transport squadrons (114 C-47s, sixty-five of which were supplied by the United States), and several liaison squadrons consisting of eight C-45s, twelve L-20 Beavers, and eight H-19 helicopters, plus another eighty-five liaison aircraft due to be delivered by the end of August 1954.[29] There were also twenty-two C-119 Flying Boxcars and two hundred American mechanics on loan to the French from the United States. By the end of the war in mid-1954, the number of French aircraft had risen to 388: 180 combat, 100 transport, and 108 liaison aircraft.[30]

The Strength and Distribution of Ground Combat Forces

Although the overall size of the CEFEO expanded from 46,513 men in December 1945 to 183,949 men in July 1954 as shown in table 2.3, the successive *commandants en chef* had to fight a constant battle to maintain the CEFEO's core strength of regular French, Foreign Legion, North African, and Senegalese units that constituted about 70 percent of the CEFEO.[31] Political and budgetary pressures at home constantly threatened to reduce the number of non-Indochinese soldiers assigned to the CEFEO. The strength of the non-Indochinese personnel of the CEFEO actually declined somewhat after reaching a peak of 72,870 men in 1947, but then rebounded strongly after the end of 1951.[32]

In August 1949, the French National Assembly made continued support for the Indochina war contingent on a pledge that no draftees would be sent to Indochina, thus further limiting the already small pool of manpower available for assignment to the theater.[33] Even so, in August 1950 the French military commitment in Indochina amounted to about half of all Regular Army forces, about half of the French Air Force, and about one-fourth of the French Navy.[34] At that time the total number of troops available for employment under French direction in Indochina was 304,883, including 150,667 French Regular Army and colonial troops (49,267 French, 18,500 Foreign Legion, 25,100 North African, 13,800 Senegalese, and 44,000 Indochinese natives) and 37,000 auxiliaries (Cao Dai, Hoa Hao, Binh Xuyen, etc.) under direct French control, plus 117,216 men under the control of the Vietnamese, Cambodian, and Laotian national armies, including 33,216 regulars, 27,000 auxiliaries, 53,000 paramilitaries (civil police, self-defense forces, rail and plantation guards, etc.), and 4,000 tribal minority soldiers (T'ai, Nung, Muong, etc.).[35]

The French forces committed in Indochina between 1945 and 1954 also included some two thousand women, some of whom were killed, wounded, and/or highly decorated. They served in army, air force, and navy commands, with the

Table 2.3. Strength of French Union Ground Forces in Indochina, 1945–1954

Nationality/Type	Dec. 1945	Dec. 1946	Sept. 1947	Dec. 1950	Dec. 1951	June 1952	March 1953	July 1954
French						51,000	54,790	55,083[b]
Foreign Legion[a]						18,000	19,079	18,710
North African/African	40,521	62,289	72,870	52,739	59,683	25,000	47,685	56,451
Indochinese Regulars	5,992	26,736	32,023	44,376	64,750	56,000	53,182	53,705
Total CEFEO	**46,513**	**89,025**	**104,893**	**97,115**	**124,433**	**150,000**	**174,736**	**183,949**
Indochinese Auxiliaries	1,000	11,509	10,109	40,817	47,088	42,000	55,439	51,772
Vietnamese National Army		8,374[c]	16,536[d]	38,376[g]	119,478	131,881	151,000	261,729[h]
Royal Cambodian Army			4,165[e]	4,500[g]	10,233	11,945	13,100	
Laotian National Army			995[f]	1,500[g]	9,179	10,849	13,000	
Total Indigenous	**1,000**	**19,883**	**31,805**	**85,193[g]**	**185,978**	**196,675**	**232,539**	**313,501**
Grand Total	**47,513**	**108,908**	**136,698**	**182,308**	**310,411**	**346,675**	**407,275**	**497,450**

a Foreign Legion units in Indochina averaged approximately 11,000–12,000 men from 1945 to 1951; b Includes 2,460 women, of whom 380 were nurses; c Includes 3,869 Europeans and 4,505 Indochinese not included in CEFEO (mostly French Navy and Air Force Europeans and local Laotian and Cambodian forces); d As of October 1, 1947; includes 1,436 French advisors; Vietnamese National Army not formally created until 1948; e As of October 1, 1947; includes 151 French advisors: Royal Cambodian Army created in 1946; f As of October 1, 1947; includes 45 French advisors; Laotian National Army not formally created until 1949; g Rough estimate; h Total for all national armies; includes 4,656 detached CEFEO advisory personnel (4,599 French) serving with national armies; Vietnamese National Army = approximately 230,000 (including 160,000 militia); Laotian National Army = approximately 27,000.

Sources: Compiled by the author from various sources, including Bodinier, ed., La Guerre d'Indochine, vols. 1 and 2; O'Ballance, The Indo-China War, 1945–1954: Lessons Learned in the Indochina War, vol. 2; and Fonds Indochine, SHAT.

Red Cross, and with the *Infirmières Pilotes et Secoristes de l'Air* (Nurse Pilots and First Aid Workers of the Air, IPSA; the Aviation section of the French Red Cross) as administrative personnel, doctors, nurses, and medical evacuation helicopter pilots.[36] Perhaps the best known outside France was a flight nurse, Geneviève de Galard, the famous Angel of Dien Bien Phu, who flew 149 medical evacuation missions in four years before being stranded in Dien Bien Phu and becoming a prisoner of war for a short time. Geneviève Grall, another nurse, was awarded the *Médaille Militaire* for parachuting twice within a month to serve under fire with isolated CEFEO units. Captain Valérie André, a doctor, parachutist, and medical evacuation helicopter and fixed-wing pilot, flew 120 missions, was credited with saving 165 lives, and was awarded the *Croix de Guerre avec Palme*. She flew another 376 missions in Algeria and became the first French female general officer in 1976.

The estimated strength and disposition of French Union forces in Indochina as of April 1, 1953, just before the Viet Minh invasion of Laos, are shown in table 2.4.

Just over a month after French forces initiated the decisive battle of Dien Bien Phu, the U.S. Military Assistance Advisory Group–Indochina estimated the French Union ground forces in Indochina to include the number and types of combat units shown in table 2.5.

Table 2.4. French Union Ground Forces in Indochina, April 1, 1953

Component	Tonkin	Annam & Plateaux	Cochin-china	Cambodia	Laos	Total
French Far East Expeditionary Corps (CEFEO)[a]	91,000	20,000	45,000	8,000	7,500	171,500[b]
Associated States Armies[a]	27,000	33,000	20,000	8,500	8,000	96,500
Associated States National Guards	6,000	4,000	10,000	4,000	5,500	29,500
CEFEO Auxiliaries	23,000	6,500	18,000	3,300	2,400	53,200
Vietnam Auxiliaries	8,000	10,000	34,000	–	–	52,000
Other Semi-Military	27,000	7,000	30,000	9,000	6,500	79,500
Totals	**182,000**	**80,500**	**157,000**	**32,800**	**29,900**	**482,200**

[a] Regulars. French Union regular forces were organized into a total of 218 CEFEO battalions (83 infantry, 7 parachute, 8 armored, 119 artillery, and 1 antiaircraft artillery) and 95 Associated States battalions (87 infantry, 4 parachute, and 4 artillery).
[b] Total includes: 51,000 French, 19,000 Foreign Legion, 17,000 African, 30,000 North African, and 55,000 native Indochinese troops. Total does not include 6,000 French personnel detached for duty with the Associated States forces as cadres and advisors.
Source: NIE- 91, June 4, 1953, document 15, annex A, in Gravel, ed., *The Pentagon Papers*, 1:400.

Table 2.5. French Union Combat Units in Indochina, December 31, 1953

Type Unit	French	Vietnamese	Laotian	Cambodian	Total
HQ Inf Div	3				3
HQ Abn Div	1				1
HQ RCT	13	6			19
HQ Abn RCT	2				2
Infantry					
Inf Bn (Std)	87	86	6	10	189
Abn Bn	6	4	1	1	12
Lt Bn (KQ)		54	7	1	62
Support Co (KQ)		14	3		17
Heavy Mortar Co		2			2
Mixed Mortar Co	2	2			4
Abn Mortar Co	1				1
Commando	1	1			2
Auxiliary Co	368	433	45	20	866
Auxiliary Commando	36				36
Artillery					
155 mm Gun Bn	1				1
155 mm Howz Bn	2				2
105 mm Howz Bn	14	5			19
155 mm Howz Btry	1				1
75 mm RR Bn	3				3
105 mm Howz Btry	19				19
105 mm Howz Plat	12	30			42
Arty Section	42	37		13	92
Armor					
Armor Bn	4				4
Tank Destroyer Bn	1				1
Amphib Bn	5				5
Lt Tank Co	4				4
Armor Car Co	15	7	1	3	26
Armored Inf Co	4				4
Miscellaneous					
40 mm AAA Bn	1				1
Lt Avn Sqdn	4	2			6

Source: HQ MAAG-Indo-China, *Indo-China Country Statement for Presentation of the 1955 MDA Program*, 20–21.

In 1953 and 1954, the striking force of the CEFEO was thus not much larger than one U.S. Army corps, and the French believed that a force twice that size would be necessary to conduct static defense and pacification operations and free the striking force for offensive operations.[37] The stabilization of the number of CEFEO effectives at a low level restricted the strategic options of the *commandant en chef* because, although the CEFEO itself contained a large proportion of Indochinese fillers, the CEFEO units were better-armed, better-trained, and generally more aggressive than the other French Union forces and thus bore the principal burden of offensive operations.

In order to satisfy nationalist demands and to free the more mobile and more capable units of the CEFEO for offensive operations, the French grudgingly consented to the formation of national armies in Viet Nam, Cambodia, and Laos. It was hoped that responsibility for territorial control and pacification could be transferred gradually to the newly formed national armies, but although they grew rapidly, the paper strength of the national armies seldom reflected the actual number of men available, and the extant units were often poorly armed and poorly trained. The new national armies were almost entirely dependent upon the French for training and logistical support, and the slow development of their effectiveness was due in large part to the reluctance of French commanders to see to their armament and training.

The first of the national armies to be organized was the Royal Cambodian Army (*Armée Royale Khmère*, ARK), which was created in 1946 with an authorized strength of five thousand men cadred by French officers and NCOs and under French operational control.[38] The ARK significantly expanded in size after the initiation of the U.S. military aid program in 1950, and by mid-1953 it had reached a strength of over thirteen thousand men. In November 1953, the French surrendered operational control of all ARK forces west of the Mekong River to Cambodian authorities. In July 1954 the French disbanded their forces in Cambodia, and the three ethnic Cambodian battalions of the CEFEO joined the ARK.

The Laotian National Army (LNA) was created in 1949 and grew from twelve hundred men in 1949 to over twenty-seven thousand in 1954.[39] Like its Cambodian and Vietnamese counterparts, the LNA relied on French advisors and French and U.S. logistical and technical support.

Created in 1948, the Vietnamese National Army (VNA) had a slow start; by May of 1951 it still had less than forty thousand men, and only twenty-four of thirty-four proposed battalions existed even on paper. Even so, the VNA quickly outgrew the ability of the Vietnamese or even the French to support it. As the U.S. military aid program to Indochina began to provide the required arms and equipment, the VNA began to expand more rapidly and assumed military responsibility for more and more territory. A separate Vietnamese General Staff was created in 1952, and General Nguyen Van Hinh, formerly a French Air Force colonel,

Table 2.6. French Union Forces in Indochina, December 31, 1953

Type	French	Associated States
Ground	187,494	292,434
Naval	9,975	992
Air	11,003	1,136
Total	**208,472**	**294,562**

Source: HQ MAAG-Indo-China, *Indo-China Country Statement for Presentation of the 1955 MDA Program*, 17.

became chief of staff. By July 1954, the VNA had a strength of over 230,000 men, of whom slightly over half were regulars. Although organized on paper with four divisions in 1954, there were no units in the VNA larger than a battalion.

Just after the beginning of Operation CASTOR at Dien Bien Phu, the *commandant en chef* in Indochina had just over half a million men available to him, as shown in table 2.6.

Naturally, the overall number of troops available to the *commandant en chef* determined the number of combat units that could be fielded at any given time. The total number of French Union infantry units available in November 1953 is shown in table 2.7.

The steady growth of the CEFEO as well as the development of the Vietnamese, Cambodian, and Laotian national armies placed a constantly growing strain on the always undermanned French logistical system in Indochina. Indeed, the

Table 2.7. French Union Infantry Units in Indochina, November 10, 1953

Type Unit	CEFEO	VNA	ARK	LNA	Total
Infantry Battalions	88	53	10	6	157
Parachute Battalions	6	4	1	1	12
Light Infantry Battalions	0	48	0	0	48
National Guard Battalions	0	16	0	0	16
Mountain Infantry Battalions	0	9	0	0	9
Separate Infantry Companies	0	3	0	0	3
Heavy Infantry Companies	0	14	0	0	14
Heavy Mortar Companies	0	4	0	0	4
National Guard Companies	0	0	16	46	62
Total	**94**	**151**	**27**	**53**	**325**

Source: O'Daniel, *Progress Report on Military Situation in Indochina as of 19 November 1953*, 25, annex B, appendix 2, enclosure 1 (Infantry Units in Indochina—10 November 1953).

requirement to support the rapidly expanding national forces was the more significant factor since the CEFEO grew rather slowly, only about 400 percent between December 1945 and July 1954. Meanwhile, the Vietnamese National Army expanded by over 1,150 percent between September 1947 and July 1954.[40]

Tactical Organization of French Ground Forces

For the most part, the French divisions sent to Indochina as part of the CEFEO in late 1945, like those in metropolitan France, were organized using tables of organization and equipment (TOEs) derived from those of U.S. Army divisions, with certain modifications, while independent regiments and battalions continued to use unique French organizational structures.[41] Originally organized to fight the Japanese, the divisions were heavy in artillery and armor and were thus ill-suited for both the guerrilla war that ensued in Indochina from 1945 to 1950 and the widespread conventional operations against the Viet Minh regular forces that followed. In any event, soon after they arrived in Indochina the major divisional formations were broken up and distributed in fixed positions throughout the country. Subsequently, the French Union forces in Indochina did not operate on a divisional basis but utilized the battalion as the basis for the formation of task forces designed with particular operational missions in mind. However, in 1953 the *commandant en chef,* Lieutenant General Henri Navarre, organized three light division headquarters to control mobile combat forces in Tonkin. Each of those division headquarters was designed to control three mobile groups (regimental combat team equivalents) as well as an armor squadron, an artillery battalion, and attached engineer and signal units.[42] Subsequently, the French developed a "Far East Infantry Division-Type 1955," but such divisions were never actually formed.

Following their transformation into territorial forces in December 1946, the combat units of the CEFEO were reorganized in March 1947. The number of European troops was reduced by elimination or replacement by Indochinese troops, and attempts were made to standardize the tables of authorized weapons and equipment to facilitate integrated operations.[43] Several types of units that could be used to form task forces were reorganized to better carry out particular types of missions. The infantry regiments were lightened and their headquarters became primarily administrative bodies responsible for support. Certain heavy elements, such as heavy infantry weapons, armored maintenance, and artillery command and observation units, were decentralized, and equipment and weapons were standardized. Subsequently, most of the elements of the French Union operational forces in Indochina, save for those formations assigned the duty of static defense of key areas and installations, were organized principally on the task force pattern, such as the mobile group (*groupe mobile,* GM), the commando group (*groupe mixte d'intervention,* GMI), or various airborne and amphibious groups.

The infantry battalion was the basic building block, both for the mobile task forces and the static defense units.[44] The March 1947 reorganization led to the creation of two unique type units, the "Infantry Battalion-Type Far East" and the "Parachute Commando Battalion."[45] On September 4, 1947, the "Infantry Battalion-Type Far East"—standardized with an authorized strength of twenty-three officers and 840 enlisted personnel—became the standard French battalion type until the end of the war.[46] Each such battalion had a headquarters and service company and four rifle companies, each of which had a headquarters, a support platoon, and three rifle platoons of three rifle squads each. The headquarters and service company, which contained the command, staff, and service elements of the battalion, was authorized four 81 mm mortars and (later) four 57 mm recoilless rifles. The battalion often was augmented by a motor transport element and a company of native auxiliaries. The support platoon of the rifle company was authorized two machine guns and two 60 mm mortars. The inclusion of four rather than the usual three rifle companies was generally judged to be essential for area operations in Indochina. This type battalion, although somewhat lighter than its European counterpart, was well-suited to mobile operations in Indochina, but it was somewhat less satisfactory in the fixed defense role, the actual organization of which necessarily depended on the number of posts to be occupied and the numbers and types of weapons to be manned.[47] Another defect lay in the reduction of organic transport and heavy weapons that made the "Infantry Battalion-Type Far East" a lighter and more mobile organization but simultaneously created greater reliance on road-bound logistical and artillery support.[48]

The organization of the "Infantry Battalion-Type Far East" headquarters and service company was frequently criticized in that it contained both operational elements designed to go forward and administrative elements designed to man the rear echelon. In most cases, a battalion was required to establish and operate a rear base composed of personnel from the headquarters and service company and personnel levied from the rifle companies. This normally amounted to about 10 percent of the available battalion personnel.[49] The lack of cadre and transport for manning the rear base reduced the operational unit's combat effectiveness, and proposals were made—but not generally adopted—to consolidate the rear bases of several units or to divide the headquarters and service company into a headquarters company for operations and a service (administrative) company to operate the rear base.[50] Local security was also a key consideration. The headquarters and service company was, in most cases, unable to provide security for the battalion command post, and combat units were required to perform that role.

Static Forces

The principal tasks assigned to the territorial, or static, forces were the protection and control of the lines of communication, the progressive "clearance" (*nettoyage*) of the areas under French Union control, and the pacification of the cleared areas by disarmament of the rebels and elimination of the causes of dissatisfaction among the people. Another operational function of those static forces assigned to occupy fixed fortified positions was to act as bait to lure the Viet Minh into the open, where they could be decisively attacked by superior French firepower and technology. Such defensive employments tied down a significant portion of the available manpower in hundreds of isolated and vulnerable fortifications.

Despite the obvious drawbacks, the French increasingly turned to fortifications as the answer to the ambushes and small-scale attacks mounted by Viet Minh guerrillas, first in the south, and after 1949 in the north as well. Along the key highway and waterway routes throughout Viet Nam the French constructed numerous fortified watchtowers and small forts surrounded by barbed wire and mines. Occupied by Indochinese troops under French officers and NCOs, these fortified positions were extremely vulnerable and the Viet Minh avoided them or overran them at will. The most extensive and well-integrated line of such fortifications was the so-called De Lattre Line, which enclosed the critical areas of Hanoi and the Red River delta in Tonkin. The fortifications of the De Lattre Line extended for some thirty-two hundred kilometers and were generally well-constructed and mutually supporting. They were backed by generous artillery support and mobile forces of regimental size to destroy those Viet Minh troops who did penetrate the outer shell. But as Douglas Pike has pointed out, the 15 million tons of concrete poured in the Red River delta in a single year of the war was of little value in defeating a mobile and determined enemy.[51]

In addition to tying down large numbers of troops and artillery support, the watchtowers and other isolated fortifications were difficult to maintain logistically. The fortifications themselves required constant repair and improvement, but French commanders were limited in what they could do by the lack of funds and the large requirements for manpower, construction materials, and heavy equipment needed for such improvements.[52] The results were thus often makeshift and unsatisfactory. The resupply of the fortified posts also posed certain problems. The isolation of most of the posts coupled with ever-increasing Viet Minh guerrilla activity made resupply by road and inland waterway uncertain, and in many cases an outpost could be resupplied only by air. Consequently, most of the outposts, depending on their degree of isolation, had to be stocked with relatively large quantities of rations and ammunition. Storage thus became a problem in the smaller fortifications, and the large stocks of supplies on hand made the outposts even more attractive targets for the Viet Minh.

The successive *commandants en chef* in Indochina recognized the drain on resources represented by the static defense forces and sought with varying degrees of success to decrease the proportion of their troops dedicated to static defense tasks while increasing the proportion of mobile forces. Peter D. Jackson has noted, "This competition between spreading forces out to provide security against small insurgent elements and to provide area control for the government, versus the need to concentrate forces for semi-conventional battles against the Viet Minh main forces, would bedevil the French the whole war."[53] In the course of 1953, Lieutenant General Navarre managed to organize a striking force of three light division headquarters, nine mobile groups, twenty-nine infantry battalions, and an airborne group of nine parachute battalions by reducing the number of battalions committed to static defenses throughout Viet Nam from sixty-five to fifty-six, evacuating the isolated base at Na San, and obtaining additional troops from France.[54] Nevertheless, by the end of the war in 1954 the French still had over two-thirds of their available combat forces tied down in static positions.[55]

Mobile Forces

The offensive component of the French strategy in Indochina required well-armed, highly mobile forces capable of seeking out and destroying the main force Viet Minh units. The mobile forces carried out clearance operations to gain area control just like the static defense forces, but their primary function was to engage the Viet Minh regular forces in sustained combat in the hope of destroying them with superior French firepower. The French sought to create a variety of mobile forces, but the desire to maximize their firepower and on-road mobility often resulted in the creation of mechanized task forces that were largely tied to fixed bases and the inadequate and vulnerable road networks found in Indochina. Even the most mobile French Union forces were heavily laden with weapons, ammunition, and a plethora of other equipment, and the French discovered, much to their sorrow, that their mechanized mobility was no match for the foot mobility of the Viet Minh. In their after-action reports, French commanders freely acknowledged that their units, organized for warfare in Europe, proved to be "ill-suited to the task of carrying on a struggle against rebel forces in an Asiatic theater of operations."[56]

The shifting of French combat units from one operational area to another, particularly from the delta to the mountains or jungle, further reduced mobility and tactical efficiency by repeatedly placing troops in areas and environments with which they were unfamiliar. Heavy, road-bound forces unprepared for rapid movement in the unfamiliar mountains and jungles produced hesitant, slow-paced operations that allowed the enemy to escape or give battle on terrain of his choosing. As late as the end of 1953, the *commandant en chef* still found it necessary to issue a bulletin that admonished: "Commanders at all echelons still suffer from a 'motor complex.' They are used to moving with vehicles which restrict them to roads and certain trails. They forget that our enemy is completely independent of motor transport and can rapidly assemble and move large forces in difficult areas where it is impossible for us to follow and give battle unless we give up our motorized transport."[57]

Indeed, only a few French commanders were willing to adopt the methods of the Viet Minh in order to beat them. One was a battalion commander nicknamed "Rice-Dried Fish" after the orders that he issued at the beginning of each operation.[58] By limiting the weight of the rations carried by his men in the field, he brought them into combat well-rested, and although his soldiers grumbled at the restricted diet, they soon appreciated the reduction in loads that his orders made possible. The alternative was to end up like the unit that participated in Operation CONDOR to relieve Dien Bien Phu, which left its base on April 13, 1954, carrying five days of rations (about thirty-three pounds) per man in their packs. By the end of the second day's march one corporal had died and twenty-five men had been evacuated due to exhaustion.[59]

The best known of the mobile task forces created to find and decisively engage the Viet Minh was the mobile group (*Groupe Mobile,* GM).[60] The typical GM was in effect a regimental combat team and was usually composed of three or four infantry battalions and a motorized artillery group reinforced by armor, engineer, and other supporting units as dictated by their proposed employment.[61] The GMs were highly effective in the deltas, but, being largely road-bound, they were of little or no use in the rugged terrain of the mountains and jungles and frequently found themselves impotent in dealing with the light, mobile Viet Minh.[62] Various proposals were made to tailor GMs for specific terrain or to create a special unmotorized type of GM for operations in mountains and jungle.[63]

Being relatively large formations, the GMs required the employment of a large part of their infantry strength for security missions, thereby reducing their effective maneuver strength. The effectiveness of a GM depended in large part on the nature of the Viet Minh units it encountered. Against small groups of Viet Minh regional or local forces a GM might prove too large and unwieldy to successfully engage the enemy before they got away. On the other hand, if a single GM encountered a more heavily armed Viet Minh regular force, it might well find itself outnumbered and outgunned and suffer the sad fate of the unlucky GM 100, which was annihilated by a superior Viet Minh force in the Mu Gia Pass in the central highlands in early 1954.

Not only were the motorized GMs tied to the limited road networks of Indochina, they were also notorious consumers of logistical support, particularly petroleum products, ammunition, and maintenance. The artillery and the headquarters elements of the typical GM were 100 percent motorized, and the infantry battalions were usually about one-third motorized.[64] In part, the high consumption of fuel and repair parts associated with the GMs stemmed from the fact that the older trucks, scout cars, half-tracks, and light tanks utilized by them, although adequate for route security and escort duties, were not specially adapted to the climate and terrain of Indochina.[65] The normal GM did not have organic service elements of its own except for a headquarters company that included a small medical unit. Quartermaster, ordnance, transportation, and other logistical support was provided by the service elements of the territorial command concerned or by units specifically placed at the disposal of the operational commander.

The heavy logistical requirements of the GMs usually demanded an operational base near the area of operations and exaggerated the dependence on ground and air lines of communication that were vulnerable to both the weather and enemy action. Moreover, the reliance on heavily mechanized infantry forces had another, more indirect, logistical consequence. As cross-country mobility decreased, there was a corresponding increase in dependence on artillery and close air support to accomplish tactical missions that just as easily could have been accomplished by small-unit fire and maneuver. This dependence in turn led to an increased consumption of artillery ammunition.[66] In one three-month period in 1952, the French artillery in Tonkin expended forty-eight hundred tons of ammunition, and nearly the same number of guns expended eighty-nine hundred tons in the same period in 1954. Similarly, in central Viet Nam artillery ammunition expenditures rose from twelve hundred tons in 1952 to twenty-two hundred tons in 1954. The use of mortar shells and grenades by the infantry expanded in the same way. As Bernard Fall noted, the pressing problems of logistical support for mechanized forces were never mastered, and "the appetites of armored vehicles mounting automatic weapons are gargantuan and insistent. The comparison between the supply of a squad mounted in a half-track and that of a squad trotting through the jungle, each man with a four-day ration of rice in a bag slung about his neck, would be ridiculous had it not proved so tragic."[67]

Amphibious and Riverine Forces

In one area the French held a significant advantage over their Viet Minh adversaries. That was in their ability to move by water, both along the coasts and on the inland waterways that were important avenues in the delta regions and elsewhere. The Viet Minh used small boats for the movement of men and supplies, and they became quite adept at placing mines and other obstacles in the waterways, ambushing river convoys, and even using frogmen to attack French vessels, but they never exploited watercraft as a means of operational mobility as did the French. The only occasion on which the French encountered an armed Viet Minh river flotilla was during a raid between Rach Gia and Ca Mau in southern Viet Nam in February 1946, when elements of the 6th Colonial Infantry Regiment met a dozen small Viet Minh vessels, one of which was armed with a 75 mm antiair-craft gun.[68]

Soon after their return to Indochina, the French began to assemble mobile coastal and riverine forces to satisfy logistical requirements of the scattered garrisons that were accessible by water, to ensure freedom of movement on the principal waterways, to secure harbors, and to conduct amphibious operations. The army eventually assumed most of the responsibility for waterborne resupply activities and some limited patrol missions, while the innovative French Naval Brigade concentrated on the formation of tactical river flotillas consisting of a selection of armored and well-armed landing craft. The vessels utilized for these tactical formations were for the most part U.S.-type landing craft modified for riverine operations by the addition of armor plating and guns ranging from 75 mm tank guns mounted in turrets to twin 20 mm or 40 mm antiaircraft guns to a variety of mortars and artillery pieces. Many of these vessels survived the First Indochina War and, manned by South Vietnamese troops, were still in active service as late as 1969.

First formed in 1946, the French riverine flotillas were redesignated in 1947 as naval assault divisions (*Division Navale d'Assault,* DNA), which became famous under their nickname, *Dinassaut.*[69] The size and composition of the *Dinassauts* differed from time to time and place to place, but the typical *Dinassaut* was a tactical grouping of watercraft consisting of a command and fire support ship (usually a Landing Craft, Infantry [LCI]), a vessel for the transportation of troops and equipment (usually a Landing Craft, Tank [LCT]), one patrol and liaison craft (usually a harbor patrol boat type), and several landing and support vessels (usually two Landing Craft, Mechanized [LCM] and four smaller Landing Craft, Vehicle and Personnel [LCVP]). Whenever possible, the *Dinassaut* also included a small landing force of navy commandos or a company of infantry. Thus equipped, the typical *Dinassaut* was capable of transporting and landing a battalion-size combat force with its equipment and supporting the operations of that force ashore by fire while simultaneously controlling the waterways in the vicinity. The *Dinassauts* were thus formidable and highly mobile tactical units when operating along the coasts, in the deltas, or in other regions accessible to shallow-draft watercraft.

The principal difficulty encountered in the use of the *Dinassaut* was the lack of sufficient suitable landing craft and the vulnerability of *Dinassaut* shore bases to Viet Minh attack. The attachment of ground combat elements unfamiliar with amphibious operations rather than providing each *Dinassaut* with its own permanent assigned infantry forces also lessened their independent action and efficiency. Although frequently ambushed by Viet Minh forces hidden along the banks of the rivers and canals, the armored landing craft possessed superior firepower and maneuverability and were generally able to overcome such attacks, especially since the Viet Minh seem to have lacked their usual tactical savvy when attacking armed French watercraft units.[70]

The *Dinassauts* were used whenever feasible to support major offensive and defensive operations and often played a key role. For example, *Dinassaut 1* provided fire support for the defense of Mao Khe in March 1951 and successfully landed the 6th Parachute Battalion just before the main Viet Minh assault. *Dinassaut 3* and a pick-up force designated *Dinassaut A* played major roles in the defense of the Day River line in May 1951.[71] The French continued to develop and use their *Dinassaut* forces and to improve the techniques of riverine warfare right up to the end of the First Indochina War. The *Dinassaut* concept was one of the more successful of the French operational innovations in Indochina, one that provided on the water that which the French forces most desired on land: superior mobility coupled with superior firepower.

To complement the very effective *Dinassaut*, French Foreign Legion elements formed combat commands using armored amphibious tractors to operate in the wetlands of the Vietnamese deltas.[72] In late 1947, the Foreign Legion's 1st Cavalry Regiment obtained several American M29C Weasels for operational testing in the Plain of Reeds. The tests worked out well, and thirty "Crabs," as they were called by the French, were obtained for each of the regiment's two squadrons. However, the unguarded two-man crews were vulnerable, and the Crabs could not carry enough infantry to provide the needed support. In October 1950, the Foreign Legion 1st Cavalry Regiment received several U.S.-made Landing Vehicle, Tank (4)s for operational testing. The LVT-4, nicknamed the "Alligator," proved a much more suitable vehicle, and in April 1953 the 1st Amphibious Group was formed consisting of a reconnaissance and rapid maneuver element of two squadrons, each with three platoons of ten Crabs, and a "shock element" of three squadrons, each with eight LVT-4s embarking a light rifle company, and three LVT(A)-4s for direct support.[73] A separate platoon of six LVT(A)-4s under the control of the amphibious group headquarters was provided for general support. A second amphibious group was subsequently formed for service in Tonkin.

Parachute Forces

The limited cross-country mobility of heavy mechanized forces and the inherent restrictions of waterborne transport led the French commanders in Indochina to place increased reliance on air mobility as the war went on. The use of airplanes and parachutes to deliver men and supplies in accordance with the concept of "vertical envelopment" offered the advantage of speed, flexibility, and surprise that French ground troops lacked for the most part. As the commander of French airborne troops in Indochina noted in his final report, "In some cases, 'the parachute-airplane' was used exclusively as a means of transport because it was the most rapid, the least tiring, the least dangerous, perhaps the only possible, means."[74] The climate, lack of suitable aircraft in sufficient numbers, a shortage of trained pilots, and the scarcity of airdrop equipment limited air transport, aerial resupply, and parachute assault operations, but such operations did provide a means of overcoming the difficulties of ground transport and were well-developed by French Union forces.

The number of available parachute infantrymen increased dramatically over the course of the war.[75] The number of qualified parachutists in Indochina rose from a few hundred in 1946 to 5,684 in 1950, and then the number almost doubled (to 10,639) in 1951, as parachute artillery, engineer, signal, and medical units were added.[76] An airborne forces command was organized in 1949, as were two airborne forces bases: the *Base Aéroportée Sud* (BAPS) at Saigon and the *Base Aéroportée Nord* (BAPN) at Hanoi. In 1950, the airborne forces command was redesignated Airborne Forces Command Indochina (*Troupes Aéroportés d'Indochine*, TAPI), and an Airborne Forces Command, North (*Troupes Aéroportés, Nord*) was created to manage airborne forces in Tonkin. By 1954, there were six parachute battalions in the CEFEO (including two Foreign Legion parachute battalions), six in the VNA, and one each in the LNA and ARK. Parachute units were generally lighter than the other infantry units deployed by the French in Indochina, although they too were often more heavily laden with weapons, ammunition, and other supplies than the Viet Minh regulars they faced. In 1946, the CEFEO parachute battalions were made up only of Frenchmen and were provided with sixty to seventy jeeps equipped with machine guns. However, by 1954 the parachute battalions were organized much like the regular infantry battalions, with four companies and a personnel complement that was about 50 percent Indochinese.[77]

As the elite troops of the CEFEO, the French, Foreign Legion, and colonial parachute infantry battalions were used in a variety of operations requiring speed and mobility. The purpose of such operations varied from providing reinforcements (Cao Bang, October 1950) to recapturing a fallen post (Dong Khe, 1950) to supporting a withdrawal (Nghia Lo, 1951).[78] About 150 airborne operations were conducted during the First Indochina War, of which fifty-two were commando actions, sixty-three were to reinforce or assist in the disengagement of outposts, thirty-three were conducted for miscellaneous reasons including search and clear operations in support of ground forces, and five were major independent operations: Operations LEA (October 1947), LOTUS (November 1951), MARION (November 1952), HIRONDELLE (July 1953), and CASTOR (November 1953).[79] Tactically, the relatively light, highly mobile parachute units were best-suited to sudden, sharp actions to gain a bridgehead or cut off Viet Minh forces. They were not well-suited for extended operations, but were often misused for exactly that in Indochina, the siege of Dien Bien Phu being the most prominent example.[80]

In the late 1950s, parachute units in most modern armies, including the French in Algeria, began to be replaced by helicopter-borne forces. Helicopters were used by the French in Indochina, but principally for medical evacuation, reconnaissance, and liaison missions. Preparations began in mid-1953 to introduce some five hundred tactical helicopters into Indochina to extract committed parachute forces and provide greater off-road tactical mobility, but at the end of the war in 1954 the French had only fifty helicopters in Indochina.[81]

Commando Forces

One other French tactical formation common in Indochina deserves special mention because of its extraordinary logistical requirements and its ability to deal with the terrain of Indochina and the Viet Minh on equal terms. The Composite Airborne Commando Group (*Groupement de Commandos Mixtes Aéroportés*, GCMA), later redesignated the Composite Intervention Group (*Groupement Mixte d'Intervention*, GMI), was created under the control of the French security services (*Service d'Espionage et Contre-Espionage*, SDECE) in 1951 and was commanded by the famous Major Roger Trinquier. By November 1953, the GMI controlled some six thousand commandos, including three hundred French soldiers, operating as guerrillas.[82] The GMI commando units usually consisted of a headquarters platoon and three combat platoons, each of which had a headquarters element and two squads. The total strength of such units was usually about one hundred men, including a French cadre of one officer, four NCOs, and a radioman plus eight Indochinese NCOs and about eighty Indochinese soldiers.[83] Although the commandos proved most effective in gathering intelligence, interdicting Viet Minh lines of communication, and attacking isolated Viet Minh units and installations, the GMI, being an elite irregular unit, was not well-favored by the conservative French commanders in Indochina and was never developed to its full potential.[84]

The logistical arrangements for commando units were somewhat different than for other types of task-organized forces. The GMI command headquarters in each territorial division included an administrative center that was designed to relieve all commando units of the administrative and local guard requirements.[85] Lightly armed, generally well-trained, and highly mobile on foot, the one-hundred-man units could remain in the field for extended periods living off the countryside with occasional aerial resupply of rations, ammunition, and other equipment. The weapons and equipment prescribed for such units were specially selected to be as light and silent as possible and included an augmented first aid pharmacy, ropes, individual shelter halves, and other equipment needed to permit extended independent operations.[86] Normally, each commando unit was authorized forty-seven submachine guns, fifteen U.S. carbines, six rifles, twenty rifles with grenade launchers, six semiautomatic rifles, and six automatic rifles as well as ten radios.[87] Despite their relatively low logistical requirements, the effort required to support the GMI units in the field proved to be significant, especially with regard to air transport. In November 1953, an average of seven parachute drops per day was required to support them.[88] In 1954, GMI units were allotted each month some fifteen hundred C-47 flight hours and close to three hundred tons of paradropped ammunition and other supplies.[89]

Auxiliary Forces

The GCMA/GMI was a special type of auxiliary unit formed by the French in Indochina. Less well-known were the many locally raised auxiliary units that formed an important part of French combat power in Indochina.[90] Raised and administered by the territorial commands, auxiliary forces were used for manning the guard towers, local defense, reconnaissance, and other missions. The typical auxiliary company consisted of five or six French cadre (perhaps one officer and four NCOs plus a radio operator) and about a hundred Indochinese auxiliaries. By the end of the war in July 1954, some 51,772 indigenous auxiliaries, organized in about eleven hundred companies, augmented the French forces in Indochina.

Throughout the First Indochina War, the leaders of the French Union forces struggled to maintain the necessary troop levels and to organize effective forces to deal with the Viet Minh threat. The debilitation of French resources in World War II, commitments elsewhere, and political resistance at home meant that sufficient resources of men, money, and materiel were not forthcoming, even after 1950, when military and economic aid from the United States became more available.

The effort to create effective forces was hampered by the application of organizational structures, equipment, and tactics better suited to the conventional European battlefield than to a guerrilla war in Southeast Asia. The assignment of a significant portion of the available forces to the static defense of fixed facilities and lines of communications consumed enormous amounts of resources and proved largely ineffective against the highly mobile Viet Minh forces. Repeatedly, heavy reliance on motorized and mechanized forces also proved unwise, and the use of parachute forces and aerial resupply were restricted by the lack of suitable aircraft and generally poor flying weather. However, in a few areas French Union leaders in Indochina were able to devise successful means of countering the Viet Minh threat. Riverine and commando forces, in particular, proved highly effective and difficult for the Viet Minh to counter or match.

3

Viet Minh Combat Forces

The Vietnamese People's Army (*Quan Doi Nhan Dan Viet-Nam*), commonly known as the Viet Minh, began its existence as a number of small, independent guerrilla bands with only the most rudimentary organization. Over time, more and larger units were formed, and a more complex administrative and tactical structure, based essentially on the triangular principle, was adopted. Combat units were organized into squads, platoons, companies, battalions, regiments, and eventually divisions, each with its complement of staff, combat, and support elements.[1] Specialized artillery, antiaircraft artillery, engineer, intelligence, signal, and logistical units were also developed, as was a so-called heavy division consisting of artillery and engineer units. Flexibility was emphasized, and even as they formed more heavily armed division-size units, the Viet Minh continued to ensure that their forces remained highly mobile. Viet Minh combat forces were often "task-organized" with elements from more than one division. By the end of the war, the Viet Minh forces in the main area of operations in Tonkin had evolved far from their guerrilla roots and constituted a powerful conventional force supported by plentiful artillery and motor transport and directed by a sophisticated and competent staff.

Higher Command and Staff Organization

The guerrilla forces led by Ho Chi Minh and Vo Nguyen Giap in northern Indochina in the final year of the Second World War scarcely required a sophisticated higher command, but with the official proclamation of the formation of the Democratic Republic of Viet Nam (DRV) by Ho Chi Minh on September 2, 1945, a Ministry of National Defense was created.[2] On November 3, 1946, control of the growing Viet Minh armed forces was placed in the hands of the Committee of National Defense (also known as the Supreme Defense Council), headed by General Vo Nguyen Giap, who also became minister of national defense at the same time, thereby consolidating his control over the Viet Minh military forces.[3] From December 19, 1946, when the Viet Minh passed over to direct action against the French, until well after the expulsion of the French from northern Viet Nam in 1954, the Viet Minh armed forces were directed by the president of the Democratic Republic of Viet Nam and nominal commander in chief, Ho Chi Minh, working through the Supreme Defense Council and the minister of national defense, General Giap, who was for all practical purposes the commander of all Viet Minh military forces.

The Ministry of National Defense acted through three main directorates—the General Political Directorate, the General Supply Directorate, and the General Staff Directorate—as shown in figure 3.1. Each of the directorates was represented down to regimental level. The functions and internal organization as well as the names of the three principal offices of the Ministry of National Defense changed over time, mostly in minor ways. The General Political Directorate was responsible for Communist political control and indoctrination in cooperation with the Political Bureau of the General Staff Directorate. The system of political control was extensive in the Viet Minh armed forces, and political commissars at all ech-

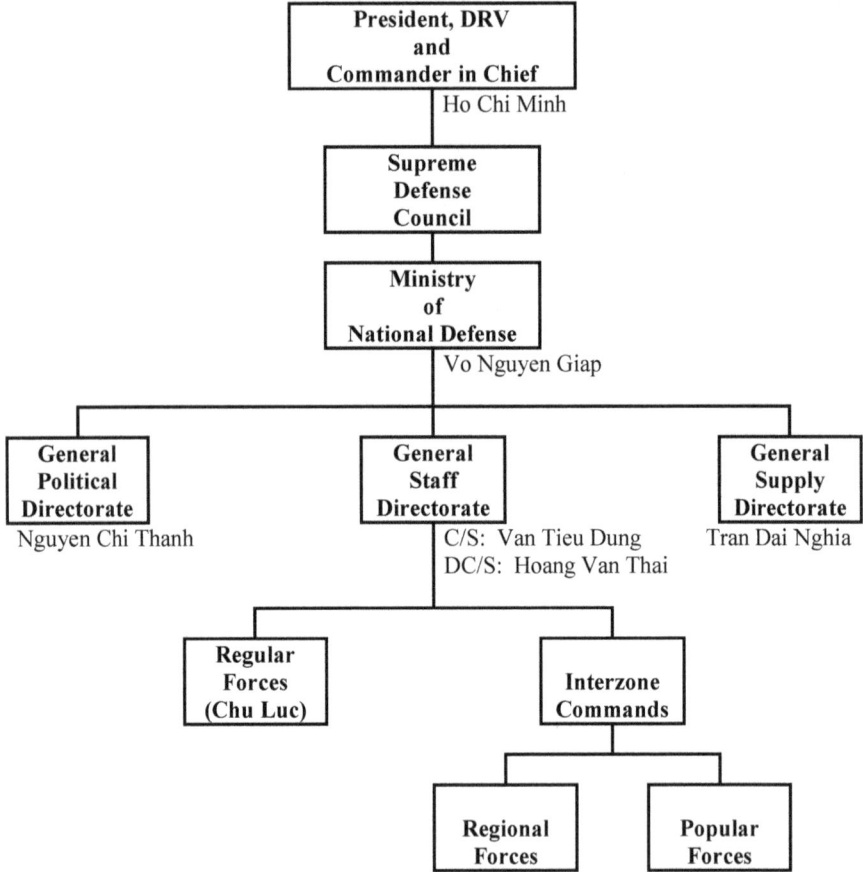

Figure 3.1. Viet Minh Command Structure, 1950–1952. (Based on Tanham, *Communist Revolutionary Warfare*, 38–39, and Fall, "Indochina—The Last Year of the War," 5 [figure 3].)

elons usually retained the final decision on matters of military as well as political importance. The General Supply Directorate was responsible for all logistical matters. Outside the Ministry of National Defense was a Ministry of Paramilitary Formations, which was also controlled by General Giap, with (in 1947) Hua Van Thai as chief of staff.[4]

The General Staff Directorate was the mechanism by which the commander in chief planned and directed the operations of the Viet Minh armed forces. In April 1947, the Viet Minh high command was relatively simple in organization and was concerned almost entirely with guerrilla operations, training, and the organization of units. The Supreme Command, as it was then called, had five major elements: an Intelligence Service; a Political Service; a Bureau for Popular Troops; an Inspector General; and a rudimentary General Staff.[5] In response to the growing size, complexity, and operational employment of the Viet Minh forces, in 1950 General Giap established a true General Staff patterned largely on the French and American model. This General Staff included a Cabinet with four sections (Local Security, Communications, Accounts, and Administration) and four principal staff sections (Personnel, Intelligence, Operations, and Supply).[6] The main focus of General Staff activity was the formation and employment of combat units.

The lack of well-trained staff officers created many weaknesses in the functioning of the Viet Minh General Staff, the weakest functional area being that of logistics. However, by 1953 many Viet Minh officers had been trained in Chinese Communist military schools, and the influence of Chinese advisors became evident with the reorganization of the General Staff to bring it more into line with Chinese organizational concepts.[7] In January 1951, the head of the Chinese Military Advisory Group (CMAG) to the Viet Minh, General Wei Guo Qing, expressed to Mao Tse-tung his dissatisfaction with the Viet Minh and proposed to reorganize and train them along Chinese lines.[8] Mao approved the proposal but urged General Wei to be patient with the Viet Minh, and in early 1951 the CMAG recommended to their Viet Minh protégés a plan for the reorganization of the Viet Minh command structure and for the training and reorganization of the Viet Minh forces. Beginning in early 1951, the structure of the three principal directorates of the Ministry of National Defense (the General Staff Directorate, the General Political Department, and the General Supply Department) was simplified, rules and regulations were streamlined, and excess personnel were transferred to combat units. The four principal staff divisions of the General Staff Directorate (Personnel, Intelligence, Operations, and Supply) were replaced by ten bureaus as shown in figure 3.2, the most important of which were the Political Bureau, the Directorate of Operations, and the Bureau of Important Affairs, which took charge of training and planning for operations at least six months ahead. In addition to the ten main bureaus, the General Staff also controlled special artillery and engineer sections and a Code Bureau. The General Staff's remaining logistical

```
                        ┌──────────────┐
                        │   General    │
                        │    Staff     │
                        │ Directorate  │
                        └──────────────┘
```

┌────────────┐ ┌────────────┐ ┌────────────┐ ┌────────────┐
│ Political │ │ Operations │ │ Important │ │Intelligence│
│ Bureau   │ │Directorate │ │ Affairs   │ │Directorate │
│   │ │   │ │ Bureau   │ │   │
└────────────┘ └────────────┘ └────────────┘ └────────────┘

┌────────────┐ ┌────────────┐ ┌────────────┐ ┌────────────┐
│   Admin   │ │ Training │ │   Armed   │ │ Popular   │
│Directorate │ │Directorate │ │   Forces   │ │ Troops   │
│   │ │   │ │Directorate │ │Directorate │
└────────────┘ └────────────┘ └────────────┘ └────────────┘

┌────────────┐ ┌────────────┐ ┌────────────┐ ┌────────────┐
│ Military   │ │ Commo &   │ │ Engineer │ │ Artillery │
│ Affairs   │ │ Liaison   │ │ Section   │ │ Section   │
│Directorate │ │Directorate │ │   │ │   │
└────────────┘ └────────────┘ └────────────┘ └────────────┘

                        ┌──────────────┐
                        │   Code   │
                        │   Bureau   │
                        └──────────────┘

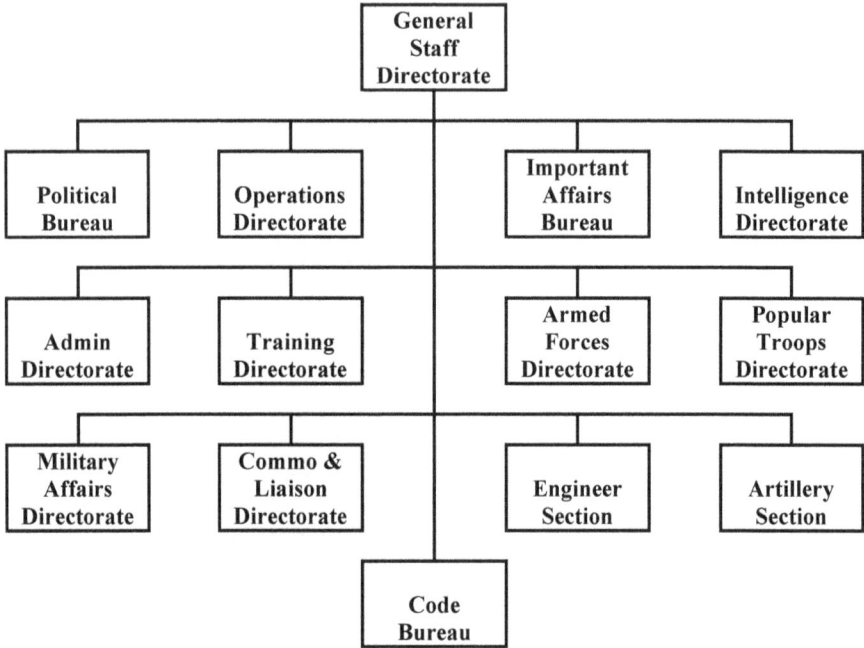

Figure 3.2. Viet Minh General Staff Directorate, 1953–1954. (Based generally on Tanham, *Communist Revolutionary Warfare*, 39–41.)

functions were transferred to the General Supply Directorate, and the reorganized General Staff, superior in training and experience to its predecessor, subsequently functioned as a field army headquarters as well as the principal military planning and coordinating element.[9]

Territorial Organization

The Viet Minh, like the French, divided Indochina into a number of geographical regions to facilitate political and military control. Administratively, the territory controlled by the Viet Minh was divided into three major defense areas: the Bac Bo (Tonkin), the Trung Bo (Annam), and the Nam Bo (Cochinchina). These regional administrations were normally bypassed as far as military affairs were concerned. However, the commander of the Southern Defense Administration (the so-called Nam Bo Command), Lieutenant General Nguyen Binh, was given extraordinary powers until, as a result of exercising those powers too vigorously, he was eliminated in 1950, ostensibly by a French patrol but probably with the connivance of higher Viet Minh authorities.[10]

From 1945 until 1948, Viet Nam was further divided into fourteen zones (*khu*) in which the Viet Minh political and military administrations were combined under the direction of a reliable military commander or Party official who worked through an Executive and Resistance Committee that controlled all political, economic, military, social, and cultural activities in the assigned area.[11] Below the zone level the territory was further subdivided into (in descending order) provinces, districts, intervillages or communes, and villages, each of which had its own Resistance Committee structure.[12]

In an effort to streamline administration, six interzones (*Lien-Khu*, LK) were created in March 1948.[13] The number of interzones, each of which theoretically controlled several zones, later increased to nine: Interzones 1, 2, and 3 in Tonkin; Interzones 4, 5, and 6 in Annam; and Interzones 7, 8, and 9 in Cochinchina. In practice, some interzones had no subordinate zones, and there were some autonomous zones directly controlled by the Ministry of National Defense.[14] After 1951, Interzones 7, 8, and 9 were collapsed into the Nam Bo Command, which was further subdivided into eastern and western zones separated by the northern channel of the Mekong River. The Nam Bo Command also controlled military and political affairs in Cambodia. The number of interzones was subsequently reduced to four (the Viet Bac Interzone covering northern and western Tonkin; Interzone 3 covering most of the Red River delta; Interzone 4 consisting of the six northern provinces of Annam; and Interzone 5 consisting of the southern provinces of Annam) plus the Nam Bo Command.[15] The First Indochina War was fought primarily in Interzones 1, 2, and 3, with some activity in Interzones 4 and 5. Interzone 4 acted as a rear base for Viet Minh forces operating to the north in the Red River delta, and Interzone 5 was a stronghold of Viet Minh support (as was Interzone 9, which covered the Ca Mau area at the tip of Cochinchina).

The Ministry of National Defense controlled major regular combat units directly regardless of the geographical area in which they might be located, but regional military affairs were managed by the command committee of the interzone or zone.[16] The typical command committee consisted of the interzone/zone commander, his deputy, and his political commissar assisted by a small staff. The interzone/zone commander and his command committee were responsible for recruiting, training, and supplying the regional forces and any regular forces located in their area that were not under the direct command of the Ministry of National Defense. They planned and conducted regional military operations and supervised the popular forces of the territorial commands subordinate to them. The interzone/zone commanders took their orders from both the Ministry of National Defense (the commander in chief through the General Staff Directorate) and the Interzone or Zone Resistance Committee, of which they were usually a member.[17]

From time to time "Front" headquarters were established to plan and conduct specific tactical operations in a given area. Front headquarters also played an important role in "preparing the battlefield" by assembling supplies, gathering intelligence, and preparing routes, fortifications, and other facilities.[18] The Front headquarters were technically temporary in nature, but they tended to become semipermanent and were subordinated either directly to the General Staff Directorate or to one of the interzones.[19] Laos, for example, was divided into three fronts: the Upper and Central Fronts subordinate to Interzone 4 (which also controlled the Binh-Tri-Thien Front) and the Lower Front subordinate to Interzone 5. Interzone 3 was divided into two fronts, the Left Bank Front and the Right Bank Front, separated by the Red River. The Northwest Front in northwestern Tonkin, where the main battles late in the war were fought, was part of the Viet Bac Interzone.

Strength of Viet Minh Forces, 1945–1954

Vo Nguyen Giap returned to Tonkin from Yunnan in late 1944, and there in the Dinh Ca valley near Cao Bang on December 22, 1944, he formed the forerunner of the Viet Minh Regular Army, the Armed Propaganda Team, with thirty-one men and three women armed with two revolvers and thirty-one rifles, thirteen of which were flintlocks.[20] Within months Giap's guerrilla forces numbered over seven hundred soldiers.[21] By August 1945, when the Viet Minh emerged into the open, they numbered some five thousand men, and after the surrender of Japan they were augmented by a number of Japanese deserters and local forces created by the Japanese that brought their strength up to about fifteen thousand.[22] By the time the French military forces began to return to Indochina in September 1945, the strength of the armed and organized Viet Minh forces had reached about thirty-one thousand, and a year later the Viet Minh forces included about sixty thousand men of the Regular Army (*Chu Luc*), twenty thousand militia (*Tu Ve*), mostly in the Hanoi area, and another fifteen thousand troops, including about two thousand Japanese deserters, in various special units (local self-defense forces, terrorist and sabotage teams, women's units, suicide squads, etc.).[23]

Recruitment was a relatively minor problem for the Viet Minh, as they found many young people eager to join the battle for the freedom of their country. Thus, after September 1945 the Viet Minh regular, regional, and local forces grew steadily, as shown in table 3.1. Initially outnumbered and outgunned, the Viet Minh soon approached numerical parity with their French opponents, and by early 1954 the ratio of Viet Minh to French Union combatants was nearly 1:1.[24] At the time of the cease-fire in July 1954, the Viet Minh forces numbered over 335,000 men and women out of a total population of about 28 million.[25] Moreover, by that time the Viet Minh forces were quite as well-armed as the French Union forces and their superior training, discipline, and enthusiasm made success possible even without the 10:1 or 15:1 numerical superiority found necessary for rebels in other insurgencies.

Table 3.1. Development of Viet Minh Strength, 1945–1954

Date	Regular Forces	Regional Forces	Local Forces	Total
September 1945	31,000	–	–	> 31,000
August 1946	60,000	20,000		95,000[a]
January 1947	47,000	56,000		103,000
March 1947	60,000	100,000		160,000
1948–1949	75,000	175,000		250,000
June 1950	120,000	40,000	85,000	245,000
Early 1951	120,000	120,000		240,000
April 1952	130,000	70,000	70,000	270,000
Summer 1952	110,000	75,000	>120,000	>305,000
May 1953	123,000	62,000	115,000	300,000
September 1953	116,000	67,000	107,000	290,000
May 1954	118,000	72,000	106,000	296,000
Mid-June 1954	120,000	76,000	106,000	302,000
July 1954	144,000	77,000	114,000	335,000
October 1954	161,000	68,000	110,000	339,000

[a] Total for August 1946 includes 15,000 Japanese deserters and other personnel.

Sources: Compiled by the author from various sources. All figures are estimates.

The Distribution of Viet Minh Tactical Units

While the strength of the various components of the Viet Minh military forces grew steadily between 1945 and 1954, the proportion of regular, regional, and local forces fluctuated from time to time as casualties occurred, new recruits were added, and new units were formed or transferred from one component to another. Their geographical distribution also varied from time to time according to operational plans and the tactical situation.

The principal areas of formation, training, and operations of the Viet Minh regular forces were in Tonkin, northern Annam, and northern Laos. The Viet Minh units operating in southern Annam, the Central Highlands, Cochinchina, Cambodia, and southern Laos were almost exclusively regional or local forces. The eighty thousand armed combat troops available to the Viet Minh in August 1946 were distributed roughly as follows: thirty-five thousand in Tonkin, fifteen thousand in northern Annam, twenty thousand in southern Annam, and ten thousand in Cochinchina.[26] One year later, in August 1947, the Viet Minh forces had forty-five thousand men in Tonkin, sixteen thousand in northern Annam, four thousand in southern Annam, eighteen thousand in Cochinchina, and eighteen

Table 3.2. Estimated Viet Minh Ground Forces Strength and Disposition, April 1, 1953[a]

Component	Tonkin	Annam & Plateaux	Cochinchina	Cambodia	Laos	Total
Regular Army[b] (*Chu Luc*)	81,000	25,000	13,000	1,000	3,000	**123,000**
Regional Forces (Full-time)	35,000	14,500	7,500	3,000	2,000	**62,000**
People's Militia (Armed)	50,000	34,000	25,000	5,000	1,000	**115,000**
Total	**166,000**	**73,500**	**45,500**	**9,000[c]**	**6,000**	**300,000**

[a] Strengths and dispositions changed during the Viet Minh incursion into Laos in April 1953. An estimated 30,000 Viet Minh regulars moved from Tonkin into Laos and an estimated 10,000 moved from Annam. By mid-May, however, it is believed that all but 15,000 of the Viet Minh regulars had returned to their base areas in Tonkin and Annam.
[b] The Viet Minh regulars were organized into six infantry divisions, one artillery division, fourteen independent regiments, and fifteen independent battalions. Regional forces were organized in forty-four battalions.
[c] Some 3,000 dissident Khmer Issaraks were also active in Cambodia.
Source: National Intelligence Estimate 91 ("Probable Developments in Indochina through Mid-1954"), June 4, 1953.

hundred in Thailand.[27] Between 1946 and July 1954, Viet Minh forces in Cambodia never exceeded a total of ten thousand, of which only about one thousand were regulars.[28] Table 3.2 depicts the situation on April 1, 1953.

Tactical Organization of Viet Minh Forces

Following the failure of an attempted uprising in December 1946, the Viet Minh retreated into the mountains of northwest Tonkin, where they reconstituted and reorganized their forces during 1947–1948. It was during this period that the Viet Minh armed forces were divided into three components, each of which had a particular mission and was equipped, disciplined, and trained to a different standard. The three components varied widely in their combat capability, but each element had its role to play in carrying out the overall strategy and plan of campaign of the Viet Minh high command. In fact, the three-fold division paralleled General Giap's concept of the three stages of the war of liberation, the Popular (Local) Forces (*Tu Ve*) being best suited to the first, or guerrilla, stage; the Regional Forces (*Bo Doi Dia Phuong Quan*) for the second stage; and the Regular Forces (*Bo Doi Chu Luc*) for the "general counteroffensive" stage. All three elements were trained to act in cooperation with each other, and each lower echelon was the principal source for recruits for the next higher echelon.

At the top of the hierarchy were the Regular Forces (*Ve Quoc Quan*, or more commonly, *Bo Doi Chu Luc*), who were reserved primarily for large-scale conventional operations under the direct control of the high command. Tracing their heritage back to the few hard-core guerrillas who accompanied Ho Chi Minh and Vo Nguyen Giap from China in 1944 and formed the first Armed Propaganda Teams, by 1950 the *Chu Luc* were being organized in units of up to division size equipped with artillery, antiaircraft weapons, and a variety of other supporting elements, including a well-organized logistical "tail." The elite *Chu Luc* were well-armed and well-trained, and by 1954 the Viet Minh regular infantry, more than a match for their French opponents, could be considered among the best in the world.[29] The Viet Minh regular soldiers, who took a special ten-point oath in which they swore sacrifice, obedience, diligence, security, and loyalty to the cause, were recruited from the ranks of the regional forces and received regular pay, uniforms, and the best food and equipment available.[30]

For the most part, the Viet Minh regular divisions and independent regiments and battalions were employed as a complete unit, although some divisions were broken down to infiltrate behind French lines. The *Chu Luc* were organized as light infantry and were equipped with small arms, light automatic weapons, and mortars. Radios, tentage, camp equipage, and other equipment normally found in the equivalent size French Union units were kept to a minimum or did not exist at all. Motor transport and heavy engineer equipment were not organic to tactical units. As a result, all *Chu Luc* units were expected to move on foot with only the aid of porters provided by the central supply services. This they were indeed able to do, over distances and with a speed that confounded the French. Mobility was the hallmark of all Viet Minh forces. Lacking both extensive combat trains and large numbers of tanks, trucks, and heavy artillery, the Viet Minh regular infantry were not restricted to the limited road networks and were in fact quite adept at cross-country movement even in the most difficult terrain. The routine dispersion and quick reaction time of the *Chu Luc* helped them to avoid French air attacks, and their lack of heavy equipment also made possible the infiltration of even division-size units around and through French defensive zones.

The second component consisted of the Regional Forces (*Bo Doi Dia Phuong Quan*), which were controlled by the commander in chief through the territorial commands. The Regional Forces were of two types: Provincial Forces, which were comparatively well-armed and well-organized, and District Forces, which had less military capability. Less well-armed and less well-trained than the regulars, the regional troops were generally employed in the region from which they were raised. The mission of the Regional Forces was primarily defensive. They opposed the French sweeps, protected the Viet Minh lines of communication, carried out guerrilla operations, trained the local guerrilla units, and provided recruits and reinforcements as well as reconnaissance, screening, and other support for the regular forces. The largest Regional Force unit was generally the battalion, although by the end of the war Regional Force regiments were organized in Tonkin with a mobility and armament nearly equivalent to that of the regular forces.[31] The Regional Force regiments formed in Tonkin consisted of three infantry battalions and some regimental support elements (a guard unit, an engineer platoon, an escort platoon, etc.).[32]

The third component consisted of the Popular Forces (also known as Local Forces, Militia, or Self-Defense Forces) (*Tu Ve*) that formed "the backbone" of the Viet Minh armed forces.[33] Such part-time guerrilla units were raised at the local (village or hamlet) level and were generally employed locally in self-defense and support tasks. The Popular Forces were divided into two categories: the *Dan Quan*, which included men and women of all ages and which had no combat capability, and the more-selective *Dan Quan Du Kich*, comprised of men between the ages of eighteen and forty-five. The *Dan Quan* were generally unarmed and were used to collect intelligence, construct roads and camps, serve as porters and guards, and occasionally conduct sabotage operations.[34] Although without uniforms and poorly armed and poorly trained, the *Dan Quan Du Kich* were organized in units of eight to fifteen men and were capable of conducting limited guerrilla-type operations. They also were used to support the regular and regional forces operating in their vicinity. The Popular Forces were controlled by the high command through the territorial command structure that at the lowest (intervillage or village) level consisted of a three- or four-man committee that made decisions regarding the defense of the village and guerrilla activities. The village committee usually was dominated by its secretary, who was normally a Communist Party member.[35]

The Viet Minh Infantry Division (Dai Doan)

Until 1947, the largest infantry unit of the Viet Minh was the regiment (*Trung Doan*), sometimes reinforced and called a "group."[36] The growth of the Viet Minh forces and a more aggressive program of offensive actions made the formation of divisions desirable, and the aid received from the Chinese Communists greatly facilitated their formation. The first Viet Minh division was the 308th "Pioneer" Division, formed in January 1947 from the 88th "Tu Vu" and 102nd "Capital" Infantry Regiments, augmented later by the 36th Infantry Regiment. The next four Viet Minh divisions (the 304th "Glory," 312th "Victory," 316th "Bong Lau," and 320th "Delta") were formed in 1950. Each of the first five divisions had an establishment of about fifteen thousand men in three infantry regiments, an artillery battalion, and supporting units. A sixth infantry division, the 325th "Binh Tri Thien," was formed in March 1951 for operations in central Viet Nam. Such divisions had a very high proportion of combat troops and only relatively small command and logistical elements. Throughout the war, the *Dai Doan* relied on large numbers of porters rather than on motor transport to meet their transport needs. In early 1951, the divisional artillery battalions were stripped away to form the

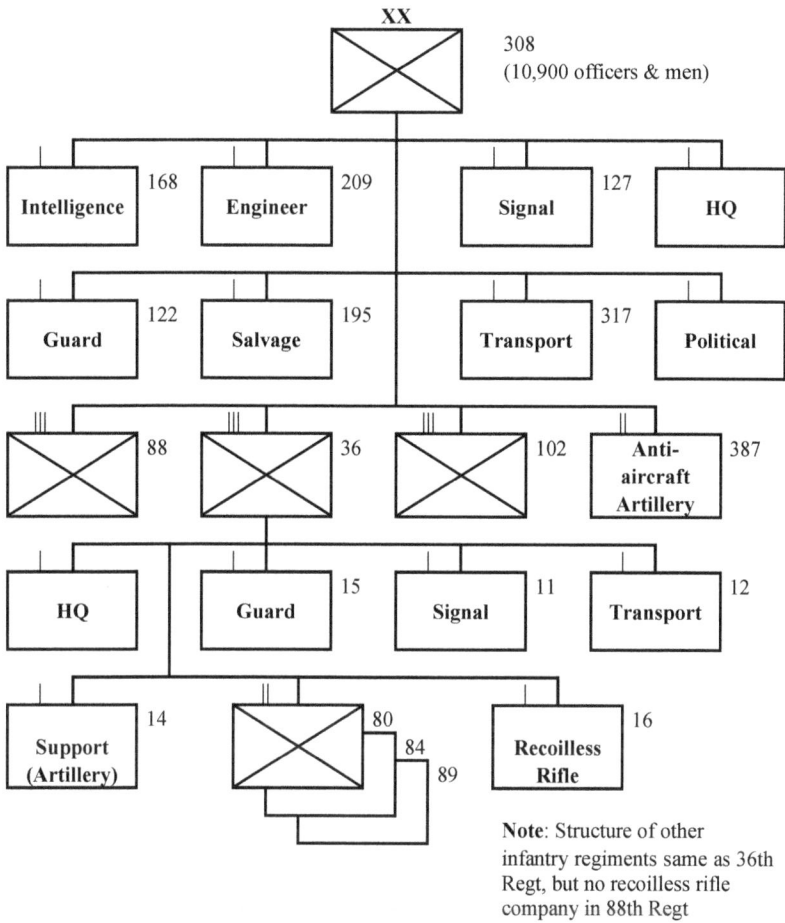

Figure 3.3. Viet Minh 308th Infantry Division, 1954. (Based on *Order of Battle: Viet Minh Army,* 3, 8–9; Fall, "Indochina—The Last Year," 4 [figure 1].)

new 351st Heavy Division, although by the end of the war some of the divisions had regained their supporting artillery battalions.[37]

By the end of 1952, the three largest Viet Minh divisions each received an organic antiaircraft artillery battalion equipped with 37 mm antiaircraft guns and 12.7 mm antiaircraft machine guns.[38] Heavy Viet Minh losses in the fighting of 1951–1952, and the desire for a more flexible organization, led to the reduction in size of the division first to thirteen thousand men and then, by 1953, to about ninety-five hundred men.[39] All but about one thousand men of the new, lighter division were in its three infantry regiments. The organization of a typical Viet Minh infantry division, in this case the famous 308th "Pioneer" Division as it existed at the end of the First Indochina War in 1954, is shown in figure 3.3.

The Viet Minh Heavy Division

In 1951, the Viet Minh formed the 351st Heavy Division on the pattern of the Soviet artillery division of World War II. Created in part from the artillery battalions formerly assigned to the infantry divisions, the 351st was originally organized with two artillery regiments (each with four 75 mm field or mountain guns and about eleven hundred men, of whom about half were porters used to carry ammunition) and one combat engineer regiment.[40] By the time of the cease-fire in July 1954, the division consisted of two artillery regiments, a mortar regiment, an antiaircraft artillery regiment, and an engineer regiment as well as a selection of service troops.[41] One artillery regiment, the 45th, had three battalions of four 105 mm howitzer batteries each, and the other artillery regiment, the 675th, had three battalions equipped with a total of eighteen to twenty-four 75 mm mountain guns and twelve 120 mm mortars. The 237th Mortar Regiment was equipped with 60 mm and 82 mm mortars. The 367th Antiaircraft Artillery Regiment had four bat-

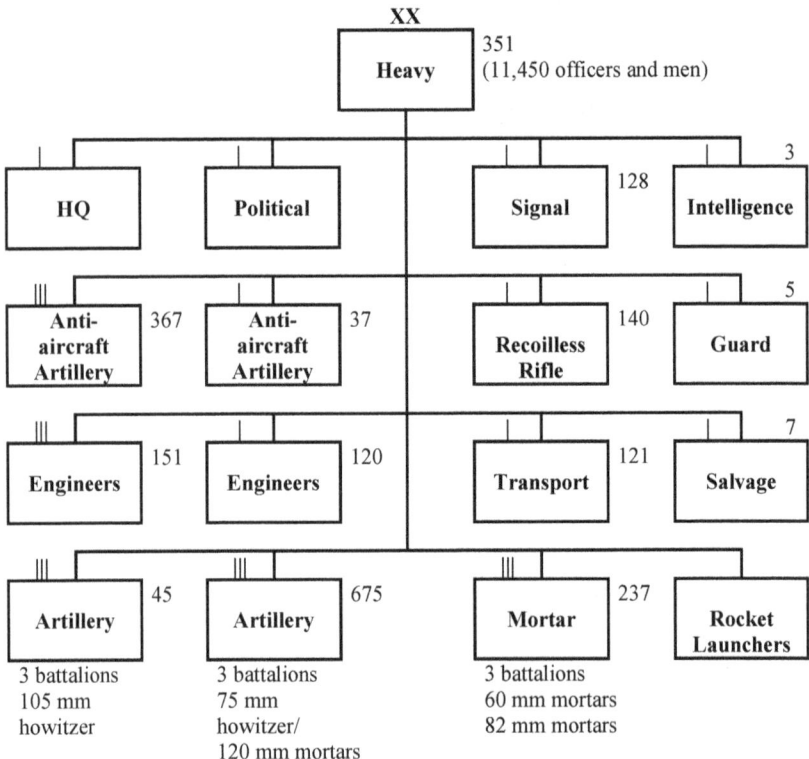

Figure 3.4. Viet Minh 351st Heavy Division, 1954. (*Order of Battle: Viet Minh Army,* 4, 13–15; Fall, "Indochina—The Last Year," 4 [figure 2].)

talions equipped with 37 mm antiaircraft guns and 12.7 mm antiaircraft machine guns. The 151st Engineer Regiment had four combat engineer battalions and a number of supporting elements. The structure of the 351st Heavy Division at the end of the war is portrayed in figure 3.4.

Although its artillery was motorized to a certain extent, the 351st Division remained much lighter and more mobile than even some French Union infantry formations. Artillery or engineer units detached to support the operations of the Viet Minh infantry divisions generally matched their infantry comrades in mobility and flexibility. When necessary, as at Dien Bien Phu, the Viet Minh artillerymen were capable of hauling even their 105 mm howitzers by hand through the densest jungle and over the steepest hills. It was this kind of mobility that French intelligence officers and commanders found incredible and that led them to seriously underestimate the capabilities of their opponent.

Subordinate Tactical Units

The regimental structure was found both in the divisional and independent regiments (*Trung Doan*) of the Viet Minh regular forces and in a limited number of Regional Force regiments, primarily in Tonkin. The *Chu Luc* infantry regiments could vary substantially. For example, in 1948, the 9th Infantry Regiment, one of the better Viet Minh regular units, had some eighteen hundred men in six battalions and was equipped with only two mortars, two 75 mm guns, and a few automatic weapons.[42] By 1951, the 9th had only three battalions but had grown to thirty-five hundred men and was equipped with twenty-four mortars, nine recoilless rifles, eighteen machine guns, and more than sixty other automatic weapons. A typical regular divisional infantry regiment had a regimental headquarters, three infantry battalions, and normally about six company-size support and service elements.[43] In September 1950, the *Chu Luc* regiments averaged about seventeen hundred men and included a thirty-man military police platoon (*Ban Chat Tu*) and a fifty-man propaganda platoon (*Ban Tu Ven Truyen*) but no supporting artillery.[44] By the end of the war, some *Chu Luc* divisional regiments also had a heavy weapons battalion equipped with 120 mm and 150 mm mortars, heavy machine guns, rocket launchers, and at least two artillery pieces.[45] The independent *Chu Luc* infantry regiments were organized in a slightly different manner from the divisional regiments. They generally lacked the engineer and transportation companies and were less well-equipped.

Battalion formations were found in both the divisional and independent regular infantry and in the Regional Forces. The *Chu Luc* infantry battalion (*Tieu Doan*) consisted of about five hundred men in a small headquarters company, three rifle companies, and, usually, a heavy weapons company.[46] The heavy weapons company was organized with a headquarters platoon, an 81 mm or 82 mm mortar platoon, and a light machine gun platoon. The *Chu Luc* battalion, commanded by a major, had few logistical personnel and usually maintained no reserve of supplies, its subordinate companies drawing what they needed directly from the regimental level.[47] The better Regional Force battalions in Tonkin were equipped with about 120 rifles, fourteen automatic rifles, four 60 mm mortars, and two rocket launchers.[48] Independent *Chu Luc* battalions and Regional Forces battalions were somewhat less well-armed and generally had slightly fewer personnel.

The regular Viet Minh infantry companies (*Dai Doi*) differed substantially from the Regional and Popular Forces companies.[49] The *Chu Luc* infantry company was authorized 165 men and usually had an actual strength of around 150 men organized into a company headquarters and three rifle platoons. Commanded by a captain or first lieutenant, the company was authorized, in addition to platoon weapons and equipment, one mortar, two rocket launchers, one heavy machine gun or 12.7 mm automatic cannon, a reserve of fifty hand grenades, six or seven mines, and variable amounts of reserve small arms ammunition, plus three pairs of binoculars and a compass. The headquarters element consisted of the commander, a political officer (a captain or first lieutenant), an executive officer (a first or second lieutenant), an adjutant (a second lieutenant), two clerks (NCOs or soldiers), one ordnance technician (an NCO or soldier), three cooks, and five runners. In contrast, the Regional Force infantry company was authorized only 132 men and usually could muster around 115 to 120. It, too, had three platoons and a headquarters element consisting of the commander, a political officer, an executive officer, and an adjutant (all without formal rank) and one clerk, an ordnance technician, three cooks, and three runners. In addition to the arms and equipment in the rifle platoons, the company was authorized one light machine gun, one rocket launcher, two grenade launchers, sixty hand grenades, about twenty mines, and variable amounts of reserve small arms ammunition as well as, in some cases, a mortar and a pair of binoculars. Popular Forces companies were much smaller and much less well-armed.

The *Chu Luc* infantry platoon (*Trung Doi*) had an authorized strength of fifty men in three fifteen-man squads (*Tieu Doi*) and a small platoon headquarters element consisting of the platoon leader (a warrant officer or second lieutenant), an assistant platoon leader (an NCO), and three clerks. In addition to the weapons and equipment in the squads, the platoon was usually authorized a light machine gun and a reserve of about thirty hand grenades, plus a light mortar. In the early days of the war, even some regular units did not have a weapon for each man, but after 1950 most squads in both the *Chu Luc* and the Regional Forces were fully armed, often with automatic weapons and hand grenades. The Regional Force infantry platoon also consisted of three squads but was authorized only forty men (twelve per squad), including the headquarters element consisting of a platoon leader and an assistant platoon leader (both without formal rank), and two clerks.

Such platoons were authorized only five or six mines in addition to the normal squad equipment.

With respect to the organization of combat forces, the Viet Minh had few inherent advantages over the French Union forces. Their one salient advantage was raw manpower. The Viet Minh forces at all levels never lacked for new recruits, and the strength of the Viet Minh grew steadily throughout the war. Although the Viet Minh initially lacked the weapons and other equipment necessary for a modern army, the Viet Minh leaders were very successful in turning that apparent disadvantage into a war-winning attribute. Ho Chi Minh and Vo Nguyen Giap structured their forces so as to accommodate the terrain on which they were to fight. By emphasizing light, flexible, highly mobile formations capable of moving quickly on foot through all types of difficult terrain, the Viet Minh leaders ensured that their forces would be far better adapted to the physical environment than were their opponent.

As the war progressed, so too did the organization of the Viet Minh combat units, which grew larger, better equipped, and capable of sustained combat operations against the French Union forces. Although the Viet Minh developed division-size units, including a heavy division, they did not permit the addition of artillery and engineer forces to hamper their operations by restricting their mobility. In the end, the Viet Minh were far more successful than the French in adapting their combat organizations to the physical and operational environment. They thus secured a significant advantage over their opponent, one that led ultimately to victory.

4

French Logistical Doctrine and Organization

The French returned to Indochina in 1945 to find the prewar territorial system of posts, depots, and workshops largely intact. This existing infrastructure was expected to provide a sound framework for the deployment of the logistical elements accompanying the French Far East Expeditionary Corps (CEFEO) because the combat forces as well as the political administration of Indochina were to be reestablished on a territorial basis. For most of the First Indochina War, this territorial system proved adequate for supporting the field forces engaged in pacifying the countryside and defending against sporadic guerrilla attacks. However, as the Viet Minh gained in strength, field operations became more widespread, of longer duration, and more complex. Such changes required both an increase in size and the adoption of new tactical methods on the part of the French Union combat elements, which in turn prompted, along with the creation of the armies of the Associated States, a corresponding increase in logistical demands and an increasing requirement for flexibility on the part of the supply services. New shops and depots were built, stocks were increased, and lines of communication were further developed. The large-scale mobile operations of the last few years of World War II in Europe had also required the French supply services to develop mobile support elements capable of rapid displacement to keep up with the combat forces as well as greater reliance on air transport as a means of supplying far-flung forces in the field.

By 1953, the battlefield in Indochina looked much more like the European battlefield for which much of the French Army was organized and equipped, but, nevertheless, Indochina remained a unique theater of war. The harsh climate, difficult terrain, and poor transportation networks were coupled with a distant overseas supply base controlled by a constantly changing, unenthusiastic, and generally parsimonious government. Moreover, the logistical challenges were significantly increased by the fluctuating number of troops supported, their dispersion and frequent movement, and their ethnic and religious diversity, as well as by the growing demands placed on a logistical system that was itself undermanned, underfunded, terribly mixed in its equipment, and hampered by antiquated procedures and regulations better suited to metropolitan France in peacetime than to Indochina in a state of war.

Logistical Policy and Doctrine

A major contributing factor to the problems that afflicted the French supply services in Indochina was the unfavorable political and economic situation in France. Even by 1954, France's political morale as well as its physical capital had not yet recovered from the shock of the Second World War. The instability occasioned by some fourteen governments in the ten years from 1945 to 1954 did little to ensure adequate systematic planning and execution of the war in Indochina. Ideological divisions within the French government as well as doubts over whether France's colonial empire ought to be retained at all hampered the adequate support of its forces in Indochina. One historian has written, "French responsibility for the direction of the war was diffuse, negligent, and contradictory," a view shared by at least one of the French *commandants en chef* in Indochina, Lieutenant General Henri Navarre, who wrote in 1957 that the failure of the French government to clearly define its goals led inevitably to "the complete lack of coordination between policy and strategy."[1]

The lack of political and strategic clarity was reflected in the logistical doctrine adopted by the French in Indochina. At its base, the conflict between the Viet Minh and the French Union forces represented the clash of two divergent military philosophies: one built on the mobility of the individual soldier; the other on the mobility of armies.[2] The adoption of one or the other of these two basic philosophies framed the corresponding logistical doctrine and, within the context of political and strategic policies, established the limits of what was possible or desirable. In general, French logistical doctrine in Indochina between 1945 and 1954 emphasized the basic principles of its contemporary American counterpart: command responsibility for logistics, impetus from the rear, and centralized control of decentralized operations. However, the French logisticians had to cope with the special problems of reconciling two very different logistical systems, neither of which was particularly well-suited to the kind of war being fought in Indochina. The static territorial support system created by the pre–World War II colonial regime was adequate for the routine support of static garrisons over fixed lines of communication relatively free from enemy interdiction. The more mobile, unit-oriented support system developed in the European theater in World War II was better suited to the highly mobile offensive operations required to find, fix, and fight the Viet Minh conventional forces. However, neither system was entirely adequate for meeting the logistical requirements of the complex strategic and tactical situation in Indochina between 1945 and 1954. Moreover, the existence of two systems only increased the complexity of logistical operations, and the two systems often did not mesh as well as might have been hoped.

Logistical Organization

Uncertain policy and doctrine were manifested in the complexity of the lines of logistical command and coordination, in the instability of logistical planning, and in the many delays and difficulties encountered in obtaining the men and materiel needed by the supply services to support the French Union forces in the field. This complexity is shown in figure 4.1, which represents only one snapshot of an ever-changing system.

French operational staffs in Indochina were organized on the well-known G-staff basis. The four principal G-staff sections (G-1 Personnel, G-2 Intelligence, G-3 Training and Operations, and G-4 Logistics) were designated in French as the *1e, 2e, 3e,* and *4e Bureau,* respectively. In Indochina, the senior French staffs added a *5e Bureau* with responsibility for propaganda and civil affairs and a *Bureau des Mouvements et Transports* responsible for transportation matters. On the other hand, the various supply services were organized on the more traditional departmental system wherein each supply service was responsible for all aspects of the management of its assigned commodities or service. Thus the *Service de l'Intendance* (Intendance Service, SI) determined requirements and procured, stored, distributed, maintained, and issued food and clothing, while the *Service du Matériel* (Ordnance Service, SM) did the same for weapons, ammunition, vehicles, and other equipment. The *Train,* considered more an arm than a service, handled transportation matters, and a separate *Direction des Essences* (Petroleum Directorate) was responsible for all petroleum products.[3] The engineer, signal, and medical corps each took care of all supply and maintenance activities connected with their particular commodities and services. In the main, the organization of the French logistical system in Indochina very much resembled its American counterpart in the years before World War II when the General Staff was limited to operational planning and coordination and the supply departments took care of all aspects of operating the supply system, including the management of their own personnel. Overall, the departmental system and the G-staff system worked together with a fair degree of harmony and effectiveness, but minor conflicts were inevitable.

Manpower was a constant concern for the CEFEO, but the question of sufficient manpower was not just one of having enough riflemen. The highly mechanized French Union forces required drivers, mechanics, and skilled technicians of every sort, all of whom were perpetually in short supply. Restrictions on the number of French personnel assigned or available for assignment to Indochina particularly affected the supply services, which were almost entirely dependent on French soldiers for trained supply and maintenance technicians, although a few Indochinese, North African, and Senegalese soldiers also served in the French logistical services, as did a fairly large number of European and Indochinese civilians. In his May 1954 debriefing, Major General Thomas J. H. Trapnell, a former

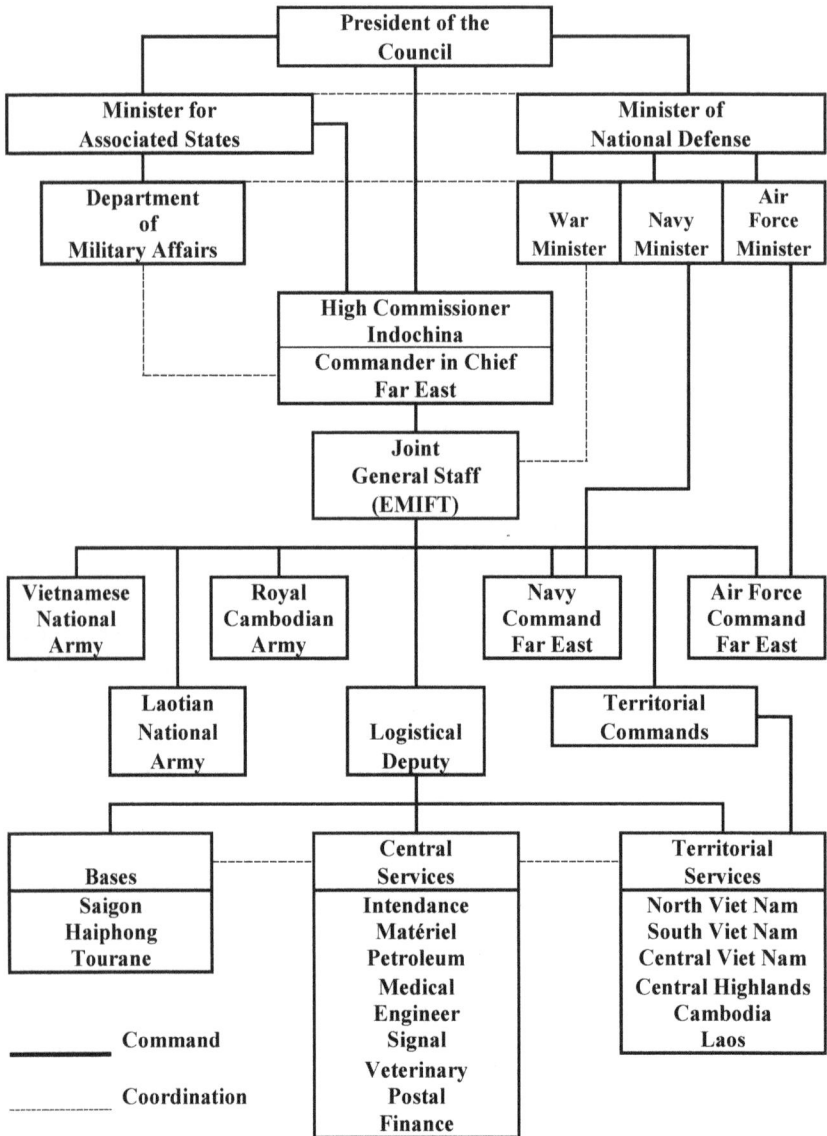

Figure 4.1. Organization of French Logistics in Indochina, 1952. (Compiled by the author from documents in box 10 H 1536, Fonds Indochine, SHAT.)

commander of MAAG-Indochina, noted, "The French Forces are handicapped by an insufficient number of units and trained specialists and consequently are unable to furnish the amount and quality of support given by comparable U.S. units."[4]

Table 4.1. Strength of French Union Service Elements in Indochina,
September 1947–March 1953

Service	Sept. 1947	Dec. 1950	Dec. 1951	March 1953
Intendance (Quartermaster)	961	1,386	1,882	1,883
Matériel (Ordnance)	2,526	4,509	5,401	5,907
Essences (Petroleum)	258	440	726	813
Train (Transport)	6,540	6,661	8,788	8,481
Santé (Medical)	2,986	3,310	4,446	4,415
Veterinaire (Veterinary)	unknown	179	216	210
Total Service Personnel	>13,271	16,485	21,459	21,709
Total FUF Supported	136,698	182,308	310,411	407,275
Service Personnel as % of Total FUF	9.7%	9.1%	6.9%	5.4%

Sources: Compiled by the author from various documents in the Fonds Indochine, SHAT, and Bodinier, ed., *La Guerre d'Indochine*, vols. 1 and 2. The numbers on the table include French, North African, Senegalese, and Indochinese personnel.

The CEFEO also included a number of female soldiers who performed logistical and other support duties. The first twenty women arrived in September 1945, and by 1954 there were 2,460 French women serving in Indochina, of whom 120 were in the air force and another thirty were in the navy.[5] They served as nurses, medical orderlies, ambulance drivers, parachute riggers, flight attendants, movie operators, and Red Cross workers. Greater use of female personnel might have alleviated the severe shortages in certain logistical specialties. In any event, the total number of service personnel assigned to the CEFEO did not keep pace with the expansion in combat personnel. While the total strength of the CEFEO increased nearly four-fold between December 1945 and March 1953, the number of logistical personnel assigned increased less than two-fold. The discrepancy appears even greater when it is recalled that the logistical services of the CEFEO also had to provide most of the logistical support for the growing national armies. Table 4.1 shows the steadily declining ratio of service personnel to the total number of troops supported.

The *Service de l'Intendance*

The French Army *Service de l'Intendance* (SI), which corresponded roughly in functions and responsibilities to the U.S. Army Quartermaster Corps, was responsible for the management of all subsistence and clothing matters, to include the determination of requirements, procurement, storage, and distribution, as well as for troop pay and certain other financial disbursements. Unlike its American counterpart, the SI was not responsible for supplying petroleum products, which in the French service were the responsibility of a separate organization, the *Direction des Essences*.

Intendance Organization and Personnel

The *Service de l'Intendance* in Indochina was organized on a territorial basis and constituted a vast network of workshops, depots, and other facilities. This territorial organization, required by the existing political and military divisions and by the terrain and operational necessity, meant that the SI had to deal with a number of territorial establishments rather than directly with field units, as they did in metropolitan France.[6] The general organization of the SI in Indochina as it existed in 1952 is shown in figure 4.2.

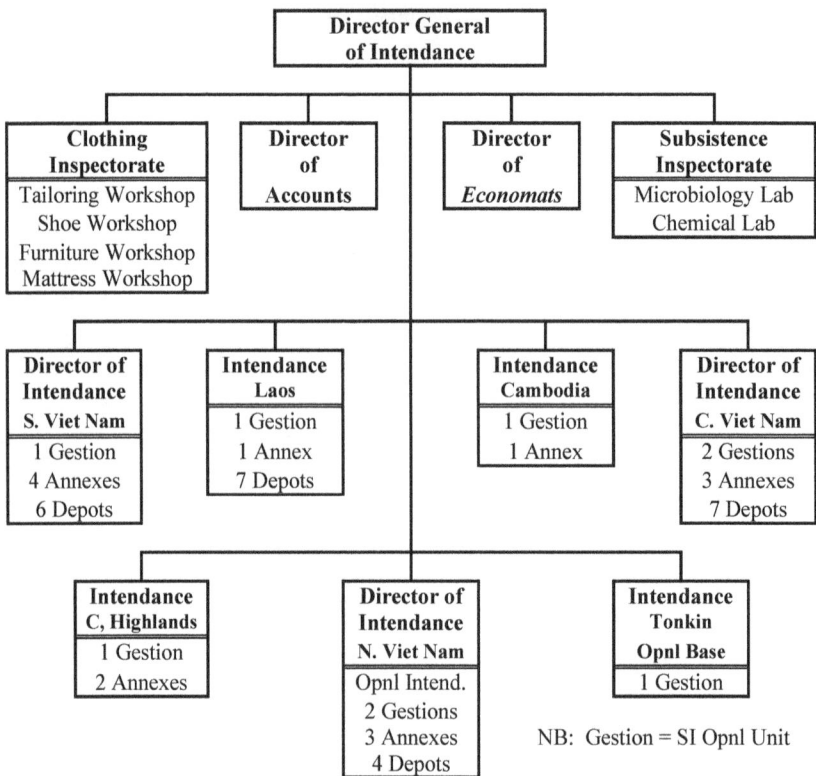

Figure 4.2. French Intendance Service in Indochina, 1952. (Compiled by the author from documents in box 10 H 1536, Fonds Indochine, SHAT, and Bodinier, ed., *La Guerre d'Indochine*, 2:52–53.)

Table 4.2. Personnel of the *Service de l'Intendance* in Indochina, January 1953

Category	Number
Intendants (Officers)	29
Administrative Officers	79
NCOs	400
Enlisted Supply Specialists (European)	387
Enlisted Non-Specialists (Senegalese and Indochinese)	756
Total Military	**1,651**
Civilians (European)	192
Civilians (Indochinese)	1,377
Total Civilians	**1,569**
Total Personnel Assigned	**3,220**

Source: 4e Bureau, EMIFT, "Note sur le service d'Intendance en Indochine," 2.

The territorial supply system of the SI was complemented by a number of exploitation groups (*groupes d'exploitation,* GE).[7] These were light, flexible, and mobile supply elements designed to support combat formations engaged in active field operations. The GE constituted the SI element in the so-called operational support groups, which also had ammunition supply, maintenance, and engineer elements. The GEs were normally co-located with the headquarters of the combat force commander, and their mission was to estimate requirements, verify demands, make issues, and relocate in accordance with the tactical situation.[8] They were task-organized and usually included a tented depot for rations, a field bakery unit, an animal park and abattoir, a small clothing depot, and a mobile retail sales facility (commissary/exchange). A GE supporting a task force of fifteen thousand men normally included one officer, twelve NCOs (of whom nine were warehousemen), a number of drivers, and about sixty Indochinese laborers.[9] In addition, each Far East infantry division was authorized a sixty-five-man divisional GE consisting of one French officer, six French NCOs, and eighteen French soldiers plus two African NCOs and thirty-eight African soldiers.[10] This was in addition to the normal authorization of three officers, eight NCOs, and twelve soldiers (all French) for the divisional quartermaster section (*Intendance Divisionnaire*).

The total number of military and civilian personnel assigned to the SI in Indochina was never large and in most cases was inadequate to the tasks assigned.[11] The number of assigned military and civilian personnel as of January 1953 is shown in table 4.2.

Adequately trained SI officers were scarce throughout the First Indochina War, and unit supply officers had increased responsibilities due to the separation of units from their bases for extended periods of time. Various *Intendance* duties were thus assigned to NCOs, and recommendations were made for increased numbers of trained personnel at the battalion level and the retention at company level of only those trained supply personnel needed to manage transfers, pay the troops, and maintain ration records.[12]

Intendance Requirements

The annual requirements for subsistence and clothing for the troops in Indochina were substantial. For example, the 1953 annual requirement for meat alone was 22,700 tons, of which only 14,550 tons could be supplied locally. The remainder was requisitioned from France and included 1,750 tons of preserved meat, 6,300 tons of frozen meat, and 100 tons of live sheep for the Muslim troops of the CEFEO.[13] Shipping shortages and other factors conspired to limit the amounts of subsistence and clothing items actually received from overseas each year.

Based on actual consumption in the 1952–1953 campaign in Tonkin and northern Laos, in October 1954, the EMIFT *4e Bureau* estimated the "normal" rate of consumption of *Intendance* items (food and clothing) in Indochina at 2.75 kilograms per man per day in both offensive and defensive operations.[14] The "extreme" rates were calculated at 2.5 kilograms per man per day (calm) and 2 kilograms per man per day (crisis). Actual consumption varied somewhat from the theoretical rates. For example, the subsistence ration alone for troops at Dien Bien Phu in 1954 was 3 kilograms per European, 2.5 kilograms per African or North African, 2 kilograms per local soldier or auxiliary, and 1.5 kilograms per Viet Minh prisoner.[15] Based on the events at Dien Bien Phu, the experts concluded that in a defensive battle reliant on aerial resupply, a fourteen-day supply of rations was probably the essential minimum safety level.[16]

Procurement of Rations and Clothing

Clothing and subsistence for French Union forces in Indochina were procured locally or imported from France or elsewhere. In 1952 alone, the SI imported some twenty thousand tons of clothing and one hundred thousand tons of rations.[17] The severe climate and poor roads of Indochina as well as active combat operations required the frequent replacement of clothing and equipment. For example, the useful life of the steel helmet in active operations was three years; of the jungle hat and fatigue shirt and trousers, four months; of canvas and rubber jungle boots, three months; and of the canvas shelter half, one year.[18] The excessively rigid local procurement regulations in force complicated the procurement of clothing and equipment. Otherwise, the supply of such items posed no particular problems. In addition to supplying the special items of clothing (such as turban cloth and *djebellahs*) required by the different types of troops in Indochina (French Army,

Foreign Legion, Algerian, Moroccan, Senegalese, Vietnamese, Cambodian, and Laotian), the SI also had to supply winter clothing to troops in Tonkin and Laos. Several initial problems, such as the far too heavy cloth used for combat uniforms and the inadequacy of the regular combat boot in the paddies and jungles of Indochina, were resolved without undue effort.[19] In 1952, the workshops directly controlled by the SI produced some 2,170,000 cloth articles, 125,000 pairs of service shoes, 10,000 pairs of paratroop jump boots, and 3,000 pairs of sandals.[20]

The procurement of subsistence was more complex. Local agricultural resources were largely limited to the production of a single crop—rice—and meat production was almost nonexistent. Consequently, local procurement of subsistence was largely limited to rice and dried fish, which, although useful for meeting the special subsistence needs of the native Indochinese troops, did not meet the special needs of European, North African, or African troops. The procurement of food for the Muslim soldiers of the French Union forces posed a particular problem. The Muslim meat ration consisted primarily of live sheep that had to be bought in Australia or North Africa and transported to Indochina at considerable expense. The sheep were issued live to Muslim troops in even the most remote posts, being transported there by whatever means were available, including by parachute.[21]

Several types of packaged rations were used by the French Union forces in Indochina. Again, special arrangements had to be made for the tastes and dietary restrictions of the various ethnic and religious groups that made up the French Union forces. The standard packaged ration types included the *Ration individuelle "Guerre"* (Individual War Ration, comparable to the U.S. K-ration), the *Ration Multiple F.O.M.* (Multiple Overseas Ration, comparable to the U.S. C-ration), the *Ration de Secours F.O.M. 101* (Emergency Overseas Ration, reserved to airborne troops), the *Ration de Secours "Guerre"* (Emergency War Ration, on trial for only two days in 1950), and the *Ration Conditionnée Spécialement Réservée* (Special Field Ration, for local troops).[22]

Several improvements were made to the existing field rations during the course of the war in Indochina. Among the improvements were better packaging designed to resist the tropical climate and the inclusion of writing paper, razor blades, and various condiments. The Multiple Overseas Ration 10 was replaced by the Multiple Overseas Ration 5, which was easier to handle and better suited to the small unit operations in Indochina. The number of menus included in the "overseas" ration was also increased from three to five for more variety.

Storage and Distribution of Rations and Clothing

The limited facilities in Indochina for the storage of food and clothing, both of which were very vulnerable to heat, humidity, mildew and other fungi, and rats and other vermin, consisted initially of prewar fixed depot facilities and tents for field storage.[23] These soon proved inadequate in capacity as well as unsatisfactory with respect to the protection of materiel. Some expansion was undertaken during the course of the First Indochina War, but adequate, safe storage for quartermaster supplies remained a problem until the end.

At the beginning of the war French Union forces ate fresh meat from local livestock, but the situation in Indochina soon required a shift to the use of imported boneless frozen meat. This in turn required the establishment of a system of cold storage facilities and the use of refrigerated trucks and containers for distribution of frozen meat to the field. The resulting system of cold storage depots, completed in 1951, consisted of large-capacity cold storage facilities for long-term storage at the major ports and depots and a number of smaller, short-term cold storage facilities located at the less important depots or near the troops.[24] The cold storage facilities available in 1952 amounted to 92,660 cubic feet, the bulk of which was located in Saigon and Haiphong.[25] Another 6,178 cubic feet of space was under construction, and plans for 1953 called for the construction of an additional 102,370 cubic feet of cold storage.

As might be expected, the distribution of rations and clothing to French Union forces in Indochina was complicated by the great distances involved, the difficult climate and terrain, the constant movement of combat units, and the fluctuation in unit strength as well as the need for secrecy and the lack of adequate training in requisition and issue procedures.[26] Nevertheless, the SI was reasonably successful in keeping the French forces well-fed and well-clothed. As one French lieutenant testified: "Despite the obvious difficulties, my company had fresh food much of the time and on occasion we even had ice; in general, clothing and individual equipment was satisfactory. The services certainly did their very best to help us endure the hardships of the campaign."[27]

In addition to distributing subsistence and clothing to the troops in the territorial commands and in the field, the SI also operated a system of retail commissaries and post exchanges that sold food, cigarettes, and other personal comfort items directly to the troops. Those *"Économats"* were conceived by *Intendant Général* Trémolet in October 1945, and on August 17, 1946, the *Service Centrale des Économats des Troupes Françaises en Extrême-Orient* was created as part of the SI.[28] The main depot was located in Saigon, and there were central storehouses at Tourane (Da Nang), Haiphong, and Kratie as well as two retail stores in Saigon and one each in Can Tho, Da Lat, Phnom Penh, Savannakhet, Kratie, Haiphong, Hanoi, and Lang Son. The main Saigon store carried fifteen hundred items.

Challenges for the Service de l'Intendance in Indochina

The challenges faced by the *Service de l'Intendance* in Indochina included the problems common to all the supply services and arose from the economic and political situation in France, the difficult climate and terrain, long distances, the inadequate transportation network in Indochina, and the lack of sufficient trained personnel as well as constant enemy guerrilla activity. The modesty of the means initially available, the wartime destruction of facilities and resources in Indochina, the limited aid available from metropolitan France (which was still suffering the economic effects of World War II), and above all the increasing number and variety of troops requiring support as the war went on all served to complicate the supply of subsistence and clothing.[29]

From the logistical point of view, the great diversity of the French Union forces in Indochina can only be viewed as a serious weakness. As Major General Thomas J. H. Trapnell, a former chief of MAAG-Indochina, noted in May 1954:

> The French Expeditionary Corps is composed of Foreign Legion, Moroccans, Algerians, Tunisians, Senegalese and a small percentage of metropolitan French volunteers. These units are diluted nearly 59 percent by native Indochinese. The Associated States Forces are composed of varieties of native Vietnamese, Laotians and Cambodians. The whole effect is that of a heterogeneous force among whom even basic communication is difficult. Troops require a variety of clothes sizes and diets. They have different religious customs, folk-ways and mores. They vary in their capacity for different tasks and terrain. Logistically, a great problem exists in the support of such troops.[30]

The SI also seems to have been particularly sensitive to the extreme diversity of the materiel employed and the fact that certain procedures and equipment developed for use in the European theater were unsuitable to a greater or lesser degree for operations in Indochina.[31] Continuous improvements and modernization took place, but some challenges were never fully met. As one director general of the *Service de l'Intendance* in Indochina noted in his final report: "Beginning with the arrival of the first elements in Indochina, the Expeditionary Corps was able to utilize an administrative organization that had been in existence for a long time. There were no problems at first, but this was not to continue. . . . The inadequacy of personnel and equipment, the enforcement of peacetime regulations applicable to France and the colonies, and the administrative procedures used by the various formations—all combined to create significant major difficulties for the Quartermaster Corps, which grew as the strength of the Army in the Far East [increased]."[32]

The rigidity of French regulations pertaining to the procurement and issue of supplies was a particular source of difficulty right to the end of the war in Indochina. The responsible SI officers acknowledged that their service did have to be modified somewhat to meet the needs of French Union forces in Indochina and that while these modifications were generally adequate, "administration remained too rigid, and the troops certainly suffered from adherence to peacetime regulations."[33] They also concluded that new regulations should be drawn that would be applicable to both peacetime garrison service as well as field service overseas in time of war.

The regulations pertaining to the local procurement of supplies were especially inflexible and thus significantly hampered efforts to supply the French Union forces with adequate food and clothing. Private (in other words, "sole-source") contracts were generally prohibited, and the various supply organizations were usually forced into inefficient competition with one another for the services of the nearest suppliers. Local procurement was thus accomplished in spite of, rather than with the assistance of, "regulations concerning local purchase in the Far East which had never been modified to meet the requirements of the war."[34] Furthermore, at the unit level the failure to simplify administrative and supply procedures placed a heavy paperwork burden on units already weighed down by operational matters. In retrospect, French SI officers recognized a number of administrative faults that should have been corrected, such as oversupply of cash to disbursing officers in forward locations, the preparation of pay records at battalion level rather than in the rear, and the impossibility of maintaining individual clothing issue records in the field during active operations.[35]

A number of minor problems also added to the difficulties of supplying food and clothing to the troops in Indochina. The task equipment available to the SI was generally rated unsatisfactory due to the variety of makes and models and the unsuitability of some equipment to the Indochina environment.[36] For example, the scarcity of dry wood in most of Indochina posed problems with the existing bakery units and field kitchens, which were wood-fired.[37] The provision of water and the issue of ice were also SI functions in Indochina, and the equipment for purifying water and making ice was generally cumbersome and immobile.[38] Moreover, the chemicals used in the treatment of water gave the water a disagreeable taste and did not remove material suspended in the water. The lack of standard widths for uniform cloth and the shrinkage of the available materials caused problems in the manufacture and maintenance of clothing.[39] The dispersion of troops in the field and the lack of adequate transportation precluded the effective deployment of clothing repair and laundry companies, and an adequate system for the maintenance of clothing in service was never established.[40] The canvas material French manufacturers used for tents and vehicle tarpaulins was not entirely satisfactory, and the field beds in use were heavy, bulky, and poorly made.[41] The standardization of issue items and improved requisitioning procedures coupled with the formation of a support base in metropolitan France that could ship directly to using units in Indochina would have done much to facilitate SI operations, but such improvements were never fully accomplished.[42] For example, despite numerous recommendations, consolidated rear area clothing maintenance facilities were never established. As the French supply officers themselves acknowledged: "There is little merit in speaking of the slowness of transportation and the difficulty of supplying remote posts. This explains why it was occasionally necessary to send urgent requests to France even when the supply situation for Indochina as a whole was satisfactory: supplies were available in some remote areas but these were in effect 'frozen' since they were inaccessible or irrecoverable. . . . In sum, there was little flexibility in the supply system."[43]

The *Direction des Essences*

The supply of petroleum products to French Union forces in Indochina was the responsibility of the *Direction des Essences en Extrême-Orient* (Direction of Petroleum–Far East, DEEO), a joint service activity controlled directly by the logistics deputy of the General Staff at the headquarters of the *commandant en chef*. The DEEO determined requirements for petroleum, oils, and lubricants (POL), managed the procurement and storage of POL products, and oversaw the distribution of POL to military units of the French Army, Navy, and Air Force in Indochina as well as to the Vietnamese, Cambodian, and Laotian national forces. Like the other supply services, the DEEO operated through the various territorial commands. The lack of any joint headquarters at the territorial command level caused some problems in that the army tended to assume control over the representatives of the DEEO, thereby causing some difficulties in supplying air force units.[44]

Overall, however, the supply of petroleum products to French Union Forces in Indochina posed few special problems. Changing requirements and the chronic shortage of storage capacity and POL containers, as well as the ground movement of POL, particularly to Laos, were managed with a fair degree of efficiency and did not seriously degrade the operational capabilities of the French forces. Security concerns were met with outstanding success considering the high vulnerability of fuel products and fuel storage areas to Viet Minh sabotage and direct attack.

DEEO Organization and Personnel

In 1947, the French petroleum supply organization in Indochina consisted solely of the central headquarters (DEEO) and two petroleum resupply companies (the *731e* and *732e Compagnies de Ravitaillement des Essences*, CRE).[45] By 1952, the DEEO had expanded significantly, as depicted in figure 4.3.

The number of personnel required to manage the French military petroleum distribution system remained relatively small throughout the war, never exceeding 0.5 percent of the total strength of the CEFEO.[46] It grew from 637 in 1950 to 826 in 1951 and then stabilized at about 942.[47] In January 1953, DEEO mili-

```
                    ┌─────────────────────────┐
                    │  Director of Petroleum  │
                    │    Far East (DEEO)      │
                    └─────────────────────────┘
```

Deputy DEEO S. Viet Nam & Cambodia	Labs and Workshops	Deputy DEEO C. Viet Nam & Laos	Deputy DEEO N. Viet Nam
Nha Be Company	Sub-Deputy DEEO Savannakhet	Lien Chieu Company	Sub-Deputy DEEO Hanoi
Phnom Penh Company	707e CRE (Tourane)	CRCs and Depots	Do Son Company
731e CRE (Phu To)		Thuong Ly Company	732e CRE (Thuong Ly)
CRCs and Depots		730e CRE (Hanoi)	CRCs and Depots

CRE = POL Resupply Co.
CRC = Composite POL Resupply Co.

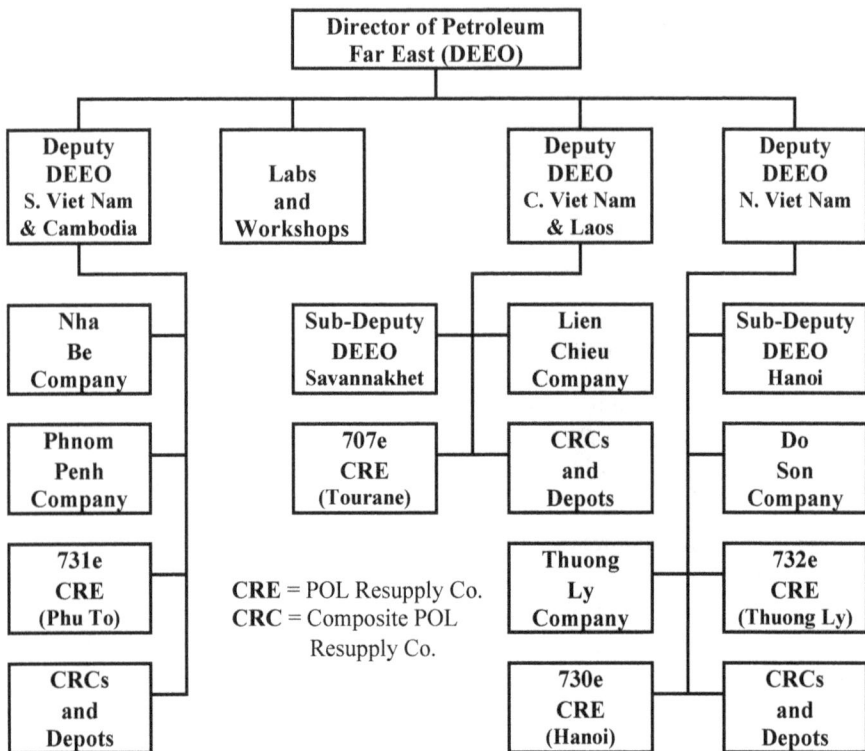

Figure 4.3. French Petroleum Service in Indochina, 1952. (Compiled by the author from documents in boxes 10 H 1525 and 10 H 1536, Fonds Indochine, SHAT.)

tary personnel strength was 821 (421 French, 120 North African, and 280 Indochinese, including thirty-two French officers and nine French female soldiers), augmented by ninety-one Indochinese civilian employees and 464 permanently assigned Indochinese laborers, for a total of 1,376 personnel.[48]

Petroleum Requirements

The director of the DEEO normally determined the annual fuel requirements at the beginning of each year, but unanticipated operational requirements usually rendered the annual projection useless. For example, the consumption of aviation gasoline by aircraft supporting Dien Bien Phu was estimated at 7,696 barrels per month in April 1954, but in May the United States loaned twenty-five C-119 transports to the French, and actual consumption was 13,949 barrels per month.[49] Based on actual consumption in the 1952–1953 campaign in Tonkin and northern Laos, in October 1954 the *4e Bureau* of the EMIFT estimated the "normal" consumption rate for POL at 2 kilograms per man per day in offensive operations, 1.05 kilograms per man per day in defensive operations at an improvised base, and 1.02 kilograms per man per day in defensive operations at an established base.[50] The "extreme" rates were 1 kilogram per man per day (calm) and 3.36 kilograms per man per day (crisis).

Consumption of petroleum products grew steadily between 1945 and 1954 as the size and operational activity of the French expeditionary forces expanded and organization of the military forces of the Associated States proceeded. The consumption of POL was only 630,110 barrels in 1950, but by 1953 it had nearly doubled to 1,201,260 barrels, and in 1954 POL consumption reached 1,712,360 barrels.[51] Losses of petroleum products due to destruction and condemnation were relatively minor. French logistical planners estimated the rate of such losses in 1954 to be about 2.04 percent per year for automotive fuel, 2.51 percent per year for aviation gasoline, and 1.66 percent per year for diesel fuel.[52]

Procurement of Petroleum Products

Until July 1953, all petroleum products used in Indochina were imported on the basis of contracts with commercial firms, principally Shell, SVOC, CALTEX, and Socone.[53] From July 1953 to July 1954, aviation gasoline was supplied through the U.S. aid program either on the basis of contracts by the U.S. Armed Services Purchasing Petroleum Agency with Shell or Standard Oil or by direct shipment in U.S. tankers from Japan, a procedure that seriously stretched the limited storage facilities available in Indochina.[54] In July 1954, the United States stopped supplying fuel and the pre-July 1953 procedures were reinstated.

Storage and Distribution of Petroleum Products

For the most part, the storage of petroleum products was accomplished by commercial firms at their fixed depots in the larger cities. However, the operational environment also required the establishment of several semipermanent major fuel depots and a number of smaller dumps scattered throughout Indochina. These storage facilities were managed by French military petroleum resupply companies and lacked the mobility found in similar POL facilities in the European environment. Each CRE maintained a reserve element that was designated an "operational depot" and that was intended to provide immediate support for combat operations. The operational depots were relatively mobile, but had only a limited supply capacity, averaging about two thousand to four thousand gallons per day.[55]

Safety levels for petroleum products at the ports were fixed at two months' supply of ground automotive fuels (diesel and gasoline) and four months' supply of aviation fuels. Petroleum storage facilities throughout Indochina were always limited. In 1953, the civilian storage capacity was 410,440 barrels, and the military capacity was 236,180 barrels, a total of 646,240 barrels.[56] When the point of maximum consumption was reached in May 1954, a storage capacity in the ports of 673,400 barrels was required, but DEEO had available a capacity in the ports of only 336,700 barrels, one-half of what was required.[57]

Security of POL storage facilities, both civilian and military, was an important consideration. The major fixed installations were protected by reinforced concrete walls, barbed wire, and exterior lighting, and field fuel dumps were protected by dispersion, earthen berms, illuminated barbed wire, and, of course, the surrounding combat forces. Surprisingly, the vulnerable major fuel storage depots were only infrequently attacked, and the few incidents involving Viet Minh sabotage or direct attack on POL depots had little or no impact on the conduct of operations.[58] The fuel depot at Phan Thiet was destroyed in a mortar attack in 1954, and the depot at Hue was burned out by incendiary shells in July 1954. Direct attack by Viet Minh forces partially destroyed the civilian and military fuel depots at Thuong Ly in June 1953 and completely destroyed the depot at Phu Tho in 1952 and that at Nha Trang in January 1954. The depot at Tourane was destroyed by civilian workers there in 1952.

All modes of transportation were utilized to distribute fuel from the major storage areas in the ports and urban areas to smaller depots and units in the field. The DEEO itself operated three small POL tankers (*petroliers caboteurs*) with capacities of 4,330, 5,770, and 13,470 barrels, and the DEEO also had constructed four two-hundred-ton tanker barges.[59] The smaller fixed fuel depots usually were located where they could be resupplied by water—for example, at Nam Dinh, Qui Nhon, Nha Trang, Vinh Long, Can Tho, and Kratie.[60] Most POL movements were made by ground transportation using civilian trucks rented from the commercial petroleum firms; however, DEEO management of civilian tank truck assets was not always adequate and on several occasions the means of moving of fuel to Laos were almost entirely lacking.[61] Some POL was moved by railroad, there being thirty-two railroad tank cars available, each of 3,730 barrels capacity.[62] Viet Minh attacks on the rail lines throughout Indochina, and particularly in Tonkin, made the movement of POL by rail quite hazardous. Operational conditions were such that the distribution of POL was much easier in southern Indochina than it was in Tonkin, and on occasion fuel had to be transported to Tonkin and Laos by aircraft despite the high cost and limited capacity of the available air transport.[63] In severe operational circumstances, fuel was even airdropped in five-gallon tins to units in forward areas, a procedure that resulted in about 20 percent of the POL being lost and in the total loss of the scarce containers.[64] The damage and loss of petroleum containers was a consistently serious problem throughout the First Indochina War and persisted during U.S. operations in Viet Nam. As of 1954, French logistical planners estimated the annual losses and condemnation of five-gallon jerricans at a rate of 8.29 percent per year.[65]

The *Service du Matériel*

The French *Service du Matériel* (SM) corresponded to the U.S. Army Ordnance Corps and performed three main tasks: the supply of weapons, vehicles, and army aircraft; the maintenance of weapons, vehicles, and army aircraft; and the supply of ammunition. The director of the French Army ordnance service in the Far East (*Directeur du Service du Matériel des Forces Terrestres en Extrême-Orient*, DIRMAT FTEO) was responsible for determining requirements, requisitioning, receiving, storing, distributing, and maintaining weapons, vehicles, repair parts, optical equipment, and ammunition as well as chemicals, animal transport gear, aerial resupply equipment, office and printing machines, and light observation aircraft.[66] In addition, the SM was responsible for the evacuation and salvage of damaged equipment and for explosive ordnance disposal.

DIRMAT FTEO Organization and Personnel

In 1945 and 1946, the DIRMAT FTEO reestablished the old pre–World War II ordnance system in Indochina by reoccupying the existing artillery repair shops in the major urban areas. The organization of the DIRMAT FTEO subsequently underwent numerous changes in response to the growing ordnance supply and maintenance workload, the evolving tactical conditions, and general modernization of the service. For example, between 1948 and 1953, the number of vehicles supported increased from 17,110 to 60,221, the number of maintenance units increased from nine to twenty-six, and the number of maintenance personnel from 7,850 to 11,599.[67] A major turning point was reached in 1949, when the DIRMAT FTEO began creating a major rebuild capability and assumed responsibility for the higher level maintenance of combat equipment, particularly armored vehicles.[68] Another major change took place in 1952 and 1953, when the DIRMAT FTEO took over responsibility from the French Air Force for the maintenance of light observation aircraft and responded to the increasing number of river craft by creating specialized units to maintain them.[69] The major elements of the French ordnance system in Indochina were in place by the end of 1952, but in 1953 the DIRMAT FTEO was reorganized as shown in figure 4.4.

As part of the 1953 reorganization a Central Supply and Purchasing Service, an Organization Section, and a Technical Section for technical studies, experiments, and the study of new materiel were added to the DIRMAT FTEO in Saigon.[70] The old General Reserve Depot was reorganized into three separate groups with different missions. The General Reserve Depot-Materiel (*Établissement de Réserve Générale du Matériel*, ERG/MAT), which consisted of the 1st General Reserve Ordnance Battalion (*1e Bataillon de Réparation du Matériel du Réserve Générale*, 1e BRMRG), with five companies located in Saigon, was responsible for

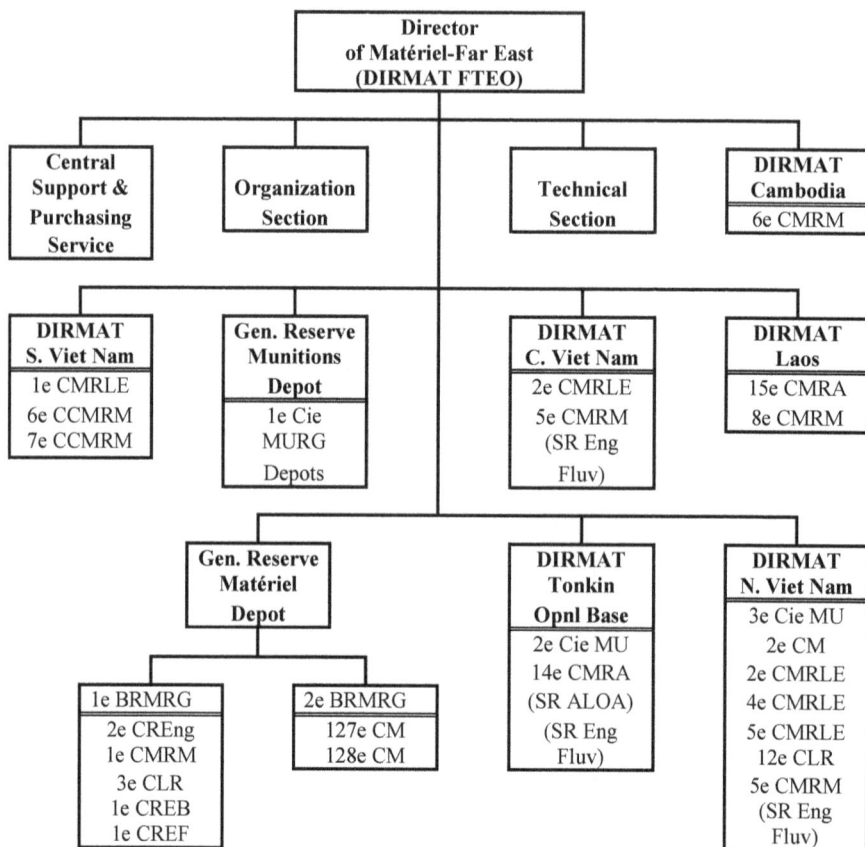

NOTE: French unit abbreviations may be found in the glossary.

Figure 4.4. French Ordnance Service in Indochina, 1953. (Compiled by the author from documents in box 10 H 984, Fonds Indochine, SHAT.)

higher level maintenance and rebuild of equipment. The 2nd General Reserve Ordnance Battalion, with elements located in both Saigon and Haiphong, was responsible for the storage and distribution of weapons, vehicles, and ordnance supplies other than ammunition. The resupply of ammunition was the responsibility of the General Reserve Ammunition Depot (*Entrepôt de Réserve Générale des Munitions,* ERG-MU), with the 1st Ammunition Company (*1e Compagnie des Munitions, 1e CM*) at Saigon and the 2nd Ammunition Company (*2e Compagnie des Munitions, 2e CM*) at Haiphong. Six territorial DIRMATs with a varying number of third-echelon maintenance units, ammunition depots, and other facilities were responsible for carrying out the functions of the DIRMAT FTEO in the field.

The changed tactical situation in northern Indochina after December 1950 required a more mobile ordnance maintenance and supply capability than was provided by the existing territorial organizations. The mobile divisional maintenance companies (*Compagnies de Réparations Divisionnaire*, CRD) that accompanied the French divisions returning to Indochina in 1945 and 1946 were soon absorbed into the territorial ordnance organization and lost their mobility.[71] The existing maintenance and ordnance supply organization operated from fixed facilities and was largely immobile and ill-suited to direct support of active operations in the field. It thus became necessary to devise new light mobile maintenance and ordnance supply organizations to support the combat forces in active operations. Operations involving full divisions were rare in Indochina, but the 1954 Far East infantry division was authorized a *Direction du Service du Matériel* (one officer, four NCOs, and five soldiers, all French) and a Foreign Legion Medium Maintenance Company (*Compagnie Moyenne de Réparation du Matériel de Légion Etrangère*, CMRLE) consisting of a total of 220 personnel (six officers, thirty-two NCOs, and 182 soldiers, of whom two NCOs and forty-eight soldiers were Indochinese).[72] Both the divisional and nondivisional Foreign Legion maintenance companies (CMRLE) were very important to the actual provision of ordnance service in the field, since most of them were organized with a heavy platoon for general maintenance support and supply and three light ordnance maintenance teams, each capable of supporting a task force.[73]

In terms of the number of personnel employed, the DIRMAT FTEO was by far the largest of the supply services in Indochina. However, the inadequate number of trained technicians remained a problem throughout the war. Between 1951 and 1954, the personnel of the DIRMAT FTEO constituted only between 2.9 and 3.4 percent of the total strength of the French Army in the Far East, a ratio that compared unfavorably with the usual ratio of 9 percent of total strength for the U.S. Army Ordnance Corps during that period.[74] Although civilian personnel additions brought the ratio up to 6–7 percent, the number of DIRMAT FTEO personnel available remained insufficient for the tasks they were called upon to perform. In November 1947, for example, the number of personnel assigned was 25 percent less than the number required and authorized.[75] Table 4.3 shows the number of military and civilian personnel employed from 1947 through 1954.

Moreover, the number of trained specialists was particularly low. The officers and NCOs of the SM in Indochina were derived from four sources: the SM in metropolitan France, the SM in the French colonies, the Foreign Legion, and a few from line artillery and infantry units.[76] In ordnance units in metropolitan France generally 80 percent of the NCOs were specialists; in Indochina the proportion was only about half that. In 1954, 40 percent of the NCOs assigned to the DIRMAT FTEO were specialists versus 78 percent in metropolitan France. This situation arose from the fact that NCOs posted to Indochina were generally of low

Table 4.3. Personnel Strength of the *Service du Matériel* in Indochina, 1947–1954

Year	Military Personnel	Civilian Personnel	Total Personnel
1947			2,661
1948	3,100	4,750	7,850
1949	4,283	4,750	9,033
1950	4,497	4,836	9,333
1951	5,536	5,938	11,474
1952	5,562	6,768	12,330
1953	6,842	4,757	11,599
1954	7,868	8,151	16,019

Source: DIRMAT FTEO, "Enseignements à tirer de la campagne d'Indochine," annex "Plan," chapter 2, page 1.

time in grade and thus had not yet attained high-level technical training. About 4 percent of the DIRMAT FTEO strength was composed of European civilians, most of whom were in clerical positions and who were only about 60 percent as effective as their military counterparts. While most ordnance personnel were quite competent, many were used to operating from fixed facilities and were thus unfamiliar with the special requirements of a more mobile environment, such as that found in Indochina. The Indochinese employees of the DIRMAT FTEO were for the most part semiskilled at best and had only about one-half the effectiveness of French personnel. The best technicians were to be found in the Foreign Legion maintenance units, which were manned by a high percentage of long-service trained specialists.

The Supply of Weapons, Vehicles, and Other Equipment

Until 1950, the French Union forces in Indochina suffered chronic shortages of equipment and were plagued by the age and diverse types of most of the weapons, vehicles, and other equipment available.[77] In 1947, for example, only 210 vehicles were received from France out of 3,682 requested; of 9,148 motors requested only 250 were received; and out of 76,639 tires requested only 10,843 arrived, of which only 6,517 were from France and half of them were used.[78] The weapons and vehicles used by the French Union forces in Indochina were drawn from the stocks of at least five countries (France, the United States, Britain, Germany, and Japan) and represented a large number of makes and models, many of which were obsolete and for which spare parts were no longer available.[79] For example, there were thirty-six different models of semiautomatic pistols among the twenty-eight thousand pistols in service, thirty-three models of rifles and carbines among the four hundred thousand on hand, seventeen types of light machine guns among the fourteen thousand in service, and sixteen models of mortars among the thirty-eight hundred on hand.[80] The large variety of models increased maintenance problems by increasing the spare parts inventory required and inhibiting the application of mass production methods in making repairs.

The commencement of American aid in 1950 permitted the initiation of a program prepared in 1949 for standardizing the arms and equipment of the CEFEO on American models, a program that was scheduled for completion by the beginning of 1952. At the same time the French planned to reinforce their Indochina forces with an additional infantry division, three groups of heavy artillery, two engineer battalions, and various transport and logistical support elements, all to be equipped by American aid. However, most of the arms and equipment envisioned in this plan was diverted to equip the newly formed armies of the Associated States.

At the end of 1951, the number of vehicles on hand included 18,000 wheeled vehicles, 2,300 armored vehicles, and 4,200 trailers. In addition, there were 230 river craft engines. The 648,000 infantry weapons on hand included 106,000 submachine guns, 468,000 rifles, 22,000 automatic rifles, 3,800 rockets, and 7,500 mortars and grenade launchers. The 748 pieces of artillery included 54 105 mm Long 1936 howitzers, 185 of the 105 mm HM2 howitzers, 106 of the 25-pounders, 21 155 mm HM1 guns, and 160 of the 40 mm Bofors antiaircraft guns. Ammunition reserves totaled about 30,000 tons, and there were 18,000 personnel parachutes and 5,800 cargo parachutes in theater. Nevertheless this impressive list of arms and equipment represented only about 70 percent of the receipts envisioned by the standardization program and only about 80 percent of the overall requirements of the CEFEO.[81] Moreover, most of the materiel on hand was badly worn and needed replacement.

By May 1953, the near total fulfillment of the U.S. aid programs for FY 1951 and FY 1952 had brought significant improvements. The number of vehicles had risen to 23,000 wheeled vehicles, 3,000 armored vehicles, and 6,000 trailers, and the number of river craft engines to 500. Some 745,000 infantry weapons were on hand, of which about 535,000 were in service, and some 730 artillery pieces were on the books, with 540 in service plus another 250 mounted in turrets in fixed fortifications. Some 18,000 personnel parachutes and 8,000 cargo parachutes were available. The only remaining serious deficiencies were in certain repair parts and communications equipment.[82]

The Storage of Weapons and Equipment

The storage of weapons and equipment was a principal function of the General Reserve Depot-Materiel (*Établissement de Réserve Générale du Matériel*, ERG/

Table 4.4. Receipts and Issues from ERG/MAT Storage Facilities, 1950–1954

Category	1950	1951	1952	1953	1954
Tons Received	32,000	38,000	79,000	105,000	125,000
Tons Issued	31,000	40,000	74,000	79,000	82,000
Total Tons Handled	**63,000**	**78,000**	**153,000**	**184,000**	**207,000**

Source: DIRMAT FTEO, "Enseignements à tirer de la campagne d'Indochine," annex "Plan," chapter 2, page 7.

MAT). While the amount of both covered and open storage available usually exceeded the theoretical requirements, the ERG/MAT was never able to organize the storage areas in a fully efficient manner due to the lack of trained personnel and the persistent shortage of materials-handling equipment.[83] For example, in 1952 the ERG/MAT had only eleven forklifts. The number of forklifts grew to twenty-three in 1953 and thirty-one in 1954, but remained only about one-half the normal requirement. Furthermore, as the war progressed consumption increased and the corresponding increase in stocks required exceeded the rate at which additional storage areas became available.[84] Thus, the total amount of covered storage available was never actually sufficient, although by 1954 there were 807,000 square feet of covered storage and 1,410,754 square feet of open storage available.[85]

The ERG/MAT was the focal point for the receipt and onward distribution of weapons, vehicles, and other equipment to the French Union forces in Indochina. Some indication of the increased depot workload occasioned by the higher tempo of operations and consequent higher consumption of materiel after 1951 is shown in table 4.4.

The Maintenance of Weapons, Vehicles, and Other Equipment

The maintenance of weapons, vehicles, and other equipment was another of the major functions of the DIRMAT FTEO and one of the most complex and difficult to accomplish. Rigid regulations and procedures, the persistent shortages of trained personnel and repair parts, the great variety of types of equipment, heavy equipment usage in a difficult terrain and climate, the wide geographical distribution of materiel, and a steady increase in the number of items to be maintained all contributed to problems in providing adequate maintenance service to the French Union forces in Indochina. The necessity of providing mobile maintenance services for combat forces in the field, the requirement to support the development of the *Services du Matériel* in the newly formed armies of the Associated States, and the special maintenance demands of river craft and light observation aircraft further compounded the problems. That the DIRMAT FTEO achieved as much as it did under the circumstances was a minor miracle.

The First Indochina War was fought with arms and equipment designed for a war in Europe rather than in the tropical climate and terrain of southeast Asia. The effect of high temperatures and high humidity on packaging, textiles, and radios and other electronic equipment significantly reduced the performance and life span of some equipment and increased the demand for those items. Many improvements and modifications to equipment were introduced to overcome the special climatic and operating conditions in Indochina. Some of these modifications resulted from the formal research and development review activity of the Technical Section of the DIRMAT FTEO and of the SM in metropolitan France, but many were the result of individual soldier initiative.

Despite their great variety and often advanced age, most of the weapons, vehicles, and other equipment available in Indochina gave good service. But some small arms and other infantry equipment had problems resulting from inherent defects, inadequate maintenance, or climate-related deterioration and required replacement or substantial modification. The standard French infantry rifle, the MAS 36, was frequently criticized for its weight, low rate of fire, and lack of accuracy, but still had to be used.[86] Some vehicles had to be modified to provide additional protection against mines and small arms fire and to permit the installation and operation of automatic weapons, such as the .50-caliber machine gun. The DIRMAT FTEO attempted whenever possible to satisfy the requests of the combat units for new items or modifications to existing equipment. Some of the new items were manufactured locally and achieved a degree of success. Particularly effective and well-received were the multiple grenade launcher for the MAS 36 rifle, the "My Tho" boat made of wood with a jeep engine, and the Type BIB-54 lifejacket.[87]

Like all other DIRMAT FTEO activities, the maintenance services were organized for the most part on a territorial basis, although some provisions were made for the mobile maintenance support of combat forces in the field. The familiar pattern of five echelons of maintenance was also followed, as shown in figure 4.5. First-echelon maintenance involved inspection, cleaning, and minor adjustments carried out by the equipment operator, and second-echelon maintenance was performed at the unit level and involved recovery, evacuation, inspection, trouble-shooting, and some replacement of parts and assemblies. Third-echelon maintenance in Indochina was carried out by the direct support units of the DIRMAT FTEO and involved recovery, evacuation, inspection, replacement of major parts and assemblies, and the repair of some assemblies carried out in fixed maintenance facilities or by mobile maintenance teams. Items submitted for third-echelon maintenance were generally returned to the using unit after they were repaired. Fourth-echelon maintenance involved the systematic repair and rebuild of equipment in general support of the third-echelon maintenance units

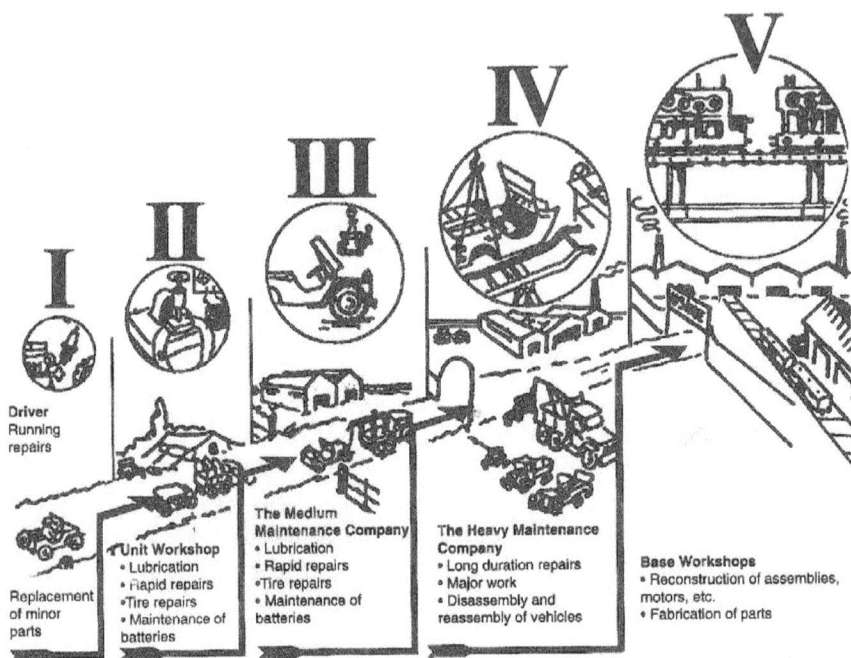

Figure 4.5. The Five Echelons of Maintenance. ("La Mission du Matériel en Indochine," *Caravelle*, 258 [November 26, 1950]: 9.)

and was generally carried out in fixed facilities by heavy maintenance units of the DIRMAT FTEO. Items repaired or rebuilt at the fourth echelon were returned to general stocks rather than to the original using unit. Fifth-echelon maintenance, also carried out by designated DIRMAT FTEO heavy maintenance units in fixed facilities, involved the complete renovation of major assemblies (such as motors or transmissions) for return to general stocks.

In the course of the First Indochina War, the DIRMAT FTEO added an additional echelon of maintenance as a means of reducing the excessive third echelon maintenance backlog. Called Third Echelon-Long Duration ("*3e échelon de longue durée*"), this intermediate category applied to vehicles and other equipment repairs that were expected to require more than thirty days to complete.[88] In such cases, the using unit lost control of the item to be repaired and was issued a replacement, as was the case when an item entered fourth-echelon maintenance. In another departure from normal procedures, the DIRMAT FTEO also authorized selected troop units to perform third-echelon maintenance. Some twenty-seven troop units, mostly armored formations and motor transport units of the *Train,* were authorized to perform third-echelon maintenance.

Table 4.5. Capabilities of Selected French Maintenance Units in Indochina

Type Unit		Echl.	Avg. No. of Items Supported	Avg. No. of Hrs. per Item	Avg. Monthly Repair Capability
Foreign Legion Medium Maintenance Company (CMRLE)		3rd	2,450	15–20	864 items 17,280 hrs.
Medium Maintenance Company (CMRM)	with military personnel	3rd	2,300	40–70	230 items 11,520 hrs.
	with civilian personnel	3rd	1,700	40–70	170 items 8,640 hrs.
Heavy Maintenance Company (CLRM)		3rd LDᵃ	1,400	70–90	140 items 13,400 hrs.
Foreign Legion Armored Engine Maintenance Company (CREBLE)		4th 5th	1,600	90–120	80 items 9,600 hrs.
Light Artillery Observation Aircraft Maintenance Section (SR ALOA)		4th 5th	30	ᵇ	Unknown

ᵃ LD = Longue Durée
ᵇ The 60-hour inspection for the L-19 required 13 maintenance hours versus 80 hours for the Morane 500. The 120-hour inspection for the L-19 required 22 maintenance hours versus 130 hours for the Morane 500.
Sources: Conference sur L'Organisation, 23–26, 30–32, and annexes IV and IV *bis*; DIRMAT FTEO, "Enseignements à tirer de la campagne d'Indochine," annex "Plan," chapter 2, pages 12–16, 24–25. The full French titles of the various types of maintenance units can be found in the glossary.

French maintenance units in Indochina were structured to handle various levels of maintenance for various types of materiel. The capabilities of selected maintenance units in Indochina are shown in table 4.5.

The principal determinants of the maintenance workload in Indochina were the quantity and the number of types of materiel that had to be supported at any given time. Throughout the First Indochina War the number of weapons, vehicles, and other pieces of equipment to be maintained grew steadily. The number of wheeled and armored vehicles, trailers, and boats alone increased four times in the seven years from 1947 to 1954, as shown in table 4.6. Fortunately, there was some corresponding reduction in the number of types of automotive items that had to be maintained. In 1949, the CEFEO fleet of twenty thousand vehicles was 73 percent U.S.-manufactured, 7 percent French-manufactured, and 20 percent British-manufactured, but by 1954 the British types had been eliminated, and the fleet of sixty thousand vehicles was 85 percent U.S. types and 15 percent French types.[89]

The requirement to support the newly formed Vietnamese, Cambodian, and Laotian national armies added substantially to the overall ordnance service workload of the DIRMAT FTEO. The DIRMAT FTEO had been responsible for all

Table 4.6. Number of Wheeled and Armored Vehicles, Trailers, and Boats in Indochina, 1947–1954

Type Items	1947	1948	1949	1950	1951	1952	1953	1954
Wheeled Vehicles	11,000	12,800	15,100	15,900	19,400	29,300	36,760	44,350
Armored Vehicles	1,000	1,200	1,650	1,950	2,340	3,170	3,610	3,590
Trailers	3,000	3,000	3,250	3,100	4,230	7,350	10,560	10,720
Boats	0	110	110	112	288	463	1,343	1,561
Total	**15,000**	**17,110**	**20,110**	**21,062**	**26,258**	**40,283**	**52,273**	**60,221**

Source: DIRMAT FTEO, "Enseignements à tirer de la campagne d'Indochine," annex "Plan," chapter 2, page 12, and tableau annexe 7. The total includes the following number of items belonging to the armies of the Associated States: 1951 = 1,500; 1952 = 7,500; 1953 = 15,000; and 1954 = 22,000.

maintenance for the armies of the Associated States before they began to form their own *Services du Matériel,* and would continue to be responsible for their fourth- and fifth-echelon maintenance support and all supplies until the cease-fire in July 1954. However, the effort to provide maintenance support for the newly formed combat units of the Associated States and to organize their maintenance services consumed even greater time and effort on the part of French maintenance officers and technicians.

The assumption by the DIRMAT FTEO of responsibility for the maintenance of watercraft and light observation aircraft also added significantly to the maintenance burden. By 1950 the number of watercraft (sampans, junks, "My Tho" boats, patrol craft, LCMs, and harbor craft) in use by the CEFEO had increased to the point that separate provisions for their maintenance were necessary. The number of watercraft to be maintained increased dramatically after 1950, reaching a total of 1,561 vessels in 1954, as shown in table 4.6.[90] The wide dispersion of watercraft and the rapid deterioration of hulls and underwater fittings due to the corrosive waters of the deltas posed significant maintenance problems.

Watercraft repair elements in several of the existing medium maintenance companies, and later one watercraft engine maintenance company at Saigon, were formed to support the CEFEO riverine fleet, but some repairs were performed by civilian firms, and there was some joint Army-Navy maintenance pooling for fourth- and fifth-echelon work.[91] The principal watercraft workshops were located at Nam Dinh, Hanoi, Haiphong, and Sept Pagodes in the north; Hue, Tourane (Da Nang), Nha Trang, and Savannakhet in the center; and Phnom Penh, Can Tho, My Tho, and Saigon in the south.[92]

Before January 1, 1953, maintenance for all French Army light observation aircraft in Indochina was provided by the French Air Force. The trusty L-4s (Piper Cubs) used in the beginning of the war were underpowered for a mountainous tropical country and were soon replaced by the French Morane 500, a notorious "hanger queen" that required many hours of maintenance.[93] Some improvement was noted when the Moranes began to be replaced by L-19s (Cessnas) received under the U.S. military aid program beginning in April 1954. To provide the necessary maintenance support, two Light Artillery Observation Maintenance Sections (*Sections de Réparation des Avions Légeres d'Observations d'Artillerie*, SR ALOA) were created in July 1953 and based at Cat Bi (Haiphong), Tourane, and Saigon.[94] Shortages of trained aircraft maintenance personnel, repair parts, and specialized tools contributed to the problems of maintaining the army's light observation aircraft in first-class flying condition.

The ever-increasing maintenance workload, coupled with shortages in trained personnel and repair parts, resulted in significant backlogs in the third-echelon repair shops. The establishment of the "*3e échelon de longue durée*" and the delegation of some third-echelon maintenance tasks to selected line units helped reduce the backlogs somewhat, as did the organization of additional mobile maintenance teams operating in the field with combat units.[95] The fourth- and fifth-echelon maintenance facilities under the control of the DIRMAT FTEO were an important source of renovated equipment for the French Union forces, but for some time they, too, remained poorly organized and were run mostly on a handicraft basis rather than by the use of assembly line methods. The situation improved significantly after the reorganization of the rebuild and renovation maintenance program in 1948 and 1949, but the DIRMAT FTEO continued to be plagued by a lack of spare parts and other necessary supplies. Nevertheless, the number of rebuilt vehicles and renovated assemblies produced by the maintenance units in Saigon, Phnom Penh, Hanoi, and Haiphong was substantial. Between 1948 and 1954, the number of vehicles rebuilt annually increased from 900 to 4,750, and the number of assemblies renovated increased from 1,000 to 13,200 annually.[96] In all, some 13,212 vehicles were rebuilt and some 62,500 assemblies were renovated during the same period.

The key to a good overall maintenance program is good operator maintenance and close supervision at the unit level. For the most part, first- and second-echelon maintenance of the French Union forces in Indochina was consistently very poor, as numerous observers attested.[97] The shortage of drivers and the lack of adequate driver training produced inadequate operator maintenance, hard usage, and frequent accidents that led to abnormal consumption of repair parts and premature washout of vehicles. On the whole, the ordnance specialists of the DIRMAT FTEO at the third, fourth, and fifth echelons performed as well as might be expected given the problems they faced. However, they did not escape criticism either.

American military observers frequently commented on the poor maintenance at all levels in Indochina, and one historian noted, "In the central maintenance depot near Saigon, thousands of tons of equipment lay scattered in disorder over 32 acres of open fields, where it was subject to the ravages of the humid South East Asian climate in which deterioration set in very rapidly."[98]

The Supply, Storage, and Distribution of Ammunition

The third major function of the DIRMAT FTEO was the supply of ammunition. At all echelons the resupply of munitions was a command function exercised through the *4e Bureau* of the General Staff, which issued the orders concerning the resupply of ammunition and coordinated the actions of the various operating organizations (DIRMAT ammunition agencies, transportation units, labor, etc.). The ammunition supply responsibilities of the DIRMAT FTEO were in fact carried out by the General Reserve Ammunition Depot (*Entrepôt de Réserve Générale des Munitions,* ERG-MU) and its subordinate staff and operating units in the various territories. The ERG-MU was responsible for the management of ammunition storage and stocks on hand, preparing plans for the ammunition service, tracking consumption, advising the commander on requirements and the establishment of stockage levels, and issuing ammunition stocks in accordance with the instructions received from the commander through the *4e Bureau.*[99] The ERG-MU was also responsible for explosive ordnance disposal services as well as the recovery of ammunition left by friendly and enemy forces on the battlefield and the maintenance and renovation of ammunition stocks.

The French ammunition system in Indochina was governed before the end of 1952 by the *Instruction sur le Ravitaillement en Munitions* of May 1, 1925, concerning the regulation of the munitions service in time of peace in the colonies. Subsequently, the *Instruction* of February 7, 1930, was applied in early 1953, but was quickly superceded by the *Instruction sur le Ravitaillement en Munitions en Indochine* of March 11, 1953.[100] In accordance with the *Instruction* of March 11, 1953, the general reserve ammunition depots were managed and operated by the ERG-MU and its subordinate ammunition companies. The 1st Munitions Company (*1e Cie Mu*) at Saigon managed the general reserve and principal territorial ammunition depots in south and central Viet Nam, the Central Highlands, Cambodia, and Laos. The 3rd Munitions Company (*3e Cie Mu*) in Hanoi managed the principal ammunition depots in Tonkin other than those of the Tonkin Operational Base (*Base Opérationnelle du Tonkin,* BOTK), which were managed by the 2nd Munitions Company (*2e Cie Mu*). The ammunition companies were organized with a headquarters detachment and six ammunition detachments, each capable of living and working independently, and were composed of specialists who oversaw the common labor made available by the commander for ammunition operations.[101] The transport available to each detachment was limited to that necessary for internal depot operations, and the general movement of ammunition was handled by transportation resources controlled by the territorial commander. The ERG-MU also controlled the "principal depots" in each of the territorial commands. Each territorial command also operated a number of secondary "sector" depots and, as the tactical situation required, might establish temporary "operational" depots in proximity to the combat units being supported. Combat units established and operated temporary ammunition dumps as required to support ongoing operations.

The changing nature of operations caused monthly ammunition expenditure levels to fluctuate, but in general there was a steady rise in consumption from 1951 to the end of the war: from fifteen hundred tons per month in 1951 to six thousand tons per month in 1954.[102] The consumption of ammunition was only loosely related to the number of weapons of various types in service at any given time. The number of fixed (positional, or fortress) and field artillery pieces in service in Indochina rose from 468 in 1951 to 693 on August 1, 1954, but the number of rounds fired increased from 331,762 in 1951 to 792,690 up to August 1, 1954.[103] In 1954, the French expended four times as many 105 mm artillery shells as they did in 1951, although the number of guns had increased only one and one-half times in the same period.

The majority of all the ammunition stored in Indochina was stored in the general reserve ammunition depots controlled by the ERG-MU.[104] In late 1952, the capacity of those facilities amounted to some 45,200 tons, the bulk of which was in four depots in Tonkin (16,200 tons at Kien An I and II, Ciments Fondus, and Do Son) and three depots in Cochinchina (17,600 tons at Khanh Hoi, Tan Tuy Ha, and Phu Tho). An additional 7,000 tons of storage capacity was available in depots in North Viet Nam (Gia Lam, Citadelle, Concession, Hai Duong, Fort Annamite, Nam Dinh, and Port Wallut) operated by the SM but not counted as part of the general reserve.

On January 1, 1953, the ERG-MU had stocks on hand of only 42,000 tons, but plans called for a 30,000-ton increase in the first few months of the year. Accordingly, plans were made to accommodate the additional tonnage by the creation of one or two new depots to serve Middle Laos (Seno and Wattay near Vientiane), the expansion of the depot at Tan Tuy Ha by 10,000 tons, the expansion of the Phu Tho depot, the placement in service of a new depot at Go Vap (7,650 tons), and the creation of a depot at Cap St.-Jacques (Vung Tau). By July 1, 1953, however, only the expansion at Tan Tuy Ha and the placement in service of Go Vap (only 6,850 tons) had been accomplished, giving the ERG-MU a total general reserve storage capacity of approximately 72,000 tons. On the same date the ammunition stocks controlled by the ERG-MU reached 75,000 tons, and an additional 45,000 tons were expected in the second half of 1953. Thus, additional expansions were planned to bring the total ERG-MU ammunition storage capacity to 80,000 tons by January 1, 1954, at which time the stocks on hand reached a total of some 83,000 tons. Ammunition stocks evacuated from Tonkin after the cease-fire in July 1954 were distributed among existing depots and by the creation of temporary depots and storage areas.

Ammunition consumption was monitored by the commander at each level by means of reviewing the stockage levels reported at the end of each month. Other than for items declared in short supply by the *commandant en chef,* the territorial commanders were free to determine the consumption and stockage levels for their commands within established limits. In gross terms, the *Instruction* of March 11, 1953, provided for a stockage level of twenty days' consumption for North Viet Nam; twenty-five days' consumption for the Northern Zone of central Viet Nam; thirty-five to forty days' consumption for South Viet Nam, the Central Highlands, and the Southern Zone of central Viet Nam; and forty-five to sixty days' consumption for Cambodia and Laos.[105] Some adjustments were possible. For example, the authorized stockage level for the Northern Zone of central Viet Nam was increased by 25 percent at the end of each summer to account for the isolation of the depot at Dong Hoi during the rainy season. For ammunition items that for various reasons could not be included in the prescribed general stockage level, the ERG-MU in Saigon maintained one-quarter of the general reserve and the BOTK and the general reserve depots of the territories stocked the remainder. Except for the depots in Tonkin, a safety level of one-sixth of the prescribed stockage level was maintained and released only in an emergency.

General reserve ammunition stockage levels rose steadily from 15,000 tons in 1951 to 37,000 tons in 1952, but jumped significantly to 83,000 tons by the end of 1953 due to the increasing intensity and changing nature of operations in Indochina.[106] The level fell precipitously from 83,000 to 53,000 tons between December 1953 and March 1954, due principally to issues of ammunition to support Dien Bien Phu and the operations in Laos and the Highlands and low receipts from overseas (only 7,500 tons from the United States), before rising again between May 1954 and the cease-fire to some 91,700 tons.

For most types of munitions, reserve stocks remained at a comfortable level through the war, but several types, notably 7.62 mm cartridges; concussion, fragmentation, and tear gas hand grenades; 60 mm and 81 mm mortar illumination rounds; and pyrotechnics of all types, were in perpetual short supply.[107] From time to time, certain types of munitions—particularly hand grenades, rockets, and fuzes—proved unreliable and caused numerous accidents. Thus their issue and use were suspended for safety reasons.[108]

The distribution of ammunition was regulated by the consumption rates and tables of allowances prescribed in the *Instruction* of March 11, 1953, and was characterized by decentralization and flexibility of operations. Ammunition resupply was carried out primarily at the territorial level, and ammunition resupply operations were decentralized to the maximum extent possible in order to reduce the distance to supported units and the exposure of ammunition convoys to Viet Minh action. The general reserve depots were replenished periodically with munitions received from overseas, primarily from France and the United States. The ERG-MU controlled the distribution, acting as a regulator for general reserve munitions. From the general reserve depots ammunition was distributed to the principal depots in the territorial commands controlled by the ERG-MU and from there to the secondary (sector) depots and on to the using units either directly or via operational depots in the field. Every effort was made to push munitions in complete units as far forward as possible toward the point of use to reduce the requirements for small, vulnerable storage sites and the need for additional personnel to handle the munitions. The operative concept was that each territorial commander should have on hand sufficient ammunition to replenish the basic loads of all units assigned to his command and to supplement the basic loads of units temporarily operating in his area. The actual physical distribution of ammunition was carried out by various modes of transport, including air transport when necessary, provided by the *commandant en chef* or a territorial commander from the transportation assets available to him.

Challenges Faced by the SM in Indochina

By far the largest and most complex of the French logistical services in Indochina, the DIRMAT FTEO faced many challenges. Active operations in a severe climate and over difficult terrain produced a heavy maintenance and ammunition resupply workload that fluctuated wildly. Shortages of personnel, and most particularly the chronic shortage of trained specialists, coupled with a hodgepodge of old and much-used equipment, significantly increased the problems of effectively maintaining the vehicles and other materiel of the French Union forces in fighting trim. The long distance from the sources of supply in France and the United States and antiquated regulations and procedures, some of which dated from 1902, only compounded the problems. However, the latter abated somewhat after January 1951, when the *commandant en chef,* Lieutenant General de Lattre, obtained the suppression of peacetime ordnance rules in favor of the simpler wartime procedures.[109]

The principal problems in ordnance supply were produced by the sheer number of line items required, the great variety of types and models of equipment, and the long order-ship times, especially for materiel obtained under the American military aid program (formally the Mutual Defense Assistance Program, MDAP).[110] Although the average order-ship time for MDAP materiel was about six months, some important items (for example, engines and assemblies for U.S.

vehicles) took two years to arrive. The receipt of equipment from metropolitan France usually required more than one year from the time the request was submitted.[111] As a consequence, high stock levels had to be maintained in Indochina despite the lack of covered storage areas and the lack of manpower. Moreover, by the time requests were filled, the requirements frequently no longer existed.

The requirement to support the various national armies placed a special additional burden on the already overworked SM. Cross-servicing agreements did little to ameliorate the problem in view of the slow development of the ordnance services of the Vietnamese, Cambodian, and Laotian armies. Until 1952, the national armies had few maintenance personnel of any type and were supported totally by the DIRMAT FTEO. From 1952 onward, they began to develop their own ordnance services with cadre furnished by the DIRMAT FTEO. The transfer of personnel and units from the DIRMAT FTEO to the national armies was completed by the end of 1953, but they remained dependent on the French for higher level maintenance and all supplies until the cease-fire.[112]

On the other hand, the French were relatively successful in reconciling the old territorial ordnance support system with the increasing demand for mobile maintenance and ordnance supply. Existing units were modified to provide mobile maintenance detachments and contact teams, and the creation of the Tonkin Operational Base (BOTK) did much to improve support of field forces in the main area of active operations. The DIRMAT FTEO also responded quite well to the new requirements for the support of light observation aircraft and watercraft. The overall assessment of the SM offered by the authors of the postwar report on lessons learned in Indochina was that "many of the imperfections noted were the result of one and the same cause, alas: our lack of means of all types, this lack being compensated for in a few areas only by foreign assistance without the over-all situation ever being able to attain the homogeneity which is characteristic of an efficient logistics system."[113]

Throughout the First Indochina War, the French and their Indochinese allies constantly sought to improve the organization and operation of their logistical service, and in some areas, notably transportation, they succeeded admirably. However, the authors of the official French report on the lessons of the war conceded: "The logistics of the war in Indochina were characterized as a constant search for remedies to situations that were as unfavorable as they were unstable. The solutions arrived at were, therefore, more often 'patch jobs' or even 'D systems' than the results of deliberate planning."[114] "D-system" was French Army slang derived from the verb *debrouiller*, meaning "to manage or shift for oneself." The logistical system of every army relies to a greater or lesser degree on scrounging, individual initiative, outright theft, and other "D-system" methods, but the French became masters of the art.

Overall, the French authorities, both at home and in Indochina, demonstrated an inability (or perhaps an unwillingness) to come to grips with the logistical problems of supporting a modern army engaged in heavy fighting against a determined and increasingly sophisticated enemy halfway around the world. For a while, peacetime regulations and a blasé contempt for the ability of the Viet Minh inhibited the search for viable solutions to the logistical problems inherent in the Indochina situation. However, French military leaders at lower levels in Indochina could not blame their misfortunes entirely on the parsimonious government at home and the lack of wisdom of the higher commanders. Almost every observer of the First Indochina War reported the lack of commitment, lackadaisical attitude, and sloppy performance of many of the officers and soldiers at the lowest levels. Of course, dedication and even heroism were to be found frequently, but on the whole the technical skill and massive amounts of modern war equipment available to the French Union forces could not compensate for the lack of enthusiasm and discipline, qualities that were so prominently displayed by their Viet Minh opponents. Once it was recognized that the Viet Minh were indeed capable of achieving their objective of driving out the French colonial regime, it was almost too late to devise effective means of countering them.

5

Viet Minh Logistical Doctrine and Organization

The First Indochina War ended in July 1954 in a clear victory for the Viet Minh. That victory was due in no small part to the successful development by the Viet Minh of an effective and efficient logistical system to support their main combat forces and the large number of regional and local guerrillas that comprised the Viet Minh armed forces. Starting with almost nothing, in less than eight years the Viet Minh built combat forces and logistical support organizations that proved able to defeat their French Union opponents. The Viet Minh had the unusual advantage of building a logistical system nearly from scratch and focusing its development on the immediate requirements of the physical and military situation. The resulting logistical system, designed and operated by a very small number of trained military logistical personnel, was characterized by comparatively low requirements; a reliance on outside sources of supply for arms, ammunition, and heavy equipment; skillful exploitation of captured materiel and local sources of supply; numerous well-dispersed logistical facilities; and numerous supply routes employing all modes of transport except air transport. Although extremely lean and mobile, the Viet Minh regular forces did have substantial logistical requirements. Food, ammunition, and a minimum level of other supplies were required to keep the *Chu Luc* units in the field for extended campaigns. They did not "live off the land," as is often alleged, but neither were they tied down by an excessive reliance on motor transport and inflexible routes. Throughout the war the Viet Minh leaders found that their most difficult challenges involved the acquisition, storage, and distribution of supplies for their combat forces. They met these challenges with determination, innovation, and flexibility.

One striking characteristic of the Viet Minh logistical system was the degree to which manpower was substituted successfully for mechanization in the distribution of supplies. The Viet Minh relied on large numbers of civilian laborers and porters for the production of food and other military supplies; the construction of roads and logistical facilities; the manufacture and repair of arms, ammunition, vehicles, and other equipment; and transportation services. Lines of communication were constructed and maintained using little equipment and many coolies, and the comparative lack of mechanized transport was made up for by the extensive use of porters and animal transport particularly well-suited to the climate and terrain of the Indochina theater of operations.

By far the most salient and consequential characteristic of the Viet Minh logistical system was its ability to adapt to the environment and to changing operational conditions. In 1946, the French Union forces had an overwhelming superiority in manpower, logistical support, and technological sophistication, but by 1954 the Viet Minh proved themselves more flexible in meeting the existing environmental and military logistical challenges. While the French logistical system remained comparatively static over the course of the eight-year struggle, the Viet Minh logistical system continually improved in effectiveness due to three main factors: continuing organizational improvements, the application of cumulative experience, and increasing Chinese Communist support. Under conditions of tremendous stress it evolved from a "cottage industry" capable at best of supporting a few thousand guerrillas to a sophisticated organization able to supply large conventional forces engaged in nearly continuous combat operations.[1] As one historian has noted, "Although the Vietminh logistic system lacked the flexibility conferred on the French by the use of air power, provided the distance was right, overall their supply system was more flexible and better suited to the terrain."[2] The triumph of the Viet Minh in the decisive battle of Dien Bien Phu was a clear demonstration of how a relatively small, primitive, and manpower-intensive logistical system, well-adapted to its physical and military environment, could outperform a larger and more sophisticated system that failed to adapt successfully to the conditions under which it had to function.

Viet Minh Logistical Doctrine

Logistical considerations permeated all aspects of Viet Minh military doctrine.[3] The offensive actions of the Viet Minh were largely directed at their opponent's logistical system, and the offensive employment of the Viet Minh regular, regional, and local forces was based in large part on their logistical needs and capabilities at any given time. Although derived in part from the Marxist-Leninist canon and the writings of Mao Tse-tung, the logistical doctrine of the Viet Minh was in the main a homegrown product based on the military thought and writings of the Viet Minh military commander, General Vo Nguyen Giap.[4] The guiding strategic philosophy of the Viet Minh was that of *dau tranh* ("struggle"), the sustained application of total military and nonmilitary force over long periods of time in pursuit of the final objective. The prospect of a drawn-out war was actually welcomed by Giap, who noted, "Only a long term war could enable us to utilise to the maximum our political trump cards, to overcome our material handicap and to transform our weakness into strength . . . to build up our strength during the actual course of fighting."[5]

The most notable characteristic of Giap's military thought was the proposition that a war of national liberation, such as the Viet Minh were fighting against the French, would be a long-term conflict in which innumerable small victories of the weaker insurgent forces against a stronger enemy would eventually produce the sought-for victory. The emphasis in Viet Minh logistical doctrine on secure base areas, on the maximum utilization of resources taken from the enemy by stealth or on the battlefield, and on general logistical austerity stemmed from the basic premise that the war conducted by the insurgents would be an extended war carried out with scant resources.

The other principal feature of Giap's military thought was the proposition that the war fought by the insurgents should proceed in three main stages. In each phase, the primary burden would be borne by armed insurgent forces of a size, composition, armament, and organization suitable for the type of combat characteristic of that particular phase. As the military analyst and historian Edgar O'Ballance has pointed out, the three-phase Viet Minh strategy was closely linked to the logistical capabilities and vulnerabilities of the Viet Minh forces at various stages.[6] Thus the first phase of "defensive" or "guerrilla" war would be fought principally by lightly armed guerrilla forces that would draw their sustenance in part from the countryside and in part from materiel captured from the enemy. Such forces would require only a small and relatively unsophisticated logistical "tail." The guerrilla forces best suited to the first stage would continue to operate in the second ("equilibrium" or "protracted warfare") stage, but they would be increasingly reinforced by more heavily armed and better trained regular forces, including supporting arms and services, which would begin to demand the formation of formal logistical support methods and organizations to ensure their ability to carry out increasingly large-scale operations. In the third and final ("general counteroffensive" or "mobile warfare") stage, guerrillas would also continue to operate, but the principal burden would be borne by the regular insurgent forces, armed and equipped to meet the enemy in full-scale mobile conventional warfare. Such forces obviously would require the support of a well-developed logistical system capable of providing a full range of supply, maintenance, and transportation services. As Giap himself put it: "The army is organised in order to defeat the enemy, therefore the formation of the army must meet the demand of the realities in fighting, and be in harmony with the strategic guiding principle and the principle of fighting in each stage of the war. The organisation must be in line with our possibilities in equipment and supply, based on the national economy and in harmony with the practical conditions of the battlefields in our country."[7]

One of the philosophical underpinnings of Viet Minh as well as Chinese Communist logistical doctrine was the idea that deficiencies in arms and equipment could be overcome by the will and enthusiasm of the soldier as an individual and of the army as a group. As formulated by Mao Tse-tung, human, spiritual, and political factors, rather than weapons and technology, are the decisive factors in a people's war.[8] From this principle stemmed the Viet Minh emphasis on indoctrination, discipline, training, and morale that served them so well in their successful struggle against the French. It was also the concept that underlay and inspired the tremendous physical efforts of thousands of Viet Minh soldiers and porters to carry tons of supplies on their backs hundreds of miles under French air attack to meet the needs of the front-line combatants. As General Giap expressed it: "Our Party educated the army to develop the fine nature of a revolutionary army to increase the political supremacy in order to make good our weakness in equipment. Hence our army succeeded, with inferior arms, in defeating the enemy who was many times stronger in weapons. It has become an extremely fine tradition of our army—to vanquish modern weapons with an heroic spirit."[9] Eventually, the more perceptive of the French commanders in Indochina came to understand the power of the human spirit to overcome material obstacles. Lieutenant General Lionel Max Chassin, a former commander in chief of the French air forces in the Far East, observed, "Even in this century of materialism and mechanization, it is always the spirit which rules, morale which wins battles."[10]

Logistical considerations, as well as the philosophy of "man-over-machine," played a key role in forming even the tactical doctrine of the Viet Minh. For example, the Viet Minh tactical principle of "close-range combat" was not only designed to avoid the effects of French supporting fires by "hugging" the French forces closely in battle, but also served to compensate for the technological inferiority of the Viet Minh forces and to economize on ammunition. In close combat, "the objective becomes larger, more clearly visible and time of fire is more prompt," and in close combat the plain and simple methods best suited to the technologically unsophisticated Viet Minh soldiers with minimal training could offset the French advantages of airpower, artillery, and mechanization.[11] As the author of one Viet Minh document expressed it: "Under the present circumstances, since we lack scientific means, we must have recourse solely to our manual skill, to our competence. To win success, we have only one method at our disposal: combat at close range."[12]

Similarly, tactical doctrine was formulated in such a manner as to relieve some of the stress on the Viet Minh logistical system. As the author of the Viet Minh document just cited noted:

> Our ammunition is limited in quantity. If we fire at long range, we shall have to fire a great quantity of ammunition to be able to destroy the enemy. We shall go against the conception that the imperialist troops have with respect to utilization of the weapons, which consists in applying a powerful density of projectiles so as to be able to place one shot in the target. We shall, on the contrary, imbue ourselves with the following principle: instead of using 100 cartridges of which only one reaches the

target, we must try to obtain the same result with a single cartridge. In this manner we can save 99 cartridges.[13]

Viet Minh Logistical Organization

Before the formation of the Viet Minh regular divisions and the beginning of large-scale Chinese Communist aid in 1950, the Viet Minh logistical system was generally small and decentralized.[14] It grew in size and sophistication with the combat forces it was designed to support, and in general a careful balance was maintained so that the available resources were properly distributed between the combat and service forces. Although capable of supporting an ever-increasing regular army and growing regional and popular forces, the Viet Minh logistical system itself remained quite small in terms of the number of military personnel assigned. Instead, the system relied on large numbers of civilians to perform necessary logistical functions, particularly the movement of supplies from one place to another. Such civilians were dragooned for a particular operation or period of time and did not have to be maintained during periods of inactivity. Already by 1950, the Viet Minh armed forces, particularly the *Chu Luc,* were no longer simple guerrilla bands able to live off the land and take their arms and ammunition from their enemy. By 1953, the *Chu Luc* was in fact a conventional regular force of over one hundred thousand men in seven divisions equipped with artillery, antiaircraft guns, radios, and trucks and supported by considerable numbers of regional and local guerrillas. Such an army required a well-articulated logistical system with established procedures for the acquisition, storage, and distribution of supplies and the service units necessary to conduct supply operations efficiently and with some degree of speed.

Viet Minh operational plans were generally worked out well in advance to permit the necessary logistical preparations, including the recruitment of porters and the establishment of stockpiles. The logistical requirements for a given operation depended on such factors as the size and type of Viet Minh forces to be employed, the distance from established bases, the plan of maneuver, and the strength and disposition of the French Union forces.[15] In general, Viet Minh logistical requirements were quite low compared to those of the opposing French Union forces. At the same time, supply discipline was high, thereby further reducing the need for excessive amounts of supplies. Wherever possible, manpower was substituted for technology—although toward the end of the First Indochina War the Viet Minh possessed substantial numbers of weapons and vehicles that consumed considerable quantities of fuel and ammunition and that required periodic maintenance by skilled technicians.

The overall number of Viet Minh personnel involved in logistical operations is not known, but given the extensive use of manpower rather than mechanization the number was probably quite large. Viet Minh authorities could draw upon most of the physically fit adult population under their control for porters, construction work, and general labor, but the principal pool of manpower for such tasks was the *Dan Quan* (Popular Forces). The size of the *Dan Quan* fluctuated from time to time, increasing during the campaign season. For example, the *Dan Quan* numbered some 70,000 men and women in April 1952 but expanded to over 120,000 in the summer of 1952, and in July 1954 French intelligence analysts estimated that the *Dan Quan* numbered some 114,000. Although unskilled labor was readily available, the Viet Minh had very few trained personnel to carry out technically demanding logistical tasks. The shortage of skilled and experienced logistical staff officers and technicians was a constant problem that was solved only by on-the-job experience and some Chinese Communist training courses.

The General Supply Directorate

The General Supply Directorate (GSD) of the Ministry of National Defense was responsible for all aspects of the logistical support of the Viet Minh armed forces, including liaison with the Chinese Communist agencies providing support to the Viet Minh and logistical planning for specific campaigns.[16] Led by its chief, Tran Dai Nghia, the GSD was organized with five principal branches, each of which was responsible for a particular logistical function, as shown in figure 5.1.[17] Although the details are not entirely clear, it seems that the branches of the GSD corresponded to what in the French Union forces were the various separate supply services (*Intendance, Service du Matériel, Train,* etc.). The offices of the various branches of the GSD were located for most of the war northwest of Hanoi in the quadrilateral Tuyen Quang–Bac Kan–Thai Nguyen–Phu Tho.[18]

The Food Supply Branch managed all aspects of the production, collection, storage, and distribution of food, including the rationing of food for both military units and civilians and the establishment of food storage facilities in the base areas, in operational areas, and along key lines of communication. The Arms Supply and Workshops Branch was responsible for the acquisition, storage, distribution, and maintenance of all weapons and also oversaw the scattered, mostly small-scale arms production facilities operated by the Viet Minh. The Ammunition Supply Branch controlled the storage and distribution of munitions received from Communist China and other outside sources and managed the small Viet Minh facilities that produced limited quantities of grenades, mines, and small arms ammunition. The Medical Supply Branch was responsible for the evacuation and treatment of Viet Minh casualties and for the acquisition, storage, and distribution of medical supplies. Until very late in the war, the Viet Minh gave medical service only a very low priority. Trained medical personnel were few and even the most basic medical supplies were in short supply.[19] The largest of the GSD's branches was the Transportation Branch, which coordinated the recruitment and

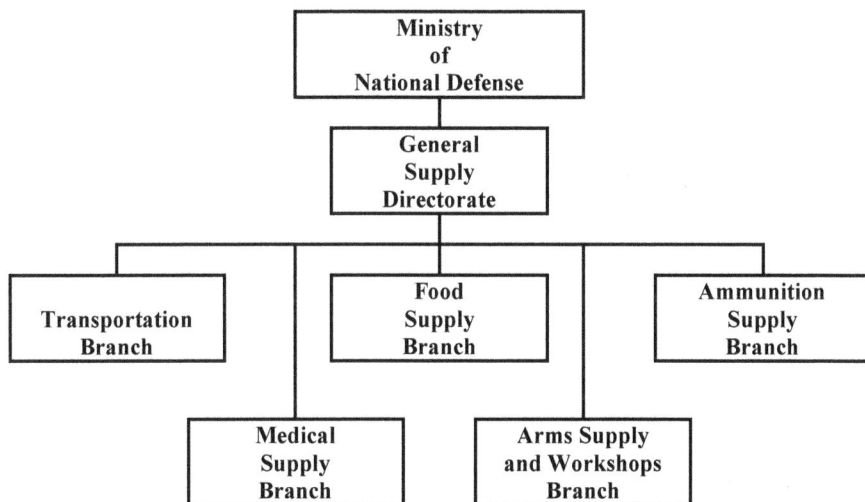

Figure 5.1. Viet Minh General Supply Directorate. (Fall, "Indochina—The Last Year of the War," 5 [figure 3]; Tanham, *Communist Revolutionary Warfare,* 38–39.)

employment of porters, the maintenance and employment of motor vehicles, and the movement of supplies by all modes.

The acquisition, storage, and issue of supplies were coordinated at the highest level of the Viet Minh armed forces by the five branches of the GSD. The plans and decisions of the GSD were implemented by Viet Minh logistical staff officers and operational logistics units at lower echelons. Staff officers at lower levels often lacked formal technical training but gained considerable practical experience in logistical operations in the course of the war. The number of standing operational logistics units in the Viet Minh was quite small, the usual practice being to assemble temporary groupings of laborers, porters, and other unskilled personnel for a specific operation or campaign. Apparently, only a relatively small number of trained supply personnel were needed to manage the depot areas and to supervise the large number of coolies involved in the receipt, storage, and issue of supplies. Supply personnel were also assigned, again in relatively small numbers, down to battalion level, although the regiment was the lowest level at which formal reserves were maintained and supply dumps established.

Viet Minh Base Areas

Viet Minh political and military doctrine stressed the importance of secure base areas from which political and military offensives could be launched against an enemy and which could serve as a secure retreat in case of reverses. The Viet Minh

concept of creating a secure rear area went well beyond a narrow military interpretation and included ensuring the political loyalty and active cooperation of the
population as well as the general economic development of the area. Some idea of
the importance to the Viet Minh of secure rear bases can be gleaned from General
Giap's *People's War, People's Army,* in which he wrote:

> One cannot speak of the armed struggle and the building of the revolu-
> tionary armed forces without mentioning the problem of the rear. This
> is an important problem of strategic significance and a decisive factor to
> the outcome of armed struggle and in the building of the armed forces.
> . . . throughout the Resistance War, the safeguarding of resistance bases
> and the consolidation of the rear were considered by our Party as of the
> utmost importance. Because they wanted to crush our leading organ and
> smash our Resistance, the French colonialists used every scheme to raze
> our resistance bases, but they suffered defeat after defeat and finally col-
> lapsed. Our armymen and people fought heroically to protect the Viet
> Bac resistance base—the main one in the Resistance War.[20]

The principal base area of the Viet Minh throughout the First Indochina War
was located in the six provinces of the Viet Bac Autonomous Region in the highlands north and northwest of Hanoi.[21] The Viet Bac included the provinces of Bac
Kan, Cao Bang, Lang Son, Ha Giang, Tuyen Quang, and Thai Nguyen. After 1949,
Communist China constituted in effect an enormous and secure rear base for the
Viet Minh, and from 1954 to 1975 all of North Viet Nam constituted the secure
rear base for the Communist guerrillas operating in South Viet Nam. The locations of the principal Viet Minh base areas are shown on map 5.1.

The Viet Bac offered defensible terrain, limestone caves for offices, workshops,
and storage areas, good concealment from aerial observation, and a friendly population. Established by Giap's Viet Minh guerrillas, the Viet Bac was already secure
and well-developed as a supply, training, and rest area by the end of 1944.[22] It subsequently became the major Viet Minh stronghold, and although raided periodically by the French Union forces, the Viet Bac remained under Viet Minh control
throughout the war. The government of the Democratic Republic of Viet Nam as
well as the headquarters and logistical agencies of the Viet Minh armed forces were
located in the Viet Bac, and it was the home base of the Viet Minh regular forces.
The main offices of the various branches of the General Supply Directorate as well
as most of the major Viet Minh storage areas were thus secure and had easy access
to the transportation routes coming from China. Although the locations of many
of the depots are known, as are the types of supplies they contained, their capacities
are generally unknown. It was to the Viet Bac that Ho Chi Minh and his followers
retreated after their temporary setback by the French in December 1946. It was in the

Map 5.1. Viet Minh Base Areas in Indochina, 1945–1954.

Viet Bac that the regular divisions of the *Chu Luc* were raised and trained, and from the Viet Bac that the important Viet Minh offensives were subsequently launched.

The other main Viet Minh base area, known as the South Delta Base, was somewhat smaller and less important than the Viet Bac base. Located in the hills and jungles of Thanh Hoa, Nghe An, and Ha Tinh Provinces south of the Red River delta in northern Annam, the South Delta Base was particularly important to the collection and distribution of rice from Thanh Hoa Province.[23] Other much smaller and less important Viet Minh bases were scattered throughout Indochina. The more important bases in Cochinchina were located in the swampy Plain of Reeds (*Plaine des Joncs*) northwest of Saigon, Thu Dau Mot Province stretching north of Saigon to the Cambodian border, Baria Province on the coast, and the entire southern tip of Indochina south of the Bassac River, otherwise known as the Ca Mau peninsula.[24]

In addition to the major base areas, the Viet Minh created a network of temporary operational bases, camps, workshops, and supply dumps throughout Indochina. Many of these facilities, particularly the supply dumps and workshops, were located in caves or other underground facilities, and almost all of them were in mountainous and forested areas that the French Union forces found difficult to penetrate. Some of these smaller supply dumps and workshops could even be moved on relatively short notice.

Throughout the First Indochina War the Viet Minh were conscientious and adept at camouflaging their administrative and logistical facilities, both the larger base areas and the forward headquarters and supply dumps. Although speaking specifically of Viet Minh guerrilla installations in Cambodia, one lecturer in 1951 described the temporary Viet Minh facilities typically found throughout Indochina during the First Indochina War:

> Installed in regions difficult of access (most often in forests), the camps are scattered over a large area and one does not discover them until one gets within a few dozen meters. There are no solid constructions; the huts are made of straw with a more or less elaborate arrangement of beds, rifle racks, ammunition dumps, and storehouses for rice. The various straw huts are used for special purposes: for offices, sleeping rooms, kitchens, hospitals, etc. In case of an enemy attack (which is generally reported in time by their agents), the Viet Minh abandon the camp after having camouflaged the important materiel in traps covered subsequently with earth and carefully camouflaged.[25]

Viet Minh Supply Operations

Very little is known of the detailed inner workings of the Viet Minh supply system beyond the obvious facts that the system was quite simple, depended on outside sources of supply, and handled a limited number of line items. It is clear that the regular Viet Minh forces had to be supplied with clothing, camp equipment, vehicles, petroleum, radios and associated gear, medical supplies, and small quantities of engineer supplies and barrier materials as well as the three principal items of concern: food, arms, and ammunition. The regional and popular forces also required food at only a slightly lower rate than the *Chu Luc,* but their requirements for all other types of supplies were considerably lower due to the much reduced allocations of weapons and ammunition. Some regional force units were provided with uniforms, but the popular forces usually wore the ubiquitous áo bà ba (black pajamas).

The Viet Minh requisition and issue system probably worked in much the same way as that of the Chinese Communist army. Staff elements determined the quantities of supply by type required for a given operation or noncombat period. The supply agencies (the five branches of the General Supply Directorate) then saw to it that the necessary supplies were stockpiled along the expected route of march or in proximity to the area of operations. Combat units, which normally carried with them only small quantities of supplies, generally just those needed for a given operation or a given period in garrison, then drew supplies as required from the established dumps. Except perhaps for food and ammunition, resupply during actual combat was rather rare; more commonly units were refitted at the end of a battle or campaign season. The Viet Minh were inveterate record keepers and no doubt a variety of requisition forms, issue documents, and periodic status reports were used to regulate the issue of supplies of all kinds.

Viet Minh Supply Requirements

Attempts to calculate the supply rate for the Viet Minh forces is fraught with difficulties, and such estimates remain largely theoretical. One estimate puts the annual requirements for a 300,000-man Viet Minh army at just over 108,775 tons of supplies (107,000 tons of rice, 670 tons of salt, 555 tons of quartermaster supplies, 550 tons of petroleum products, and a small amount of engineer materiel).[26] The daily supply requirements of the individual Viet Minh soldier were considerably less than those of the French Union soldier, perhaps even only one-third as much. It has been estimated that at the time of Dien Bien Phu, the daily supply requirement of the Viet Minh soldier was around 3.3 kilograms per man per day versus 9 kilograms per man per day for the French Union soldier.[27]

Rations

Other than arms and ammunition, the principal logistical concern of the Viet Minh was the supply of food. Although the diet of the Viet Minh soldier was limited by Western standards, the total quantities of rice, salt, and other food-stuffs required by the Viet Minh armed forces were considerable. The normal diet of rice and salt was supplemented whenever possible by *nuoc mam* (a potent fish sauce very high in protein), fruits and vegetables, vegetable oils, and small quantities of salted fish. Sugar, tea, eggs, poultry, and meat were scarce. French control of the major rice-producing areas resulted in some modifications of the diet of the Viet Minh, including the substitution of corn, potatoes, and cassava for rice.[28]

A detailed breakdown of the Viet Minh ration during the First Indochina War is not available, but the allowance for dry rice has been estimated at 750–800 grams (1.65–1.76 pounds) per day during combat operations.[29] At such rates, a regular Viet Minh infantry division with a nominal strength of ten thousand officers and men would require about 12 short tons of uncooked rice per day at the full (800 gram) consumption rate, or about 8.5 short tons per day at the reduced (750 gram) rate. Ten short tons of uncooked rice per day per division could thus be considered a realistic average on a yearly basis. Detailed estimates of the authorized ration for the Viet Cong soldier during the Second Indochina War are available and are probably quite close to the actual Viet Minh figures. In the period 1959–1964, the Viet Cong guerrilla in combat received a ration consisting of 750 grams of dry rice, 750 grams of seasonings (salt, *nuoc mam*, peppers, etc.), and 300 grams of vegetables, plus two kilograms per month of meat.[30] The authors of *Viet Cong Logistics* give the Viet Cong ration around 1967 as 1,983 grams (4,110 calories) per day, consisting primarily of dry rice (750 grams; 2,630 calories) and manioc (904 grams; 1,090 calories).[31] They also note that rice constituted about 40–50 percent of the weight and approximately 70 percent of the calories of the Viet Cong soldier's diet, state that Viet Cong porters received 1.2 kilograms of rice per day, and compare the Viet Cong soldier's daily allowance of 4,110 calories to the 3,955-calorie diet considered necessary for a growing boy.[32] Overall, the Viet Minh soldier was adequately fed, although local, temporary shortages of rice and the general lack of variety in the diet of the Viet Minh soldier did result in a high frequency of beriberi and other nutritional deficiency diseases that at times affected up to half of a unit's men.[33]

The Food Supply Branch of the General Supply Directorate was responsible for the overall coordination of the acquisition and distribution of rice and other food items to the Viet Minh forces in the field and in the base areas. However, the primary responsibility for the supply of rations lay with the unit commander at the company level and above.[34] The Viet Minh soldier of the First Indochina War habitually carried about three kilograms of rice (about four days' rations) in a long, narrow bag (the *boudin,* or sausage) looped around his neck.[35] His Viet Cong counterpart in the Second Indochina War normally carried two days of roasted rice and five days of normal (raw) rice in the same manner.[36] Normally, rice and other ration items were acquired as close as possible to the place where they would be consumed in order to minimize transport and storage problems. The required stockage level maintained by Viet Minh units from 1945 to 1954 is not known, but Viet Cong units between 1959 and 1967 normally maintained a ten- to thirteen-day supply of rice at the regimental level and a thirty-day supply at the division or regional rear services level.[37]

The quantity of rice allotted for daily consumption by each Viet Minh soldier was only part of the overall requirement since the Viet Minh regulars were normally paid in rice, thus providing them with a means of supporting their families or supplementing their own diet by the barter of rice for other commodities or its sale.[38] A Viet Minh battalion commander captured by the French alleged that the scale of payments included a basic allowance of 1.6 kilograms per day for each superior officer and political commissar and 1.2 kilograms per day for all other officers and soldiers, augmented by an additional monthly allowance of 9 kilograms for each superior officer and political commissar, 7 kilograms for each junior officer, and 2 kilograms for each soldier, plus an additional premium of 1 kilogram per month for each officer and soldier with over three years of service.[39] Viet Minh general officers received the equivalent of 25 kilograms of rice per day as pay.[40]

The acquisition and distribution of rice and other foodstuffs was a major problem for Viet Minh supply officers throughout the First Indochina War. Units of company size and larger utilized troops unfit for combat duty to cultivate crops and raise animals for the unit's own use.[41] The main area of operations for the *Chu Luc* was in northern Tonkin, not a major rice-producing area, and by February 1950 the French had gained control over most of the rice-producing areas of the Tonkin delta. The other principal rice-producing areas of Indochina were in Cochinchina, which was for the most part also under French control. The Viet Minh stronghold in the Trans-Bassac was a major rice-growing area, but the Viet Minh had no means of transporting the surplus of the Trans-Bassac to their regular combat units in Tonkin.

General Supplies and Petroleum Products

Viet Minh requirements for clothing and other general supplies and equipment were limited. An entire Viet Minh infantry division probably required only about thirty tons of clothing and other general supplies annually.[42] Each soldier of the *Chu Luc* probably received only one uniform and one pair of canvas shoes per year. Most carried some sort of canteen and a pouch for rations, extra ammunition, and personal items, but steel helmets and web gear were not common, although the characteristic Viet Minh pith helmet was ubiquitous. Viet Minh requirements for construction and barrier materials were also minimal. They used some barbed wire, but obtained the timber and other materials for the repair and construction of camps, bridges, and roads locally or did without. The Viet Minh apparently had little or no construction equipment (graders, dump trucks, rock crushers, etc.) and only limited amounts of hand tools such as saws, axes, picks, and shovels. Even with such minimal equipment the Viet Minh engineers, using large numbers of coolies, were able to accomplish a good deal.

Viet Minh requirements for gasoline and other petroleum products were also quite limited, being required mainly for the fleet of trucks used to move supplies from China to the Viet Minh rear depots. In May 1953, U.S. intelligence officers estimated that the amount of gasoline required for the Viet Minh forces was about forty-five tons per month.[43] That estimate was based on gasoline as the fuel for all Viet Minh trucks, although some of them were fueled with charcoal. No estimate could be made of the amounts of lubricants and other Class III items required. The only source of petroleum products for the Viet Minh, other than small amounts obtained by theft or capture from the French, was Communist China, and presumably the bulk of the gasoline and other petroleum products was loaded directly into the using vehicle at the Chinese end of the supply route rather than being stockpiled in the Viet Minh base areas in northern Tonkin.

Arms and Ammunition

The supply of arms and ammunition was a major preoccupation of Viet Minh logisticians and commanders. For most of the First Indochina War, the Viet Minh forces were equipped with a hodgepodge of captured or locally manufactured weapons. When the Democratic Republic of Viet Nam was formed in August 1945, the Viet Minh regular forces numbered some forty thousand men but had weapons for only about 75 percent of the troops.[44] In all, the armament available to the Viet Minh in August 1945 included around 34,000 rifles, 600 submachine guns, 700 other automatic weapons, 150 mortars, 50 light artillery pieces, and 12 armored vehicles.[45] Those weapons represented arms formerly held by the French colonial militia, stocks handed over by the Japanese to the Vietnamese, materiel parachuted to the Viet Minh by the Americans during World War II, and the greater part of the armament of the Japanese forces in Tonkin seized by the Nationalist Chinese and subsequently sold to the Viet Minh. Not only were these weapons insufficient for the needs of the growing Viet Minh regular forces, they were also a well-worn mix of American, British, French, German, Japanese, Chinese, and Russian models. General Giap later claimed that in late 1945 his forces were armed with at least sixteen different types of rifles, ranging from 1905 Russian models to new U.S. M1 Garands.[46] Aside from their lack of reliability, such an array of different weapons presented a significant problem in ammunition resupply by virtue of the mixture of calibers.

The only immediate options available for the acquisition of more arms and ammunition were to capture them from the French, purchase them on the open market in Hong Kong or Bangkok, or manufacture them in homegrown workshops. General Giap elected to pursue all three courses simultaneously, and by the time open conflict with the French broke out in December 1946, the Viet Minh regular forces numbered over sixty thousand men in Tonkin alone and had formed about fifty regiments of three battalions, each of which was armed with five hundred rifles, thirty submachine guns, fifteen other automatic weapons, and two or three mortars, and had grouped their heavy weapons in artillery units.[47] The French subsequently captured the arms of four or five battalions during the battle for Hanoi in late 1946, but the reversion of the Viet Minh to guerrilla warfare allowed them to economize on arms and ammunition.

Although the negotiations for a cease-fire between the French and the Viet Minh in 1947 came to naught, the French negotiating proposal gives some indication of French perceptions of Viet Minh resources at the time. Among the conditions offered by the French for a cessation of hostilities in early August 1947 was the proposal that in return for reductions in the French forces the Viet Minh should assemble and place under mixed Franco–Viet Minh control armaments totaling some 15,000 rifles, 550 submachine guns, 345 light machine guns and automatic rifles, 90 heavy machine guns, 31 mortars, and 18 radios.[48] The French proposal, presumably based on an estimate of what arms the Viet Minh did possess, also provided for the delivery to the mixed storage sites of 100 cartridges per rifle or submachine gun, 500 cartridges per automatic weapon, and 50 rounds per mortar. An equal amount of arms and ammunition were to be placed under joint control by November 1, 1947.

With the failure to reach a negotiated settlement with the French, the Viet Minh pressed forward with the organization and armament of military forces capable of carrying out General Giap's three-stage strategy. Until 1950, the principal means of acquiring additional arms and ammunition was to capture them from the French Union forces. Only with the advent of Chinese Communist support in 1950 were the Viet Minh able to begin standardizing their armament and to obtain heavy weapons, such as 105 mm howitzers and 37 mm antiaircraft guns. By the end of the war in July 1954, the Viet Minh regular forces were nearly as well-armed as their French opponents, with significant stocks of modern American- and Soviet-type small arms, automatic weapons, artillery, antiaircraft guns, and even a few tanks, and many of the Viet Minh weapons were newer than—and in many cases superior to—those available to the French.

The requirements and consumption rates for Viet Minh arms and ammunition are difficult to determine due to the lack of reliable experience data and authorization tables. One U.S. intelligence agency estimated the authorized armament of a ten-thousand-man Viet Minh infantry division around May 1953 to include an unknown number of pistols, about 3,150 rifles, 260 submachine guns and machine guns, twelve antitank guns and bazookas, fifty-four 60 mm mortars, thirty 81 or 82 mm mortars, an unknown number of 120 mm mortars, twenty-seven 12.7 mm antiaircraft machine guns, eighteen 75 or 105 mm guns/howitzers, and two 20 mm antiaircraft guns.[49] Presumably, weapons destroyed, rendered inoperable, or lost in combat were replaced on a one-to-one basis as required.

The Viet Minh apparently did not have any formal regulations specifying the allocation of ammunition or the size of the basic load or unit of fire for various weapons, but the ammunition requirements of a Viet Minh infantry division with artillery support have been estimated at a minimum of five short tons of ammunition per day of combat.[50] The amount of ammunition carried by the individual Viet Minh combatants and weapons crews probably varied enormously, but may have been around 70 rounds per rifle, 390 rounds per light machine gun or automatic rifle, and 15 rounds per 81/82 mm mortar.[51]

The principal strengths of the Viet Minh logistical system were its adaptation to the physical and operational environment and its flexibility. One of the more persistent myths about the Viet Minh, a myth that also persists in regard to the contemporary North Korean and Chinese Communist forces in Korea, is that they lived almost entirely off the countryside and obtained what little arms and equipment they possessed by capturing it from the enemy. While it is true that the Viet Minh generally subscribed to the ninth of Mao's "Ten Commandments"—"Use the material and the personnel of the enemy to reinforce your own troops and your own resupply"—and made excellent use of the materiel that they did capture, particularly during the early years of the war, the eventual size and sophistication of the Viet Minh armed forces required a formal logistical system with established sources of food, clothing, arms, ammunition, vehicles, and other equipment and established lines of communication.[52] This was a fact that General Giap himself knew well but saw fit to pass over for ideological reasons in his observation that, "From the military point of view, the Vietnamese people's war of liberation proved that an insufficiently equipped people's army, but an army fighting for a just cause, can, with appropriate strategy and tactics, combine the conditions needed to conquer a modern army of aggressive imperialism."[53]

The fact is that the Viet Minh logistical system expanded and developed in direct proportion to the growth and increasing sophistication of the combat forces it was designed to support. The escalation of the regular Viet Minh forces to division-size units and large-scale conventional warfare operations was matched by the development of a larger and more complex supply and transportation system. Overall, the Viet Minh mastered the challenges of logistics in the First Indochina

War much better than did their French Union opponents once due allowance is given for the disparity in resources ultimately available to the two sides. Brigadier General Chapelle, the commander of the French transport forces in Indochina, summed up the situation when he wrote after the war: "The armed forces of the adversary were adapted to the country. Their logistical needs were very reduced. Their displacements were made on foot. But the Viet Minh were strongly aided by the civil population and knew the countryside perfectly."[54]

6

The Opposing Transport Systems

The most difficult logistical task in Indochina was undoubtedly the movement of men and materiel. Transportation, always the key to logistics, was made difficult for both sides in Indochina by a number of factors, including the hostile climate, difficult terrain, great distances, and an aggressive enemy, which affected the organization, plans, and operations of each side differently. In addition, the French Union forces suffered from long strategic lines of communication, inadequate support from the government at home, and a strong dose of hubris that blinded them to the true capabilities of their enemy. Nevertheless, they were relatively successful in overcoming most of the challenges to providing transportation support to the garrisons and to the combat forces in the field, and in some areas, particularly the utilization of inland waterways and air transport, there were some very positive innovations. The Viet Minh, on the other hand, were in their native element, and their transport system was characterized by heavy reliance on raw manpower, careful planning and coordination, and flexible use of all available modes of transportation. Thus, the Viet Minh transport system proved well-suited to the physical and operational environment. After some initial failures, the system proved fully capable of supporting the complex offensive operations of the main Viet Minh battle forces effectively and efficiently.

The French Transport System

Organization and Personnel of the French Transport Services

The staff organization for transportation planning and supervision in Indochina was somewhat different from that employed elsewhere in the French Army. In Indochina the transportation unit commanders did not act as staff transportation officers as they did in France and North Africa.[1] Instead, the transportation unit commander assigned an officer to the General Staff section responsible for transportation planning and coordination. At the highest staff level in Indochina this responsibility was vested in a special Transport Bureau (*Bureau Mouvement Transport,* BMT), independent of the *4e Bureau* but working closely with it under the direction of the deputy for logistics (*sous-chef logistique*) of the EMIFT.[2] There was also a *Bureau Transport* in the staff of each of the territorial commands. A representative of the transportation unit commander was assigned to the *Bureau*

Transport in each case. This centralization of control over transport had some drawbacks but was absolutely necessary for coordinating the transport activities of the several services (army, navy, and air force) and modes (human, animal, truck, rail, water, and air transport), given the degree to which requirements exceeded the available transportation assets and the fact that many transportation support operations were "joint" in nature.

Military transportation operations in Indochina were the responsibility of the commandant of the *Train* of the Far East Expeditionary Corps (*Train du Corps Expéditionnaire en Extrême-Orient, Train*), which controlled all of the headquarters support, human and animal transport, motor transport, traffic regulation, Army watercraft, and aerial resupply units in the theater.[3] The missions assigned to the *Train* included support of the various major headquarters, traffic control, the movement of personnel and supplies, transportation-related training, and the support of tactical movements by the combat units. As the war progressed, the *Train* was assigned a number of additional primary and secondary missions. The primary missions added were the planning and execution of human and animal transport, river transport, and aerial resupply. Secondary missions included route reconnaissance, security patrols in the pacified zones, exploitation of the port of Saigon, and participation in various operations. The physical and tactical situation in Indochina required the addition of armed security elements as well as more and better communication equipment to cover the long distances and to control the civilian transportation augmentations that were commonly employed.[4]

Initially organized for European-type operations, the *Train* proved adaptable to the physical and tactical environment in Indochina, placing greater emphasis on air and inland water movements, improved radio communications and liaison, and new procedures for traffic control and security.[5] The operational efficiency of the *Train* in Indochina suffered, as did that of the other logistical services, from the climate, the distance from its base in metropolitan France, the high turnover of personnel, and the mixed ethnic composition of its personnel, but, on the other hand, the *Train* did maintain a 90 percent vehicle availability, and its losses were relatively light.[6]

The *Train* of the CEFEO was formed in North Africa in the summer of 1944 and underwent several reorganizations in France before being deployed to Indochina under the command of Lieutenant Colonel Chabert.[7] The first elements of the thirty-four-hundred-man *Train* began to arrive at Saigon in October 1945 and were immediately employed in the Saigon area. The first casualties of the *Train* were suffered during an ambush on the route to Cambodia on November 18, 1945.

By November 1946, the *Train* included some five thousand men and two thousand vehicles.[8] At the end of 1946 the *Train* was reorganized on a territorial basis

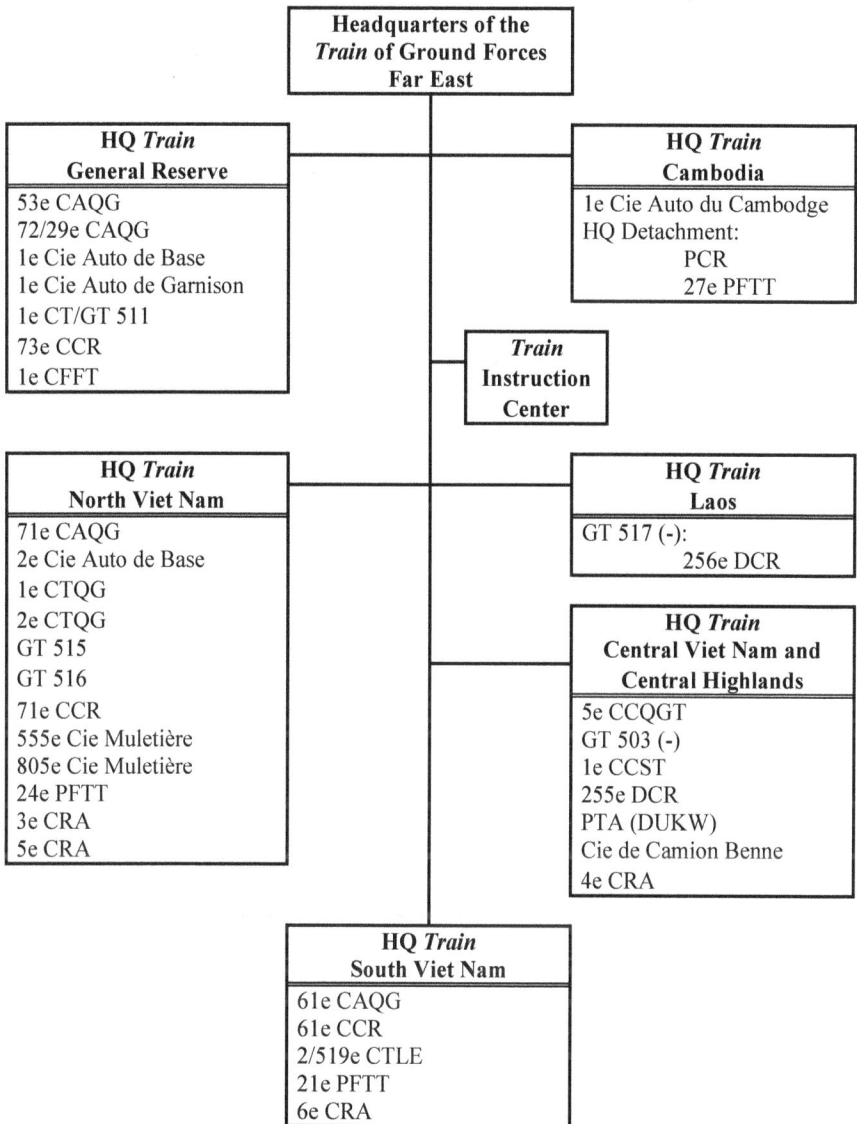

Figure 6.1. Organization of the *Train* in Indochina, 1953–1954. (Compiled by the author based on Couget, *Le Train en Indochine,* passim. Medical units belonging to the *Train* in Indochina are not shown. Full designations of units, abbreviated here, can be found in the glossary.)

to correspond to the territorial command organization of French ground forces. Four major elements were established: a general reserve; the *Train* of Ground Forces–North Viet Nam in Tonkin; the *Train* of Ground Forces–South Viet Nam with headquarters in Saigon; and the 1st Cambodian Car Company (*1e Compagnie Automobile du Cambodge,* 1e Cie Auto du Cambodge), which was attached to the *Train* of Ground Forces–South Viet Nam.[9] Subsequently, separate *Train* organizations were established for central Annam (April 1947), Laos (May 1947), and Cambodia (February 1953). The *Train* subsequently underwent several reorganizations as units were created, dissolved, renumbered, and shifted from one territorial command to another. The organization of the *Train* as it existed in 1953–1954 is shown in figure 6.1.

Despite the great demands placed upon it, the *Train* in Indochina never exceeded nine thousand military personnel. However, it did employ large numbers of Indochinese civilians, and most of the military movements in Indochina, particularly cargo movements, were carried out using civilian transport. Thus, a true picture of the number of personnel involved in military transport operations in Indochina would have to include the civilians employed by the *Train* itself, prisoners of war (PIMs) who were used by the French for labor, and the innumerable civilian employees of the commercial trucking and shipping firms, the railroads, and the civilian airlines, all of whom contributed to the movement of men and materiel. In general, the trend was to reduce the number of Europeans in the units of the *Train* by substituting Indochinese. In April 1947, there were 6,430 military personnel assigned to the *Train* (5,213 Europeans and 1,127 Indochinese); by December 1950 the overall military strength had increased only slightly, to 6,621 (4,425 Europeans and 2,236 Indochinese). The military strength of the *Train* peaked in December 1951 with 8,788 military personnel (5,174 Europeans and 3,614 Indochinese), but by March 1953 the number had declined somewhat to 8,481 (4,659 Europeans and 3,822 Indochinese).[10]

The French Military Transport System in Indochina

The French military transportation system in Indochina can be divided conveniently into two major segments. The first segment consisted of the lines of air and sea communication converging from overseas on three major reception centers: Saigon, Haiphong, and Tourane (Da Nang). The second segment consisted of internal lines of communication radiating out from the three major reception centers to the garrisons and combat units in the field.

The performance of the converging segments of the transportation network hinged on the availability of air and ocean transport and the great distances involved. It could be influenced by the authorities in Indochina only by the establishment of priorities. The two principal currents of maritime transport to Indochina originated in metropolitan France and North Africa, one and a half months away by sea, and in the United States, two months away by sea. The two major currents were supplemented by deliveries by sea from Japan, which took approximately eight days. The delivery of supplies to Indochina from overseas was always slow and did not always conform to the sense of urgency being experienced in Indochina. In reality, the order-ship time for supplies from metropolitan France was closer to four months than to one and a half, a situation that argued for the maintenance of a four-month safety level in theater.[11] Air delivery from France and the United States was reserved for passengers and a small amount of high-priority cargo. The converging lines of air and sea communication terminated in Indochina at one of the three major base areas: Saigon and Tourane, which acted as transit bases, and Haiphong, which was both a transit base and an operational base. The amount of cargo received at the three bases from overseas amounted to some 361,000 tons in 1951, some 360,000 tons in the first eleven months of 1952, and over 535,000 tons in 1953 (Saigon, 391,752 tons; Haiphong, 131,191 tons; and Tourane, 12,783 tons).[12]

The second segment of the distribution system in Indochina was by far the more difficult segment and involved the use of all available modes of transport: highway, rail, coastal and inland water transport, air, and even human and animal transport in the more remote regions. The onward movement of supplies from the major reception centers necessarily involved multiple handling and the use of progressively more difficult and less efficient transport means. Cargo movements to and within Indochina in 1953 are shown in table 6.1.

In 1953, the internal transportation system in Indochina had sufficient capacity and flexibility to meet the needs of the French Union forces. However, the system overall was subject to delays caused by the seasonal monsoons, and some areas, particularly in northwest Tonkin and northern Laos, were either so remote or so isolated by enemy forces that resupply was possible only by air, and certain coastal locations, such as Dong Hoi in central Viet Nam, were almost totally isolated during the rainy season. As a consequence, it was necessary to stockpile reserves at critical points. The high level of operations in Tonkin and the distance from the major logistical facilities in Saigon led to the creation in 1952 of the Tonkin Operational Base (*Base Opérationnelle du Tonkin,* BOTK) at Haiphong, directly subordinate to the *commandant en chef,* to act as the major *entrepôt* for support of the combat forces in northern Viet Nam. Both the BOTK and the Haiphong reception base were supplied whenever possible by direct shipment from overseas (France, the United States, and Japan) rather than by transshipment from Saigon. Vientiane, augmented by Xieng Khouang and backed by Hanoi, also became an important redistribution center for Upper Laos, which had to be supplied primarily by air during much of the year.[13]

The provision of transport service in Indochina was expensive, the more so

Table 6.1. Cargo Movements to and within Indochina, 1953

From	To	Mode	Metric Tons
From Overseas			
France	Saigon	sea	199,778
	Saigon	sea	191,974
Other overseas areas	Haiphong	sea	131,191
	Tourane	sea	12,783
Within Indochina			
Phnom Penh	Poipet	railroad	7,200
Kratie	Savannakhet	highway	28,852
Saigon	Nha Trang	coastal water	874
	Nha Trang	railroad	107,000
	Tourane	coastal water	57,829
	Haiphong	coastal water	150,581
	Hanoi	air	751
	Dalat	railroad	3,200
	Ban Me Thuot	highway	28,137
	Phnom Penh	highway	2,744
	Phnom Penh	inland water	6,567
	Kratie	highway	14,644
	Kratie	inland water	22,926
	Seno	air	795
Tourane	Dong Hoi	coastal water	11,509
Hanoi	NW Tonkin & Laos	air	45,908
Haiphong	Hanoi	highway	42,444
	Hanoi	railroad	464,000
	Moncay	coastal water	14,667

Source: "EMIFT, 3e Bureau, Enseignements à tirer de la campagne d'Indochine, Fasc. III, 98," [Saigon, 1955], map "Transport de Fret (En Tonnes) Pour l'Année 1953," facing page 258. Some tonnage is counted more than once. For example, cargo arriving at Saigon by sea might have been transshipped to Haiphong by coaster and then forwarded to Hanoi by highway. Such cargo was counted at each stage of its journey.

because of the required use of air transport to supply many isolated locations. The costs for internal transport for French Union ground forces in Indochina increased from 9 million francs in 1952 to 12 million francs in 1953 and totaled some 8.3 million francs in the first six months of 1954 alone.[14]

Human and Animal Transport

In certain regions of Indochina, particularly the mountainous parts, resupply could be accomplished only by air, porters, or animal transport. The carrying capacity of human and animal transport was limited, and both men and animals were vulnerable to the harsh climate, rugged terrain, and diseases prevalent in Indochina. Nevertheless, both sides made considerable use of both porters and pack animals. The French Union forces often relied on porters to move cargo in the more remote areas, but they never utilized porters to as good effect as did the Viet Minh. A porter could transport one box of 105 mm ammunition (four complete rounds), one box of twenty 2.36-inch rockets, or, with the aid of a "chogie stick," two boxes of 60 mm mortar ammunition (a total of ten rounds) nineteen to twenty-two miles in a day.[15] In rough terms, twenty porters could carry the same load as one U.S. GMC truck.[16]

Mules, packhorses, and even water buffalo were used by the French Union forces in Indochina for transport purposes. The CEFEO maintained two pack mule companies (*Compagnie Muletière*) in Tonkin and five pack mule detachments in central Viet Nam to supply isolated outposts and accompany infantry columns, but pack mule transport proved ineffective. The mules did not fare well in the terrain and tropical climate of Indochina, as they suffered from the heat and had difficulty moving in the dense jungle and rice paddies.[17] Furthermore, the available pack equipment was poorly designed, and the Indochinese did not get along well with the mules, preferring to use water buffalo or small horses for transporting goods. Mule trains were also extremely vulnerable to attack and required significant support (forage, veterinary service, etc.), which led the authors of the postwar study of lessons learned in Indochina to conclude that the movement by pack train of heavy weapons was impractical, and that the pack mule trains ought to be replaced by aerial resupply.[18] One commander of the *Train* noted, "Two or three transport helicopters could have easily replaced a mule company."[19] Despite their drawbacks, mules were marginally more capable than porters, at least in terms of their carrying capacity and endurance. For example, a healthy mule could carry a load of 176 pounds a distance of fifty miles in one day.[20]

Motor Transport

Highway transport throughout Indochina was precarious due to the poor roads and ever-present prospect of enemy ambush. For the most part, all movement at night was prohibited and daytime highway movements in most areas had to be supported by costly clearance and escort operations. Moreover, Viet Minh control of large areas of Indochina made interterritorial highway movements all but impossible. The limited road network of Indochina, which ranged from dense in the delta areas to nonexistent in the mountainous regions, was perpetually in poor condition and required intensive and difficult repair efforts.

The majority of highway movements in Indochina were carried out by the motor transport units of the *Train*. The motor transport battalions (*Groupements de Transport*, GT) in Indochina consisted of a small headquarters platoon (twenty NCOs and drivers plus battalion officers), which had minimal administrative functions, and two or three motor transport companies (*Compagnies de Transport*, CT). The motor transport companies (about one hundred NCOs and drivers plus company officers) consisted of three or four motor transport platoons and a small headquarters platoon, a security element, and a signal element.[21] The security elements were usually equipped with scout cars or half-tracks. There were normally an equal number of security elements and motor transport platoons, but many officers recommended two armored vehicles per platoon and three elsewhere in the company for a total of nine. Most of the motor transport companies were authorized sixty task vehicles (twenty per platoon), many of which were U.S. Dodge or GMC 2.5-ton, 6x6 models capable of carrying twenty-five men or up to five tons of cargo on good roads, although in Indochina the normal load was closer to two tons.[22]

Despite their limitations, the motor transport units of the *Train* achieved a significant volume of highway movements. In 1949, for example, some 9,000 task vehicles moved 60,000 men and some 34,000 tons of cargo.[23] Overall in 1953, some 116,821 tons were moved by highway transport in Indochina. The tonnages moved over the poor roads of Indochina during the war by individual motor transport units were equally impressive. In 1946–1947, the four motor transport companies (240 trucks) directly controlled by the headquarters of the CEFEO covered some 3.1 million miles, carried 73,000 passengers, and hauled some 160,000 tons of cargo at a cost of thirty-two killed and sixty-three wounded.[24] Between September 1946 and July 1954, the men of the 1st Cambodian Car Company drove some 6.82 million miles and carried 920,000 passengers and 100,000 tons of cargo.[25] Even the motor transport companies of the national armies achieved good results. In 1952, the transport company of the 4th Vietnamese Infantry Division was the only truck company in the Central Highlands and had the mission of resupplying scattered posts and civilian locales and providing operational transport of men and supplies. Under the command of Captain Balabeau and with a staff of one French and two Vietnamese lieutenants and French NCOs as platoon leaders, the company trained 415 drivers in addition to its own personnel and drove some 1,620,000 task miles plus another 380,000 miles in training and internal support with never more than five vehicles deadlined at any one time, winning themselves thirteen letters of congratulations and seventeen individual citations.[26]

Railroads

Indochina's railroads were decidedly inferior to those of Europe, and the use of railroads for the movement of supplies was restricted by the limited number of established routes, the limited infrastructure, and the characteristics of the available locomotives and rolling stock. In 1953, only about 50 percent of the total rail net in Indochina, divided into four unconnected sections, was usable.[27] Despite the many drawbacks of the Indochina rail system, it remained an important means of moving large tonnages. In 1953 alone, some 580,944 tons moved by rail.

The railroads in Indochina were operated by government employees and civilians, but military railway engineers were used to maintain the right-of-ways, bridges, tunnels, and other facilities. The 1st Far East Railway Engineer Company was established in July 1946 at Nha Trang and was attached to the 5th Engineer Regiment as the 5/10th Far East Railway Engineer Company on November 1, 1946.[28]

The rail lines were vulnerable to sabotage and direct Viet Minh attack. Between May and October 1950, the Viet Minh made some 10.5 miles of cuts in the rail lines, mostly of five hundred to forty-five hundred yards in length.[29] Due to the complaints of Vietnamese civilians, the Viet Minh subsequently switched their emphasis to direct attacks on the motive power and rolling stock using large contact-detonated or electrically detonated mines. To reduce the incidence and impact of Viet Minh sabotage and direct attack, the French authorities ran three or four trains together under armed escort, the resulting convoy being called *une rafale*.[30] Each train hauled four hundred to five hundred tons of cargo. The French 4th Dragoons, among other units, provided the railway escort detachments.

Coastal and Inland Water Transport

The movement of military personnel and cargo in Indochina by coastal shipping or by inland water transport was relatively cheap, easy, and secure, at least in the great deltas of the Mekong and the Red Rivers. Sufficient commercial watercraft were available, and for the execution of certain military water movements the *Train* established riverine units equipped with landing craft (usually thirty-ton-capacity LCMs) and protected by armed escort vessels. French transportation officers in Indochina also experimented with a variety of amphibious vehicles, including the DUKW (an amphibious GMC 2.5-ton truck), the M29C cargo carrier (known as the "Crab"), and the LVT-4 (known as the "Alligator").[31] The DUKW soon proved unsuitable, but a number of them continued to be used, particularly in central Viet Nam. The Crab and Alligator proved better suited to amphibious combat operations in Indochina.

The inland water transport units of the *Train* were formally established in 1951.

Two river craft companies (*Compagnies Fluvial de Transport du Train,* CFTT) were formed, each consisting of four river craft platoons (*Pelotons Fluvial de Transport du Train,* PFTT) of one officer, eighty NCOs and men, and eight Landing Craft, Mechanized (LCM).[32] The PFTT were of two types: "Base" and "Normal."[33] The base-type platoons had civilian crews except for the commander and his deputy, who were both military personnel. They were usually unarmed and were not equipped with radios. The LCMs of base platoons were employed individually in the security of the ports, as lighters for the loading and discharge of ships, and in other harbor tasks. The normal-type platoons were manned entirely by military personnel and were organized with three elements: a command group consisting of the commander and his second in command, a transport echelon consisting of four groups of two LCMs, and a reserve element consisting of two officers and twenty-four men who provided the internal services for the platoons and replacements or reinforcements for the crews of the transport echelon boats. Each of the LCMs of the normal-type platoons was armed with two 7.5 mm machine guns and an automatic rifle in addition to the individual weapons of the crew. Each LCM was also equipped with a radio, and each of the four groups had a more powerful radio.

The principal task vessels of the PFTT in Indochina were the LCM-3 and the LCM-6. These vessels were generally of American manufacture, but some inferior, nonstandard LCM-6s were built by the French in Indochina. Both types of LCM were capable of carrying about sixty fully equipped troops with accompanying gear or one thirty-ton tank. The LCM-3 had a cargo capacity of about thirty tons of cargo (twenty to twenty-five tons on long trips), and the LCM-6 had a cargo capacity of about sixty tons or two fifteen-ton tanks. Both the LCM-3 and the LCM-6 had an operating speed of about eight knots. A variety of other river craft were also utilized for various tasks. The most notable of these was the "My Tho" boat, a small wooden craft about the size and capacity of a Landing Craft, Vehicle and Personnel (LCVP). The My Tho boats were manufactured locally and were powered by a jeep engine. They proved quite successful.

The river craft platoons of the *Train* were assigned to support tactical operations, to carry out general administrative movements of personnel, cargo, and equipment, and to perform a variety of secondary tasks. When called upon to support tactical operations, the river craft platoons were normally grouped with a naval amphibious group and might be utilized to transport infantry, haul supplies, evacuate wounded men and damaged materiel, or provide patrols for the surveillance of waterways. Patrol missions and direct participation in combat assaults were normally performed by the riverine elements of the French Navy, the famous *Dinassaut* (*Division Navale d'Assaut*), but river craft units of the *Train* sometimes participated. The most common employment of the PFTT, however, was the general movement of personnel and cargo in accordance with instructions received from the *2e Section* of the territorial *Train* headquarters or the *4e Bureau* of the territorial General Staff. The possibility of Viet Minh mines or direct attack from the riverbanks generally required the employment of river craft in convoys accompanied by armed escort vessels, even for administrative movements in "safe" areas.

The lack of formal training in small boat and landing craft operations and maintenance significantly reduced the efficiency of the army riverine units, but most of the military cargo transported by coastal vessels and inland watercraft in Indochina was carried in civilian vessels. Security considerations required that the circulation of civilian river craft in Indochina be regulated by the military authorities and carried out generally in convoy. Military authorities prescribed the routes, times, and loading of all civilian riverine convoys, and military cargo was given priority at all times.[34]

Overall, a total of 235,460 tons moved by coastal watercraft and 29,493 tons moved by inland watercraft in 1953. The individual riverine platoons also achieved significant results. Between its establishment in 1953 and July 1954, the 27e PFTT, attached to the 1st Cambodian Car Company, covered some 4,960 miles and moved some 2,000 passengers and 1,000 tons of cargo.[35]

Air Transport and Aerial Resupply

Although comparatively insignificant at the beginning of the First Indochina War, French air transport capability improved dramatically, both in volume and technique, as the war went on. The movement of personnel and supplies by air offered the advantages of speed and flexibility, surmounted the difficulties of terrain, and made possible operations outside the zones controlled by French ground forces. However, the available military air transport fleet—even augmented by the available civil air transport—was never sufficient for the needs of the theater, and frequently poor flying weather and the lack of suitable landing fields as well as shortages of parachutes and other equipment limited the use of air transport and aerial resupply. French air capabilities were further limited by inadequate maintenance stemming from poor procedures, the lack of qualified personnel, and a general lack of interest in improving the situation.[36] Despite the importance of air transport to French Union operations, the general decrepitude of French airfields was often noted by French reporters as well as American observers. The French correspondent Lucien Bodard described Mao Mai airfield in Tonkin in 1947 as:

> bareness, penury itself. The smell of old army stores pervaded everything; everywhere there was the aftertaste of a neglected barracks. The men, surrounded by these decaying hangars and their heaps of old iron, displayed a kind of weariness, a kind of deliberate carelessness. And yet, so long as they did not look as though they were working, and so long as it

amused them to, how arduously these mechanics, old sweats with a heavy accent, toiled over their engines. So did the pilots, slim young men with a horror of seeming earnest. They were all expert tinkerers: nothing was organized, and everyone shifted for himself.[37]

One of the most significant French operational innovations of the First Indochina War was the "air-land base" (*base aéro-terrestre*), the isolated strongpoint supplied entirely by air that acted as a fortified operational headquarters and logistical support center for combat forces operating deep in enemy territory. Dien Bien Phu was perhaps the best known of these bases. Seno in central Laos was another important *base aéro-terrestre*, particularly in the winter of 1953–1954.[38] In 1952, some eighty to 120 drop zones were supplied by air each month, and on average about sixty outposts were resupplied exclusively by air at any given time.[39]

As might be expected, the weather limited the air transport of men and supplies as well as the tactical employment of airborne forces in Indochina, but the principal constraints were the limited number of suitable transport aircraft and crews and the perpetual shortage of parachutes and related equipment. Even so, some installations and operations could be supplied by no other means and required a maximum application of the available military and civil aviation resources. Toward the end of the war, many isolated units could be supplied only by airdrop or paradrop, and the tonnage of airdropped and paradropped supplies for all of Indochina increased accordingly from an average of 1,700 tons per month in January–November 1953, to 2,200 tons in December 1953, to 4,700 tons in March 1954, to 7,000 tons in April 1954.[40] The period of greatest intensity was reached during the battle of Dien Bien Phu, when a total of 30,000 tons—the equivalent of 12,000 truckloads—were delivered by air to French Union forces throughout Indochina.[41] Between November 20, 1953, and May 7, 1954, 20,860 tons of cargo were delivered to Dien Bien Phu, some 6,584 tons of which were airlanded before the loss of the airfields. The other 14,276 tons were airdropped or parachuted over the course of the entire 169 days of the operation, and amounted to about 100 kilograms per minute, or about 124 tons per day, and required almost 80,000 parachutes, plus airdrop rigging.[42]

Military transport aircraft were controlled by the French Air Force headquarters in Indochina. The number and quality of the transport aircraft available grew steadily throughout the First Indochina War but were never sufficient to meet the ever-increasing air transport and airdrop needs of the French Union ground forces. In November 1947, for example, the three available transport groups could muster only seventeen C-47s and thirty-five ancient Amiot AAC 1 Toucans (a French-built version of the German Junkers Ju 52), of which twenty-seven were inoperative.[43] By May 1953, the air transport fleet in Indochina consisted of three transport groups: GT 2/64 "Anjou" at Tan Son Nhut near Saigon, with detachments at Gia Lam-Hanoi and in central Viet Nam, Laos, and Cambodia; GT 1/64 "Bearn" at Nha Trang, with detachments at Tan Son Nhut, Gia Lam, and Tourane; and GT 2/62 "Franche Comté" at Do Son near Haiphong, with an operational detachment at Bach Mai-Hanoi.[44] The three transport groups were authorized a total of only fifty C-47 and five AAC 1 transports, but were augmented from November 1952 to March 1953 by twenty-nine C-47s from France and twenty-one C-47s borrowed from the United States. Losses, particularly over Dien Bien Phu in the first months of 1954, were heavy, and the Viet Minh conducted several daring raids on French air transport bases in Tonkin that resulted in heavy losses.[45] An augmentation of C-119 transports with American crews arrived during the last months of the war, and at the time of the cease-fire in July 1954 the French air transport fleet in Indochina included one hundred C-47s, twenty-four C-119s, and twelve other transport aircraft.[46]

The perpetual shortage of transport aircraft required the French authorities to rely heavily on the temporary augmentation provided by the civil air transport firms operating in Indochina. By the end of the war, civilian aircraft and pilots were used even for the most dangerous missions, such as the resupply of commando units and the support of Dien Bien Phu. The civilian pilots, already thoroughly familiar with flying conditions in Indochina, became very experienced at military formation flying and air delivery techniques and were a valuable supplement to the limited military air transport. However, as late as November 1953, the French authorities still had not instituted effective procedures for the control of the available airlift, military or civilian, and there were no definitive procedures to regulate the flow of cargo and establish priorities.[47] The lack of effective airlift control procedures prevented the efficient concentration of available assets and often necessitated the temporary requisitioning of civilian aircraft for military tasks.

A variety of transport aircraft were used for air transport and parachute operations in Indochina. The characteristics of the principal aircraft and helicopters employed are shown in table 6.2.

The French Air Force in Indochina initially employed a number of Amiot AAC 1 Toucan cargo planes. These were gradually replaced by the American-manufactured C-47 Dakota, known to most Americans as the "Gooney Bird" and perhaps the most successful transport aircraft ever designed. At the end of 1953, the American aid program began to deliver a number of the new C-119 Flying Boxcar transports, which had greater power and rear clamshell doors, and following the cease-fire a number of French Nord 2501 transports were delivered. A few British Bristol 170 Freighters belonging to commercial airlines in Indochina were also employed and proved particularly useful for the air transport of heavy equipment. The most notable achievement of the Bristol Freighters was the delivery of ten M24 Chaffee light tanks to Dien Bien Phu in what was called Operation RONDELLE II.[48] The French command in Indochina established the requirement

Table 6.2. Characteristics of Transport Aircraft and Helicopters Used by the French in Indochina

Aircraft	Type	Speed	Range/Combat Radius	Armament/Remarks
Transport Aircraft				
Bristol 170 Freighter	twin engine transport	153 mph	700 miles	unarmed; 44 troops; 8,950 lbs. cargo; heavy lift; 2-man crew
Douglas C-47 Dakota; Skytrain	twin engine transport	185 mph	860 miles	unarmed; 28 paras + 7 containers; 18 stretchers; 5,850 lbs. cargo; 3-man crew
Fairchild C-119 Packet; Flying Boxcar	twin engine transport	180 mph	> 1,100 miles	unarmed; 42 troops + 10 containers; 34 stretchers; up to 12,000 lbs. cargo; heavy lift; 5-man crew
Amiot AAC 1 Toucan	three engine transport	135 mph	800 miles	unarmed; 18 troops; 12 stretchers; up to 5,000 lbs. cargo; 3-man crew
Nord 2501 Nordlatlas	twin engine transport	198 mph	930 miles	unarmed; 45 troops; up to 18,500 lbs. cargo; heavy lift; 3-man crew
Helicopters				
Hiller H-23 Raven	light helicopter	87 mph	135 miles	unarmed; 2 passengers; 2 external litters; 1-man crew
Sikorsky S-51	light helicopter	85 mph	150 miles	unarmed; 2 passengers; 2 external litters; 1-man crew
Sikorsky H-19 Chickasaw	cargo helicopter	112 mph	360 miles	unarmed; 8 passengers; 6 litters + attendant; 2,405 lbs. cargo; 2-man crew

Sources: Compiled by the author from various sources, including Leonard Bridgman, ed., *Jane's All the World's Aircraft, 1952–53* (New York: McGraw-Hill, 1953), and Fred Hamil and others, eds., *The Aircraft Year Book for 1950* (Washington: Lincoln, 1950). Performance characteristics are for aircraft with normal combat loads and are only approximate due to variance in models and dates of manufacture. Speed given is approximate cruising speed. Range given is the maximum one-way distance with a normal load of fuel and cargo.

for a cargo plane capable of landing or taking off with a two-ton load of personnel or equipment on short (less than 150 yards) unimproved landing strips, and the French aeronautical designer Louis Breguet actually designed such an airplane, but the French Air Force was not interested.[49]

The Toucan and the Dakota were only capable of carrying or airdropping personnel and light equipment, and even the Dakota (which had a greater load capacity than the Toucan) often needed to make as many as twelve passes over the drop zone to deliver its cargo, a procedure that increased its vulnerability to enemy antiaircraft fire. Both aircraft required that the cargo be loaded and unloaded or dropped from side-opening doors. Theoretically, the AAC 1 had the same capacity as the C-47, but its slower rate of climb and the antiquity of the available aircraft required lighter loads in mountainous country, and normally an AAC 1 carried only thirteen parachutists versus twenty-four for the C-47.[50]

The C-119 and the Nord 2501 were capable of delivering heavy loads and vehicles in packages of over one ton. The C-119 could deliver a load of six to seven tons in one pass over the drop zone. It was considered excellent for dropping parachutists and could carry and drop heavy equipment, such as bulldozers and 105 mm howitzers. Two groups of twenty Nord 2501s began to operate before the end of 1954, and each Nord 2501 could carry forty paratroopers or heavy cargo like the C-119.[51]

The helicopter, which proved so characteristic an element of the Second Indochina War, was still something of a novelty during the First Indochina War. Although helicopters held the promise of overcoming many of the obstacles to the movement of men and supplies in Indochina, they were employed by the French in very small numbers and almost entirely for medical evacuation purposes. The first two Hiller H-23 ambulance helicopters were delivered to Saigon in April 1950.[52] The delivery of additional medical evacuation helicopters was delayed due to the priority given to forces in Korea, but by 1952 ten were available.[53] On December 31, 1953, the French forces in Indochina had eighteen helicopters on hand (six Hiller H-23As; five Hiller H-23Bs; three Westland-Sikorsky WS-51s; and four Sikorsky S-55s), which had already accumulated a total of 4,821 flying hours, evacuated 4,728 casualties, and rescued nineteen pilots and three observers who had been shot down.[54] However, the French were already in the process of shipping the Westland-Sikorsky WS-51 helicopters back to France due to insurmountable maintenance support problems.[55] The army organized a helicopter training command in early 1954, built a heliport in Saigon, and made plans to acquire one hundred helicopters by the end of the year. The plan was to activate GT 65 with a twenty-five-machine light helicopter squadron, a twenty-five-machine medium helicopter squadron, and a maintenance squadron. However, only twenty-eight helicopters had arrived by the end of 1954, and American military aid personnel, who were supplying the helicopters, advocated "a more modest approach to the helicopter force build up for the French Land Forces."[56]

The small number of available machines and pilots as well as the lack of a well-developed understanding of helicopter operations limited the use of the helicopter in Indochina to medical evacuation and rescue work. As a result, they played an insignificant role in the logistics of the First Indochina War. However, by July 31, 1954, French helicopters in Indochina had flown some 7,040 hours in 5,400 sorties and had evacuated 10,820 sick and wounded men and rescued thirty-eight downed airmen and eighty escapees.[57]

French airborne forces, which participated in only a minor way in the great Allied airborne operations of World War II, were fully developed and came into their own in Indochina, spurred by the nature of the "war without front," an extensive theater of operations, plentiful drop zones, and the absence of enemy airpower. Throughout the First Indochina War, the French airborne forces grew in size and continually developed their technique. From a few hundred infantry paratroopers in 1946, the French airborne forces in Indochina grew to 10,639 qualified parachutists in 1951, with growing numbers of specialists (artillery, engineers, signals, and support troops).[58] By 1954, the airborne forces available in Indochina included six parachute battalions in the CEFEO, six Vietnamese National Army parachute battalions, one Laotian parachute battalion, one Cambodian parachute battalion, and smaller units from the other services.

The French Union airborne forces in Indochina were not subordinated to the territorial commands and were thus responsible for their own logistical support. In 1949, they were organized under an Airborne Forces Command, and two airborne bases were established. The *Base Aéroportée Sud* (BAPS) at Saigon and the *Base Aéroportée Nord* (BAPN) at Hanoi provided headquarters facilities and all necessary logistical support for the available parachute units. In 1950, the Airborne Forces Command was redesignated as Airborne Forces Command Indochina (*Troupes Aéroportés d'Indochine*, TAPI) and an Airborne Forces Command, North, was created to control airborne forces in Tonkin. From 1953, liaison teams from the airborne forces worked with the various territorial command headquarters to plan and coordinate airborne operations.

The limited number of transport aircraft available, coupled with the requirement to support a large number of outposts and operational bases almost entirely by airlanding, airdropping, or paradropping supplies, restricted the use of airborne combat forces primarily to defensive rather than offensive operations. It also precluded large airborne operations, and thus most airborne operations in Indochina involved only one parachute battalion at a time.[59] As a rule, a parachute battalion, consisting of some six hundred effectives, dropped from one wave of twenty-six to thirty transports.[60] The experience gained in earlier airborne operations led the *commandant en chef* in the summer of 1952 to establish a requirement for sufficient transport aircraft to lift three parachute battalions (about twenty-four hundred men) at one time, as the Viet Minh had been successful in escaping from traps when fewer than three parachute battalions were used to close off their routes of escape.[61] This would require about one hundred C-47 aircraft, but at the time only fifty C-47s and twenty-two older Ju 52 transport aircraft were available. However, the necessary one hundred C-47s did become available by November 1952.

Throughout much of the First Indochina War, parachutes and airdrop equipment were in short supply. Basically, every man and every one hundred kilograms of cargo dropped required one parachute.[62] Given the heavy use of paradrops to support isolated garrisons and combat forces in the field, the perpetual shortage of parachutes demanded a maximum effort on the part of airborne forces to recover parachutes after an operation. After every jump, one-fourth to one-third of the paratroopers spent up to half a day just recovering the parachutes. This imposed a significant burden on the parachute units and supporting logistical personnel.[63] The shortage of parachutes also increased the importance of free-drop techniques. As early as 1950, about 40 percent of the air-delivered tonnage was free-dropped, and the use of free-drop techniques made possible a gain of up to 12 percent in the useful tonnage delivered by air.[64] Increased French production and American aid deliveries of parachutes and airdrop equipment provided some relief by the end of the war.

Not only were the parachutes and other airdrop equipment used in Indochina expensive and generally in short supply, but the great variety of such materiel greatly complicated the work of the French aerial resupply units. French industry was unable to supply parachute releases suitable for the 118-mile-per-hour speed of the C-47, so about 80 percent of the parachutes used in Indochina were supplied by the United States under the MDAP.[65] Although many of the technical problems associated with the design and manufacture of parachutes, particularly the heavy-drop parachutes required for equipment and supplies, were resolved during the First Indochina War, some problems were never satisfactorily overcome. For example, the increasing strength of Viet Minh antiaircraft defenses later in the war made delayed-opening drops from higher altitudes a necessity, but a truly effective delayed-opening device capable of ensuring reasonable accuracy of the drop and reliable opening of the parachute was not perfected before the ceasefire.[66] The lack of reliable delay fuzes resulted in as much as 50 percent of some drops failing to hit the designated drop zone.[67] Parachute loads with malfunctioning delay fuzes often were destroyed on impact, and occasionally the results were even more tragic, as when the defective parachutes and their loads fell indiscriminately, destroying friendly bunkers and killing friendly personnel. The ground lighting of drop zones and temporary landing fields was yet another problem not resolved satisfactorily before the end of the war.

Parachute assaults and the air transport of men and supplies required the highly skilled services of aerial resupply units to repair and pack parachutes, to marshal supplies for aerial delivery, and to rig equipment for air transport and paradrop. At the beginning of the war, one aerial resupply platoon, controlled by the airborne forces, was sufficient to perform such tasks for all of Indochina. But as the utilization of air transport and airborne forces increased, it was necessary to increase and reorganize the aerial resupply units. In 1948 an aerial resupply company (*Compagnie de Ravitaillement par Air,* CRA) was created, and by the end of

Table 6.3. Aerial Resupply Units in Indochina, September 1953

		Personnel		Monthly Capacity		
Unit	Location	Military	POWs	Normal (tons)	Max (tons)	Para-troops
CRA du Nord	Hanoi Base	253	400	2,475	5,000	2,500
	Cat Bi Annex	Personnel, etc., furnished from Hanoi				
CRA du Centre	Tourane Base	129	200	750	4,000	2,000
	Seno Annex	62	100	1,350	1,500	750
	Vientiane Annex	40	100	500	500	150
SRA du Sud	Ba Queo Base	40	100	350	1,000	500
TOTAL		524	900	5,425	12,000	5,900

Source: 1e Section, 4e Bureau, EMIFT, "Instruction relative à l'organisation générale au ravitaillement par Air des F. T. d'Indochine: Annexe No. II," [No. 441/4/1, Saigon, September 15, 1953], in folder "EMIFT, 3e Bureau, Operations: Dien Bien Phu, 4e Bureau Materials," box 10 H 1176, Fonds Indochine, SHAT. The CRA were located near, but not on, major airfields.

the war four such companies were in operation. Table 6.3 shows the distribution and capacity of available aerial resupply units in September 1953. In January 1954, the aerial resupply units in Indochina were reorganized, and from February 1954 the CRA were distributed as follows: 3e CRA at Gia Lam near Hanoi, 4e CRA at Tourane in central Viet Nam (detachments at Seno and Vientiane), 5e CRA at Cat Bi near Haiphong, and 6e CRA at Ba Queo near Saigon.[68]

Each CRA was authorized about three hundred trained military personnel and was augmented by some four hundred to five hundred Indochinese laborers (mostly Viet Minh prisoners of war, PIMs, who worked exclusively with cargo loads) and over two hundred trucks per company, giving it a capability of handling 150 to 200 tons of air cargo per day.[69] Each CRA was normally divided into three teams: a Reception and Packaging Section, which supervised the receipt of cargo and its rigging by teams of PIMs; a Loading Section, which loaded the aircraft; and a large Equipment Section, which maintained the parachutes and other airloading, airdrop, and paradrop equipment.[70] However, it should be noted that an increase in the company's strength did not produce an increase in capability; it was necessary to create additional CRAs to increase the overall aerial resupply capability in the theater.

The French were highly successful in overcoming many of the obstacles to effective and efficient aerial support of their forces in Indochina. Effective staff and operating organizations were developed to plan and execute air transport, and techniques were developed to minimize the impact of climate, terrain, and an aggressive enemy. However, persistent shortages of trained personnel and specialized equipment, particularly aircraft and parachutes, limited what could be accomplished. Excited by the advantages inherent in air transport unopposed by enemy counterair operations, the French came to rely too heavily on what was in reality a very thin and fragile rope, and in the final analysis air transport and aerial resupply, which many French military leaders saw as the key to victory in Indochina, turned out to be a major factor in their ultimate defeat.

The Viet Minh Transport System

The Viet Minh transport system demonstrated a clear sense of purpose, great determination, and substantial innovation in the movement of men and supplies. The hardy Viet Minh soldier required few and relatively simple supplies and thus early in the war Viet Minh transport requirements were much lower than those of the French. However, by 1950–1951, the emergence of division-size units and of extended offensive campaigns required the Viet Minh to plan and execute the movement of their forces and supplies with great care, the more so because the assembly of large numbers of porters and the relatively slow speed of their overland movement demanded detailed planning, route reconnaissance, the establishment of way stations, and close coordination far in advance of the operation to be supported.

Initially, the Supply section of the General Supply Directorate (GSD) of the Ministry of National Defense played the principal role in determining transport requirements and preparing the transport plans needed to support combat operations. In the reorganization of 1953, central management of Viet Minh military transportation matters and associated operational planning responsibilities were passed to the Transportation Branch of the GSD. The largest of the Viet Minh logistical services, the Transportation Branch organized porters, oversaw the operation of motor transport assets, and handled other transportation matters.

The Construction and Maintenance of Routes

The Viet Minh spent the first half of the war destroying roads, bridges, railways, and other transportation facilities, but with the advent of Chinese Communist aid in 1950 they found it necessary to initiate a program for the repair and improvement of existing routes and the construction of new routes in the areas under their control as well as those leading to the areas in which they intended to conduct operations.[71] Chinese and Viet Minh engineers oversaw this effort, but large numbers of conscripted Indochinese coolies provided the actual labor.[72] The techniques employed were primitive, and the equipment and construction materials available were basic, but the Viet Minh road and bridge builders displayed great determination and achieved considerable success despite French aerial interdiction efforts. Once formed, the 151st Engineer Regiment of the 351st Heavy Division usually detailed elements to maintain and improve the main supply routes for each campaign, tasks for which they were often complimented by the Viet Minh leadership.[73]

Major effort was directed at improving the routes into northern Viet Nam from China to facilitate the delivery of supplies. There were four main entry routes from Communist China, with an estimated total capacity of 2,350 long tons per day under ideal conditions, but in May 1953 the estimated monthly tonnage forward was only about 1,000 tons.[74] The busiest entry route in 1950 and 1951 was the truck route from Nanning to Chennan-kuan (Na Cham) opposite Lang Son and then along the old French frontier route (RC 4) northwest to Cao Bang. The generally poor condition of this route led to the development of a second truck route running in an arc northwest from Nanning toward Kunming but turning south at Tientung to Cao Bang and then on to Bac Kan, the main Viet Minh supply center.[75] The third entry route utilized the narrow-gauge railroad from Kunming three hundred miles south to Hokow near Lao Kay, with onward movement by trucks and porters. The fourth major entry truck route crossed the China–Viet Nam border near Ha Giang. In 1952, the Chinese began construction of a good, all-weather road from Kokiu south of Kunming to the Vietnamese border town of Phong Tho near Lao Kay and then on southwest to Lai Chau. Completed in late 1953, this route enabled the Viet Minh to support their divisions threatening northern Laos and played an important role in the Dien Bien Phu campaign.[76]

The road network under Viet Minh control in Tonkin and northern Annam probably totaled at least 930 miles and included two critical north-south arteries: RC 3 from the Chinese border through Cao Bang and Bac Kan to Thai Nguyen and RP 12 from the rice-producing area around Thanh Hoa north to Hoa Binh. RC 3 was the focal point of French air interdiction efforts in the early fall of 1952, when, despite the best efforts of the Viet Minh, French air attacks managed to reduce the traffic from China into Tonkin to only about one hundred tons per month versus the one thousand tons per month carried on RC 3 before July 1952. The Viet Minh restored the route to its previous capacity in the fall and winter of 1952.[77]

Whenever possible the Viet Minh "doubled" their lines of communication by developing temporary parallel routes to minimize the effects of French interdiction. For example, RP 12 from the plain of Thanh Hoa to Hoa Binh was "doubled" by another (temporary, unnumbered) route through the mountains farther west.[78] Alternate bridges and river crossing sites were also prepared whenever possible, and routes and crossings were well-camouflaged and later protected by antiaircraft artillery. Similar techniques were used in the construction of the network of roads leading from the Viet Minh rear areas to Dien Bien Phu in late 1953 and early 1954. To further avoid observation and attack by French aircraft, nearly all movements were made at night or in periods of inclement weather.

Although the Viet Minh were able to considerably improve the transportation routes in their main area of operations in Tonkin and northern Annam, movement between the various regions of Indochina remained extremely difficult. Couriers traveling from the Trans-Bassac region at the southern tip of the Indochinese peninsula to the Viet Bac in northern Tonkin usually required five months to make the journey on foot.[79] A similar journey in reverse awaited the North Vietnamese soldiers who would travel south over the famous Ho Chi Minh trail during the Second Indochina War. In fact, the network of roads, paths, trails, and stopover camps in eastern Laos and Cambodia that constituted the Ho Chi Minh Trail was first developed during the war against the French and was utilized to provide some limited support for the Viet Minh cadres in Cochinchina.[80] An interesting experiment was conducted in the summer of 1956 when a one-hundred-man South Vietnamese Army unit followed the trace of the Ho Chi Minh Trail along the Annamite Chain from RN 9 (at the approximate latitude of Hue) to Qui Nhon, a distance of 250 miles by air but 450 miles on the ground, in fifty actual marching days. The party received eight aerial resupply drops but lived mostly off the countryside. They usually marched only in the mornings since the afternoon rainstorms made the streams impassable. They concluded that such a party could cover the trail in thirty days at an average of fifteen miles per day, if the troops were unencumbered.[81]

Porters

The Viet Minh skillfully utilized all of the modes of transport at their disposal, including porters, animal transport, trucks, coastal and inland water transport, and railroads. Although there is no firm evidence to suggest that the Viet Minh had access to air transport, some French officials claimed that small amounts of cargo were flown in to the Viet Minh from Communist China.[82] Porters, however, were the backbone of the Viet Minh transportation system and were used extensively in every area of Indochina throughout the First Indochina War and after. In the early days of the war the Viet Minh armed forces requisitioned civilian laborers locally as required to meet their needs. But beginning in November 1949, the Viet Minh leadership implemented a program of obligatory military service and tried to mobilize the entire civilian population to support what was rapidly becoming a conventional modern war.[83]

The porter system was placed on a more regular basis in 1951 when the Viet Minh government decreed that all able-bodied peasants, male and female, must contribute three months of labor per year to the Viet Minh logistical effort.[84] The GSD Transportation Branch organized an "auxiliary service" of porters to move supplies from depot areas to forward supply dumps and troop units. The auxiliary service was structured along paramilitary lines, with companies of about 140 porters drawn from a prescribed geographical area.[85] Each auxiliary service company consisted of three sections, each with three groups of fifteen coolies. Auxiliary service companies or parts thereof were activated as required to meet operational requirements and could be called upon only by the GSD, the GSD Transportation and Food Supply Branches, interzone commanders, or other high-level agencies.

Operationally, the supporting Viet Minh porters were organized in "convoys" protected by armed escorts.[86] The escorts provided security for the porters and sometimes created diversions to distract French Union forces while the porters slipped by an observation post. The porters marched mainly at night over routes offering good cover and concealment. The established routes were cleared, smoothed out, and maintained. They usually were divided by relay posts called *trams*.[87] The night's march usually ended at a *tram*, which often was equipped with crude facilities for cooking and shelter and at which the porter convoy hid and rested during daylight hours.

The normal load of the Viet Minh porter was about fifty pounds, carried over a distance of up to fifteen miles in a twenty-four-hour period.[88] The general capabilities of Viet Minh porters with respect to different cargoes carried over various types of terrain are shown in table 6.4. The amount of cargo that could be handled by one porter increased substantially if bicycles were used.[89] The famous Viet Minh "cargo bicycle" had no pedals or chain, and was normally pushed along with the aid of a horizontal stick attached to the frame rather than being ridden. One bicycle porter could move his load about twenty-five kilometers per day.[90]

The number of porters employed by the Viet Minh on a given campaign varied according to the circumstances, but the total, as well as the ratio of porters to combat troops, could be quite high. One analyst has calculated that in order to move five tons of supplies over a distance of fifty miles, each porter carrying thirty pounds over a distance of 9.3 miles per day, a force of 3,585–27,835 porters would be required.[91] A twelve-thousand-man Viet Minh division on a forced march of fifteen days duration required *for its rations alone* around fifteen thousand porters.[92] Some reports placed the number of Viet Minh porters used to support the three Viet Minh divisions during the three-month battle for Hoa Binh in the winter of 1951–1952 at between 150,000 and 160,000 men and women.[93] During their campaign in the T'ai region of northwestern Tonkin in the fall of 1952, the Viet Minh were reputed to have employed some thirty thousand porters, a ratio of one porter for every soldier supported.[94] Another Viet Minh division is reported to have required forty thousand porters to meet its needs in a simple operation, and the two Viet Minh divisions operating in Laos in the spring of 1953 are said to have been supplied by a force of forty-five thousand porters.[95] J. Wallace Higgins estimated that in the eight major battles between the battle for RC-4 in 1950 and Dien Bien Phu in 1954, the Viet Minh employed some 1,541,381 "transport porters" who worked a total of 47.8 million man days in all.[96]

The advantages to the use of porters in Indochina were several. Porters were

Table 6.4. Typical Viet Minh Porter Loads and Distances

Terrain Type	Miles Per 24-Hour Period		Load (lbs.)	Supply Type
	Day	Night		
Level	15.5	12.4	55	Rice
Level	15.5	12.4	33–44	Arms
Mountains	9.3	7.5	29	Rice
Mountains	9.3	7.5	22–33	Arms

Source: Based on Higgins, *Porterage Parameters and Tables*, 6 (table I).

plentiful, they were able to overcome almost any physical obstacle, and they were relatively undetectable from the air when observing normal march discipline. On the other hand, porters posed their own problems. For one thing, they were usually required to carry their own provisions in addition to their cargo since the requisitioning of food from the local areas through which Viet Minh units passed was generally avoided whenever possible to avoid antagonizing the civilian population.[97] As Bernard Fall has pointed out, the average daily rice ration for a porter was 1.76 pounds; thus, on a journey of 310 miles requiring about fifteen days of marching a porter would consume half of the 55 pounds he might carry, thus reducing his cargo load to only 28.6 pounds.[98] On longer trips a porter might eat 90 percent of what he could carry.[99]

The Viet Minh porter system also had a significant impact on Viet Minh strategic planning and operations. Since the *Chu Luc* were almost entirely dependent on civilian porters for the movement of their supplies, the timing and tempo of offensive operations were dependent on the seasons. The five months most favorable for offensive military operations in northern Indochina were November, January, February, March, and April. Due to the seasonal monsoon, the months of May through September were generally too wet and muddy for easy cross-country movement. December and June were the rice-planting months and May and October were the harvest months. During the planting and harvesting seasons, all able-bodied men and women were needed to perform the critical agricultural work, and thus were unavailable for carrying military supplies.

A system dependent on large numbers of coolies drafted from their homes and fields for periodic service as porters was difficult to maintain. Enthusiasm for such work was not high. Heavy loads, long distances, absence from home, fatigue, disease, and strafing by French aircraft were not conducive to happy porters, and the GSD Transportation Branch often had to struggle to keep the porters on the job until the mission was finished.[100] Management of the porter system was made even more complex and unpopular by policies that called for porters to be "activated" for only fourteen days at a time, of which seven were "carrying days" and seven were allotted for traveling from and to the home village. Indeed, in certain areas, such as the T'ai region in northwestern Tonkin, the population successfully evaded such service, and the required number of porters was usually obtained only under coercion despite Viet Minh propaganda regarding the glorious exploits of the dedicated *Dan Cong*. The levying of an agricultural population for labor, especially a large proportion of the remaining able-bodied population in areas already combed for combatant males, also had the potential of disrupting the all-important business of planting and harvesting rice. As one French authority noted: "The arrival of Chinese automotive equipment revolutionized the enemy's military transportation system. It resulted in the country's roads being put into good condition and removed the terrible strain off the country insofar as the levying of coolies was concerned for forming up the troop combat trains."[101]

Animal Transport

The Viet Minh used a variety of types of animal transport, including horses, water buffaloes, and even elephants, although they preferred human porters for overland movements because they were hardier, easier to manage, and more flexible. While a cart drawn by a water buffalo could move an average load of 770 pounds about 7.5 miles in a twenty-four-hour period, and a horse-drawn cart could move an average load of 473 pounds a distance of 12.4 miles in the same amount of time, carts were often impractical due to the terrain and the ease with which they could be spotted from the air.[102] In 1953, pack animals were used extensively to shuttle supplies around sections of road in the Viet Minh base areas made impassable by French air attacks.

Motor Transport

Despite continued reliance on hordes of porters, after 1950 the Viet Minh increasingly depended on motor transport for the movement of ammunition and other supplies and equipment, mainly from China to depots in the Viet Minh base areas in northern Tonkin. Only in exceptional circumstances, such as the Dien Bien Phu campaign, were the available Viet Minh trucks used to transport personnel or to move supplies forward from the depots into the combat areas. The Viet Minh truck fleet began with fifty–sixty trucks abandoned by the French during their evacuation of Cao Bang and Lang Son in 1950.[103] In 1951, the Viet Minh still had less than one hundred trucks, mostly taken from the French, but by 1953 the number had risen to nearly one thousand.[104] Most of the motor vehicles used by the Viet Minh after 1951 were supplied by Communist China, and they included large numbers of American trucks captured in Korea and subsequently refurbished by the Chinese. The Chinese may also have supplied most of the drivers, at least up to 1953–1954. By the end of the war in 1954, the Viet Minh probably had over two thousand trucks in service.[105] Of course, not all of those trucks were available at any given time since the wear and tear on the relatively small Viet Minh truck fleet was tremendous. Spare parts were always scarce, and there were few trained mechanics.

About one-third of the Viet Minh motor transport was assigned to one or another of the nine companies of the three-thousand-man 16th Truck Regiment (*Trung Doan 16*), which was controlled by the GSD Transportation Branch.[106] The principal mission of *Trung Doan 16* was the movement of supplies and equipment from China to the depots in the Viet Minh base areas in northern Tonkin.[107] The routes over which *Trung Doan 16* operated were divided into three "relays"—Viet Bac, Central, and Northwest—under the control of the Transportation Branch, and each relay had its own administrative, technical, and transport sections.[108] Guards and convoy conductors were provided by a separate armed unit directly controlled by the Transportation Branch. The Viet Minh truck regiment was not employed as a unit. Instead, each company, which had ninety to a hundred men and about thirty-five task vehicles as well as its own maintenance section, was assigned its own self-contained operating segment of the line of communication.[109] Consequently, drivers became very familiar with the routes over which they operated and were generally able to drive at night without headlights.[110] On the other hand, such a segmented system required repeated transloading of cargoes, which was very inefficient even with the large number of coolies available. The fragmentation of the routes from China to the Viet Minh base areas was necessitated by the fact that the damage caused by French air attacks on bridges and other transportation choke points naturally divided the routes into segments.[111]

The Viet Minh task vehicles were mainly American or Russian 2.5-ton models. The more powerful American GMC "deuce and a half" was used in the more difficult mountainous areas, for example between Cao Bang and Bac Kan, while the Soviet GAZ-51 Molotova was operated on the easier terrain of the central relay.[112] A typical load for the GAZ-51 was thirty bags of rice at 132 pounds per bag, or ten drums of gas at 341 pounds per drum, or eighty 75 mm artillery shells or 240 81 mm mortar rounds.[113]

Water Transport

Small motor vessels and sailing junks were important means of moving supplies from mainland China and Hainan to the coastal areas of Tonkin and northern Annam and, to a lesser degree, all along the Indochinese coast from the Gulf of Tonkin to the Gulf of Siam. This coastal traffic, which was important principally for the movement of military supplies between Interzone 4 and Tonkin and between Interzone 5 and Cochinchina, increased during the favorable sailing season, reaching as much as one hundred to two hundred tons per month.[114]

Despite the deployment of a blockading force of both ships and Catalina flying boats, the French never entirely succeeded in shutting down the movement of Viet Minh supplies by sea. The Viet Minh also made maximum use of available inland water routes, mostly in northern Annam, although the French were able to control waterborne traffic on the major rivers and in the great river deltas to a great degree. The movement of men and supplies by sampan was more important in the southern regions of Indochina than it was in the northern areas that were the main operational areas of the war. The use of small boats for ferries, however, was important everywhere.

Railroads

The Viet Minh made what use they could of the limited railroad trackage under their control in Tonkin and northern Annam. In December 1951, the Communist Chinese advanced their rail line from Nanning to Chennan-kuan (Na Cham) on the Vietnamese border near Lang Son, but there was no actual rail connection into Tonkin from anywhere in China.[115] Major restoration of the rail system in northern Viet Nam and reconnection with the Chinese rail system did not occur until after the 1954 cease-fire and was accomplished mainly by the Chinese.[116]

Some sections of the Haiphong–Yunnan rail system and of the main north-south coastal trunk line that were under Viet Minh control were restored, but for the most part the restored sections were used for small rail cars that were pushed by coolies running barefoot on the ties and ballast.[117] Each coolie pushed along a six-mile section of track and was paid 2,000 Viet Minh *piastres* per night. The pace was relatively quick, about 6–7.5 miles per hour, and on the downhill slopes the coolies hopped aboard for the ride. In some cases, jeeps or trucks fitted with flanged wheels were used as motive power. For example, trucks with flanged wheels ran on the short segments of railroad between Bao Ha and Yen Bay in Tonkin and near Quang Ngai and Qui Nhon in Annam.[118]

The heavy reliance of Viet Minh logisticians on porters for the movement of supplies was considered by many Western observers to be a weakness, but in reality the use of porters was perfectly adapted to the terrain of Indochina and capitalized on the large but untrained manpower pool available to the Viet Minh. Porters could go where trucks could not, and they proved generally invulnerable to French air and ground interdiction. More significantly, although difficult to manage, after a few initial failures the porter system proved more than adequate to meet Viet Minh needs. The adaptability of the Viet Minh logistical system was further demonstrated by the effective use of motor transport once it became available in sufficient quantities.

While the Viet Minh porters slipped through the jungles and mountains with relative ease to support their combat forces in the areas of operations, the French Union forces struggled to support their wide-spread garrisons and operational units by land, water, and air. The terrain, climate, and poor transportation infrastructure restricted movements and often meant that isolated units went days without resupply. The wear and tear on both equipment and personnel were heavy, and in the end the results proved unsatisfactory for the French, who, unlike the Viet Minh, failed to adapt adequately to the existing physical and operational environment.

7

French Sources of Supply

In 1945, the French Union forces seemed to have an enormous advantage over the Viet Minh with respect to the acquisition of war materiel. France was an industrial nation with direct access to the production of the other major Western industrial powers. Moreover, France controlled the principal resources of Indochina itself as well as the facilities necessary to process them for use. But to some degree the French advantage was illusory because neither the French nor the Viet Minh would have been able to pursue the war in Indochina without outside assistance. Although possessed of enormous potential resources, including those of its colonies in Africa and Asia, France had suffered heavily in World War II and the French economy was in shambles. Hard pressed to restore the economy of metropolitan France, the French were clearly unable to sustain a major war effort in Indochina without help. That aid became available after 1950 in the form of massive American financial and material support, including aircraft, watercraft, arms, ammunition, and a vast array of other war supplies.

Local Production and Procurement

The local resources of Indochina were limited principally to foodstuffs and other raw materials. Rice, fish, animals, coal, charcoal, and construction materials were available and were acquired in considerable quantities, particularly by the *Service du Matériel* (SM) and the engineers.[1] The advantages of local procurement included rapid delivery to the site of use, support of the indigenous economy, and the development of safe sources of supply in the event of failures in deliveries from overseas. On the other hand, local goods were often more expensive than the same items purchased in France or on the world market. Increased local production of the military materiel required by the French Union forces would have significantly improved the timely supply of critical items, but the French authorities, following a long-standing colonialist policy, declined to develop a local military equipment industry in Indochina. The reason advanced for this policy was that locally produced military goods might more easily fall into Viet Minh hands, but the real reason was that the French wished to keep Indochina dependent on France.[2] In September 1951, the U.S. Military Assistance Advisory Group–Indochina (MAAG-Indochina) and the American legation in Saigon suggested that some simple items of military equipment be manufactured in Indochina to reduce the quantity of materiel to be shipped across the Pacific. French resistance to the suggestion was strong, and the U.S. authorities eventually decided that an effort to force the issue would be unproductive.[3]

Procurement on the World Market

In the immediate post–World War II period, the French authorities in Indochina attempted to purchase some of the enormous amounts of military equipment declared surplus or simply abandoned by the U.S. and British forces in Asia. Purchasing missions were established in Manila, Singapore, New Delhi, and Calcutta, and a significant amount of war surplus was purchased before anticolonialist opposition cut off such sources of supply.[4] The Americans were generally reluctant to approve such purchases, but the British were more accommodating.[5] The Indian market was well-provided with foodstuffs, clothing, and tires, but Indian laborers refused to load such material on ships bound for Indochina. In 1947, such surplus stocks were turned over to the new national governments (India and Pakistan), and thus the French were denied access to them altogether. A purchasing office was also maintained in Tokyo by the Department of the Associated States, which made direct purchases on the Japanese market for the French Union forces in Indochina. The postwar revival of the Japanese economy made such purchases possible at good prices, and the delivery time for some items difficult to obtain from France (parachutes, radio equipment, and spare parts) was much reduced.[6] Some supplies were also purchased in Australia and elsewhere.

Procurement from France and the French Union

Local production and purchases on the world market met only a small percentage of the overall requirements for the French Union forces. In the first years of the war, as a matter of policy as well as a matter of necessity, the bulk of the war materiel required by the French Union forces in Indochina was obtained from metropolitan France or the other states of the French Union. In 1951 alone, some 289,000 tons of supplies were imported from France and North Africa, and in 1952 the total rose to 323,780 tons.[7] French forces in metropolitan France obtained supplies and equipment through the central directions of the supply services under the Ministry of War. However, the forces in Indochina obtained their requirements through the Military Affairs Directorate of the Overseas Ministry, which budgeted for and conducted its own procurement operations.[8] The directorate passed demands to civil providers or in some cases through the War Ministry to the central directions of the various military supply services. However, the personnel of the Military Affairs Directorate lacked experience in military procurement, and long delays occurred in the provision of critical items to the troops in Indochina, particularly in the early years of the war. Annual supply plans of fifty thousand to sixty thousand lines (individual items), the long budget lead time, and the problems of French industry just recovering from the war contributed to delays of eighteen to twenty-four months on obtaining supplies for the forces in Indochina.[9] The delays in acquiring needed supplies were compounded by the frequent delays in passing the annual budget. At the end of the 1951 budget year, for example, only 50 percent of the requirements had been filled due in part to the delays that had occurred in passing the budget.[10]

The logistical support of the French Union forces in Indochina was carried out under rigid peacetime budgeting procedures and in an economy that had yet to recover from World War II and that was also on a thoroughly peacetime basis. The supply and equipment requirements for the forces in Indochina were addressed in the form of an annual campaign plan and an annual supply plan submitted by the *commandant en chef* in Indochina to the Military Affairs Directorate.[11] The campaign plan was submitted on July 1 for the following year and was essentially a financial plan for the ground forces in Indochina (the navy and air force elements were included in the budgets of their respective ministries) and expressed the supply plan in financial terms. The campaign plan was used to establish the annual budget for Indochina and was recalculated by the Military Affairs Directorate to accommodate known budget constraints and the possibilities of supply. The supply plan set forth the actual requirements by supply line item. Since the determination of requirements took place a minimum of six months before the execution of the supply plan, there were often many discrepancies between the plan and reality. For example, in July 1950 the estimate was made that in 1951 only five thousand rounds of 105 mm ammunition would be required per month and that there would be no significant engineer work. However, the increased intensity of operations in Tonkin actually resulted in a monthly expenditure of over thirty thousand rounds of 105 mm ammunition and several million francs worth of concrete fortifications.[12] Similarly, the estimate for 1952 was for 687,000 rounds of 105 mm HM2 ammunition but consumption was actually only 580,000 rounds, and the 1953 estimate was set at 500,000 rounds but actual consumption turned out to be 514,000 rounds.

Such a process was not convenient, either to the government or to the commander in the field, but it resulted from the peacetime economy of France and the changing conditions on the battlefield in Indochina. The problems might have been alleviated by the stocking of adequate reserve supplies in Indochina, but such stockpiling was not possible due to the low productive capacity of French industry at the time.[13] The *commandant en chef* could, of course, submit emergency requests for supplemental supplies, and he did so on numerous occasions. However, the long order-ship time for supplies and equipment from France and the uncertain availability of specific items generally made this a futile effort.[14] The establishment of a rear supply base in France for Indochina would have been of great use. Such a rear supply base for ammunition was set up at Miramar, but no such base was ever created for other supplies and equipment, with the result that deliveries were irregular and additional storage facilities had to be created in Indochina.[15]

The delays in deliveries from metropolitan France and North Africa to Indochina were due not only to the long distances involved and the delays in budgeting and procurement. Active opposition to the war in Indochina was promoted by the French Communist Party and by other left-wing groups that were able to slow down movements of cargo to the ports and the loading of that cargo aboard ships bound for Indochina. Moreover, a French parliamentary inquiry determined that about 40 percent of all the equipment sent to Indochina from France was sabotaged by sugar in the gasoline tanks, broken wiring, or emery oil in the transmissions.[16] On the other hand, several French cities, notably Bordeaux, collected money to purchase helicopters for the evacuation of French wounded in Indochina.

Logistical Support from the United States

From mid-1950 to the end of the war in July 1954, the United States was the principal source of military equipment and supplies for the French Union forces. In May 1954, one former chief of MAAG-Indochina estimated that "indigenous production is practically negligible," and that only about 30 percent of the hard items needed by the French Union forces was provided by French procurement agencies, the remainder being provided through U.S. military aid.[17] Even then, most of the materiel provided by the French themselves was of U.S. manufacture and obtained during World War II or from postwar U.S. surplus stocks. Although entirely dependent on American support to continue the war, the French were rude and ungrateful recipients of American largesse. For their part, although eager to prop up their NATO ally and to pursue the anti-Communist crusade in Asia, U.S. leaders were uncomfortable with the idea of supporting a failed colonial regime and with providing millions of dollars' worth of equipment and supplies to a client who refused to consider seriously any American suggestion.[18] In fact, the goals of the two countries in Indochina were very different. France sought to retain control over her colonies, while the United States was instead focused on containing the spread of Communism. Ultimately, the decision to aid the French in Indochina and to establish a military assistance advisory group there began the direct involvement of the United States in a war that would last a quarter of a century and cost more than fifty-four thousand American lives.

The Origins of U.S. Involvement in Indochina

The strained relationship between France and the United States with respect to Indochina went back to American opposition to the French colonial regime in

Indochina during and immediately after World War II, a matter that has engendered considerable historical debate. In his several works on Indochina, Bernard B. Fall, reflecting a French perspective, portrayed the American opposition to the French as strong and premeditated.[19] More recently, Ronald H. Spector has taken a contrary view, noting that "the view that the United States deliberately limited and delayed its help to the French during the Japanese takeover is incorrect," and that, although opposed to the restoration of French colonial rule in Indochina, President Franklin D. Roosevelt did permit limited support to the French.[20] In any event, the French perception that the United States deliberately abandoned them to the Japanese and then worked with the Viet Minh to prevent the restoration of French control in Indochina did much to sour relationships between France and the United States in the postwar period.

From the beginning of the Second World War until 1950, American policy toward the French in Indochina might indeed be described as thoroughly antipathetic. President Roosevelt himself led the anti-Vichy, even anti-French, opposition and limited assistance to the French regime in Indochina before and during World War II. Roosevelt's distaste for French colonial rule in Indochina seems to have been largely personal, but it was translated into policies that inhibited French resistance to the Japanese.[21] In a memorandum to Secretary of State Cordell Hull on October 13, 1944, President Roosevelt stated, "We should do nothing in regard to resistance groups or in any other way in relation to Indochina," and less than a month later, on November 3, he instructed American field commanders in Asia to refuse "American approval . . . to any French military mission being accredited to the South-East Asia Command."[22]

French efforts to obtain aircraft, weapons, and other equipment from the United States or elsewhere before the Japanese moved into French Indochina on September 22, 1940, were also stymied. For example, the efforts of the French commander in Indochina, General Georges Catroux, to strengthen his position against Japanese demands by obtaining the 120 modern fighter aircraft and the antiaircraft artillery already bought and paid for by the French government were brought to naught when the U.S. government prohibited shipment of the equipment to Indochina.[23]

Once the French had taken up arms against the Japanese, President Roosevelt refused to sanction low-level French participation in U.S. intelligence and commando operations in Indochina, and the few joint Franco-American operations that did take place were mostly unsuccessful since the Indochinese were wary of the French members of the teams and refused to help.[24] According to Bernard Fall, President Roosevelt directed his military commanders in China to deny support to the scattered and starving French forces even when they were overrun by the Japanese in March 1945 and were fighting for their very existence against the common enemy.[25] In fact, the U.S. forces in China had very little to give, and although opposed to the restoration of the French colonial regime in Indochina, President Roosevelt did permit limited support of the French.[26] To his credit, Lieutenant General Claire L. Chennault, commander of the U.S. Fourteenth Air Force in China, apparently provided limited supply drops and some fighter cover to the retreating French troops in northern Tonkin through May 1945.[27] Chennault later wrote that when "orders arrived from Theater headquarters stating that no arms and ammunition would be provided to French troops under any circumstances . . . I carried out my orders to the letter but I did not relish the idea of leaving Frenchmen to be slaughtered in the jungle while I was forced officially to ignore their plight."[28]

Once the war was over, the attempts of the French to resume their military presence in Indochina were frustrated for a time by the lack of available transport, a lack that some French leaders attributed (with some justification) to malice on the part of their erstwhile allies.[29] Even before the war ended, President Roosevelt refused to approve the allocation of shipping to move a French expeditionary corps to Southeast Asia.[30] When, despite all obstacles, the French regained a foothold in Indochina and attempted to supply their forces there with some of the surplus materiel left in Asia by the British and American forces, they again met with opposition.[31] The British were somewhat more sympathetic and provided the French forces recently returned to Indochina with some eight hundred U.S. Lend-Lease jeeps and trucks as well as other materiel.[32] President Truman approved the transfer only because repatriation of the vehicles to the United States would have been impractical, but in general the U.S. government continued to oppose such aid. For example, until 1950 American-built propellers installed on British aircraft had to be removed when such aircraft were sent to the French in Indochina.[33] In September 1945, the French commander in Indochina, Lieutenant General Philippe Leclerc, found General Douglas MacArthur in Tokyo apparently willing to provide much-needed supplies and equipment, but only if he received the orders to do so from Washington.[34]

The brief flirtation of the United States with the Viet Minh in 1945 and 1946 also created a very negative impression on the French that has even yet to be dispelled. The desire to defeat the Japanese and American anticolonialist sentiment combined to produce a degree of American cooperation with Ho Chi Minh and his nationalist movement. Although the degree of cooperation and the amount of arms and equipment provided to the Viet Minh by the American Office of Strategic Services (OSS) were small, the public approbation of the Viet Minh greatly offended the French, who had hoped for more from their old ally. The French complained bitterly that the Viet Minh had been able to seize control of large parts of Indochina in 1945 only because they had been supplied by the OSS with arms and ammunition, but Ronald Spector notes that the effect was mainly psychological and that "arms received during World War II accounted for only about

12 percent of the estimated 36,000 small arms in Viet Minh hands in March 1946 and only about 5 percent of the weapons available to them at the start of the war against the French in December 1946."[35] On the other hand, the humiliating treatment of French prisoners of war and the public encouragement of the Viet Minh by American officers in the immediate postwar period provided more than sufficient grounds for French suspicion and distrust of American motives.[36]

The Decision to Aid the French

At best, American attitudes toward the French in Indochina were ambivalent until the late 1940s. Even after the United States abandoned Uncle Ho, little effort was made to aid the French in retaining their colonial empire in Asia. However, as the Cold War with the Soviet Union began to take shape, the U.S. State Department and Joint Chiefs of Staff (JCS) recognized that Indochina was an area of vital strategic interest to the United States, and France came to be viewed as a lynchpin of the NATO alliance facing the Soviets in Europe. The situation began to change dramatically in 1949 with the successful Soviet testing of an atomic bomb and, more importantly, the victory of Mao Tse-tung's People's Liberation Army over the Chinese Nationalist troops of Chiang Kai-shek at the end of the year. The outbreak of the war in Korea in June 1950 and the subsequent intervention of the Chinese Communists in that conflict in October 1950 completed the transformation. Thereafter, the United States acted forcefully to assist the French Union forces against the Viet Minh as part of an overall effort to stop the Communist tide in Asia. As Lieutenant General Henri Navarre, one of the last French *commandants en chef* in Indochina, later wrote: "The Americans finally realized the danger of Communism in Southeast Asia, which led them to modify their point of view on the war in Indochina. In place of an impious 'colonial war,' they promised a holy war against Communism."[37]

On October, 6, 1949, the U.S. Congress passed "An Act to Promote the Foreign Policy and Provide for the Defense and General Welfare of the United States by Furnishing Military Assistance to Foreign Nations," subsequently known as the Mutual Defense Assistance Act of 1949, which established the Mutual Defense Assistance Program (MDAP) to provide American arms, military equipment, and training assistance to friendly countries worldwide. Although the bulk of the first appropriations under the Act went to NATO allies and to Greece and Turkey, Section 303 of the Act authorized $75 million to be used "in the general area of China," and in January 1950 Congress appropriated that amount.[38]

On February 4, 1950, the French government announced formal ratification of the Elysée Agreements granting independence within the French Union to the so-called Associated States, and on the following day the United States recognized the governments of Viet Nam, Cambodia, and Laos. Although reluctant to call upon the United States for assistance, following an interarmy conference at Paris in February 1950, the French drew up initial lists of equipment needed in Indochina, and on March 16, 1950, those lists, which included arms and equipment worth some $94 million, were presented by the French government to the U.S. embassy in Paris as a formal request for American aid.[39] The lists included $11 million worth of ammunition, $32 million worth of automotive equipment, $2 million in medical supplies, $8 million in engineer equipment, and $8 million worth of signal equipment. The lists were later modified to accommodate the changing military situation in Indochina (the emergence of the main Viet Minh regular battle force) and General Jean de Lattre's plans to reinforce the CEFEO and develop the National Armies of Viet Nam, Cambodia, and Laos.

Meanwhile, on March 1, 1950, the JCS recommended the allocation of $15 million in Section 303 funds to Indochina, and President Harry Truman approved that recommendation on March 10.[40] The same day, President Truman asked the JCS to study the situation in Indochina and forward its recommendations. The JCS responded in a memorandum for the Secretary of Defense dated April 10, 1950, and recommended "early implementation of military aid programs for Indochina, Indonesia, Thailand, the Philippines, and Burma."[41] They also recommended the allocation of $100 million for the military portion of the aid program under Section 303 of PL 329 for Asia in the coming fiscal year (FY 1952). Given the recent debacle in China, where enormous amounts of U.S. military aid had fallen into Communist hands, the JCS urged that the following conditions be applied to aid to Indochina:

a. That United States military aid not be granted unconditionally; rather, that it be carefully controlled and that the aid program be integrated with political and economic programs; and

b. That requests for military equipment be screened first by an officer designated by the Department of Defense and on duty in the recipient state. These requests should be subject to his determination as to the feasibility and satisfactory coordination of specific military operations. It should be understood that military aid will only be considered in connection with such coordinated operational plans as are approved by the representative of the Department of Defense on duty in the recipient country. Further, in conformity with current procedures, the final approval of all programs for military materiel will be subject to the concurrence of the Joint Chiefs of Staff.[42]

The JCS also recommended the immediate formation of "a small United States military aid group in Indochina" to fulfill the requirements set forth in paragraph 9b of the memorandum.[43] The bottom line was that the JCS recommended "the provision of military aid to Indochina at the earliest practicable date under a program to implement the President's action approving the allocation of 15 million dollars [of MDAP aid] for Indochina and that corresponding increments of political and economic aid be programmed on an interim basis without prejudice to the pattern of the policy for additional military, political and economic aid that may be developed later."[44] In early June, the JCS recommended and President Truman approved an additional $16 million in MDAP aid to Indochina in FY 1950.[45] The JCS also recommended that Indochina receive first priority among all the Asian military aid programs.

Initial Military Aid to the French

Following the Communist Chinese capture of Hainan Island at the beginning of May 1950, President Truman approved the allocation of $10 million to pay for the shipment of urgently needed military supplies to Indochina. The decision was announced by the secretary of state to a meeting of the French ministers on May 8, and on May 24 both the French government and the governments of the Associated States (Viet Nam, Cambodia, and Laos) were informed of the U.S. decision to establish an economic aid mission in Indochina. President Truman acknowledged his decision publicly two days after North Korean forces attacked the Republic of Korea, when he issued a press release on June 27, 1950, condemning the Communist action and outlining the measures that the United States would take to aid South Korea and prevent further Communist aggression in Asia. As part of those actions, President Truman "directed acceleration in the furnishing of military assistance to the forces of France and the Associated States in Indo China and the dispatch of a military mission to provide close working relations with those forces."[46]

Three days later, on June 30, the same day U.S. ground forces were committed to combat in Korea, the first shipments of American aid arrived in Saigon aboard eight old C-47 transports loaded with spare parts, and by July 30, equipment sufficient for twelve infantry battalions was en route by ship to Indochina.[47] The C-47s were turned over by their American pilots to the French at Tan Son Nhut airport, and the SS *Steelrover,* carrying the first load of heavy weapons and infantry equipment, docked in Saigon on August 10.[48] Meanwhile, a French aircraft carrier was scheduled to take on forty F6F fighters in California in September and another French ship was scheduled to transport eighteen LCVPs, six LSSLs, and other cargo from the United States to Indochina.[49]

Earlier, on July 15, 1950, a joint U.S. State Department–Defense Department MDAP survey mission headed by John F. Melby of the State Department and Major General Graves B. Erskine, USMC, arrived in Saigon to study the situation and determine the role that the United States might play.[50] The members of the survey mission concluded that there could be "no over-all solution to the Indochina problem without a military solution as a primary requisite," but that "this military solution can in no sense be decisive without the application of political and economic techniques to the problem."[51] They also found that the existing aid program was inadequate. For his part, Major General Erskine noted "the absolute interdependence of the military, political, and economic problems in the country; the mutual distrust and lack of good faith between French and Indochinese at all levels; and the lack of offensive spirit in the French high command and the poor strategic distribution and use of its forces," and he also expressed his doubts that "the French authorities have sincerely put forth their best efforts to train and equip a Vietnamese army and thus remove one of the great sources of distrust now existing."[52] The survey team also recognized the key to French victory or defeat in Indochina, stating: "The French and the Indochinese must be persuaded, wherever necessary, to rise above their own parochial interests by realizing that these interests can be served by the establishment of a community of interests dedicated to the independence, integrity, welfare, and prosperity of the peoples concerned. Any division in this community of interests is and will continue to be the nourishment upon which the Communists will feed."[53]

U.S. Military Aid Deliveries to the French

The Chinese Communist intervention in the war in Korea in the fall of 1950 served to accelerate the provision of American aid to the French in Indochina, but for almost a year deliveries under the existing plans were slow, due in part to the lack of production facilities, machine tools, and raw materials as well as labor problems; at the end of FY 1951, for example, only 444 of the 968 promised jeeps had been delivered and only 393 of the 906 promised 2.5-ton trucks.[54] Although U.S. MDAP deliveries were admittedly slower than desired, the French constantly misrepresented the progress achieved and criticized "the amount and timeliness of American aid," perhaps in an effort to justify the deteriorating military situation in Indochina.[55] The editors of *The Pentagon Papers* opined that such "complaints probably reflected less genuine U.S. shortcomings than French resentment of American efforts to advise, screen, inspect, and verify, and sheer frustration."[56] Yet, despite the slowness of American deliveries, the French were unable to keep up with the distribution of the material within Indochina, although many observers credited the influx of American equipment with contributing to the French victories in the first half of 1951. In fact, the chief of MAAG-Indochina, Brigadier General Francis G. Brink, personally flew to Tokyo in January 1951 to obtain critical supplies for the French units engaged at Vinh Yen, and in June 1951, when French stocks of 105 mm ammunition ran dangerously low during the battle for Phat Diem on the Day River, Brink again personally intervened to arrange for the French to draw ammunition directly from the U.S. Far East Command depots.[57]

Following the successful visit of General de Lattre to the United States in September–October 1951, U.S. military aid deliveries were speeded up—as U.S. Army Chief of Staff General J. Lawton Collins had personally assured de Lattre they would be. From November 1951, deliveries were quite steady, delivery time was reduced, and the number of items in critical short supply in Indochina declined.[58] Between October 1951 and February 1952, a total of 130,000 tons of equipment, including 53 million rounds of ammunition, 8,000 vehicles, 650 combat vehicles, 200 aircraft, 3,500 radios, and 14,000 automatic weapons were received by the French from American sources.[59] Overall, deliveries in 1951 from the United States and from U.S. stocks in Japan totaled some 95,000 tons and then rose to 110,000 tons in 1952, and by February 1953 some 137,200 long tons—the equivalent of 224 ship-loads—of American equipment had reached Indochina.[60] That materiel included 900 tracked combat vehicles, 15,000 wheeled vehicles, nearly 2,500 artillery pieces, 24,000 automatic weapons, 75,000 small arms, and almost 9,000 radios, as well as 160 F6F and F8F fighters, 41 B-26 light bombers, 28 much-needed C-47 transports, 155 aircraft engines, and 93,000 bombs for the French air forces in Indochina.[61]

Some of the supplies obtained from the United States were acquired by direct dollar purchases made by the French purchasing mission in the United States, but most of the materiel was provided gratuitously by the U.S. government under the Mutual Defense Assistance Program, and after 1953 under the Military Support Program (MSP), both of which depended on credits authorized by the U.S. Congress. The equipment and supplies provided under the MDAP and MSP generally came from military depots in the United States, but some materiel, especially ammunition, vehicles, and Air Force spare parts, was issued from U.S. depots in Japan, thereby significantly reducing the shipping time by about six months.

In his May 3, 1953, debriefing, the former commander of MAAG-Indochina, Major General Thomas J. H. Trapnell, noted:

> The U.S. has greatly contributed to the success of the French in hold-ing Indochina from the beginning. In January 1951, material was rushed from the docks of Haiphong to the battlefield of Vinh Yen, then being fought under the personal direction of Marshall De Lattre himself. Since then, delivery of aid has kept pace with changing French needs, often on a crash basis, down to the present heroic defense of Dien Bien Phu. U.S. aid has consisted of budgetary support, furnishing of end items, mili-tary hardware, and of technical training teams. The magnitude and range of this contribution is shown by the following very few examples. All of these figures are as of 31 March this year [1953].
>
> a. 785 million dollars has been allocated for the budgetary support of the French Expeditionary Force and the Vietnamese Army. This will assist in

Table 7.1. Value of U.S. Military Assistance Program for Indochina, 1950–1956 (in U.S. $)

Categories	Army	Navy	Air Force	Total MAP
Equipment	461,696,000	58,790,000	128,002,000	648,488,000
Aircraft	1,067,000	7,235,000	55,518,000	63,820,000
Ships	2,011,000	17,778,000	–	19,789,000
Tanks, Vehicles, and Weapons	155,848,000	2,681,000	3,274,000	161,803,000
Ammunition	205,936,000	26,218,000	63,668,000	295,822,000
Electronics and Communications	32,946,000	2,445,000	1,710,000	37,101,000
Other Equipment and Supplies	63,888,000	2,433,000	3,832,000	70,153,000
Services	4,064,000	1,389,000	46,000	61,088,000
Repair and Rehab of Equipment	4,049,000	1,156,000	46,000	5,251,000
Pack/Crate/Handling/Transport	–	–	–	55,589,000
Training	15,000	233,000	–	248,000
Total (excluding credit financing and excess stocks)	**465,760,000**	**60,179,000**	**128,048,000**	**709,576,000**
Excess Stocks (Acquisition Cost)	**15,993,000**	**5,130,000**	**759,000**	**21,882,000**

Source: "Indochina," *Journal of Military Assistance* 14, no. 80 (December 1961): 124.

    meeting budgetary requirements for pay, food, and allowances for these troops.

    b. Under MDA Programs, a total of more than 784 millions of dollars has been programmed for the years 1950–54. Of this, more than 440 million dollars' worth of military end items have been received.

    c. To date, 31 March 1954, 441 ships have delivered a total of 478 thousands of long tons of MDA equipment to Indochina.[62]

With the inactivation of the CEFEO on April 28, 1956, the U.S. military assistance program was terminated, and all the remaining MAP-provided equipment was supposed to revert to the U.S. government, but the French kept the best of it and left the rest for the armed forces of the Republic of Viet Nam. The cumulative MAP totals are shown in table 7.1.

Between 1950 and 1954, the United States provided the French Union forces in Indochina with an astounding amount of arms and equipment, in all more than 1.5 million measurement tons, not including aircraft and naval vessels that arrived under their own power.[63] As the authors of the U.S. Joint Chiefs of Staff history of the period stated: "When the United States entered the picture in 1950 French Union forces were indifferently armed with largely obsolescent World War II equipment. Long and hard usage in the humid climate of Indochina, together with improper and inadequate maintenance, had made much of this equipment nearly unserviceable. Between 1950 and 1954 the French and native troops were almost completely reequipped with modern weapons and vehicles."[64]

Included in the total of equipment and supplies provided by the United States to the French in Indochina between 1950 and 1954 were 1,880 tanks and combat vehicles, 30,887 motor vehicles, 361,522 small arms and machine guns, 5,045 artillery pieces, over 500 million rounds of small arms ammunition, and over 10 million artillery shells.[65] In addition, the French Navy in Indochina received some 106 vessels, including two light aircraft carriers (CVA) and large numbers of patrol and landing craft.[66] Aircraft delivered under the MDAP between 1950 and 1954 included: twenty-seven for the army (twelve L-20 and fifteen L-19 liaison/observation planes); thirty-three for the navy (four AU-1 [F4U-7] fighter-bombers, eighteen F6F fighters, five JRF fighters, and six PB4Y-2 Privateer long-range maritime patrol bombers); and 245 for the air force (eighty B/RB-26 light bombers, 101 F8F fighters, three C-119 transports, twenty-six C-47 transports, six C-45 utility transports, four L-20 liaison/observation planes, and twenty-five H-19 helicopters).[67]

Article 1719 of the Geneva Accords, which ended the First Indochina War on July 20, 1954, severely restricted the supply of arms and equipment to the former belligerents by outside parties. The shipment to Indochina of new types of arms, ammunition, and equipment was forbidden, and worn-out or defective materiel could be replaced only on a one-for-one basis and then only through designated control points.

U.S. Military Assistance Advisory Group–Indochina

The second criterion established by the JCS for aid to Indochina, the creation of a military assistance advisory group to monitor the delivery of U.S. materiel, took some time to set in operation, in part due to French reluctance to accept such an advisory group. As the JCS historians noted:

> The French gave the American plan a chilly reception; they wanted American arms with no strings attached. Their views indicated a desire that the United States simply fill French orders for equipment without attempting to influence types or quantities of material or how it was employed. General Marcel Carpentier, French Commander-in-Chief in Indochina, said that he "would welcome" a United States military mission but wished it to be as small as possible and part of the attaché group at the American legation in Saigon. Although he "would welcome" representatives of the Associated States in the receiving and distributing apparatus, only the French High Command "would be equipped [to] receive and stock American materiel for Indochina."[68]

Despite French misgivings, the first elements of the U.S. Military Assistance Advisory Group–Indochina (MAAG-Indochina) arrived in Saigon on August 3, 1950. The MAAG was formally organized on September 17, and assembled in the Saigon-Cholon area on November 20. Earlier, on October 10, Brigadier General Francis G. Brink, USA, assumed command as the first chief of MAAG-Indochina.[69]

Brigadier General Brink's principal responsibility was to manage the flow of military aid to the French and (later) the Associated States, but military training of the forces of the Associated States remained in French hands. Thus, the main function of MAAG-Indochina was "to make sure that equipment supplied by the United States reached its prescribed destination and that it was properly maintained by French Union forces."[70] The allocation of aid to the Associated States had to be made through the French, and the French prohibited the MAAG from controlling the dispensing of supplies once they were in Indochina. At least one French commander in chief in Indochina, General Henri Navarre, considered "any function of MAAG in Saigon beyond bookkeeping to be an intrusion upon internal French affairs," and, as the editors of *The Pentagon Papers* proclaimed:

> Even though it would have been difficult beyond 1952 to continue the war without American aid, the French never permitted participation by U.S. officials in strategic planning or policy making. Moreover, the French suspected the economic aid mission of being over-sympathetic to Vietnamese nationalism. The director of the economic aid program, Robert Blum, and the DCM of the American Embassy, Edmund Gullion, were subjected to French criticisms of their pro-Vietnamese views, although the American Ambassador, Donald Heath, remained staunchly pro-French. Thus, French officials insisted that American assistance be furnished with "no strings attached" and with virtually no control over its use. Underlying this attitude was a deep-seated suspicion that the United States desired to totally supplant the French, economically as well as politically, in Indochina.[71]

Although the French had the final say on the use of the materiel provided, MAAG-Indochina was charged with providing advice and with conducting inspections in the field to observe how the American-supplied weapons and other equipment were being maintained and utilized. However, MAAG-Indochina proved unable to perform even the minimum functions assigned to it inasmuch as the French, never eager for U.S. advice, limited the MAAG to "order-taking in the commercial sense."[72] Accordingly, Brigadier General Brink was directed to not assume any training or advisory responsibilities toward the armies of the Associated States, and "from the outset, the French rigorously limited end-use inspections of MAAG to a small number of carefully prescribed visits."[73]

Despite the restrictions imposed by the French on American observation, examination, and advice-giving, the members of the MAAG did their best to aid the ungrateful and obstinate French. Major General Trapnell, the second chief of MAAG-Indochina, observed, "The use of MDAP equipment has not generated any critical training problems, however a need exists for management training to encompass stock control; organization of depots and other procedural-type activities."[74] He went on to state:

> Generally, maintenance standards of MDAP equipment are below those of the U.S. Armed Services, although within well-trained units employing equipment in the intended manner, favorable comparisons may be reached. Since many of the personnel of the French Union Army begin their careers as illiterate peasants, completely unskilled, the training and indoctrination task toward better maintenance is evident. MAAG visiting teams proffer such guidance as is feasible. Specific notification of superior, as well as unsatisfactory units, are made officially to the French military authorities. Under the existing terms of reference, MAAG has no authorized direct contact with armed forces of the Associated States.[75]

Although the task of overseeing the distribution and use of U.S. equipment provided to the French in Indochina was enormous, MAAG-Indochina remained small throughout its existence. The total authorized strength upon activation in 1950 was 128 men, but the initial complement was only sixty-five officers and men and one civilian clerk.[76] By July 20, 1954, when Article 16 of the Geneva Accords fixed the number of advisors in the MAAG, there were only 342 personnel assigned.[77] Although the Army provided the chief and most of the officers and men assigned, MAAG-Indochina was a joint service activity with representatives from the U.S. Navy and U.S. Air Force.

Unfortunately, few of the officers and men assigned to MAAG-Indochina spoke French, and the French military authorities in Indochina actively obstructed their efforts.[78] French pique at their dependence on American aid was manifested in a number of petty ways. For example, MAAG-Indochina personnel received very little assistance in either their living arrangements or in the conduct of their duties, which after all did involve the coordination of U.S. aid to the French in Indochina.[79] Of greater consequence, however, was that: "MAAG officers were not given the necessary freedom to develop intelligence information on the course of the war; information supplied by the French was limited, and often unreliable or deliberately misleading. The French resisted repeated U.S. admonitions that the native armies of the Associated States be built up and consequently they did not create a true national Vietnamese army. With some minor exceptions, the French excluded American advisors from participating in the training for the use of the materials being furnished by the U.S."[80]

What MAAG-Indochina personnel did see of French logistical operations was not pleasing, and the officers of the MAAG frequently complained of the waste and sloppy supply accounting of the French.[81] U.S. Air Force and Navy MAAG officers, who had somewhat freer access to French air and naval bases, also complained of the lack of safety precautions and the poor quality of French maintenance efforts. The air force advisors were particularly shocked by the "standard French procedure of drinking while working" and also observed that French aircraft were often too dirty to inspect thoroughly before flight, and navy advisors found vessels turned over to the French in good condition to be rusty and dirty and the French sailors themselves "sloppy and unkempt."[82]

The successive commanders of MAAG-Indochina reported the reluctance of French authorities in Indochina to permit U.S. examination of how and where they were using MDAP materiel and other deficiencies in French organization, staff work, and performance. In his May 3, 1954, debriefing, Major General Trapnell stated:

> Although Navarre demands that his requirement for U.S. equipment should not be challenged by this MAAG, the fact is that the small inadequate French staff handling this function is not capable of accurately presenting requirements for Indochina. Were it not for the screening which these requests undergo by MAAG, material would be wastefully supplied, and many critical and sudden shortages would occur. . . . Lack of command supervision is obvious in all echelons, the best evidence of which is the absence of command inspections and maintenance inspections of equipment of commanders. End-use inspections by members of this MAAG frequently reveal that higher commanders have never made an inspection of equipment in their subordinate units. Shortage of personnel is another contributing factor which cannot be overcome except through more extensive support from metropolitan France.[83]

The problem apparently went deeper than personal incompetence or neglect on the part of French commanders and staff officers. Major General Trapnell also noted: "A significant weakness on the part of the French is their failure to project their system of field operations and staff planning beyond their experience in Indochina. *Imagination is frequently lacking. Also evident is the fact that their limited experience in World War II has stunted their overall development in modern warfare.* This is basically the reason underlying their poor staff work, logistics and operational plans. In addition, the French are sensitive and touchy and loath to accept advice. We frequently encounter outdated techniques dating back to Colonial campaigns and World War I."[84]

Aid to the Associated States

A major area of Franco-American disunity was aid to and training of the armed forces of the Associated States. The development of viable national armies in Viet Nam, Cambodia, and Laos that could assume responsibility for area defense and free French forces for offensive action was a key part of the French policy in Indochina, but the process was one that the French found expedient to drag out for political reasons. From the beginning, U.S. authorities recognized that the political interests of France and those of the Associated States were not only different but mutually exclusive.[85] MAAG-Indochina commanders, such as Major General Thomas J. H. Trapnell, recognized that the French had little confidence in their allies and were unlikely to push forward the creation of the national armies without American prodding.[86] Such prodding was most unwelcome. Although the only source of arms and equipment for the proposed national armies was the United States, the French insisted on controlling their distribution. As the U.S. Joint Chiefs of Staff history of the period notes:

> Commissioner Pignon flatly informed the United States that France, and not the Associated States, must control distribution of arms. In Pignon's view, the "operations of receiving and distributing important quantities of material involve a series of complex technical problems which only the French military services can resolve at this time." Since the French Commander-in-Chief in Indochina was responsible for the conduct of military operations, he must direct the distribution of materials. The French lists would be prepared by the French commander, acting in his capacity as Chief of Staff of National Defense for each Associated State, and "There can be no question of changing this established program (procedure)."[87]

The French were particularly reluctant to arm the new national armies with the best equipment, and they objected strenuously to any direct U.S. aid to the governments or to the military forces of the Associated States, maintaining that the complex problems of the supply of arms and equipment could only be managed by French military personnel.[88] When U.S. aid was being discussed in early 1950, the French *commandant en chef* in Indochina, General Marcel Carpentier, was quoted in the *New York Times* on March 9, 1950, as saying, "I will never agree to equipment being given directly to the Vietnamese. If this should be done I would resign within twenty-four hours. The Vietnamese have no generals, no colonels, no military organization that could effectively utilize the equipment. It would be wasted, as in China, the United States has had enough of that."[89]

The real reasons for French opposition to direct aid were pride and the desire to maintain control over the national armies. However, there may have been some substance to their claim that the Indochinese lacked the ability to deal with the influx of new materiel since U.S. advisory reports on the national armies were generally pessimistic.[90] However, the French were even more adamant in their opposition to the United States providing training for the armies of the Associated States that would allow them to use the better weapons and equipment effectively, and they were successful in preventing such training almost to the end. Lieutenant General John W. "Iron Mike" O'Daniel, the third chief of MAAG-Indochina, discussed the matter with the French general Paul Ely, the French high commissioner and *commandant en chef* in Indochina, in June 1954 and obtained an informal agreement for U.S. participation in the training of the Vietnamese national forces.[91] O'Daniel then drew up a comprehensive plan for U.S. advisory efforts at all levels. In July, he requested that the MAAG-Indochina staff be increased before August 11, when the Geneva limits on the introduction of new personnel went into effect, but the JCS refused to go along.[92] It was not until December 13, 1954, nearly six months after the Geneva Accords ended the war, that a formal agreement was signed by General Ely and General J. Lawton Collins, a former U.S. Army chief of staff and then special representative of the United States in Viet Nam with ambassadorial rank.[93] Thus, the First Indochina War ended before the enormous training resources of the United States could be brought into play to help create effective anti-Communist armies in Viet Nam, Cambodia, and Laos.

Assessment of the U.S. Aid Program

The decision to provide military aid and establish a military assistance advisory group in Indochina was made "in spite of the U.S. desire to avoid direct involvement in a colonial war, and in spite of a sensing that France's political-military situation in Indochina was bad and was deteriorating. Moreover, predictions that U.S. aid would achieve a marked difference in the course of the Indochina War were heavily qualified."[94] As noted in *The Pentagon Papers*, the French resisted U.S. efforts and failed to take full advantage of the generosity of their ally:

> The French were able to resist pressures from Washington and through the MAAG in Saigon to create a truly Vietnamese army, to grant the Vietnamese more local autonomy and to wage the war more effectively. MAAG was relegated to a supply function and its occasional admonitions to the French were interpreted by them as interference in their internal affairs. Even though by 1954, the U.S. was financing 78% of the costs of

the war, the French retained full control of the dispensation of military assistance and of the intelligence and planning aspects of the military struggle. The expectation of French victory over the Viet Minh encouraged the U.S. to "go along" with Paris until the conclusion of the war. Moreover, the U.S. was reluctant to antagonize the French because of the high priority given in Washington's planning to French participation in the European Defense Community. France, therefore, had considerable leverage and, unless the U.S. supported Paris on its own terms, the French could, and indeed did, threaten not to join the EDC and to stop fighting in Indochina.[95]

In point of fact, even the very first assessments of the aid program were not sanguine. In his report of the July 1950 military mission to Saigon, rendered on August 5, 1950, Major General Erskine noted that the core of the problem was "a deep-seated hatred and distrust of the French by the population that precluded their cooperation in the prosecution of the war" and that "the amount of aid and the scope of the assistance thus far requested by the French were inadequate to the needs of the situation."[96]

Nor was the ultimate result an unqualified success. As noted in *The Pentagon Papers*, "The decision to begin military assistance to France and the Associated States of Indochina was not made under the illusion of great expectations. In April 1950, the Joint Chiefs would go no further than to say that prompt delivery of the aid would do no more than create the 'possibility of success.'"[97] Although the French logistical situation was much improved by American support, the efficiency of the logistical services remained adversely affected by the diversity of personnel and equipment, the dispersion of the combat and support forces, the lack of reliable reinforcement, and a host of minor logistical difficulties.[98] The U.S. personnel assigned to MAAG-Indochina were baffled by the failure of the French to use the enormous quantities of military materiel being supplied by the United States.[99] Of course, the massive amount of mechanized equipment was part of the problem rather than part of the solution: it contributed to the restriction of French Union forces to the few available roads and thus to their vulnerability to guerrilla attack. Moreover, the French were unable to maintain the equipment adequately and were unwilling to accept U.S. advice and maintenance assistance. Thus, the results of the decision to aid the French can be characterized only as mixed. As noted in *The Pentagon Papers*: "Although implementation of the decision was partially successful in that it enabled the French to continue the military campaign in Indochina to the time of the Geneva Accords, military assistance was by and large a failure as an instrument of U.S. policy: the U.S. neither assured the French a military success, influenced the political situation to advantage, nor prevented the loss of North Vietnam to the communists at Geneva."[100]

And when all was said and done, the French were not particularly grateful for the efforts made by the United States on their behalf. Although dependent on American support, French authorities at all levels resented American suggestions on political, economic, and military matters, and such advice "often put them in a white-hot fury."[101] French military authorities in Indochina were particularly resistant to MAAG-Indochina "end-use" inspections and whenever possible they avoided them, delayed them, or simply faked them.[102] In a classic bit of understatement, Lieutenant General O'Daniel, the head of the U.S. Joint Military Mission to Indochina in early 1954, noted: "The French are sadly lacking in know-how in many fields, including planning and maintenance matters. They are proud and sensitive to criticism. They need help."[103]

After the war, Lieutenant General Henri Navarre petulantly complained that the materiel provided by the United States was unsuitable for counterguerrilla warfare and was thus actually a disservice to the French cause.[104] General Navarre's distaste for American equipment appears to have been a postwar development. On January 28, 1954, he expressed to Lieutenant General O'Daniel his concern over delays in receiving what he considered to be "essential equipment," noting at the same time that he had been criticized in the Paris press for allowing the United States to participate in the war effort in matters other than supply.[105] The French were particularly put out to find that the Viet Minh often were equipped with newer or better models of U.S. equipment provided by the Chinese Communists from stocks captured from the Nationalist Chinese or in Korea. Bernard Fall, among others, reflected the French view and charged that the equipment and supplies provided by the United States were too heavy, too old, or unsuited to the Indochinese situation, observing, "The belated influx of large amounts of American equipment—equipment that was largely unsuited to the kind of war being fought there—could, of necessity, affect very little the eventual outcome of that war."[106] Of course, Fall was correct; the outcome of the First Indochina War was determined more by French *hauteur*, incompetence, and lack of will than by the types or quantities of the equipment provided by the United States.

The Cost of the War

The First Indochina War was not cheap. France, the Associated States, and the United States expended some $10 billion in eight years.[107] The French reportedly spent about 250 billion francs per year on the war, and their total expenditure may have amounted to around U.S.$7 billion.[108] To the amount expended by the French must be added the very substantial amounts of direct military and economic aid provided by the United States, which totaled about $2.753 billion between May 1950 and July 1954.[109] That sum was distributed in several programs:

Military Assistance (MDAP)	$1,308 million
Financial Support of French Budget	$1,285 million
Military Support Program	$75 million
Defense Support Program	$95 million
Total Cost to U.S.	$2,763 million[110]

The proportion of the cost of the war borne by the United States increased steadily from 1950 to 1954. In 1950–1951, the U.S. provided the equivalent of about 15 percent of the French expenditure on the war, and by mid-1952 that percentage had risen to about 33 percent.[111] In September 1953, the U.S. reluctantly agreed to underwrite up to 70 percent of the French war effort in Indochina, and in return the French were required to reinforce their forces in Indochina from France, complete the training of the Vietnamese National Army by 1954, and consider American views on strategy.[112] In FY 1954, the United States provided about 78 percent of the total cost of the French war effort.[113] One French newspaper even wryly suggested, "The Indochina War had become France's number one dollar-earning export," and one French correspondent on the scene later wrote: "That great flow of dollars which meant that in the end the Indochinese war cost France almost nothing: indeed, it has even been said that she made a profit out of it. The notorious billion francs a day (and later it was to be well over a billion) was paid to an ever-increasing extent by the taxpayers of the New World."[114]

On March 29, 1954, Admiral Arthur W. Radford, then chairman of the U.S. Joint Chiefs of Staff, prepared a memorandum for the President's Special Committee on Indochina recapitulating his discussions with his French counterpart, General Paul Ely, regarding the situation in Indochina.[115] The exchanges between Admiral Radford and General Ely were quite frank. Admiral Radford reported that he "presented to General Ely our views in regard to expanding the MAAG to assist the French in training the Vietnamese, indicating to him the importance which we attach to this action, first, to obtain better results, secondly to release French officers for combat service," but that "General Ely was most unsympathetic to any encroachment on French responsibilities or significant expansion of the MAAG. The reasons given related to French 'prestige,' possible lack of confidence in French leadership by the Vietnamese, 'the political situation in France,' etc."[116] Radford concluded that "the French are disposed firmly to resist any delegation of training responsibilities to the U.S. MAAG."[117]

For his part, General Ely "made quite a point of explaining with 'great frankness' actions on the part of the United States which were causes of friction."[118] According to Admiral Radford, the points mentioned specifically were:

a. Americans acted as if the United States sought to control and operate everything of importance; that this was particularly true at lower levels and in connection with FCA operations.

b. The United States appears to have an invading nature as they undertake everything in such great numbers of people.

c. French think that McCarthyism is prevalent in the U.S. and actually is akin to Hitlerism.

d. Americans do not appreciate the difficulties under which the French must operate as a result of two devastating wars.

e. Many Americans appear to favor Germany over France.

f. U.S. administrative procedures are enormously wasteful, irritating and paper heavy.

g. In Germany the U.S. forces have the benefit of better weapons and most modern techniques, whereas the French forces do not.

h. In connection with offshore procurement, the U.S. appeared to lack confidence in the French in the manufacture of most modern weapons and equipment.[119]

Admiral Radford "endeavored to set the record straight on each of these particulars and stressed the fact that Americans were growing very impatient with France over its lack of action on the EDC [European Defense Community] and German rearmament and French tendencies to overemphasize their prestige and sensitivities."[120]

American analysts at the time and later have also noted defects in the way U.S. aid to the French in Indochina was handled. For example, the editors of *The Pentagon Papers* in 1971 highlighted six points of criticism of the U.S. policy toward Indochina. They were:

1. The United States mistakenly acted on the belief that U.S. and French goals were similar and that the French would follow U.S. advice and, once the war was over, would allow Vietnam, Cambodia, and Laos to become free and independent states.

2. The United States failed to recognize the flaws in its policy and failed to seek alternatives that might have produced a more favorable outcome for the United States.

3. The suppression of alternatives led to "a circularity in and reinforcement of existing policies" that constantly "forced choices between 'bad' and 'worse.'"

4. The United States failed to bargain effectively with the French, giving them most of what they asked for without insisting that they live up to the preconditions the United States wished to impose or even permit monitoring of the use and disposition of the aid provided.

5. The United States was easily manipulated by misinformation provided by

the French and others, who found that crying "The Reds are coming" was particularly effective for getting the United States to do what they wanted.

6. The United States failed to weigh the costs of the effort against the potential gains, failed to analyze the "domino theory" thoroughly, and failed to ask the key question: "How important is Indochina to the vital interests of the United States?"[121]

Concluding his March 29, 1954, memorandum, Admiral Radford noted that he was "gravely fearful that the measures being undertaken by the French will prove to be inadequate and initiated too late to prevent a progressive deterioration of the situation in Indo-China," and that "if Dien Bien Phu is lost, this deterioration may occur very rapidly due to the loss of morale among the mass of the native population. In such a situation only prompt and forceful intervention by the United States could avert the loss of all of South East Asia to Communist domination."[122]

The defects of U.S. policy aside, the most serious obstacles to the effectiveness of the U.S. military assistance program were the French themselves. As the JCS historians noted, the French high command in Indochina was "burdened by pre–World War II staff thinking and a cumbersome logistics apparatus that resulted in waste of material and unrealistic equipment requests. MAAG officers found that the French supply organization lacked an efficient and centralized stock control system and hence had no provision for lateral redistribution. The French would submit requisitions for a given item on the basis of a shortage existing at one installation. Investigation would reveal an oversupply of the same item at another installation. These operating procedures placed a heavy burden on the American logistics system."[123]

Moreover, the MAAG often was forced to deny French requests for equipment based upon "the fact, known to MAAG but rarely recognized by the French, that the desired items could not be properly maintained or utilized with existing facilities and personnel. The French were wasteful and haphazard in their maintenance practices and were sensitive to criticism and offers of technical advice."[124] In the end, the U.S. Joint Chiefs of Staff concluded in 1954 that "the furnishing of material and other types of aid to France through the medium of MDAP has proved to be too time-consuming and cumbersome because of all the criteria and administrative procedures involved."[125]

While by 1954 U.S. military aid constituted the major portion of all the resources applied by the French in Indochina and had surely delayed a Viet Minh victory, the overall conclusion reached by the editors of *The Pentagon Papers* was that "the effectiveness of the United States assistance program as an instrument of United States policy—quite aside from the outcome of the war—was thus quite low."[126] In fact, the United States, desperate to hold the line against the spread of

Communism in Asia following the defeat of the Nationalist Chinese by Mao's Red Army, allowed itself to be manipulated by the French, who received a cornucopia of military equipment with which to pursue their efforts to maintain political, economic, and military control over their Indochinese colonies while constantly assuring the U.S. government of their intentions to grant them full independence at the earliest possible time. The failure of the U.S. government to correct these defects in policy formulation and execution helped to seal the fate of the French in Indochina and led the United States into a conflict that would last for the following quarter century.

8

Viet Minh Sources of Supply

Like the French, the Viet Minh could not have sustained the war without outside support. Until the triumph of the Chinese Communists over the nationalist forces of Chiang Kai-shek in late 1949, the Viet Minh struggled to obtain the minimum amounts of food, arms, ammunition, and other war supplies needed to keep them in the fight. Initially, they lacked all types of materiel, but in time they became adept at exploiting every possible source for the supplies needed by their ever-growing military forces. Throughout the war, the Viet Minh captured and stole from the French Union forces; purchased food, clothing, arms, ammunition, gasoline, vehicles, and other equipment on the local market and from Nationalist China, Thailand, the Philippines, Hong Kong, and even the United States; and produced war materiel in their own workshops, even though the territory they controlled did not have the industrial base necessary to support a large-scale protracted war.

After 1950, the Viet Minh received substantial support from the Chinese Communists in the form of arms, ammunition, transport, petroleum products, and other supplies as well as—most importantly—technical expertise and secure facilities for the organization and training of their forces. Other Communist countries, notably the Soviet Union and East Germany, also provided some military supplies, but the bulk of the war materiel used by the Viet Minh was obtained from Communist China in return for raw materials and other considerations. The scarcity and diversity of weapons, ammunition, and other equipment that hampered Viet Minh logistics in the early years of the war were thus overcome as time went on by Chinese aid and a program of standardization on Soviet/Chinese models that eliminated many of the problems posed by a hodgepodge of military hardware.[1] During the critical last four years of the war, the period of large-scale conventional operations, the Viet Minh were nearly as well-armed and well-supplied as the French, and the Viet Minh leaders freely admitted that they would not have been able to pursue the war to a successful conclusion in only eight years had they not had the generous logistical support provided by Communist China.

Arms Acquired as a Result of World War II

The Viet Minh began their war against the French in 1945 with a miscellany of weapons, ammunition, and other military equipment obtained during and immediately after World War II from a variety of sources, including the Japanese, the

Americans, the Nationalist Chinese, and even the French.[2] Some weapons were stolen or seized in small-scale military operations, and others were purchased. For example, the Viet Minh captured five rifles from the Japanese garrison at Dong Mu at the end of December 1944, the arms of eighty Japanese soldiers at Dinh Ca on April 10, 1945, and the weapons of five hundred Indochinese auxiliaries at Quang Yen near Haiphong on July 10, 1945.[3]

At the end of World War II, some Japanese soldiers and even whole units turned over their weapons to the Viet Minh, but some authorities argue that the Japanese did not turn over any significant quantities of arms and ammunition directly to the Viet Minh. For example, one Vietnamese authority has argued: "Contrary to what some maintain, the Japanese never gave any of their arms to the Vietminh. During the first days immediately after their surrender, the Japanese inclined to the idea of offering part of their arms and equipment to the Vietminh, but they changed their minds when Vo Nguyen Giap, en route from Viet-Bac to Hanoi, attacked their garrison at Thai Nguyen on August 17, 1945. The Japanese thereafter burned all their commissariat stores and later on handed over to the Chinese at Haiphong 400,000 tons of arms and ammunition."[4]

However, the Viet Minh certainly took the opportunity presented by the confusion at the end of the war to pilfer Japanese weapons stores and may have made deals with individual Japanese soldiers and commanders for various types and quantities of munitions. Historian King C. Chen has noted: "On some occasions the Japanese sold arms through private channels to the Viet Minh. . . . In Annam, the Japanese either gave arms to the Bao Dai government . . . or simply burned their weapons. In other parts of Vietnam, the Japanese handed over equipment to the Viet Minh."[5] And the authors of "Early Days: The Development of the Viet Minh Military Machine" maintain that:

> With the mass surrender of many Indochinese garrisons (including that of the Palace of Representatives in Hanoi, who yielded 200 carbines and a large supply of grenades), together with the donation of equipment by the retreating Japanese forces (including a windfall for the VM when a stock of weaponry—intended for China, but which had been held at Haiphong by the French in 1940—was handed over by the Japanese. This included numbers of AA guns, AT guns, and Russian 7.62mm rifles with AT rounds), by the end of 1945 estimates of weaponry in VM hands included: 35,000 small-arms (rifles, carbines, pistols, etc.), 1,350 SMGs [submachine guns], 200 mortars, [and] 54 artillery pieces (of various types).[6]

Indeed, there is a good deal of other evidence that large, direct transfers from the Japanese to the Viet Minh took place.[7]

Despite later French claims that during and even after World War II the United

States provided the Viet Minh with the arms and equipment that leavened their resistance to French control of Indochina, the amounts of such aid were minuscule. In March 1945, representatives of the U.S. Army Air Forces Air Ground Aid Service offered (and later delivered by paradrop) to Ho Chi Minh radios, small arms, and medical supplies in return for Viet Minh assistance in recovering downed Allied pilots and gathering intelligence.[8] Several Office of Strategic Services (OSS) teams were inserted to coordinate Viet Minh guerrilla operations against the Japanese, gather intelligence, and assist in the rescue of Allied pilots, and they too provided small amounts of arms and other supplies to the Vietnamese guerrillas.[9] In the immediate postwar period, the U.S. position hardened, and the Viet Minh leader, Ho Chi Minh, appealed several times to the United States for aid, but received no reply.[10]

The quantity and types of materiel supplied by U.S. agencies to the Viet Minh in the last days of World War II were relatively insignificant in comparison to the arms and equipment the Viet Minh obtained from the French, the Japanese, and the Chinese Nationalists. French sources also indicate that of the thirty-six thousand small arms held by the Viet Minh in March 1946, only about 12 percent were obtained during World War II, and by the start of open warfare against the French in December 1946 the proportion had declined to 5 percent.[11] French intelligence agents also supplied Ho's forces with weapons during World War II, and the Viet Minh acquired a number of weapons from the Vietnamese puppet forces set up by the Japanese. The main effect of the U.S. contacts with the Viet Minh was to give the appearance rather than the reality of U.S. support to the Viet Minh in their later struggle to free themselves from French colonial rule, and Ho Chi Minh skillfully exploited the relationship.[12] Even Bernard Fall, one of the more severe critics of U.S. aid to the Viet Minh, concluded, "In any case, American material aid to Ho was of a minor nature and probably had not been the subject of a high policy decision."[13] As the JCS historians noted, "the subsequent French assertion that the OSS had 'armed' the Viet Minh was an exaggeration."[14]

The arms and other equipment provided to the Viet Minh by the Nationalist Chinese were far more important to the subsequent success of the Viet Minh than the relatively minor contributions of either the Japanese or the Americans. As early as 1943, several hundred Viet Minh had been trained by the Nationalist Chinese at Liuzhou in Guangxi and in Tonkin, and some weapons also had been obtained from the Nationalists.[15] The Viet Minh acquired a major portion of the French and Japanese stocks of arms and equipment in Indochina by purchasing them from the Nationalist Chinese general Lu Han, whose 180,000-man army was assigned to occupy Tonkin and northern Annam and to disarm the Japanese.[16] Using the gold collected from the population of Tonkin during the "Week of Gold" in September 1945, the Viet Minh purchased from General Lu Han some 3,000 rifles, 50 automatic rifles, 600 submachine guns, and 100 mortars of American manufacture as well as French and Japanese weapons amounting to some 31,000 rifles, 700 automatic weapons, 36 artillery pieces, and 18 light armored vehicles.[17] The Chinese Nationalists allegedly even sold some of their new American Lend-Lease weapons to the Viet Minh.[18] In addition to pure avarice, the Chinese Nationalists apparently also were motivated by the desire to control Haiphong, important to Chinese trade with Indochina, and perhaps to replace the French as the arbiters of Indochina.[19] Even after the removal of their occupation troops from Tonkin and Annam, the Nationalist Chinese continued to sell arms and other equipment to the Viet Minh, most of which was delivered by sea from Pak Hoi, Canton, or Hong Kong.[20] The Nationalist Chinese had an office in Pak Hoi that oversaw the sale and delivery of materiel purchased by the Viet Minh. Payment was usually in gold, rice, tin, or opium.

Captured Materiel

The Viet Minh set a high priority on obtaining the arms and equipment of French Union units that they overran, and a significant proportion of the better weapons used by the Viet Minh in the first half of the war was captured from the French. For example, in their retreat from Cao Bang in October 1950, the French lost 13 artillery pieces, 125 mortars, 950 machine guns, 1,200 carbines and submachine guns, and over 8,000 rifles, plus 450 trucks destroyed or abandoned.[21] On the other hand, French raids and major clearing operations frequently netted considerable quantities of Viet Minh arms, ammunition, and other equipment.

Of course, the Viet Minh captured ammunition as well as weapons. Until they began to receive significant quantities of arms and ammunition from the Communist Chinese in 1950, the Viet Minh were perpetually short of ammunition, particularly mortar and artillery shells. However, there was no great disparity reported between the number of weapons captured from the French and the amount of ammunition available for those weapons.[22] In addition to capturing arms and equipment from the French on the field of battle, the Viet Minh encouraged the theft of such materiel and even established a formal price table for stolen equipment.[23] General Giap himself later noted the inadequacy of efforts to import arms and ammunition or to manufacture them locally, and stated: "The greatest difficulty to be solved was the equipment problem. . . . The sole source of supply could only be the battlefront: to take the material from the enemy to turn it against him. While carrying on the aggression against Viet Nam the French Expeditionary Corps fulfilled another task: it became, unwittingly, the supplier of the Viet Nam People's Army with French, even U.S. arms. In spite of their enormous efforts, the arms factories set up later on with makeshift means were far from being able to meet all our needs. A great part of our military materials came from war-booty."[24]

Local Procurement and Production

Although clearly aware of the inadequacy of local production to meet their war needs, the Viet Minh devoted considerable effort to obtaining the maximum output from the slender local resources. They proved themselves masters of innovation and determination, and throughout the war an important portion of Viet Minh weapons, ammunition, and other supplies were locally produced, often with the help of Japanese, and later French Union, deserters.

The one item of supply in which the Viet Minh were nearly self-sufficient was food. For example, salt was an important component of the Viet Minh ration, and the estimated twenty thousand tons per year that the Viet Minh required was probably obtained entirely from coastal areas under their control.[25] However, rice was the principal foodstuff required, and the Viet Minh needed about 1.4 million tons of milled rice to feed the estimated 10 million people under their control in 1951, plus another sixty thousand tons for the Viet Minh military forces. Rice production in Viet Minh–controlled areas in 1951 totaled about 1.5 million tons, but a large proportion of that amount was grown in the Trans-Bassac and could not be redistributed to Tonkin, where it was needed to make up a 10–15 percent shortfall. Consequently, the Viet Minh had to conduct military operations to seize rice in areas nominally under the control of the French, obtaining probably twenty thousand to thirty thousand tons per year in that manner. In areas under their own control, the Viet Minh obtained the rice required in the form of a tax that left the farmer only enough rice to feed his family and to seed the next crop. This agricultural tax in kind was later stabilized at a rate of 15 percent.[26]

Rice was the basis of the entire Viet Minh economy—the Viet Minh even calculated their budget in kilograms of rice. Naturally, the Viet Minh were always concerned about the supply of rice, and from time to time French operations threatened the flow of rice to the Viet Minh. For example, in 1950 the French nearly succeeded in starving out the Viet Minh, and one Viet Minh minister later told the French correspondent Lucien Bodard: "It was dreadful. I was ill with hunger, and for months on end I was very weak. Not only rice was lacking but everything—there was no salt left, no medicines, no clothes. What quantities of men died in those days among the terrible mountains. Morale was affected from top to bottom. The French had us by the throat."[27] However, as the Viet Minh expanded their control over key areas in Tonkin and Annam and as Chinese support increased after 1950, the situation improved.

The limited industrial production facilities and major commercial markets of Indochina were almost all under French control, but some Viet Minh requirements were met with goods acquired in Indochina. Viet Minh agents were active in the marketplaces of towns and cities under French control. They bribed or blackmailed French Union soldiers and civilians to steal supplies for them, and they also purchased items—ostensibly nonmilitary in nature, such as medicine, cloth, machinery, and household goods—on the open and black markets.[28] Viet Minh agents probably also exploited the black market that existed in the territory under Viet Minh control, a market in which American as well as French goods were obtainable if the buyer had the exorbitant price. Black market items of particular interest to the Viet Minh included medical supplies, bicycle tires and tubes, flashlight batteries, compasses, and binoculars.[29] Later in the war, the Viet Minh also managed to take advantage of the scandalous situation with respect to the difference in exchange rate between the Vietnamese *piastre* and the French *franc* and used the profits to buy arms and equipment.[30]

As part of his overall strategy for the formation and equipping of Viet Minh fighting forces, General Giap initiated the establishment of numerous small arsenals and workshops scattered throughout the territory controlled by the Viet Minh, particularly in the safe base area of the Viet Bac, and even in French-held areas. In 1947, there were three major Viet Minh arms factories: one at Phu Tho in northern Tonkin, one in Annam, and one at Thap Muoi in Cochinchina. The largest of these factories was that at Thap Muoi, which employed some five hundred workers, including a number of Japanese prisoners of war and German deserters from the CEFEO.[31] In one large Viet Minh arms factory in Tonkin women comprised 15 percent of the workforce, and much of the equipment (including a six-cylinder Chrysler marine engine) was of French or American manufacture.[32] By October 1950, the Viet Minh had established an arsenal in every province they controlled and a workshop in every district.[33]

Many of the early workshops were established in old French or Japanese arsenals or in converted railroad workshops.[34] For example, the Phan Dinh Phung company, which had facilities located in China, southeast of Hanoi, and in Thai Nguyen, produced infantry weapons and small arms ammunition with the aid of Japanese technicians, while the Bai Thuong company produced automatic weapons, as did the Van Ly company located twenty-four miles south-southeast of Nam Dinh. In Annam, workshops and factories were located at Quang Ngai, Phu My, Phu Cat, Gia Long, Da Le, Co Bi, and Cong Son.[35] These workshops made repairs and produced crude but usable small arms, light automatic weapons, small arms ammunition, mines, and grenades. In some cases, the shops were quite small, mobile, and primitive; in others, they included sophisticated machine tools and elaborate fixed facilities. The workshops in Viet Minh–controlled territory employed up to five hundred persons, but those in French-held areas were smaller, employing only ten to fifteen.[36] The workers in Viet Minh arms factories included some Chinese workers. For example, several Chinese were reported to have worked in Viet Minh repair shops near the border town of Tra Linh in 1947–1949.[37]

Despite limited amounts of precision tools, power, and raw materials, the

Viet Minh workshops were surprisingly productive, causing one French observer, referring to the workshops discovered by the French in the limestone mountains near the Day River in the fall of 1949, to exclaim, "We were cognizant of their existence, but we had no idea of the quality of their organization and of their equipment, nor of their capacity insofar as production of mines was concerned."[38] In the first half of 1948, the shops in one area produced 38,000 grenades, 30,000 rifle cartridges, 8,000 light machine gun cartridges, 60 rocket launcher rounds, and 100 mines, and those in another area produced 61 light machine guns, 4 submachine guns, 20 semiautomatic pistols, and 7,000 cartridges.[39]

One outstanding characteristic of the Viet Minh effort to produce their own arms and equipment was the enthusiastic and innovative spirit with which the task was approached. The Viet Minh workers demonstrated an ability to turn every available item to some military use. Chlorate of potassium, permitted for the curing of hams, was used for the production of explosives; unexploded French ordnance was salvaged for raw materials; and Viet Minh divers recovered old Japanese shells from the open sea. The Viet Minh even produced flying bombs launched from ramps and manufactured from empty aluminum liquid air containers obtained cheaply in the French-controlled towns.[40]

Enthusiasm and innovation notwithstanding, the quality of the arms and ammunition turned out by these workshops was generally quite low. Viet Minh–produced munitions were frequently unreliable due to the use of explosives and propellants salvaged from French duds, old Japanese bombs, and similar sources that had been exposed to the elements. All Viet Minh mines, with the exception of some captured from the French, were locally manufactured and were about 60 percent duds due to crude workmanship and unstable explosives subject to the effects of the humid weather conditions.[41] Viet Minh–produced hand grenades usually contained a weak charge and were about 20 percent duds, while the locally produced shaped charge rockets for the U.S. 2.36-inch rocket launcher (the bazooka) proved about 80 percent defective.[42] None of the Viet Minh factories were capable of producing artillery pieces or artillery ammunition, and such materials became available to the Viet Minh only after the Chinese Communists began to provide regular support.

Although the quality of such homemade material was generally poor and the amounts produced were insufficient to meet Viet Minh needs, the multitude of small munitions factories and workshops did play an important role in supplying the growing Viet Minh forces with arms and ammunition in the early days, and they were lauded by General Giap, who later wrote, "In circumstances of extreme hardship and privation, the workers in the arms-factories raised to new heights the heroic and creative spirit of the Vietnamese working class, overcoming very great material and technical difficulties in order to turn scrap-iron into weapons for our troops to exterminate the enemy."[43]

Procurement on the World Market

In November 1945, Viet Minh agents established what can only be called a purchasing office in Bangkok, Thailand.[44] With the complicity of the Thai government and the assistance of General Hsiang Ying, the former deputy commander of the Chinese Communist New Fourth Army then resident in Bangkok as the representative of the Chinese Communist Party, the Viet Minh purchased for shipment to their forces in Indochina significant quantities of arms and other equipment in small lots from Thai, Chinese, Indian, and Malay sellers and in larger lots from Europeans and Americans.[45]

Most of this materiel came from Japanese stocks surrendered to the Allies or from British and American stocks parachuted to resistance movements in Thailand and China during World War II. One of the major sellers was the firm of Kovit, which also supplied the Khmer-Issarak rebels and which in February 1947 engaged to provide 10,000 rifles to the Viet Minh. At the end of March 1947, the Viet Minh purchased some 10,000–15,000 rifles, 1,000 submachine guns, 20 machine guns, 500,000 cartridges, and 10,000 grenades in Thailand, and soon thereafter a Viet Minh agent obtained (for 22.4 kilograms of gold) 166 rifles, 2 machine guns, 1 automatic rifle, 5 mortars, and about 30,000 cartridges. Those munitions were forwarded to Cochinchina by water or overland transport and were subsequently redistributed to Viet Minh forces throughout Indochina. Despite strong efforts, the French were able to intercept only a fraction of the munitions and other supplies purchased for the Viet Minh in Thailand. In 1948 the Thai government adopted an anti-Communist policy, and tolerance of Viet Minh purchasing activities was ended, but until 1950 the Viet Minh openly maintained an office for the purchase of American-made equipment and medical supplies within one block of the U.S. Information Service office in Bangkok.[46] As late as May 1953, U.S. intelligence agencies estimated that the Viet Minh were still receiving as much as twenty-five tons of military supplies per month from purchases made in Thailand.[47]

Hong Kong was another important source of European and American weapons and medical supplies for the Viet Minh, who often settled their black market accounts with opium obtained in northern Laos.[48] In 1947, the Viet Minh permanent representative in Hong Kong was Le Xuan, who occupied himself particularly with the purchase of weapons.[49] The purchases in Hong Kong (as well as in Thailand) were often paid for with gold, opium, or rice.[50]

The Viet Minh also obtained American arms and other equipment in the Philippines, under conditions that remain somewhat unclear. The Indochina expert Bernard Fall maintained that such material was flown to Viet Minh airfields near Vinh and Thanh Hoa in northern Annam in unmarked aircraft flown by American pilots, and that the same planes and pilots were subsequently found operating as "privately chartered aircraft" for the Laotian government. According to Fall, the French National Intelligence Service (*Deuxième Bureau*) established a network of agents and informants in the Philippines that reported the departure of ships and airplanes bound for Viet Minh territory, and the French forces in Indochina subsequently intercepted and destroyed several such ships and planes, thereby reducing such traffic after 1947.[51]

Support from the Soviet Union and Its Satellites

Despite the traditional links between the Vietnamese Communists and the Soviet Union, Soviet support for the struggle of the Viet Minh against the French can be described as lukewarm at best. The Soviet Union and its European satellites provided little or no direct aid in arms, equipment, or other supplies, and indeed the Soviet Union did not even recognize Ho Chi Minh's government until January 30, 1950, and also refused to support the Democratic Republic of Viet Nam's bids for United Nations membership in 1948 and 1951.[52] However, the victory of Mao's Communist forces over the Nationalist Chinese at the end of 1949 spurred Soviet interest in the Viet Minh as a counterweight to the Chinese. That interest seems not to have produced any significant material support for the Viet Minh until after the Indochina cease-fire in July 1954, even though a fund of $500 million to support the Viet Minh war effort was established by the Soviet Union and the other Communist Bloc countries on March 28, 1954.[53] However, East Germany is reported to have provided small gifts of drugs and medical supplies as early as 1952, and already by the end of 1953 eastern European newspapers were reporting that the Viet Minh had placed orders with East Germany for some 32 million marks worth of trucks, tracked vehicles, and optical instruments.[54] Eastern European Communists also provided technical expertise to the Viet Minh. A French commando raid on a Viet Minh mine factory just south of the village of Kaskos on the Song Be River in the Mekong delta on July 11, 1952, killed two Czechoslovakian technicians and netted a pile of plans and technical notices in Czech.[55]

Support from Communist China

The defeat of the Chinese Nationalist forces by Mao's People's Liberation Army (PLA) in 1949 opened the possibility of Chinese Communist aid to their comrades struggling against the French in Indochina. After 1949, the Chinese Communists became a major source of arms, ammunition, vehicles, gasoline, and other supplies for the Viet Minh. The Viet Minh were probably capable of conducting guerrilla and terrorist activities for an indefinite period without outside logistical assistance, but only the continuous supply of arms, ammunition, and other supplies from Communist China permitted the Viet Minh regular forces to engage in large-scale conventional offensive operations. Although the Chinese-supplied materiel represented only about 20 percent of the total supplies available to the Viet Minh, that 20 percent consisted of those items essential for the Viet Minh to challenge the French in open, direct combat, particularly artillery, antiaircraft guns, and motor transport.[56]

Early Contacts and Aid

Until 1949, relations between the Indochinese Communist Party and the Chinese Communist Party (CCP) were limited, as the CCP was intensely focused on defeating the Nationalists of Chiang Kai-shek and seizing control of mainland China.[57] Ho Chi Minh and other Viet Minh leaders had lived and worked with the Chinese Communists for many years before and during World War II, and the personal contacts made during that period were exploited fully during the Viet Minh war for independence. However, there is no evidence of substantial CCP technical assistance to the Viet Minh up to 1947, although the Hong Kong sub-bureau of the CCP did provide the Viet Minh with funds on an irregular basis.[58]

The CCP–Viet Minh relationship became more active after 1947. In the spring of 1947, Liao Cheng-chih, head of the CCP's South China Bureau, visited the Viet Bac, and in June 1947 Major General Fang Fang also visited the Viet Minh base area. Both men attended the Viet Minh conference held at Soc Giang on August 1, 1947, and subsequently the Yueh-Kwei Border Democratic United Army was placed temporarily under Liao's command to cooperate with the Viet Minh.[59]

Until September 1949, Ho Chi Minh repeatedly denied that any support agreements existed between the Viet Minh and the Chinese Communists.[60] But even before the Chinese Communist triumph over the Nationalists, the Viet Minh received some small-scale aid in arms and equipment through contacts with local Chinese Communist guerrilla units in south China.[61] For example, as early as September 1947, the Viet Minh arranged for the purchase of some 12 million *piastres* worth of equipment from the Communist Chinese for shipment to the Viet Bac.[62] However, significant quantities of Chinese aid did not begin to reach the Viet Minh until early 1950.

Origins of the Chinese Military Aid Program

The Chinese Communist Second Field Army arrived on the borders of Tonkin in late 1949, chasing some thirty thousand bedraggled Nationalist troops before them.[63] Then, on January 18, 1950, the Chinese Communist government formally recognized the Democratic Republic of Viet Nam. The previous month, the Chinese Communists had sent a military mission to the Viet Bac to determine what assistance was needed by the Viet Minh, and a Viet Minh military delegation headed by Nguyen Dai Chi had visited Beijing.[64] The result was a formal "Sino-Vietnamese Trade Agreement on Military Supplies" concluded on January 18, 1950, that provided for the sale by China to the Viet Minh of 150,000 Japanese rifles, 10,000 American carbines, and a large quantity of ammunition, the first increments of which arrived in Tonkin in mid-March.[65]

The Viet Minh leader, Ho Chi Minh, arrived in Beijing on January 30, 1950, and was fêted by high-level Party officials. Ho told them of the situation in Viet Nam and asked for additional Chinese aid, whereupon the Chinese leaders agreed to provide what he requested. In April 1950, Ho specified his needs, which included the establishment of a military training school in China, the sending of Chinese military advisors to Viet Nam, and the supply of weapons.[66] The Chinese again agreed, and Liu Shaoqi, then the first vice chairman of the CCP, was charged with implementation of the aid program. Liu delegated responsibility for working out the details to General Chen Geng, then commander of the PLA XX Army Corps.[67]

In November 1950, Ho traveled to Nanning to meet with Chinese and Soviet leaders and apparently worked out yet another Sino-Vietnamese agreement whereby the Viet Minh would obtain from China munitions, machine tools, and medicine in return for timber and rice. A similar agreement was reportedly signed in November 1951, and it was also reported that a Viet Minh–Chinese–Soviet agreement was concluded in 1951 whereby China and the Soviet Union would supply the Viet Minh with munitions, technical assistance, and industrial equipment.[68]

In late April 1951, Hoang Van Hoan was sent to Beijing as ambassador of the Viet Minh, and in July 1951 a fourteen-member Viet Minh delegation led by Hoang Quoc Viet arrived in Beijing to negotiate a "Sino-Vietnamese Friendship Agreement" that called for the Chinese to provide technicians, medicine, and training for Vietnamese students in return for Vietnamese agricultural products and minerals.[69] A "Sino-Vietnamese Goods Exchange Agreement" was subsequently signed by Hoang Minh Giam and Chou En-lai in Beijing in July 1952. The Viet Minh ambassador in Beijing, Hoang Van Hoan, negotiated a supplement to the agreement, which was signed in May 1953 and provided for Chinese support for the Viet Minh fall offensive in 1953 and for the treatment of wounded Viet Minh soldiers in China. The agreement was renewed for additional quantities in 1954.[70]

From 1950 onward, French and other Western sources repeatedly reported that the Viet Minh and the Communist Chinese had concluded a full-blown military alliance. However, the best evidence seems to be that no such formal pact was ever concluded. King C. Chen suggests that the successive Sino-Vietnamese trade agreements, which called for the delivery of Chinese military goods in exchange for Vietnamese raw materials, were probably the "military alliance" in question.[71]

The Scope of Chinese Logistical Support

The exact quantities and nature of the war materiel and other supplies provided to the Viet Minh by the Chinese Communists between 1950 and 1954 is not known, and the figures cited by various authorities differ widely. It appears that the amounts of arms, ammunition, and other equipment and supplies procured by Viet Minh liaison and purchasing agents in South China remained fairly limited during 1950 and early 1951.[72] The authors of a French retrospective on the operations in northern Tonkin in the fall of 1950 put the amounts provided by the Chinese in 1950 at a total of 3,983 tons, including 1,020 tons of weapons and ammunition, 161 tons of military clothing, 20 tons of medicines and medical equipment, 71 tons of materiel for the production of weapons, 2,634 tons of rice, and 30 Molotova trucks.[73]

Estimates of monthly tonnages are equally diverse. The number and volume of shipments increased in the summer of 1951, following establishment of the "Aid to the Viet Minh Committee," and then increased again with the completion of the Nanning–Chennan-kuan rail line in October 1951. American intelligence sources reported that in November 1951 alone over 3,000 tons of military materiel reached the Viet Minh from Communist China.[74] On January 23, 1952, French authorities in Saigon reported that in the last four months of 1951 the Viet Minh had received from the Chinese some 4,000 tons of weapons, including 100,000 hand grenades, 10,000 75 mm shells, 10 million cartridge cases, a large quantity of Soviet-made explosives, many Skoda rifles, 75 mm guns of Russian and Chinese manufacture, and some German-made guns, and it was also reported that Chinese aid in 1952 included some 40,000 rifles, 4,000 submachine guns, 450 mortars, 120 recoilless rifles, 45–50 antiaircraft guns, and 30–35 field guns.[75] In June 1953, the CIA estimated that the Viet Minh were receiving about 400–500 tons of military supplies per month from China, but a more recent estimate by Michael W. Clodfelter puts the monthly tonnages much lower: about 10–20 tons per month in 1951, 50 tons per month in 1952, 600 tons per month in 1953, and 1,500–4,000 tons per month in 1954.[76]

Clearly, the quantity of arms and equipment received by the Viet Minh from Communist China increased after the Korean armistice was signed on July 27, 1953, but the impact may not have been as immediate or as dramatic as Bernard Fall (who was in Hanoi in the summer of 1953) implied when he later observed, "The increased weight of new materiel . . . for the Viet-Minh forces made itself readily felt immediately after the Korean cease-fire."[77] In the six-week period from September 1 to October 10, 1953, only an estimated 1,080 tons of military supplies were delivered to the Viet Minh from Communist China, an amount that, although about the same as the monthly average for 1952, was actually slightly less than the average one thousand tons per month delivered between January and September 1953.[78]

Table 8.1. Arms Supplied to the Viet Minh by Communist China, 1950–1952 (Est.)

Weapon	1950	1951	1952
Rifles	50,000	18,000	40,000
Automatic Weapons	245	1,200	4,000
Mortars (81 and 122 mm)	30	150–200	450
Recoilless Rifles	–	50	120
Antiaircraft Guns	8	unknown	40–50
Artillery Pieces	36	unknown	30–35

Source: Compiled by the author from various sources, including Miller, "'A Handful of Rice?,'" 110; O'Ballance, *The Indo-China War*, 141n2; Fall, *Le Viet-Minh*, 195; Spector, *Advice and Support*, 125; Serieye, *Le Viêt-Minh*, 9.

The monthly tonnages represented a variety of arms and other supplies. Reliable sources estimated that about 75 percent of the Chinese aid consisted of munitions and petroleum products, the remaining 25 percent being arms, medical supplies, and signal equipment.[79] One French authority claimed that the materiel received by the Viet Minh from Communist China in the last six months of 1952 alone included: 20 105 mm artillery pieces, 10,000 rounds of 105 mm artillery ammunition, 15,000 rounds of mortar ammunition, 2,000 submachine guns, 1 million rounds of 12.7 mm heavy machine gun ammunition, 80 heavy machine guns, 300 tons of signal equipment and medical supplies, 130,000 pairs of footwear, 350 trucks, and (for the entire year of 1952) 1.5 million liters of gasoline.[80] In 1953, about 300 of the 1,000 tons of materiel that reached the Viet Minh each month from Communist China were in arms, ammunition, or the materials for producing them.[81] Some idea of the numbers and types of weapons received on a yearly basis is provided by the data in table 8.1.

The total amount of military equipment and supplies provided by the Chinese to the Viet Minh was substantial. According to Qiang Zhai, between April 1950 and mid-1954, the Chinese Communists supplied the Viet Minh with some "116,000 guns and 4,630 cannons, and equipped five infantry divisions, one engineering and artillery division, one antiaircraft regiment, and one guard regiment."[82] The materiel supplied by the Chinese was provided on very generous terms, payments being deferred if the Vietnamese could not make them.[83]

The Chinese-supplied materiel was of diverse origins. Early deliveries consisted mainly of Chinese copies of Soviet small arms and automatic weapons and a few Czechoslovakian bazookas. Soviet-made trucks and weapons were first discovered by French forces during a raid on Phu Tho, a Viet Minh supply center in the Viet Bac, in late November 1952. However, about 95 percent of the arms and equipment provided by the Chinese to the Viet Minh between 1950 and 1954 was of American manufacture.[84] The American small arms, automatic weapons, mortars, ammunition, vehicles, radios, and medical supplies provided to the Viet Minh represented stocks taken by the Chinese Communists from the Nationalist Chinese or captured from U.N. forces in Korea and subsequently refurbished in Chinese arsenals. In some cases, the American weapons received by the Viet Minh were newer or better models than the U.S.-made weapons available to the French. For example, the Chinese provided the Viet Minh with American 75 mm recoilless rifles while the French had to make do with the older 57 mm models. Since both sides used American equipment in considerable quantities, the Viet Minh were able to obtain repair parts by capturing or stealing them from the French.

Nanning in Kwangsi Province, some two hundred kilometers northeast of Lang Son, and Kunming in Yunnan Province were the two main bases from which the Chinese Communists supplied the Viet Minh.[85] Other important Chinese supply facilities supporting the Viet Minh were located at Ping-hsiang and Chennankuan, near the Tonkin border in Kwangsi, and Meng-tzu in Yunnan. Many of the weapons received by the Viet Minh from the Chinese had been reworked at the old 53rd Arsenal in Kunyang in Yunnan Province, which the Chinese renovated and equipped with Soviet-supplied machine tools to produce several types of light weapons. Renamed the "Arsenal of the Southwest," the Kunyang facility focused on the support of the Viet Minh and the Communist guerrillas in Burma.[86] Two Chinese arsenals in Canton also produced grenades, rifles, machine guns, and other light arms for the Viet Minh after 1951.[87]

The General Supply Directorate of the Viet Minh Ministry of National Defense was responsible for coordinating all supply matters and maintained contact with Viet Minh liaison teams in Communist China, the most important of which was the office set up in Nanning on February 10, 1950, to manage the delivery of Chinese equipment to the Viet Minh.[88] Smaller liaison teams were located at Chinese supply installations just across the border from Tonkin. The Nanning mission arranged the procurement of all types of supplies from the Chinese. For their part, in the summer of 1950 the Chinese Communist government appointed General Li Tien-yu, deputy commander of the Kwangsi Military Region, to head a logistical committee responsible for the preparation and transfer of food, ammunition, and medical supplies to the Viet Minh, and in early 1951 the Chinese Communists set up the "Chinese Committee for Aid to Vietnam," which, with the assistance of numerous smaller agencies, coordinated deliveries to the Viet Minh.[89] Following the July 1952 agreement, a "Sino-Vietnamese Control Committee for Goods Exchange" was established to oversee the shipment of goods under the existing agreements. China's Teng Tzu-hui was appointed chairman of the committee, with the Viet Minh's Hoang Quoc Viet and Vo Van Giam as vice chairmen, and twelve transportation teams were set up to work under the direction of the committee.[90]

The Chinese authorities were not entirely satisfied with the management of the supplies that they so generously provided to the Viet Minh. Rather, they saw "economic mismanagement at the top . . . corruption among lower-level Viet Minh cadres in charge of financial matters as well as negligence and waste of the materials provided by China."[91] Twice, in April and May 1951, Liu Shaoqi was compelled to communicate to Ho Chi Minh "the importance of punishing those officials who had violated financial rules and discipline," telling him that "many Chinese materials, including munitions, transmitter-receivers, and X-ray equipment were left unattended either by roadsides or in caves in Vietnam."[92]

To facilitate the movement of supplies to their client, the Chinese made great efforts to improve the highways and rail lines on their side of the border leading from the major supply centers into Indochina, and the U.S. intelligence assessment in December 1950 was that "it appears likely that if the Viet Minh forces (aided by China) gain complete control of the border highlands, they will be able to develop supply lines from bases in China to the northern edge of the Tonkin Plain."[93] The principal land routes used to ship materiel to the Viet Minh were by highway from Tung Hsing to Mon Kay; by rail from Kunming in Yunnan to Hokow and then by numerous roads and trails to the border towns of Lao Kay and Ha Giang; and by rail from Nanning to Chennan-kuan (Na Cham), and thence by truck via Ping-hsiang to Dong Dang and from there south to Lang Son and north to Cao Bang. The latter route was by far the most important; nearly three-quarters of the Chinese supplies entered Indochina at Ta Lung and moved by way of Cao Bang, Nguyen Binh, Bac Kan, and Thai Nguyen to Viet Minh forces in the west or around the Tonkin delta to forces in the south.[94]

The improvement of the road network on the Chinese side of the frontier involved more than one hundred thousand Nationalist Chinese prisoners and Tonkinese coolies working with their hands and small baskets. More than half of them died, but four roads, suitable for heavy trucks and guns, were completed in only a few months. Those paved and gravel roads led from Nanning to key points on the frontier at Lao Kay, Cao Bang, Lang Son, and Mon Kay. In late 1953–early 1954, a new road opened from Meng-tzu in Yunnan via Lai Chau to the Dien Bien Phu area. Further improvement of the roads from the Chinese railheads into Tonkin by early 1952 permitted the delivery by truck of supplies to within twenty miles of the French lines.[95]

In 1950, the railroad from Kunming to Hanoi, which had been torn up on the Chinese side of the border during World War II, ran only halfway from Kunming to the Tonkin border, and it was not fully restored until 1958. Consequently, the rail route from Nanning to Chennan-kuan was the most important and most active of the rail lines used by the Chinese to supply the Viet Minh during the First Indochina War. Construction of this important Chinese rail line, which linked to the Hunan–Kwangsi railroad, was about 60 percent complete by the fall of 1939, when the Japanese invasion of Kwangsi brought work to a halt. In September 1950, the Chinese Communists applied some two hundred engineers and thirty thousand coolies to the job, and the work was completed in October 1951. With the extension of the Kwangsi railroad to Na Cham on the Tonkin border, Nanning became the most important center for supplying the Viet Minh, and the flow of supplies to the Viet Minh was substantially increased, although the actual physical connection of the Kwangsi and Indochinese rail systems was not completed until 1955.[96]

Military cargoes for the Viet Minh also moved by sea from the Chinese ports of Yulin and Haikow on Hainan Island, from Chin-chow-wan, and from Wei-chow-tao to Viet Minh–controlled areas near Haiphong, Nghe An, Quang Tri, Quang Ngai, and Tourane (Da Nang). An inland waterway capable of handling shallow-draft twenty-five-ton junks also ran from Nanning to close to the border.[97]

There is scant evidence to suggest that the Chinese and Viet Minh made any considerable use of air transport, but in the summer of 1953 the newly built airports at Nanning, Lungchow (now Longzhou), and Lang Son were opened to traffic and some twenty to thirty Soviet-made transports operated out of them.[98] The airfield at Lang Son was, of course, in Tonkin, and thus some Chinese supplies may have been delivered to the Viet Minh by air.

The Chinese Military Advisory Group

Given the lack of technical and higher staff skills among the Viet Minh early in the war, the advisors, technicians, and training provided by the Chinese Communists were of major importance to the development of the Viet Minh armed forces, particularly the Viet Minh logistical system. Before 1950, the role of technical advisor was filled by deserters from the Japanese forces in Indochina and by deserters from the Foreign Legion or other French Union units. About two thousand Japanese soldiers deserted to the Viet Minh at the end of World War II, and there were still five hundred to eight hundred of them with the Viet Minh in late 1950. The Japanese deserters served as military instructors and technical specialists and helped to organize the first Viet Minh armaments workshops. In October 1945, the Viet Minh forces also included about fifty Foreign Legion deserters, most of whom were working on radios or vehicles, or as "doctors."[99]

The Viet Minh seized power in Hanoi in August 1945, and in March 1946 the one-thousand-man 1st Regiment of the Communist Guangdong and Guangxi People's Force, led by its commander, Huang Jingwen, and its political commissar, Tang Caiyout, under heavy pressure from the Nationalist Forty-Sixth and Sixty-Fourth Armies, took refuge in Tonkin, where they were supported by the Viet Minh, who asked in return that they help train the Viet Minh forces.[100] The 1st Regiment subsequently developed a plan to send officers to train Viet Minh cadres, and, according to Qiang Zhai, "by July 1947, over 830 officers and soldiers from the Viet Minh army had received training in the camp of the First Regiment and a force of 1,000 overseas Chinese organized and incorporated into the VM."[101] The 1st Regiment returned to China in August 1949 to establish a base area and help Mao's forces crush the Nationalists in North China. The relationship between the 1st Regiment and the Viet Minh was an important first step toward Chinese Communist support of the Viet Minh struggle against the French. Qiang Zhai offers the opinion that even though "Mao was preoccupied with the struggle against Chiang Kai-shek in Manchuria and North China," the sheltering of the 1st Regiment by the Viet Minh "was important because it strengthened the link between the two revolutionary movements and paved the way for their future cooperation."[102]

In April 1950, Ho Chi Minh formally requested the assignment of Chinese military personnel as advisors at Viet Minh army headquarters and at the division level, and as commanders at the regimental and battalion levels. Chinese Communist leaders agreed to provide the advisors at the army and division levels but declined to assign any Chinese officers to command Viet Minh units, and on April 17, 1950, the CCP Central Military Commission authorized the establishment of a Chinese Military Advisory Group (CMAG) to assist the Viet Minh army headquarters and three divisions and to set up an officers' training school.[103] The CMAG was formally established in Nanning in late July 1950, and General Wei Guo Qing (a veteran of the Long March) was named chairman, with Mei Jia Sheng and Deng Yi Fan as deputy chairmen. The initial CMAG contingent consisted of seventy-nine advisors and their assistants, in all 281 persons. The military experts needed as advisors were selected from the PLA's Second, Third, and Fourth Field Armies.[104]

The CMAG, led by General Wei Guo Qing and accompanied by General Chen Geng, left Nanning on August 9, 1950, and reached Viet Minh headquarters at Quang Nguyen, near Cao Bang, on August 12.[105] Chinese advisors were immediately sent to the Viet Minh 304th, 308th, and 312th Divisions, and later in the year advisors were also sent to the 316th Division and the 351st Heavy Division. At about the same time, General Li Tien-yu, deputy commander of the Guangxi Military Region, was named to head the committee responsible for providing the organization and transportation of food, ammunition, and medical supplies to the Viet Minh. Two special field hospitals were also established to treat the Viet Minh wounded.

Even before the CMAG was activated, the CCP had already begun to provide training and advisors to the Viet Minh forces. Arthur J. Dommen has written:

> With the onset of the rains in June 1950, the Viet Minh sent its battalions to Chinese training camps in the region of Wenshan, Long Tcheou, and Chingshi. The troops, without arms, crossed the border on foot and

once in China were transported by truck. Clothed in new uniforms, they followed an intensive training course for three months under Chinese instructors. The Viet Minh used these troops to form an entirely new military organization. From 2,000 men, the Viet Minh regiment rose to 3,578 men. At all echelons, these regiments were henceforth supported by heavy equipment, signals, and headquarters units. Some 20,000 men rotated through this training in 1950 alone.[106]

At about the same time (June 1950), the CCP had assigned General Chen Geng as senior military advisor and representative to the People's Army of Viet Nam (PAVN).[107] However, General Chen Geng left Indochina to become the deputy Chinese commander in Korea in November 1950, and the post of senior advisor to the Viet Minh was not filled until October 10, 1953, when the CCP Central Committee named General Wei Guo Qing, the chief of the CMAG, to the post.[108]

Large-scale reorganization, training, and re-equipment of Viet Minh soldiers in Communist China did not begin until 1950, but, as already noted, some Viet Minh soldiers were sent to China for specialized training in infantry, artillery, and armored tactics and in communications, engineering, maintenance, and other technical skills as early as 1947 and 1948. The principal Chinese training centers for Viet Minh troops were in Guangxi and Yunnan Provinces. Engineers were trained in Nanning, and tank troops (never employed as such until the very end of the war) were trained at the armored vehicle school at Wu Ming. The Chinese also provided important training for Viet Minh staff officers as well as troop commanders and noncommissioned officers. In addition, large numbers of Chinese Communist training manuals were translated into Vietnamese and provided to the Viet Minh.[109]

The Chinese training facilities established in Guangxi and Yunnan in February 1950 reportedly were capable of handling fifteen thousand to twenty thousand Viet Minh personnel at one time for a three-month period of training and equipment.[110] The Communist Chinese Second Field Army played an important role in the process by providing access to artillery ranges at Tsin-tsi and Lungchow (now Longzhou) and other training facilities in Guangxi Province and by helping to train the 304th, 308th, 312th, 316th, and 320th Viet Minh Divisions.[111] By the summer of 1950, perhaps twenty thousand Viet Minh soldiers had received such training, and in March 1952, U.S. intelligence sources reported that some sixty thousand Viet Minh troops had been trained, equipped, and reorganized in the Chinese centers.[112]

Additional Chinese advisors and specialist troops, such as antiaircraft crewmen, artillery experts, engineers, and truck drivers, soon followed the initial contingent of the CMAG, and by November 1950 U.S. intelligence sources believed that Chinese Communist technicians had been integrated into Viet Minh units and that a number of nontechnical Chinese personnel, thought to be from the border regions, had entered the Viet Minh forces.[113] In March 1952, U.S. intelligence sources reported that the Chinese and Viet Minh had established a joint staff with Soviet advisors in Nanning and that an advanced echelon of that joint staff was with the Viet Minh headquarters in Tonkin, assisting in operational planning and overseeing the Chinese Communist advisors "known to be with Viet Minh units of all types down to company level."[114] The influence of such advisors was said to have been evident in "the Chinese-type infiltration and deep penetration tactics employed at Hoa Binh."[115] Bernard Fall also maintained that there were around three hundred Soviet advisors in Indochina, although there seems to be little evidence to support such a claim.[116]

With the signing of a truce in Korea in July 1953, French and American leaders were concerned that veteran Chinese troops might be redeployed for direct intervention in Indochina. Wellington Koo, the Nationalist Chinese ambassador to the United Nations, had already reported in early May the existence of a Soviet–Chinese–Viet Minh agreement by which the Soviets would supply the arms for five divisions and the Chinese would send three hundred thousand men into northern Indochina.[117] The report was denied by the Communists and denounced as a lie. In the summer of 1953, the Chinese Communist military council did send General Hsiao Ke to Cao Bang to head a new 228-man Chinese military training mission to the Viet Minh, and on October 17–20, 1953, General Li Tien-yu, then chief of staff of the Guangxi Military Region, traveled to Nanning to confer with General Giap and reach an agreement on the shipment of additional war materiel and the protection of the Lang Son airfield.[118] General Li subsequently was put in charge of Vietnamese military affairs in 1954.

The number of Chinese military personnel who supported the Viet Minh in Indochina is unclear, but probably has been greatly exaggerated by Bernard Fall and others, who claim that some twenty thousand to thirty thousand Chinese "volunteers" entered Tonkin to fight alongside the Viet Minh. Although Fall agreed that the Chinese were restricted principally to logistical roles, he did credit the reports of Chinese troops manning the Viet Minh guns around Dien Bien Phu. One American author, Robert B. Rigg, who himself had served with the Communist Chinese guerrillas after World War II, also alleged the presence of Chinese "volunteers" in Indochina. A French author, Claude Guigues, put the number of Chinese advisors assigned down to regimental and even battalion level in 1950 and 1951 at five thousand to six thousand and noted that by 1953 the number had decreased significantly and that Chinese advisors were found only in some divisions and attached to the various elements of the Viet Minh high command as political and administrative advisors. The size of the Chinese advisory effort has been estimated elsewhere at four thousand to six thousand men in June 1951 and seven thousand to eight thousand men in 1952. In March 1952, the number of such Chinese advisory and technical personnel was estimated by American intelligence sources to be around fifteen thousand, and PLA detachments were believed to be garrisoning some towns on the border, including Cao Bang and Lang Son. In September 1952, one thousand Chinese medical personnel were sent to Indochina, and an undetermined number followed in 1953 and 1954.[119]

In his book on Dien Bien Phu, Jules Roy noted that the statements of America's Secretary of State John Foster Dulles and France's Lieutenant General Henri Navarre regarding the large numbers of Chinese advisors in Indochina were probably "inspired simply by the desire to explain away their failures by attributing them to extraneous causes."[120] In reality, only a relatively small number, perhaps half the number given by Fall, of Chinese Communist advisors and technicians were stationed in Tonkin to advise the Viet Minh on political and military matters and to assist the Viet Minh in the care, use, and maintenance of the equipment provided by Chinese aid.[121] Apparently some Chinese soldiers did play a more active role by driving trucks, performing engineer work, and manning antiaircraft guns, notably at Dien Bien Phu. However, the French were unable to confirm the presence of Chinese combat troops at the time since no Chinese bodies were found and no Chinese prisoners were taken.[122] Both the Chinese and the Viet Minh denied the reports of Chinese advisors and technical personnel serving with the Viet Minh, and as late as February 1, 1954, French authorities still reported that as of that date no Chinese had been captured or even seen in the forward areas, although Lieutenant General Navarre told Lieutenant General O'Daniel that he believed the Chinese were present in the rear areas.[123] In December 1964, Joseph Zasloff interviewed a high-ranking French intelligence officer from the Indochina war who denied that there were any Chinese "volunteers" in Indochina, as confirmed by the fact that the French never took any Chinese prisoners.[124]

One important question concerns the degree to which the Chinese advisors dominated the strategic and operational decision-making of the Viet Minh. In an article in the *Journal of Military History* in 1993, historian Qiang Zhai asserted that the planning and direction of Viet Minh operations, particularly the campaigns along the border in late 1950, in northwest Tonkin in 1952, and at Dien Bien Phu, were in the hands of Communist Chinese advisors and that Viet Minh strategy and tactics were transferred directly from Chinese models.[125] A similar view is held by the American historian Douglas Porch. In his review of Howard R. Simpson's book on Dien Bien Phu, Porch argued, albeit unconvincingly, that the Chinese, not General Vo Nguyen Giap, were responsible for directing the battle of Dien Bien Phu.[126] Porch also alleged that Chinese military advisors intervened in 1953 to cause Giap to redirect his offensive away from the delta to the northwest highlands of Tonkin.[127] Qiang Zhai and Porch necessarily denigrate the independent role and reputation of General Giap, and they both almost certainly exaggerate the importance and impact of the Chinese advisory effort.

The Chinese Communists did have a significant influence on the operational decisions of the Viet Minh, if for no other reason than that after 1950 they controlled the bulk of the physical resources needed to mount extended operations. But it is also quite clear that the Viet Minh reserved to themselves the final decision on all political and military aspects of the war against the French and that General Giap was "the man in charge of the war."[128] Long after the war, former Viet Minh commanders freely admitted that many Chinese soldiers had served in their units, but they all vehemently denied that the Chinese advisors had dominated the strategic planning and operational conduct of the war.[129] Having interviewed General Giap and other Viet Minh military leaders, all of whom were indignant at the suggestion that they took orders from the Chinese, Jules Roy concluded that the pride of the Viet Minh and their natural antipathy for the Chinese would have limited Chinese influence in any event.[130]

While most eager to receive Chinese support and assistance, Ho Chi Minh, for one, was not blind to the negative aspects of the arrangement, even at the very beginning of the relationship. In March 1946, soon after Ho acceded to internal pressures within his government to temporarily dissolve the Indochinese Communist Party and then sought an accommodation with the French, pro-Chinese elements within the Democratic Republic of Viet Nam criticized him severely, which prompted him to declare:

> You fools! Don't you realize what it means if the Chinese stay? Don't you remember your history? The last time the Chinese came, they stayed one thousand years!
>
> The French are foreigners. They are weak. Colonialism is dying out. Nothing will be able to withstand world pressure for independence. They may stay for a while, but they will have to go because the white man is finished in Asia. But if the Chinese stay now, they will never leave.
>
> As for me, I prefer to smell French shit for five years, rather than Chinese shit for the rest of my life.[131]

As the struggle to throw out the French became more difficult, Ho found it expedient to accept not only Chinese material support but advisors as well. And throughout the 1950s and 1960s, the Vietnamese Communists willingly accepted the aid of their Chinese comrades to fight first the French and then the South Vietnamese government and its ally, the United States. The relationship was described by Ho himself as one of "comrades plus brothers," and it was only in 1970, as the Second Indochina War began to wane and relationships between China and the United States started to thaw, that the Sino-Vietnamese relationship began to deteriorate.[132]

Given that the Chinese Communists had only recently defeated their Nationalist rivals and seized control of the Chinese mainland and, after June 1950, were deeply involved in the war in Korea, why did Mao Tse-tung divert considerable military resources to aid the Viet Minh? The historian Qiang Zhai explains Beijing's Indochina policy as "the result of a convergence of geopolitical realities, ideological beliefs, personality, and political circumstances." Support of the Viet Minh offered an opportunity to resist the United States, which Mao considered to be "the primary threat to China's security and revolution," and to define China's identity or image in the world. Mao also apparently felt a "sense of an international obligation and mission to assist a fraternal Communist party and to promote anti-imperialist revolution in Asia." The latter impulse was reinforced by the fact that during the Chinese civil war of the late 1940s, the Viet Minh government had provided sanctuary for Chinese Communist troops forced to flee from Nationalist attacks, and Mao subsequently "stressed the importance of reciprocating friendship."[133]

U.S. Perceptions of Chinese Aid to the Viet Minh

It did not take long for U.S. intelligence agencies to discover that the Chinese Communists were supporting the Viet Minh in a substantial way. On February 27, 1950, the National Security Council reported, "The presence of Chinese Communist troops along the border of Indochina makes it possible for arms, material and troops to move freely from Communist China to the northern Tonkin area now controlled by Ho Chi Minh. There is already evidence of movement of arms."[134] On December 29, 1950, the Central Intelligence Agency reported:

> The Chinese Communists have been training and equipping large numbers of Viet Minh troops in China and are supplying the Viet Minh considerable amounts of materiel. A small number of Chinese Communist advisory personnel wearing Viet Minh uniforms probably are already serving with the Viet Minh forces. In fact, official French sources report that Chinese Communist troops are already in Tonkin in some strength. Although the ability of the Chinese to furnish military equipment is limited, they should be able to make available to the Viet Minh enough small arms and artillery to give the Viet Minh a distinct superiority over present French forces. Viet Minh capabilities continue to be enlarged faster than the French have expanded their own.[135]

Seven months later, the CIA was slightly more optimistic regarding Chinese support of the Viet Minh. The CIA analysts noted that the Viet Minh were dependent on the Chinese for logistical support; that some ten thousand Chinese personnel were serving as cadre, technicians, and advisors to the Viet Minh; and that, although the number of Chinese personnel in Tonkin was increasing, "the Chinese Communists while apparently maintaining roughly the same level of material assistance as of last December, have not intervened directly or with substantial 'volunteer' forces or noticeably stepped up arms aid."[136] They estimated that should the Chinese leaders decide to intervene directly in Indochina, "roughly 100,000 Chinese Communist field force troops could now be made available and logistically supported," although only for "short offensive operations of about one week at a time, passing to the defensive during the intervals for replenishment of supplies." They also noted that the rugged terrain and poor road network along the Sino-Vietnamese border would limit the forces that could be deployed, and that "Chinese Communist logistical capabilities for offensive operations are gradually increasing." Moreover, they assessed that Chinese capabilities for an invasion of Indochina would increase significantly two months after a Korean armistice was signed.

By 1952, it was clear that the military situation in Indochina had become one of stalemate, and that "increased U.S. aid to the Franco-Vietnamese forces has been an essential factor in enabling them to withstand recent communist attacks. However, Chinese aid to the Viet Minh in the form of logistic support, training, and technical advisors is increasing at least at a comparable rate. The prospect is for a continuation of the present stalemate in the absence of intervention by important forces other than those presently engaged."[137] Nevertheless, in June 1953 the CIA was still reporting that: "Small Chinese Communist units reportedly have entered the mountainous northwest sections of Tonkin on several occasions to assist the Viet Minh against French-supported native guerrillas, but no Chinese Communist troops have been identified in forward areas."[138]

For both the French and the Viet Minh, the most significant sources of arms and other military supplies were external, and neither side could have pursued the war as long as they did without such external support. The arrival of the Chinese Communist forces on the Indochinese border in the fall of 1949 significantly changed the nature of the war for both the Viet Minh and the French. For the Viet Minh, the acquisition of arms and other military materiel was greatly facilitated and made possible the contemplation of large-scale operations to throw the French Union forces out of Tonkin and the rest of Indochina. For the French, the situation became uncertain: Would the Chinese Communist forces stop at the border or would they continue on into Indochina to assist the Viet Minh directly? Lieutenant General Henri Navarre, the French *commandant en chef* in 1953 and 1954, later wrote: "Until then the enemy had envisioned only the objectives of the guerrilla. All that would change if China provided them with the strength which they lacked. For France the hour of decision had arrived: to win the war by applying the necessary resources before the Chinese aid took on a more important character or to end the war by a political arrangement."[139]

Pro-Communist Western commentators vehemently denied that Viet Minh acceptance of Chinese Communist materiel, training, and advisors compromised their independence or changed the nationalist nature of the struggle in any way.[140] But on an international level, the aid provided to the Viet Minh by the Chinese Communists provoked a reaction in the West that ensured that the Indochina conflict would subsequently be viewed not as a war of nationalists against their colonial masters but as part of the international struggle between Communism and the Western democracies.[141] The major result of this change in attitude was that the United States made available to the French massive quantities of economic and military aid. Moreover, it provided the Chinese with a means of influencing events on her borders and of tweaking the West without direct intervention. From the Viet Minh perspective, the victory of the Chinese Communists over the Nationalists ended their geographical isolation and opened a conduit to the outside world and particularly to the socialist countries from which they hoped to obtain much-needed support.

The military impact of Chinese aid was felt as early as May 1950, as General Giap began to properly outfit his new regular divisions and to improve the armament of the regional and local guerrillas, who received the cast-off equipment of the *Chu Luc*. The substantial support received from the Chinese also encouraged Giap to proceed to the third, or "general counteroffensive," stage of his strategy, the direct confrontation of the French Union forces in conventional offensive operations on a major scale. The new equipment provided by the Chinese was certainly felt in the battle for the French garrisons on the Chinese frontier in September 1950, in which the newly re-equipped Viet Minh forces won an important victory over the French. The increased quantities of arms and other supplies received by the Viet Minh from Communist China after the Korean War cease-fire on July 27, 1953, further improved the Viet Minh combat effectiveness and capability for sustained offensive operations. But as important as Chinese military aid was to the Viet Minh war effort, it was perhaps not sufficient. In May 1953, analysts in the office of the U.S. Army assistant chief of staff G-2 concluded: "Even if greater tonnages than that could be transported, such aid would not assure the Viet Minh of a capability of ultimate military victory. A change in the type of Chinese Communist aid, with provisions of air power, heavy artillery or troops, would be required to enable the Viet Minh to defeat the French Union Forces."[142]

In any event, high levels of Chinese aid to the Viet Minh aroused in the French the fear that they might actually lose the war and at the same time provided them with a convenient excuse for their own shortcomings and inability to stem the Viet Minh tide.[143] The response of French officials in Indochina was to seek additional outside assistance rather than to correct their many internal deficiencies of policy, strategy, and execution. In terms of the gross tonnage of materiel supplied, the United States provided far more aid to the French Union forces in Indochina than the Communist Chinese provided to the Viet Minh, but in the end, the amount of aid mattered less than what was done with the aid. On the whole, the Viet Minh seem to have been much more successful in employing the arms, ammunition, and other supplies received than were the French. Indeed, the massive quantities of heavy weapons, ammunition, vehicles, aircraft, and other supplies delivered by the United States seem to have lulled the French Union forces into a false sense of superiority even as they were overwhelmed by the difficulties of storing, maintaining, and bringing this equipment to bear against the Viet Minh.

Despite the work of Qiang Zhai and others, opinion remains divided over the degree to which Chinese support of the Viet Minh was a decisive factor in the First Indochina War.[144] The Vietnamese Communists and their backers remain reluctant to acknowledge the importance of Chinese support, and the lack of access to Chinese and Indochinese sources by Western historians has limited understanding of its impact. On balance, however, one must conclude that the supplies, training, and advice given by the Chinese Communists to their Viet Minh comrades was a decisive element in the ultimate victory of the Viet Minh over the French. As one pair of biographers of Chairman Mao have written: "It was having China as a secure rear and supply depot that made it possible for the Vietnamese to fight for 25 years and beat first the French and then the Americans."[145]

9

The Shape of Battles to Come

The first logistical campaign of the Indochina war encompassed the struggles of both the French and the Viet Minh to develop an effective strategy for the war and to build the combat and support forces needed to carry out that strategy. Although those struggles continued throughout the war, they were particularly characteristic of the period from August 1945 to December 1950. From the logistical point of view, the campaign was primarily an internal one for both sides. The first battle of the campaign was the effort by both the French and the Viet Minh to develop sufficient effective combat forces to prevent their opponent from gaining a quick victory. Although weakened by the Second World War, the French appeared to hold an initial advantage with limited but relatively well-armed and well-trained forces available for commitment in Indochina. However, their opponent, the Viet Minh guerrilla army, had gained strength and experience opposing both the French and the Japanese during the war, and they held much of the ground. Although poorly armed and lacking resources, the Vietnamese nationalist coalition led by Ho Chi Minh had what the French-led forces did not, an inspiring cause: national freedom and independence.

As the necessary military forces were assembled and trained, the strategies of both the French and the Viet Minh began to gel, and both sides undertook a number of operations that foreshadowed the remaining course of the war. In October 1947, the French launched Operation LEA, the first of a series of major offensives against the Viet Minh bases in northern Tonkin. For their part, the Viet Minh ended the period with the first major test for their newly formed main battle force, a large-scale attack on the French outposts on the Chinese border in the fall of 1950 that resulted in a crushing defeat for the French Union forces in northern Tonkin. Both Operation LEA and the battle of Route Coloniale 4 (RC 4) and the Chinese frontier posts established patterns that would dominate the First Indochina War in its two succeeding phases: the campaign for the base areas and the campaign for control of the lines of communication.

The Uneasy Peace, August 1945–December 1946

On March 9, 1945, the Japanese ended their joint condominium with Vichy France in Indochina by disarming and interning the French troops, some of whom resisted and were killed, captured, or driven north into southern China, where they were interned by the Nationalist Chinese.[1] The Japanese coup seriously impaired French authority and prestige in Indochina, and the emperor of Annam, Bao Dai, subsequently proclaimed himself emperor of all Viet Nam and formed a feeble and corrupt puppet government under Japanese influence. The Bao Dai regime quickly demonstrated its inability to govern, and the Japanese assumed direct control. Meanwhile, the nationalist guerrillas of Ho Chi Minh and Vo Nguyen Giap refused to support the Bao Dai government, and the Committee for the Liberation of the Vietnamese People was formed with Ho as president and achieved considerable success in opposing the Japanese occupation forces in Tonkin.

The American atomic bombing of Hiroshima and Nagasaki in early August 1945 was soon followed by the surrender of Japan, although Japanese forces continued to hold their positions in Indochina and elsewhere. On August 10, 1945, Ho Chi Minh ordered a national uprising against the Japanese, partly in the hope of forestalling the return of the French to Indochina. The nationalist revolt was immediately successful in the north, and on August 25, 1945, Emperor Bao Dai abdicated in favor of the new nationalist government of Ho Chi Minh, which was formed on August 29. The fragmented Vietnamese nationalist elements in the south were less successful in seizing control from the Japanese, but they too accepted Ho's leadership. At Hanoi on September 2, 1945, Ho Chi Minh proclaimed the complete independence of Viet Nam and the establishment of the Democratic Republic of Viet Nam.

The Return of French Forces to Cochinchina

In mid-1945, there were some fifty thousand Japanese troops in Indochina. In accordance with the decisions of the Allied powers at the Potsdam Conference in July 1945, the British were assigned to receive the surrender of the Japanese forces in southern Indochina (south of 16 degrees North latitude) and the Nationalist Chinese were to perform a similar function in the north. Accordingly, British troops under Major General Douglas D. Gracey, accompanied by a very small contingent of French troops, arrived in Saigon on September 12, 1945. The occupation by British forces was unpopular, and they were obliged to use the surrendered Japanese forces to help maintain law and order. In the north, the Nationalist Chinese under General Lu Han rapidly occupied Tonkin, disarmed the Japanese, and settled in for a profitable exploitation of the powers vested in them by the Allies.

The Potsdam conferees made no provision for the return of Indochina to French control. Indeed, every obstacle was placed in the path of the French, who naturally wished to reinstate their authority in Indochina as quickly as possible. The Nationalist Chinese, eager to maintain their dominance over northern Indochina, were opposed to the return of the French. The United States, following a policy established by President Franklin D. Roosevelt, was generally opposed on the grounds of anticolonialism.[2] The British were marginally more sympathetic.[3] The principal problem for the French was logistical: how to transport to Indochina the forces needed to restore their colonial regime. Since the Allies refused to allocate the shipping necessary to transport a French expeditionary force, the French had to use a few of their own scarce naval vessels to transport the initial contingents to Saigon. On August 28, 1945, the designated French commander for Indochina, Lieutenant General Philippe François Marie de Hauteclocque (*dit* Leclerc), still in Ceylon, sketched for the designated high commissioner, Vice Admiral Georges Thierry d'Argenlieu, still in Paris, the attitudes of the Allies and his plans for the use of the French cruisers *Béarn* and *Ville de Strasbourg* to move sufficient troops to Saigon to reoccupy the area south of the 16th Parallel, noting: "All this is conditional on a single principal factor: the ships and the means of debarkation. . . . None of the Allies will actually aid us in reoccupying Indochina, in particular no senior commander will consent to provide aircraft or shipping north of the 16th Parallel without the orders of his government."[4]

The first contingent of French troops arrived at Saigon on September 23, 1945, and proceeded to reoccupy the public buildings and to reestablish French authority. Another small group arrived at Cap St. Jacques (Vung Tau) on October 2, and on October 22 the main elements of the French Far East Expeditionary Corps (*Corps Expéditionnaire Français d'Extrême-Orient*, CEFEO), including the 2nd Armored Division, began landing in Saigon. The attempt to reestablish French control of Indochina was met with active opposition by Vietnamese nationalists of all political persuasions, but the British authorities, as well as the recently surrendered Japanese forces, assisted the French in their initial efforts to regain control in the south, and by November 1945 all strategic points in Cochinchina had been retaken. In March 1946 the British formally relinquished control of southern Indochina to the French.[5]

In the north, the Viet Minh cooperated with the Nationalist Chinese occupation forces that to some degree supported Vietnamese nationalist aspirations against the French for their own reasons. In order to disguise the Communist influence in his nationalist government, Ho Chi Minh dissolved the Communist Party on November 11, 1945, and elections were held in January 1946 for a National Assembly. Ho Chi Minh presented his new government as a coalition of nationalist interests, but as time went on the Communists became increasingly dominant. However, the Vietnamese Communist Party was not reestablished formally until March 1951, when it reemerged as the Vietnamese Workers' Party (*Dang Lao Dong Viet Nam*). By that time, Ho Chi Minh and his Marxist supporters had all but eliminated independent, non-Communist elements in the nationalist movement.

The Search for a Negotiated Settlement

In order to regain control of northern Viet Nam, the French had to reach an agreement with both the Nationalist Chinese and the government of Ho Chi Minh. On February 28, 1946, they signed an agreement with the Nationalist Chinese by which France ceded its extraterritorial rights in China, guaranteed rights for Chinese nationals in Indochina equivalent to those of French citizens, and granted certain favorable trade concessions to the Chinese. In return, the Nationalist Chinese agreed to evacuate their occupation forces from northern Viet Nam and permit the French to return.

Meanwhile, the French planned in secret an operation to reoccupy Indochina north of the 16th Parallel. Operation BEN TRÉ involved the embarkation at Saigon of some twenty-one thousand troops of the 9th Colonial Infantry Division and the 2nd Armored Division on February 27–March 1, 1946, to sail for Haiphong and an eventual linkup with a small force that was to be airlifted into Hanoi.[6] The French armada arrived at Haiphong on March 6, expecting Chinese cooperation with the landing. However, the Nationalist Chinese feared becoming caught up in an open conflict between the French and the Viet Minh and opened fire on the French ships to prevent a landing. Both sides suffered casualties before the Chinese forced them to come to terms and a cease-fire was arranged.

Meanwhile, on the same day, Ho Chi Minh and the French high commissioner reached an agreement in their ongoing negotiations that called for the establishment of Viet Nam (minus Cochinchina, the status of which was to be decided by a referendum) as a free state in a future Indochinese Federation within the French Union.[7] In return, the French were to be permitted to reenter Tonkin with less than two divisions. The French entered Haiphong on March 8 and Hanoi on March 18. Soon thereafter, they reoccupied Tourane (Da Nang), Hue, Lang Son, Phong Sa Ly, Sam Neua, Lai Chau, Mon Cay, and other key towns in Tonkin and northern Annam.

The terms of the March 6 agreement were left purposefully vague, and neither side really accepted them as a final solution. A series of conferences in the spring and summer of 1946 failed to clarify the outstanding issues. Ho Chi Minh traveled to Paris in May 1946 to complete the details of the agreement but was met with delay and evasion on the part of the French. The discussions were ended by the declaration in early June 1946 of an independent republic by pro-French elements in Cochinchina. One further attempt at a peaceful solution was made in September 1946, when the French and Viet Minh agreed to a modus vivendi that was designed to permit the restoration of French economic and cultural influence in the north in return for more liberal French policies. The modus vivendi, like the March 6 agreements that preceded it, did not clearly spell out a plan for Vietnamese unity or independence and ultimately proved no more successful as a basis for a final political settlement. Despite the continued hope of reaching some long-term agreement on the political fate of Indochina, relations between the French and Viet Minh soon began to deteriorate. The French proceeded with their military reoccupation of the country, and the Viet Minh plotted to eliminate the French presence once and for all.

The Outbreak of Open Warfare

The half-hearted attempts to reach a political accommodation began to fall apart in November 1946.[8] Neither side kept the agreements scrupulously, and small-scale incidents were common. Tensions ran particularly high in the key Tonkinese port city of Haiphong, where the French were eager to reestablish control over the customs operations in an effort to stem the flow of arms and equipment to the Viet Minh. Open conflict was precipitated by the announcement by Colonel Debès, the French commander in Haiphong, that the French would take over the customs service as of October 15.[9] The Viet Minh waited and plotted, and on November 20 scattered fighting broke out in Haiphong between the Viet Minh and French forces. Senior authorities on both sides in Tonkin sought to restore the situation, but Colonel Debès, encouraged by the *commandant en chef,* General Jean-Étienne Valluy, in Saigon, struck the Viet Minh with all the force at his disposal, including a naval bombardment of the Vietnamese sections of the city that resulted in over six thousand Vietnamese casualties.[10] After several days the French gained control of Haiphong and the surrounding area, and on November 23 the French ordered the Vietnamese to evacuate their section of Haiphong under threat of further reprisals.

Neither side wanted nor was ready for an open break, and Ho Chi Minh is reported to have observed, "Neither France nor Vietnam can afford the luxury of a bloody war."[11] However, the Haiphong incident clearly demonstrated that the attempts to reach a negotiated settlement of French and Viet Minh differences were doomed. The total collapse of the search for a political solution came on the night of December 19–20, 1946, when the Viet Minh self-defense fighters (*Tu Ve*) in Hanoi precipitated open warfare by attacking the Hanoi electric plant and other French installations in the area. The Viet Minh leadership had indeed called for a nationwide surprise attack on the French on December 19, but at the last minute Vo Nguyen Giap, having learned that the French were alerted to the coming attacks, canceled the planned operations. Overzealous Viet Minh supporters in Hanoi proceeded with the assault anyway, and the Viet Minh leadership had no option but to execute their plans at a disadvantage.[12]

Although the *Tu Ve* apparently acted contrary to the explicit orders of the Viet Minh high command, the die was cast. Forewarned of the coming attack, the French quickly took control of Gia Lam airfield and the central part of Hanoi.

After massacring forty Europeans and carrying off some two hundred as hostages, the Viet Minh, no match for the well-armed and well-trained French troops, withdrew from the city. The following day, December 21, Ho Chi Minh called for a general uprising against French colonial rule that met with widespread support throughout Viet Nam, but the French acted quickly and efficiently to secure the key towns and villages in Tonkin, forcing the Viet Minh to retreat into the countryside.

The Reoccupation of Tonkin

Following the events in Haiphong and Hanoi in November–December 1946, General Valluy moved to regain full French control of Tonkin and northern Annam. By late January 1947, French troops had retaken most of the major towns and cleared the vital road between Haiphong and Hanoi that had been blocked by the Viet Minh. In early February, the isolated garrison in Hue, under siege for six weeks, was relieved by French forces moving up from Tourane, and another French armored column relieved the besieged town of Nam Dinh in the Red River delta in early March. By the end of March, control had been reestablished over most of the urban areas of Tonkin and Annam, with the exception of Vinh, an important town on the border of the Viet Minh base area in the southern delta. During the summer of 1947, the French paused to deal with increased Viet Minh guerrilla activity in southern Viet Nam, but they again seized the initiative in the autumn and moved north to the Chinese border, clearing large parts of the Viet Minh stronghold in the Viet Bac region and inflicting heavy casualties.

Attempts to reach a negotiated settlement did not end with the battles for Haiphong and Hanoi. In April 1947, Ho Chi Minh received the distinguished French sociologist Paul Mus as an emissary of the new French high commissioner, Émile Bollaert, but the meeting ended in failure. Subsequently, while actively fighting the Viet Minh, the French sought to construct a competing movement that would counteract the Viet Minh appeal to nationalist sentiment. The attempt was frustrated by French unwillingness to concede any substantial measure of control to the Vietnamese, much less to grant independence. Proposals such as High Commissioner Bollaert's September 1947 promise of "liberty within the French Union" were never laid out clearly, and Vietnamese nationalists who showed an interest in vague French promises found themselves the special targets of Viet Minh vengeance. By permitting diehard conservative colonialists to determine the course of affairs, the French stymied the efforts of moderate nationalists to build an effective movement that would appeal to the Vietnamese population. In 1948, the French opened negotiations with former emperor Bao Dai that resulted in the Elysée Agreements of March 8, 1949, which nominally unified the three parts of Viet Nam (Tonkin, Annam, and Cochinchina) into a single state, with Bao Dai as chief of state. Viet Nam and the separate kingdoms of Cambodia and Laos were to constitute the Associated States of Indochina within the French Union. The Elysée Agreements did not, however, grant complete Vietnamese independence. For example, foreign policy would continue to be controlled by the French. Moreover, the corrupt and unpopular Bao Dai government was clearly unable to compete with the dedicated Viet Minh for the support of Vietnamese who wanted national independence. Nevertheless, the Elysée Agreements went into effect in February 1950, and the new state of Viet Nam was soon recognized by Great Britain, the United States, and other nations allied with the West.

The Viet Minh Return to Their Base Areas

Driven from Hanoi in December 1946 and from most of the other urban areas of Tonkin and northern Annam in the early months of 1947, the Viet Minh withdrew to the rugged mountains and dense jungles of the Viet Bac, a region incorporating parts of the provinces of Thai Nguyen, Bac Kan, and Tuyen Quang between Hanoi and the Chinese border. The Viet Bac would serve as the temporary capital and principal logistical and training base of the Viet Minh until their ultimate victory in the summer of 1954. Another smaller (but still important) base was established in the rich rice-producing region around Thanh Hoa in northern Annam, and lesser bases were scattered throughout Tonkin, Annam, and Cochinchina. In these secure base areas, which were raided but never seriously threatened by the French, the Viet Minh undertook the long and difficult process of recruiting, arming, and training the regular military forces that would be needed to face the French Union forces in an all-out battle for the independence of Viet Nam. Although their efforts focused on the building of the regular forces (*Chu Luc*) and providing for their logistical support, the Viet Minh meanwhile made good use of their regional and local guerrilla forces to harry the French. Infiltration, subversion, sabotage, ambush, and small-scale attacks were conducted by Viet Minh guerrillas throughout Viet Nam. As time went on, these minor actions evolved into larger, more sustained attacks that were intended not only to weaken the French Union forces militarily, but also to weaken their will to continue the struggle. All the while the Viet Minh, not the French, retained the initiative.

The Development of French Strategy in Indochina

French strategy in Indochina had two main objectives: to restore French control over the people and territory that had fallen under Viet Minh domination, and to decisively engage and destroy the Viet Minh military forces. Pursuit of these twin objectives produced a bifurcated strategy with both defensive and offensive components that were neither entirely compatible nor particularly well-suited to the nature of the conflict. The defensive and offensive elements of the French strategy in Indochina competed with each other for scarce manpower and logistical resources, and the emphasis shifted between the two elements from time to time in accordance with the political and military situation. In developing their strategy for the defeat of the Viet Minh insurgency, the French both underestimated their Viet Minh opponent—particularly with respect to his logistical capabilities—and failed to grasp "the essential Viet Minh techniques of revolutionary guerrilla warfare."[13]

The defensive component of the French strategy in Indochina focused on the protection of key areas and lines of communication and the use of small-scale offensive operations to gradually eliminate Viet Minh control over the countryside. It thus seems to have been little more than an application of the old methods of colonial conquest and control. Soon after their arrival in October 1945, General Leclerc's mechanized forces quickly struck out and secured the key population centers in Cochinchina and southern Annam but did not decisively engage the Viet Minh guerrillas, who continued to control the countryside. The French then sought to apply the well-tried "oil slick" (*tache d'huile*) method that had proven successful in Morocco in the 1920s and elsewhere. This method—it could hardly be called a strategy—involved the creation of secure centers from which the pacification forces spread outward to incorporate gradually the areas held by the rebels.[14] The key tactics of the oil slick strategy involved the division of enemy-held territory into small sectors or squares, which were then carefully cleared or "raked over" by forces who knew the area well or were led by those who did. The oil slick method required comparatively large numbers of troops to conduct the raking over and then keep the area clear of rebel forces. It also required a willingness to get out into the paddies, swamps, jungles, and mountains. Although the oil slick method, combined with interdiction of Viet Minh supply lines and attempts to destroy Viet Minh base areas, remained at the heart of operations against the Viet Minh right up to the end of the war in 1954, the French never had either the manpower or the will to make it fully effective.

The offensive element of the French strategy involved the use of well-armed mobile forces to seek out and destroy the main Viet Minh military forces. Such operations required good intelligence; a high degree of operational mobility; relatively large, well-trained combat forces; and effective logistical support, all of which the French lacked in various proportions throughout the war. Bringing a wary and elusive enemy to bay was not an easy task, and the search of many French commanders for the "single decisive battle" remained a fantasy until Dien Bien Phu, and then it was the French and not the Viet Minh who were caught in the trap and exterminated.

Time was an important factor in both aspects of the French strategy. The war in Indochina was unpopular at home and thus had to be won in the shortest possible time before the French government and public became entirely disillusioned. Time was also a factor with respect to the assistance provided to the Viet Minh by Communist China beginning in 1949–1950. The impact of such aid in quantity was certain to reduce the French chances of success, and thus its prospect placed upon the French strategists a requirement for a quick knockout blow against the Viet Minh before the full weight of Chinese logistical support could make itself felt. In the end, time ran out for the French before such a blow could be struck.

Both the defensive and offensive components of the French strategy were profoundly affected by logistical considerations. The defensive element focused on the protection of key French logistical assets (such as lines of communication and logistical support facilities), and the resupplying of a large number of isolated outposts, characteristic of the defensive strategy first in the south and later in the north, was a critical factor. A major part of the offensive strategy was clearly aimed at the interdiction of Viet Minh lines of communication and the destruction of their logistical bases, and the timing, size, and duration of offensive operations were almost entirely decided on the basis of logistical considerations, the most important of which was the availability of transport to move French Union forces to the area of operations and to keep them supplied.

The competing defensive and offensive elements presented French strategists and commanders with an operational dilemma. The chronic shortage of French Union combat forces and logistical resources did not permit the effective, simultaneous accomplishment of the twin objectives of clearing and protecting the vital rear areas and mounting offensive operations to engage and destroy the main Viet Minh forces. The assembly of forces for an offensive operation invariably exposed the areas from which they were drawn to increased Viet Minh infiltration and subversion, a process that the French referred to as "the rot" (*la pourissement*). Even after the French commanders in Indochina recognized that the critical battle of the war would be fought against the Viet Minh regular forces in Tonkin, French Union manpower continued to be drained off for the static defenses of the Red River delta and continued clearance operations in Cochinchina and Annam. Thus, the competing requirements of the defensive and offensive elements in the French strategy was the crucial problem that the French commanders in Indochina were never able to resolve satisfactorily and that became their nemesis.

In 1948, limited manpower and insufficient operational transport severely restricted the strategic options of the French commanders in Indochina and compelled them to choose between completely clearing Cochinchina or striking directly at the main Viet Minh concentration in Tonkin.[15] Eventually, the French chose to force the issue in the north, but although southern Indochina clearly became a secondary theater of operations after 1947, the Viet Minh guerrillas in Cochinchina and southern Annam maintained a high level of activity that required the French to maintain sizable forces in the south to protect vital areas and lines of communication, thus weakening the forces that could be applied to offensive actions in the north. The pacification effort in southern Indochina proceeded slowly with the help of the Cao Dai and Hoa Hao religious sects and other Vietnamese elements estranged from the Viet Minh, but it was still not completed when the crucial battles were fought and lost in Tonkin.

Until the arrival of a new *commandant en chef,* Lieutenant General Roger Blaizot, in mid-1948, the lack of resources restricted operations in Tonkin. The French did secure the critical land route between Haiphong and Hanoi and extended their control over parts of the vital Red River delta, including the important Catholic sees of Bui Chu and Phat Diem.[16] Operations outside the delta area were limited to minor improvements in the outposts along the Chinese border and a brief effort to gain the support of the anti–Viet Minh tribal groups in the highland areas northwest of Hanoi.[17]

Before leaving Paris, Lieutenant General Blaizot obtained the promise of twelve additional combat battalions for Indochina, and meanwhile a program for augmentation of the French units in Indochina with native personnel had begun.[18] As the personnel situation began to improve, the French were able to reoccupy Son Tay, Viet Tri, Hung Hao, and adjacent areas to the south, thereby linking together the French positions along the Red and Black Rivers, which could henceforth be resupplied by inland water transport, thus releasing scarce French air transport for other uses. These operations also split in two the area held by the Viet Minh by placing the French squarely astride the Viet Minh lines of communication from the Viet Bac to northern Annam.

By the beginning of 1949, the French position had improved considerably. The pacification program in the south was progressing in a satisfactory manner, and the situation in the Red River delta was also improving slowly. However, the Viet Minh were increasing their pressure on the outposts along RC 4, and the monthly resupply convoys became costly major operations.[19] The situation in central Annam also remained tenuous, as the Viet Minh infiltrated well-armed guerrilla forces into the Central Highlands, making RC 9 from Dong Ha on the coast to Savannakhet in Laos extremely hazardous, and into the coastal villages, where only six French battalions had to cover some 186 miles of coastal plain.

Concerned by the steady progress of Mao Tse-tung's Communist forces against their Nationalist opponents in China, Lieutenant General Blaizot proposed a plan for a major effort in Tonkin to weaken the Viet Minh as much as possible before the Red Chinese reached the Sino-Vietnamese border and were in a position to provide massive support to the Viet Minh. In February 1949, the French high commissioner in Indochina, Leon Pignon, rejected Blaizot's plan in favor of increased pacification activities in Cochinchina and Annam to ensure the success of ongoing efforts to form a pro-French Vietnamese government under Emperor Bao Dai. However, the French government at home, alarmed by the steady advance southward of the Communist Chinese, reversed Pignon's decision in March 1949, and the first stage of Blaizot's plan, to gain firm control of the rice-producing area of the Red River north of the Haiphong–Hanoi line, was set in motion. Subsequent stages of the plan called for the reduction and consolidation of isolated garrisons on the Chinese border, the positioning of blocking forces at the southern exits from the highlands, and the establishment of advanced offensive bases at Thai Nguyen, Phu Tho, and Yen Bay to be used by mobile forces that would be assigned the mission of penetrating and destroying the Viet Minh base areas north of Hanoi.

The overall Blaizot plan was approved in June 1949, and as the first major reinforcements arrived from France, the French Union forces in Tonkin moved north of Hanoi to occupy Bac Ninh, Phu Lang Thuong, Vinh Yen, and Phuc Yen. However, following the departure from Indochina of Lieutenant General Blaizot on September 2, 1949, the reinforcements were increasingly diverted to pacification duties in the south, and the French offensive in Tonkin stalled. At the same time, the Viet Minh further increased their offensive activity and seized Pho Lu, some 18.6 miles south of the border outpost of Lao Kay, isolating that French position and permitting the Viet Minh to reestablish their overland connections with northern Annam. The Viet Minh also stepped up their attacks against the French lines of communication linking the outposts along the Chinese border in the northeast. French losses on the September and October 1949 resupply convoys on RC 4 were so heavy that they were forced to rely on air transport to provide the five hundred tons of supplies required by the border posts each month.[20]

The difficulties of supplying the border posts preoccupied the French command in Tonkin, and during most of 1950 the French were unable to mount any substantial offensive action to interrupt the flow of supplies from Communist China to the Viet Minh or to directly attack the Viet Minh forces or their base areas. And despite the best efforts of the French Union forces, the Red River delta became increasingly vulnerable to heavy Viet Minh infiltration. French installations and supply lines as well as the rice fields and centers of friendly population in the delta were prime targets for Viet Minh guerrilla attacks. These developments, coupled with the prospect of a Communist victory in China and the potential establishment of supply and training bases for the Viet Minh just over the border in China, prompted the French to undertake a thorough review of their strategic position.

In May 1949, a study group under General Georges Revers, the French Army chief of staff, arrived in Indochina, studied the situation on the spot, and made a number of recommendations regarding the French strategy in Indochina. Among the measures proposed by General Revers were the withdrawal of French forces from the vulnerable, isolated outposts along the Chinese border and their concentration in what was called *Viet-Nam utile* ("useful Viet Nam"), the urban centers and the rich rice-producing delta of the Red River, which the Viet Minh had to control in order to feed their troops and loyal population in the highland areas of Tonkin.[21] He pointed out the obvious problem of resupplying the border posts should the roads to them be closed and the posts themselves come under Viet Minh attack.[22] General Revers also recommended that before offensive operations were undertaken against the Viet Minh base areas, the French should thoroughly secure the deltas of both the Red River and the Mekong and turn them over to Vietnamese administrators, whose authority would be backed by the new Vietnamese National Army, which he also recommended should be armed and trained at once. The recommendations of the Revers report were never formally adopted, in part because the report was leaked to the Viet Minh, but eventually many of the actions recommended by General Revers were taken out of necessity.

At the end of 1949, General Marcel Carpentier, then *commandant en chef* in Indochina, assigned Major General Marcel-Jean-Marie Alessandri to command in Tonkin. Alessandri believed the effort to engage and defeat the Viet Minh in a single decisive battle would remain futile unless the Viet Minh main forces could be enticed to fight for some crucial objective. Consequently, he chose to strengthen French control over the Red River delta, which contained the one item absolutely essential to the Viet Minh—rice—in the hope of either starving the Viet Minh into submission or forcing them into a battle in which superior French firepower and mechanized mobility could be applied decisively.[23] In the end, Major General Alessandri's strategy failed due to the lack of sufficient troops to effectively clear the delta area and prevent further Viet Minh infiltration, the lack of a positive program to attract the loyalty of the Vietnamese population, and the massive support of the Viet Minh by the Chinese Communists. However, his efforts did significantly reduce the flow of men and supplies from the delta to the Viet Minh regular forces in their bases north and south of the Red River delta and probably precipitated the unsuccessful Viet Minh campaigns against the delta in 1950 and 1951.[24]

The Development of Viet Minh Strategy

The overall objective of Viet Minh military strategy was clear from the beginning. It was to ensure that the political objective of *doc-lap* ("independence") was decisively achieved. The Viet Minh political and military leaders understood that the achievement of independence from a French colonial regime backed by formidable modern military forces could not be accomplished quickly, but only by the slow erosion of French military power to the point at which it could be overcome in a final determined push. Consequently, Viet Minh strategy developed along the lines of a three-stage process, with deliberate escalation from one stage to the next only when the conditions were right and suitable Viet Minh forces were available.

In general, the Viet Minh strategy throughout the war was offensive in orien-

tation, a defensive stance being taken only as necessitated by the prevailing political or military conditions or in local situations. With the return of French forces
to southern Indochina in September 1945, the Viet Minh temporarily adopted
a defensive strategy in Cochinchina and southern Annam in order to concentrate on opposing French efforts to regain control of Tonkin and northern Annam.
The failure to obtain a negotiated settlement and the serious setback in the battles
for the Haiphong-Hanoi area in November and December 1946 also put the Viet
Minh on the defensive in the north and brought with it the recognition that their
relatively weak and poorly equipped forces would have to be strengthened considerably before resuming an offensive posture.[25]

In early 1947, the Viet Minh leaders retired to their bases in the Viet Bac and
began developing a strategy and the forces to support it. Initially, the plan was to
employ the regional and local guerrilla forces to tie down and harass the French
throughout the country while suitable regular Viet Minh forces were organized,
armed, and trained in the secure base areas. The overall military strategy adopted
by the Viet Minh was based on the writings of Mao Tse-tung as interpreted by the
secretary general of the Indochinese Communist Party, Truong Chinh. The emi-
nent French historian Bernard Fall maintained that the principal source of the
well-known three-phase Viet Minh strategy was Truong Chinh's 1947 book, *The
Resistance Will Win*, a reformulation of Mao's *On Protracted War*.[26] While Truong
Chinh may well have been the theorist, Vo Nguyen Giap was undeniably the one
who translated theory into action.

The basic concept underlying Viet Minh strategy was that any war of liberation against the French would proceed in three phases: an initial defensive period
(known as *phong ngu*) in which the still-weak Viet Minh forces would be capable
of only limited guerrilla action against the French, who would hold the towns and
lines of communication in a tight grip; an interim period of stalemate, or equilibrium (known as *cam cu*), once the Viet Minh forces had reached a level of parity
with the French; and a final, decisive period of all-out conventional warfare that
Giap referred to as the "general counteroffensive" (known as *tong phan cong*), in
which the Viet Minh regular forces (*Chu Luc*) would meet the French head-on,
defeat them, and win the independence of Viet Nam from colonial rule.[27] The first
two phases were to be carried out primarily by Viet Minh regional and popular
(local) guerrilla forces, the newly organized Viet Minh regular forces being held
back for the final decisive phase. In point of fact, the war proceeded in much the
way General Giap envisioned, and very little adjustment was required in the basic
Viet Minh strategy once the initial glitches were worked out. The advent of massive Chinese aid in 1949 and 1950 made possible the acceleration of the second
and third phases of the Viet Minh strategy. Thus, the "guerrilla" phase extended
from 1946 to 1950, the unexpectedly brief "protracted war" stage from 1951 to
1952, and the decisive final phase of "mobile warfare" from 1953 to 1954.

As noted, a good deal of Giap's military strategy was derived from the writings of Mao Tse-tung. Perhaps the most important principle adopted from Mao was the emphasis on the "security of the rear." In its larger meaning, the "security of the rear" involved the total effort to win over the people to the cause and to ensure their active engagement in supplying the rebel armed forces with information, manpower, and logistical support.[28] The great emphasis on the creation of a network of secure rear bases from which both the *Chu Luc* and the Viet Minh guerrilla forces could operate was a manifestation of this principle. At the same time, the principle of the "security of the rear" shaped Viet Minh offensive operations by focusing attention on the potential vulnerability of the enemy's rear areas. Thus, the Viet Minh strategy included subversion, sabotage, ambush, and direct attacks in the areas under nominal French control in order to weaken both the capability and the will of the French and the Vietnamese population under their control to resist.

Another important Viet Minh application of the principle of the "security of the rear" was the emphasis placed on careful preparation of the battlefield. Viet Minh operational doctrine called for careful reconnaissance and intelligence-gathering regarding potential targets and elaborate stockpiling of food, ammunition, and other supplies near and en route to the intended area of operations. Such intensive preparations often involved the creation or improvement of transportation routes and advance supply dumps as well as actual fortification of key terrain in the objective area. In general, the regular combat forces were not assigned to perform such activities. It was in these activities that the regional and popular militia forces were most useful.

Time was also a factor in the Viet Minh strategy. Patient by nature and determined to succeed no matter what the cost or time required, the Viet Minh basically hoped for a prolonged war that would permit them to assemble, arm, and train the regular forces needed for the final "general counteroffensive" phase. General Giap maintained that, in theory, the transition to the "general counteroffensive" would not take place until Viet Minh forces were superior to those of the enemy and both the military and international political situation favored the Viet Minh. When the conditions were right, "mobile warfare will become the principal activity, positional warfare and guerrilla warfare will become secondary."[29] Giap then went on to state the problem posed for the French by such a strategy: "The enemy will pass slowly from the offensive to the defensive. The *blitzkrieg* will transform itself into a war of long duration. Thus, the enemy will be caught in a dilemma: he has to drag out the war in order to win it and does not possess, on the other hand, the psychological and political means to fight a long drawn-out war."[30]

The operational execution of the Viet Minh strategy depended on a set of simple tactical principles that could be understood by every soldier, excellent intelligence, and detailed planning.[31] The tactical operations of the Viet Minh regular divisions generally took one of two forms: large-scale coordinated offensives or elaborate long-range feints to deceive the French high command. Both types of action required long-range movement of large forces over difficult terrain, often far from supporting bases, and thus demanded careful logistical planning, thorough preparation, and a distribution system of some complexity.[32] After some initial failures in the period 1950–1952, Viet Minh logisticians proved fully capable of meeting the challenges presented by such large-scale conventional operations.

The Shape of Battles to Come

The principal focus of the efforts of both the French and the Viet Minh during the first logistical campaign of the war in Indochina was the development of a strategy and the forces to carry out that strategy. For the most part, combat operations were limited to the recovery of key urban areas and lines of communication and the clearance and pacification of key rural areas by the French and the conduct of infiltration, subversion, sabotage, ambushes, and small-scale guerrilla attacks on isolated outposts by the Viet Minh. However, two major operations were conducted during the period that foreshadowed the two succeeding logistical campaigns of the First Indochina War. Operation LEA, launched by the French on October 7, 1947, with the objective of decapitating the Viet Minh leadership and destroying the Viet Minh logistical infrastructure in the Viet Bac, was but the first of several full-scale offensives by both sides to seize control of major base areas held by the enemy. It thus was the first major engagement of the "battles for the base areas" that would consume much of 1951 and 1952. In the fall of 1950, the Viet Minh initiated another major engagement. Designed to cut off and eliminate the French outposts strung out along the Chinese border in northern Tonkin, the fight for Route Coloniale 4 and the French posts on the border heralded the coming campaign for control of the lines of communication that would characterize 1953 and 1954.

Operation LEA (October–November 1947)

By mid-1947, the French forces in Indochina had achieved considerable success in suppressing guerrilla operations in the south and had recovered the principal urban areas and substantial parts of the vital Red River delta in the north. Expressing a desire to press the struggle against the Viet Minh rebels to a quick conclusion, a desire prompted by pressures from the French government at home and the growing prospect of a Communist victory in China, the French high commissioner in Indochina decided on May 19, 1947, that a major military effort should be made in Tonkin in the fall.[33] On July 23, the *commandant en chef* of French forces in Indochina, Lieutenant General Jean-Étienne Valluy, defined the general objective of the fall campaign as the decapitation of the political and military organism that directed Viet Minh activities throughout Indochina. The commander of the French troops in northern Indochina (*Troupes Françaises en Indochine du Nord,* TFIN) subsequently began the detailed planning that would lead to Operation LEA.[34]

The physical objectives of Operation LEA were located in the quadrilateral Lang Son–Cao Bang–Chiem Hoa–Thai Nguyen north of Hanoi in Tonkin. Centered on the village of Bac Kan, this area was the heart of the Viet Minh base in the Viet Bac and contained important political and military headquarters, training areas, and depots as well as the greater part of the Viet Minh regular combat forces then in the process of formation. This Viet Minh redoubt was linked to China by two main routes: from Bac Kan north through Cao Bang to Tsin Tsi and from Tuyen Quang northwest through Lao Kay to Hokow. The Viet Minh defenses of the area faced to the south and were organized in depth. Good cover and concealment were available, and many of the Viet Minh installations in the objective area were heavily fortified.

The proposed area of operations, shown on map 9.1, was in terrain very difficult for mechanized military operations. The largely uncharted area consisted of steep mountains with many narrow defiles and was heavily forested. The principal roads were RC 3 from Thai Nguyen north through Chu Moi and Bac Kan to Cao Bang and RC 4 from Lang Son northwest along the Chinese border to Cao Bang. Both of these routes were restricted by the surrounding mountains and forests and by the numerous ravines and watercourses that had to be crossed on inadequate bridges. They were thus ideal for ambushes and for delaying actions. The available water routes along the Red, Clear, and Gam Rivers were subject to floods and torrents as well as to enemy ambushes from the banks and required experienced guides with recent knowledge of the sandbars and channels. The sparse civilian population of the region, mostly tribal minorities such as T'ais, Nungs, Meos, Thos, and Muongs, made on-the-spot recruitment of labor difficult, and the lack of food resources in the area required that any force operating there be resupplied from its distant fixed bases over the limited and very precarious transportation routes.

The primary objective of Operation LEA was to kill or capture the Viet Minh leadership. The other two major objectives were to cut the flow of arms from China to the Viet Minh base areas in northern Tonkin and to destroy the Viet Minh military forces and installations in the objective area. The latter two objectives were essentially logistical in nature, designed to cripple the Viet Minh ability to supply their growing forces by cutting their supply lines to China and destroying the Viet Minh depots, workshops, and materiel located in the Viet Bac. Operation LEA was also intended to restore French control of the important towns of Cho Moi, Bac Kan, and Cao Bang and thus reopen RC 3 and RC 4 to French forces, which were to reestablish the French presence in the hill regions of Tonkin.

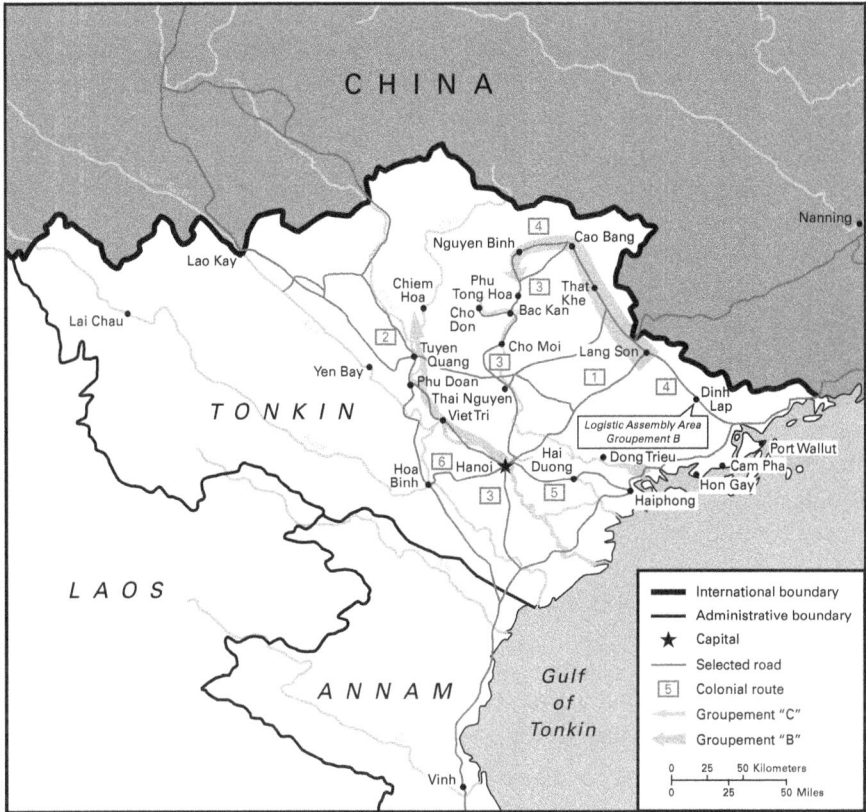

Map 9.1. Operation LEA, October–November 1947.

The concept of Operation LEA was that of a three-pronged advance converging on the center of the objective area around the town of Bac Kan. *Groupement S,* consisting of two parachute infantry battalions (twelve hundred men) under Lieutenant Colonel Henri Sauvagnac and reinforced by an airborne engineer platoon and an airborne surgical team, was to initiate the operation with a parachute assault on Bac Kan and the nearby villages of Cho Don (twelve miles west) and Cho Moi (twenty miles south). The main effort was to be conducted along a northern axis of advance by *Groupement B,* commanded by Colonel André Beaufre. *Groupement B,* a strong motorized ground element that included the 5th Moroccan Rifle Regiment (three infantry battalions), half (three armored squadrons) of the Moroccan Colonial Infantry Regiment, an artillery group (three battalions), an engineer battalion, and a transportation battalion, was to move by road from Lang Son northwest along RC 4 to link up with a parachute infantry battalion (not part of *Groupement S*) to be dropped at Cao Bang. From Cao Bang *Groupement*

B would move southwest via Nguyen Binh to link up with *Groupement S* at Bac Kan, 140 miles from Lang Son. The third element, *Groupement C*, commanded by Lieutenant Colonel Pierre Communal, was to be an amphibious force consisting of three infantry battalions and two artillery batteries transported by three *Dinassauts*. This force was to move aboard landing craft from Hanoi up the Red and Clear Rivers to Tuyen Quang and then up the Gam River to Chiem Hoa, and thence overland to attack the Bac Kan area from the south and west.

Operation LEA eventually involved nearly sixty thousand French Union troops, including three parachute infantry battalions, most of the French air forces in Indochina, and several small naval detachments. The ground combat forces employed in the operation were obtained for the most part by withdrawing defensive forces from the Red River delta and particularly from the Hanoi sector, which contributed three of its five battalions. In addition, the commander in Tonkin received from southern Indochina four infantry battalions, two armored squadrons, one group of mountain artillery, and a battalion of engineers as well as an air transport group, a fighter group, and the means necessary to form the three *Dinassauts*. Several of the ground combat elements coming from the south were newly formed or inexperienced with combat in the highlands and had to receive supplementary training.

The Viet Minh forces in the objective area probably did not exceed fifty thousand men but included the bulk of the regular forces in the process of formation and training as well as nearly all of the Viet Minh leadership and trained staff, administrative personnel, and logistical forces. These forces were familiar with the area of operations and well-prepared to conduct an all-around defense on ground of their own choosing amid their own supply dumps.

The logistical preparations for Operation LEA carried out by the French Union forces were unprecedented in Indochina. The assembly of the forces for *Groupement B* alone involved the concentration in the area of Dinh Lap of some 9,000 combat troops, 1,000 coolies, 600 animals, 700 vehicles, and 3,200 tons of supplies. The ports, highways, and other transport facilities in Tonkin were unprepared to handle such massive movements. Theoretically, such a concentration should have taken five months; in reality it was achieved in less than a month by taking extraordinary measures, including the establishment of temporary debarkation points and bases at Hon Gay, Cam Pha, Port Wallut, Pointe Pagode, and Khe Tu. The preparatory operations were later deemed "*un véritable tour de force*" and spoke well of the efficiency of the *4e Bureau* of the TFIN and the Haiphong base and of the hard work of the participating units.[35] The latter faced severe logistical problems, including the lack of vehicles and other equipment, occasioned by their movement direct from operations in the south. Poor weather during the last half of September further complicated matters.

The original date for the beginning of Operation LEA was October 1, 1947, but the operation had to be postponed to October 7 in order to complete the assembly of *Groupement B*. Despite the prospect of a typhoon, the French airborne elements conducted a well-executed parachute assault on the three villages of Bac Kan, Cho Don, and Cho Moi on the morning of October 7. Another parachute infantry battalion, the 1st Battalion, Provisional Parachute Half-Brigade (*1e Bataillon de la Demi-Brigade de Marche Parachutiste*, 1e Bn, DBMP), was dropped on Cao Bang on October 9. At Bac Kan the paras narrowly missed capturing Ho Chi Minh and General Giap, who fled from their headquarters, leaving the papers on which they were working laying on the table.[36] They did, however, succeed in capturing the main Viet Minh radio broadcasting station and large stores of food and munitions. Despite the initial shock of the parachute assault, the Viet Minh quickly recovered, and by the third day of the operation they had regrouped and surrounded the paras, who were forced to conduct an all-around defense while awaiting the arrival of *Groupements B* and *C*.

The mechanized ground element, *Groupement B*, was divided into five subgroups and included two battalions of Moroccans prepared to follow the main column mounted on mules. The column departed Lang Son on October 7 and intended to move forward twenty-four hours per day, with the subgroups leapfrogging one another. However, the road-bound forces of *Groupement B* quickly found their progress along RC 4 slowed by Viet Minh delaying operations. Bridges and culverts were destroyed, trees were felled into the roadway, harassing attacks were made, and the heavy French forces, lacking off-road mobility, found themselves slowed to a snail's pace. Unable to deploy his available infantry and firepower to maximum advantage, Colonel Beaufre repeatedly had to halt and deploy his forces to clear obstructions and Viet Minh ambush sites. Consequently, the mechanized column took six days to cover 130 miles along the narrow roads before being halted altogether by a determined Viet Minh stand just ten miles north of Bac Kan on October 13. It was not until the early afternoon of October 16, following a hard three-day fight, that Colonel Beaufre's column linked up with Lieutenant Colonel Savagnac's paras eleven miles north of Bac Kan.

The amphibious element, *Groupement C*, also found the going slow. Encountering sandbars and other obstructions, the boats moved slowly up the Red and Clear Rivers. When one *Dinassaut* ran aground only nine miles from Hanoi, Lieutenant Colonel Communal decided to continue his mission with the remaining two *Dinassauts*. The reduced force reached Phu Doan on October 12 and Tuyen Quang the next day. One of Communal's three infantry battalions, a light commando battalion, was immediately dispatched up the Gam River, but after traveling nineteen difficult miles the troops had to disembark and continue their march overland. They reached Chiem Hoa on October 17. The onward march toward Bac Kan had to be made at a pace much too slow to trap the alert and mobile Viet Minh, who escaped to the northwest, and it was not until October 19 that the amphibious element linked up the paras and mechanized column south of Bac Kan.

Following the link-up on October 19 and until November 10, the French Union forces engaged in Operation LEA proceeded to harrow the Viet Minh stronghold, destroying the enemy's forces and seizing his command posts, depots, and radio installations. The newly won positions at Cao Bang, Bac Kan, Cho Moi, Tuyen Quang, and Chiem Hoa were secured, as were the lines of communication along RC 4, RC 3, RC 3 bis, and the Clear River, and political action was set in motion to win over the local Tho population to the French side.

The costs of Operation LEA were high, and the results were less than expected. The Viet Minh leadership was neither killed nor captured, and although Viet Minh communications with the Chinese Communists were temporarily inconvenienced, they were by no means cut off. However, the operation did result in significant material losses for the Viet Minh. Thus, although the achievement of objectives fell short of what had been envisioned, the French success in Operation LEA was substantial.[37] Tactical surprise was achieved by the parachute assault of *Groupement S,* and French intelligence regarding the enemy's dispositions and resources for once proved accurate. The Viet Minh government was disrupted, and the Viet Minh military forces were, at least temporarily, battered and dispersed. The principal Viet Minh supply route to China through Cao Bang was cut, the northeastern sector of the Viet Bac redoubt was seriously dislocated, and an important part of the Viet Minh war industry, supplies, and propaganda instruments were lost. The amount of arms and equipment taken by the French significantly slowed the Viet Minh effort to organize and equip their regular forces. General Giap himself estimated that Viet Minh losses by the end of October amounted to about two-thirds of his depot stocks. The operation almost certainly preempted a Viet Minh offensive campaign and set back General Giap's plans for some time. Furthermore, the strong French effort impressed the Chinese Communists and disrupted Viet Minh efforts to win over the various tribal groups and factions. French influence was extended to the heart of the Viet Minh stronghold, and the important centers of Tuyen Quang, Cao Bang, Bac Kan, the mines of Thinh Tuc and Luc Nam, Sept Pagodes, Dong Trieu, and Lao Kay were restored to French control, and RC 3 and RC 4 were opened, at least temporarily, to French highway traffic.

French casualties in the autumn 1947 campaign were officially put at 242 killed, 2 drowned, 41 missing, and 586 wounded.[38] The hard fighting and inconclusive results lowered French morale, and the operation placed such a strain on the already worn French equipment that another major operation was out of the question for some time. The toll for the Viet Minh was even heavier: perhaps 7,200 killed, 1,000 taken prisoner, and an unknown number wounded. The Viet Minh materiel losses were also substantial. The French seized or destroyed ten munitions factories with all their tools and finished materials; five radio sets, including the main "Voice of Viet Nam" broadcasting station; printing presses; numerous command posts; two cadre schools; thirty military camps; numerous depots and storage sites containing large quantities of food, clothing, weapons, and other equipment; and a variety of machine tools and raw materials. The booty also included about one thousand tons of various types of ammunition and explosives, eight artillery pieces, ten machine guns, ten mortars, fifteen automatic rifles, one thousand rifles and carbines, four submachine guns, and twelve pistols.[39] The fifteen hundred tons of arms and munitions taken represented about two years' supply at the then-current Viet Minh replacement rates.[40]

Operation LEA foreshadowed many aspects of the future battles for the base areas in Tonkin. From the French perspective, the objectives chosen were largely logistical in nature, the operation required careful logistical preparation, and the results achieved were mainly the degradation of the Viet Minh logistical capabilities. From the Viet Minh perspective, Operation LEA involved a fight to protect key logistical installations and vital supply lines, and the damages suffered were mainly logistical as well. The success of their efforts to delay the French mechanized and waterborne columns and to minimize the destruction of their base areas hinged in large part on the mobility not only of the Viet Minh combat elements but of their logistical elements as well, a mobility that was achieved mainly by the application of manpower rather than of mechanization.

Among the many errors of Operation LEA that the French would repeat elsewhere was their haughty underestimation of their opponent. Expecting to meet relatively light resistance from a few thousand poorly armed and poorly trained guerrillas, the French forces were surprised to meet instead some fifty thousand well-disciplined regular troops who, despite their inferiorities in training and equipment, put up a determined and skillful fight. Lieutenant General Valluy would not be the last French *commandant en chef* in Indochina to seriously underestimate his foe. Speed of execution was another key factor in Operation LEA, but the heavy French ground and water elements were simply unable to move fast enough. Even the surprise drop of French paratroops on the Viet Minh headquarters at Bac Kan was not quick enough to catch the elusive Viet Minh leaders. On the other hand, the Viet Minh demonstrated a capacity for quick reaction and rapid movement on difficult terrain. Even the Viet Minh supply depots proved to be highly mobile, their effective alert systems and the ready availability of large numbers of porters and a few trucks enabling them to evacuate an area in a very short period of time.[41]

For their part, the Viet Minh took seriously the lessons they learned during Operation LEA and worked hard to ensure that their errors were not repeated. Deficiencies in command and control were soon worked out by the creation of a staff system and the reorganization of the separate Viet Minh *Chu Luc* battalions into regiments and eventually divisions. But the most important lesson revealed by Operation LEA was that the new Viet Minh regular units required the support of an effective and efficient logistical system—one without which they could scarcely hope to engage the French Union forces successfully.

Following Operation LEA, the French refocused their efforts on pacification of the territory already under their control. However, they did conduct two further operations northwest of Hanoi before the end of 1947. Operation CEINTURE, which began on November 17 and ended on December 22, was conducted along the southern edge of the Viet Minh stronghold between Tuyen Quang and Thai Nguyen. Moving out simultaneously from a number of points on the periphery of the objective area (Tuyen Quang, Viet Tri, Hanoi, Sept Pagodes, Cho Chu, and Cho Moi), the one airborne, two amphibious, and seven light infantry *groupements* assigned to the operation succeeded in clearing most of the objective area of Viet Minh forces and capturing large quantities of supplies, but the Viet Minh avoided a decisive engagement and reoccupied the area when the French units withdrew.[42] The other operation, which had more positive and lasting results, involved the use of two T'ai battalions with French officers to clear the Fan Si Pan Mountains between the Red and Black Rivers. This was T'ai country, and the Viet Minh were forced to avoid the area for several years.

For some time following Operation LEA the French continued to hold the key towns in Tonkin and a string of outposts along the Chinese border, but their control of the countryside remained tenuous. By early 1948, military operations, except for patrols, were no longer aggressively pursued, and in effect the border was unguarded from Lao Kay to Cao Bang. A small garrison was left at Bac Kan, but it proved difficult to resupply and operationally insignificant and was abandoned in August 1948. However, by late 1949 the French began to realize that Tonkin would be the decisive area of operations and they began to shift the emphasis of their military operations from the pacification of Cochinchina and southern Annam to Tonkin.[43] This recognition was forced in large part by the arrival of Chinese Communist forces on the border and the growing strength of the Viet Minh as aid from China began to arrive in quantity. At the same time, the Viet Minh began to increase the frequency and intensity of their attacks on the French outposts along RC 4 and the border with China.

The Battle of Route Coloniale 4, Fall 1950

Operation LEA contained a warning regarding the difficulties of movement along the lines of communication in and near the Viet Minh base areas in Tonkin, and especially along RC 4, which paralleled the Chinese border and was the main supply route for the French outposts scattered along that line to threaten the Viet Minh supply lines to Communist China. The final major engagement of the first logistical campaign of the war in Indochina would be fought for control of those

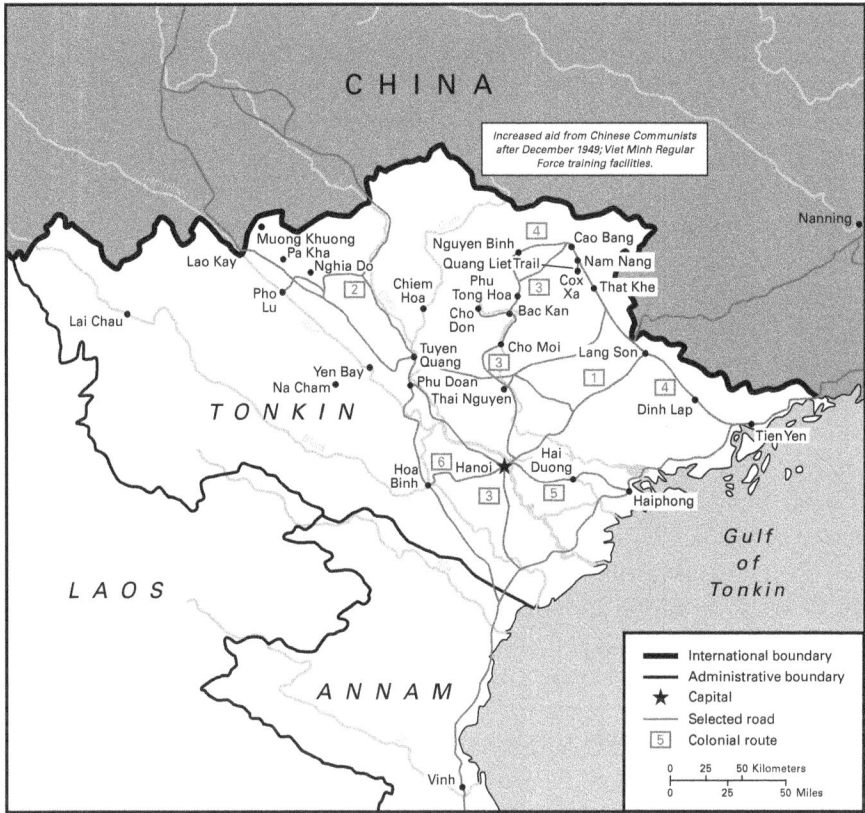

Map 9.2. The Battle of Route Coloniale 4, Fall 1950.

lines of communication. As one French officer wrote, "No battle had greater consequences there than that of Colonial Road No. 4."[44] And, it might be added, no battle of the period before 1950 would demonstrate more clearly the character the war in Indochina would assume in its final stage in 1953 and 1954.

Following their offensive into the Viet Bac in the fall of 1947, the French exercised a tenuous control over the border with China from strongpoints at Lao Kay, Cao Bang, and Lang Son (shown on map 9.2) as well as a number of smaller outposts in the Black and Red River valleys and strung along RC 4. During 1948 and 1949, the outlying garrisons became increasingly difficult to resupply.[45] After December 1949, Viet Minh activity rendered the normal supply route for the French border posts, RC 4 (by then known as "the bloody road," *la route sanglante*), unusable on a regular basis except from Tien Yen to That Khe, although the road south of Lang Son (RC 1A) continued to carry daily traffic. Already in 1948, one French sergeant had predicted: "This road [RC 4] will get us all. The

Viets shoot us like rabbits. I've been in six big ambushes already. Twice I've been in trucks that were burned out—look at my hand. Done rare."[46] The French correspondent Lucien Bodard later wrote: "Already, all through 1949, the R.C. 4 had been in its death throes. Each convoy had been a battle, a harder, longer battle than the last. It was not ambushes any more, but head-on collisions: now the Viets were standing up and blocking the road. All the troops on the frontier had to be thrown in, in a full-blown war, for every convoy. This went on for weeks. Every peak had to be won in succession, and every yard of the road. Then one day there was no getting through."[47]

The victorious Chinese Communist columns reached the Vietnamese border in December 1949, and almost immediately the flow of supplies to the Viet Minh increased. The winter of 1949–1950 was thus a period in which the Viet Minh efforts to build a conventional military capability began to achieve considerable success, and General Giap began to contemplate the use of his new regular forces in conventional mobile warfare.[48] The additional arms and equipment, as well as the use of Chinese training facilities in Guangxi Province, permitted General Giap to accelerate his program for the reorganization and rearmament, and by the summer of 1950 those efforts were far advanced. Some seventy-six battalions were involved and over twelve thousand new recruits from northern Annam alone were incorporated in the Viet Minh regular forces.[49] The *Chu Luc* battalions were reformed into regiments, brigades, and later divisions, and already by mid-September 1950 General Giap had formed two infantry brigades and nine independent regiments as well as a number of engineer and transportation units.[50]

Even in early 1950 the regular Viet Minh forces were nearly equal to the French Union forces in numbers and were increasingly capable of conducting extended campaigns, substantial Chinese military aid was in prospect, and the French were showing definite signs of weakness due to insufficient reinforcements, dispersion, and logistical difficulties.[51] The facts were generally known to French intelligence officers, who estimated that the Viet Minh had more than thirty battalions in place along RC 4, twice as many battalions as the French Union forces had there.[52] Moreover, the contents of the top-secret Revers report of May 1949 were leaked to the Viet Minh, who saw in it the growing weakness of the French Union forces and the deteriorating will of the French government and people to support the war in Indochina and were thus encouraged to hasten the French retreat by testing their newly formed regular forces against the areas lying on the fringes of French control.[53]

Thus, the conditions seemed ripe for the commencement of the third phase of General Giap's tripartite strategy, the "general counteroffensive," although the Viet Minh leader recognized that his forces were still at a disadvantage with respect to command and control, firepower, and staff expertise.[54] Doubt as to the preparation of the Viet Minh forces for the final all-out campaign against the French was even stronger within the Vietnamese Communist Party, and General Giap's view that his forces were ready and the "general counteroffensive" should begin in 1950 only narrowly prevailed.[55]

Giap's choice of the French border posts as the objective of the first major test for his new regular units was dictated almost entirely by logistical considerations. The elimination of the French outposts along RC 4 would reduce the threat to the Viet Minh supply lines into Communist China, permit the Viet Minh to expand and consolidate their rear base in the Viet Bac and link it firmly with the training and storage areas in southern China, and remove the threat to Giap's flank and rear if, as he intended, he later moved south to challenge the French for control of the vital delta region. Furthermore, the area of operations would be close to his bases of supply and thus would not overstrain his still immature logistical system. On the other hand, the precarious logistical situation of the weak and isolated French outposts, linked only by a poor road controlled by the Viet Minh and able to be reinforced only by parachute, would almost certainly guarantee a stunning victory for the new *Chu Luc* battalions and regiments, thus giving them the confidence needed to face the French Union forces in earnest.[56]

General Giap's plan for taking the French outposts along the Chinese border was rather simple. First, the Viet Minh forces under Nguyen Binh in southern Indochina would launch diversionary attacks in their area to prevent the movement of French reinforcements to Tonkin from Cochinchina. Then a series of preliminary operations would be conducted in early 1950 around Lao Kay and along RC 4 to season the new units and uncover any critical faults. The main effort could then be launched in the fall of 1950 against the French border posts along RC 4. First, the Viet Minh would attract French attention by surrounding and threatening Cao Bang and That Khe. They would then move to seize and hold Dong Khe, the seizure of which would cut the road connection between Cao Bang and That Khe and force the French to take one of three very undesirable options: (1) evacuate the threatened outposts overland, (2) try to keep the threatened outposts resupplied by air, or (3) attempt to reinforce the threatened outposts by road or air. Regardless of the French response, continued Viet Minh pressure on RC 4 and the outposts themselves would ensure that in the end the French would abandon their positions altogether.[57]

In January 1950, fifteen Viet Minh battalions undertook an offensive against the French outposts in the Black River valley.[58] Code-named Operation LE LOI after the Vietnamese king who had once expelled Chinese invaders, the Viet Minh offensive failed to take any of the French outposts but did succeed in reopening Viet Minh communications between the Viet Bac and northern Annam and provided valuable staff and combat experience to the new Viet Minh units.[59] Following a short pause, the Viet Minh undertook an even larger offensive, Operation LE HONG PHONG I, against the outposts surrounding Lao Kay in the Red River valley in February–April 1950. The newly formed Viet Minh 308th Division first overran the isolated mud and log outpost of Pho Lu, overwhelming the single 150-man French company of defenders with a massive assault by some five thousand to six thousand troops in nine or ten battalions. The French attempted to reinforce the doomed company at Pho Lu with a parachute infantry company, but it was dropped twenty miles from its objective, attacked by two Viet Minh battalions, and only barely managed to fight its way to safety, being forced to abandon its dead on the field. The extrication of the parachute infantry company was made possible only by the sudden appearance of six French fighters that strafed and bombed the onrushing Viet Minh. The para company commander, Captain Dubois, was killed and the second in command, Lieutenant Planet, was subsequently accused (perhaps unjustly) of cowardice by the commander in chief, General Carpentier.[60] The next Viet Minh thrust was directed at Nghia Lo, another satellite of Lao Kay. The isolated company-size post was attacked by the 308th Division in March, but Nghia Lo was saved by the parachute insertion of the reinforced 5th Parachute Battalion. General Giap declined to force the issue with the paras, and in April 1950 the 308th Division and its supporting army of coolies returned to the Viet Bac and prepared for one last test before the major offensive in September.

On May 25, 1950, four *Chu Luc* battalions of the 308th Division, supported by artillery, attacked the French garrison at Dong Khe on RC 4. The Viet Minh forces overran the three French infantry companies defending Dong Khe on May 27, and by the following day all French resistance had ceased. The French responded on the morning of May 28 with a parachute assault by the 3rd Colonial Parachute Battalion. Surprising the Viet Minh, the paras retook the fortifications of Dong Khe in hard hand-to-hand combat. The battle for Dong Khe was costly for both sides. The Viet Minh lost some three hundred soldiers, two howitzers, three machine guns, and many small arms. The French lost all but one hundred men of the battalion that had held Dong Khe, along with all their equipment and a number of the paras of the relief force.

In general, the French believed these isolated outposts to be invulnerable to Viet Minh attack since they did not believe the Viet Minh had the tactical and logistical skill necessary to assault them directly without Chinese assistance.[61] Nevertheless, in the course of 1950 French engineers worked to improve the airfields at Lang Son, Cao Bang, and That Khe as well as the smaller fields at Dong Khe and Na Cham in order to resupply the outposts more readily by air should they be cut off on the ground. Indeed, throughout the summer of 1950 the French effort to resupply their garrisons on the Sino-Vietnamese border became ever more difficult and costly, and the key posts of Lao Kay and Hoa Binh became so isolated that at times they could be supported only by air.[62] Each ground resupply convoy became a major combat operation, often consuming more resources than it delivered. Convoys from Lang Son to Cao Bang had to contest every mile with the increasingly strong and bold Viet Minh, and RC 4 became the *voie sacrée* of Indochina.[63] The French commander of the border region, Colonel Vicaire, was compelled to tell the organizer of one "superconvoy": "The whole thing is a failure. Your convoy was so heavy and so slow that it has consumed everything it was meant to carry in. Instead of bringing gasoline, for example, it had to be given some from the wretched little reserve at Caobang so as to get back to Langson."[64] Lucien Bodard observed, "By the end of this period the garrison at Caobang came to look upon the arrival of the trucks of the convoys with horror, and they called their crews the locusts, for as they ate everything they possessed on the outward journey, they fell upon the meager provisions of the legionaries."[65]

On September 1, 1950, twelve of the forty regular French combat battalions in Tonkin were stationed along the Chinese border. Lang Son at the eastern end of the line was the main French base for the defense of the border region and had a garrison of about four thousand men, including a high percentage of service troops. The core of the Lang Son defense forces was a mobile operational group commanded by Lieutenant Colonel Maurice Le Page and consisting of four battalions drawn from the 8th Moroccan Rifle Regiment and the 3rd Moroccan Armored Cavalry Regiment. The area northeast from Dinh Lap to Cao Bang was manned by four battalions plus an artillery group, four armored troops, and five thousand partisans. Cao Bang, with a garrison of two or three infantry battalions and several hundred administrative and logistical troops, anchored the center section and was supported by satellite outposts at Dong Khe and That Khe, each of which was held by a Foreign Legion battalion, for a total force of about four thousand. At the far northwestern end of the border line was Lao Kay, which had a garrison of some two thousand to three thousand men, including its four company-size outposts at Muong Khuong, Pa Kha, Nghia Lo, and Pho Lu.

Despite the growing evidence that the French outposts on the Chinese frontier were about to be isolated and eliminated by the increasingly strong Viet Minh forces, the French refused to evacuate them as recommended in the top-secret Revers report of May 1949 lest the French should suffer a serious loss of face.[66] Instead, they continued to believe that "the victory seemed to be in reach, as if you only had to stretch out your hand for it. It was the brief moment when the French believed that they were about to win the race against the clock. . . . Period of illusions!"[67]

The final battle for RC 4 and the French outposts began on September 16 when well-trained Viet Minh forces supported by 120 mm mortars and artillery again attacked the French outpost at Dong Khe. Dubbed Operation LE HONG PHONG II by General Giap, the renewed Viet Minh offensive involved the five *Chu Luc* regiments that had participated in Operation LE HONG PHONG I reinforced by ten new infantry battalions and a complete artillery regiment. Dong Khe fell on September 18, thus separating Cao Bang and the northern posts from those to the south toward Lang Son. The Viet Minh forces employed in the sweep of the French posts along RC 4 included the recently formed 165th and 174th Infantry Regiments, which would be the base regiments of the new 312th and 316th Divisions, respectively.[68]

The assault on Dong Khe was accompanied by renewed Viet Minh offensive activity in the northwest around Lao Kay. The shock of the Viet Minh success at Dong Khe and the renewed threat to Lao Kay caused the French commanders to decide to concentrate their forces around Lao Kay and abandon the posts along RC 4 north of Lang Son.[69] They carried out the consolidation around Lao Kay without difficulty, but the decision to abandon the posts along RC 4 resulted in disaster. Colonel Pierre Charton, the commander of the Cao Bang garrison, was ordered to abandon his motor transport and other heavy equipment and evacuate his twenty-six-hundred-man force plus five hundred civilians toward Dong Khe, which was to be retaken by a mobile task force of thirty-five hundred Moroccan troops commanded by Lieutenant Colonel Maurice Le Page advancing north from That Khe.[70] Colonel Charton decided against orders to save his trucks and heavy equipment, and at dawn on October 3 he evacuated Cao Bang and marched south over the narrow, restricted eighty-five-mile road toward Dong Khe.[71] The retention against orders of the artillery and trucks restricted the withdrawing column to the road, and the Viet Minh took full advantage of the French handicap by blowing bridges and laying ambushes. After one day, the column from Cao Bang had advanced only nine miles. Meanwhile, the Le Page task force, outnumbered three to one, had moved up RC 4 to a position south of Dong Khe and doggedly guarded their section of the route. Too late, the remnants of the Cao Bang force abandoned their trucks and heavy equipment on October 5 and left the main road at Nam Nang, moving south along the Quang Liet trail to join Le Page's Moroccans in the hills around Dong Khe. But time and luck ran out for both forces. The Moroccans left RC 4 on October 3 and moved to link up with the Cao Bang survivors southwest of Cox Xa. It was there that the combined Cao Bang–Moroccan task force was wiped out by the Viet Minh on October 7. Three parachute battalions, inserted to support the doomed forces of Charton and Le Page, only narrowly escaped the trap.

Panic ensued all along the frontier. That Khe was abandoned on October 10, the refugees fleeing southward along RC 4 with the 3rd Colonial Parachute Battalion (which had been dropped on October 6 to help gather the remnants of the Cao Bang disaster) acting as rear guard. The withdrawal from That Khe nearly matched the retreat from Cao Bang as an unmitigated disaster. The Viet Minh kept the retreating column of troops and civilian refugees under constant harassment, and the 3rd Colonial Parachute Battalion lost all but five men. On October 17, Lang Son, which had yet to be attacked and which was admirably suited for a prolonged defense, was abandoned along with thirteen hundred tons of supplies.[72] By the end of October 1950, all of northern Tonkin was in Viet Minh hands and the last remaining obstacles to a free flow of Chinese Communist arms, ammunition, and other military equipment to the Viet Minh were obliterated. Only the key post of Lao Kay at the northwestern end of the line remained. The French *commandant en chef*, General Carpentier, decided to evacuate Lao Kay as well, leaving the timing of the withdrawal to the discretion of the garrison commander, Colonel Coste. Showing considerable nerve and professional skill, Coste led his forces out from Lao Kay on November 3 and successfully fought his way through to Lai Chau.

Even General Giap seemed surprised by the rapid collapse of the French position on the Chinese border, and he failed to exploit his successes vigorously.[73] Once the withdrawals were completed, the French Union forces held only the heart of the Red River delta, the narrow coastal strip from Haiphong north to Mon Cay, and the high ground to the northwest between Than Uyen and Nghia Lo. However, the posts guarding the Red River delta held firm and the French continued to oppose strongly any Viet Minh encroachment in that vital area.

The battle for the French outposts along RC 4 was a total disaster for the French. The defeat at Dong Khe alone cost the French 7 battalions, and in a period of only three weeks the French Union forces overall lost 8 battalions, 13 artillery pieces, 125 mortars, 90 rocket launchers, 160 machine guns, 380 automatic rifles, 1,209 submachine guns, 8,222 rifles, and large stocks of rations, ammunition, and other supplies—enough to completely outfit an entire Viet Minh division of 15,000 men.[74] The premature evacuation of Lang Son resulted in a particularly rich bonanza for Giap's troops. The French engineers responsible for the destruction of the enormous stocks of food, clothing, medical supplies, arms, and ammunition at Lang Son never received the necessary written orders to blow them up, and aircraft were subsequently unable to do the job. The materiel abandoned to the Viet Minh at Lang Son included some ten thousand 75 mm shells, four thousand new submachine guns, and hundreds of gallons of gasoline, "an incalculable treasure of military stores."[75] The stunning defeat of the French was later characterized by Bernard Fall as "their greatest colonial defeat since Montcalm had died at Quebec."[76]

The Viet Minh claimed to have eliminated some 10,000 French Union troops. Bernard Fall put the total quantitative losses at 6,000 troops, 13 artillery pieces, 125 mortars, 450 trucks, 3 armored platoons, 940 machine guns, 1,200 submachine guns, and more than 8,000 rifles. Most of the 6,000–8,000 French Union troops lost were taken prisoner.[77]

The loss of the frontier posts also severely affected French morale and precipitated a sharp exchange of accusations between the politicians and the soldiers. One French correspondent on the scene later wrote: "The catastrophe of the Chinese border in 1950 can be explained only by the generals' irresponsible foolery and all the tricks they played on one another during the preceding months, at every possible and imaginable level. The greatest danger lay in the fact that beneath their selfish motives each was equally convinced that he was right and that he was acting in the best interests of France and the Expeditionary Forces: this meant that both cast all restraint aside and became capable of anything whatever."[78]

On December 4, Leon Pignon, the French high commissioner in Indochina, ordered the families of French civil and military personnel in Tonkin to prepare to be evacuated on short notice.[79] The same month, both Pignon and General Carpentier were recalled, and on December 17 the powers of both offices were combined and entrusted to General Jean de Lattre de Tassigny. The shock of the defeat brought some change in attitude on the part of the French public, and the government subsequently agreed to send additional reinforcements and supplies to Indochina. The defeat also accelerated plans for the formation of a new Vietnamese National Army to provide the manpower needed to attend to the pacification duties, thus releasing the CEFEO to concentrate in Tonkin to deal with the main Viet Minh threat.

From the Viet Minh perspective, the campaign was a qualified success. All of the major objectives were attained, and the new *Chu Luc* forces had proven themselves capable of successfully engaging the French Union forces in an extended fight. Despite significant casualties, morale and confidence were enhanced.[80] Perhaps more importantly, the Viet Minh logistical situation was greatly improved. The supply lines to China were cleared, and the supplies and equipment captured by the Viet Minh during the battle for the Chinese border posts greatly augmented their military strength by providing the means to outfit additional regular units. In April 1949, the Viet Minh had twenty regular battalions in Tonkin; by June 1951 the number had grown to seventy-eight regular battalions.[81] But the easy victory along RC 4 masked certain problems that remained in Viet Minh organization and staff work, particularly in the organization of logistical support, and would embolden General Giap to commit his still immature forces to an all-out offensive in 1951 that would end very differently.

The disaster on the Chinese frontier in October 1950 certainly made clear the extent to which Chinese Communist training and logistical support had strengthened the Viet Minh and made the French position in Tonkin extremely precarious. As one participant put it: "We did not perceive this general picture of the aid given until the smashing blow we received at the frontier zone in October of 1950. . . . It was during the course of this difficult battle . . . that we became cognizant of the transformation the Viet Minh had undergone; it was then that we discovered that they were well equipped with automatic weapons, mortars, and ammunition."[82]

But the Viet Minh achievement of a rough parity in number of troops and armament was not the only dramatic change that took place between December 1946 and December 1950. By the end of 1950 the French had lost not just their outposts on the Chinese border, they had also lost the campaign to form an effective strategy and the combat and supporting forces to implement it. The Viet Minh, however, had carefully articulated a strategy well-suited to the physical and operational environment. And, having clearly determined the ends that they wished to achieve, they were well on the way to creating the forces necessary to the success of their strategy. The Viet Minh had won the first logistical campaign of the war and had also seized the initiative, which they would retain until their final victory in 1954.

10

The Campaign for the Base Areas

The second logistical campaign of the First Indochina War involved a struggle for control of the base areas held by the two sides and reached its greatest intensity between December 1950 and July 1953. At the end of 1950, the newly formed regular divisions of the Viet Minh were committed in a sustained campaign to gain control over the resources of the Red River delta. Extended conventional operations revealed the limitations of the still immature Viet Minh command and logistical systems, and in a series of hard-fought battles at Vinh Yen, Mao Khe, and the Day River in the first half of 1951, the French successfully defended the loyal population and rice production of the delta but were unable to deliver a knockout blow. The Viet Minh were forced to retreat to their base areas, lick their wounds, and revert temporarily to guerrilla warfare while they rebuilt their forces and reformulated their strategy for defeating the French. Meanwhile the French initiated their own series of operations designed to seize the Viet Minh strongholds in the Viet Bac and elsewhere. Those efforts ranged in scope from small-scale commando raids, such as the very successful Operation MARS on the Gulf of Thailand in March 1951, to full-scale coordinated offensives by French Union airborne, waterborne, and ground elements, such as Operation LORRAINE (October 1952) and Operation HIRONDELLE (July 1953). Offensive operations against the Viet Minh administrative and logistical centers achieved varying degrees of success but failed to strangle the Viet Minh.

The Fight for the Red River Delta, 1951

The sudden collapse of the French outposts on the Chinese frontier in late 1950 created among the Viet Minh leaders a false confidence in the preparedness of their regular forces for extended conventional campaigns against the French Union forces in Tonkin. With most of northern Tonkin in their hands, their bases in the Viet Bac secure, and the supply line from Communist China choked with new weapons and other equipment, General Giap and the other Viet Minh leaders were certain the time had come to launch the final offensive against the French colonialists.[1] Viet Minh hopes were so high that Viet Minh propagandists took up the cry that Ho Chi Minh would celebrate Tet 1951 in Hanoi.[2] That the commanders and staff officers of the *Chu Luc* still had much to learn, particularly in the field of planning and executing the logistical support of major operations, was borne out by their subsequent defeat in the series of battles for the control of the vital Red River delta in the winter and spring of 1951.

In December 1950, the most able of the French *commandants en chef* in Indochina, General Jean de Lattre de Tassigny, assumed command and proceeded to complete and improve the defensive measures initiated by his predecessor, General Marcel Carpentier, who had sought to protect the Tonkin delta and to provide a secure base for French offensive operations through a system of fortified positions supported by mobile forces for offensive operations. The energetic General de Lattre, often considered the greatest French soldier of his generation, immediately recognized the crucial importance of the delta region and acted to secure it.[3] He strengthened the line of fortified posts ringing the delta and thus created what came to be called the "De Lattre Line," a 110-mile string of small, mutually supporting fortifications that enclosed a triangular area running west from the sea north of Haiphong to a point around Viet Tri and then southeast to the sea again near Phat Diem (shown on map 10.1). By mid-summer 1951, some six hundred posts had been completed, and another six hundred were finished by the end of the year.[4] Another inner line of fortifications some thirty-one miles long was constructed in an arc twenty-two miles outside Haiphong, which contained critical bases, airfields, and port facilities. De Lattre reorganized his mobile combat elements to create strong, flexible reserves and greater offensive punch in the form of mechanized "mobile groups" and supported the creation of specialized commando units for long-range counterguerrilla and intelligence-gathering operations.[5] He also made the first serious efforts to organize a Vietnamese national army capable of taking over some of the burden of defending against the Viet Minh. General de Lattre also stressed the greater integration of air and ground operations and succeeded in opening the valves of American material aid for the French Union forces in Indochina, aid which amounted to over 400 billion francs by July 1954.[6]

Unlike his predecessors, whose decisions were closely monitored by the political authorities in Paris, General de Lattre combined the offices of both high commissioner and *commandant en chef* in Indochina and thus had the advantage of conducting operations when, where, and in whatever strength he saw fit and thus could capitalize on temporary Viet Minh weaknesses.[7] Although his solution to the operational problems in Tonkin required more men than were available and thus required the French to voluntarily cede some outlying posts and peripheral areas to the Viet Minh, he was partially successful in restoring the military balance in the north in 1950–1951 and succeeded in reviving French morale.[8] General de Lattre's premature departure in late 1951 and subsequent death from cancer in Paris in January 1952 were critical blows to the French effort to maintain their position in Indochina by force of arms. His principal intention had undoubtedly been to create the conditions favorable for offensive action, but his successors

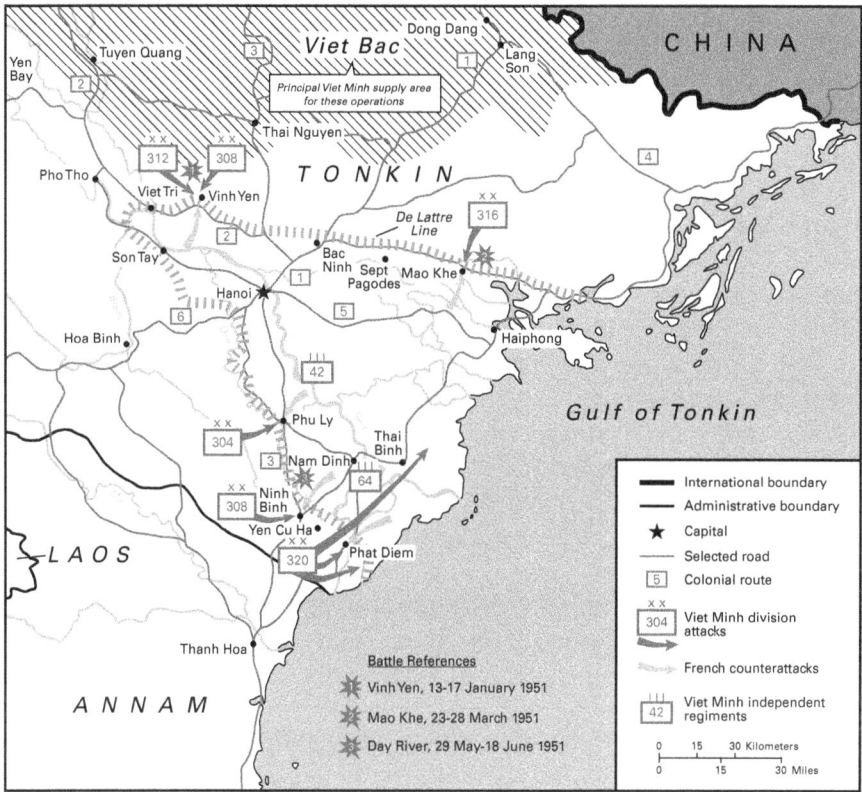

Map 10.1. The Viet Minh Offensives against the Red River Delta, 1951.

tended to focus on the defensive elements of his plans and increasingly abandoned the initiative in Tonkin to the Viet Minh.[9]

The Battle for Vinh Yen, January 1951

The French commander in Tonkin in 1950, Major General Marcel-Jean-Marie Alessandri, had stressed the clearance and pacification of the rich rice-producing areas of the Red River delta in order to deny to the Viet Minh both recruits and the rice essential to the maintenance of the growing Viet Minh regular forces. Major General Alessandri's program had been somewhat successful in reducing the number of recruits available to the Viet Minh and had cut about in half the amount of rice they were able to obtain.[10] Thus, even after their great success in seizing the French forts on the Chinese border and opening their supply lines to China, the Viet Minh continued to suffer from their lack of access to the rice of the delta that was used not only to feed the *Chu Luc* but to pay their bills. The only solution was to mount a direct attempt to seize control of the resources of the Red River delta.

As the French border posts fell or were evacuated at the end of 1950, General Giap repositioned his recently tested troops for a strike at the delta. The Viet Minh forces were arrayed in three main groups to the north, west, and south of the French perimeter. Giap eventually assembled five divisions (sixty-five infantry, twelve artillery, and eight engineer battalions) facing the French defensive line around the delta.[11] The 308th and 312th Divisions were west of the delta near Vinh Yen, the 316th Division on the coast north of Haiphong, the 320th Division south of the delta, and the 304th Division in reserve in the Viet Bac.

Giap quickly discovered that his existing logistical system was incapable of supporting the divisions in place and that the French defenses were too strong for a hasty attack. He thus postponed his assault on the delta until he could complete the preparation of his combat forces and stock the logistical bases on which they would have to depend. By early 1951, all the political and military preconditions for launching the "general counteroffensive" phase seemed to be in place. Moreover, the shortages of manpower and rice were beginning to bite and could only be relieved by gaining control over the populous and fertile delta. The arrival of the energetic General de Lattre and the increasing American aid to the French decided the issue for General Giap, who directed his first blow against the town of Vinh Yen.

By mid-January 1951, the green Viet Minh 308th and 312th Divisions were poised to begin Operation HOANG HOA THAM I, aimed at Vinh Yen at the northern tip of the delta, only thirty miles northwest of Hanoi.[12] The French strongpoints in and around Vinh Yen were manned by some six thousand French Union troops, including the two thousand men of Mobile Group 1 (*Groupe Mobile 1*, GM 1). On the evening of January 13, 1951, two regiments of the 308th Division began the five-day battle for Vinh Yen by crossing the Red River, overrunning the small French outpost at Bao Chuc, and establishing themselves on the hills surrounding Vinh Yen.[13] The following morning, GM 1 was ordered to clear the Viet Minh from Bao Chuc, but four miles from Vinh Yen the column was ambushed and lost half its strength.[14] The survivors barely escaped back into Vinh Yen under cover of the French air forces and artillery. Meanwhile, elements of the Viet Minh 312th Division occupied the hills to the northwest of Vinh Yen, and on the night of January 14–15 the two Viet Minh divisions overran most of the remaining outposts, bottling up the surviving French defenders inside Vinh Yen and opening a gap in the French defensive line to the east.

On January 14, General de Lattre flew into Vinh Yen to obtain a firsthand assessment of the situation. Taking charge of the battle in person, de Lattre ordered into the area the bulk of the available French airpower in Indochina and began the transfer by air of troops from southern Indochina to reinforce the delta area and relieve the hard-pressed defenders of Vinh Yen. The available reinforcements were hastily organized into a second mobile group (GM 3), and the reorganized GM 1 was recommitted to drive the Viet Minh from key terrain in the hills around Vinh Yen. Once GM 1 was entangled with the Viet Minh, de Lattre committed GM 3 on January 15 to block the gap that had opened to the east of Vinh Yen. This was done successfully by seizing key terrain in that area. General Giap had committed twenty-one battalions (some twenty-two thousand combat troops) to the fight. The French air forces came into full play on January 15, and by the 17th the Viet Minh were forced to withdraw in the face of superior French firepower after having suffered heavy losses of between fifteen hundred and six thousand dead and five hundred taken prisoner.[15]

The battle for Vinh Yen, which has been called the first conventional battle of the First Indochina War, clearly demonstrated that the new Viet Minh regular divisions were not quite ready for direct confrontation with the French. U.S. intelligence analysts concluded that Viet Minh staff planners had failed to coordinate the attacks over wide areas, which would have prevented the French from concentrating their reserves; Viet Minh artillery support was limited; and the Viet Minh had almost no protection against French air attacks, particularly those involving the use of napalm.[16] In an after-battle critique on January 23, 1951, General Giap admitted some of his own faults and criticized his troops for failing to push frontal attacks against the French positions aggressively, but he singled out the civilian porters who provided his transport service for special praise.[17] Indeed, the Viet Minh porters merited such praise. More than 180,000 porters had played some role in supporting the Viet Minh attack on Vinh Yen, working some 2 million man hours and bringing into the battle area over five thousand tons of food, weapons, and ammunition.[18] But as the subsequent battles in the delta would show, the Viet Minh logistical services were not yet perfected, and the overworked porters would prove unable to keep the frontline troops supplied adequately.

For their part, the French Union forces were unable to exploit their success at Vinh Yen due to the lack of the necessary manpower, airpower, and cross-country mobility and were thus forced to consolidate their position and wait for the next Viet Minh attack.[19] The French Union forces had faced their own logistical problems in the fight for Vinh Yen, and the narrow French victory would probably have been impossible without the logistical support provided by the United States. The hard-pressed French defenders were protected from the onrushing Viet Minh infantry by American-made napalm bombs, and critical supply shortages were made up only after Brigadier General Francis G. Brink, the U.S. Military Assistance Advisory Group–Indochina (MAAG-Indochina) commander, flew to Tokyo and intervened directly with U.S. Far East Command headquarters for the shipment of supplies, particularly 105 mm artillery ammunition, direct from U.S. depots in Japan to Tonkin.[20]

The Battle for Mao Khe, March 1951

Neither side had fully recovered before General Giap, undeterred by the poor showing of his forces at Vinh Yen, resumed his offensive against the delta. Operation HOANG HOA THAM II was intended to cut the French off from their major port of Haiphong only twenty-five miles from the battle line, and Giap's decision of where to attack was strongly influenced by logistical considerations.[21] The Viet Minh offensive was aimed at the critical French port and supply center of Haiphong and its connection with Hanoi, and Giap's own supply problems would be greatly eased if he were to attack the northern face of the French defensive perimeter since it was closer to his own bases in the Viet Bac and in China.[22] The newly formed 316th Division, along with elements of the 308th and 312th Divisions, opened the operation on March 26 with an attack focused on the mining town of Mao Khe. There were three French battalions in the area, but the main blow fell most heavily on the single French-Vietnamese battalion defending the Mao Khe coal mines. Although outnumbered three to one, the French Union troops put up a spirited defense.[23] The pithead of the mine itself was held by a company of Tho tribesmen commanded by a Vietnamese lieutenant and three French NCOs who held out until a French parachute infantry battalion arrived to relieve them.[24] Casualties were high on both sides: the French defenders lost over 25 percent of their effectives, and the Viet Minh lost 1,500 killed and 483 captured.[25] Once again, Giap's forces had proved unready for direct confrontation with the troops of the French Union, and Giap himself had underestimated the effect of French airpower and parachute forces as well as the firepower that French naval forces in the area could bring to bear.[26]

The Battle of the Day River, May–June 1951

Although the attacks on Vinh Yen and Mao Khe were both repulsed with heavy losses, the Viet Minh leaders remained eager to engage the French in a decisive battle. The two previous attempts had been aimed at Hanoi and Haiphong, respectively, but for his third attempt Giap decided on a more limited objective. Operation HA NAM DINH, as it was called, was aimed at seizing the rice-rich anti–Viet Minh Catholic provinces of Ha Nam and Nam Dinh in the southwestern corner of the Red River delta, the occupation of which would be a major blow to French control of the delta region and would provide the Viet Minh with access to the rice that they so desperately needed.[27]

The terrain of the proposed area of operations was ideal for a surprise attack. The southwestern face of the De Lattre Line followed the east bank of the Day River. The western bank of the Day River, from which the Viet Minh were to launch their attack, towered over the flat plains of the delta east of the river and was honeycombed with numerous caves that provided excellent cover and concealment for the Viet Minh attackers. However, the Day River itself was a key terrain feature in the area of operations and decidedly favored the French. The river was navigable and thus permitted the employment of *Dinassauts,* which were to play a key role in interdicting the supply lines of the Viet Minh.

Giap's plan of attack involved the better part of four divisions. The 312th Division actually opened the campaign by creating a diversion at the northwestern corner of the delta perimeter during the month of April 1951 and alternately threatened to march against Vinh Yen or Nghia Lo in the T'ai country. The 304th and 308th Divisions were assigned to conduct strong diversionary attacks against Phu Ly and Ninh Binh, respectively, to pin down French reserves, while the main effort was made by the 320th Division against the weak French posts between Ninh Binh and the sea, focusing on the key town of Phat Diem and ultimately aimed at linking up with Viet Minh guerrilla elements northeast of the town of Thai Binh. This time Giap sought to prepare the battlefield somewhat more carefully by infiltrating the 42nd and 64th Independent Infantry Regiments into the delta behind the French line along the Day River to attack French installations in the rear areas and disrupt the movement of troops and supplies to the front. The timing of the Day River offensive was determined almost entirely by logistical considerations. General Giap hoped to begin the action in late April or May so that his preparations and troop movements could be made during the dry season. The main attack was to take place just before the onset of the southwest monsoon. Thus, any successes could be protected from French air and ground interference and, should the attack fail, his forces could withdraw under cover of the rain and mist.[28] However, a Viet Minh attack on the southwestern face of the delta perimeter was a major logistical undertaking. Just moving some sixty thousand to seventy thousand combat troops into position was an extremely difficult task, particularly in view of the fact that the Viet Minh staff skills were still of a comparatively low order. Movements were largely restricted to the hours of darkness in order to avoid observation and attack by French air forces. One division (the 308th), some ten thousand combat troops supported by forty thousand porters, had to be moved from Mao Khe in late March right around the entire perimeter of the delta to a point opposite Ninh Binh in time for the Day River offensive.[29] The approach march was further complicated by inadequate staff work, the inability to obtain rice en route in the quantities expected, and the early onset of the monsoon in early May.[30] Moreover, peasants in the area proved unexpectedly uncooperative and refused to supply food to the Viet Minh, making the porterage of additional quantities of rice over long distances necessary. Thus, moving the troops into position and supplying them at some distance from their main bases in the Viet Bac took nearly two months, and the attack did not begin until the end of May rather than in late April as Giap had hoped. The Viet Minh logistical system came close to collapsing altogether under the strain and was able to provide only the minimum essentials to keep the Viet Minh moving forward; indeed, some units refused to move at all until their logistical needs were met.[31]

The French did not expect an attack on the southwestern corner of their defense line, and when the battle opened on May 29, 1951, with violent Viet Minh attacks from the front and rear against the Day River positions, the French were taken by surprise. As at Vinh Yen and Mao Khe, the initial Viet Minh attack achieved a high degree of success. The 304th Division crossed the Day River on May 29 and routed the French outposts around Phu Ly while the 308th Division overran the French outposts and entered the town of Ninh Binh despite the valiant delaying action that cost the life of General de Lattre's only son.[32] On May 29–30, the 320th Division crossed the river and began the main attack by destroying a number of small French outposts south of Ninh Binh.

General de Lattre responded forcefully and within two days had committed to the battle additional forces amounting to two divisions, including three mobile groups, four artillery groups, an armored group, and a parachute infantry battalion. By June 1, the battle had begun to turn against the Viet Minh as Giap's forces moved out onto the open plains of the delta and thus became more vulnerable to French air attacks and artillery fire. On the whole, Giap's generalship in the Day River battle was quite poor. Having committed all of his forces simultaneously, Giap no longer had a significant reserve with which to exploit local successes. The 320th Division also encountered unexpectedly strong resistance from the pro-French Catholic militia, which slowed Viet Minh progress until French reinforcements could be brought up. The two independent Viet Minh regiments previously infiltrated into the delta, the 42nd and 64th, were unsuccessful in blocking the French reinforcements in part because they, too, were observed and harassed by the Catholic militia. But perhaps the most important factor that halted the Viet Minh drive was French control of the Day River over which all of the Viet Minh men and supplies had to pass. Acting in concert with the French air forces, the *Dinassauts* operating on the Day River effectively cut the supply lines to the three Viet Minh divisions east of the river, and the Viet Minh attack soon ground to a halt due to the lack of food and ammunition.

On the night of June 4–5, the battle of the Day River reached its climax around the key post of Yen Cu Ha, which changed hands several times. By June 6, the French were clearly in control and French interdiction of the tenuous Viet Minh supply lines across the Day River began to determine the course of the battle. Unable to supply his forces east of the river, General Giap was forced to withdraw them, and on June 10 the Viet Minh began to fall back into the hills to the west of the river. By June 18, the battle of the Day River had ended in yet another costly defeat for the Viet Minh and another narrow victory for the French defenders of the Red River delta.

The true dimensions of the Viet Minh defeat on the Day River have never been revealed. The Viet Minh probably lost about one-third of the troops they committed to the fight, and most authorities put Viet Minh losses at around ten thousand, of which one thousand were taken prisoner.[33] General Giap had made two major mistakes. First, he had failed to foresee the degree to which his supply lines across the Day River would be vulnerable to French air and riverine forces. Second, he had failed to anticipate the strong resistance of the Catholic militia forces in the area that slowed his own forces and hampered the efforts of the Viet Minh units previously infiltrated into the delta. Either miscalculation was sufficient to doom the Viet Minh attack to failure; their combination nearly brought disaster.[34]

Although they had been able to interdict the enemy's supply lines decisively, the French defenders of the Day River line had faced a number of severe logistical challenges of their own. The Viet Minh 42nd and 64th Regiments, infiltrated into the delta before the battle began, posed a serious threat to the French rear areas and lines of communication to the Day River front, a threat that did not become a critical factor only by virtue of the unexpectedly stout resistance of the Catholic militia units. Supply shortages, particularly a critical shortage of 105 mm howitzer ammunition, had again proven to be a problem that required the aid of the United States to resolve. At one point during the battle there were only six thousand artillery shells available in all of Indochina, and the lack of reserve ammunition had delayed the French counterattack for eight days.[35] Brigadier General Brink had flown once more to Tokyo and again arranged for the direct issue of 105 mm ammunition from U.S. Far East Command depots direct to the French defenders.[36]

Aftermath of the 1951 Viet Minh Offensives

The failure of their 1951 offensives against the Red River delta came as a great shock to the Viet Minh leaders. The unsuccessful attacks on Vinh Yen, Mao Khe, and the Day River line had cost them some twenty thousand of the newly armed and newly trained *Chu Luc* as well as the temporary loss of the initiative in Tonkin.[37] Fortunately, the French remained too weak to follow up their successful defense, and the Viet Minh once again retired to their base areas in the Viet Bac to refit and rethink their strategy and operational procedures, especially the problems of supplying large forces far from the established base areas.

A good deal of the responsibility for the failure of the 1951 offensives belongs to General Giap. Recriminations within the Viet Minh leadership were severe, and Giap retained his position only with difficulty, being spared the humiliation of removal only because the decision to proceed to the "general counteroffensive" phase of the war had been a collective decision of the entire Viet Minh party leadership.[38] In point of fact, the scapegoat for the failures of 1951 turned out to be

Nguyen Binh, the semiautonomous Viet Minh guerrilla commander in Cochin-china. Nguyen Binh was unfairly accused of having failed to indoctrinate his men thoroughly and of not having acted aggressively to pin down French forces in southern Indochina. In reality, he was probably condemned mainly for being too independent, and the Viet Minh leadership may have played a duplicitous role in his death. Nguyen Binh was killed when his party ran into a French patrol as they made their way back to Cochinchina from a meeting with Ho Chi Minh and General Giap in the Viet Bac.[39]

In any event, Giap's generalship in the 1951 campaign was not of a high order. The decision to commit the *Chu Luc* in all-out offensive operations against the French before they were entirely ready was in large part due to his personal insistence. His campaign plan, involving as it did the sequential commitment of his forces around the French defense perimeter guarding the vital Red River delta, played into General de Lattre's hands by permitting the French to concentrate their forces to defeat each Viet Minh thrust in turn.[40] It must be noted, however, that given the still immature staff and logistical capabilities of the Viet Minh regular forces, a simultaneous, coordinated assault by five divisions all around the delta was probably not a realistic possibility. In any event, Giap's handling of his divisions in the sequential battles of the 1951 campaign did not exhibit the coordination, flexibility, and decisiveness of his later engagements against the French Union forces.

Giap also demonstrated a fault that is usually attributed to the French: a serious underestimation of his foe. Encouraged by his great successes in the battles along RC 4 in late 1950, Giap seems not to have recognized that in General de Lattre he faced a French commander who was much more vigorous and skilled than his predecessors. Furthermore, in 1951, and indeed throughout the First Indochina War, General Giap, by all accounts a brilliant strategist and organizer, seems never to have fully understood the potential of French air and naval power. Having no experience with the use of close air support, parachute troops, or heavily armed naval forces, Giap repeatedly found himself surprised by their mobility and effects. The difficulties of positioning his forces and keeping them supplied adequately under attack from French air and naval forces during the 1951 campaign were lessons that Giap grasped only weakly, and on several occasions before and after 1951 he failed to anticipate the employment of French air and naval forces, underestimated their effectiveness, and failed to take adequate countermeasures.[41] Giap would exhibit the same blind spot when faced with the far greater air and naval power of the United States in the Second Indochina War.

Perhaps the greatest weakness revealed by Giap's 1951 offensive campaign was his failure to correctly assess the logistical difficulties of the campaign and the inability of his logistical system to meet them. The battles for Vinh Yen and Mao Khe were fought on the northern edge of the French delta perimeter in close proximity to the Viet Minh supply installations in the Viet Bac. Even so, the Viet Minh experienced often severe problems in keeping up with the demand of front-line units for food, ammunition, and other supplies. The more complex battle for the Day River line—far from their bases and with lines of communication from the Viet Bac, across the Day River, and in the open country of the delta east of the river subject to intense French air, water, and ground interdiction—resulted in an overload on the Viet Minh logistical system and consequent loss of the battle. The timing of the engagements of the 1951 campaign revealed the fact that about one month was the minimum amount of time required to establish the forward logistical support base for each committed division.[42] In large part, the explanation of why Giap did not mount a simultaneous assault by all five of his divisions on the French perimeter lies in the inability of the Viet Minh commanders and staff officers to plan, coordinate, and execute the logistical support for such an operation. In 1951, the Viet Minh logistical system was incapable of accomplishing such a feat; in 1954, they would win the war by virtue of their ability to do so at Dien Bien Phu.

One other logistical defect of the Viet Minh forces in 1951 that is often overlooked is that they were still inadequately equipped and supplied for a major confrontation with the very strong French Union forces that faced them. From December 1949 until the late fall of 1950, Chinese Communist support of the Viet Minh was plentiful, but it declined once the Chinese intervened in Korea and found themselves faced with their own logistical problems. The battle for the frontier posts in the fall of 1950 had been won by the Viet Minh, and large quantities of weapons, ammunition, and other supplies were captured from the French. However, losses in the subsequent campaign in 1951 against the delta perimeter were enormous. The Chinese had warned the Viet Minh to move forward cautiously.[43] That advice was ignored, and the stunning defeats at Vinh Yen, Mao Khe, and the Day River ensued. As a consequence, the Viet Minh were forced to revert to something less than an all-out conventional war against the French until they could again build up their forces and stockpiles.

For their part, the French regarded the battles for the Red River delta in 1951 as glorious victories. In fact, the battles were inconclusive and provided the Viet Minh an opportunity to discover problems in organization, command and control, staff work, and logistics that, once corrected, would make them all the more formidable.[44] However, the May 1951 Viet Minh attacks against the Day River line would be their last attempt to penetrate into the Tonkin delta by direct assault, although they did continue to infiltrate the delta and conduct an active guerrilla campaign in the French rear areas.[45] Between July 1951 and July 1954, they also carried out a number of significant commando raids on French base areas, including destructive raids on the French airfields at Gia Lam, Cat Bi, and Do Son in early 1954; the destruction of ammunition depots at Kien An in March 1953 and at Phu Tho in June 1954; and the destruction of fuel depots at Do Son in 1953,

Thuong Ly in June 1953, and Nha Trang in January 1954. However, after June 1951 the roles would be reversed, and it would be the Viet Minh defending their vital bases against the offensive actions of the French Union attackers.

The Attack and Defense of the Viet Minh Base Areas

The campaign for the base areas was by no means a one-sided affair. Even while maintaining their defensive perimeter around the critical delta region in Tonkin, the French planned and executed a number of minor and major offensives aimed at penetrating and destroying the Viet Minh supply and administrative bases in the Viet Bac, around Thanh Hoa south of the Red River delta, in Annam, and in Cochinchina. The first major operation of this sort, Operation LEA (described in chapter 9), took place in 1947, and one of the more successful of the early operations was the amphibious raid on July 19, 1949, directed against the large Viet Minh depot of railway equipment at Tam Quan in central Viet Nam in which the French raiders destroyed six locomotives, 240 railroad cars, and one repair shop.[46]

Such offensive operations continued to the very end of the war. Two of these attacks against the Viet Minh base areas are worthy of detailed examination: Operation LORRAINE, a full-scale coordinated offensive into the Viet Bac base areas in October 1952, and the last and most successful airborne raid of the war, Operation HIRONDELLE, directed at Viet Minh facilities around Lang Son in July 1953. In each of these operations the French attempted to capitalize on their superior firepower and air mobility to seriously cripple the Viet Minh logistical system by invading and destroying its rear bases.

Operation LORRAINE, October–November 1952

Operation LORRAINE involved some thirty thousand French Union troops and was the largest and most complex of the direct French attempts to invade the Viet Minh rear bases.[47] Directed at both the Viet Minh depots north of Hanoi and the lines of supply to the Viet Minh forces operating in the T'ai country of northwestern Tonkin (see map 10.2), Operation LORRAINE did not achieve its pre-established goals. Large quantities of Viet Minh supplies were captured and destroyed, but the French seriously overextended themselves and failed to accomplish the key objective of forcing General Giap to withdraw his three divisions from their offensive in the Black River region in order to save his supply bases. Operation LORRAINE underscored both the difficulties of penetrating the Viet Bac to deliver a fatal blow to the Viet Minh logistical system and the problems associated with providing adequate logistical support to extended French Union forces connected to their own bases by a vulnerable road network and limited aerial resupply means.

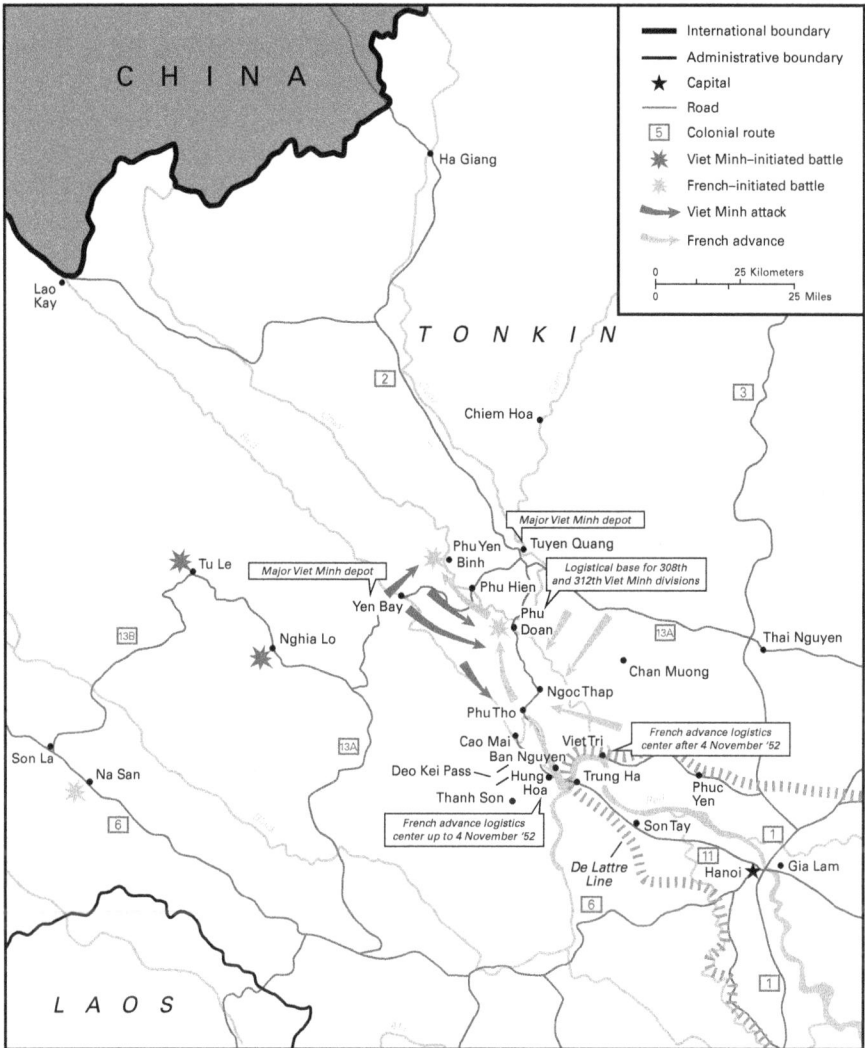

Map 10.2. Operation LORRAINE, October–November 1952.

In mid-October 1952, the Viet Minh launched a full-scale offensive far from their bases in the Viet Bac against the French posts covering the upper reaches of the Black River in the difficult T'ai country of northwestern Tonkin. By the end of October 1952, they were fully engaged, having committed to the operation the majority of their regular forces, including the 308th, 312th, and 316th Divisions reinforced by elements of the 351st Heavy Division. Having taken the key French outpost of Nghia Lo northwest of Hanoi on October 17, General Giap proceeded to regroup and resupply his forces for the continuation of the offensive.

The Viet Minh divisions operating in northwestern Tonkin were supplied from their bases in the Viet Bac, the main supply line running from Tuyen Quang via Yen Bay, and were supported by more than twenty thousand porters.[48] Before moving his divisions toward the Black River, General Giap had anticipated a possible French action in his rear, and he had thus left behind one regiment (the 176th) from the 316th Division and one regiment (the crack 36th) from the 308th Division to guard the important depots around Yen Bay and Tuyen Quang. These two *Chu Luc* units were supported by a number of regional and local force elements scattered about the area. At the time they were seized by the French (November 9–12, 1952), the rear bases and depots of the 308th and 312th Divisions (and of the 141st and 209th Independent Regiments) near Phu Doan were guarded by about two hundred men each, and reinforcements available to the Viet Minh within twenty-four to forty-eight hours from Phu Doan included two to three battalions at Yen Bay and one battalion at Tuyen Quang.

Unable to counter the Viet Minh offensive in northwestern Tonkin directly, Lieutenant General Raoul Salan, who replaced General de Lattre as *commandant en chef* in January 1952, decided to launch an offensive of his own against the Viet Minh rear bases. This offensive, code-named Operation LORRAINE, began on the night of October 28–29, 1952, with the objectives of penetrating and seizing the Viet Minh supply bases in and around Phu Tho, Phu Doan, and Yen Bay north of Hanoi and of destroying any enemy supplies and facilities found there. Lieutenant General Salan hoped that a major offensive against the Viet Minh rear areas would also result in the termination of the Viet Minh offensive in the Black River area by cutting off the flow of supplies to the divisions deployed there and forcing their return to the Viet Bac to defend their bases. In all, some thirty thousand French Union troops were involved in Operation LORRAINE between October 28 and December 6, 1952. The major units assigned to the operation included four mobile groups, an airborne task force, and supporting armor, artillery, engineer, signal, service, and *Train* elements.[49]

On October 27, 1952, Colonel Louis Dodelier, the acting commander of the 1st Provisional Division of Tonkin (*1e Division de Marche du Tonkin,* 1e DMT), was designated as the commander for Operation LORRAINE and received his instructions regarding the operation. Those orders envisioned that the operation would be conducted in two phases. During the first phase, the assigned forces would move up the south bank of the Red River in the general direction of Phu Tho–Yen Bay, creating a large bridgehead west of the Black River and north of the line La Phu–Thanh Son and securing the route leading from Hung Hoa to the pass of Deo Kei. The operation would then develop quickly to the southwest to destroy the Viet Minh depots in the area of Thanh Son–Thuc Luyen and to the north toward Phu Tho. The second phase of the operation, to be conducted "on order" around November 4 after taking Phu Tho, would threaten Yen Bay from both the north and south while a strong covering force was maintained to the west and southwest of Hung Hoa. The operation was to take place without waiting for the concentration of all the necessary forces and thus was expected to unfold sequentially as the additional forces scheduled to take part became available in Tonkin. Following destruction of the Viet Minh depots in the Phu Doan area, the French Union forces were expected to permanently occupy the Red River valley in the region and continue operations against the Viet Minh as the situation warranted.

Operation LORRAINE actually unfolded in four phases quite different from the original two-phase concept of the operation. Phase I, October 28–November 3, involved the seizure of Phu Tho by the mobile task force advancing from Trung Ha and the establishment of the bridgehead north of the Red River. Phase II was conducted between November 4 and 8 and involved the movement of the second mobile task force north from Viet Tri and the clearance of RC 2 from Viet Tri north to Ngoc Thap and a linkup with the Trung Ha task force. Phase III of the operation was carried out between November 9 and 13 and involved the northward movement along RC 2 of the combined ground elements to a linkup with the airborne and riverine task forces for the seizure of Phu Doan and onward movement to Phu Hien, some one hundred miles north of the De Lattre Line. In Phase IV, between November 14 and 26, rather than permanently occupying the region as originally planned, the French Union forces gradually contracted their bridgehead north of the Red River and withdrew to safety in Viet Tri under heavy Viet Minh pressure.

Phase I, October 28–November 3, 1952

Launched without waiting for the concentration of all the forces that were to participate, Operation LORRAINE began on the night of October 28–29, 1952, and unfolded progressively to the northwest as the necessary forces became available. French Union elements, including GM 1 under the command of Lieutenant Colonel Fonclare, GM 3 under the command of Lieutenant Colonel Vincent Moneglia, and Armored Sub-Task Force 2 under Major Henri Spangenberger, crossed the Black River at Trung Ha and proceeded along the river north via Hung Hoa, encountering only sporadic Viet Minh resistance. Elements of GM 3 crossed the Red River on November 2 and established a bridgehead immediately to the east of Phu Tho. On November 3, the 2nd Muong Battalion occupied Phu Tho without resistance. Meanwhile GM 5, commanded by Lieutenant Colonel Ruyssen, and GM 4, commanded by Lieutenant Colonel Kergaravat, began operations around Ban Nguyen and Cao Mai, respectively, and a battalion of GM 1 conducted a raid on November 3, destroying Viet Minh installations and depots near Thanh Son.

Initially, and up to the enlargement of the Hung Hoa bridgehead, the French logistical services were centered on Son Tay, and a surgical team was deployed at Trung Ha. The selection of Son Tay as the logistical center for the operation was dictated by the existence at Son Tay of the territorial ammunition and petroleum depots. Thus, it was necessary only to raise the stockage levels at the existing depots and add a quartermaster element (*groupe d'exploitation de l'Intendance, GEI*). As a precaution, another small depot of ammunition and petroleum was established at the beginning of the operation on the east bank of the Black River across from Trung Ha. As the first phase of Operation LORRAINE unfolded, it soon became necessary to position logistical resources west of the Black River due to the depth of the penetration and to avoid the necessity for units to cross the Black River at Trung Ha, where the bridge was of limited capacity. Subsequently, the logistical center for Operation LORRAINE was moved forward to Hung Hoa, which offered a good beaching area on the Red River 6.5 miles from the village and possessed the requisite security conditions and storage capacity. Accordingly, Hung Hoa was provided with a resupply center replenished by water and an ordnance contact team, one section of which was left at Trung Ha. The surgical team temporarily remained near the Trung Ha airfield, which was being reconditioned.

Phase II, November 4–8, 1952

Following the decision of the commander to move north of the Red River in the direction of Phu Doan, the second phase of Operation LORRAINE involved the enlargement of the bridgeheads north of the Red River around Phu Tho and Cao Mai followed by a converging action to gain control of RC 2 from Viet Tri north to Ngoc Thap. The second phase then ended with the abandonment of the restricted Hung Hoa–Phu Tho axis in favor of a transfer of all forces to the north of the Red River between Viet Tri and Ngoc Thap. In the course of the movement from Phu Tho and Cao Mai to RC 2, the French Union forces faced serious encounters with two battalions of the Viet Minh 176th Regiment of the 316th Division and were obliged to expend considerable engineer effort to recondition RC 2 between Viet Tri and Phu Lo.

The decision to abandon the Trung Ha–Phu Tho axis of advance in favor of an advance along RC 2 north from Viet Tri presented several logistical problems. The relocation of the logistical centers on the Trung Ha–Phu Tho axis—particularly the resupply center at Hung Hoa from which some three hundred tons of supplies were evacuated by truck to Son Tay in less than eight hours—and the establishment of a new logistical center at Viet Tri were major undertakings and also involved moving the pontoon bridge at Trung Ha to Viet Tri. Pending the renovation of RC 2 west of Viet Tri, which was not completed until November 11, the logistical support for most of the units operating north of the Red River around Phu Tho and Cao Mai had to be provided by parachute drop due to the difficulties of crossing the Red River at Phu Tho.

Phase III, November 9–13, 1952

The third phase of Operation LORRAINE involved the raid on Phu Doan and the subsequent movement up RC 2 through Phu Hein. The ground forces involved in this phase of the operation were divided into two task forces: Task Force "Bonichon" had the mission of covering RC 2 from Viet Tri to Ngoc Thap, and Task Force "Dodelier" was charged with leading the drive toward Phu Doan and on to Phu Hein. The armored task force directly under the command of Colonel Louis Dodelier, the commander of the 1e DMT and of Operation LORRAINE itself, overcame Viet Minh delaying actions on March 9 and arrived near Phu Doan at 1400 hours. Trailing Colonel Dodelier's armored task force were two additional armored mobile groups stretched out along RC 2 between Ngoc Thap and Phu Doan to cover the road and mop up around Phu Doan itself. Meanwhile, three battalions of the 1st Airborne Task Force (*1e Groupement Parachutiste*, 1e GP), under the command of Lieutenant Colonel Pierre Ducournau, successfully conducted a parachute assault in the Phu Doan area on the morning of November 9, linked up with riverine forces ascending the Chay River (from the Clear River), and established a bridgehead around Phu Doan before linking up with the armored column commanded by Colonel Dodelier. The combined forces then proceeded to uncover and capture or destroy the numerous Viet Minh supply storage areas in the region.

The airborne portion of the combined attack on Phu Doan was known as Operation MARION and began with the parachute assault of the 1st and 2nd Foreign Legion Parachute Battalions (*1e et 2e Battalions Étrangers Parachutistes*, 1e BEP and 2e BEP) and the 3rd Colonial Parachute Battalion (*3e Bataillon de Parachutistes Coloniaux*, 3e BPC) north of the Chay River opposite Phu Doan at 1030 hours, November 9, with the objective of closing RC 2 to Viet Minh traffic and destroying Viet Minh installations in the region.[50] The jump was made with no opposition and minimal jump casualties (one killed, sixteen injured, ten evacuated by helicopter), and by 1500 hours the paras linked up with the riverine forces moving up the Chay River. The paras were then ferried across the Chay by the *Dinassaut*, established a bridgehead around Phu Doan, and two hours later linked up with the armored column advancing north on RC 2. Between November 10 and 14 they cleared the banks of the Chay River, forcing two battalions of the Viet Minh 176th Regiment and 105 mm howitzers and 120 mm mortars of the 351st Heavy Division to fall back northward along RC 2.

With the Phu Doan area firmly in friendly hands, the operation was continued on November 13 to the north along Route Provinciale 11 (RP 11). The joint armor-airborne force occupied the crossroads village of Phu Hien north of Phu Doan, and elements of that group subsequently advanced as far north as Phu Yen Binh, some forty miles northwest of Phu Doan and almost one hundred miles from the De Lattre Line. Meanwhile on November 13, a strong combined arms task force blocked RC 2 north to Tuyen Quang about twelve miles north of Phu Doan, and a similar task force of about five battalions took up a blocking position astride RP 13A about ten miles from Yen Bay and just east of the interposing ridgeline.

At the beginning of the third phase of Operation LORRAINE the logistical support of the units involved was concentrated at Viet Tri: the resupply center, ordnance contact team, and surgical team at Viet Tri "West" and a maintenance repair element at Viet Tri "East." Once RC 2 was opened, a second maintenance repair section and the surgical team moved forward to Ngoc Thap, and a maintenance contact team pushed on up to Phu Doan. The requirements for aerial resupply diminished significantly during the course of the third phase of the operation, being used only to support the combined armor and para force advancing on Phu Hien. Following the conclusion of the action at Phu Doan, it was planned to create an advance depot at Ngoc Thap that would eventually relieve the congestion on RC 2 between Viet Tri and Ngoc Thap. However, this project was not carried out once the decision was taken on November 14 to withdraw the forces engaged north of Ngoc Thap.

Phase IV, November 14–26, 1952

Both Tuyen Quang and Yen Bay were major Viet Minh supply centers, and the seizure of either one would have dealt General Giap a staggering blow. However, Lieutenant General Salan, estimating that taking Yen Bay and Tuyen Quang was probably beyond the capability of the available French Union forces, declined to try for either prize and instead decided on November 14 to terminate the operation and withdraw his forces south toward Ngoc Thap. Dictated in part by the enormous logistical resources required to keep his heavily mechanized forces operating far from their fixed bases, Salan's decision to terminate Operation LORRAINE with a staged withdrawal southward was also contingent on the fact that the operation had failed to provoke the desired reaction from General Giap. Moreover, by absorbing all of the available reserves, Operation LORRAINE deprived the French high command of a mobile reserve with which to influence the action in the far more critical T'ai country and Red River delta.

The fourth and final phase of Operation LORRAINE thus involved the withdrawal of all forces from Ngoc Thap southward to Viet Tri and the termination of the operation on November 26. Initiated on November 14 by the withdrawal of French Union forces north of Ngoc Thap, this phase of the operation took the form of a slow contraction of the bridgehead between the Clear and Red Rivers and ended on November 25–26 with all French Union forces withdrawn behind the concrete barrier of the De Lattre Line.

The withdrawal of the French Union forces southward along RP 11 and RC 2 from beyond Phu Hien toward Ngoc Thap began on November 15 and ended on November 17 only after a heavy engagement near the Chan Muong Pass on RC 2 involving the crack Viet Minh 36th Regiment of the 308th Division and two French mobile groups (GM 1 and GM 4). The village of Chan Muong lay in a 2.5-mile-long gorge, and the Viet Minh ambush, which was conducted with a 0.6-mile-long kill zone along RC 2 immediately south of Chan Muong, produced a savage hand-to-hand fight in which both sides suffered heavy losses.[51] The struggle lasted throughout the afternoon of November 17 before the Viet Minh broke off around 1630 hours. However, the French rear guard was violently attacked at Chan Muong at 1830 hours and was subsequently forced to continue its withdrawal from Chan Muong to Thai Binh under heavy attack, losing one tank, six half-tracks, and two jeeps. By 2230 hours, all French forces had been withdrawn south of Ngoc Thap and were assembled in the area of Go Cay–Phuc Loc–Phu Lo.

Subsequently, strong elements of the Viet Minh 36th Regiment attacked two French Union units on the right flank on the night of November 23–24. One of the units repulsed the attack, but the other was overrun.[52]

At the beginning of the fourth and final phase of Operation LORRAINE, the logistical elements withdrew by echelon to Viet Tri, where they remained until the end of the operation. The surgical team and maintenance repair section returned to Hanoi on November 27. The resupply center at Viet Tri "West," containing about 450 tons of supplies, was evacuated by truck in twenty-four hours on November 27–28, the ammunition being removed to Phuc Yen and the rations and petroleum to Hanoi.

Results of Operation LORRAINE

Operation LORRAINE resulted in substantial personnel losses for both sides. French Union casualties during the operation were reported as 82 killed, 250 wounded, and 199 missing, the bulk of them occurring between November 9 and 17.[53] Viet Minh personnel losses were reported as 171 killed (by body count), of which 153 were regulars from the 36th Regiment of the 308th Division and the 176th Regiment of the 316th Division.[54] French authorities estimated that overall the Viet Minh lost about seven hundred killed in action and about the same number of wounded. The number of Viet Minh taken prisoner was fifty-nine, of which twenty were regulars and thirty-nine were regional force troops.

The Viet Minh materiel losses were serious but not disastrous. The list of materiel seized by the French Union forces at Tay Coc, Phu Doan, and elsewhere during Operation LORRAINE was substantial but scarcely merited the resources thrown into the operation by the French. As usual, the Viet Minh were forewarned and managed to remove a considerable portion of the supplies in the depots around

Phu Doan before the French arrived. Nevertheless, the balance sheet for Operation LORRAINE contained a large number of items seized by the French Union forces. Among those items recovered and evacuated to the rear were 3 recoilless rifles, 2 120 mm mortars, 14 81 mm mortars, 40 60 mm mortars, 22 machine guns, 30 automatic rifles, 100 submachine guns, 23 bazookas (2.36-inch rocket launchers), 500 rifles, 400 rounds of 105 mm HM2 ammunition, 80 rounds of 120 mm mortar ammunition, 1 jeep (quarter-ton truck), 2 Molotova trucks, about 5 tons of rice, 20 tons of salt, and 10 tons of cinnamon. Materiel destroyed on site included more than 152.5 tons of munitions and explosives, including 25,000 grenades, 1,200 rounds of 120 mm mortar ammunition, 4,200 rounds of 81 mm mortar ammunition, 1,800 rounds of 60 mm mortar ammunition, 1,500 rounds of 57 mm recoilless rifle ammunition, 800 rounds of 75 mm howitzer ammunition, 1,500 mines of various types, and 500,000 cartridges of various calibers, numerous weapons (including about 500 rifles), 1 Molotova truck, numerous tools (shovels, picks, etc.), 1 grenade workshop, and 1 ton of leather.[55]

The capture of at least three relatively new Soviet-made GAZ-51 Molotova trucks was a significant indicator of the growing sophistication of the Viet Minh logistical system as Chinese aid expanded. Well-adapted to the physical environment of Tonkin, the sturdy 2.5-ton Molotovas were a major enhancement of the Viet Minh logistical capability, and eventually over eight hundred of them would be supplied by Communist China.[56] The historian Bernard Fall erroneously attributed the discovery of the first two Molotovas to Lieutenant Marion, a tank platoon leader in GM 1. Fall wrote that Marion had noted unusual tire tracks going off the Phu Doan–Yen Bay road and had followed them to discover the trucks hidden under palm branches.[57] Marion, a descendant of Francis Marion, the "Swamp Fox" of American Revolutionary War fame, later stated that the trucks had actually been discovered by elements of GM 4.

Despite the prospect that the French offensive into the Viet Bac might produce significant materiel losses, General Giap had refused to allow his offensive in the T'ai country to be terminated by the return of forces to defend his bases as the French had hoped. Following his usually successful method of requiring each unit to carry out its mission as best it could without reinforcement, Giap had left the forces in place in the Viet Bac to fend for themselves. Having anticipated that the heavily mechanized French Union forces would be hard-pressed to sustain a major advance into the Viet Bac, particularly a coordinated advance to his key logistical centers at Thai Nguyen and Yen Bay, General Giap relied on his two reserve *Chu Luc* regiments to block the French advance and declined to return any major portion of his forces on the Black River to defend his bases.

From the French point of view, Operation LORRAINE did achieve some larger strategic successes in addition to the destruction of Viet Minh supplies, equipment, and facilities. The French commander of Operation LORRAINE, Colonel

Dodelier, reported that the operation had profoundly disorganized the Viet Minh regional system around Phu Tho; isolated two battalions of the 176th Regiment of the 316th Division; obliged the enemy to return from northwestern Tonkin one of his best regiments, the 36th Regiment of the 308th Division, on which heavy losses were inflicted; and imposed on the enemy the necessity of engaging at the end of the operation his last available strategic reserves, a battalion of the 246th Regiment and the Viet Minh headquarters guard regiment.[58] In fact, the 36th Regiment of the 308th Division appears to have been one of the two *Chu Luc* divisional infantry regiments left behind by General Giap to guard his rear areas when he began his foray into the T'ai country in mid-October, the other certainly being the 176th Regiment of the 316th Division. Thus, the 36th Regiment was not obliged to return from northwestern Tonkin, as Colonel Dodelier indicated. The identity of the so-called Viet Minh headquarters guard regiment is uncertain, but the reference may be to the 148th Independent Regiment. In April 1952, U.S. order of battle analysts believed the 148th Independent Regiment to be at Yen Bay and the 246th Independent Regiment to be at Thai Nguyen.[59]

Colonel Dodelier also stated that although the Viet Minh leaders had probably foreseen an attack on their rear bases as a reaction to their campaign in the northwest, the rapid movement of French Union forces on Phu Doan menacing the major supply centers of Yen Bay and Tuyen Quang had succeeded in surprising the enemy, who did not have time to evacuate his depots. Such operations at a distance of over sixty miles from the De Lattre Line would, he believed, force the Viet Minh to live in fear of future operations of a similar nature and would have a negative psychological effect on the Viet Minh troops and the civilian population under Viet Minh control.[60]

The French capacity for self-deception remained strong. While Dodelier's optimistic evaluation of the achievements of Operation LORRAINE was not without some elements of truth, the fact is that the operation was a failure. The Viet Minh offensive on the Black River was not seriously affected, no major Viet Minh forces were returned to the Viet Bac, and no decisive engagements were fought. While the Viet Minh rear areas had been thrown into considerable turmoil and substantial quantities of arms, ammunition, and other supplies were captured or destroyed, the materiel losses inflicted on the Viet Minh were nowhere near proportionate to the resources committed to the operation by the French. Indeed, those resources, particularly the air transport capability consumed, might have been better used in reinforcing the isolated French strongholds in northwestern Tonkin and in increasing the pacification effort in the delta, which continued to be increasingly infiltrated by the Viet Minh.

Both the French and the Viet Minh learned important strategic, tactical, and logistical lessons from Operation LORRAINE. For the French, the handling of the mobile groups in mountainous terrain distant from their fixed bases of supply pointed to the need for greater coordination of the efforts of all arms as well as to the need for more effective logistical planning. An appreciation of the difficulties of maneuvering the heavy mechanized columns and their logistical support elements on the narrow roads and mountainous terrain of the Tonkin highlands was reinforced, and the value of light, mobile, and fast-moving units was once again underscored. In his report on the operation, Colonel Dodelier noted that the command post of a mobile group normally displaced with about sixty vehicles, that an artillery group formed a column of some eighty vehicles and numerous trailers, and that an infantry battalion trailed in its wake a substantial number of coolies, who lengthened the columns on the roads and inflated immeasurably the size of defensive positions. But he also noted that while in certain cases the logistical trains of French units might be reduced, any draconian reduction in the number of coolies was only hypothetical as long as the European soldiers were required to operate for prolonged periods in the hard climate of Indochina.[61]

Colonel Dodelier also noted that airborne forces did not provide the optimum solution inasmuch as their rapidity of action was constrained by the necessity of assembling and collecting the parachutes following a drop, which could take as much as forty-eight hours when the drop zones were scattered, as at Phu Doan, and by their lack of transport (either trucks or coolies), which limited their ability to maneuver and their firepower. On the other hand, according to Dodelier—himself an armor officer, not a parachutist—the armored elements involved in Operation LORRAINE performed perfectly, and their success argued for the augmentation of the French Union forces in Tonkin by additional tank squadrons teamed with specially trained infantry.[62]

On the other hand, Bernard Fall noted, "The very size and heaviness of the units involved in the offensive made the restoration of roads and bridges an overriding condition of movement and slowed down the whole operation to a crawl."[63] He also remarked that the French engineers had to work with commercial-type bulldozers exposed to enemy fire since there was not a single tank-dozer in all of Indochina. The engineer operations associated with Operation LORRAINE indicated the need for additional engineer capability, particularly bridging and river-crossing resources.[64] The value of the riverine forces that participated in the operation was also considered high, and the cooperation of the navy and the efficiency of the coordination between ground and riverine elements was judged to be superior. In a final note, Colonel Dodelier pointed out some of the lessons learned with respect to the resupply of ground forces by parachute. His observations are all the more interesting in view of the subsequent difficulties faced in the aerial resupply of the garrison at Dien Bien Phu in early 1954. Among the problems with aerial resupply in Operation LORRAINE cited by Dodelier were a disconcerting tendency for supplies to be dropped in the wrong place or to miss the assigned drop zones, as well as the problems of air-to-ground communications and the precise coordination of aerial resupply operations.[65]

American observers, particularly the chief of MAAG-Indochina, Major General Thomas J. H. Trapnell, who was responsible for the massive American military aid program, were disappointed with the failure of Operation LORRAINE and believed the French had bungled a good chance to inflict a stunning defeat on the Viet Minh by holding on to Phu Doan and thereby eventually forcing Giap into a decisive battle for his rear areas under conditions favorable to the French.[66] However, such opinions tended to overemphasize French numerical superiority and failed to account for the fact that the heavy French Union forces required enormous amounts of supplies that could only be brought up over the limited road network that was subject to continued Viet Minh interdiction. Indeed, it was just this logistical consideration that forced the termination of Operation LORRAINE before it achieved all of its stated objectives. The maintenance of some thirty thousand heavily mechanized troops one hundred miles from their bases and depots posed logistical problems that the French Union forces were not equipped to solve. Lieutenant General Salan's decision to terminate the operation and fall back to the De Lattre Line was also dictated in large part by the fact that continued operations in the Viet Bac would monopolize the scarce air transport that was desperately needed to resupply the isolated positions under threat in northwestern Tonkin and elsewhere.[67]

This time, General Giap had correctly assessed the logistical aspects of the war. His own lines of communication and the flow of supplies to his offensive forces on the Black River were practically unaffected by Operation LORRAINE, and his estimate that the French could not sustain a major drive into the Viet Bac was proven correct. In any event, although the French Union troops engaged in Operation LORRAINE uncovered and destroyed or carried away an enormous amount of arms, ammunition, and other supplies, the overall Viet Minh supply situation was not seriously affected in view of the extensive stockpiles already developed and the continuing high level of support provided by Communist China. Thus, Giap's decision to refuse to terminate his Black River offensive and return his three divisions to fight for their bases in the Viet Bac turned out to be the correct one. Giap would continue to have to fight to keep his lines of communication open, but his rear bases would never again face a coordinated all-out assault such as Operation LORRAINE.

Thus, Operation LORRAINE, launched on the basis of logistical considerations, was likewise terminated based on logistical factors. The largest and perhaps most complex operation of the First Indochina War was from first to last a logistical battle, one in which the still somewhat primitive logistical system of the Viet Minh proved more effective than the sophisticated and highly mechanized system of the French by virtue of the greater flexibility and better adaptation of the

Viet Minh system to the physical environment and the enormous consumption of resources attendant on the French system. This disparity in weight and flexibility would be further demonstrated in the operations that followed in northwestern Tonkin in 1953 and 1954.

Operation HIRONDELLE, July 1953

Operation LORRAINE failed to achieve its main objectives, but Operation HIRONDELLE (SWALLOW) in July 1953, one of five major airborne operations conducted during the First Indochina War, was perhaps the most successful of the French operations against the Viet Minh rear areas.[68] Operation HIRONDELLE was in effect an airborne commando raid, but it was a raid that required the use of three parachute infantry battalions in recognition of the fact that the Viet Minh rear areas could no longer be attacked without major force commitments. As Operation MARS, conducted in October–November 1951 in Rach Gia Province in southwestern Cochinchina, had shown, with good intelligence and good operational security the use of parachute forces offered an excellent prospect of achieving tactical surprise, the key element in successful operations against Viet Minh rear areas.[69] Although limited in scope, Operation HIRONDELLE was based on sound intelligence and was both well-planned and well-executed. It thus achieved its objectives and yielded results proportionate to the resources expended.

The principal objective of Operation HIRONDELLE was to find and destroy the stocks of weapons, ammunition, and other supplies stored in the important Viet Minh depots located in the caves of Ki Lua near Lang Son. The operation was part of Lieutenant General Navarre's plan to keep the Viet Minh off balance and on the defensive and was also intended to demonstrate to the Americans that the French Union forces were still capable of offensive action and thus merited the continued logistical support of the United States. After a careful analysis of all available information, the French intelligence service posited that three key factors would influence the course of Operation HIRONDELLE: (1) the nature and size of the enemy depots targeted; (2) the possibility of intervention by enemy forces; and (3) the terrain along the route to be used by the parachute task force during its withdrawal from the objective area (see map 10.3).[70]

In general, the area of Lang Son was known to contain a number of important depots for the receipt of war materiel provided by the Chinese Communists. It was also assumed that as of July 8, 1953, the Lang Son depots were swollen by virtue of the fact that in the preceding month French air forces had been successful in cutting the supply lines from the Lang Son area to the Viet Minh forces elsewhere in Tonkin. Although the precise number of storage locations in the objective area and the exact quantity of materiel in each was unknown, it was determined that the three most important depots in the area were the caves of Nhi Thanh and Tam

Map 10.3. Operation HIRONDELLE, July 1953.

Thanh north of the Ky Cung River and the cave of Chua Tien south of the river. It was estimated that the Tam Thanh cave held about 105 tons of supplies and that the Nhi Thanh depot was full but the tonnage unknown. The depot at Chua Tien was estimated to contain some thirty-six tons of supplies. It was subsequently discovered during the course of the operation that such limestone caves provided excellent storage sites when located near roads, being easy to access and protected from aerial observation and attack. Since the supplies were not easily seen and not subject to aerial attack, the Viet Minh did not follow standard storage practices, and gasoline, ammunition of various types, and weapons were all stored in the same gallery.

French intelligence estimated that as of July 8, Viet Minh reaction capabilities in the area of Lang Son–Loc Binh included immediate reaction by the existing depot guards and one battalion from Lang Son on D-day, a coordinated reaction by three regional force battalions and one *Chu Luc* battalion in two to three days, and a possible intervention by Chinese Communist frontier forces after D+1. The French also estimated that all or part of the Viet Minh 308th Division could reach the Lang Son region in four days, and there was the added possibility of an intervention by an indeterminate number of Chinese Communist frontier forces.

Aerial reconnaissance and aerial photography interpretation were used to analyze the nature of the terrain around Lang Son and along the proposed withdrawal route, with a view to selecting drop zones and determining the existing obstacles, possible travel times, and repair work required to make RC 4 usable. This analysis proved generally accurate, although aerial photography did not reveal all of the obstacles and the time required to repair RC 4 from Tien Yen to Loc Binh was slightly underestimated, requiring forty-eight rather than the anticipated thirty-six hours. In general, the withdrawal route (RC 4 from Lang San through Loc Binh and Dinh Lap to Tien Yen), except for the final twelve miles nearest Tien Yen, was characterized by many destroyed bridges and culverts that required engineer work to make the route passable for vehicular traffic.[71]

The mission assigned to Brigadier General Jean Gilles, the commander of Operation HIRONDELLE, was to conduct on D-day, July 17, 1953, a rapid surprise airborne raid on the Viet Minh depots at Lang Son situated north of the Ky Cung River (those south of the river were to be attacked by aircraft) and destroy any enemy weapons, ammunition, or other supplies found there.[72] After the destruction of the depots, the parachute troops were to withdraw rapidly along RC 4 toward Tien Yen. Meanwhile, a ground element was to be moved by sea from Haiphong to Pointe Pagode and pushed up RC 4 toward Lang Son as rapidly as possible to be in position 4.5 miles northwest of Dinh Lap no later than noon on D+1 to link up with the paras and cover the withdrawal of the combined force to Tien Yen.

The French authorities recognized that the success of the operation hinged on totally surprising the enemy and on the rapidity with which the enemy supplies and equipment could be destroyed and the friendly troops withdrawn. Accordingly, the plan called for a parachute assault on drop zones adjacent to the objectives as early as possible on D-day. The paras would then immediately proceed to find and destroy as much enemy materiel as possible before withdrawing rapidly down the RC 4 to Loc Binh, south of the Ky Cung River, by the morning of D+1. To speed the operation, the parachutes used by the elements dropped on Lang Son were to be abandoned and those of the units dropped south of the Ky Cung River were to be recovered by the advancing ground element, which was assigned the primary mission of covering the withdrawal of the paras. Both the paras and the ground element were to be evacuated by sea from Pointe Pagode to Haiphong at the end of the operation.

French naval elements received the missions of transporting the ground elements from Haiphong to Pointe Pagode and landing them; transporting supplies from Port Wallut to Pointe Pagode; and reembarking the parachute and ground elements at Pointe Pagode and transporting them to Haiphong. French Air Force elements in northern Viet Nam were instructed to give absolute priority to supporting Operation HIRONDELLE; to provide transport aircraft for the jump and resupply; to provide close air support to prepare and protect the parachute assault, isolate the drop zone, maintain contact, and intervene with aerial fires on request; to maintain constant aerial observation of the zone of operations and possible axes of advance for Viet Minh (or Chinese) relief forces; and to provide liaison and aerial evacuation support as required.

Several diversionary actions were also planned to attract the attention of the Viet Minh regular and regional forces in the area and to deceive the enemy as to the route by which the paras were to withdraw. These diversions included action by the 2nd Provisional Division of Tonkin (*2e Division de Marche du Tonkin*, 2e DMT) in the area north of Phu Lang Thuong and Luc Nam and by subsector forces west of Mon Cay.

Operation HIRONDELLE was executed speedily and without major deviation from the plan. The destruction of enemy supply installations was completed only nine hours after the parachute assault, and the para task force linked up with the ground element advancing from Point Pagode thirty hours after the completion of the destruction of the Viet Minh depots. Altogether, the operation lasted just three days and sixteen hours. All forces involved in the operation were back within the De Lattre Line by July 20.

Overall, the Viet Minh resistance in the area of operations was characterized by extreme slowness and a confusion of orders and reaction plans.[73] Thus, Operation HIRONDELLE met with very little organized resistance and reconfirmed the observation that in their deep rear areas the Viet Minh seldom kept their defense plans up to date and employed few defensive measures other than hiding their depots underground and moving only at night. The actual Viet Minh response to Operation HIRONDELLE can be divided into three main phases. During the first phase (July 17) the Viet Minh agents in place rendered contradictory reports, and thus the parachute assault met with only light resistance by scattered Viet Minh troops in the objective area, resulting in five Viet Minh killed and one Viet Minh automatic rifle captured. The entrance to the depot cave at Tam Thanh was defended by several guards from the Viet Minh supply services, but the intervention of French aircraft soon put an end to the weak resistance. On the afternoon of July 17, the head of the French ground element advancing on RC 4 was taken under fire by a section from Viet Minh *Dai Doi 35* about two miles southeast of Chau Son with minimal effect. The Viet Minh apparently feared an extension of the operation to other nearby depots and consequently attempted to organize a defense of Ta Lai that consisted of an antiaircraft artillery company and twenty depot guards to defend the entrance to the cave depot. A group of diverse elements, mainly young volunteers, was organized to defend the road to Na Chan, and an appeal was made to Chinese Communist troops to protect the route from Dong Dang to Na Chan.

The second phase of the Viet Minh reaction took place on July 18. Having learned that morning that the French raiders had retired toward Loc Binh on the evening of July 17, the commander of the regional forces around Lang Son named a commission to examine the situation. The commission subsequently made a summary listing of the materiel lost, conducted a severe interrogation of the local population to uncover traitors, and assigned to the commander of the local Viet Minh guerrilla forces the mission of moving in the direction of Loc Binh in the hope of barring the route to the withdrawing French forces.

The final phase of the Viet Minh reaction came on July 19, when, having finally realized that the French were executing a general withdrawal along RC 4, the Viet Minh commander attempted to engage the French forces with regional forces from Hai Ninh, who were given orders to harass the French columns. Regional force companies from Hai Ninh were echeloned between Dinh Lap and Tien Yen but did not dare act on their own authority and awaited orders. The only real action came on the afternoon of July 20, when the tail of the ground element column was harassed by Viet Minh elements echeloned along RC 4 about 7.5 miles northwest of Tien Yen.

The French logistical support for Operation HIRONDELLE was as meticulously planned as the tactical deployments.[74] The various supporting services operated in conjunction with the operational command posts established at Hanoi (for the airborne elements) and Tien Yen (for the ground elements). Staff supervision of all logistical matters connected with the operation was exercised by the *4e Bureau Opérationnel* (the logistical staff section of the Operation HIRONDELLE field headquarters). The supply center for the operation was located at Tien Yen, and all arrangements for the internal management of the base were delegated to the designated base commander. Guard personnel, rations, and lodging in the rear area were the responsibility of the commander of the Coastal Zone Command (*Zone Côtière*). Viet Minh prisoners of war held in camps at Tien Yen (sixty-three men) and Khe Tu (sixty-one men) constituted a labor pool for use by forces involved in Operation HIRONDELLE or by the *Zone Côtière*.

Intendance support was provided from the depot operated by the *Gestion d'Hanoi* and a ration depot located at Tien Yen. Each parachutist carried one combat ration on his person, and two days of Ration 102 were held in reserve. Plans called for aerial resupply of rations beginning on D+1. Rations for the troops of the ground element (one ration in the course of consumption and one combat ration in reserve for each man) were carried by the individual or on unit transport, and plans called for the resupply of rations after noon on D-day from the depot at Tien Yen.

Supporting ammunition depots were located at Port Wallut (main) and Tien Yen (secondary). Infantry ammunition was allocated at a rate of one unit of fire per battalion carried on unit transport.[75] One unit of fire for each artillery piece (175–200 rounds) was maintained within the fortified camp at Tien Yen. Tank and scout car units were authorized one unit of fire carried on the unit vehicles.[76] Requests for resupply of ammunition approved by the operations section of the *4e Bureau Opérationnel* were filled by the secondary depot at Tien Yen on a twenty-four-hour basis.

Maintenance facilities (to third echelon) were established at Tien Yen by the 2nd Section, 3rd Foreign Legion Medium Repair Company (*2/3e Compagnie Moyenne de Réparation de la Légion Étrangère*, 2/3e CMRLE), reinforced by a ten-ton wrecker. Units were responsible for emergency repairs and evacuation of vehicles in their zone of action, but assistance was provided by the 2/3e CMRLE on the orders of the *4e Bureau Opérationnel.* The prescribed axis of evacuation was along RC 4 to Tien Yen, with items requiring fourth-echelon repairs being evacuated by 2/3e CMRLE by sea to Haiphong. Minor repairs to signal equipment were the responsibility of the using unit with assistance and spare parts provided by the signal element attached to the operational command post. Requests for replacement radios were routed through the *4e Bureau Opérationnel.*

A basic petroleum allocation of four refills per vehicle or engine was established, and requests for petroleum products were filled by the secondary fuel depot established at Tien Yen. No containers were loaned. Engineer supplies were obtained by requests addressed to the *4e Bureau Opérationnel* and filled by the territorial depot at Haiphong.

Arrangements for aerial resupply were managed by the *4e Bureau Opérationnel,* but the limited air transport means available restricted aerial resupply to ammunition, medical supplies, batteries, rations (combat or *FOM*), and rice. Once the operation was launched, requests for resupply by units of the airborne task force were made by coded radio messages indicating the desired drop zone, the receiving unit, and the necessary radio frequencies.

Medical support of the operation was provided by a surgical team located at Tien Yen, by the hospital at Haiphong, and by the Hôpital Lanessar in Hanoi. Units were responsible for evacuating casualties to the surgical team at Tien Yen, with onward evacuation to Haiphong upon the request of the chief surgeon of the surgical team to the *4e Bureau Opérationnel.* Helicopter evacuation was also available, with requests routed through the *4e Bureau Opérationnel*. Requests for resupply of medical items were also handled by the *4e Bureau Opérationnel*, with the chief surgeon of the surgical team at Tien Yen prepared to provide light resupply to units by helicopter or Morane fixed-wing aircraft.

A major part of the success of Operation HIRONDELLE can be attributed to the effective use made of the limited air, ground, and water transport available to support the operation. The effectiveness of the plans and execution of transportation support for Operation HIRONDELLE reflected very favorably on the professionalism and hard work of the personnel of the transportation staff section (*Bureau Mouvements Transports*, BMT) managing the operation.[77] In general, the transportation resources available to support Operation HIRONDELLE were quite limited. A total of forty–six GMC 2.5-ton trucks and ten Dodge 6x6 trucks were made available by the *Train* and the *Zone Côtière*, but only about forty trucks were available at any one time. Rail assets were also utilized during the positioning phase. For example, the 2/5e REI was moved by rail from Yen Vien to Haiphong for embarkation. Water transport assigned to the operation included four navy LCMs for riverine logistical movements between Port Wallut and Tien Yen and one navy LST, five navy LCTs, and the commercial steamship *Gascogne* for coastal movements between Haiphong and Pointe Pagode. Very effective traffic control within the operational area was provided by one platoon (three traffic control posts) of the 71st Traffic Control Company (*71e Compagnie de Circulation Routière*, 71e CCR).

In general, the coordination and cooperation of ground and naval forces was excellent and coastal movements were carried out without incident. However, the loading of the *Gascogne*, which made two round-trips between Haiphong and Pointe Pagode during the positioning phase and two more during the evacuation phase, was slow (1.5 hours for 850 men) due to the configuration of the ship and the care taken by Tonkin Operational Base (*Base Opérationnelle du Tonkin*, BOTK) to count each embarking soldier one by one. BOTK, which for security reasons was not informed in advance of the troop movements in support of Operation HIRONDELLE (other than those affecting units in Haiphong), also experienced difficulties in providing billeting for the twenty-four hundred troops waiting to be embarked at Haiphong as well as in supplying dunnage and water.

Transportation operations during Operation HIRONDELLE proceeded in three phases: (1) the positioning of the forces; (2) the movement of troops and supplies during the operation itself; and (3) the termination of the operation and evacuation of the forces engaged. Strenuous efforts were required of transport personnel during all three phases, but they resulted in a high degree of success achieved with limited means. The positioning of the forces for Operation HIRONDELLE involved some 3,600 men, 80 vehicles, and 120 tons of supplies. This phase of the operation was influenced by the need to preserve secrecy, the limited water transport available, the precarious nature of the ground route (RP 18) from Haiphong to Tien Yen over which only a limited number of vehicles could be moved each day, and the requirement to put in place all forces on D-day without any pre–D-day movements. For example, the scarcity of available water transport required that forty of the GMC trucks to be involved in the operation move overland on RP 18 from Haiphong to Tien Yen. However, this movement could not begin before D-day and no more than twenty trucks could utilize the route each day. Thus, the assembly of the major portion of the motor transport for the operation was delayed in arriving in the area of operations until the morning of D+2. The movement of support elements by sea, on the other hand, was completed by 1000 hours on D-day, some three hours ahead of schedule.

Movements during the course of the operation itself were characterized by the absolute priority accorded the movement of the tactical units; the speed and short duration of the operation, which did not provide time to assemble additional transport; and the requirement to use a single line of communication (RC 4) that was in poor condition, had limited capacity, and contained many obstacles and detours. The condition and limited capacity of RC 4 greatly hampered highway operations. For example, transit of the Dinh Lap–Khe Tu section required eight hours, and thus each vehicle could only make two round-trips per day at most.

The necessity of repairing the roadway as the ground elements moved forward slowed the progress of the operation to the speed of a bulldozer or of a man afoot. The tactical situation for the advancing ground forces also made it impractical (and unwise) to move the combat forces forward on trucks, and thus the motor transport was mainly of benefit to the follow-on echelons. For reasons of economy, the use of trucks during the withdrawal of the combined para and ground elements was restricted to the movement of units fully assembled and ready to move in sufficient numbers to justify the commitment of the motor transport. Furthermore, the danger of serious accidents on the poor roads, especially considering the fatigue of both the vehicles and the drivers, restricted most troop movements to daylight hours. For example, the poor state of the roadway produced as many as eighty-six flat tires for forty trucks in a single day, and the drivers worked practically without sleeping for the first three nights of the operation.

The recovery phase was executed in a minimum amount of time without waiting for the withdrawal to protected areas of all the engaged units. The evacuation of the committed forces had to be carried out without creating additional burdens for the infantry security forces and involved some two thousand men—the paras—in addition to those put in place by ground and sea transport.

Maintenance support provided to the motor transport elements engaged in Operation HIRONDELLE was excellent, but some difficulties were encountered in the supply of rations and petroleum products. For administrative reasons the ration and POL depots were not co-located on the southwest bank of the Pho

Cu River at Tien Yen with the troops and vehicles of the *Train* to be supported, thus causing delays in refueling and provisioning the drivers. Also, the scarcity of motor transport and the high mobility of the combat units assigned to the operation created difficulties in effecting the required resupply movements, since tactical movements took priority over logistical movements.

Two major lessons were learned during Operation HIRONDELLE with respect to transportation support. First, it was noted that a complex coordinated operation cannot unfold properly unless meticulously planned, but meticulous planning does not preclude flexibility if the combat and logistical forces are accustomed to working as a team. The second lesson was that the speed of transport movements is not solely a function of the number of vehicles available, but also depends on the state of the available routes and the efficiency of the traffic regulation on those routes.

Overall, Operation HIRONDELLE was a stunning success for the French Union forces. The operation proceeded rapidly and smoothly, achieving all of its objectives with minimal friendly casualties. In all, some five thousand tons of Viet Minh equipment and supplies, much of it Chinese and Russian in origin, were destroyed. French Union casualties in the operation were light. Combat losses amounted to only one man killed and six wounded, the majority of friendly casualties (four dead and 102 incapacitated) being due to heat stroke.[78] Nineteen men were injured in the jump itself, and casualties from accidents included four killed, thirty-one injured, and one missing in a truck accident in the 57th Vietnamese Battalion (*57e Bataillon Vietnamien*, 57e BVN).

Viet Minh losses during Operation HIRONDELLE were substantial, although Lieutenant General Navarre later called the destruction of the Viet Minh depots "*malheureusement trés partielle*" (unfortunately very partial).[79] Viet Minh personnel losses included twenty-one killed and five wounded. About 450 civilians were evacuated from the operational area to zones controlled by the French. Some fifty-five pounds of documents were destroyed and another five pounds were recovered for subsequent evaluation. The materiel losses of the Viet Minh were heavy, and the weapons, ammunition, and other equipment destroyed by the French included 250 cases of Skoda automatic rifles (4 per case, for a total of 1,000) and 2 separate Skoda automatic rifles; 13 MAT 49 submachine guns; 10 Thompson submachine guns; 45 chargers for automatic rifles and submachine guns; 6 American .30-caliber carbines; 4 U.S. rifles; 230 rifles and pistols of various makes; 1 ton of various munitions; 4 GMC trucks; 2 Molotova trucks; 17,655 cubic feet of diverse materiel (55 truck engines, gear boxes, etc.); 250 tires; 4,754 gallons of gasoline; 15 electric motors; 8 machine tools (lathes, etc.); 1 electric generator; 1 telephone switchboard; 4 telephones; 4 typewriters; 20,000 pairs of shoes (of Chinese manufacture); 141 cubic feet of cloth; 1 ton of tea; 500 cartons of cigarettes (Russian); and other miscellaneous items.[80]

The success of Operation HIRONDELLE was due to two major factors: the total surprise of the enemy and the rapidity with which the destruction of the objectives and the withdrawal of the committed troops was effected.[81] The complete surprise of the Viet Minh was due to a number of factors, including the choice of an objective far from friendly bases; the secrecy of preparations (small number of planners, limited copies of orders delivered by hand or opened only at sea); deception measures, including the issuance of false orders; confinement of the paras after they were briefed on the operation; the absence of all prepositioning movements; and the violence and simultaneity of the airborne and ground action. The speed of execution of the operation was due to the intense efforts of the participants, sustained day and night for the duration of the operation. For example, the paras, having made the parachute assault on Lang Son, moved thirty-seven miles entirely on foot in only thirty hours. Some of the ground element units moved forward more than thirty-four miles from their debarkation point at Pointe Pagode in less than thirty hours, while the engineers repaired more than thirty-seven miles of RC 4 in forty hours of uninterrupted work. The motor transport units of the *Train* operated constantly day and night for four days, with time out only for necessary repairs and resupply.

Operation HIRONDELLE was one of the few French operations against the Viet Minh base areas that met all three of the criteria for success: sound target intelligence, detailed and secret preparations, and rapid execution.[82] Target intelligence for HIRONDELLE was excellent, and the outcome of the operation revealed that it was better to attack a number of well-reconnoitered targets with several battalions than to raid a small, often improperly identified installation with a single company or platoon. In large measure, the success of Operation HIRONDELLE was due to the stringent security measures that were taken to prevent the Viet Minh from learning of the planned raid. The plans were made in absolute secrecy by the task force commander and one intelligence officer, and the operations orders were drawn up only after July 15. Participating units were alerted at 1400 hours on July 14 and confined to their quarters. The commander of the airborne troops briefed the operation at 1500 hours on July 16, and subordinate commanders had just one hour to conduct their own briefings. The first aircraft took off at 0700 hours on July 17.

General Giap's offensives against the vital Red River delta in 1951 demonstrated the danger and futility of attempting major offensive operations with forces inadequately prepared for the logistical problems of mounting large, extended operations far from the established bases of supply, particularly if those operations were directed against a well-supplied and competent defender. However, the abortive 1951 offensives served an important purpose for the Viet Minh by pointing out the work still to be done in creating an effective logistical staff and working out effective methods for the support of large-scale offensives. The lessons presented to General Giap and his subordinate commanders were well-learned, and subsequently the Viet Minh logistical system was to demonstrate a continually improving capability to plan and execute the logistical support of large-scale, extended operations far from its bases in the Viet Bac.

The success of French Union operations against the Viet Minh base areas was contingent on careful preparation, the achievement of a high degree of surprise (in turn dependent on good operational security), and the rapidity with which the operation was carried out. On the whole, all of these conditions were seldom met and many of the French operations, such as Operation LORRAINE, found the enemy well-prepared to oppose the invading force and having already removed an important part of his supplies and equipment to more secure locations. Moreover, the logistical burdens of large-scale operations into the Viet Minh rear areas were heavy, and as Operation LORRAINE (and before it, Operation LEA) demonstrated, the results achieved were seldom commensurate with the resources committed. On the other hand, when the necessary criteria of success were met, as in Operation MARS and again in Operation HIRONDELLE, the French Union forces were able to inflict considerable damage on the Viet Minh logistical system with relatively small forces and with minimal friendly losses. Despite the successes achieved, overall the French operations designed to cripple the Viet Minh by the seizure and destruction of their logistical bases failed to produce the desired results and, in fact, did very little to slow the buildup of the Viet Minh regular forces or hamper their offensive operations.

Vo Nguyen Giap and Ho Chi Minh, 1942. (Author's collection.)

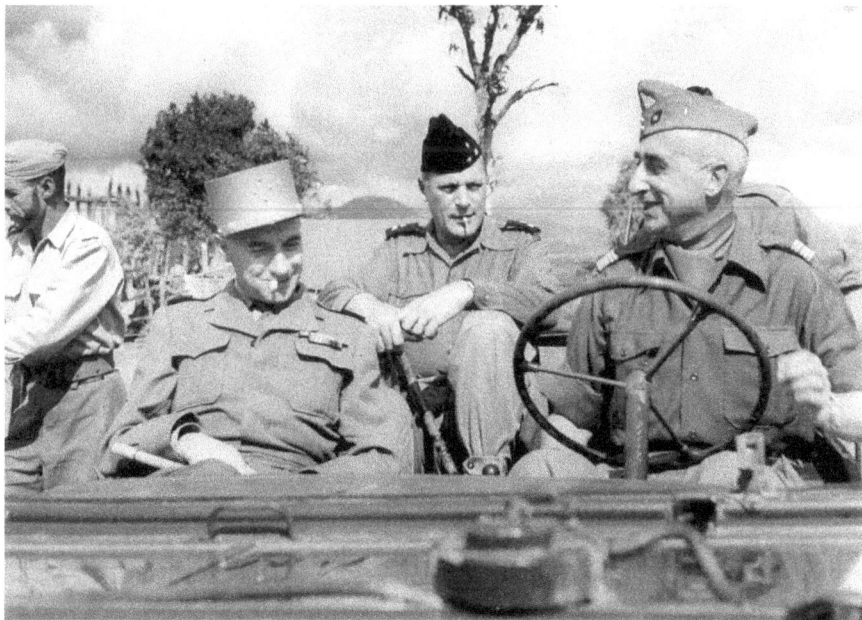

Generals Henri Navarre and René Cogny with Colonel Christian de la Croix de Castries (*left to right*) in Laos near the end of 1953. (Courtesy of Raymond Cauchetier/Rue des Archives, Paris, France/The Granger Collection, New York, New York.)

American half-track delivered at the port of Saigon in 1951. (Courtesy of Établissement de Communication et de Production Audiovisuelle de la Défense, Ivry-sur-Seine, France.)

Lt. Gen. John W. O'Daniel, chief of the USMAAG-Indochina, April 1954–October 1955. (Courtesy of the U.S. Army Center of Military History, Fort Leslie J. McNair, District of Columbia/U.S. Army photograph.)

Molotova truck and Viet Minh supply cave captured during Operation
HIRONDELLE, July 1953. Many of the crates bore Chinese markings.
(Courtesy of Établissement de Communication et de Production
Audiovisuelle de la Défense, Ivry-sur-Seine, France.)

French *base aéro-terrestre* on the Plaine des Jarres, Laos, 1953. (Courtesy of
the U.S. Army Military History Institute, Carlisle Barracks, Pennsylvania.)

Aerial view of Dien Bien Phu, November 1953. Note the C-47s on the airfield (*center*). (Courtesy of Établissement de Communication et de Production Audiovisuelle de la Défense, Ivry-sur-Seine, France.)

Preparing rations for parachute drop to Dien Bien Phu at Gia Lam Airfield, Hanoi, April 1954. (Courtesy of Établissement de Communication et de Production Audiovisuelle de la Défense, Ivry-sur-Seine, France.)

Tank reassembly line at Dien Bien Phu. (Courtesy of Établissement de Communication et de Production Audiovisuelle de la Défense, Ivry-sur-Seine, France.)

Paradrop to a French patrol, 1953. (Courtesy of the U.S. Army Military History Institute, Carlisle Barracks, Pennsylvania.)

C-119 paradrop, Muong Sai, Laos, February 1954. (Courtesy of the U.S. Army Military History Institute, Carlisle Barracks, Pennsylvania.)

More than twenty thousand pack-bikes served the Dien Bien Phu campaign. (Courtesy of Vietnam Pictorial/Vietnam News Agency, Hanoi, Vietnam.)

During the Second Indochina War, Viet Cong porters used bicycles similar to those used by the Viet Minh. (Courtesy of the U.S. Army Military History Institute, Carlisle Barracks, Pennsylvania.)

Supplies coming down the Ho Chi Minh trail

Trucks of the Viet Minh Transport Department crossing a stream en route to Dien Bien Phu. (Courtesy of *Vietnam Pictorial*/Vietnam News Agency, Hanoi, Vietnam.)

The 308th Viet Minh Division enters Hanoi on GAZ-51 trucks, October 10, 1954. (Courtesy of *Vietnam Pictorial*/Vietnam News Agency, Hanoi, Vietnam.)

11

The Campaign for the Lines of Communication

The third logistical campaign of the First Indochina War encompassed the battles for control of the lines of communication. Although control of the limited roads and waterways of Indochina was a major objective of both sides throughout the war, the struggle reached its greatest intensity, particularly in the critical area of operations in Tonkin, between late 1952 and May 1954. As the Viet Minh turned from challenging the French for control of the vital Red River delta to extended operations in the remote regions of northwestern Tonkin far from the bases of either side, the interdiction of the opponent's supply lines became even more important, and the success of any given operation came to hinge on the degree to which one side or the other could keep their forces in the field adequately supplied. In the end, the manpower-intensive logistical system of the Viet Minh proved more resilient and better adapted to the terrain and operational conditions than the heavily mechanized French support system, which became increasingly dependent on the use of always scarce and often unreliable air transport.

Throughout the war the interdiction of French ground and water communication was a major component of Viet Minh strategy. Sabotage and ambush proved effective means for the generally weaker Viet Minh to deny to the French the use of Indochina's limited surface transportation network. Despite the expenditure of enormous resources of men and materiel, the French Union forces were unable to guarantee the free and continuous use of ground or water transport to supply their scattered and often isolated forces. At the same time, French efforts to interdict the Viet Minh lines of supply, principally by the use of airpower, achieved only limited success. The growing size and technological sophistication of the Viet Minh forces, as well as the decision to conduct extended operations far from their bases in the Viet Bac, increased the vulnerability of the Viet Minh logistical system to French interdiction efforts, but at the same time the Viet Minh became increasingly adept at masking their logistical movements.

In a succession of extended operations around Hoa Binh (November 1951–February 1952), in the T'ai country of northwestern Tonkin (October–December 1952), and in Upper Laos (April–May 1953) the Viet Minh demonstrated their ability to support large conventional forces far from their fixed bases of supply. Relying on porters as their principal means of transport, the Viet Minh were able to move men and supplies freely in areas devoid of improved roads and despite French air superiority. For the French, operations in the remote regions of Tonkin and Upper Laos posed the problem of supporting numerous small defensive outposts almost entirely by air. Although the French achieved some successes, notably at Na San in 1952–1953, the strain of maintaining their lines of communication to their defensive outposts were enormous.

In the hope of maximizing the impact of their advantage in air transport and reducing the burden of supporting numerous isolated outposts, in mid-1953 the French launched a series of vigorous offensive operations designed to isolate the main Viet Minh combat elements and force upon them a decisive battle under unfavorable logistical conditions. The centerpiece of such operations was the "air-land base" (*base aéro-terrestre*), also known as the "hedgehog" (*hérrison*), a strongly fortified camp established and supported entirely by air and used both as a base of operations for forays against the Viet Minh lines of supply and as bait to entice the Viet Minh to concentrate their forces and engage in a decisive battle. The French strategy achieved some minor successes in south and central Viet Nam but led eventually to Operation CASTOR, the establishment of a fortified advance base in northwestern Tonkin beginning in November 1953, the first stage of the decisive battle of Dien Bien Phu, which would ultimately result in the major Viet Minh victory that brought the war to an end.

French Convoy Operations, 1945–1954

Throughout the First Indochina War, the French sought to make maximum use of the limited road and waterway network in Indochina, while the Viet Minh endeavored to make such usage as costly as possible if not stop it altogether. The Viet Minh were past masters at the art of sabotage and sudden, unexpected guerrilla-type attacks on highways and waterways. The ambush of tactical and logistical convoys by Viet Minh guerrillas, or even by units of the *Chu Luc*, became a salient characteristic of the war. Viet Minh ambushes were almost always carefully planned and prepared in detail.

The standard procedure was not only to stop and destroy the target element, but also to engage and destroy any forces sent to the relief of the force under attack.[1] Accordingly, the typical Viet Minh ambush involved the coordinated action of three elements. A stationary blocking force would set up the ambush at a suitable site, usually in an area that provided good cover and concealment for the ambushers and where the maneuver and speed of the target were restricted. The second, or main element, was then posted on both sides of the road if possible, some 500–1,000 yards down the road from the blocking force. Once the target convoy had been halted by the blocking element, the second element attacked the convoy's flank from their concealed and covered positions. A third element was usually posted even further back down the road and was assigned the mission of blocking any retreat from the ambush site and of ambushing any relief forces that might be dispatched. The size of such ambushes might range from the attack of a small convoy by a Viet Minh regional or local force squad up to major ambushes by six thousand regular troops along a one- to three-mile stretch of highway.[2] The French discovered that their troops and vehicles could take fire at any time at ranges of up to one thousand yards or might be ambushed even immediately after a friendly patrol had passed through the area safely.[3]

The success of such actions depended on security to hide the ambush from French ground and air reconnaissance and on rapid, violent execution to overwhelm the defenders with surprise and superior firepower. Often the Viet Minh ambushers disguised themselves as civilians, as friendly troops, or even as women. The same deception measures continued to be used by the Viet Cong during the Second Indochina War. In August 1968, a U.S. convoy from Long Binh to Tay Ninh was caught in a large ambush near Go Dau Ha. The Viet Cong were in plain sight along both sides of the road, disguised as friendly regional force soldiers who smiled and waved to the passing convoy before putting it under a withering fire. The mining of roads used by the French Union forces was also highly successful. In early 1954, the French lost an average of thirty vehicles and fifty men killed or wounded each week due to Viet Minh mines.[4]

More often than not, the Viet Minh ambushers succeeded in interdicting the surface routes used by the French. The French Union forces tried various countermeasures, including the lengthening of convoys to prevent all vehicles being caught in the kill zone, but until the end of the war the mining and ambush of highway and inland water movements was an effective Viet Minh tool.

Ambush of the Ban Me Thuot Convoy, December 1945

Highway motor transport operations were a primary function of the units of the *Train* of the French Far East Expeditionary Corps (*Corps Expéditionnaire Français d'Extrême-Orient*, CEFEO). The first *Train* units arrived at Saigon on October 24, 1945, and the first *Train* casualties (two wounded) were taken in the course of an ambush on the road from Saigon into Cambodia less than a month later, on November 18.[5] The first fatal casualties among the *trainglots* occurred on December 20, 1945, during an ambush of a convoy returning from Ban Me Thuot to Saigon.[6] Although a small and unimportant encounter in and of itself, the ambush of the Ban Me Thuot convoy on December 20, 1945, stands as a classic example of a type of combat action that would become all too familiar to French Union soldiers over the next nine years.

During December 1945, the recently arrived CEFEO undertook to clear the roads in the Central Highlands of southern Annam leading to the town of Ban

Me Thuot. On December 16, a resupply convoy consisting of twenty-five vehicles from two platoons of the *Train* (1st Platoon, 171st Transport Company, and 3rd Platoon, 271st Transport Company) left Gia Dinh on the outskirts of Saigon bound for Ban Me Thuot. The convoy arrived at its destination without incident on December 18, unloaded, and prepared to depart for Saigon at daybreak on the 20th. However, on the night of December 19–20, Ban Me Thuot came under Viet Minh attack, and the convoy did not depart until 0800 hours. At 0845 hours, three miles south of the town, the convoy was caught in a strong Viet Minh ambush in an area of dense forest where both sides of the road were bordered by impenetrable thorns and vines. At a turn in the road, the head of the column suddenly encountered a roadblock of fallen trees. The infantry escort immediately set out to clear the ambush site on foot with the aid of the drivers and covered by automatic rifles and the machine guns ring-mounted on the trucks. Viet Minh automatic weapons fire swept down on the halted convoy, but several of the trucks at the head of the convoy succeeded in driving away. However, the driver and NCO machine gunner of the leading vehicle were killed just at the moment their truck hit a second obstacle of stumps and rocks. With the exception of the men manning the machine guns, the remaining convoy personnel took shelter in the ditches and returned fire at the unseen enemy. Meanwhile, the escort rushed to clear the second roadblock. An NCO took the place of the dead driver of the first truck, but he soon fell, as did the driver of another truck who was attempting to reposition his machine gun. The column was thus completely immobilized, and the enemy rained grenades upon it from all sides.

The convoy commander, returning down the line, succeeded in getting the two last GMC trucks to make an acrobatic detour under a hail of bullets. The two drivers rushed back to Ban Me Thuot to seek assistance. The situation of the transport element and its escort rapidly became tragic as hidden Viet Minh snipers adjusted their fire, and French losses mounted. Around 1130 hours, the relief column from Ban Me Thuot surged forward with two armored cars, a half-track, and a group from the Light Intervention Corps transported on the two trucks that had earlier escaped the ambush. The enemy immediately ceased fire and melted into the jungle. The attack had cost the convoy seven killed and six seriously wounded, but the tribulations of the column were not yet at an end. The following day, on the return route to Saigon, it encountered another ambush from which it was able to extricate itself after a half-hour of combat. Two additional *trainglots* were wounded.

The scenario of the Ban Me Thuot convoy would be replayed many times before the end of the First Indochina War. None of these small ambushes of resupply convoys constituted a significant loss to the French Union forces as a whole, but taken together, the accumulation of ambush losses amounted to a significant destruction of men and equipment. More importantly, the threat of such actions inhibited the full use of the limited highways of Indochina and forced the French to rely increasingly on aerial resupply to meet their logistical requirements, a task which the French air forces in Indochina could not possibly accomplish with the limited transport aircraft and pilots at their disposal.

Route Security

The security of the land lines of communication throughout Indochina was a continuing problem for the French. Most importantly, the attempt to provide secure movement over the roads and waterways tied down a significant number of French Union troops in static, isolated, and vulnerable outposts and thus diminished the French capacity for offensive operations. To counter the Viet Minh interdiction of the highways and waterways, the French were obliged to develop a number of preventive measures and counterambush techniques. Despite the application of significant amounts of men and materiel, none of these measures to minimize Viet Minh sabotage and ambush operations was able to guarantee the French unrestricted use of surface transport in the theater.

Responsibility for security of the highway routes as well as for the regulation of military and civilian motor transport and the establishment of supporting facilities was assigned to the various territorial commanders. From the start it was recognized that the extent of the road network, the difficult terrain through which most of the roads passed, and the limited manpower resources available meant that most routes could be secured only during daylight hours (if at all) and that the control of those routes would have to be ceded to the Viet Minh at night. Given that concession, the French authorities sought to control the lines of communication by four principal methods: the establishment of fixed outposts and watchtowers to protect key routes by observation and fire; the use of patrols to clear roads and the use of larger combat formations to establish and hold secure corridors; the use of mobile forces, often armored, to intervene as required; and the institution of a variety of traffic regulation and convoy defense measures to maximize the security of movements over the contested routes.[7]

To maintain observation over key land routes, the French established a chain of manned watchtowers along critical roads.[8] First employed in Cochinchina beginning in 1948, the watchtower system was later extended to Annam and to a lesser extent in Tonkin. The watchtowers, usually constructed of timber or masonry at a cost of about $3,000 each, were set up along a stretch of road within sight of one another (normally about one kilometer apart) and manned by five or six Indochinese auxiliary soldiers led by a French NCO or junior officer.[9] The families of the men manning the towers usually lived nearby, thereby increasing the squalor and decreasing the security of the post. "Mother towers," larger and with increased firepower, were established at greater intervals and were manned by regular troops and equipped with periscopes, electric generators, armored firing ports, and turrets.[10] Theoretically, the posts were supported by artillery, but the Viet Minh soon learned to mount diversionary attacks on outposts near the main objective. The resulting multiple calls for fire usually ensured that the post under main attack was inadequately supported.

The missions of the men assigned to these towers were to prevent the Viet Minh from cutting the road, to protect local facilities, to observe movements, to assist friendly vehicles, and to contribute to the protection of vehicles in case of attack. In the event of an ambush, the nearest watchtower sounded the alarm and prevented additional vehicles from entering the danger area while mobile reaction forces moved to the relief of the elements under attack. Initially, the system worked quite well, but after the Viet Minh obtained shaped-charge rockets from Communist China in 1950, the system in central Viet Nam began to fall apart. The shaped-charge projectiles could penetrate the masonry watchtowers, and the garrison of a threatened tower usually preferred to abandon their post rather than risk certain destruction. In any event, it was obviously impossible to establish a full chain of watchtowers on every important road in Indochina.

To supplement the system of watchtowers, the French also found it necessary to institute a number of other physical measures to provide additional security on the roads. They found that paving the roadways made it more difficult for the Viet Minh to plant mines or booby traps. In contested areas trees and brush were cleared up to 100–200 yards from each side of the road and the cultivation of tall crops (corn, sugar cane, etc.) in those areas was prohibited. In extreme cases, it became necessary to clear the inhabitants from villages located less than five hundred yards from the road, but such measures were adopted reluctantly due to the ill-will created among the displaced villagers.

All routes, even those in relatively secure areas, had to be patrolled regularly on foot or by vehicle to prevent or discover Viet Minh sabotage and potential ambushes. This was normally accomplished by one of two principal methods. Even well-traveled routes in reasonably well-pacified regions usually belonged to the Viet Minh at night and thus had to be cleared each morning. The French did try to patrol roads at night with armored forces equipped with infrared night vision devices, but the attempts proved unsuccessful due to the technical limitations of the night vision equipment. Another technique considered was the use of armored or motorized patrols equipped with powerful searchlights. The French also attempted to employ fast-moving night convoys and achieved some success as long as no mines were encountered and the procedure was not attempted repetitively along the same route.[11]

Daily "road-clearing" operations were conducted by foot and vehicular patrols as a tactical operation, the troops on foot being necessary to discover and disarm any mines and booby traps. The normal road-clearing procedure was to have Moroccan, Algerian, or Senegalese troops walk the route in front of the armored vehicles manned by French soldiers, although the non-European troops did not much appreciate this method, which exposed them to disproportionate danger from Viet Minh mines and booby traps.[12] Such operations in secure areas might involve only a squad, but in more hazardous areas they might require one or two infantry battalions supported by armor, artillery, aircraft, and engineers. Such was the case in May–June 1954 for the daily opening of RC 5 between Hanoi and Haiphong in the vicinity of Ban Yen Nhan. Vital and frequently used roadways were cleared daily, while some secondary routes were opened only at irregular intervals. Routes in particularly insecure areas might be opened only for a specific tactical operation or not at all. In some cases, the usual daily road-clearing operation was insufficient to guarantee the security of the route. It then became necessary to employ the more costly and time-consuming method of establishing a "secure corridor" by clearing the areas along the route with combat troops. Usually such a security cordon was kept in place only long enough to pass a convoy over the route, but in some cases a secure corridor might be maintained for several days. In other cases, it proved impossible to maintain a secure corridor. For example, in Tonkin at the beginning of 1954, not a single secure corridor could be guaranteed, and at noon on March 12 a company-size convoy escorted by a platoon of half-tracks was nearly wiped out near Ban Yen Nhan on the road between Hanoi and Haiphong, even though the road had been "opened" early in the day.[13]

In addition to providing the troops to conduct daily road-clearing operations and establish secure corridors as needed, the territorial commands also maintained detachments of infantry and armor on alert to respond to incidents along the routes and rescue ambushed convoys. The territorial commands also maintained radio nets that were invaluable for maintaining control of the routes. Major convoys normally were equipped with their own radio nets that provided necessary internal convoy communications and permitted the territorial command to track the progress of the convoy. Whenever possible, aircraft conducted route reconnaissance, relayed radio traffic, and attacked Viet Minh ambushes.

Traffic Regulation

The various highway routes in Indochina were classified into one of four categories: Normal, Controlled, Regulated, or Prohibited.[14] Normal routes could be used day and night by all types of vehicles operating alone or in groups. Controlled routes could be utilized only during fixed hours of daylight and after the road had been declared "clear." Single vehicles or convoys could run freely during the periods a Controlled road remained "open." Regulated routes were open only on certain days and then only to military or civilian vehicles furnished with an "integration ticket." When the security cordon on such routes was continuous, vehicles might be allowed to proceed singly or in groups at prescribed intervals (the "continuous flow" or *courant de transport* method). If a route were used regularly, the "continuous flow" method discouraged enemy attacks since it limited the number of vehicles that might be caught in an ambush at any one time and place. However, it did require good driver discipline (and a lot of nerve) to proceed alone through dangerous areas, and isolated vehicles were admittedly exposed to easy capture by only one or two enemy soldiers. If the security cordon were not continuous, the normal method was to organize the vehicles in escorted convoys of fifteen to twenty vehicles per serial. Prohibited routes could not be used at all except in the case of active operations.

No control measures were necessary for Normal routes, but on Controlled routes the drivers had to obtain the necessary authorization to proceed from a control post at either end of the route where travel authorizations were verified. Of course, the control measures were most detailed and onerous for travel on Regulated routes. Vehicles operating on Regulated routes under the continuous flow method were dispatched over the route at fixed intervals of one or two minutes and were controlled en route by traffic regulation units. The more secure escorted convoy method used on the more dangerous routes involved what was for all intents and purposes a coordinated combat operation with fixed schedules, checkpoints, full communications, and support available on call. In general, it was found desirable to restrict such convoys to fewer than 100–130 vehicles.

Traffic regulation was an assigned function of the *Train,* which provided specialized units to maintain order on the routes, facilitate movements, and ensure the necessary communications and coordination. Traffic regulation units as well as maintenance teams and mobile radio units were infused in the flow of vehicles operating over Regulated routes under the continuous flow rules. The same services were provided in the case of escorted convoys, but were integrated into the operation under the direction of the designated convoy commander. Among the fixed traffic regulation facilities operated by the *Train* were the terminals, which operated in the convoy assembly areas or at the departure point for Regulated routes and which were headed by an officer of the *Train.* Control posts were established at the exits from towns and villages or at other designated points along the route to check off the vehicles using the route and to verify their travel documents. Required halting places were established along the Regulated routes to permit the reassembly of convoy serials and to maintain control over the movement of the convoys. Routes that required more than a day to traverse were provided with way stations where the drivers could rest, obtain a hot meal, obtain medical treatment, or fix their vehicle.

In addition to controlling military highway operations, the French authorities in Indochina had to make provision for the free circulation of civilian traffic in order to maintain the economic life of the country. Rules for the movement of civilian as well as military traffic were made by the territorial commanders, and in general the movement of civilian vehicles was conducted using the same methods as for military vehicles. When integrated into military convoys (as on a Regulated route), the civilian vehicles came under the orders of the convoy commander.

The "Operational Convoy"

From the beginning to the end of the war, the insecurity of the highways in Indochina obliged the French to consider all motor transport operations as tactical movements. That is, all motor transport activity was conducted under "alert" conditions regardless of the presumed security of the area through which it was traveling, the size of the elements moving, or the type of movement (cargo, troops, etc.).[15] Unit (troop) movements by road particularly subscribed to the "movement on alert" procedures. Although resupply vehicles might be integrated into a troop movement convoy, it was always the troop unit commander who was responsible for the execution of the movement and for the associated security measures.[16] In coordination with the commander of any elements of the *Train* participating, the troop commander prescribed the organization of the convoy and all security measures to be taken in the case of an ambush. The vehicles of the troop unit were normally grouped in the center of the convoy with all troops embarked on the trucks ready to dismount and maneuver to defeat any ambush. Armored cars posted at the tail of the convoy were normally used to protect broken-down vehicles and return them to their position. Elements of the moving unit were used to protect the rear of the convoy in the absence of the escorting armored cars.

As time went on, the improving security situation on the roads in Cochinchina permitted the gradual elimination of restrictions on vehicular movements, but in Tonkin the constant infiltration of Viet Minh units even into the interior of the delta region required ever more stringent control methods to ensure the security of friendly highway traffic.[17] The French situation in northern Tonkin began to deteriorate seriously in early 1948 as the Viet Minh increased their pressure against the outposts along RC 4, and for a time in 1948 the French had to suspend convoy operations in northern Tonkin altogether due to a lack of manpower. They chose instead to open a few key roads just long enough to pass through a convoy.[18] By 1949, the concept of the "operational convoy" was developed as a solution to the problem of forcing through resupply convoys to the isolated outposts in northern Tonkin.[19] In essence, the concept involved treating what were essentially logistical movements as full-blown combat operations with attendant fire and air support plans as well as the integration of infantry, armor, and artillery into the convoy itself. The success of such convoy operations was dependent on good reconnaissance and effective communications, particularly between the convoy and any supporting aircraft or artillery units.

A typical "operational convoy" from Lang Son to That Kien moved at about ten miles per hour and took three to five days to complete.[20] By mid-1950, the time required to move an operational convoy from Lang Son to Cao Bang (a distance of 124 miles) required a full two weeks.[21] The convoy began with the assembly of the convoy vehicles and support elements at a departure staging area. Normally, the convoy was organized with an armored escort (one or two armored vehicles with infantry support aboard) in the front, followed by the operational command post with communications links to the bases and to other convoy elements. The operational command post often included an artillery liaison detachment and direct fire artillery pieces. Next came the *Train* command post, which included a traffic regulation detachment, a radio vehicle, and a GMC truck loaded with infantry support. The main body of the convoy consisted of a variable number of serials of ten to twelve task vehicles (cargo trucks) each. Bringing up the rear was a trail element composed of a command post, radio vehicles, wreckers, and an armored escort.[22] "Operational convoys" normally were provided with air cover and could call for assistance to combat forces maintained on alert at the departure base or elsewhere along the route. It was not unusual for such convoys to have to fight for every mile of the route.

Riverine Convoys

The Viet Minh were also adept at impeding the use by French Union forces of the inland waterways of Indochina. Ambushes, often at bends in the river or canal where the French craft were only five to ten yards from the bank, and the use of mines were common.[23] The steps taken by the French to ensure the security of inland waterway movements in Indochina were very similar to those taken for highway movements. Some inland waterways were protected by outposts and watchtowers sited at intervals, but the establishment of secure corridors was possible only on the Saigon, Mekong, and Bassac Rivers and along certain stretches of the Red River. Except on the most heavily used waterways or the broader rivers, riverine movements generally required the use of convoys escorted by armed vessels and preceded by minesweepers.[24]

The French Navy developed standard procedures for escorted riverine convoys.[25] A typical riverine convoy formation is shown in figure 11.1. The armed riverine convoys organized by the French Navy should not be confused with the famous *Dinassaut*, river craft combat units of the French Navy organized to support ground operations along the waterways of Indochina.[26] The procedures employed called for careful planning of all riverine convoy operations, including coordination with supporting air and artillery forces, although U.S. observers rated French coordination of support as poor. The U.S. MAAG-Indochina commander, Lieutenant General O'Daniel, for one, observed, "There is an obvious lack of coordination in joint operations, and small craft troop convoys in ambush

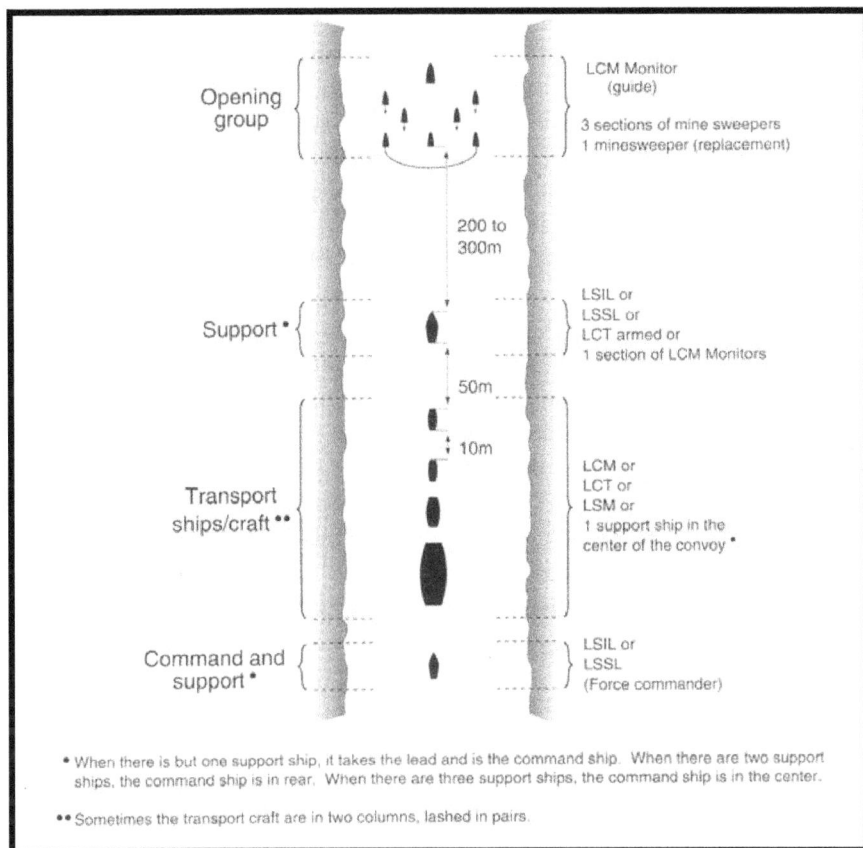

Figure 11.1. Typical French Riverine Convoy in Tonkin. (*Lessons Learned in the Indochina War,* 2:176 [figure 17].)

country have not received either observation or air support, either of which would normally ensure a safe journey, barring the ever present threat of mines."[27]

Normally, riverine convoys were organized with an "opening group" consisting of an LCM Monitor (an armored, armed LCM) as guide, three sections of minesweepers, and one relief minesweeper followed by the "main body" sailing two hundred to three hundred yards back and consisting of fire-support vessels (LSSLs or LSILs, heavily armed LCTs, or sections of LCM Monitors) and the transport vessels (LSMs, LCTs, LCMs, or other types of cargo craft).[28] If only one support vessel were available, it usually carried the force commander and took station at the head of the main body. If two were available, one was posted at the head of the main body and the other, carrying the force commander, followed the main body. If three were available, the command vessel took position in the center of the main body. The distance between vessels in a riverine convoy varied, but fifty yards between larger vessels and ten to twenty yards between smaller vessels was common. Whenever possible the convoy proceeded in two parallel columns, and the cargo craft were often lashed in pairs. Army resupply LCMs of the *Train* participated in many operational movements in central Annam and Tonkin, in which case they were integrated into the formation under navy control. Occasionally, LCMs of the *Train* carried out operational movements alone. On such occasions it was necessary to provide small patrol craft to scout ahead of the boat convoy.

Riverine convoys often were supported by aircraft for reconnaissance and close air support, and the technique of reconnaissance by fire by the escort vessels was common and generally quite effective in causing the Viet Minh attackers to disclose their positions prematurely. Embarked marine infantry were prepared to conduct a hasty assault landing to clear any Viet Minh ambush. In particularly hazardous areas, the convoys proceeded with all stations manned and the personnel alert. In the event an ambush was encountered, the convoy and its escort vessels immediately laid down a heavy volume of fire on the suspected Viet Minh position and surged forward to break through the ambush site as rapidly as possible in what was known as the "Ball of Fire" method. Such actions required the rapid establishment of fire superiority, which in turn required sufficient numbers of armed and armored escort vessels that in fact were not always available. Experience and training permitted the movement of such convoys even at night, when any potential Viet Minh ambusher would be at a disadvantage in that the flash of his weapons could be seen better.

The Costs of Convoy Operations in Indochina

The effort to control the land lines of communication in Indochina imposed a heavy burden on the French Union forces, both in terms of the resources required to protect the routes and convoys and in terms of the casualties and equipment losses suffered. The cost of securing installations and routes only increased as the war dragged on due to the gradual improvement in Viet Minh capabilities and the extension of their influence into new areas.

Keeping the roads open to traffic required a significant proportion of the available French Union combat manpower in Indochina. Well over a third of the infantry forces available in Indochina, fixed or mobile, were used for guard duties.[29] Even the mobile groups had to use about one-quarter of their personnel to protect command posts, artillery positions, and the heavy equipment. In March of 1953, for example, both the French and the Viet Minh had about ninety maneuver battalions available in Tonkin, but the French had to assign sixty-five of their battalions to protect their rear areas and lines of communication, thus leaving only twenty-five battalions for mobile offensive operations.[30] Even in reasonably secure areas, the equivalent of one infantry battalion and one artillery battery were required to maintain control of a twelve-mile section of road that the Viet Minh could threaten with only one company.[31] In the more dangerous areas, it often was necessary to cordon the area surrounding the roadway and conduct a clearance operation, which was very costly in terms of time and the manpower required. As one French battalion commander noted, "If movements were slow, it was less because of the difficulty of the terrain than because we had to search everything, see everything, go through everything, and distrust everything."[32] Convoy escorts also required significant resources. A convoy of two hundred vehicles might require an escort force of up to five infantry battalions, two artillery groups, and two squadrons of armored cars, and even a small convoy usually required an escort consisting of the better part of two infantry battalions.[33]

A study made of road security requirements on four selected routes in Tonkin during the first half of 1954 determined that the cost of opening sixty miles of road for six to ten hours per day averaged three to ten men killed, wounded, or missing.[34] On the routes studied, the defensive posts were spaced about three to five miles apart and required a manning of about thirty to fifty combat troops per mile. Daily road-opening operations required about sixteen men per mile. The study concluded that the costs of controlling an axis of communication, in terms of time and manpower, was exceptionally high, particularly if the area through which the route ran had not been thoroughly pacified, and thus it was less costly to pacify the area than to control only the roadways.[35] Alternatively, it was found that it might be more desirable to open the routes only as they were needed, although opening a route for a specific operation also required a good deal of engineer support. One sector commander noted: "There must be some greater return from the effort made to extend control over an area than merely being able to resupply posts whose main purpose is to keep the line of communication open. A commander must be prepared to relinquish control of the routes that are not absolutely indispensable to him, even if this means that certain selected routes will have to be forcibly reopened for a specific operation and kept open throughout its duration."[36] The soundness of this view was borne out by the reopening of part of RC 2 for Operation LORRAINE and of RP 59 for Operation MOUETTE.

It should come as no surprise that the men who operated on the dangerous highways and inland waterways of Indochina were no less valorous than their comrades in the infantry, armored forces, or artillery or that they suffered high casualties in performing their mission. In the course of the war the 511th Transport Group (*Groupe de Transport 511*, GT 511), which operated in Cochinchina, Laos, and the Central Highlands, earned a division-level unit citation and 381 individual citations. GT 516, operating in Tonkin, earned four unit citations (two of which were Army-level) and 927 individual citations while losing thirty-eight men killed in action, twenty-six missing in action, and sixty-seven wounded in action.[37] The *Train* in Tonkin in three years (1948–1950) lost forty-nine men killed, fifty-two missing, and sixty-six wounded.[38] Most of the losses were accumulated in small increments over time, but a few major ambushes were catastrophic. The most infamous incident was the destruction of Mobile Group 100 in the Mu Gia Pass in the Central Highlands in June 1954. GM 100, composed principally of a French battalion that had recently been transferred to Indochina from Korea, was annihilated by the Viet Minh and lost nearly 1,100 men (50 killed, 253 wounded, and 771 missing), 240 vehicles, and an entire artillery group (sixteen 105 mm howitzers).[39]

French Interdiction Efforts

While struggling to protect their own lines of communication, the French Union forces also expended enormous efforts to interdict Viet Minh supply lines. The use of naval and riverine forces to control Viet Minh water traffic and the use of French-led guerrilla forces to block Viet Minh surface transport achieved some success, but air interdiction proved to be less successful than might have been expected, given the total French air superiority in Indochina. Difficult flying conditions, the lack of sufficient aircraft and pilots, terrain that provided excellent cover and concealment, and effective Viet Minh countermeasures limited the impact of French air interdiction. Although the French inflicted considerable damage and restricted Viet Minh movements in certain areas for limited periods of time, in the end they failed to stop either the movement of supplies from Communist China to the Viet Minh rear depots or the onward movement of supplies from the rear areas to the forward areas of operation.

Control of the Waterways

The French naval and armed riverine forces available to interdict Viet Minh river and coastal traffic were formidable. Even so, the territory to be covered was enormous, nearly 25,500 miles of rivers and nearly 1,900 miles of canals, and the task of impeding Viet Minh use of the complex web of inland waterways was practically impossible, although the French patrol forces were able to control many of the major arteries.[40] Consequently, the Viet Minh were able to use small junks and sampans to move men and materiel on the rivers, canals, and streams of Indochina throughout the war. Coastal interdiction was the responsibility of the French Navy, which had available two aircraft carriers with four dive-bomber and fighter-bomber squadrons embarked as well as a number of land-based aircraft, such as Catalina flying boats that were used for coastal surveillance.[41] Despite a decided advantage in surface vessels and naval reconnaissance and strike aircraft, the French were never entirely successful in totally shutting down the Viet Minh coastal junk traffic, despite the fact that between 1948 and 1952 alone French naval forces stopped and searched some thirty thousand junks and sampans, seizing or destroying over seventeen thousand of them with their cargoes, including 4,000 tons of rice, 2,500 tons of salt, and 284 tons of sugar, plus arms, medicines, and other war materiel.[42] One junk stopped on January 28, 1954, had aboard 1 million Viet Minh *piastres* and a cargo of opium and was en route to obtain hospital supplies.[43]

French Guerrilla Operations

Soon after assuming his post as *commandant en chef* in December 1950, General de Lattre decided to apply some of his scarce resources to the Franco-Vietnamese guerrilla groups operating behind enemy lines. In December 1951 he brought in the well-known guerrilla leader Major Roger Trinquier to command these forces, and by late 1953 there were some twenty thousand French cadre and native guerrillas operating under Trinquier's command.[44] These formations, known as Mixed Native Commando Groups (*Groupes Commandos Mixtes Autochtones,* GCMA) and after December 1953 as Mixed Intervention Groups (*Groupes Mixtes d'Intervention,* GMI), had been in existence for some time but had not been looked upon favorably by most high-level French commanders, probably because of their unorthodox methods of operation and the fact that they tended to drain off the more adventuresome junior officers and NCOs.[45]

Although normally too weak to influence ongoing combat operations or to completely shut down Viet Minh lines of communication, the GCMA/GMI were very effective at long-range reconnaissance and posed a substantial threat to the security of the extended Viet Minh supply lines in the remote areas of northwestern Tonkin. They were an effective use of scarce resources and were greatly feared by the Viet Minh. In mid-1953, some fifteen thousand French and Vietnamese guerrillas were operating in the Viet Minh rear, and General Giap was forced to dedicate as many as ten of his regular force battalions to countering them.[46] Major Trinquier himself claimed that by August 15, 1954, the Viet Minh had deployed fifteen *Chu Luc* battalions, fifteen regional force battalions, and seventeen regional force companies to counter the GMI in their rear areas.[47] Although the GCMA/GMI tied down considerable numbers of Viet Minh troops, forcing them to do what the French had been forced to do for so many years—guard their depots and supply lines—the GCMA/GMI were never very successful in actually interdicting the Viet Minh supply lines, primarily because they could not remain in one area long enough to effect a permanent cut in a supply line without being engaged by a superior Viet Minh force.[48] During the battle of Dien Bien Phu, for example, the GMI tied down three times their own number of Viet Minh troops but were unable to hamper the flow of supplies to the Viet Minh forces surrounding Dien Bien Phu.

The GCMA/GMI had to be supported almost entirely by air, and as their numbers grew they placed an increasingly heavy burden on the limited French air transport services. In 1954, the fifteen thousand French-led guerrillas operating in northeastern Laos and northwestern Tonkin consumed about two hundred tons of supplies per month while tying down seven Viet Minh battalions in January, eleven battalions in March, twelve in April, and perhaps fourteen battalions in May. During the same period, the fifteen thousand men encircled at Dien Bien Phu immobilized twenty-eight Viet Minh infantry battalions, but consumed an average of two hundred tons per *day*.[49]

The success of the GCMA/GMI peaked in October 1953, when French-led guerrillas recruited in the Red River region reoccupied the area around Phong Tho and its airfield and seized Thai Nguyen and held it for seven months. One of the most spectacular GCMA/GMI operations began on October 3, 1953, when a French-led guerrilla force composed of six hundred T'ai and Meo tribesmen and a French paratroop platoon descended on the key Viet Minh supply center at Lao Kay near the Chinese border.[50] The Lao Kay raid was very successful, but interest in the use of French-led guerrilla forces subsequently waned even though they continued to attract the allegiance of increasing numbers of natives.[51] Under terms of the Geneva cease-fire agreements in 1954, the French were not permitted to resupply the GCMA/GMI, many of which continued to operate independently until they were picked off one-by-one by the Viet Minh.[52] In retrospect, despite their poor record as an interdiction force, the GCMA/GMI were a good "cheap" solution to the problem of tying down the Viet Minh, and the failure of the French high command to fully exploit their potential was one of the major mistakes of the war.

Air Interdiction

Despite the total absence of any Viet Minh airpower, the French air forces in Indochina were plagued with a number of handicaps that served to limit the effectiveness of all types of air operations.[53] First, the number of first-class airfields was limited, and the construction of new airfields was slow, difficult, and costly. Consequently, there were only five first-class all-weather airfields to cover all of Indochina. Second, the weather in Indochina severely restricted operations in many areas, and the French weather reporting system was generally limited. For example, the infamous drizzle in Tonkin, known to the French as *crachin* ("spit"), generally made early morning air sorties from the bases in Tonkin impossible. The difference in weather conditions between regions also meant that a sortie might be launched from Hanoi in good weather only to find the target in northwestern Tonkin totally socked in. Third, the maps available were generally inadequate for flight operations and increased the dangers of flying in bad weather. Fourth, the available radio guidance and navigational beacon systems were inadequate for normal flying conditions and even worse for night and bad-weather conditions. Finally, most French airmen complained of the command system in Indochina, which they felt subordinated the air forces to the ground commanders to a degree that seriously limited the effective employment of airpower. They particularly complained that the resources expended on close air support of ground forces might have been used more effectively in interdiction and other missions, although the inadequacies of the French ground combat forces and the political necessity of minimizing the number of casualties obviously required that a large proportion of the available tactical aircraft be utilized in the close air support role.[54] Even so, the coordination between French ground and air forces was generally adequate. All French tactical aviation in Indochina, including naval aircraft, was controlled by three regional commands (North, South, and Central), known as Tactical Air Groups (*Groupements Aériens Tactiques*, GATAC). A separate GATAC temporarily covered Laos in 1953–1954. The GATACs were commanded by a French Air Force brigadier general, and Air Force liaison officers and forward air controllers were assigned to most of the ground combat elements.

The lack of sufficient numbers of suitable aircraft and of trained pilots severely hampered the French air interdiction campaign. Throughout the war the French had far fewer reconnaissance aircraft, fighter-bombers, and light bombers than were necessary to meet the challenges of an air interdiction campaign against the elusive Viet Minh. Bernard Fall noted, "If much of the Indochina war was fought on a thin shoestring, the air war was fought on one that was also badly frayed, and had to be held together by knots at several places."[55] In 1946, the French had to rely on some sixty old British Spitfire fighters whose wood and canvas components often disintegrated in mid-flight, and until 1950 the French bomber forces consisted mainly of French variants of old German Junkers Ju 52 Toucan tri-motors, transports that were "converted" to bombers by the simple expedient of rolling the bombs and napalm canisters out the side door.[56]

Between October 1951 and February 1952, the United States supplied the French with some two hundred aircraft, and by early 1953 the Americans had provided another 160 F6F and F8F fighters, 41 B-26 light bombers, 28 much-needed C-47 transports, 155 aircraft engines, and 93,000 bombs for the French air forces in Indochina.[57] But even after the United States began to supply the French in Indochina with aircraft, the numbers and types remained inadequate for the job. In particular, the lack of strategic bombardment aircraft made the interdiction of Viet Minh supply lines close to the Chinese border nearly impossible. For example, there were never any medium strategic bombers except for a few French Navy PB4Y-2 Privateers, which replaced the older PBY5A Catalinas in 1951 and 1952. In 1954, there were in Indochina two patrol squadrons of Privateers (24F at Tan Son Nhut and 28F at Haiphong), each with seven aircraft.[58] In addition, Squadron

8S, based at Cat Lai near Saigon, provided reconnaissance with Sea Otters and Loire 130s.

The inadequacy of the total number of reconnaissance and ground attack aircraft available in Indochina was compounded by the age of the available aircraft and poor maintenance, which meant only about 75 percent of the planes were available at any given time.[59] Moreover, the constantly increasing numbers and efficiency of Viet Minh antiaircraft artillery units kept the French aircraft at higher altitudes than were necessary for good bombing results and also required the diversion of aircraft for flak suppression.

Flak suppression, close air support, and interdiction of Viet Minh lines of communication were tasked to French Air Force and French naval air force units in Tonkin and off the coast. A large part of the flak suppression and close air support mission was performed by French carrier-based tactical aircraft. From 1947, the French had one or two small escort (CVE) or light (CVL) aircraft carriers deployed off Indochina. The *Dixmude* (CVE, twelve aircraft) first took station in 1947, the *Arromanches* (CVL, thirty aircraft) in November 1948, the *La Fayette* (CVL, twenty-six aircraft) in 1951, and the *Bois Belleau* (CVL, twenty-six aircraft) in April 1954.[60] Various types of carrier-based aircraft were embarked, including Douglas SBD-6 Dauntless and Curtiss SB2C Helldiver dive-bombers; Grumman F6F Hellcat and F8F Bearcat fighters; and Chance Vought F4U Corsair fighter-bombers.

The French air forces in Indochina had attempted sporadically to interdict Viet Minh troops and supply movements from the beginning of the conflict, principally by bombing bridges and conducting armed reconnaissance strikes along the lines of communication; however, it was not until 1952 that the French instituted a formal program of intensive air interdiction against the Viet Minh supply routes.[61] Directed principally against the supply routes leading from Communist China to the Viet Minh rear areas, the campaign concentrated on two types of targets: fixed facilities, such as truck parks and storage areas, and sections of road that were difficult to bypass. Most of these targets lay in the triangle formed by the towns of Lang Son, Cao Bang, and Bac Kan. The French effort increased significantly in the later stages of the war, particularly after the United States began supplying aircraft and munitions. Total bombing tonnages rose from 834 tons for all of 1949 to some 12,800 tons in the last seven months of the war.[62] The French claimed considerable success, including the reduction in the flow of supplies from China to the Viet Minh from 1,500 tons to only 250 tons per month.[63] But even had they been politically inclined to attack directly the Chinese installations supplying the Viet Minh, the French did not have the means available in Indochina to do so, and thus throughout the later stages of the war Chinese Communist supplies for the Viet Minh flowed south to the Sino-Vietnamese border unimpeded.

Viet Minh Counterinterdiction Methods

Although the Viet Minh had no air force whatsoever and as far as is known the Chinese Communist air forces did not intervene in Indochina, the French Air Force had little success in creating any more than a temporary disruption of the Viet Minh transport system by aerial interdiction. The territory to be covered was simply too large, the demand for close air support too great, the French air assets too few, and the Viet Minh countermeasures too effective. As one contemporary French observer lamented, "We have never been able, despite precision bombardment, systematically and effectively carried out along the two main roads used for delivering Chinese aid, to stop outright the regular transports or those which are in movement during an operation; we have simply retarded their movements for two or three weeks at most, particularly along R.C. 3, north of Bac Kan, or the 'Lorraine' operation which we conducted at Phu Doan."[64] The best example of the futility of French air interdiction efforts is their failure to shut down RP 41, the main Viet Minh supply route into the Dien Bien Phu area.[65]

Like their North Korean comrades of the same era, the Viet Minh became masters of cover and concealment on the march, and they proved innovative and determined in repairing such damage to their lines of communication as the feeble French air forces were able to inflict. In any event, the Viet Minh transport system, built as it was on the use of porters, was far too flexible and mobile to be successfully interdicted from the air. Viet Minh truck transport in the rear areas was more vulnerable, however, and the French obtained some success with the use of French-led guerrilla forces (GCMA/GMI) to interdict Viet Minh supply routes on the ground.

Given the rugged terrain in most of Tonkin, the key area of operations, the French experienced great difficulty in locating the many small groups of porters moving over numerous protected trails. The problem was compounded by excellent Viet Minh march discipline and camouflage technique. Viet Minh soldiers and coolies were well-trained to disperse and seek cover and concealment whenever French aircraft appeared. Each man usually carried a small wire disk on his shoulders that was used for affixing grass, branches, and other camouflage materials that were constantly improved by the man next in line and changed as necessary to conform to the foliage in the area traversed. As one frustrated French airman noted:

In my career I have had the opportunity to fly over Moroccan, Italian, German, even English adversaries. I never had such a sensation of complete emptiness as above the rebel territory. I assume that the Viet-Minh have a very well organized patrol network because it was extremely seldom that an enemy detachment was surprised, even during drills and on the far-off rear. Surprise can only be achieved by skimming the ground, but after the time is taken to regain altitude and to maneuver for a strafing movement the enemy has disappeared. There is only one phase of the battle when the Viet-Minh come into the open: for the attack.[66]

The Viet Minh measures taken to protect their lines of communication from French air interdiction were not particularly innovative, but they were highly effective. The counterinterdiction methods used by the Viet Minh in Indochina were nearly identical to those being used at the same time by the North Koreans and Chinese Communists in Korea, and there can be little doubt that information and suggestions for defeating air interdiction were exchanged. Comparatively limited Viet Minh supply requirements and their reliance in forward areas on highly mobile porters who could move over primitive trails or directly through the mountains and jungles rather than on motor transport restricted to vulnerable improved roads provided a certain inherent immunity to aerial observation and attack.

The relatively small size and the dispersion of Viet Minh units, even in the key areas of operations in Tonkin, also decreased the effectiveness of French aerial bombardment and strafing. Compared to a European theater of operations, the density of combatants in Indochina was extremely low, probably in the neighborhood of only one combatant from both sides to every two square kilometers.[67] Before the great expansion of the Viet Minh logistical system due to the growing support of Communist China after December 1949, the Viet Minh simply did not provide lucrative targets for the application of a determined air interdiction campaign. Even after the Viet Minh logistical system became larger—and in some respects more conventional—dispersion, the restriction of most movement to the hours of darkness or limited visibility, and strict march and camouflage discipline protected the Viet Minh. The construction of alternate routes and the development of better methods for the quick repair of damaged roads and bridges also served to limit the effects of French air attacks, and as the war reached its final stages the Viet Minh employed increasingly larger numbers of antiaircraft artillery guns to protect their supply lines and key logistical installations.

The destruction of fixed transportation facilities, such as roads and bridges, was extremely difficult in the technical sense and had very little permanent effect. Considerable effort was required just to cut a road at one or two critical points. Perhaps thirty to forty bombs were required to make just one road cut.[68] The French soon discovered that it was more profitable to attack roads along the sides of mountains than to destroy bridges that were quickly rebuilt, and they also discovered that it was necessary to follow up with strikes to harass Viet Minh road repair crews. The high sortie rates and bomb tonnages required, increasingly effective Viet Minh antiaircraft artillery, and the enormous manpower available to the Viet Minh for making repairs made bridge destruction and road-cutting attacks more and more difficult and less and less effective as the war entered its later stages. In reality, the French air attacks on Viet Minh roadways became little more than harassment. The Viet Minh quickly shifted to alternate routes and developed very effective repair techniques. Repair crews frequently were stationed at critical points along the supply routes, and using primitive hand tools and large numbers of coolies, the Viet Minh were able in most cases to repair a damaged bridge or resurface a cratered roadway in a matter of hours. One visitor to the Viet Minh base area in the Viet Bac was told that the repair of a single bomb crater required fifty man-nights and that the coolies assigned to road repair worked about four hours per night for two pounds of rice.[69]

Similarly, the dispersion and camouflage of Viet Minh vehicle parks and supply depots lessened the impact of French air operations against such facilities. The identification of such targets required careful analysis of aerial photography and the correlation of a wide variety of often unreliable intelligence reports. In some cases, a building targeted as a Viet Minh ammunition dump might prove to be nothing more than a grass shack containing several hundred hand grenades. Once genuine targets were located, they usually required a large tonnage of bombs to destroy, and often required ordnance that the French did not possess or could not deliver. For example, an attack on the key Viet Minh transportation node at Tuan Giao during the battle for Dien Bien Phu required upward of ninety-eight tons of bombs.[70] The destruction of such economic targets as dams and canal dikes required 2,000-pound bombs, but the only French bombers available, B-26 light bombers, could only carry 1,000-pound bombs. The effect produced by two 1,000-pound bombs was not equivalent to the effect produced by one 2,000-pound bomb.

In the end, the French advantage in technology failed to overcome Viet Minh determination and manpower just as U.N. technology had failed to overcome North Korean and Chinese Communist determination and manpower in Korea. As one French officer observed: "We failed in Indochina as regards the attack on communication networks which is so important in a western theater of operations. Surely, after very heavy expenditure in our potential, we were successful in curbing, sometimes markedly, the routing of reinforcements and supplies. But the use of thousands of coolies to repair the gaps, the installation of numerous diversions, installation of revetments on the waterways, the utilization of covers and of night permitted the army of masses to win over technology."[71]

The Battle for Hoa Binh, November 1951–February 1952

Following the repulse of the Viet Minh direct attacks on the Red River delta perimeter in 1951, General de Lattre sought to gain the initiative by launching a major offensive to sever the Viet Minh north-south communication route between the

Viet Bac and the South Delta Base area around Thanh Hoa on the coast south of the Red River delta, a move he hoped would precipitate a set-piece battle in which the superior French air and artillery firepower could grind up the Viet Minh regular units.[72] Although de Lattre considered two other Viet Minh supply centers— Thai Nguyen north of the De Lattre Line and Thanh Hoa south of the delta—as possible targets, he chose to focus on the town of Hoa Binh on the Black River because of its political importance and accessibility.[73] The seizure of Hoa Binh— a key node on the Viet Minh lines of communication from the Viet Bac to the rich rice-producing areas south of the Red River delta—would not stop the movement of men and supplies between the two regions, but de Lattre hoped to slow the movement of new artillery, trucks, and ammunition manufacturing machinery to the Viet Minh South Delta Base. Moreover, Hoa Binh was the capital of the Muong, who were allied with the French, and General de Lattre was eager to influence the 1952–1953 budget debates in the French National Assembly as well as to demonstrate to the Americans that the French could put to good use the new equipment being received from the United States.[74]

The town of Hoa Binh lay on a small plain surrounded by hills some forty-five miles west-southwest of Hanoi and twenty-five miles from the De Lattre Line, as shown on map 11.1. Hoa Binh was connected to the French bases in the delta by two main surface supply lines: RC 6, which wound through difficult terrain from Xuan Mai on the De Lattre Line, and a water route via the Black River from Viet Tri. The third key French supply line was the aerial route from the bases in the delta to the airstrip at Hoa Binh. All three routes were vulnerable to Viet Minh attack. At the beginning of the operation, RC 6 was little more than a jungle trail, having been ravaged by both the Viet Minh and the French air forces, and was subject to Viet Minh ambushes. Although navigable from Trung Ha to Hoa Binh by French river craft, the Black River route also offered numerous ambush sites. The airfield at Hoa Binh was likewise subject to attack by Viet Minh artillery and antiaircraft fire from two overlooking hills.

The first phase of the French offensive in the Muong country, Operation LOTUS, was launched at dawn on November 14, 1951, with an assault by three French parachute infantry battalions and a section of 75 mm guns on the Hoa Binh airfield.[75] The paras, dropped in three waves, met only light resistance, and within twenty-four hours the town was firmly under French control.[76] Meanwhile, the French initiated operations to clear both RC 6 and the Black River routes into Hoa Binh. The task force on RC 6, consisting of fifteen battalions, reached Hoa Binh in only two days, as did the riverine task force of some twenty landing craft moving up the Black River from Trung Ha. Having cleared the road and river routes into Hoa Binh, the French proceeded to establish a string of strongpoints on each axis. Outposts were established on the west bank of the Black River, key garrisons being located at Ap Da Chong, Notre Dame Rock, and Tu Vu. Of the

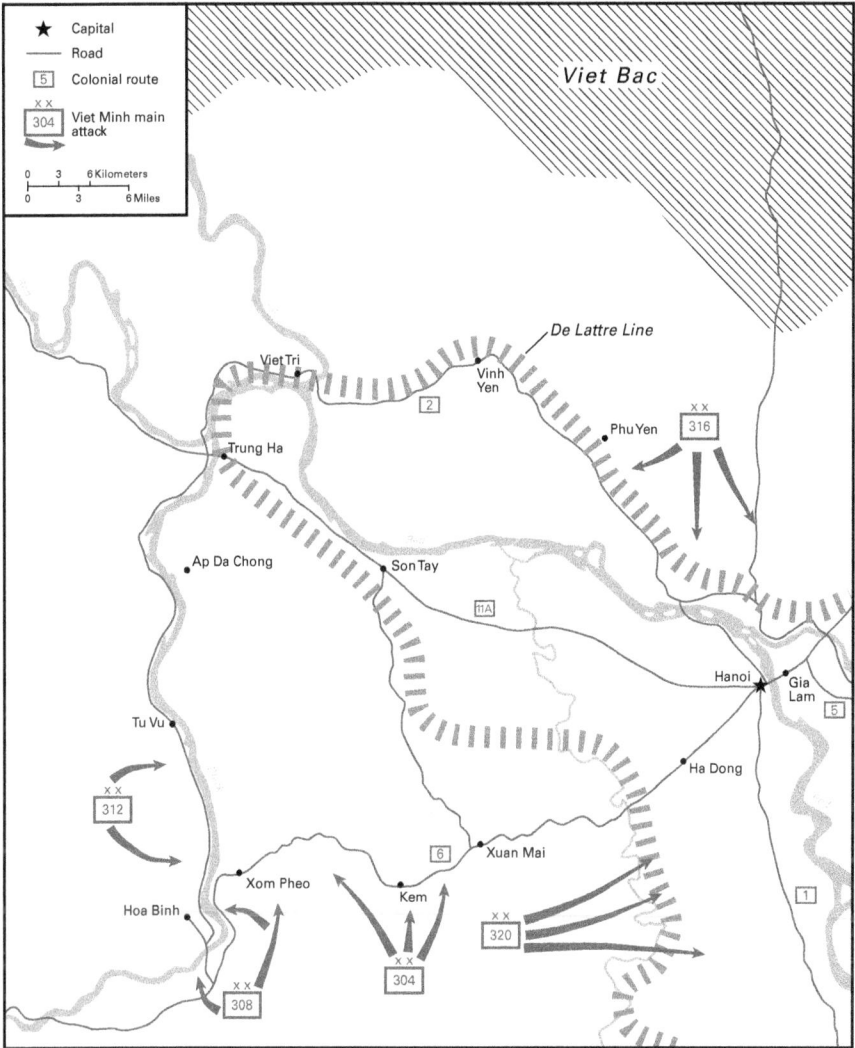

Map 11.1. The Battle for Hoa Binh, November 1951–February 1952.

ten outposts established along RC 6, the most important were at Xuan Mai, Kem, and Xom Pheo, each of which subsequently became the scene of a savage battle in miniature in which supplying the outposts became more difficult than supplying Hoa Binh itself.[77]

The French action was successful initially but provoked a Viet Minh reaction that eventually involved some 40,000 Viet Minh troops.[78] After a month's delay to position his units and arrange the necessary logistical support, General Giap threw the 304th, 308th, and 312th Divisions, supported by the artillery of the 351st Heavy Division, against the posts guarding the French lines of communication rather than directly against Hoa Binh. The 312th Division was ordered to attack the posts along the Black River, and the 308th Division was directed to assist the 312th Division and to menace Hoa Binh. The 304th Division was assigned to harass the French outposts on RC 6 from the south while, as a diversion, the 316th Division (north of the delta) and 320th Division (south of the delta) were ordered to step up their infiltration of the Red River delta. The 316th and 320th Divisions subsequently laid siege to key provincial towns in the delta, including Thai Binh and Nam Dinh.

Giap began his counteroffensive on December 9 by mounting a strike against Tu Vu, one of the outposts guarding the Black River convoys. In a savage "human wave" attack, two regiments of the 312th Division drove the two Moroccan companies defending the post from their position, destroyed the tanks, artillery, and fortifications of Tu Vu, and then withdrew, leaving four hundred Viet Minh dead on the battlefield.[79] The French outposts along the west bank of the Black River each became the scene of brutal fighting, and the French situation quickly began to deteriorate. On November 20, General de Lattre was invalided home to France; he died in Paris on January 11, 1952. His place was taken by Lieutenant General Raoul Salan, who responded to the rising French casualties and deteriorating morale by withdrawing the outposts on the west bank of the Black River. During November and December 1951, the French riverine forces managed to keep open the Black River supply line at a very heavy cost, but on January 12, 1952, a Viet Minh ambush with mortars and automatic weapons hidden along the riverbank south of Notre Dame Rock sank four patrol boats and one LSSL and forced the other vessels, all seriously damaged, to turn back. The Viet Minh annihilated the entire convoy and effectively closed the Black River route to Hoa Binh.

Simultaneous with the attacks on the Black River outposts, the Viet Minh started to seal off the French ground supply line to Hoa Binh. On January 8, the 304th Division and the 88th Regiment of the 308th Division began to attack the outposts along RC 6. The infantry battalion, artillery battalion, two armored battalions, and engineer group guarding the outposts progressively lost ground to the Viet Minh attacks, and by mid-January the road between Xuan Mai and Hoa Binh was closed. Lieutenant General Salan subsequently decided to reopen the twenty-five-mile stretch of RC 6 between Xuan Mai and Hoa Binh, but the effort took eleven days (January 18–29) and required twelve infantry battalions and three artillery groups.[80]

The Viet Minh also sought to draw the noose tighter around Hoa Binh itself, occupying the heights around the town and bringing the airfield under intermittent artillery fire. The increasing quantity and accuracy of Viet Minh antiaircraft fire further restricted use of the landing strip, and the French lost a half-dozen aircraft on the approaches to the field or on the runway itself. The five French Union infantry battalions and one artillery group guarding Hoa Binh held on, but the French attempts to resupply the remaining outposts along the Black River and RC 6 and to reopen the main supply corridors resulted in significant casualties and materiel losses. Finally, at the end of January, Lieutenant General Salan elected to abandon the effort and evacuate Hoa Binh.

The evacuation from Hoa Binh, Operation AMARANTH, was planned as a three-stage withdrawal of the twenty-thousand-man garrison along RC 6 and the Black River conducted in leapfrog fashion, one unit holding a key terrain feature long enough for the others to pass through.[81] Operation AMARANTH began on the evening of February 22, with more than two hundred heavily loaded trucks, more than six hundred porters carrying supplies for the combat forces, and almost one thousand Muong civilians being ferried across the Black River by landing craft. The French blew up some 150 tons of supplies that they were unable to evacuate. The combat forces crossed the river at 0600 hours on February 23, and the column, supported by tactical aircraft and artillery (which fired some thirty thousand rounds between February 22 and February 24), began to withdraw along RC 6 toward Xom Pheo. The Viet Minh reaction was delayed, but the withdrawal soon became a fighting retreat as the main column fended off Viet Minh ambushes and the French units struggled to hold each successive post long enough to pass through the column. Meanwhile, the riverine forces also had to fight their way north and east down the Black River to safety within the De Lattre Line at Viet Tri.

The battle of Hoa Binh in fact turned out to be the "meat grinder" that General de Lattre had envisioned, but it ground up both sides. By the time the French withdrew from Hoa Binh, the battle had consumed most of the available French reserves in Indochina. More than sixteen infantry battalions and three artillery groups were committed without achieving the principal objective of blocking Viet Minh use of the north-south lines of communication, the Viet Minh having built a bypass around Hoa Binh within thirty days of the French occupying the town.[82] Nevertheless, the new French *commandant en chef,* Lieutenant General Salan, was generally satisfied with the operation, which had resulted in some 22,000 Viet Minh casualties and only 1,588 French casualties.[83] However, the French failure to hold Hoa Binh induced serious doubts in the minds of France's American suppliers as to France's long-term will and ability to continue the struggle to victory over the Communist Viet Minh.[84] More importantly, the battle demonstrated the severe logistical problems faced by the French Union forces in trying to operate at a distance from their bases in the Red River delta, but the French leaders chose to ignore the lesson and continued to seek a decisive set-piece battle with the Viet Minh in far northwestern Tonkin.

The Viet Minh could claim the battle for Hoa Binh as a victory. Despite heavy Viet Minh casualties, the lines of communication between the Viet Bac and the

South Delta Base were interrupted only temporarily. As Lucien Bodard later wrote: "Holding Hoabinh meant strangling the Viets. Leaving it meant giving them back total freedom of movement. From that time on not only were they sure of their supply lines but they could also maneuver their divisions all around the delta in a kind of hide-and-go-seek for the attack of that rapidly diminishing territory."[85]

The battle for Hoa Binh also provided a severe test of the recently reorganized Viet Minh logistical services and of the Viet Minh divisions fully equipped with new Chinese equipment and American weapons captured by the Chinese Communists in Korea. The fighting around Hoa Binh in December 1951 and January 1952 saw the introduction by the Viet Minh of a "two-platoon" system in which, to ensure adequate logistical support, each Viet Minh division was organized into two task forces, each of which would fight until its supplies were exhausted and then be relieved by the other, which had meanwhile received replacements and resupply from the rear. The "two-platoon" system allowed the Viet Minh to sustain their offensive against the French forces around Hoa Binh for eight weeks, whereas previously the *Chu Luc* had been unable to remain in action much longer than five or six days, with each period of action usually followed by a two-month recovery period.[86]

While the Viet Minh regular units engaged around Hoa Binh tested the new system and gained additional experience in facing French air and artillery firepower, the Viet Minh logistical services, forced to respond quickly to an unexpected operation, had functioned quite well, although their limited ability to respond to changes in the tactical situation at short notice remained a key shortcoming.[87] For some three months, the Viet Minh logisticians had supported successfully a force of over three divisions (some seventy thousand men), an effort that required the opening of new routes and the establishment and operation of many new depots in the battle area. The size and complexity of the undertaking can be judged by the fact that some 150,000–160,000 porters are said to have been employed.[88]

"War in the Empty Lands"

General Giap as well as his combat commanders and logisticians took the lessons of Hoa Binh and the earlier battles around the French perimeter in Tonkin to heart and worked diligently to further improve training and staff work. Giap recognized that although his forces grew stronger each day, he could not reasonably expect to achieve a final victory over the French by battering against the strongly held positions ringing the Red River delta. He also recognized that despite their seeming abundance of resources, the French had only a limited capability for supporting major forces outside the delta, although they were obliged to defend outlying areas such as Laos as well as friendly tribal groups such as the T'ai and the Muong. Consequently, the French might be expected to react to Viet Minh operations in the more remote regions of northwestern Tonkin and Upper Laos even though they would be at a disadvantage. Accordingly, from mid-1952 onward, General Giap followed a strategy, perhaps recommended by the Chinese Military Assistance Group, emphasizing offensive operations in northwestern Tonkin, Laos, and the Central Highlands designed to engage the French Union forces far from their bases and under conditions favorable to the Viet Minh.[89] For their part, the French reacted much as Giap expected, drawing on their scanty reserves of men and air transport to reinforce isolated garrisons in the remote areas, to create new bases from which ground and airborne forces could operate against the Viet Minh columns, and to attempt to interdict the extended Viet Minh supply lines and thus bring the wide-ranging *Chu Luc* columns to a halt.[90] Unable to run the elusive Viet Minh to ground, the French eventually turned to using their isolated outposts in northwestern Tonkin and Upper Laos as bait to entice the Viet Minh into a decisive battle.

For both sides the key to victory in this "war in the empty lands" was the establishment and maintenance of extended lines of communication from their distant rear bases to the area of operations. Because the use of the existing roads and waterways was generally denied to both sides, the Viet Minh relied on hosts of porters moving stealthily over forested mountain trails, while the French depended upon air transport to keep their forces supplied. Both porters and air transport had their faults and were vulnerable to enemy counteraction, and both the French and the Viet Minh sought to exploit the enemy's logistical weaknesses as much as possible. Thus, the "war in the empty lands" in fact was largely a battle for the control of the lines of communication.

Operations in the T'ai Country, October–December 1952

Several weeks before the French operations against Hoa Binh began, the Viet Minh launched an offensive of their own in the T'ai country. General Giap committed the Viet Minh 316th Division against the major French outpost at Nghia Lo, but the French responded by reinforcing the garrison by air on October 3, 1951, and the next day they dropped two parachute infantry battalions on Giap's flank, forcing him to withdraw back toward the Red River.[91] The first round at Nghia Lo was undoubtedly a victory for the French, but it was also an engagement that imbued the French leaders with a false sense of the value of quick air reinforcement and a mistaken appreciation of the willingness of the Viet Minh regular force units to stand and fight.[92] Such mistaken appraisals only served to reinforce the French willingness to hazard their isolated garrisons as bait to draw the Viet Minh into a decisive battle. The Viet Minh, however, recognized in the unsuccessful Nghia Lo operation not only their own limitations, but also French weaknesses that could be exploited profitably.

In October 1952, having regrouped and rebuilt his forces, General Giap launched a general offensive into the T'ai country of northwest Tonkin to win a major political and psychological victory by eliminating the French outposts along the low Fan Si Pan mountain range between the Red and Black Rivers. The outpost line was anchored by Nghia Lo, the T'ai tribal center that had survived a Viet Minh attack in October 1951. On October 11, 1952, the Viet Minh 308th, 312th, and 316th Divisions crossed the Red River on a forty-mile front north of Yen Bay and advanced in three columns.[93] The center column, composed of the crack 308th Division, was aimed at Nghia Lo. On the right (west), the 312th Division headed for Gia Hoi, a small outpost ten miles northwest of Nghia Lo, and on the left (east), the 316th Division made for Van Yen. The 148th Independent Regiment screened the attacking divisions to the north, moving in a wide arc on the axis Than Uyen–Dien Bien Phu as shown on map 11.2.

On October 15, the 312th Division invested Gia Hoi, and Lieutenant General Salan, realizing at last the danger facing his isolated garrisons, reacted by dropping the 6th Colonial Parachute Battalion (6e Bataillon de Parachutistes Coloniaux, 6e BPC) at Tu Le, fifteen miles northwest of Gia Hoi and twenty-five miles northwest of Nghia Lo, to screen a withdrawal to the stronger outposts south and west of the Black River. At 1700 hours on October 17, the 308th Division struck at Nghia Lo. Battered by a heavy mortar preparation and a determined Viet Minh infantry assault, the French garrison was overrun in less than one hour, at a cost of seven hundred French Union casualties. The loss of its anchor caused the collapse of the entire French line astride the Fan Si Pan ridge, and under heavy pressure the French survivors, screened by the sacrifice of the 6e BPC, fell back to another line of outposts behind the Black River.[94]

The line south and west of the Black River was guarded by several strong outposts, the most important of which were, from northwest to southeast, Lai Chau, Son La, Na San, and Moc Chau. The French subsequently concentrated their forces at the two heavily defended airheads of Lai Chau (the T'ai capital) and Na San on an open plateau near the Black River and prepared for the inevitable Viet Minh attack. However, by early November the strain was beginning to tell on the still-inadequate Viet Minh logistical system. Slowed by logistical problems, the Viet Minh divisions did not reach the French line behind the Black River until mid-November.

The 308th Division in the center came to a halt just short of the fortified French camp at Na San on November 23.[95] Believing there to be less than two thousand men holding the antiquated brick fort at Na San, General Giap initiated a series of disastrous frontal attacks that were all repulsed with great losses for the Chu Luc.[96] The French estimated over fifteen hundred dead Viet Minh around the camp, but the fruitless attacks on Na San may have cost the Viet Minh some seven thousand casualties, more than half of the 308th Division.[97] Meanwhile, to the south, the

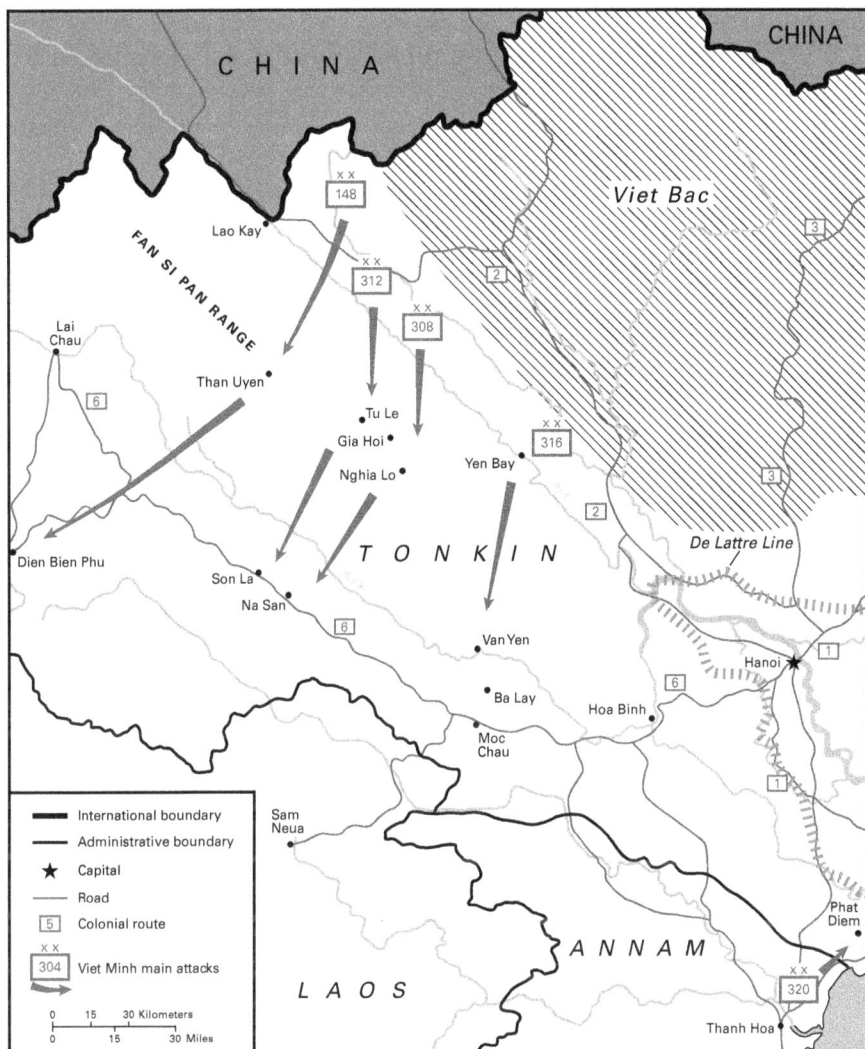

Map 11.2. The Viet Minh Campaign in the T'ai Country, Fall 1952.

316th Division occupied Van Yen and stopped ten miles farther on, near Ba Lay, which the French were rapidly turning into a major strongpoint to block access to the delta. To the north, the 316th Division bypassed Lai Chau and struck at the small French-led garrison at Dien Bien Phu, which fell on November 30. By early December, the Viet Minh drive toward Sam Neua had overrun the French outposts on the Laotian border. The Viet Minh divisions had "covered 180 miles in six weeks without using a single road or a single motor vehicle," but in doing so they had finally outrun their logistical support and were forced to halt—in large part due to the problems of recruiting the necessary porters from the uncooperative T'ai.[98] The increasingly desperate Viet Minh supply situation was compounded by the better flying weather after mid-November that permitted the French air forces, largely ineffective throughout October and early November, to increase their efforts to interdict the already-strained Viet Minh supply lines.[99]

Having withdrawn his forces into the strongpoints behind the Black River in mid-October 1952, Lieutenant General Salan sought to counter Giap's advance toward Laos by reinforcing the garrisons at Lai Chau, Na San, and Moc Chau and by launching his own coordinated offensive, Operation LORRAINE, against the Viet Minh bases in the Viet Bac. As described earlier, Operation LORRAINE, which ended on November 26, failed to achieve either of its principal objectives: the destruction of the Viet Minh logistical base and the forced withdrawal of the three Viet Minh divisions in northwestern Tonkin. Even so, General Salan was particularly pleased by the bloody defeat inflicted on the Viet Minh at Na San in late November and claimed to have delayed any Viet Minh invasion of Laos by four months at least.[100]

Once again the Viet Minh logistical system had been exercised to the limits of its capabilities, and in the process had gained valuable experience. Recruiting the horde of porters required to move supplies forward had not been easy in the unfriendly T'ai country, nor had the management of the many small groups of plodding porters been easy under even scattered French air attacks.[101] Nevertheless, the Viet Minh supply services had proven able to support a major extended operation far from their bases in the Viet Bac. The Viet Minh campaign in the autumn of 1952 had involved some thirty thousand men in a two-month operation at a distance of some one hundred miles from the Viet Bac; the next campaign, in the spring of 1953, would involve forty thousand men in a two-month operation at twice that distance.[102]

The Invasion of Laos, April 1953

Between late December 1952 and March 1953, neither side initiated any large-scale combat operations, and Indochina experienced one of the quieter periods of the war (although small-scale operations continued throughout the country). Having been stymied in his first invasion of Laos by the inadequacies of his logistical services, General Giap planned to rest his three divisions in northwestern Tonkin during the first quarter of 1953, but in December 1952 the 320th Division mounted an attack on Phat Diem, one of the Catholic centers in the Red River delta. The French reacted quickly and had no sooner beaten off the attack on Phat Diem than they were faced by an even more serious Viet Minh offensive in the Central Highlands. In January 1953, the Viet Minh 84th and 95th Independent Regiments attacked the French outposts around An Khe on RC 19 and threatened to overrun the key towns of Kontum and Pleiku. The apparent objectives of this offensive were to sever French north-south communications at the narrow waist of Indochina and to gain control of Kontum and Pleiku, which dominated the region. The French quickly committed three parachute infantry battalions to the area, and after some hard fighting the Viet Minh threat was diminished for the time being.

The diversion of French Union forces to deal with the Viet Minh threat in the T'ai country and Upper Laos in the fall of 1952 had left the vital Red River delta open to further infiltration by the Viet Minh in a process that came to be called *la pourrissement du delta* ("the rotting of the delta").[103] Thus, while fighting off minor attacks in the Central Highlands, the French concentrated on clearing operations in the Red River delta. Meanwhile, General Giap prepared to resume the offensive. With the 312th Division at Dien Bien Phu, and the 308th and 316th Divisions around Moc Chau, Giap's combat forces were well-positioned for a number of offensive options. He could easily continue the offensive into Laos, attack the southwestern face of the De Lattre Line, try again to take Na San, strike at Lai Chau, or simply remain in place and secure his north-south supply lines from the Viet Bac to Thanh Hoa.[104] Unable to determine which course Giap might take, the French could only wait and hope to be able to react effectively when the time came.

Laos, defended by the ten-thousand-man Royal Laotian Army and supported by some three thousand French advisors and logistical personnel, was a tempting prize.[105] Until late 1952, Laos had remained relatively untouched by the war. Four Viet Minh infantry battalions (the 80th, 81st, 82nd, and 83rd) were stationed in Laos but generally avoided extended contact. Instead, they concentrated on training the pro-Communist Pathet Lao forces of Prince Souphanouvong, who had established a shadow government under Viet Minh protection in the Viet Bac in August 1950.[106] The political stakes of a successful invasion of Laos were high, and from General Giap's perspective the risks were low.[107] The opposing forces were small and could be reinforced or supported logistically only with great difficulty. In the event of a setback, the Viet Minh could melt into the difficult terrain of Upper Laos under cover of the monsoon, which would begin in May. Furthermore, continued operations in Upper Laos would have the distinct advantage of stretching French airpower to its limits. By virtue of the greater distances involved, the French would be unable to bring to bear massive close air support and interdiction forces, and their air transport forces would be hard-pressed to meet minimum requirements.

General Giap thus chose to resume his offensive into Laos. This time the Viet Minh logisticians were given three months to make their extensive preparations, in hopes of avoiding some of the problems that had plagued the aborted Viet Minh invasion of Laos in December 1952. Having failed to take Na San, which he hoped to use as a forward logistics base for his invasion of Upper Laos, Giap instead chose Dien Bien Phu and Moc Chau as the principal forward depots for the 1953 campaign. The forward base at Moc Chau was developed and stocked with weapons and ammunition moved directly to Moc Chau from Communist China by truck.[108] Large numbers of reliable porters were recruited outside the uncooperative T'ai region and assembled at the forward logistical bases. Rice and other foodstuffs were stockpiled in depots along the three planned invasion routes with the assistance of the pro-Communist Pathet Lao.

On April 9, 1953, the Viet Minh 312th Division at Dien Bien Phu, the 308th Division at Na San, and the 316th Division at Moc Chau swept south on three separate axes into northern Laos, as shown on map 11.3.[109] On the western flank, the 312th Division at Dien Bien Phu headed down the Nam Ou River toward Luang Prabang, while on the eastern flank, the 316th Division moved from Moc Chau toward Vientiane via Sam Neua and the Plain of Jars (*Plaine des Jarres*). In the center, the 308th Division left one regiment to contain the French airhead at Na San and moved forward along the Nam Seng River prepared to support either the 312th Division drive toward Luang Prabang or the 316th Division drive toward Vientiane. The 308th Division was not committed toward the Plain of Jars until the French evacuated Xieng Khouang on April 19 to move to Jars Camp. Supported by an additional column composed of elements of the 304th Division and by some four thousand Pathet Lao troops, the Viet Minh invaders kept the French and Laotian defenders off balance by covering as much as twenty miles per day through the rugged mountains and by shifting their direction of advance several times. The prepositioned rice caches and some two hundred thousand porters kept the advancing Viet Minh columns fully supplied.

Two regiments of the Viet Minh 312th Division were delayed by late supply deliveries and losing their way as well as by the gallant thirty-six-day defense of Muong Khoua by a Laotian battalion commanded by a French captain, sacrificed to protect the withdrawal of the other French and Laotian outposts in the region.[110] Ordered to hold out for two weeks against the bulk of the 312th Division, the garrison of Muong Khoua stretched the defense for nearly five weeks, but there were only four known survivors. Some of the other retreating outposts fared little better: the garrison of Sam Neua, ordered to evacuate its position on April 12, lost all but 180 of its 2,400-man complement in its 110-mile retreat to the west. In all, the withdrawal from northern Laos in the spring of 1953 cost the French Union forces the equivalent of five French and Laotian battalions.[111]

Despite the sacrifice of the garrison of Muong Khoua, by April 30 the elements of the 312th Division had bottled up three French battalions and miscellaneous Laotian units in the royal capital of Luang Prabang. Meanwhile, the 308th and 316th Divisions had surrounded the ten battalions manning the newly created French base in the Plain of Jars southeast of Luang Prabang. The relatively small

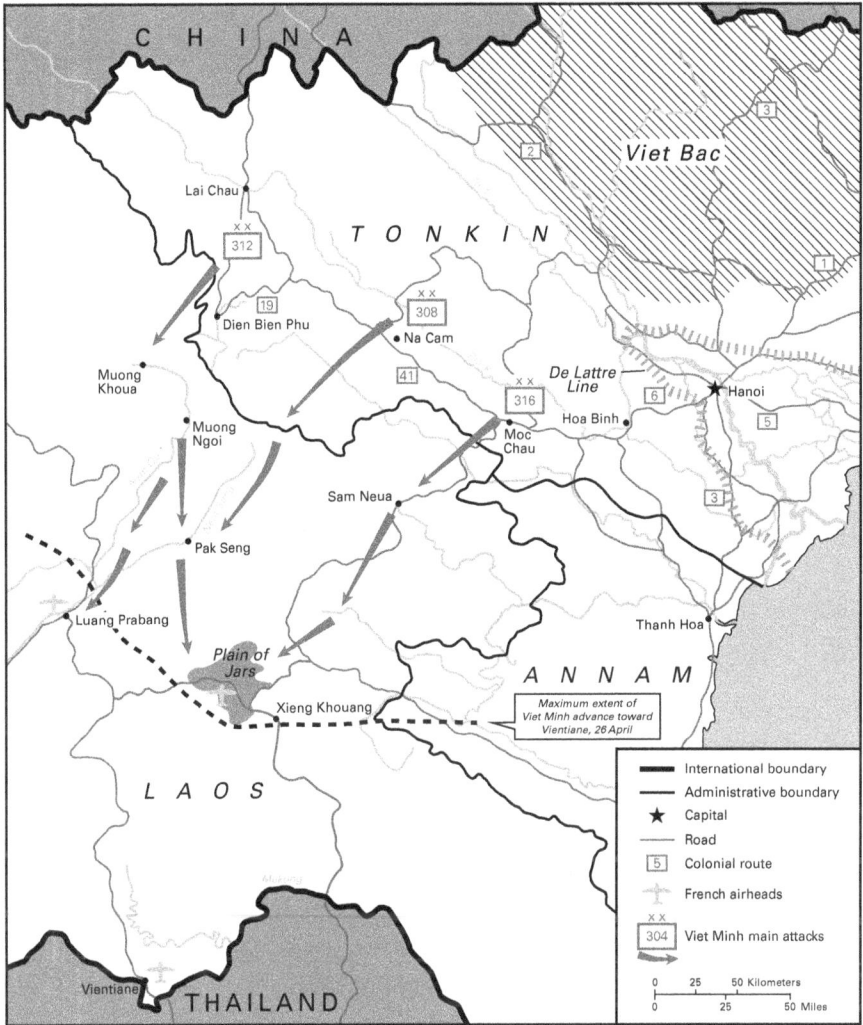

Map 11.3. The Viet Minh Invasion of Laos, April 1953.

(eighteen miles by fifteen miles) Plain of Jars lay astride the most likely axes of advance toward Vientiane. On April 19, the French, noting the probable commitment of the 308th Division toward Vientiane rather than Luang Prabang, evacuated their position at Xieng Khouang, twenty miles east of the Plain of Jars, and established Jars Camp on the plain. The subsequent effort by the French to reinforce Jars Camp monopolized most of the available air transport in Indochina. The fortified base was over five hundred air miles from Hanoi and nearly one thousand air miles from Saigon, and the air transport priority given to the camp left the ten-thousand-man force at Na San, for example, temporarily bereft of aerial resupply. On the night of April 26, two Viet Minh divisions mounted a hasty attack on the uncompleted camp but were repulsed with heavy casualties. A smaller attack on Luang Prabang also miscarried, and with the onset of the rainy season General Giap began on May 7, 1953, to withdraw his exhausted forces to his bases in Tonkin, leaving behind the 308th Division to harass the French and oversee the establishment of caches of rice and other supplies to be used in any subsequent operations in Upper Laos.[112]

The invasion of Upper Laos in April 1953 was a strategic success for the Viet Minh. Although the major Viet Minh objectives in Laos remained in French hands, Lieutenant General Salan had been forced to shift significant combat forces from the delta and other vital areas in order to defend Luang Prabang, Jars Camp, and Vientiane. He also had been forced to apply most of his air transport resources just to keep the garrisons in Laos supplied, thereby demonstrating that any major threat far from the French bases was sure to reduce their ability to support other areas adequately. These unfavorable omens regarding French logistical capabilities become even more sinister when considered alongside the greatly improved capabilities of the Viet Minh logistical services demonstrated by their successful support for over a month of three advancing Viet Minh divisions at a distance of over one hundred miles from their advance depots.[113] As one authority has noted, "The campaign in Laos amply demonstrated that Giap had forged a maneuverable and well-balanced regular force, led by officers of talent and high morale, accustomed to exacting forced marches and exhibiting great logistical ingenuity."[114]

Neither contestant was able to deliver a knockout blow in the campaign for control of the lines of communication. However, the Viet Minh were able to deny to the French Union forces the free use of much of the surface transportation network of Indochina and made movements on the remaining roads and waterways extremely difficult and costly. The French were forced to adopt restrictive and expensive convoy methods supported by large numbers of static defense troops and mobile escort and relief forces which themselves often fell victim to Viet Minh sabotage and ambushes. Largely restricted to the use of air transport to supply their many isolated outposts and even their larger mobile forces, the French found they did not have sufficient aircraft or pilots to meet their needs fully.

On the other hand, after a rough initial learning period, the Viet Minh were able to successfully support their major combat forces in extended operations far from their bases. Although relatively slow, the Viet Minh transport system, composed as it was of well-disciplined porters able to traverse even the most difficult off-road terrain under the threat of French aerial observation and attack, proved flexible and effective. French attempts to interdict the long columns of Viet Minh porters generally failed due to difficult flying conditions, inadequate numbers of suitable aircraft, and effective Viet Minh countermeasures. At Hoa Binh in 1951, in the T'ai country in 1952, and in Upper Laos in 1953, the Viet Minh operated at the end of very fragile supply lines reaching back as much as two hundred miles to their main logistical bases in the Viet Bac. Even so, the French, with complete air superiority and a host of other resources, were unable to stop the flow of supplies to the advancing Viet Minh divisions. The streams of porters continued to plod forward, bypassing French blocking forces on jungle trails and avoiding aerial interdiction by strict march and camouflage discipline. French air force efforts to stem the flow of supplies from Communist China to the Viet Minh rear depots were similarly ineffective. The French naval and riverine forces achieved somewhat greater success in interdicting Viet Minh coastal and river transport but were unable to stop such traffic altogether. Even the highly mobile French-led GCMA/ GMI, excellent as intelligence-gatherers, proved to be of little value in the campaign for the lines of communication.

Around Hoa Binh in October–December 1951 and again in the T'ai country and Upper Laos a year later, the Viet Minh logistical services were stretched to the breaking point and limited General Giap's tactical and strategic options. However, the Viet Minh quickly learned from their mistakes and the invasion of Laos in the spring of 1953 demonstrated clearly that their logistical system could fully support major combat forces in extended operations far from their bases. The same operations offered to the French a demonstration of the limitations of their own logistical system. While Na San and other isolated posts could be reinforced and maintained by air, the difficulties, costs, and risks of such logistical undertakings were enormous. Unable to use the existing roads and waterways freely, the French relied increasingly on air transport, but at Hoa Binh in November 1951 and again at Na San in late 1952 and early 1953, the Viet Minh gave ominous demonstrations of their growing antiaircraft artillery capabilities.

In the end, the more basic transportation system of the Viet Minh proved to be superior to the highly mechanized French system despite the enormous resources applied by the French to interdict the Viet Minh supply lines. By mid-1953, the Viet Minh had built a logistical support system well-adapted to the operational environment and fully capable of meeting the needs of their combat forces in the decisive Tonkin theater of operations despite French air interdiction. As U.S. Army intelligence analysts subsequently concluded, "The history of the Viet Minh campaign clearly shows that sustained interdiction of main lines of transportation and communication in Indochina will not defeat an enemy guerrilla force capable of developing such a profuse net of supply lines over mountain trails and by waterways that its dependency on any one artery becomes relatively unimportant."[115]

12

Planning and Buildup for the Battle of Dien Bien Phu

Foreshadowed by the establishment, successful defense, and eventual evacuation of the fortified airhead at Na San in the summer of 1953, and interrupted by diversions that dissipated logistical support, the operations around Dien Bien Phu between November 20, 1953, and May 7, 1954, reflected aspects of all three logistical campaigns of the war in Indochina. The objectives, forces committed, timing, and duration of the battle were all clearly dictated by logistical considerations, and Dien Bien Phu became the ultimate test of the efficiency and effectiveness of the logistical systems devised by the French and by the Viet Minh during the preceding eight years of war. The outcome of the battle hinged primarily on poor French intelligence, overconfidence, and tactical blunders, but logistical factors, particularly the difficulties faced by the French in resupplying their forces adequately and the success of the Viet Minh in doing so despite French air interdiction, also played an important role. The surrender of the French defenders of Dien Bien Phu was quickly followed by the Geneva agreements, a cease-fire in July 1954, and the last major French operation of the war, Operation AUVERGNE, to protect their withdrawal from Tonkin, itself a major logistical undertaking.

The political, strategic, and tactical details of the creation of the French *base aéro-terrestre* at Dien Bien Phu (Operation CASTOR) and the ensuing battle are well-known and need not be repeated here.[1] The focus here is on the logistical aspects of the battle as seen from both the French and the Viet Minh perspective. What were the logistical requirements of both sides and to what degree were they met? What impact did interdiction operations have on logistical support? What were the major logistical constraints and difficulties and how were they overcome or not overcome? And finally, which side proved best able to meet the logistical demands of the battle and why?

The Phases of the Battle of Dien Bien Phu

From the logistical point of view, the operations at Dien Bien Phu between November 20, 1953, and May 7, 1954, can be divided into two main phases—the "buildup" phase and the "active battle" phase—corresponding to the changing tactical situation and divided by effective loss of the main airfield on March 14, 1954.

Each phase can be further subdivided into three periods, based again on the tactical situation and particularly on the volume and efficiency of the aerial resupply operations in support of the entrenched camp.

The buildup phase extended from the initiation of Operation CASTOR on November 20, 1953, to the beginning of the Viet Minh assault on March 13, 1954.[2] From November 20, 1953, to January 25, 1954, the focus was on the establishment of the *base aéro-terrestre* at Dien Bien Phu. The second period, extending from January 26 to February 24, 1954, was coterminous with the raid of the Viet Minh 308th Division toward Luang Prabang in Upper Laos and saw a sharp decline in the supply levels at Dien Bien Phu. The final period of the buildup phase ran from February 25 to March 13, 1954, and was characterized by strong efforts to rebuild the stockage levels of the camp that had fallen due to the diversion of air transport in support of forces in Laos over the preceding month. Throughout the buildup phase, the main airfield at Dien Bien Phu remained available, and both cargo and personnel were delivered by airlanding as well as by airdrop and parachute, and the evacuation of the wounded and of used parachutes, refillable containers, and damaged equipment was possible.

Logistically, the active battle for Dien Bien Phu began with the effective closure of the main airfield on March 14, 1954, and extended to the fall of Dien Bien Phu to the Viet Minh on May 7. The loss of the main airfield was a major blow to the defenders of Dien Bien Phu and forced all personnel and cargo to be delivered by less efficient airdrop and parachute methods. Thus, throughout the active battle phase the French logistical situation steadily declined as poor weather and an increasingly unfavorable tactical situation combined to reduce the flow of supplies to only a portion of the base's daily requirements. Like the buildup phase, the active battle phase can be subdivided into three periods. During the last half of March 1954, the logistical effort was concentrated on rebuilding the supply levels in the camp that had fallen precipitously during the combat operations of March 13–15. During April, aerial resupply operations and the recovery of airdropped and parachuted materiel became increasingly difficult, as the French perimeter steadily contracted and the Viet Minh antiaircraft artillery forced the French transports to higher altitudes, resulting in a loss of accuracy in the supply drops and the loss of an increasing proportion of the supplies parachuted to the camp. The climactic final period of May 1–7 saw the virtual strangulation of the French defenders and their ultimate capitulation to the Viet Minh attackers.

The Navarre Plan

The events that would lead to the decisive battle of Dien Bien Phu began on June 28, 1953, when Lieutenant General Henri Navarre assumed command of the French Union forces in Indochina from Lieutenant General Raoul Salan. The situation at that time was not encouraging. The political situation in France was decidedly unfavorable and was characterized by confusion, lack of direction, and lack of will to either abandon Indochina or provide the resources necessary to retain it. French public opinion had turned against the war, and relations with the Associated States and with France's principal supporter, the United States, were unsteady. Navarre subsequently condemned the conduct of the war by the French government, writing: "Such was the conduct of the war by the Government. It can be summarized in one word: nothing. No goal was fixed for the struggle. No policy was defined, either vis-à-vis the Associated States or with regard to our American allies. No coordination was established among the ministries interested in Indochinese affairs. The morale of the nation was left exposed without defense to every shift in the situation. The Army was not provided the necessary cadres, troops, or matériel. She was stabbed in the back by a treason against which not a single measure was taken."[3]

The military situation in Indochina was equally uncertain. Northern Tonkin, including most of the posts on the border with China, was under Viet Minh control, as were significant portions of the coastal areas of northern Annam and several major enclaves elsewhere. The vital Red River delta region was heavily infiltrated to the point where internal movement by the French Union forces was often restricted. During the spring and summer of 1953, most of the Viet Minh 320th Division successfully infiltrated through the De Lattre Line to join the 42nd, 46th, and 50th Independent Regiments operating behind French lines in the delta.[4] Land communication between Cochinchina and Tonkin was extremely unreliable, and the French Union forces available in Tonkin could probably have held a perimeter of only 95–125 miles.[5] The demands of area and route security in Cochinchina prevented the transfer of additional forces to Tonkin, and additional reinforcements from metropolitan France were not to be expected. Although the French assumed that the end of the war in Korea would bring no substantial increase in Chinese Communist aid to the Viet Minh, it should have been clear that the Korean armistice in late July 1953 would free the Chinese Communists to increase their support to the Viet Minh, who would thus be able to exert even more pressure on the already overextended French Union forces.[6]

Lieutenant General Navarre made a realistic appraisal of the French situation in Indochina and concluded that he had insufficient mobile combat forces to defeat the Viet Minh in the near term and that the forces he did have were far too cumbersome to bring the Viet Minh to bay. To correct these deficiencies, Navarre adopted a plan left to him by Salan and modified it to suit his concept of how to eliminate the Viet Minh guerrillas behind French lines and destroy the Viet Minh main battle forces. What came to be called the Navarre Plan assumed that the Viet Minh would hold the upper hand in northwestern Tonkin and Upper Laos during the 1953–1954 campaign season and that the French forces would not be sufficiently prepared for a final campaign to defeat the Viet Minh until 1954–1955, with a final mopping-up phase during the 1955–1956 campaign season.[7] Accordingly, the plan, unveiled on June 16, 1953, divided Indochina into a northern and a southern theater of operations and called for the French Union forces to assume a defensive posture in the north during 1953–1954 in anticipation of a major Viet Minh offensive either against the French position in the Red River delta or in northwestern Tonkin and Upper Laos. Meanwhile, the French Union forces would undertake a series of raids and spoiling attacks to throw the Viet Minh off balance and would initiate major offensive campaigns to clear the Viet Minh guerrillas from the Tonkin delta and from Annam and the Central Highlands.

To generate the manpower necessary for his plan, Navarre hoped to reconstitute a mobile operational reserve by eliminating isolated outposts and requesting an additional twelve infantry battalions, one engineer battalion, and one artillery group as well as additional air and naval forces from metropolitan France. However, Lieutenant General Navarre's request for twenty-five additional transports, fifty more bombers, and a considerable number of helicopters (plus the necessary crews and maintenance personnel) was refused outright. As he later related, the French government's response was delivered in February 1954 by General Pierre Fay, the chief of staff of the French Air Force: "Not one man. Not one plane!" (*Pas un homme. Pas un avion!*)[8] Another major aspect of the Navarre Plan was to place greater reliance on the growing Vietnamese National Army to secure the country-side and thus release French combat units for mobile operations.[9] Concurrently, steps would be taken to instill a greater aggressive spirit in the somewhat demoralized French Union forces.

The Navarre Plan was to be carried out in two phases. The first phase was intended to pacify the zones under French control and clean up several peripheral areas, and was to take place during the summer and early fall of 1953. In the second phase, during the 1953–1954 dry season, the French would preempt the expected Viet Minh offensive and occupy Viet Minh territory south of Vinh, in Annam.[10] Accordingly, Lieutenant General Navarre initiated the first phase in June 1953 with a number of small offensive operations to counter the renewed Viet Minh threat to the Red River delta and throw the enemy off balance.[11] A very successful airborne raid on the Viet Minh supply center at Lang Son in mid-July (Operation HIRONDELLE, discussed in chapter 10) was followed at the end of the month by the less successful Operation CAMARGUE along the central Annam coast to clear out Viet Minh–held fortified villages threatening the use by the French of RC 1. Between July 28 and August 4, as many as thirty French Union battalions took part in Operation CAMARGUE, but their target, the Viet Minh 95th Regiment, successfully avoided a decisive engagement and withdrew northward into its base area south of the Red River delta, leaving behind over two hundred dead and four hundred prisoners.[12] In early August, the garrison of the air-land base at

Na San was successfully evacuated to free up resources for other areas, and from late August into October a series of comparatively large antiguerrilla operations were conducted within the Tonkin delta perimeter (Operations TARENTAISE, CLAUDE, and BROCHET). In early October, a commando raid on the key Viet Minh transportation center of Lao Kay on the Chinese border produced mixed results. At the end of the rainy season, General Giap created the impression that he intended to break through the De Lattre Line from around Phu Tho. The Viet Minh moves were a feint, and on October 14, 1953, Lieutenant General Navarre launched Operation MOUETTE, aimed at the Viet Minh supply center at Phu Nho Quan south of the delta. More than six mobile groups supported by tanks and amphibious elements encircled the Viet Minh 320th Division and mauled it badly, but the stubborn defense put up by the Viet Minh 48th and 64th Regiments provided sufficient time for the Viet Minh to evacuate most of their supplies from Phu Nho Quan before the operation ended on November 7.[13]

Na San and the Concept of the *Base Aéro-Terrestre*

The Viet Minh offensive in northwestern Tonkin in the fall of 1952 prompted the creation of French strongholds at Lai Chau, Na San, and Moc Chau. Moc Chau fell to the Viet Minh 316th Division in November 1952, and General Giap then ordered the 308th Division to take Na San. Two costly frontal attacks, on November 23 and again on November 30–December 2, failed utterly. The final assault, on the night of December 1–2, cost the Viet Minh fifteen hundred dead, and overall the Viet Minh suffered some seven thousand casualties in their unsuccessful attempts to take Na San.[14]

With a garrison of some twelve thousand troops, Na San was still holding out in the summer of 1953, but it had outlived its usefulness and was tying down more troops and air transport than it was worth. Upon taking command in Tonkin, Major General René Cogny had urged Lieutenant General Navarre to evacuate the fortified camp and thus release the troops, air transport, and other resources for use elsewhere, particularly in the still-threatened Tonkin delta.[15] Moreover, it had become clear that the camp was no longer effective as a means of blocking Viet Minh movements into Laos since the Viet Minh had developed a bypass to the north via Tuan Giao, Dien Bien Phu, and the valley of the Nam Ou River to Luang Prabang. Cogny called Navarre's attention to the new bypass in a letter dated July 2, 1953, in which he noted, "I am persuaded of the inefficacy of Na San to impede the movements of the Viet Minh toward Laos."[16] Accordingly, Navarre ordered that Na San be abandoned, and the garrison was slowly reduced from twelve thousand men to about five thousand before the French surreptitiously evacuated the remaining troops by air between August 8 and 13 in one of the most successful air withdrawals of the war. General Giap apparently remained unaware of the withdrawal and thus missed a chance to turn the operation into a debacle by a determined attack while the evacuation was under way.

Interpretations of why General Giap missed such an opportunity vary widely. Jules Roy states that the evacuation was in fact observed while in progress, but that the message to Giap's headquarters was delayed by a radio operator's mistake.[17] Edgar O'Ballance speculates that Giap was under the mistaken impression that there were still some twelve thousand French troops at Na San and that they were moving out for an attack on Hoa Binh.[18] Phillip Davidson attributes Giap's inactivity to the fact that the Viet Minh were not prepared to respond quickly during the rainy season, but he also alludes to a French signal deception operation that led the Viet Minh radio intercept service to believe the increased air traffic into the camp was for the purpose of bringing in reinforcements.[19] In any event, the French got away clean.

Nevertheless, the evacuation of Na San was not a total success. Large quantities of ammunition, rations, and other supplies, such as precious pierced steel planking, had to be destroyed or left for the Viet Minh.[20] More importantly, the successful defense of the camp against determined Viet Minh assaults and the speed and smoothness of the camp's evacuation contributed to the mistaken conclusion that an air-land base (*base aéro-terrestre*) offered a viable means of blocking Viet Minh movements by providing a safe base for French-led guerrilla operations against the Viet Minh lines of communication as well as excellent prospects for enticing the Viet Minh into the set-piece battle that French commanders had long sought. The other major advantage of the *base aéro-terrestre* concept from the French perspective was that the use of air transport to supply them freed the French forces from the difficult problem of securing a surface line of communication. Such strongly defended "hedgehogs" (*hérrisons*)—resupplied by air and protected, if attacked, by close air support—seemed to be excellent means of increasing the insecurity of the Viet Minh rear areas.[21]

The euphoria created by the successful defense and evacuation of Na San masked the negative aspects of the *base aéro-terrestre* concept. Those who espoused the concept conveniently forgot that even the most successful of such bases, Na San, had tied down large numbers of French combat and support troops and a good deal of the scarce French air transport available in Indochina without immobilizing even an equivalent number of Viet Minh troops. The Viet Minh simply sealed off such camps and bypassed them with impunity. Moreover, the concept depended on the assumption that the Viet Minh, due to inadequate artillery, antiaircraft artillery, and logistics support, would be either unable to concentrate their forces to take a properly fortified camp, or, if they were able to do so, would expose themselves to superior French air and artillery firepower.[22]

The concept of the *base aéro-terrestre* had been a favorite of Lieutenant General Navarre's predecessor, Lieutenant General Raoul Salan, but Navarre himself saw that Na San had been a sinkhole for resources and freely admitted that as a means of blocking Viet Minh movements into Laos it had been a failure.[23] Indeed, Navarre was not a strong advocate of the *base aéro-terrestre* concept in general, calling it *"une solution médiocre,"* although the only one available.[24] In any event, Navarre's misgivings were not strong enough to forestall his willingness to gamble the French hegemony in Indochina on yet another fortified camp deep in enemy territory and supplied solely by air—at Dien Bien Phu.

The Defense of Laos

As the winter of 1953–1954 approached, it was obvious that Lieutenant General Navarre's plan had thus far failed to achieve either of its twin objectives: the elimination of Viet Minh guerrillas behind French lines or the destruction of the main Viet Minh battle forces. From Navarre's perspective, the Viet Minh had three possible courses of action for the 1953–1954 campaign season: a general attack on the French positions in the Tonkin delta; an offensive in Annam and Cochinchina, either along the Mekong or along the coast or perhaps in both areas simultaneously; or the resumption of their drive toward the upper Mekong in Laos. The latter appeared to be the most dangerous, both politically and militarily, but the French government refused to provide Navarre with clear instructions regarding the defense of northern Laos.[25] On July 24, 1953, he was ordered by the National Defense Council to defend Laos, if possible, but to give priority to preserving intact the CEFEO.[26] As Bernard Fall noted, "In strictly military terms, the evacuation of northern Laos would have greatly simplified Navarre's problem of overextended supply lines and forced the enemy to fight close to the French airbases and away from his own supply centers."[27]

Lieutenant General Navarre and other senior French military officers argued against defending Upper Laos, but the Laotians were a willing member of the French Union, and for political reasons they could not be left unprotected. Thus, Navarre was left to make his plans without the necessary political guidance and priorities and with predictable results. The ambiguity of the instructions given to him with respect to the defense of Laos was an important factor in the subsequent defeat at Dien Bien Phu. A clear statement that he was not obliged to defend Laos did not arrive until December 4, 1953, one day after he had issued orders announcing that he intended to defend Laos at all costs from the new *base aéro-terrestre* at Dien Bien Phu.[28]

Among the options ruled out by Lieutenant General Navarre were an attack on the Viet Minh administrative center at Thai Nguyen, fifty miles from Hanoi (similar to Operation LEA in 1947); an armored thrust to seize the Viet Minh supply center of Yen Bay, one hundred miles from the De Lattre Line (similar to Operation LORRAINE in November 1952); and the establishment of an air-land base closer to the De Lattre Line that could be supported, if necessary, by armored forces from the delta (as Operation HIRONDELLE against Lang Son had been supported in July 1953).[29] Having rejected the option of invading the Viet Minh bases in the Viet Bac once again, Navarre focused his attention on bringing the main Viet Minh forces to battle in northwestern Tonkin, a course of action that would presumably protect Upper Laos while providing an opportunity to eliminate the Viet Minh main battle forces once and for all. Should the Viet Minh choose to invade Laos once again, as seemed likely, their most probable course of action would be to move toward Luang Prabang from their existing base at Tuan Giao.[30] The close-in defense of both Luang Prabang and Vientiane was impractical and thus, as Navarre himself later wrote, the only viable solution was to interdict the Viet Minh invaders by implanting an entrenched camp astride their approach routes.[31]

The French position at Lai Chau in the Black River valley was strongly held and thus closed off the more northerly route toward Luang Prabang. The other potential route ran from Tuan Giao to Luang Prabang by way of the Nam Ou valley. On this southern route, the best blocking site appeared to be at Dien Bien Phu, situated in a small valley scarcely ten miles long by six miles wide and located fifty-five miles south of Lai Chau, between Tuan Giao and the Laotian border. The establishment of a major fortified camp astride the potential invasion route at Dien Bien Phu could serve as a base for French-led guerrilla forces and possibly as a base for bombers attempting to interdict the lines of communication from Communist China to the Viet Minh bases in northern Tonkin.[32] Navarre realized that such a base might not prevent all Viet Minh movements into Laos, but he had some reason to expect that its existence might draw General Giap into the set-piece battle for which the French had long hoped.[33]

It was thought that a *base aéro-terrestre* at Dien Bien Phu might also serve to deny to the Viet Minh the opium crop of northwestern Tonkin and Upper Laos upon which they relied to finance their purchases of materiel from Communist China and other suppliers. The economic importance of the opium crop of Upper Laos to the pro-French T'ai and Meo tribesmen as well as to the Viet Minh has long been known, as has the involvement of the French secret services in manipulating the opium trade to generate funds for various clandestine operations.[34] More recently, Douglas Porch has emphasized the role played by the French in the opium trade. He maintains that the establishment of the base at Dien Bien Phu in November 1953 had as its immediate objective the protection of a French special operations program among the pro-French T'ai partisans.[35]

The Planning of Operation CASTOR

From the beginning, the senior French commanders were not in agreement regarding either the desirability of establishing a *base aéro-terrestre* at Dien Bien

Phu or what role such a base might play if it were established. The *commandant en chef,* Lieutenant General Navarre, and his staff apparently felt Dien Bien Phu was the best place and that a fortified base there would act as a bulwark against a Viet Minh movement into Upper Laos. On the other hand, the French commander in Tonkin (*Forces Terrestres du Nord Viet-Nam, FTNV*), Major General René Cogny, and his staff were opposed to the Dien Bien Phu base on the grounds that it would not prevent the Viet Minh from marching on Laos but would divert critical resources from the defense of the delta.[36] Moreover, if the Dien Bien Phu base were to be established, Cogny was of the opinion that it should serve primarily as a rest and resupply center for French-led guerrillas operating against the Viet Minh lines of communication.[37] French Air Force commanders, too, were opposed to the establishment of a large base that would have to be resupplied entirely by air at a distance of over two hundred miles from the main airfields in the Red River delta. Colonel Jean Louis Nicot, the commander of French air transport in Indochina, stated flatly that he could not guarantee the required flow of supplies to Dien Bien Phu.[38]

Despite the misgivings of many of the key players and specific instructions from the French government to avoid "extravagant" operations, planning for Operation CASTOR, as the occupation of the Dien Bien Phu base was named, went forward under the direction of Lieutenant General Navarre's chief planner, Colonel Louis Berteil.[39] On December 3, 1953, *two weeks after the operation began,* the operations plan was finally sent to Major General Cogny, from whose command many of the combat troops and most of the logistical support for the operation were to come.[40] As outlined by Berteil and his associates, the plan contained several significant faults, not the least of which was the siting of the proposed *base aéro-terrestre* so far from the supporting French airfields and in a rather small valley dominated by the surrounding hills and mountains. Lieutenant General Navarre and his subordinates were not unaware of the implications of those defects but elected to proceed anyway. Navarre later characterized the distance of Dien Bien Phu from the French airfields in the Tonkin delta as "a very grave inconvenience" (*un trés grave inconvénient*).[41] The deficiencies were also clearly recognized by the Viet Minh commander, General Giap, who later remarked: "Dien Bien Phu was a very strong fortified entrenched camp. But on the other hand, it was set up in a mountainous region, on ground which was advantageous to us, and decidedly disadvantageous to the enemy. Dien Bien Phu was, moreover, a completely isolated position, far away from all the enemy's bases. The only means of supplying Dien Bien Phu was by air. These circumstances could easily deprive the enemy of all initiative and force him on to the defensive if attacked."[42]

The poor location of the Dien Bien Phu base might not have proven quite so disastrous had the French planners not also made several tragic miscalculations concerning their enemy.[43] French intelligence officers in the fall of 1953 were convinced that the Viet Minh continued to lack the logistical wherewithal to support a sustained campaign far from their bases. This view led them to conclude that any Viet Minh concentration in the area of Dien Bien Phu would be very slow and that the Viet Minh would be able to maintain a siege of Dien Bien Phu by no more than two divisions for only a very short time.[44] Furthermore, the intelligence officers and operational planners assumed that the Viet Minh would be unable to mass enough heavy artillery in the area to outgun the French artillery with which they planned to equip the garrison. And even if the Viet Minh did succeed in hauling forward a significant number of guns, it was believed that they would be unable to keep them supplied adequately with ammunition and would quickly fall victim to the superior French artillery and airpower.[45] Thus, Colonel Berteil and his associates confidently assumed that the logistical problems that the Viet Minh would have to overcome made it probable that any Viet Minh attack on Dien Bien Phu would be fought according to the following scenario: a movement phase of several weeks followed by an approach and reconnaissance phase of six to ten days, followed in turn by an attack phase of only a few days, and ending with the failure of the Viet Minh offensive.[46] Bernard Fall later wrote, "The underestimation of the Viet-Minh's capabilities was perhaps the only *real* error made by the French Commander-in-Chief in planning for the Indochina campaign of spring, 1954."[47] Such faulty assumptions and miscalculations were to have appalling consequences.

Not only did the French planners of the Dien Bien Phu operation underestimate the logistical capabilities of the Viet Minh, they seriously underestimated their own logistical requirements while simultaneously overestimating their ability to supply the proposed *base aéro-terrestre* by air. Logistical planning by the *4e Bureau,* EMIFT, assumed the garrison would consist of twelve infantry battalions, one artillery group plus another six batteries of 105 mm HM2 howitzers, one 120 mm mortar company, two platoons of M24 tanks, one engineer company, and one maintenance company, plus, of course, the necessary headquarters and support units, for a total strength of around thirteen thousand men.[48] Basing their calculations on a required daily supply rate of six kilograms per man, the planners concluded that at least 78 metric tons would be required each day. The planners also assumed that six F8F fighter-bombers would be based at the Dien Bien Phu airfield and would require, on the basis of four sorties per day, four tons per day per aircraft (or 24 tons per day total), making the daily maintenance requirement a total of 102 tons. In addition, they also assumed that an augmentation of 1.5 kilograms per man per day (a total of 19.5 tons per day) would be required during intensive combat and that the air-land base at Dien Bien Phu would probably undergo only five days of intensive combat and would thus require another 97.5 tons to be stockpiled at the base before such combat took place. Moreover, the *4e Bureau* planners proposed to put in place before the battle a reserve of two days' supplies (156 tons). Thus, it was envisioned that the daily maintenance (supply) rate for Dien Bien Phu would be 102 tons and that an additional 253.5 tons (the two-day reserve and the augmentation for five days of intensive combat) would have to be stockpiled at the base before intensive combat began.[49] In addition, the *4e Bureau* planners had to take into account the transport of replacement personnel into the entrenched camp. A normal replacement flow for a force the size of the Dien Bien Phu garrison would have been about one hundred men per day.[50] A C-47 could carry twenty-five parachutists, thus four aircraft per day would be required for personnel replacements by parachute alone.

At the same time, operational planners in the *3e Bureau*, EMIFT, were calculating the air transport needed to support the Dien Bien Phu base under conditions of limited visibility.[51] Their calculations assumed a garrison of only ten thousand men (versus the thirteen thousand estimated by the *4e Bureau*) and six fighter-bombers. They also assumed that operating under poor visibility conditions between a well-equipped departure airfield and a forward operational field outfitted with Very High Frequency (VHF) radio and an omni-directional radio beacon, one could count on handling four aircraft per hour. Using C-47 aircraft, four aircraft per hour equated to 10 short tons (9.1 metric tons) per hour. They also assumed that the airfield at Dien Bien Phu would be operational only eight hours each day due to the morning fog that did not lift until around noon. Thus, the planned airlift capacity of the Dien Bien Phu airfield would be only about 73 tons per day, or 29 tons per day less than the daily maintenance requirement established by the *4e Bureau* planners *and 11 tons per day less than the calculations of the 3e Bureau itself!*[52] The *3e Bureau* planners claimed that 84 tons per day were sufficient for the maintenance of ten thousand men and six fighter-bombers, but they did not even address the 253.5 tons of reserve supplies that would have to be stockpiled, much less account for the three-thousand-man discrepancy between their figures and those of the *4e Bureau*. Simple mathematics show that given the daily airlift capacity at Dien Bien Phu, it would be impossible to meet the daily maintenance requirement set by either *Bureau*, much less stockpile the supplies designated by the *4e Bureau*.

Moreover, the *3e Bureau* planners apparently did not consider either the auxiliary airfield south of the main Dien Bien Phu position or the airdrop/parachute delivery of supplies in their calculations of the airlift capacity at Dien Bien Phu. The assumption was, of course, that the main airfield would remain available throughout the operation. Thus, the planning figures forecast disaster, and the 73 tons-per-day limitation on deliveries by air, of itself, should have created grave doubts as to the ability to maintain the proposed Dien Bien Phu base entirely by air. As it turned out, over the 169 days of operations at Dien Bien Phu an average of 124 tons per day (over 1.5 times the planned figure) were delivered to the camp by air, an amount that still proved to be inadequate (see table 12.2 below).

Air Transport Resources

The key to successful execution of the plans for Operation CASTOR was effective, sustained aerial resupply. However, the tonnages actually required could not be delivered by the limited air transport resources available to the French Union forces in Indochina. Five main elements are necessary to any aerial resupply effort: adequate airfields, suitable aircraft, trained crews, skilled teams to prepare the cargo for movement by air, and reliable parachutes and associated airdrop equipment. In the fall of 1953, the French clearly lacked the airfields, transport aircraft, and crews necessary to support an operation of the size of that proposed for Dien Bien Phu while simultaneously maintaining the many isolated camps throughout Indochina that relied on aerial resupply. At best, the number of available aerial resupply companies and the quantity and reliability of the available parachutes and airdrop equipment that would be needed were marginal. Moreover, air operations in northern Indochina were made even more difficult by poor maps, inadequate navigational aids, and frequent poor flying weather. These known deficiencies in the key elements needed to support the proposed operation made the decision to proceed with Operation CASTOR all the more irrational. And while they could do nothing about the weather, the French apparently chose to do nothing about the poor maps and inadequate navigational aids, things they might have improved with some effort.

Airfields

It should have been clear to the French planners that air transport operations in support of Dien Bien Phu would be hampered not only by the distance of the camp from the existing airfields in the Tonkin delta (about two hundred miles), but also by the fact that the number of departure airfields was limited. Only three main airfields were available: Gia Lam and Bach Mai outside Hanoi and Cat Bi outside Haiphong. A few smaller fields existed but were inadequately equipped to handle major air transport operations. Practical considerations of cost, time, and engineering prevented the construction of new fields nearer to Dien Bien Phu. At Dien Bien Phu itself, there were two airstrips, both of limited capacity and requiring substantial engineering work before they could be used for sustained air transport operations. The main airstrip just northwest of the center of the proposed camp had been used by the Japanese in World War II. An auxiliary strip was located just to the north of what was to become the isolated southern outpost of ISABELLE.

The configuration of the terrain around the proposed camp limited the potential volume and accuracy of personnel and supply parachute drops. In addition to allowing the Viet Minh to gain direct observation of the drop zones and to position their antiaircraft guns in a tight ring around the camp, the high hills surrounding the narrow valley in which the fortified base was to be located restricted the possible approach routes and limited the number of aircraft that could operate over the camp at any one time.

Once the operation began, it soon became obvious that the size of the Dien Bien Phu airhead was inadequate to permit simultaneous drops of cargo and personnel as well as bombing and antiaircraft artillery suppression.[53] Since close air support operations were rightfully given a high priority and flak suppression was indispensable, no supplies could be dropped while bombing and strafing of the Viet Minh positions was under way. Since the air transports were operating at the limits of their effective range, they were unable to loiter for any considerable period of time waiting for tactical air operations to conclude, and they were thus sometimes forced to return to their bases with their cargoes still aboard.

Transport Aircraft

The number and quality of the military transport aircraft available in Indochina were never sufficient to meet the air transport needs of the French Union ground forces, and the situation was to become acute during the Dien Bien Phu operation. The three available transport groups (1/64 *Béarn*, 2/64 *Anjou*, and 2/63 *Sénégal*), commanded by Colonel Jean Louis Nicot, were authorized a total of only fifty C-47 Dakotas and five ancient Amiot AAC 1 Toucan transports, but by March 1953 they had been augmented by twenty-nine C-47s from France and twenty-one C-47s borrowed from the United States.[54] In March 1954, a further augmentation of twenty-four C-119 transports with American crews arrived, bringing the total number of transports in Indochina to one hundred C-47s, twenty-four C-119s, and twelve other transport aircraft.[55]

In addition to the military transport aircraft available, the French authorities in Indochina relied heavily during the Dien Bien Phu operation on the temporary augmentation provided by the civilian air transport firms operating in Indochina. Almost all the military transport aircraft were dedicated to the support of Dien Bien Phu, and commercial aircraft handled other necessary deliveries.[56] Of course, the total number of aircraft on the books by no means represented the total number available. Combat losses, mechanical problems, normal maintenance, delays in the receipt of parts, and crew losses served to reduce the number of sorties that could be flown each day. French aircraft maintenance was notoriously poor, and Colonel Nicot could count on only about a 56–75 percent serviceability rate.[57]

Some air transport assets were also required to provide minimal support to the many isolated camps elsewhere in Indochina, several of which could only be resupplied by air. On February 18, 1954, well after Operation CASTOR was under way, a number of transports were diverted from the major effort to build up supply levels at Dien Bien Phu to provide emergency air transport support to the airland bases at Muong Sai, Luang Prabang, and on the Plain of Jars in response to

the Viet Minh 308th Division's incursion. This prompted the chief of the FTNV
Bureau Mouvements Transports to prepare a memorandum outlining the status of
the various means of transport available to FTNV.[58] He concluded that the critical
element was air transport, which at that time was insufficient to support thirty-
five thousand men exclusively by air, as was required. Immediate augmentation
was needed, and among the measures recommended to accomplish that end were
increasing the number of flying hours between overhauls for the C-47 fleet; the
addition of ten C-119s and ten C-119 crews so as to be able to perform a total of
fifteen C-119 missions per day in northern Viet Nam; government facilitation of
the importation and use by civil aviation companies of new aircraft, such as the
Nord 2501, as well as facilitation of their efforts to obtain aircraft and parts from
the nationalized aircraft factories in France; and augmentation of the capabilities
of the aerial resupply companies, particularly completion of the establishment of
the 5th Aerial Resupply Company (*5e Compagnie de Ravitaillement par Air*, CRA
5) at Cat Bi, which had been delayed for financial reasons.[59]

Several types of transport aircraft were used in Indochina. By 1954, the antiquated Amiot AAC 1 Toucan had all but been eliminated, and the workhorse of
the French air transport fleet was the familiar C-47 Dakota. The C-47 was sturdy
and reliable, but its cargo capacity was limited to only 2.5 short tons, and all cargo
had to be loaded or discharged from side-opening doors, which made it necessary
for a C-47 airdropping or paradropping cargo to make as many as twelve passes
over a drop zone to deliver its load, a procedure that increased its vulnerability to
enemy antiaircraft fire.[60] At the end of 1953, the American aid program began to
deliver a number of the new C-119 Packets, better known as the "Flying Boxcar."
With a capacity of about six short tons, the C-119 had greater power and was capable of delivering heavy equipment, such as bulldozers and 105 mm howitzers as
well as cargo packages of over one ton. The C-119 also had the advantage of clamshell doors in the rear that facilitated the discharge of cargo either on the ground
or by parachute, and the plane was considered excellent for dropping parachutists.
Its ability to deliver its load in only one pass over a drop zone was a major plus. A
few British Bristol Freighters belonging to commercial airlines in Indochina were
also employed.[61] The Bristol had clamshell doors in the nose and was used only for
airlanded cargo, particularly vehicles and other "heavy lifts." Of the total tonnage
delivered to Dien Bien Phu, 31.4 percent would be airlanded by C-47s and Bristols, 28.1 percent would be airdropped or parachuted by C-47s, and 40.5 percent
would be airdropped or parachuted by C-119s.[62]

Crews

Of course, the aircraft were useless without crews, and transport crews as well
as fighter and bomber crews were worked to exhaustion over Dien Bien Phu. At

the beginning of the operation in November 1953, Colonel Nicot had only ten French C-119 crews and fifty-two other French Air Force crews for the ten C-119s and seventy C-47s he was authorized.[63] The situation did not improve substantially during the course of the battle for Dien Bien Phu. In April 1954, many crews logged over 150 flying hours, three times what was considered normal for heavy combat flying.[64] Many of the dangerous air transport missions over Dien Bien Phu were flown by French civilian airline crews and by American civilian C-119 crews working for the Civil Air Transport Corporation, which was generally known to be a U.S. Central Intelligence Agency front organization. The French civilian crews were trained in military air transport operations, including formation flying and airdrop/paradrop procedures. The American C-119 crews were ostensibly American civilians, but they included several U.S. Air Force pilots quietly assigned to CAT to gain knowledge of air operations in Indochina in case the United States should intervene. The CAT pilots were paid $2,000 per month, but their contracts did not require them to fly in "combat" situations. Even so, they often took greater chances than the French military crews, a fact that did not escape the notice of the men on the ground that they were supporting.[65] Between April 24 and May 1, at a critical stage in the effort to keep Dien Bien Phu supplied, the American C-119 civilian crews were pulled off the Dien Bien Phu run for diplomatic reasons. During the final week of the garrison's existence, both American and French civilian crews refused to fly missions over Dien Bien Phu unless flak suppression was increased. It was not a question of their courage, which had been proven many times; the Viet Minh antiaircraft artillery fire had simply become overwhelming.

Aerial Resupply Units

Transport aircraft only carried the men and cargo to their destination. Parachute assaults and aerial resupply operations such as Dien Bien Phu also required the highly skilled services of aerial resupply units to repair and pack parachutes, marshal supplies for aerial delivery, and rig and load equipment for air transport, airdrop, and paradrop. In Indochina, these highly skilled services were found in the aerial resupply companies (*Compagnies de Ravitaillement par Air*, CRA), which were under the control of the *Commandement des Troupes Aéroportées en Indochine* (TAPI).[66] Each CRA was authorized about 250–300 trained military personnel augmented by some 400–500 Indochinese laborers, often Viet Minh prisoners of war (PIMs), and over 200 trucks.[67] The personnel of each CRA were normally divided into three teams: a Reception and Packaging Section that supervised the receipt of cargo and its rigging by teams of PIMs, a Loading Section that loaded the aircraft, and a large Equipment Section that maintained the parachutes and airdrop equipment.

Initially, the *CRA du Nord*, with its headquarters at Gia Lam airfield near Hanoi, three parachute maintenance and packing sections at the Airborne Base, North (*Base Aéroportée Nord*), a little over a mile from Bach Mai airfield outside Hanoi, and a detachment at Cat Bi airfield near Haiphong handled all air cargo for Dien Bien Phu. In September 1953, the *CRA du Nord* had 253 military personnel augmented by 400 PIMs and a normal monthly capacity of handling some 2,475 short tons of cargo and some 2,500 personnel parachutes.[68] In January 1954, the aerial resupply units in Indochina were reorganized, and from February 1954 Dien Bien Phu was supported by the 3e CRA at Gia Lam and Bach Mai and the 5e CRA augmented by three platoons from the 4e CRA (normally based at Saigon) at Cat Bi.[69]

The supplies prepared by the CRA for delivery to the units at Dien Bien Phu were issued from the depots of the Tonkin Operational Base (*Base Opérationnelle du Tonkin*, BOTK) and from the Ground Forces North Viet Nam (*Forces Terrestres du Nord Viet-Nam*, FTNV) territorial depots. Temporary depots were established near the departure airfields to facilitate the preparation of loads for delivery to Dien Bien Phu. At Gia Lam airfield alone there was one depot with 1,700 short tons of ammunition, another with 270 short tons of mines, another with 250 short tons of engineer supplies, another with 130 short tons of miscellaneous items, and yet another with over 14,000 cubic feet of petroleum products on hand to meet the needs of Dien Bien Phu.[70] Similar stockpiles of rations, clothing, medical supplies, spare parts, and radio equipment were maintained.

By and large the CRAs performed their job in an outstanding—some might even say heroic—manner. Colonel Langlais, the para commander at Dien Bien Phu, had few good words for the staff officers ensconced in comfortable billets in Hanoi, Saigon, and Da Lat, but he lauded the superhuman efforts of "those who delivered our daily bread: the riggers and the parachute packers confined in their stuffy hangers."[71] Nevertheless, mistakes were made, and some cargo was lost due to poor packing. On April 14, 1954, for example, a much-needed replacement electric generator was destroyed when it was dropped into the camp improperly packaged.[72] The same drop included numerous five-gallon cans of gasoline, also much needed, which were filled to the brim. On impact the cans burst open and the precious gasoline was lost.

Parachutes and Airdrop Equipment

The final key elements in any successful aerial supply operations are reliable parachutes and associated airdrop equipment. Throughout the First Indochina War, parachutes and airdrop equipment were in short supply and were subject to various technical limitations. Basically, one parachute was required for every man or for every 220 pounds of cargo dropped, but there was also an inherent loss of net cargo tonnage to parachute rigging materials since each 220 pounds of cargo required about twenty-seven pounds of parachute material and accessories.[73]

Table 12.1. Utilization of Cargo Parachutes in Support of Dien Bien Phu

Period	Large Parachutes (500 m², 1 ton)	Small Parachutes (50 m², 100 kg)	Remarks
Nov. 20, 1953– Jan. 25, 1954	1,867	22,679	307 malfunctions
Jan. 26–Feb. 24, 1954	506	181	23 malfunctions
Feb. 25–March 13, 1954	570	553	8 malfunctions
	820	34,262	Instantaneous; 96+ malfunctions
	0	376	25-sec. delay; 160+ malfunctions
March 14–May 7, 1954	0	20,611	40-sec. delay; 1,755+ malfunctions
	0	504	50-sec. delay; 41+ malfunctions
Total Chutes Used	**3,763**	**79,166**	**More than 2,390 malfunctions**

Source: Sauvagnac, *Report of December 20, 1954,* annex 4. Until March 14, all parachutes were recovered; thereafter none were. See also Windrow, *The Last Valley,* 681n58, and Plating, "Failure at the Margins," 63n36.

Increased French production and American aid deliveries of parachutes and air-drop equipment provided some relief, but the high demand created by the effort to support Dien Bien Phu and the fact that after the end of March 1954 none of the parachutes could be recovered nearly outstripped the available supply. Some idea of the number of parachutes required to support Dien Bien Phu and of their reliability is provided in table 12.1.

The effort to keep Dien Bien Phu alive with parachuted supplies was made possible only by the steady delivery of American parachutes to Indochina. Most of those parachutes were supplied from U.S. stocks in Japan and were obtained through the good offices of the chief of the U.S. MAAG-Indochina. On April 18, 1954, Lieutenant General Navarre himself wrote to the chief of the MAAG to thank him for obtaining parachutes sufficient to allow the French to maintain the level of deliveries to Dien Bien Phu of around one hundred large G-12 chutes and one hundred A-22 containers per day.[74] Navarre went on to request even greater efforts to obtain at least one thousand G-12 chutes and A-22 containers delivered at Haiphong every ten days beginning on June 15, as well as forty thousand smaller G-1A parachutes delivered at Haiphong by May 25, and then sixty thousand per month from June 15. The parachutes and containers requested were intended to meet an expected minimum requirement of 270 tons of cargo delivered to Dien Bien Phu each day (90 tons per day by large G-12 parachutes and A-22 containers and 180 tons per day by small G-1A parachutes).

The Buildup of the *Base Aéro-Terrestre*

Operation CASTOR began at 1035 hours, November 20, 1953, with a parachute assault by about twenty-two hundred men of three battalions of the Airborne Group (*Groupement Aéroportée*, GAP) commanded by Brigadier General Jean Gilles to seize control of the Dien Bien Phu valley. Upon landing, the paras of the 6th Colonial Parachute Battalion (*6e Bataillon de Parachutistes Coloniaux*, 6e BPC) encountered what in retrospect they may have considered a fateful logistical omen: they were opposed by soldiers of the Viet Minh 148th Independent Regiment wearing French paratroop camouflage uniforms.[75] The assault troops were reinforced during the next two days, bringing the total number of personnel to 4,560 men. In the course of the initial assault operations, the paras lost fifteen killed and fifty-three wounded; the Viet Minh lost ninety men in all.[76]

Beginning on December 1, the paras were relieved by other French Union ground forces and returned to their bases near Hanoi. On December 7, the Northwest Operational Group (*Groupement Opérationnel Nord-Ouest*, GONO) was established to command the operations at Dien Bien Phu, and the troop level reached ninety-six hundred men. By that time, the camp had taken essentially the form shown on map 12.1. The new camp was supported exclusively by airdrop and parachute until repairs to the main airfield were completed on November 25. Thereafter, men and supplies were airlanded (until March 14, 1954) as well as airdropped and parachuted. Tables 12.2 to 12.4 provide an overall picture of the total tonnage delivered to Dien Bien Phu by air during the entire operation, the average daily supply rate maintained during the various phases of the operation, and a breakout of the average daily supply rate by supply category. The three tables are based on contemporary French official documents that, as might be expected, vary somewhat, both in periodization and data elements.

In the first eighteen days of Operation CASTOR, the buildup of men and materiel proceeded according to plan and about one hundred tons of supplies and equipment arrived at the camp by air each day.[77] The following fortnight saw the evacuation of the fortified French camp at Lai Chau (Operation POLLUX); the accelerated movement of personnel into Dien Bien Phu, notably GM 9; and air transport operations focused on the delivery of engineer materials for the fortification of the camp and the reconstruction of the airfield. Between December 7 and 25, the transports delivered some 4,680 men, and another 3,470 men were evacuated from the area by air. Cargo deliveries averaged about 170 short tons per day during the same period. Between December 25, 1953, and January 25, 1954, GONO continued to develop the fortified camp and received GM 6 and various service elements. In accordance with the logistical plan, about two hundred tons of cargo were delivered by air to Dien Bien Phu each day during the period.

As of January 25, 1954, the French Union forces manning the *base aéro-*

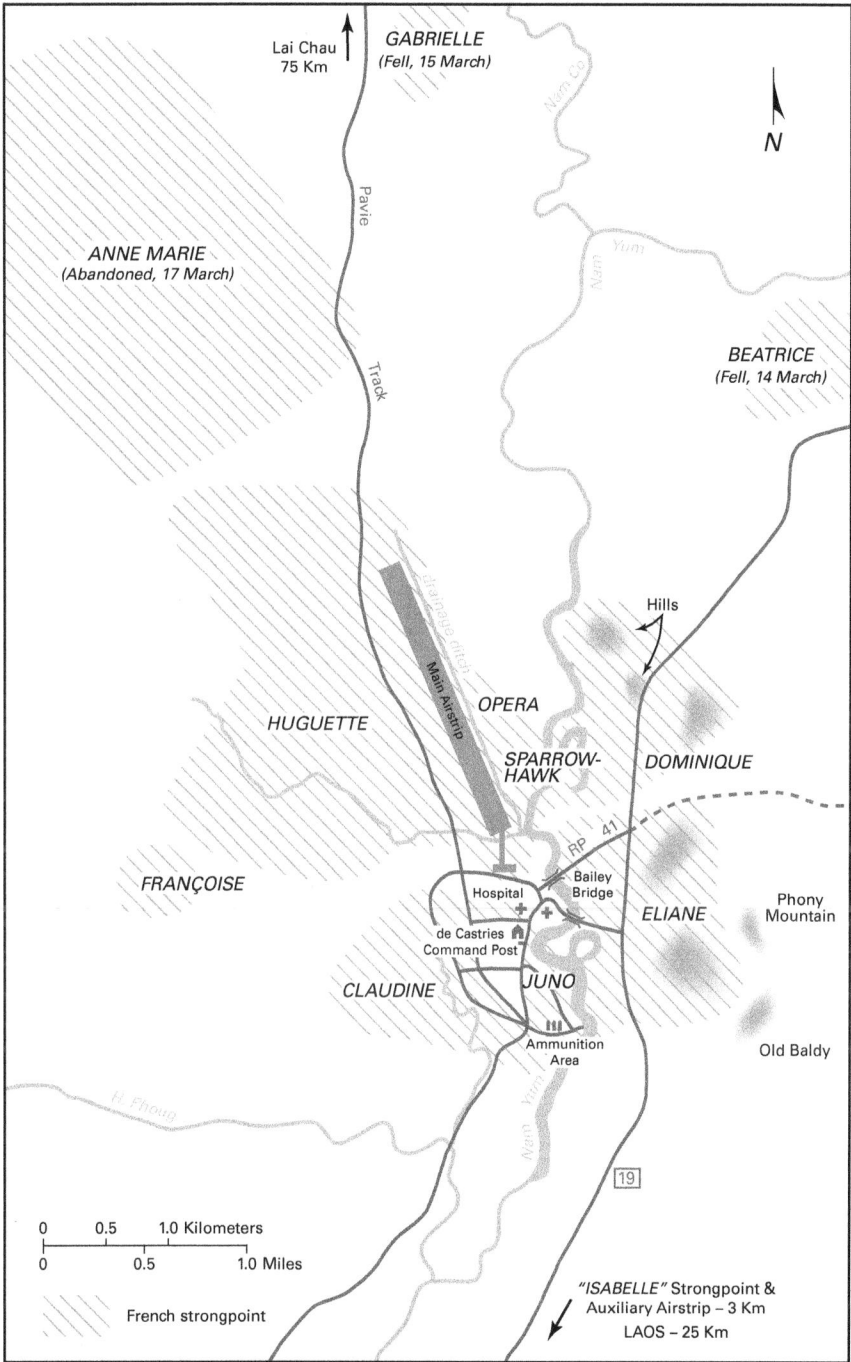

Map 12.1. The *Base Aéro-Terrestre* at Dien Bien Phu.

GABRIELLE
(Fell, 15 March)

Lai Chau
75 Km

Pavie

ANNE MARIE
(Abandoned, 17 March)

Track

BEATRICE
(Fell, 14 March)

N

Hills

Main Airstrip

OPERA

HUGUETTE

SPARROW-
HAWK

DOMINIQUE

RP 41

FRANÇOISE

Hospital

Bailey
Bridge

Phony
Mountain

de Castries
Command Post

ELIANE

CLAUDINE

JUNO

Ammunition
Area

Old Baldy

19

0   0.5   1.0 Kilometers
0   0.5   1.0 Miles

French strongpoint

"ISABELLE" Strongpoint &
Auxiliary Airstrip – 3 Km
LAOS – 25 Km

Table 12.2. Air Transport Deliveries to Dien Bien Phu

Period	Unit	Type of Aircraft	Method			Conditions	Total Tonnage Delivered	Average Daily Tonnage
			Tons Landed	Tons Dropped	Tons Parachuted			
Build-Up Phase								
Nov. 20, 1953–Jan. 25, 1954 (67 days)	CRA 5	C-119	0	1,602.6	2,067.0	day, low alt	3,669.6	157
	CRA 3	C-47 Bristol	4,383.4	440.4	2,024.0	day, low alt	6,847.8	
Jan. 26, 1954–Feb. 24, 1954 (29 days)	CRA 5	C-119	0	112.0	506.0	day, low alt	618.0	64
	CRA 3	C-47 Bristol	1,229.7	2.1	14.4	day, low alt	1,246.1	
Feb. 25, 1954–March 13, 1954 (17 days)	CRA 5	C-119	0	161.0	570.0	day, low alt	731.0	103
	CRA 3	C-47 Bristol	970.5	0	50.2	day, low alt	1,020.7	
Active Battle Phase								
March 14, 1954–May 7, 1954 (55 days)	CRA 5	C-119	0	0	2,744.0	day, low alt	3,404.9	122
					147.1	night, low alt		
					36.3	day, low alt, w/ftr cover		
					477.5	day, mdm alt, delayed		
	CRA 3	C-47	0		1,480.2	day, low alt	3,321.5	
					4.1	day, mdm alt, no delay		
				5.3	12.3			
					1,819.6	day, mdm alt, delayed		
Total (169 days)			6,583.6	2,323.3	11,952.7		20,859.6	124

Source: Sauvagnac, Report of December 20, 1954, annex 5. All tonnages are in metric tonnes, rounded to nearest tenth. See also Windrow, The Last Valley, 706.

Table 12.3. Average Daily Supply Rate at Dien Bien Phu

Dates	Average Daily Supply Rate	Daily Supply Rate by Supply Category											Remarks
		Munitions		Engineer		Intendance		POL	Med	Sig	Ord	Misc	
		Inf	Arty	PSP	Misc	Food	Misc						
Build-Up Phase													
Nov. 20, 1953–Jan. 25, 1954	15.3	1.69	2.53	1.20	3.50	3.10	0.02	0.78	0.03	0.13	0.10	2.21	Establishment
Jan. 26, 1954–Feb. 24, 1954	5.0	0.60	0.50	–	0.34	2.20	0.01	0.77	0.03	0.07	0.04	0.40	VM 308th Div raid in Laos; decline of artillery ammo levels
Feb. 25, 1954–Mar. 13, 1954	8.0	0.45	2.40	–	1.10	2.50	0.02	1.00	0.02	0.08	0.03	0.33	Rebuilding of artillery ammo levels
Active Battle Phase													
Mar. 14, 1954–May 7, 1954	11.8	1.80	4.20	–	0.35	2.30	0.01	0.27	0.14	0.13	0.11	0.42	Battle of Dien Bien Phu

Source: Baubeau, "Aspects logistiques de la bataille de Dien Bien Phu," table ("Taux Moyens Journaliers d'Entretien à Dien Bien Phu"). Average daily supply rate and daily supply rates by supply category are given in kilograms per man per day. The figures represent estimates based on the materiel delivered to Dien Bien Phu divided by the number of men present in the camp. The actual rates were probably somewhat lower due to the fact that as the operation progressed the proportion of the cargo delivered but not recovered for use steadily increased. Miscellaneous includes vehicles. Before the operation began, French planners estimated that the required daily supply rate would be six kilograms per man per day. The average daily supply rate for the active battle phase of the operation includes an additional two kilograms per man per day to account for efforts to rebuild reserves not reflected in the breakout by supply category.

Table 12.4. Percentage of Average Daily Supply at Dien Bien Phu by Supply Category

| Supply Category | Build-Up Phase | | | Active Battle Phase |
	1st Period Nov. 20, 1953– Jan. 25, 1954	2nd Period Jan. 26– Feb. 24, 1954	3rd Period Feb. 25– March 13, 1954	March 14– May 7, 1954
Small Arms Ammo	11.0	12.0	5.6	18.0
Artillery Ammo	17.0	10.0	30.0	42.0
Engineer Supplies	30.8	7.0	13.7	3.5
Food & Clothing	20.2	44.2	31.2	23.1
POL Products	5.3	15.0	12.0	2.7
Medical Supplies	0.3	0.6	0.2	1.4
Signal Supplies	0.8	1.4	1.0	1.3
Ordnance Supplies	0.6	0.8	0.4	1.2
Miscellaneous	14.0	8.0	4.0	4.5

Source: Baubeau, "Aspects logistiques de la bataille de Dien Bien Phu," table ("Taux Moyens Journaliers d'Entretien à Dien Bien Phu [h/j]").

terrestre at Dien Bien Phu included the operational headquarters (GONO), a garrison headquarters, two mobile groups and one airborne group headquarters, twelve infantry battalions, two 105 mm artillery groups, one 155 mm battery, two 120 mm mortar companies, two armor platoons (ten M24 tanks), two engineer companies, and various service elements.[78] In all, on January 25 the garrison included about 13,200 men: 4,400 Europeans, 2,550 North Africans, 250 Africans, 3,600 Indochinese (of which 1,400 were auxiliaries), and 2,400 PIMs.[79] In addition to the weapons organic to the units present, the camp was supplied with an additional twenty-six automatic rifles, seventy-five light machine guns, twenty-five heavy machine guns, and thirteen mortars (60 mm and 81 mm) as well as forty-four jeeps, forty-seven Dodge trucks, twenty-six GMC trucks, one ambulance, and three bulldozers.[80] By January 25, sufficient cargo had been delivered to bring the supply levels of the new *base aéro-terrestre* up to nine days of rations, eight days of POL, about 875 rounds of small arms ammunition per weapon, roughly 200 rounds per 75 mm recoilless rifle, about 960 rounds per 105 mm howitzer, roughly 700 rounds per 155 mm howitzer, and about 600 rounds per 120 mm mortar.[81]

Overall, between November 20, 1953, and January 25, 1954, aerial cargo deliveries to Dien Bien Phu averaged 157 tons per day, for a total of almost 10,517 tons during the period, of which 4,383 tons were airlanded, 2,043 tons were airdropped, and 4,091 tons were parachuted. The largest proportion of the total tonnage delivered, about 30.8 percent, consisted of engineer supplies, including sufficient pierced steel planking to cover the main airfield to a length of about

3,775 feet. Ammunition (28 percent) and rations (20.2 percent) formed the bulk of the remaining tonnage. Deliveries by air were sufficient during this period of the buildup phase to maintain an average daily supply rate of 15.3 kilograms per man per day.[82]

The second period of the buildup phase was marked by the raid of the Viet Minh 308th Division into Laos that began on January 27, 1954. Support of the existing Laotian outposts and the movement of reinforcements into northern Laos to foil the Viet Minh advance required a significant part of the available air transport. The number of troops at Dien Bien Phu reached 14,450 men on January 26, but aerial cargo deliveries to Dien Bien Phu between January 25 and February 24 averaged only 64 tons per day for a total of just over 1,864 tons during the period, of which 1,230 tons were airlanded, 114 tons were airdropped, and 520 tons were parachuted. The largest proportion of the total tonnage delivered, about 44.2 percent, consisted of rations, and petroleum products (15 percent) and ammunition (22 percent) constituted the bulk of the remaining tonnage. Reduced deliveries of supplies to Dien Bien Phu lowered the average daily supply rate to only five kilograms per man per day between January 26 and February 24.[83]

The final period of the buildup phase was characterized by efforts to rebuild the supply levels that had declined as a result of the diversion of air transport to Laos. On February 24, the *commandant en chef* ordered first priority on air transport shifted back to Dien Bien Phu, and in the seventeen days that remained before the first Viet Minh assault on March 13, some 1,250 men and about 1,752 tons of supplies and equipment were delivered, an average of about 103 tons per day. Of the total tonnage, 971 tons were airlanded, 161 tons were airdropped, and 620 tons were parachuted. Special efforts were made to rebuild ammunition stocks, and about 30 percent of the total tonnage delivered during the period consisted of artillery ammunition. A considerable portion of the delivered tonnage was also devoted to rations and other quartermaster supplies (31.2 percent), engineer materiel (13.7 percent), and petroleum products (12 percent). The average daily supply rate during the period crept back up to eight kilograms per man per day, and by March 13, 1954, supply levels in the Dien Bien Phu depots stood at nine days of rations, eight days of POL, about 900–1,200 rounds of small arms ammunition per weapon, and about 700–1,225 rounds per artillery/mortar tube.[84]

Major Diversions

A number of events elsewhere in Indochina created crisis conditions requiring the diversion of critical air transport and other resources that might otherwise have gone to support of the *base aéro-terrestre* at Dien Bien Phu. The evacuation of the French Union garrison of Lai Chau in mid-December 1953 as well as the Viet Minh invasion of the Central Highlands and Middle Laos in December 1953 and of Upper Laos in January–February 1954 required significant air transport assets. Viet Minh infiltration in the Red River delta demanded a response and seriously threatened the flow of cargo from the port of Haiphong to the departure airfields near Hanoi. The Viet Minh also directly reduced the number of available transport aircraft by successful commando raids on the departure airfields. The various abortive efforts, such as Operation CONDOR, to break through the Viet Minh encirclement of Dien Bien Phu also absorbed additional air transport resources. Finally, Lieutenant General Navarre's decision to proceed with a major offensive in central Viet Nam, Operation ATLANTE, while the operation at Dien Bien Phu was still in progress ate up what little reserves of manpower, logistical support, and air transport remained.

Toward the end of the war, many isolated units could be supplied only by airdrop, and the tonnage of airdropped supplies for all of Indochina increased accordingly, from an average of 1,700 tons per month in 1953, to 2,200 tons in December 1953, to 4,700 tons in March 1954, to 7,000 tons in April 1954.[85] Between November 20, 1953, and January 20, 1954, activities outside Dien Bien Phu required the delivery by air of some 9,000 short tons of supplies, but the period of greatest intensity for air transport operations in Indochina was reached between January 20 and May 7, 1954, when a total of 30,000 short tons (11,000 short tons for Dien Bien Phu and 19,000 short tons for other locations), the equivalent of 12,000 truckloads, were delivered by air to French Union forces throughout Indochina.[86]

Operation POLLUX

Lai Chau, the capital of the T'ai Federation, was an important base for the defense of northwestern Tonkin. It was the headquarters of the Northwest Operational Zone (*Zone Opérationnelle Nord-Ouest*, ZONO), commanded by Lieutenant Colonel André Trancart, and was the center for French-led guerrilla operations against the Viet Minh. The decision to abandon the base at Lai Chau was dictated in part by the difficulties of supplying it exclusively by air inasmuch as the small airfield was often flooded and was described as "the only airfield in the world where aircraft could be shot down by antiaircraft artillery firing down on them."[87] The movement of the Viet Minh 316th Division toward Lai Chau precipitated the evacuation of the garrison (Operation POLLUX). Some units were flown out on December 10, 1953, and some three hundred short tons of ammunition and forty vehicles were destroyed. Over four hundred mules and packhorses were also left for the Viet Minh who entered Lai Chau on December 12. Of the 2,101 men of the garrison who attempted to withdraw on foot toward Dien Bien Phu, mostly T'ai irregulars accompanied by French advisors, only about one hundred reached the safety of French lines.[88]

The Defense of Seno-Savannakhet

On December 22, 1953, just over a month after Operation CASTOR began, General Giap ordered the Viet Minh 101st Regiment (325th Division) and 66th Regiment (304th Division) to strike west from their bases in north-central Annam with the aim of penetrating to the Mekong River in central and southern Laos and cutting communications between Tonkin and southern Viet Nam. The Viet Minh easily brushed aside GM 2, which was hastily sent from Hue to block them, and by Christmas Day 1953, the 101st Regiment had reached the Mekong River at Thakhek and cut Indochina in two. The French responded by rushing men and supplies from Tonkin and southern Viet Nam to the Seno-Savannakhet region, where they intended to establish a fortified base for the defense of central and southern Laos.[89] Meanwhile, the 66th Regiment moved toward the French airfield at Seno, taking the French outposts along the road through the Central Highlands one by one and, on January 24, 1954, mauling GM 51, which had been sent to assist the isolated garrisons.

The logistical base at Seno-Savannakhet around which the defense of central Laos was organized had an airfield with a 5,250-foot runway that was in the process of being lengthened. The base was connected to Dong Ha in central Viet Nam by RC 9, which ran for some 186 miles through difficult terrain subject to Viet Minh infiltration. It was also connected to Saigon in southern Viet Nam by RC 13, a narrow, 518-mile route limited to about 150–160 vehicles per day by the ferry at Stung-Treng. Seno-Savannakhet was also connected to southern Viet Nam by the Mekong River, which was navigable during low water only up as far as Kratie. Although denied the use of RC 9 by three unusable bridges and the danger of Viet Minh ambushes, the French used all modes of transport simultaneously to assemble men and materiel in the Seno-Savannakhet area as quickly as possible.

Five parachute infantry battalions, two parachute artillery batteries, and one mobile surgical team moved by air from Haiphong to Seno in six days (December 25–30) using only five or six civilian aircraft of various types. One Moroccan *tabor* (infantry battalion), one artillery battery, two Laotian infantry companies, and one truck element flew from Lak Sao in northern Laos to Seno in a single day (December 26) using ten C-47s. GM 1, which was still in action in the Red River delta on December 28, moved from Haiphong to Saigon by sea in six days and then, reinforced by a maintenance platoon and a *Garde Républicaine* (national police/gendarmerie) detachment, proceeded by road from Saigon to Seno in only five days. Another mobile group (GM 51) and an additional tank platoon moved by water up the Mekong to Kratie in six days and then by road to Seno in another three days. In all, between December 25, 1953, and January 12, 1954, the garrison at Seno-Savannakhet was reinforced by five parachute infantry battalions, eight infantry battalions, two Laotian infantry companies, two artillery groups, two parachute artillery batteries, one battery of 105 mm howitzers, three platoons of armor, one engineer company, one mobile surgical team, one mobile maintenance platoon, a detachment of the *Garde Républicaine,* and miscellaneous headquarters and support elements. The results demonstrated what the French were able to accomplish under stress, but the diversion of both combat units and air transport seriously degraded French defensive capabilities in other areas and particularly decreased the air transport available for the continued buildup at Dien Bien Phu.

Despite his strong and rapid response, Lieutenant General Navarre soon learned the futility of even the most formidable blocking position in a country devoid of roads and against an enemy who had little need of them. The Seno-Savannakhet base was saved from direct attack by the gallant stand of two parachute infantry battalions at Hine Siu, but the Viet Minh simply bypassed the garrison. By mid-January, Viet Minh forces had thoroughly infiltrated the Central Highlands as well as central and southern Laos and had even surrounded Voeune Sai in northeastern Cambodia. At the end of April 1954, four Viet Minh regular battalions were still ranging through southern Laos and northern Cambodia, gathering food and organizing bases for future operations.[90] French control of the Central Highlands was subsequently restricted to a small pocket around Ban Me Thuot and Da Lat following the annihilation in the Mu Gia Pass of GM 100 by elements of the Viet Minh 108th and 803rd Regiments on June 24, 1954. Composed of French volunteers recently arrived from Korea, GM 100 was caught in a large ambush between An Khe and Pleiku and lost over two hundred vehicles, most of a 105 mm artillery group, and five hundred men, including the group commander.[91]

The second phase of General Giap's plan for the invasion of Laos involved the use of the Viet Minh 308th Division, which moved south from its positions near Dien Bien Phu on January 27, 1954, advancing toward Luang Prabang in four columns.[92] Again, Lieutenant General Navarre was forced to scramble in order to position forces in Upper Laos to counter the incursion by the 308th Division. GM 7 (four battalions) and a parachute infantry battalion were transported by air to Luang Prabang on February 13, and the priority for air transport was shifted from the buildup at Dien Bien Phu to support of the fortified camps at Muong Sai and Luang Prabang and on the Plain of Jars. The five French Union battalions at the important air-land base at Muong Sai had to be supplied entirely by air, and between November 20, 1953, and February 24, 1954, over 1,289 tons of cargo were delivered to Muong Sai by air, of which 894.2 tons were airlanded, 84.4 tons were airdropped, and 310.8 tons were parachuted.[93]

The 308th Division came into contact with some French Union elements but did not launch a full-scale assault. However, the Viet Minh invasion of northern Laos caused Lieutenant General Navarre to fritter away his remaining mobile reserves in a number of small airheads. With first priority on air transport shifted to Laos, insufficient airlift was available to continue the steady accumulation of stocks at Dien Bien Phu and indeed the necessary stockage levels could not be maintained. Between January 26 and February 24, 1954, only 1,864 short tons arrived at Dien Bien Phu (about 64 short tons per day) due to the priority given to the support of Muong Sai and the attempt to thwart the 308th Division's drive toward Luang Prabang.[94] The scarce available airlift might better have been used to ensure an adequate buildup at Dien Bien Phu, where the decisive battle of the war was soon to occur.

Viet Minh Infiltration of the Red River Delta

Even while his major units ravaged Laos and besieged the French air-land base at Dien Bien Phu, General Giap continued operations elsewhere. In February 1954, the Viet Minh 320th Division began a major infiltration of the southern corner of the Tonkin delta, and by March all three of its regiments were inside the French perimeter.[95] The Viet Minh infiltrators and guerrillas within the De Lattre Line caused considerable disruption and carried out several operations that directly impinged on the ability of the French to support Dien Bien Phu by air. On the night of March 3–4, 1954, thirty Viet Minh commandos attacked the Gia Lam airfield outside Hanoi. They destroyed a workshop and damaged ten transport planes. In an even more daring raid on Cat Bi airfield near Haiphong on the night of March 6–7, sixty Viet Minh commandos crept through the sewers and attacked the airfield, destroying one light bomber and six light observation aircraft and damaging three light bombers.[96]

By late March, the French were experiencing daily attacks along the length of the vital Hanoi–Haiphong highway (RC 5) that threatened the continued logistical support of Hanoi and the large units supplied from the depots in and around Hanoi. The Haiphong–Hanoi railroad line was also mined every night, but the French nevertheless pushed through six trains per day from Haiphong to Hanoi.[97] These attacks on transportation facilities deep in the French rear areas seriously threatened the movement of supplies to the Hanoi airfields for onward delivery to Dien Bien Phu.

Operation CONDOR

Operation CONDOR began in December 1953 as a plan for pursuing the Viet Minh whom the *base aéro-terrestre* at Dien Bien Phu was sure to displace.[98] The original plan called for an operation involving some fifty-five hundred men who would move north toward Dien Bien Phu from northern Laos. Various parts of the plan were implemented piecemeal, but by the end of April 1954, Operation CONDOR had been transformed into a scaled-down attempt to rescue the doomed garrison of Dien Bien Phu. Under the overall command of the French

Army's Colonel Then, some 3,088 Legionnaires, Laotians, and GCMA/GMI guerrillas gallantly stumbled forward but were unable to overcome the difficult terrain
or the Viet Minh forces ringing Dien Bien Phu.[99] The exhausting effort was called
off after Dien Bien Phu fell to the Viet Minh on May 7. About all that was achieved
was a further degradation of the airlift to the besieged garrison and the exhaustion
and loss of many men in the relief forces.

From the start, Operation CONDOR promised to be a black hole for logistical
resources, and airlift in particular. The original plan would have required a support tonnage of about sixty tons per day and over one hundred C-47s. Even the
scaled-down rescue attempt demanded at least forty-five tons per day, which, with
the 150 short tons per day required at Dien Bien Phu, could only have been met
by stripping all of Indochina of transport aircraft. Colonel Nicot, the French air
transport commander, reluctantly stated that it might be possible to support both
Dien Bien Phu and Operation CONDOR if every transport in Indochina except
for two C-47s at Seno could be used. Even the arrangement of ground logistics
was a major problem. The terrain over which the CONDOR forces were to move
was devoid of roads and required the use of porters or pack animals, but on April
17 Colonel Then reported that he was unable to recruit the necessary five hundred porters "even by force" and that the 150 mules and pack saddles required also
could not be obtained. Lieutenant General Navarre subsequently provided five
hundred prisoners of war (PIMs) for use as porters as well as the mules and pack
saddles from bases in the Tonkin delta, but their delivery only placed additional
burdens on the overworked air transports.

Operation ATLANTE

Lieutenant General Navarre's plan to defeat the Viet Minh by eliminating the Viet
Minh guerrillas behind French lines and the destruction of the main Viet Minh
battle forces in northwestern Tonkin and Laos had thus far proven a failure. Nevertheless, with major Viet Minh forces ranging freely throughout Laos and the Central Highlands and on into northeastern Cambodia, with increasing Viet Minh
infiltration of the vital Tonkin delta, and with a major operation already under
way at Dien Bien Phu, on December 12, 1953, Lieutenant General Navarre issued
orders for a major operation around Tuy Hoa on the coast of south central Viet
Nam, an area long held by the Viet Minh and of little strategic importance.[100] His
stated objective was to draw off Viet Minh regular forces from the main theaters of
operations in northwestern Tonkin and Laos, but Navarre apparently ignored the
fact that General Giap had consistently demonstrated that he would not abandon
successful operations to reinforce threatened locations or forces (as during Operation LORRAINE, for example).

Launched on January 20, 1954, Operation ATLANTE quickly devoured the few remaining combat reserves available in Indochina and placed additional burdens on the already overworked French logistical services. After some initial success, the fifteen-thousand-man force soon became bogged down. During its second phase after March 15, some thirty-three French Union battalions struggled to find and fight some seventeen Viet Minh battalions, of which only nine were *Chu Luc* units.[101] Although Operation ATLANTE obviously diverted men, materiel, and air transport from critical areas where they were urgently needed, Lieutenant General Navarre persisted even against the advice and complaints of his senior commanders. For example, Major General René Cogny, the French commander in Tonkin, forcefully pointed out the adverse effects of Operation ATLANTE on the Dien Bien Phu operation. Cogny would have preferred to use the few available reserves to mount small operations against the Viet Minh base areas and lines of communication in the hope of relieving some of the pressure on Dien Bien Phu.[102]

The Situation on March 13, 1954

By March 13, 1954, the buildup of the *base aéro-terrestre* at Dien Bien Phu had progressed haltingly but satisfactorily. Substantial numbers of troops, equipment, and supplies had been delivered and the construction of the fortified *hérrison* had proceeded apace. The forces supported on March 13 included some 14,450 men in twelve infantry battalions; six batteries of 105 mm howitzers (twenty-four guns); one battery of 155 mm howitzers (four guns); two companies of 120 mm mortars (twenty mortars); two squadrons of M24 Chaffee tanks (ten tanks); two companies of engineers; two quad-.50-caliber antiaircraft machine guns; and miscellaneous support troops. These support troops included a detachment of the 2nd Foreign Legion Armored Maintenance Company (2e CRBLE); a detachment of the 2nd Section, 5th Foreign Legion Medium Maintenance Company (2/5e CMRLE); Petroleum Depot No. 81 and the 730th Gasoline Supply Company (DE 81; 730e CRE); a detachment of the 3rd Munitions Company (*3e Cie Mu*); the 1st Quartermaster Operational Exploitation group (GEO No. 1); various signal, medical, security, and Air Force units, and a mobile field brothel.[103] Additional troops, equipment, and supplies would be delivered to the French Union forces at Dien Bien Phu after March 13, but to no avail. Planning errors, inadequate air transport resources, poor terrain selection, and, above all, underestimation of the enemy had already sealed the fate of the *base aéro-terrestre* at Dien Bien Phu as well as the fate of the French imperium in Indochina.

13

The Limits of Aerial Resupply

The active battle for Dien Bien Phu began on March 13, 1954, with sustained Viet Minh assaults on the isolated positions to the north of the main camp. The Viet Minh attack continued until March 15 and resulted in the fall of strongpoints BEATRICE and GABRIELLE and the loss of almost two of the twelve French Union infantry battalions present. Heavy French defensive fires from seven artillery batteries and two heavy mortar companies reduced the level in the ammunition depots severely, some 700 tons of artillery ammunition alone being consumed.[1] Cargo deliveries during the March 13–15 assaults were limited to only 306 tons, of which 173 tons were ammunition. Personnel movements also were limited: 116 men arrived and only 19 casualties were evacuated.[2] Between March 16 and 29, the defenders struggled to reorganize and reinforce the position. The average daily tonnage rose to 123 tons during this period, and a total of 1,727 tons of supplies arrived, of which 1,053 tons were ammunition.[3] Two additional battalions (997 men) parachuted into Dien Bien Phu between March 16 and 29.

The opening round of the active battle for Dien Bien Phu presaged the course of events that would ensue in the following weeks. The Viet Minh seized the initiative and slowly tightened the noose encircling the defenders of Dien Bien Phu. Meanwhile, the French Union forces struggled to maintain their defensive perimeter and their aerial lifeline to the outside. As time went on, the Viet Minh steadily reduced the former and degraded the latter. In the end, the limitations of aerial resupply of a *base aéro-terrestre* became obvious to all.

The Loss of the Airfield

The major logistical event during opening phases of the active battle was the closing of the airfields to normal traffic. Indeed, the loss of the Dien Bien Phu airfields was perhaps the beginning of the end for the *base aéro-terrestre*. As Colonel Pierre Langlais later reflected, "That fact must be taken into account if one wishes to understand the course and the psychology of the battle."[4] Viet Minh artillery and mortar fire on the main airfield reached a level that no longer permitted its regular use after March 20. The auxiliary airfield just north of strongpoint ISABELLE was also rendered unusable at the end of March by Viet Minh artillery fire. Subsequently, all personnel replacements, supplies, and equipment had to be delivered by airdrop or parachute.

The loss of the Dien Bien Phu airstrips not only reduced the amount of cargo that could be delivered to the garrison, it adversely affected other logistical matters as well. The consequent inability to evacuate casualties was particularly grave. By late March, the evacuation of the wounded had become extremely difficult. The evacuation aircraft landed, loaded the wounded aboard on the run, and took off as soon as possible, sometimes even leaving the navigator and radio operator on the ground if they had descended to help load the wounded.[5] The last evacuation plane got out on March 26, and the last aircraft to land at the main strip was a medical evacuation C-47 that landed at 0345 hours on March 28 and was destroyed by Viet Minh artillery fire at 1300 hours the same day while awaiting a minor repair, stranding the crew, including the flight nurse, Lieutenant Geneviève de Galard, who became famous as the Angel of Dien Bien Phu.[6] The French had a limited number of helicopters based at Muong Sai in northern Laos that they used to support Dien Bien Phu, primarily by evacuating casualties. The use of helicopters for medical evacuation and other purposes had to be abandoned on March 23 due to the heavy Viet Minh artillery and antiaircraft fire.[7] A total of 168 men were evacuated between March 13 and 26.[8]

In addition to the suffering of the wounded and the deaths due to lack of definitive treatment of serious wounds, the inability to evacuate casualties meant that an increasing proportion of the supplies delivered went to support noncombatants. More significantly (from a purely logistical point of view), the inability to return to Hanoi and Haiphong the used parachutes, containers, and specialized equipment, such as the insulated containers in which blood plasma was dropped, created severe problems. For example, Dien Bien Phu surgeon Paul Grauwin noted that until April 1954 he received blood packed in ice in insulated cases, but after the loss of the airstrip the cases could not be returned to Hanoi and within two weeks the entire supply of such cases in the rear area depot was exhausted.[9] Subsequently, blood and ice were dropped separately and seldom reached the hospital together. Because there were no other means of preserving the fresh blood, it went bad within twenty-four hours and became useless.

Despite the growing intensity of the Viet Minh antiaircraft artillery that ringed the camp, until the end of March airdrop and parachute operations remained relatively unaffected, and until the advancing Viet Minh infantry actually overran the airfields they continued to be used as drop zones for personnel and both airdropped and parachuted cargo. Normal drop altitudes were maintained, albeit with some difficulty, and the accuracy of the drops remained generally fair. Only a small quantity of the dropped supplies fell to the Viet Minh, and during this period an average of not more than 4 percent of the tonnage dropped was lost to malfunctions.[10] However, as the Viet Minh gained direct observation of the camp and brought the drop zones under direct artillery and automatic weapons fire, it became more and more difficult for the defenders to recover the materiel dropped or parachuted into the camp, especially at night. Consequently, Brigadier General Christian de Castries, the Dien Bien Phu commander, recommended on March 18 that all cargo be dropped directly on the strongpoints rather than on centrally located drop zones.[11]

Even with the loss of the airfield and the diversion of a significant part of the available airlift to the delivery of reinforcements and the dropping of napalm on the enemy (330 tons in fifty-five sorties), the tonnage delivered between March 14 and 30 was about 1,900 tons, or an average of 112 tons per day.[12] During this period the French high command estimated that 90–96 tons per day were necessary to sustain the *base aéro-terrestre* at Dien Bien Phu.[13] About 25 percent of the total tonnage was delivered by C-119, and three 105 mm artillery pieces and several other large pieces were parachuted with complete success, an exceptional result when one considers that such "heavy drops" were still being experimented with in France.[14]

"April Is the Saddest Month"

The month of April 1954 was the critical period in the French effort to supply the *base aéro-terrestre* at Dien Bien Phu. The onset of poor flying weather hampered flight operations through northern Indochina, and the increasing quantity and accuracy of Viet Minh antiaircraft fire forced the transports to higher drop altitudes that, with the use of unreliable delay devices, resulted in a substantial decrease in the accuracy of the drops and the consequent loss of an increasing proportion of the cargo to the enemy or to damage. Simultaneously, the Viet Minh artillery increasingly dominated the camp and the Viet Minh infantry steadily tightened their grip, thereby reducing the number of available drop zones and bringing those that remained under direct fire. In view of the growing exhaustion of the defenders, it became almost impossible to recover the greater part of the dropped supplies, and the besieged camp slowly began to starve.

The Weather

Poor flying weather over northern Indochina during the month of April 1954, compounded by the lack of state-of-the-art weather forecasting service and of sufficient up-to-date navigational aids, played a major role in reducing the amount of cargo that could be delivered to Dien Bien Phu by either day or night. On numerous occasions during the month, the transports left their delta bases only to find that the poor weather conditions over Dien Bien Phu forced them to return home without dropping their loads. For example, on April 27 twenty C-47s had to return to their bases with full loads due to clouds over the mountains, and the following day twenty-two transport sorties had to be aborted due to storms.[15] The unfavorable weather made the calibration of parachute delays difficult, and poor visibility and high surface winds over the camp also added to the inaccuracy of the parachute drops.[16] Torrential rains and the ensuing mud that covered the camp made the recovery of the dropped loads nearly impossible. The gallant and experienced transport pilots could brave the flak and find the minuscule drop zones, but there was little they could do to overcome the weather.

Viet Minh Antiaircraft Fire

One of the more significant errors the planners of the Dien Bien Phu operation made was to underestimate the potential volume and accuracy of the Viet Minh antiaircraft artillery, which proved to be the major factor in limiting aerial resupply of the encircled base.[17] The number of Viet Minh antiaircraft guns eventually deployed around Dien Bien Phu far exceeded the French estimates, and the Viet Minh gunners were much better than had been expected. According to some reports, the Viet Minh antiaircraft guns were manned primarily by Communist Chinese soldiers with only a few Viet Minh officers and men. A large number, perhaps as many as twenty thousand, Chinese troops did assist the Viet Minh in various ways, mainly as truck drivers, mechanics, and in other technical positions, and may well have helped to man the antiaircraft guns around Dien Bien Phu.[18]

Already in early March 1954, French radio intercepts and other intelligence sources had revealed the presence of at least eighty 37 mm antiaircraft guns and one hundred 12.7 mm antiaircraft machine guns in the hills surrounding Dien Bien Phu.[19] As of March 22, French and American intelligence sources were reporting the equivalent of four Viet Minh antiaircraft gun battalions near Dien Bien Phu.[20] During the battles for the HUGUETTE strongpoints on April 4–5, the French intercepted Viet Minh radio requests for the delivery of another antiaircraft artillery regiment of sixty-seven 37 mm antiaircraft guns from Communist China.[21] Well-hidden from the marauding French fighters and bombers, the Viet Minh flak batteries were also well-supplied with ammunition. The French possessed the Viet Minh logistics codes, and in early March they learned that the Viet Minh had at least forty-four thousand rounds of 37 mm ammunition in place around Dien Bien Phu.[22]

The Viet Minh flak became so heavy and so accurate that many of the older American C-119 pilots asserted that the flak over Dien Bien Phu was heavier than anything they had encountered in Korea or even over the Ruhr in World War II.[23] Indeed, the Viet Minh antiaircraft artillery fire became of such great concern that on April 26 General Henri Charles Lauzin, the commander of French air forces in Indochina, assigned first priority to flak suppression over even close air support and interdiction missions.[24] French aircraft losses over Dien Bien Phu justified General Lauzin's action; in April alone the French lost eight planes to Viet Minh flak, with another forty-seven severely damaged.[25] In all, the French aircraft losses at Dien Bien Phu numbered 48 aircraft shot down, 14 destroyed while landing or on the ground, and 167 damaged by flak.[26] The French naval air arm, which flew just over one-third of the combat missions over Dien Bien Phu, lost nine aircraft and five officers and two enlisted men killed or missing.[27]

The volume and effectiveness of the Viet Minh antiaircraft artillery fire was a major factor in reducing the ability of the French air transport forces to keep the garrison of Dien Bien Phu adequately supplied, since it was the proximate cause of the decreasing accuracy of the parachute drops. Lacking sufficient numbers of the more capacious and faster C-119 transports as well as sufficient fighter and bomber aircraft to fully suppress the Viet Minh flak, the French had to adopt different and less effective methods for dropping and parachuting supplies to the beleaguered camp. On March 29, Colonel Nicot ordered his C-47s to adopt the procedure of high-altitude daylight parachute drops using pyrotechnic delays of local manufacture.[28] At first it was possible to use twenty-five-second delays from an altitude of five thousand feet, but the murderous Viet Minh antiaircraft fire required the use after April 5 of forty-second delays from eight thousand feet. Parachute drops from such altitudes with the unreliable delay devices resulted in inaccurate drops and significant losses of cargo, perhaps as much as 20–30 percent.[29] The C-119s, relatively invulnerable due to their speed and ability to discharge their cargo in one pass over the camp, continued to drop at normal altitudes until April 20, when the Viet Minh were able to move their antiaircraft guns closer to the camp.[30] The accuracy of Viet Minh antiaircraft fire during the daylight hours also prompted the delivery of some cargo at night despite the known inaccuracy of night cargo drops and the fact that most personnel drops were made at night. Night drops continued to be made at two thousand feet.

Shrinkage of the Drop Zones

The increasing decline in the accuracy of parachute drops to Dien Bien Phu was also due in part to the progressive shrinkage of the area under French control. Once the Viet Minh began their siege operations around the camp in mid-March, the surface area of the base shrank rapidly. Between March 13 and May 7, the fortified camp shrank from an area of 1,180 acres to only 321 acres.[31] As the main French position became smaller, the pilots of the transports found it increasingly difficult to release their loads at the proper point during their rapid transit over the camp. Isolated strongpoint ISABELLE was an even more difficult target; a C-47 at stall speed would cross all of ISABELLE in just two seconds.[32] Colonel Nicot complained: "My pilots experienced difficulties in finding the DZ and in seeing its markers. . . . It is difficult to maintain a split-second course and to fly at night at only 300 meters above the bottom of the valley. The pilots are subjected to automatic weapons fire coming from all directions, and bursts of tracer bullets converge on the pilots who are also blinded by Viet-Minh illuminating shells, searchlights, and Bangalore torpedoes. The planes also are severely buffeted by the shock waves of the exploding enemy shells and by the friendly shells that are being fired."[33]

Consequently, more and more of the men and cargo parachuted to the besieged camp fell outside the French perimeter and into the hands of the Viet Minh or into areas inside the French perimeter such as minefields where they could not be recovered. On April 13, Brigadier General de Castries complained to Major General Cogny that in the previous twenty-four hours at least eight hundred artillery rounds, the cargo of five C-119s, had been "delivered to the enemy."[34] The losses in materiel were compounded by the fact that the Viet Minh fired the misdropped munitions at the Dien Bien Phu defenders.[35]

April Deliveries

Despite poor weather, inaccurate drops, and the difficulties of collection, supplies continued to get through to the defenders of Dien Bien Phu during the period from March 30 to April 26. On March 30 the Viet Minh renewed their attack, and by April 5 they had captured four of the strongpoints on the eastern face of the camp and one of the strongpoints on the north. The French artillery consumed some five hundred tons of ammunition during the period, despite the fact that fewer tubes were firing since the Viet Minh had put seven 105 mm and one 155 mm pieces as well as nine 120 mm mortars out of action.[36] Moreover, several of the camp's ration and ammunition dumps were destroyed. The new restrictions on parachute drops and the diversion of a part of the available air transport to troop drops (364 replacements) and napalm missions caused the daily tonnage delivered between March 30 and April 5 to drop to about 100 tons per day, for a total of about 800 tons, of which about 75 percent was ammunition.[37] However, 100 tons per day were inadequate to maintain the desired stockage levels in the besieged camp. To replenish the Dien Bien Phu depots it was necessary to secure a steady 200 tons per day for at least twenty days, but the tactical situation did not permit that, and the deliveries were more on the order of 30 tons one day and 312 the next.[38] In fact, the desired average of 200 tons per day was attained only during a short period between April 9 and 16 thanks to exceptionally good weather.

Between April 5 and May 1, the Viet Minh increased the pressure on the northwest face of the position. However, the weather was relatively favorable until late April, and the tactical situation remained fairly calm, permitting the delivery of a total of 3,553 tons of cargo, an average of 136 tons per day.[39] Of the total, 2,124 tons (almost two-thirds) were munitions, while rations represented most of the remainder. Some 2,006 men—the 2nd Foreign Legion Parachute Battalion (*2e Bataillon*

Étrangère Parachutistes, 2e BEP) and 750 individual replacements—also arrived during the period. A good portion of the individual replacements were general volunteers without prior parachute training, but losses due to poor landings were few.[40] The increased tonnage permitted a slight increase in the GONO supply levels by April 26, but there remained a shortfall of about 64 tons per day needed to meet the two hundred tons per day minimum and the situation remained critical with respect to rations and small arms ammunition.[41] The tonnage delivered between April 9 and 26 was 3,500 tons, for an average of 145 tons per day, about 50 tons per day short of the established goal, and the all-time high tonnage day was April 15, when 250 tons were dropped.[42] The worst day was undoubtedly April 28; the weather was beautiful, but ISABELLE received only 22 tons and the main camp received nothing at all.[43]

Only a major increase in the number of daily transport sorties could provide the needed relief, but aside from the lack of aircraft and crews it should be noted that the departure airfields were already operating at near maximum capacity, the sky over the valley of Dien Bien Phu was saturated, and the troops on the ground were increasingly limited in their ability to recover the cargo that fell within the camp.[44] The increasingly dangerous Viet Minh antiaircraft fire obliged Colonel Nicot on April 26 to order even the C-119s to adopt the high-altitude parachute methods, and the loss of cargo increased to an average of 30 percent.[45] Some 480 tons were thus parachuted to the garrison by C-119 using the delayed-opening technique, and on May 6 the delay was lengthened to fifty seconds. Low-altitude C-119 drops continued, but with heavy fighter protection to suppress the Viet Minh antiaircraft fire. Studies were made of dropping 1-ton loads using delayed opening, but the recovery of such heavy loads had become beyond the capability of the defenders.[46] Despite the best efforts of the French air transport service, the maximum possible logistical support had become insufficient; the supply situation at Dien Bien Phu had "become catastrophic."[47]

The End of the Battle

The last period of the active battle, from April 27 to the fall of Dien Bien Phu on May 7, was characterized by a notable increase in the numbers and accuracy of the Viet Minh antiaircraft guns that made airdrop and parachute operations even more difficult than they had already become. On April 30, the supply levels within the camp still amounted to three days of rations; 450–600 rounds of small arms ammunition per weapon; 875 rounds per 105 mm howitzer; 300 rounds per 155 mm howitzer; and 300 rounds per 120 mm mortar.[48] From May 1, the nibbling of the Viet Minh at the peripheral strongpoints around the main center of resistance accelerated. For some time, the entire central position itself, as well as strongpoint ISABELLE, constituted the drop zone, and there remained few points not under enemy infantry fire. After May 4, the transports continued to drop cargo even though it was known that most of it would not be recovered. It was hoped that the Viet Minh would thus be deceived as to the real conditions within the camp. The ability of the troops on the ground to recover the airdropped supplies became less and less sure and their suffocation increased. To make matters worse, the heavy rains at the end of April undermined the shelters and thus added to the loss of supplies, especially rations. The situation of the wounded became entirely untenable, and their condition quickly reached the point of tragedy. On the morning of May 4, Brigadier General de Castries signaled Major General Cogny:

> Our provisions of all kinds are at their lowest. . . . We don't have enough ammunition to stop enemy attacks or for harassing fire. . . . It appears no effort is being made to remedy this situation. . . . I'm told of the risks run by air crews when every man here runs infinitely greater risks. . . . There cannot be two weights and measures. . . . The night drops must begin at 20 hours instead of 23 hours. . . . The morning hours are lost because of fog and the planning for night drops, with the inevitable long intervals between aircraft [that] permit only ridiculous results. . . . I absolutely need provisions in massive quantities. . . . The very small state of the center of resistance, the fact that our elements on its edge can't leave their shelters without coming under fire from snipers and recoilless rifles means that more and more of the cases dropped are no longer retrievable. . . . The lack of vehicles, the lack of coolies, oblige me to use extremely exhausted units for recovery purposes. . . . The result is detestable. It also causes losses. . . . I can't even count on retrieving half of what is dropped. But the quantities that have been sent to me represent only a very small portion of what I've requested. This situation cannot go on.[49]

The final series of Viet Minh assaults began on May 5 and were sustained until the defenders of Dien Bien Phu were submerged. Between May 1 and 7, more than 800 tons, over 100 tons per day, were dropped to the camp, but more than 40 percent was lost.[50] About 200 tons were parachuted in on May 6, of which 120 tons constituted the last munitions drop.[51] Due to the heavy enemy fire, the defenders were able to gather in only a small part of the final drops. At 1000 hours on May 7, 1954, Brigadier General de Castries called for a halt to further ammunition drops.

In all, between March 13 and May 7, the second and final phase in the existence of the *base aéro-terrestre* at Dien Bien Phu, French air transports dropped 258.8 tons of napalm around Dien Bien Phu, delivered 3,879 personnel (most by parachute), evacuated 168 personnel (nearly all wounded) from the camp, and delivered a total of 6,995.7 tons of cargo, of which about two-thirds were ammunition.[52] The cargo tonnage delivered during this final logistical phase of the battle for Dien Bien Phu included: 1,784.9 tons of small arms ammunition, 2,491.8 tons of artillery ammunition, 135.6 tons of barbed wire, 11.6 tons of pickets, 129.2 tons of miscellaneous engineer supplies, 51.7 tons of miscellaneous ordnance supplies, 1,670.7 tons of rations and clothing, 131.7 tons of medical supplies, 87.1 tons of signal items, 197.3 tons of petroleum products, and 45.3 tons of miscellaneous items. An average daily delivery of 122 tons was maintained throughout the active battle phase, and altogether it appears that during the active battle phase not more than 10 percent of the total tonnage was lost.[53] If one assumes the strength of the garrison between March 13 and May 8 to have been about eleven thousand men, the average daily supply rate was about 9.8 kilograms per man per day, a reasonable amount.[54] But it was not enough.

Logistical Operations at Dien Bien Phu

The difficult struggle of the French air transport service to supply Dien Bien Phu by air is only part of the overall logistical story of the *base aéro-terrestre*. The internal logistical organization of the garrison and the activities of the various supply services are also important aspects of the operation. In particular, engineer operations and the activities of the quartermaster (*Intendance*) and ordnance (*Matériel*) services merit detailed examination.

Overall direction of the logistical support of the garrison of Dien Bien Phu was the responsibility of the *4e Bureau* of Brigadier General Christian de Castries's GONO headquarters. However, from the end of March 1954 onward, effective command of the besieged camp was exercised by Lieutenant Colonel Pierre Langlais and the "parachute Mafia."[55] The key decisions regarding the defense of the base and provisions for its supply were made in the daily morning briefing at 0900 hours attended by Langlais, paratroop Lieutenant Colonel Marcel Bigeard (Langlais's "deputy" for counterattacks), a representative of Brigadier General de Castries, Colonel Guy Vaillant (the artillery commander), Major Jacques Guérin (the air force representative), and Major de Brinon (the officer in charge of supply operations).[56] At this meeting supply requirements and the existing stockage levels were reviewed and schedules for air resupply were worked out. Combat actions required to facilitate the internal movement of supplies within the camp were also discussed. Requisitions and status reports were then radioed to Hanoi and Saigon and preparations were made to receive and distribute the day's expected deliveries.

The Recovery of Airdropped and Paradropped Supplies

One of the most difficult problems facing the defenders of Dien Bien Phu after March 13 was the recovery of airdropped and paradropped supplies. Collecting the supplies by hand was a dirty, dangerous, and exhausting task, and only a portion of the tonnage dropped could actually be recovered by ground personnel. As the size of the camp decreased, it became more and more difficult to recover even those supplies airdropped or parachuted within the French perimeter, since many of the loads fell into the minefields and barbed wire or into areas under direct Viet Minh small arms, automatic weapons, and artillery fire. Night drops made the pallets and containers difficult to find in the dark. To compensate for the almost certain loss of a part of each drop of medical supplies to the camp, the medical supply personnel in Hanoi multiplied surgeon Paul Grauwin's requisitions by ten to ensure that he received at least a minimum of what he needed.[57]

The problem of collecting the parachuted supplies was made even more difficult by the progressive loss to Viet Minh fire of the few vehicles within the camp. The water-cooled, front-mounted engines of the available vehicles were very vulnerable to being punctured by bullets and shell fragments. The last three trucks were rendered inoperative by Viet Minh artillery fire on the night of April 21–22, and subsequently all supply drops had to be gathered entirely by hand.[58] With the loss of motorized transport the centralized logistical system within the camp dissolved, and what few supplies could be recovered were used by the unit in whose area they fell. Without vehicles, the heavier one-ton loads posed particular problems, since they could not be moved intact and had to be broken down on the spot. The heavy loads posed additional dangers to the recipients in that they were sure to draw heavy Viet Minh fire, and they occasionally fell on the bunkers, crushing the structures and killing the occupants. At the request of Brigadier General de Castries heavy drops were discontinued on April 1, but they were resumed (on his request) on April 9 in a proportion of 10–20 percent of total tonnage.[59]

In his memoir, surgeon Paul Grauwin provided several striking descriptions of the hardships endured by the men assigned to the duty of collecting the parachute drops, some of whom in fact died from overexertion.[60] Many of the gatherers also died from Viet Minh artillery, automatic weapons, or small arms fire. The Viet Minh often mortared the area when a supply drop was under way and then zeroed their weapons on the fallen packages so as to be able to deliver a heavy volume of fire on anyone so foolhardy as to try to collect them later.[61] Many of the parachuted supplies were collected by the PIMs, who, despite the opportunity to escape or obtain weapons, performed their difficult task with commendable integrity and in the process suffered extremely heavy casualties.[62] Under such conditions it is not surprising that a high proportion of the materiel dropped to the garrison during the last month of the siege went uncollected. Surgeon Grauwin later wrote: "After the fall of Dienbienphu, I saw hundreds of packages still intact in the barbed wire, in the mine fields, beyond our forward positions, in the river: shells, ammunition, rations, medical supplies. Who could collect them? It would have taken a suicide squad."[63]

The internal distribution of rations, water, ammunition, and other essentials was equally onerous. Initially, the troops of each strongpoint collected the air-dropped supplies and placed them at central locations, where they were picked up during the night by truck and transported to the chief of the camp's *4e Bureau* (Captain Mehay), who then directed their distribution to the units.[64] At first, the system worked well, but the progressive loss of motor vehicles made it necessary for each strongpoint to retain supplies dropped in their area for their own use, a practice that resulted in great waste and imbalances. Even after March 18, when supply drops began to be made directly on the strongpoints, it was necessary to distribute the collected supplies among the units. Following the destruction of the last trucks, the distribution process involved dangerous and exhausting work by small groups of men operating mostly at night and carrying the supplies on their backs through the maze of trenches and barbed wire under Viet Minh artillery and mortar fire. At the end, the exhausted men were unable to pick up even the containers that fell at their feet.[65] Again, Grauwin provides a graphic description of the almost superhuman effort required of those men assigned to the carrying parties:

> It was nearly four in the morning. . . . I heard more footsteps in the passage—the squelch of many feet in the mud, and lowered voices. I went back to the entrance of my shelter to find myself face to face with curious beings covered with mud, carrying packages on their shoulders. . . . The men in the detail moved slowly, one by one. They were almost naked, with nothing but a pair of shorts which had lost any color they had had; they were completely covered with mud, drying in patches on their chests, wet and shiny on their legs, thighs, and abdomens. Their feet were also bare, as their boots had long ago been sucked down by the mud. On the left shoulder, some carried a case of ammo, others a box of rations, others a jerry can of water. They leaned against the wall with their right hands. The same expression of utter weariness and deadly resignation was visible on all their faces. Sometimes they stopped a moment, glancing at me like dead men, then turned toward the shelters on the other side from which came the smells of blood and ether, which they did not recognize. Then they started off again, mechanically.[66]

One of the most difficult of the Dien Bien Phu strongpoints to resupply was HUGUETTE 6. There were no trenches between the different HUGUETTE positions, and after mid-April resupplying HUGUETTE 6 required a major combat operation. During the night of April 14–15, a carrying party of fifty PIMs protected by most of the remaining troops of the 1st and 2nd Foreign Legion Parachute Battalions (*1e et 2e Bataillons Étrangères Parachutistes,* 1e and 2e BEP) attempted to move by way of the Pavie Track to resupply HUGUETTE 6. Pinned down for four hours in the two hundred meters of open terrain between HUGUETTE 1 and

HUGUETTE 2 by Viet Minh artillery and machine gun fire from the hulk of a destroyed C-46 on the airfield, the party finally got through to HUGUETTE 6 at 0230 hours, having lost heavy casualties and most of the supplies en route.[67] Occasionally, the effort was expended willingly and brought high rewards. Such was the case on April 30 when a patrol from the Foreign Legion's 1st Battalion, 13th Demi-Brigade, made a very successful raid on the Viet Minh trenches south of ELIANE 2, a raid that was only incidental to their main mission of recovering two crates of *Vinogel* that had fallen into no-man's land.[68]

Engineer Operations

The moonscape of craters, barbed wire, and collapsed bunkers through which the Dien Bien Phu carrying parties struggled resembled a scene from the trench systems of World War I Flanders more than the neatly laid-out fortified firebases familiar to American soldiers of the Second Indochina War. The engineering effort required to fortify the isolated *base aéro-terrestre* was tremendous, and the amount of engineer supplies absorbed by the camp constituted a major part of the total supplies delivered to the base by air. Even so, the French defenders failed to make maximum use of the engineers and construction supplies available.[69] Until late in the battle little effort was made to provide adequately protected firing positions for the artillery and mortars or to construct adequate shelters for the troops and supplies. In part, this failure to adequately fortify the camp was due to the usual underestimation of Viet Minh capabilities. On the other hand, the amount of engineer supplies and man-hours required to properly protect the camp were far beyond anything that might have been possible.

Even the meager fortifications originally planned for Dien Bien Phu required an enormous amount of materiel. At the established scales of the time, the construction of a combat bunker for one automatic weapon required about fifteen tons of engineer materiel and protecting one squad from enemy 105 mm artillery required about thirty tons.[70] A properly entrenched battalion position required fifty-five squad bunkers and seventy-five automatic weapons positions, or about 2,775 tons of engineer materiel plus another 500 tons of barbed wire and accessories.[71] The Dien Bien Phu engineer, Major André Sundrat, calculated that to adequately fortify the camp for the originally envisioned garrison of ten infantry battalions and two artillery groups about thirty-six thousand tons of engineer materiel would have been required, most of which would have to have been flown in since the area surrounding Dien Bien Phu was almost devoid of usable timber or other construction materials.[72]

In fact, Sundrat's engineers did collect some twenty-two hundred tons of wood from the surrounding area, but most of the engineer materiel consumed at Dien Bien Phu was delivered by air, particularly during the first phase of the operation,

Table 13.1. Engineer Matériel Delivered to Dien Bien Phu by Air, November 20, 1953–May 7, 1954

Category/Item		Quantity	Gross Tonnage
Wood	Beams	12,870 linear meters	130
	Rafters	4,250 linear meters	
	Boards	600 square meters	
	Stakes	60	
	Scantlings	240 linear meters	
Ventilators		20	5
Paving Material		21,000 square meters	12
Clamps (i.e., timber dogs)		9,400	10
Defensive Matériel (barbed wire, etc.)		–	3,000
Construction Steel		118 linear meters	4.5
Bulldozers	D.4–R.4	5	70
	Accessories and Spare Parts	–	8
Chain Saws		21	3
Electrical Matériel	Electrical generators	15	17
	Battery chargers	5	
	Accessories and 14,700 meters of electric cable		
Water Purifiers		–	16
Explosives	Pétards	–	23
	Slow Match	3,200 linear meters	
	Detonation Cord	5,300 linear meters	
	Fuses and Detonators	2,400	
	Bangalore Torpedoes	290	
Bailey Bridge Elements		–	44
Miscellaneous Tools		–	30
Hardware (nails, bolts, pegs, etc.)		–	4
PSP	Sheets	22,800	510
	Pickets	15,450	
Sandbags		550,000	160
Corrugated Iron and Armor Plate		–	20
		Total	**4,066.5 tons**

Source: Letter, Colonel Legendre (Chief Engineer, FTNV) to Major General Cogny (Commander, FTNV), undated [1954], table (Tonnage de matériel du Genie expédié à Dien Bien Phu). Tonnage is given in metric tons.

when approximately 31 percent of the total air-delivered tonnage was devoted to engineer supplies.[73] As it turned out, only about four thousand tons of engineer supplies were delivered to Dien Bien Phu, barely enough to protect the headquarters command post, the signal center, and the X-ray room of the underground hospital.[74] The balance of the engineer tonnage estimated as needed by Major Sundrat, 32,000 tons, would have required at least 12,800 C-47 sorties, and with the small number of C-47s available in Indochina it would have taken five months of delivering nothing but engineer supplies to satisfy the requirement. The types and amounts of engineer supplies actually delivered to Dien Bien Phu are shown in table 13.1.

The lack of suitable local materials and of the airlift necessary to fly in all of the engineer supplies needed resulted in dangerous compromises in the construction of the camp's supporting and defensive works. For example, the lack of suitable stone required the abandonment of all thought of masonry or concrete work as well as of adequate sanitary drainage and flood control projects.[75] The drainage of the main airstrip was effected using fascines rather than the 88,300 cubic feet of stone that would have been required. On February 15, 1954, Brigadier General de Castries complained to Major General Cogny that the lack of engineer supplies, particularly barbed wire, made it impossible to complete certain desirable improvements in the defensive positions, such as the construction of internal barbed wire enclosures between the strongpoints, and permitted only meager provision of the interval strongpoints between the hills to the east of Dien Bien Phu and the supply depot area.[76] In the same message, de Castries also expressed concern that the supply depots located in the valley bottom near the Nam Yum would be flooded during the rainy season, as in fact they would be. Eventually it was decided to protect the low-lying depots by constructing new supply storage areas on the steep western slope of the hill on which strongpoint DOMINIQUE was located. The repositioning of the depots meant that the 2.5-ton trucks would have to cross the Nam Yum. Major Sundrat's engineers thus had to build a Bailey bridge to connect the new depot area with the main headquarters and administrative area of the camp west of the river.[77] Map 13.1 shows the central area of the *base aéro-terrestre* in which the headquarters, supply dumps, maintenance shops, hospitals, and other logistical facilities were located.

Despite the progressive loss of skilled personnel, the destruction caused by Viet Minh artillery fire, and the lack of materiel, the Dien Bien Phu engineers continued to repair and improve the fighting positions, shelters, and logistical facilities of the camp right up to the end. On May 5 they enlarged the hospital again and dug new supply bunkers, and on May 6, under heavy fire, they laid new planking on both the Bailey bridge and the wooden bridge.[78] On May 7, when Dien Bien Phu fell to the Viet Minh, the electric generators and the water purification plant were still operating thanks to the extraordinary and innovative efforts of the men of the 31st Engineer Battalion (*31e Bataillon du Genie,* 31e BG).[79]

Intendance Operations

The receipt, storage, issuance, and accounting for all rations, clothing, and other quartermaster items at Dien Bien Phu was the responsibility of the FTNV *Direction d'Intendance,* which was represented on the ground by Exploitation Group No. 1 (*Groupement Opérationnelle d'Exploitation 1,* GEO 1), composed of one officer, three NCOs, thirteen French soldiers, and a detachment of PIMs provided by GONO headquarters.[80] GEO 1 was deployed to Dien Bien Phu on November

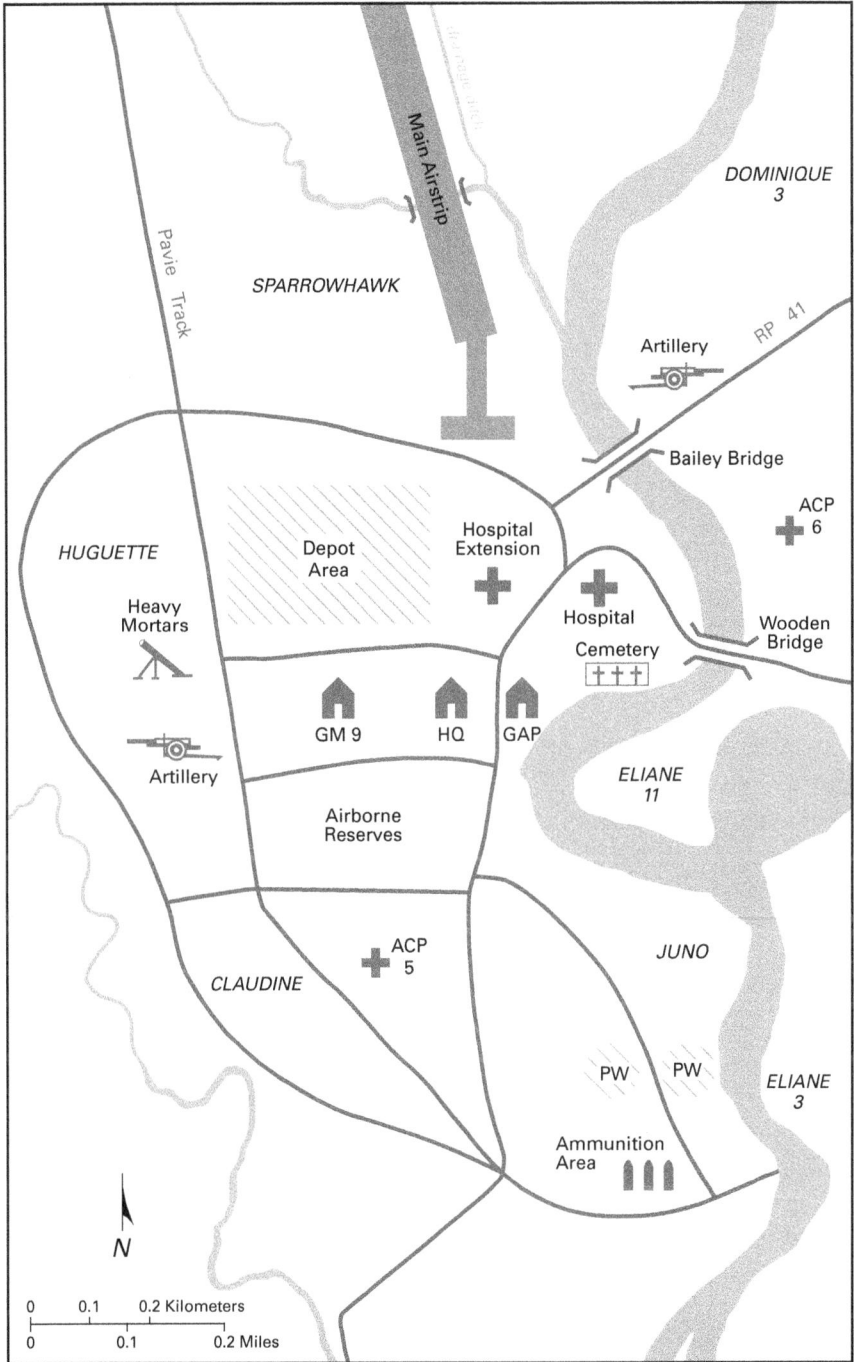

Map 13.1. Central Area of the *Base Aéro-Terrestre* at Dien Bien Phu.

Table 13.2. Average Daily Ration Strength at Dien Bien Phu

Period	European	North African	African	Indo-chinese	Indo-chinese Auxil.	PIM	Total
Build-Up Phase							
Nov. 20–Dec. 7, 1953	1,244	109	3	2,604	405	420	**4,785**
Dec. 8–25, 1953	3,245	2,017	7	3,362	2,075	1,744	**12,450**
Dec. 26, 1953–Jan. 25, 1954	4,244	2,529	125	3,525	1,348	2,123	**13,893**
Jan. 26–Feb. 24, 1954	5,138	2,933	202	2,487	1,320	2,547	**14,627**
Feb. 25–March 12, 1954	4,903	2,802	202	2,385	1,384	2,450	**14,126**
Active Battle Phase							
March 13, 1954	4,950	2,797	203	2,334	1,419	2,444	**14,137**
April 20, 1954	3,008	1,440	756	no report	3,939	no report	**11,500**

Source: Faivre Report, table 2 ("Effectifs Ravitaillés"). The last day for which exact figures are available is March 13, 1954. Ration strength on April 20, 1954, is estimated and thereafter unreported.

26, 1953, following repair of the main airstrip, although a small detachment had arrived with the first aircraft to land on November 23. Backup support for GEO 1 was provided by the FTNV *Direction de l'Intendance* and the Tonkin Operational Base. Supporting detachments were also established at Gia Lam airfield (one officer, two NCOs, and six men from January 1, 1954) and Cat Bi airfield (one NCO and two men from March 1). These detachments from the FTNV *Gestion d'Intendance* provided liaison with the CRA and helped to expedite the movement of rations and other supplies to Dien Bien Phu.

At the peak, nearly fifteen thousand French, North African, African, and Indochinese soldiers, auxiliaries, and PIMs were supported by GEO 1. The average daily ration strength at various times between November 20, 1953, and May 8, 1954, is shown in table 13.2. As the battle for Dien Bien Phu progressed, so did "internal desertion" within the camp. Hundreds of Algerian, Moroccan, and Vietnamese soldiers left their units in the line and took refuge in caves along the banks of the Nam Yum, foraging at night for food and other supplies. These "Rats of the Nam Yum" continued to be carried on the official ration strength of the garrison.

It should be noted that each group had its own special ration requirements. The North Africans, for example, were mostly Muslim and had to be supplied with mutton rather than pork products, while the Indochinese personnel subsisted mainly on rice, dried fish, and vegetables. The European soldiers, of course, had to have their bread and wine ration. The different weights of the normal French Army ration for each group were: Europeans, 2.18 kilograms; North Africans, 1.73 kilograms; Africans, 1.92 kilograms; Indochinese, 1.43 kilograms; Indochinese auxiliaries, 0.95 kilograms; and PIMs, 0.9 kilograms.[81]

All *Intendance* items, including fresh and combat rations, clothing, *Economat* stocks, and miscellaneous quartermaster supplies, were delivered to Dien Bien Phu by air. Between November 20, 1953, and May 8, 1954, some 3,930 tons of regular rations, 9.5 tons of clothing and miscellaneous items, and 32 tons of *Economat* items were delivered, a total of 3,971 net tons.[82] This amounted to an average daily delivery of 23.3 net tons of rations (including *Economat* items) against an established maintenance requirement of 19 tons per day. Among the total quantities of rations landed, dropped, or parachuted into Dien Bien Phu were: 6,194 combat rations, 22,760 reserve/survival rations, 199,760 rations of bread (*pain de guerre*), 473 tons of hardtack (*pain biscuité*), 25 tons of canned fish, 119 tons of canned meat, 195 tons of frozen deboned meat, 12.5 tons of canned sausages, 791 tons of rice, 875 tons of fresh fruits and vegetables, 65 tons of canned vegetables, 43 tons of dried vegetables, almost 60,000 gallons of wine, and about 8,480 gallons of *Vinogel*.[83] The clothing and miscellaneous quartermaster items provided during the course of the operation included: 18 water bags (Lister), 10 waterproof bags, 523 blankets, 10 pairs of jump boots, 12 pairs of leather laces, 5 pairs of combat trousers, 15 metal buckles, 2 rattan tables, 8 rattan armchairs, 15 camp cots (U.S.), 15 mattresses, 30 bed sheets, 15 mosquito nets, 15 mosquito net crossbars, 16 cushions, 12 metal mess kits, 12 forks, 12 coffee spoons, 12 glasses, 16 knives, 1 hospital tent, 9 hospital tents (CD), 6 wall tents (DT), 5,595 pounds of candles, 6,195 pounds of soap, and 100 armored vests.[84] Most of the items appear to have been for Brigadier General de Castries's headquarters mess. Armored vests, which might have prevented many casualties among the defenders of Dien Bien Phu, particularly among the exposed artillery crews, were not even requested until April 14. Obtained from the U.S. forces in Japan, the first delivery of armored vests was attempted on April 26, but they fell into the Viet Minh lines. On April 27, two hundred vests were successfully parachuted to the main position and another one hundred to strongpoint ISABELLE.[85] Martin Windrow has described the belated six-hour Christmas dinner of the paras of GAP 2 as consisting of "fresh cold cuts, roast beef with fried potatoes, French cheeses, gateaux, good wines, even champagne."[86]

During the assault phase of Operation CASTOR from November 20 to 26, 1953, all personnel subsisted exclusively on combat rations. With the opening of the main airstrip on November 26, normal (administrative) rations began to arrive, and from November 30, 1953, up to March 13, 1954, all troops at Dien Bien Phu were provided the normal ration augmented by fresh fruits and vegetables and prepared in company messes. Every effort was made to ensure that the defenders of the *base aéro-terrestre* received exactly the same rations as those troops located in the rear areas. Combat rations were utilized only for troops on patrol or engaged in operations outside the camp perimeter.

Despite the desperate situation of the camp and the severe shortage of available airlift, the officers of the besieged garrison were not denied all the little comforts of life. Some of the *Economat* items delivered to Dien Bien Phu by air are shown in table 13.3.

After the Viet Minh assault began on March 13, it became increasingly difficult to prepare the normal administrative ration, and the defenders of Dien Bien Phu ate hot or cold rations as best they were able. After March 25, the normal ration was the combat ration supplemented by hardtack, *Vinogel,* and additional quantities of jam, sugar, chocolate, canned meat, and canned vegetables. Beginning on March 17, fresh onions were provided as an antiscorbutic, and whenever conditions permitted fresh fruits and vegetables were delivered by parachute. Between April 2 and May 8, some twenty-five tons of fresh fruits and vegetables were parachuted into the base.[87] Brigadier General de Castries ordered the cessation of all parachute drops except for rations as of 1600 hours, May 7, but for several days following the surrender (until May 13), the French transports continued to parachute four plane-loads a day of combat rations, rice, drugs, and ice to Dien Bien Phu in hopes that some of the supplies might be used for the French Union wounded.[88]

When the Viet Minh assault began on March 13, the authorized ration strength of the garrison was 14,137 men, and the ration depots at Dien Bien Phu had on-hand 13.6 rations (seven normal rations and 6.6 combat rations) for each authorized European, North African, and African soldier, and thirteen rations for each authorized Indochinese person.[89] The actual ration status as of 1700 hours, March 13, 1954, included, among other things: 44,680 combat rations, 19,055 additional rations of bread (*pain de guerre*), 6,800 kilograms of hardtack (*pain biscuité*), 1,480 kilograms of roasted coffee, 1,200 kilograms of green tea, 2,650 kilograms of sugar, 2,580 kilograms of salt, 45,220 kilograms of rice, 14,300 kilograms of canned meat, 12,200 kilograms of fresh fruits and vegetables, 900 liters of *nuoc mam*, 14,700 liters of wine, and 48,000 packets of cigarettes. On March 13 there were also three days' rations in the units, of which one day was the combat ration.

Information regarding the precise stockage levels at Dien Bien Phu after March 14 is sketchy due to imprecise figures as to the daily ration strength and the fact that after April 2 the GONO *4e Bureau* no longer tracked the levels but only the quantity of ration items on hand as of 1900 hours daily. Moreover, after March 20 strongpoint ISABELLE, which earlier had drawn its rations from the central depot, was supplied separately by parachute and supplies began to be dropped or parachuted directly onto the various strongpoints of the main camp as well and

Table 13.3. *Economat* Items Delivered to Dien Bien Phu

Quantity	Item
135 1-liter bottles	Aperitifs
72 bottles	Champagne
72 75-cl bottles	Fine Wine
148 75-cl bottles	Cognac and Rum
7,680 66-cl bottles	French Beer
1,000 120-gr tins	Canned Sausages
432 250-gr tins	Pâtés
400 1-kg tins	Tripe
36 1-liter tins	Meat Concentrate (*Viandox*)
480 250-gr tins	Powdered Milk
6,720 450-gr tins	Sweetened Condensed Milk
10,000 1/6-liter bottles	Fruit Juice
980 1-kg tins	Asparagus
500 1-kg tins	Mushrooms
742 1-kg tins	Endive, Peas, and Beans
600 1-kg tins	Sauerkraut
8,200 1-kg tins	Tomato Concentrate
500 1-kg tins	Potatoes
500 1-kg tins	Canned Fruit in Syrup
60 1-kg tins	Mustard
588 packets	Cookies
24 1-liter tins	Syrup
8,500 1-kg boxes	Sugar Cubes
500	Wooden Pencils
810 packets	Airmail Envelopes
1,720 tablets	Airmail Writing Paper
14,660 packets	Razor Blades
768 tubes	Shaving Creme
220 bars	Shaving Soap
1,020	Toothbrushes
2,952 tubes	Toothpaste
6,140 bars	Soap
250 packs	Lighter Flints
12,000 packets	Cigarettes
949 500-cl bottles	Eau de Cologne

Source: *Faivre Report*, table 3 ("Denreés d'ECONOMAT").

were thus not accounted for by GEO 1. After March 14, the level of ration reserves in the depots at Dien Bien Phu quickly declined from fourteen to six days of supply and then, after April 11, seemed to stabilize at two days of supply.

In mid-April, rations stocks at Dien Bien Phu reached critically low levels as priority for air transport was given to reinforcements, ammunition, and medical supplies. On April 7, ration stocks were entirely depleted except for those in the hands of the units, and on April 11 the combat units were authorized to consume one of the three reserve rations they maintained on their positions.[90] On April 14, fires ignited by Viet Minh artillery shells destroyed more than 300 kilograms of cheese, 700 kilograms of tea, 700 kilograms of coffee, 450 kilograms of salt, 110 kilograms of chocolate, and 5,080 combat rations.[91] A few days earlier, the camp's entire tobacco reserve was set on fire, causing the camp to smell "as if it were smoking a gigantic pipe."[92]

On April 14 the garrison went on short rations. The last warm food was eaten by the troops in strongpoint ISABELLE on April 19, and the following day there remained only enough food for the severely wounded.[93] On April 26 another 26,200 rations were lost when another ration depot was set afire, and on April 29 the garrison officially went to half rations.[94] By the end of April even the Europeans were surviving on rice and *nuoc mam* mixed with canned meat.[95] By April 30 the ration stockage level within the camp had improved slightly but still amounted to only three days of supply.[96] In addition to the amount necessary to meet normal daily consumption requirements between April 2 and May 8, additional rations were parachuted to the garrison in an attempt to rebuild stockage levels in the depots. The additional items included 357,245 combat rations, 123,480 rations of bread (*pain de guerre*), 102,045 kilograms of hardtack (*pain biscuité*), 60 kilograms of chocolate, 31,500 packets of cigarettes, 3,150 kilograms of coffee, 7,319 kilograms of fats (lard, cooking oil, etc.), 2,434 kilograms of canned fish, 6,000 kilograms of dried fish, 33,356 kilograms of canned meat, 24,956 kilograms of onions, vegetables, and fruits, 178,680 kilograms of rice, 8,010 kilograms of sugar, 5,280 kilograms of salt, 1,008 kilograms of jam, 2,080 liters of *nuoc mam,* 130 liters of rum, 8,727 liters of *Vinogel,* and 6,200 kilograms of ice for the hospital.[97] These amounts were delivered above the normal consumption requirements and constituted more than double the combat rations and more than one and one-third the rice required for the effective ration strength of the garrison. Thus, despite losses due to errant parachutes and loads that could not be recovered, the troops at Dien Bien Phu were apparently well-supplied with rations despite short periods when daily deliveries faltered. Again, surgeon Paul Grauwin was an expert eyewitness: "Food was seldom lacking. Sometimes it was impossible to collect the packages of foodstuffs, and the can of rations had to be shared out among ten, twenty, occasionally but not often, thirty men. But that never went on for more than two days at the outside. Supplies were collected during a lull, and rations once more became normal—if you can call canned stuff normal. Always canned stuff, cans of meat paste, carrots and other vegetables, cans of crackers. . . . After a time the stomach categorically refused to absorb all this canned stuff. But you had to eat something."[98]

Operations of the Service du Matériel

Personnel of the *Service du Matériel* arrived at Dien Bien Phu on November 20, 1953, and continued to provide weapons supply, maintenance, and ammunition support for the *base aéro-terrestre* until its fall on May 7, 1954. The first to arrive were elements of the 3rd Munitions Company (*3e Compagnie des Munitions, 3e Cie Mu*), which operated the ammunition depot.[99] Consisting of the commander, Lieutenant Jourdonneau, four NCOs, twenty-seven Legionnaires, and one Vietnamese civilian, the 2nd Section, 5th Foreign Legion Medium Maintenance Company (*2/5e Compagnie Moyenne de Réparation de la Légion Étrangère*, 2/5e CMRLE), augmented by a detachment from the 2nd Foreign Legion Armored Maintenance Company (*2e Compagnie de Réparation d'Engins Blindés de la Légion Étrangère*, 2e CREBLE), arrived on December 4 and subsequently handled the issue and maintenance of vehicles and weapons for the garrison. A team from the 11th Medium Maintenance Company (*11e Compagnie Moyenne de Réparation du Matériel*, 11e CMRM) provided maintenance support for the garrison's artillery. Backup support was provided by the *Direction du Matériel*, FTNV. The Dien Bien Phu maintenance area was established at the junction of strongpoints CLAUDINE and HUGUETTE 2 and was dug in and integrated with the defense of the camp. Maintenance operations were conducted under the same difficult conditions faced by the rest of the garrison; the 2/5e CMRLE lost eleven men killed in action and ten seriously wounded out of a total complement of just thirty-seven officers and men.[100]

The *Service du Matériel* elements at Dien Bien Phu eventually supported seventeen battalions of infantry, two 105 mm artillery groups, one 155 mm battery, three companies of 120 mm mortars, and ten M24 tanks. Despite the restricted tables of allowances, there were some 193 major end items to be managed.[101] Throughout the battle for Dien Bien Phu, the *Service du Matériel* managed to maintain a fill level of about 80 percent on infantry weapons and 90 percent on artillery.[102] After the airfields were closed to airlanded cargo, Dien Bien Phu continued to receive replacement weapons by parachute drop. Among the many items parachuted to the beleaguered garrison were three 105 mm HM2 howitzers, two 75 mm M20 recoilless rifles, two 57 mm M18 recoilless rifles, and seventeen 120 mm mortars.[103]

The 2/5e CMRLE, supported by detachments from 2e CREBLE and 11e CMRM, was responsible for the maintenance of all weapons and vehicles within the garrison. Between November 26, 1953, and May 7, 1954, the maintenance units at Dien Bien Phu used or delivered some twenty-three tons of vehicles, fifty tons of spare parts, twenty-four tons of artillery materiel, and sixty-two tons of light weapons.[104] At its height, the pool of weapons and vehicles to be maintained included 24 105 mm HM2 howitzers, 4 155 mm HM1 howitzers, 10 M24 tanks, and some 183 wheeled vehicles (48 jeeps, 86 trucks, and 49 other vehicles).[105] Up until February 20, 1954, the maintenance personnel in Dien Bien Phu completed a total of 225 vehicular repair jobs (on 80 jeeps, 149 Dodge and GMC trucks, 17 armored vehicles, and 9 other vehicles).[106]

Perhaps the most unique accomplishment of the *Service du Matériel* at Dien Bien Phu was Operation RONDELLE II, the air movement and reassembly of ten M24 tanks delivered to the camp between December 18, 1953, and January 15, 1954.[107] The brand-new eighteen-ton Chaffee tanks were disassembled in Hanoi, flown to Dien Bien Phu aboard C-47s and Bristol Freighters, and reassembled in an open-air "production line" established by the 2/5e CMRLE, reinforced by elements of the 1st Maintenance Battalion (*1e Bataillon de Réparation du Matériel,* 1e BRM) from Saigon, under the direction of Lieutenant Bugeat.[108] Each tank was broken down into eighty-two pieces. The heaviest piece of the tank was the hull, which weighed just over five tons and could only be transported by specially modified Bristols.[109] Two Bristols and five C-47 sorties were required to deliver each tank. One tank was reassembled every two days, and the first three-tank platoon was ready for action on December 25.

Ammunition, engineer materiel, and rations were the high tonnage items handled at Dien Bien Phu. Ammunition resupply operations within the garrison, including operation of the ammunition depot, were the responsibility of the 3rd Munitions Company, the first elements of which parachuted into Dien Bien Phu on the first day of Operation CASTOR. Commanded by Lieutenant Léonard, the *3e Cie Mu* was manned primarily by PIMs, who remained faithful to the end despite heavy casualties suffered at the hands of their former Viet Minh comrades.[110] Between November 20, 1953, and January 25, 1954, the company was occupied with the establishment and organization of the operational ammunition depot and the development of the distribution system for ammunition within the camp. The main ammunition depot at Dien Bien Phu was located at the southern end of the main position, and by the beginning of March 1954 it had a capacity of two thousand tons of ammunition in three sections, with a total of seventy-two protected cells, each of which was further subdivided to limit the effects of fires and explosions.[111]

Ammunition for Dien Bien Phu was prepositioned for aerial movement at the aerial resupply companies at Gia Lam, Bach Mai, and Cat Bi airfields. About 11,454 tons of ammunition were so placed, of which a total of 7,220 tons were actually delivered to Dien Bien Phu.[112] During the period of the actual battle for

Dien Bien Phu between March 14 and May 7, 1954, about 42 percent of all the cargo airdropped or parachuted to the garrison was artillery ammunition, and another 18 percent was small arms ammunition.[113]

The expenditure of artillery ammunition in the defense of Dien Bien Phu was quite heavy despite the uncertainties of delivery by air and the difficulties of recovering parachuted ammunition during the later stages of the battle. During the buildup phase (November 20, 1953–March 13, 1954) the French Union artillery expended twenty-five thousand rounds of 105 mm howitzer ammunition, thirty-five hundred rounds of 155 mm howitzer ammunition, and ten thousand rounds of 120 mm mortar ammunition. During the active battle phase (March 14–May 7, 1954), artillery ammunition expenditures rose to seventy thousand rounds of 105 mm, five thousand rounds of 155 mm, and twenty-eight thousand rounds of 120 mm ammunition.[114]

Sustained heavy ammunition expenditures and restricted resupply by air meant that the defenders of Dien Bien Phu were frequently on the verge of exhausting their stocks of ammunition. As a result, every effort was made to conserve ammunition by curtailing fire. On February 4, 1954, the *4e Bureau,* FTNV, informed Dien Bien Phu that the garrison would have to reduce its ammunition expenditures in view of the support requirements generated in Laos by the incursion of the Viet Minh 308th Division. This restriction was doubly unfortunate in that it restricted French artillery fire just at the time the Viet Minh artillery was being installed around Dien Bien Phu and was at its most vulnerable.[115] As a consequence, the Viet Minh were able to position their artillery without facing the full force of the French artillery already in place. Once in their protected positions the Viet Minh guns proved relatively immune to French counterbattery fire regardless of the number of rounds fired at them. The amounts of ammunition delivered to Dien Bien Phu during the period January 26–February 24 were inadequate to maintain the desired stockage levels, and the garrison never really recovered before the Viet Minh assaults began on March 13.

On March 13, the depots at Dien Bien Phu contained 27,400 rounds of 105 mm, 2,700 rounds of 155 mm, and 22,000 rounds of 120 mm mortar ammunition.[116] That first night of the Viet Minh assault, the French consumed over 6,000 rounds of 105 mm ammunition, about one-fourth of their total stock on hand in the Dien Bien Phu depots.[117] In the heavy fighting on March 31, the garrison completely expended its stocks of hand grenades and 81 mm mortar shells. One of the worst days for the garrison was April 6. The ammunition stocks were down to only 7,500 rounds of 105 mm, 371 rounds of 155 mm, and 1,500 rounds of 120 mm mortar ammunition, barely enough for one night's serious firing.[118] There were no more mines or 60 mm mortar shells, and that evening the supply of flares was exhausted. To ice the cake, a flight of three C-119s dropped their eighteen tons of howitzer ammunition into the Viet Minh lines and at 1425 hours a French fighter-bomber dropped its bombs in error on one of the ammunition storage areas inside Dien Bien Phu, destroying a thousand rounds of 105 mm ammunition. Two days later, three C-119s dropped another nineteen tons of 105 mm and 120 mm shells into the Viet Minh lines.[119] By May 1, there were only 14,000 rounds of 105 mm, 275 rounds of 155 mm, and 5,000 rounds of 120 mm mortar ammunition in the Dien Bien Phu depots.[120]

Around noon on May 7, 1954, the Viet Minh 308th Division broke through to the center of the main French defensive position at Dien Bien Phu, and by nightfall the battle was over except for a last desperate sortie by the Algerians and Legionnaires of strongpoint ISABELLE that ended in failure at 0153 hours on May 8. Thus ended fifty-six days of heroic defense and an extraordinary 169-day logistical effort. Although the French failure to hold their fortified base at Dien Bien Phu must be attributed primarily to poor intelligence work, overconfidence, and tactical blunders, the difficulties of resupplying the base by air also played a part. The logistical support of the garrison rested entirely on a single method—aerial resupply—a method of great utility and flexibility but subject, nevertheless, to several limitations. Those limitations were compounded by the strenuous efforts of the Viet Minh to degrade the effectiveness of the air bridge to Dien Bien Phu by attacking the rear area airfields and the highways and rail lines that fed supplies to them. Although the French were able to deal quite successfully with the Viet Minh incursions in the rear areas, they could not cope successfully with the progressive deterioration of the terminus of the air bridge at Dien Bien Phu; it was the loss of the airfields and drop zones at Dien Bien Phu itself that most seriously reduced support of the garrison. As the number and size of the available drop zones diminished, the effectiveness of the parachute drops declined geometrically, and in the final stages it became necessary to send each soldier's daily combat ration to his individual hole—a task that was nearly impossible. Thus, despite the generally adequate functioning of all the various stages along the route, the supporting services of FTNV, the aerial resupply companies, and the air transports, the entire logistical system, resting as it did on a single method of transport, proved extremely vulnerable not only to enemy action but to the vagaries of the natural environment as well. Limited numbers of airfields and suitable aircraft; crew shortages, exhaustion, and losses; shortages and the technical deficiencies of the available parachutes and associated equipment; the terrain surrounding the camp and the weather; Viet Minh antiaircraft fire; losses due to inaccurate drops; and the inability of the troops on the ground to recover the materiel dropped all contributed to reduce the amount of cargo that actually reached the troops encircled at Dien Bien Phu.

The aerial resupply of the *base aéro-terrestre* at Dien Bien Phu required a maximum application of the available military and civil aviation resources in Indochina. Between November 20, 1953, and May 7, 1954, aircrews flew 10,400 air missions in support of Dien Bien Phu (6,700 supply and transport missions and 3,700 combat missions), of which 1,267 were flown in French Navy aircraft.[121] French air transports operated some 27,000 hours in delivering airlanded cargo to Dien Bien Phu, some 10,000 hours in returning materiel to the rear bases, and some 4,300 hours in airdropping and parachuting supplies into the camp.[122] A total of 20,859.6 tons of supplies and equipment were delivered to Dien Bien Phu (6,583.6 tons, including 105 vehicles and 10 tanks, airlanded; 2,323.3 tons air-dropped; and 11,952.7 tons parachuted), and another 800 tons of materiel were returned to bases in the delta.[123] This amounted to an average of 124 tons per day, or about 100 kilograms per minute (not counting personnel).[124]

Could more have been done if the French had simply had a greater number of transport aircraft? The answer is no. As historian John D. Plating has written: "To be sure, the leading cause of French defeat was logistical bankruptcy, but not in matters of strict quantity, but rather in the quality of the aerial delivery."[125] A simple augmentation of the number of transports involved would not have been sufficient to ensure that the necessary tonnages were delivered due to two factors: the saturation of the departure airfields (the theater airfield infrastructure never having been designed for air operations of such magnitude) and the saturation of the sky over Dien Bien Phu itself.[126] Moreover, after eight weeks of heavy combat without relief the defenders of Dien Bien Phu reached a state of exhaustion that itself reduced their ability to gather up a significant portion of the supplies that did fall within their lines, thus further contributing to their suffocation. In the end, there was little the logistical specialists in Hanoi and Haiphong and on the ground at Dien Bien Phu could do about the limitations of air transport and the difficulties of gathering supplies that deprived the French commanders of the flexibility required to overcome the principal faults in the defense: poor intelligence, over-confidence, and tactical blunders.

14

The Triumph of the Porters

The story of logistics at Dien Bien Phu is the story of the limitations of the French aerial resupply effort, but it is equally the story of the triumph of the Viet Minh logistical system, and in particular of the thousands of porters who provided the backbone of Viet Minh strategic and tactical mobility. Substantially improved after its poor performance in the battles on the perimeter of the Tonkin delta in late 1950, the Viet Minh logistical system remained seriously underestimated and held to ridicule by the French, who were incapable of believing that a system relying on manpower rather than mechanization might just be the optimum solution for the logistical difficulties faced in Indochina, especially if it were in the hands of determined and innovative operators. The Viet Minh victory at Dien Bien Phu proved decisively not only the combat capability of the People's Army but also the ability of the Viet Minh logistical system to support that army in a major extended campaign even under the threat of air interdiction.

The improvement of the Viet Minh logistical system in the two years preceding the battle of Dien Bien Phu had been steady and impressive. Morale was high, and staff expertise had improved dramatically over the poor standards demonstrated in the failed battles on the perimeter of the delta in 1951. The delivery of large amounts of weapons, ammunition, trucks, gasoline, and other supplies from Communist China since late 1950 had substantially improved Viet Minh combat capabilities, particularly with respect to field artillery, mortars, and antiaircraft artillery. The Viet Minh engineers and thousands of coolies had labored long to improve the road networks and storage facilities in the rear areas, and Viet Minh transportation capabilities had been greatly enhanced by the reorganization and expansion of the porter service and its augmentation by at least six hundred trucks obtained from the Chinese. Important improvements in Viet Minh signal communications, particularly the receipt of a large number of American-made radio sets from the Chinese Communists, had also served to improve the logistical support of forward units by providing a reliable means of transmitting requests and instructions.[1]

The Viet Minh commander, General Vo Nguyen Giap, understood clearly that the key to defeating the French at Dien Bien Phu lay not only in a successful concentration and sustainment of his main battle forces in the area but also in weakening the French defense of Dien Bien Phu by a concurrent series of attacks and feints in other vulnerable areas that would cause Lieutenant General Henri Navarre to disperse his remaining reserves and scarce air transport assets to meet the widespread threats elsewhere.[2] At the same time, Giap had to maintain the pressure on the French rear areas in the delta by increased guerrilla activity while also being prepared to once again defend his own rear areas. Giap also understood that any campaign against the French base at Dien Bien Phu would have to involve artillery fire to destroy the airstrips and antiaircraft fire to harass the inevitable fleet of transports. As he stated, "Everything was brought into play to hinder enemy supply and gradually stop it altogether."[3]

The decision to concentrate their main battle forces at Dien Bien Phu and engage the French in what might turn out to be the decisive battle of the war was in fact a risky gamble for the Viet Minh high command.[4] If the French occupation were a feint and the garrison were quickly evacuated, as the one at Na San had been, the major part of the Viet Minh combat forces would be perched at the end of a very long and very vulnerable supply line and perhaps unable to respond to a major French incursion into the Viet Bac or elsewhere.[5] However, the immediate problem was how to deal with the rapidly growing French base in the valley of Dien Bien Phu astride the routes into northern Laos. Giap and his staff officers recognized, as the French apparently did not, the vulnerability of the *base aéro-terrestre* planted so far from its supporting bases and dependent entirely on supply by air. Dien Bien Phu offered the alluring prospect of an early decisive engagement that might, coupled with efforts on the diplomatic front, finally convince the French that their best course would be to leave Viet Nam forever.[6] It was an opportunity not to be missed, but it also posed significant logistical problems for the Viet Minh, who themselves would have to maintain a major force for some time at a great distance from their bases in the Viet Bac over poor roads and under French aerial observation and attack.

Although General Giap anticipated a short campaign and a quick victory that would preclude most of the logistical problems associated with an extended campaign, many of his staff logisticians shared the doubts of the French intelligence officers about their ability to sustain a large battle force so far from their own bases, but all were agreed that the prize was worth the gamble.[7] In the end, the Dien Bien Phu campaign was perhaps longer than Giap had anticipated, but revolutionary zeal and careful calculations produced the desired victory. When the question of whether or not the timely concentration of the required combat forces and supplies around Dien Bien Phu would be possible was put to him directly, the Viet Minh director general of supplies noted that the task would be difficult but could be accomplished if thousands of Viet Minh supporters could be mobilized and inspired to accomplish the staggering task.[8]

The Viet Minh Concentration on Dien Bien Phu

French intelligence officers and operational planners were convinced that the Viet Minh were logistically incapable of concentrating significant forces around the *base aéro-terrestre* in the isolated valley of Dien Bien Phu, and, if they were able to do so, they would be unable to sustain a significant force there for very long in a general attack. For Lieutenant General Navarre and his staff officers, the thought of a sustained assault by the better part of four Viet Minh divisions was "a utopian project"; they expected to be faced with only one reinforced division at most, perhaps a dozen battalions with a few heavy guns.[9] American observers generally concurred with the French assessment. The chief of the U.S. joint military mission in Indochina, Lieutenant General John W. "Iron Mike" O'Daniel, visited Dien Bien Phu on February 3, 1954, and subsequently reported: "I feel that it can withstand any kind of an attack that the Viet Minh are capable of launching. However, a force with two or three battalions of medium artillery with air observation could make the area untenable. The enemy does not seem to have this capability at present."[10] But what the precise staff college calculations of the limits on an army supplied by porters did not allow for was the determination and ingenuity of their enemy. As Jules Roy acknowledged: "Nobody believed in the strategic mobility and logistics of the Vietminh. Nobody, or scarcely anybody, in the French Army had enough imagination to guess at the enemy's cunning and wisdom."[11]

To the great misfortune of the defenders of Dien Bien Phu and the ultimate loss of French hegemony in Indochina, General Giap was indeed able to mass the better part of four divisions and a considerable number of heavy artillery pieces and antiaircraft guns around Dien Bien Phu some 310–435 miles by road from their home bases and to sustain them there in extended combat for fifty-six days. He did so by careful planning, ingenuity, flexibility, and the determined efforts of thousands of Viet Minh soldiers, porters, and other supporting personnel. As Giap himself later told a French visitor: "The [French] Expeditionary Corps was strategically surprised because it did not believe we would attack—and we attacked; and it was tactically surprised because we succeeded in solving the problems of concentrating our troops, our artillery and our supplies. This [French] way of reasoning was logical, but of a too-formalistic logic. We did construct our supply roads; our soldiers knew well the art of camouflage; and we succeeded in getting our supplies through."[12]

In the end, it would be the French who were unable to maintain the logistical pace of the battle, not the Viet Minh. The persistent French intelligence underestimation of Viet Minh capabilities and intentions is all the more surprising in view of the fact that (as reflected in U.S. intelligence summaries of the period) the French intelligence service, which had the Viet Minh supply codes and regularly monitored Viet Minh transmissions, had every indication that the Viet Minh had significant logistical capabilities in northwestern Tonkin in the fall and winter of 1953–1954 and probably intended to use them.[13] As early as the first week of November 1953, French intelligence sources reported that the Viet Minh depots around Hoa Binh were receiving significant quantities of submachine guns, mortar and small arms ammunition, and detonators, supposedly for issue to the Viet Minh units south of the De Lattre Line, but capable of being diverted up RP 41.[14] The same report noted that the Chinese had moved some thirteen hundred drums of gasoline to the border for early delivery to the Viet Minh. The following week, the same sources noted that the Viet Minh 316th Division, then in the Dien Bien Phu area, had sufficient supplies of all types for a four-month operation, including enough rice to support the division for two months.[15] In mid-December, French intelligence officers reported that the Viet Minh continued to move troops and supplies toward Dien Bien Phu and were apparently planning to supply eighty thousand rations a day in the area. By the end of December, the French were certainly aware that the Viet Minh had improved their logistical capabilities sufficiently to sustain prolonged operations around Dien Bien Phu, and that they had sufficient transportation to move large quantities of supplies up the Black River valley.

At the same time, there were indications that the Viet Minh were moving artillery and antiaircraft guns into the Dien Bien Phu area and had amassed stockpiles of 12.7 mm and 37 mm antiaircraft artillery ammunition in their depots near Tuan Giao. The same report noted that the Viet Minh headquarters at Tuan Giao had requested four hundred barrels of gasoline for their artillery prime movers. Despite the gathering evidence, at the beginning of January 1954 the French were still uncertain as to whether or not the Viet Minh would make an all-out attack on Dien Bien Phu. In mid-January, French intelligence officers reported that the Viet Minh were continuing "an unprecedented logistical effort" in moving supplies to the Tuan Giao–Dien Bien Phu area, and estimated that the rate at which supplies were arriving in the area was as much as 150 tons per day over the previous month, with about one-third of the total tonnage being ammunition.[16]

Throughout January 1954, the Viet Minh continued to move supplies into their base at Tuan Giao and gave a high priority to the stockpiling of artillery and mortar ammunition there. On February 18, French radio research (signals intelligence) units intercepted Viet Minh orders increasing the flow of supplies into the Dien Bien Phu area from fifty to seventy tons per day.[17] And by the end of February, even the French were convinced that the Viet Minh had assembled enough supplies (including rice to supply eighty thousand men for a month) in the Dien Bien Phu area to permit sizable Viet Minh forces to operate in the area through the rainy season.

However, the Viet Minh concentration was not without its difficulties, troubles that were apparent even to the French. By mid-February, the poor road network in the region, the high rate of sickness, low morale among the porters, and the perpetual shortage of trained supply personnel had begun to take their toll on the Viet Minh logistical system. But the French nevertheless concluded that the Viet Minh logistical activity around Tuan Giao seemed to indicate that they intended to prolong their operations in northwestern Tonkin. During the first week of March, they were forced to acknowledge that the sustained stockpiling by the Viet Minh in the Tuan Giao–Dien Bien Phu area had created for the Viet Minh the capability of conducting an indefinite siege of Dien Bien Phu. They acknowledged that the concentration provided the Viet Minh with a "substantial supply base for prolonged operations against French-sponsored guerrillas and for future operations into northern Laos, and indicates an apparent Viet Minh effort to shift the center of their logistic base westward from the Delta area."[18] The same report also noted that the Viet Minh were constructing a road around Dien Bien Phu that would facilitate the movement of their artillery in support of operations against the French defenses in the valley. As of March 13, French intelligence officers were estimating that the Viet Minh had sufficient supplies of all classes on hand in the Dien Bien Phu area to support fifty thousand men for two months. Nevertheless, the French General Staff in Hanoi still refused to believe the Viet Minh artillery could sustain a battle of more than five or six days against two or three centers of resistance.[19]

By mid-March, all uncertainty regarding Viet Minh intentions had evaporated. French intercepts of Viet Minh radio traffic had revealed that the Viet Minh were planning to supply rice to ninety thousand men in the northwestern highlands, including seventy thousand men in the area of Dien Bien Phu.[20] The movement of food supplies to Dien Bien Phu had reached the level of seventy tons per day, and it was also known that two tons of medical supplies had been sent forward and that two hundred tons of ammunition were to be delivered to the Viet Minh forces around Dien Bien Phu during the second week in March.[21] It was estimated that as of March 12, the Viet Minh had stockpiled about four thousand tons of supplies, exclusive of food, in the Tuan Giao area, an amount that gave them a logistical capability in excess of their estimated manpower available for assaults against the French forces at Dien Bien Phu.[22]

In fact, the Viet Minh preparations were completed by the first week of March 1954.[23] The artillery had been hauled forward and installed in protected positions in the hills surrounding Dien Bien Phu, the flak batteries were sited, and the necessary food and ammunition stocks were in position immediately to the rear of the combat forces. The Viet Minh forces assembled included thirty-three battalions of infantry (twenty-seven around the camp itself and six, augmented by regional and local forces, along the routes leading to Dien Bien Phu), one regiment of 105 mm howitzers (twenty-four guns), one regiment of mountain artillery (fifteen 75 mm guns and twenty 120 mm mortars), a large number of mortars and recoilless rifles, three battalions of engineers, and one regiment of antiaircraft artillery (about thirty 37 mm antiaircraft guns plus around one hundred 12.7 mm and 20 mm antiaircraft machine guns).[24] The accumulated ammunition stocks near Dien Bien Phu amounted to some five thousand 75 mm shells, fifteen thousand 105 mm shells, twenty-five thousand mortar shells, and forty-five thousand rounds of 37 mm antiaircraft ammunition.[25] With an estimated 49,500 combatants in the Dien Bien

Phu area, supported by 31,500 logistical personnel and another 23,000 supporting troops along the supply lines to the front, the Viet Minh enjoyed a manpower advantage of five-to-one over the defenders of the fortified camp.[26] They also held the dominant terrain on the prospective battlefield. Given these advantages, on March 13 General Giap launched a sustained effort to destroy the French *base aéro-terrestre* at Dien Bien Phu and with it the French domination of Indochina.

Viet Minh Transport Operations

The Viet Minh won the battle of Dien Bien Phu along the roads and tracks leading to the besieged camp. Thousands of Viet Minh engineers and coolies struggled to repair the existing routes and to construct new roads for the tens of thousands of porters and hundreds of trucks that moved forward the weapons and supplies for what appeared to be the decisive battle of the war. In the final analysis, the Viet Minh triumph was gained by the multitude of individual soldiers and civilian coolies building or repairing roads through difficult terrain, pushing bicycles loaded with supplies, carrying mortar tubes on their backs, or driving trucks over poor roads under constant French air attack. Perhaps the most difficult task was moving forward the artillery and placing it in position in the hills overlooking Dien Bien Phu. The last stage, from the end of the track to the firing position, was done almost entirely by hand using levers, chocks, drag ropes, and block and tackle.[27] General Giap himself memorialized the drivers, porters, and other supply personnel who supported the Dien Bien Phu operation when he wrote:

> The Vietnamese people, under the direct leadership of the committees of supply for the front, gave proof of great heroism and endurance in serving the front. Truck convoys valiantly crossed streams, mountains and forests; drivers spent scores of sleepless nights, in defiance of difficulties and dangers, to bring food and ammunition to the front, to permit the army to annihilate the enemy. Thousands of bicycles from the towns also carried food and munitions to the front. Hundreds of sampans of all sizes, hundreds of thousands of bamboo-rafts crossed rapids and cascades to supply the front. Convoys of pack-horses from the Meo highlands or the provinces headed for the front. Day and night, hundreds of thousands of porters and young volunteers crossed passes and forded rivers in spite of enemy planes and delay-action bombs.[28]

Development of Viet Minh Supply Routes

The Viet Minh advance headquarters and supply headquarters for the Dien Bien Phu campaign were located at Muong Phan, but the main logistical staging area

Map 14.1. Viet Minh Supply Routes to Dien Bien Phu.

for the support of Viet Minh forces in the Dien Bien Phu area was at Tuan Giao at the junction of RC 6/RP 41 with RP 41A, fifty miles northeast of Dien Bien Phu.[29] As shown on map 14.1, the Viet Minh main supply route (MSR) ran from Cao Bang and Dong Dang (in the Nan Quam Pass near Lang Son) on the northern border of Tonkin with China through the main depot areas in the Viet Bac to merge at Tuyen Quang, and from there the MSR ran along RC 13A through Yen Bay to connect with RC 6 at Co Noi and thence up RC 6/RP 41 to Tuan Giao.[30] From Tuan Giao the MSR ran straight to Dien Bien Phu on RP 41A. The total road length of the MSR from Cao Bang to Dien Bien Phu was about 217 miles, most of which passed through very difficult mountains and jungle.[31]

Three secondary routes from the Chinese border to Tuan Giao were also utilized by the Viet Minh. One crossed the Sino-Vietnamese border at Thanh Thuy and ran through Ha Giang on RC 2 to join the MSR at Tuyen Quang. Another crossed the border at Lao Kay and ran along the Red River to join the MSR at Yen Bay. The French intelligence services reported in early January 1954 that the tonnages being moved over this route were small and relatively unimportant.[32] At the end of 1953, the Viet Minh with Chinese assistance opened a good, all-weather road from Kokiu, south of Kunming, through Ban Leng to the border town of Phong Tho.[33] Following the evacuation of Lai Chau by the French in mid-December 1953, the Viet Minh were able to extend the new road on through Lai Chau to Tuan Giao. On January 8, 1954, U.S. intelligence sources reported (based on French reports) that the Viet Minh were believed to be using a new supply route from Ban Leng in China through Lai Chau to Tuan Giao and that the route was expected to be open to light vehicular traffic by the end of January.[34] A month later, the French estimated that two thousand tons of rice and fifty tons of salt, enough to support eighty thousand men for a month, would be moved over the Ban Leng–Tuan Giao route in February, if the Viet Minh could arrange for the necessary transport.[35] The so-called Pavie Track, which ran from Lai Chau directly to Dien Bien Phu, was also utilized to a limited extent. Yet another important Viet Minh supply route ran up the Ma River valley from Thanh Hoa to Tuan Giao. It was over this route, some 350–400 miles cross-country, that perhaps 76 percent of the rice consumed by the Viet Minh troops at Dien Bien Phu was carried by thousands of porters.[36]

The critical segment of the Viet Minh supply route was the last fifty miles of RP 41A from Tuan Giao to Dien Bien Phu. At the beginning of the campaign RP 41A was little more than "a mule track," and the Viet Minh were obliged to build what amounted to an entirely new motor road some sixty-two miles in length through the hills from Tuan Giao to the hills around Dien Bien Phu to accommodate the movement of heavy artillery, trucks, and thousands of porters. In late November 1953, the Viet Minh 151st Engineer Regiment (351st Heavy Division) was assigned the mission of renovating RC 6/RP 41 from Son La to Tuan Giao.[37] The 151st Engineers subsequently extended their efforts to the critical segment of RP 41A between Tuan Giao and Dien Bien Phu and were reinforced in January 1954 by the 88th Infantry Regiment (308th Division), five thousand recruits of the newly formed 77th Infantry Regiment, and over ten thousand civilian coolies.[38] Subsequently, the new 154th Engineer Regiment from Nghe An Province was also committed to maintain the route, which suffered from the monsoon rains and constant French air attacks.[39] The main part of the work was completed by January 16, and the Viet Minh engineers then began what Colonel Pierre Langlais called "*un travail de titan*," the construction of trails in the immediate vicinity of Dien Bien Phu to permit the movement into position of the Viet Minh artillery.[40] That onerous task, some thirty-one miles of roads, was completed in six weeks despite the mountainous jungle terrain.

The expected onset of the monsoon rains in the spring of 1954 gave the ever-optimistic French commanders hope that the Viet Minh concentration on Dien Bien Phu would still come to naught. On March 24, the FTNV commander, Major General Cogny, wrote to Lieutenant General Navarre, "The rainy season, now close at hand, will compromise his [Giap's] communication lines and will pose a major obstacle to the development of his field fortifications."[41] Navarre, who even toyed with the idea of artificially inducing the rains by seeding the clouds over Tonkin, hoped that the heavy spring rains would seriously hamper the Viet Minh logistical effort by making the road from Lai Chau impassable, but only the French air operations were thwarted by the poor weather.[42] In reality, the monsoon degraded French air interdiction and air transport operations far more than it impeded the Viet Minh porters.

Due to the unceasing efforts of the Viet Minh engineers and the civilian labor units, the roads leading from Lai Chau and Tuan Giao toward Dien Bien Phu were generally well-maintained despite French bombs and heavy rains.[43] French intelligence officers reported that as of April 25 the road network used by the Viet Minh leading to Dien Bien Phu from the delta area was in excellent condition.[44] Indeed, in late April the roads from Lang Son and Cao Bang on the Chinese border to the interior were being improved, presumably to facilitate the increased movement of supplies from Communist China to the Viet Minh forces around Dien Bien Phu.[45]

The Porters

Manpower was the basis of the Viet Minh transportation system, and porters played a major role in the victory at Dien Bien Phu. The total number of porters employed cannot be determined with any precision, in part due to confusion over the area being considered, the constantly changing number of porters employed, and the fact that labor units were often employed as porters. The numbers usually cited range from around 33,500 to more than 260,000.[46] In late December 1953, French intelligence reports estimated that the Viet Minh were employing 30,000 to 40,000 porters (as well as two hundred trucks) in northwestern Tonkin.[47] By the time the Viet Minh attack on the camp began in mid-March, the number of porters employed in direct support of the Dien Bien Phu operation probably numbered around 70,000, and the total number of logistical personnel involved in the operation, including uniformed Viet Minh and Chinese logistical personnel, was about 300,000.[48]

The carrying capacity of each porter was greatly increased by the use of modified bicycles known as *xe thô*.[49] The French had known for some time that the Viet Minh were using bicycles as a means of transport, and in late December 1953, French intercepts of Viet Minh radio messages revealed that some two thousand bicycles were on their way toward Dien Bien Phu.[50] With only a few minor modifications, such as the use of wooden struts to strengthen the frame and front fork and the extension of the handlebars with a bamboo pole, a bicycle pushed by one man could carry as much as 440 pounds, perhaps ten times what a man could carry on his back for an extended period.[51] A 440-pound load was more than most elephants could carry. French calculations regarding Viet Minh logistical capabilities erred in not considering the increase in tonnage provided by the use of bicycles.

In any event, the number of porters employed was quite large, their loads were heavy, and the quantity of cargo moved into the battle area by porters was substantial. The bulk of the materiel moved by porters was rice, and the principal source of rice for the forces besieging Dien Bien Phu was in Thanh Hoa Province in coastal Annam, some 350–400 overland miles from Tuan Giao.[52] Significant quantities of rice also were supplied by Communist China. During February and March 1954, the Viet Minh objective was to move seventy tons of rice per day by porters over the route from Ban Leng via Lai Chau to the Tuan Giao area, although in the first week of March they were averaging only about ten tons per day.[53] By the end of March, the French estimated that an average of twenty tons of rice per day flowed over the Ban Leng–Lai Chau–Dien Bien Phu route, but there were also reports of shortages of porters.[54]

The porterage effort was not easy. Many of the Viet Minh porters died along the route from French air strikes, accidents, or diseases, such as cholera and malaria, caught in the unhealthy climate and difficult terrain along the way.[55] By the end of March 1954, illness and shortages of medical supplies were a constant problem. It was all the Viet Minh authorities could do to recruit and retain sufficient porters to keep the supplies moving toward Dien Bien Phu. But what the French considered impossible, the Viet Minh managed to do; the Viet Minh porters triumphed over every obstacle.

Viet Minh Motor Transport

While porters certainly played an important role at every stage on the lines of communication to Dien Bien Phu, the Viet Minh also relied heavily on motor transport to move forward the guns, ammunition, rations, and other supplies needed by their forces.[56] By the end of 1953, the number of trucks available to the Viet Minh was about six hundred to eight hundred.[57] By mid-February 1954, the number had increased to between one thousand and fifteen hundred, of which about eight hundred were Russian-made Molotova models. The rest were American GMC or Dodge 2.5-ton trucks captured from the French or provided by the Chinese Communists from stocks captured from the Nationalists or in the Korean War.[58] French intelligence sources estimated that if all of the available trucks were used to move supplies from the Chinese border to depots in the Viet Bac, the

Viet Minh could move at least two thousand tons per month by truck alone.[59] The use of trucks to move weapons, ammunition, and other heavy supply items was by no means restricted to the Viet Minh rear areas. French observers at Dien Bien Phu often reported hearing trucks, and in the week before the garrison fell the French estimated that the Viet Minh were operating some 405 trucks in the immediate vicinity of Dien Bien Phu.[60] However, about 350 of the trucks were assigned to the Viet Minh 16th Truck Regiment, whose mission was the movement of supplies from the Chinese border to the Viet Minh rear depots.[61] The nine companies of the 16th Truck Regiment, each with about one hundred men and thirty-five trucks, operated over a given segment of the main supply routes, the terminal points of each section being determined by bridges, ferry sites, passes, or other choke points likely to be cut by French air interdiction. A similar system was employed by the Communist forces in Korea and had the advantage of thoroughly familiarizing the drivers with their stretch of the route to the point that they could often drive the route at night without headlights. Such a system required the transloading of cargo at the segment termini, but the manpower necessary to manage such transfers was not a problem. Each section was assigned thirty to forty trucks, a number of coolies to transload cargo and repair the roads, and teams of special porters to fill in when the roads were cut.[62]

Frequent intelligence reports stated that many of the trucks involved in supporting the Viet Minh, both in the rear areas and at the front, were operated by Chinese drivers. For example, during the last week of April 1954, French intelligence sources reported that up to two hundred Chinese drivers were operating trucks hauling supplies from the Chinese border to the main Viet Minh depots in the Viet Bac.[63] No doubt Chinese drivers were employed, but many of the drivers were Vietnamese like Tha, a driver interviewed by Jules Roy, whose description of Tha's experiences provides a striking view of the difficulties faced by the Viet Minh drivers engaged in the movement of supplies by truck in late April 1954:

> At the wheel of his GMC loaded with 105-mm shells, driver Tha gritted his teeth. The mud came up over the hubs, and it was impossible to move without engaging the two live axles in ruts which the wheels refused to leave, as if they were deep rails. To repair tire covers torn by the sharp ridges of the road surface, a bolt would be inserted into the hole and a nut screwed on. The day before, on a hairpin bend in the Fa Dinh Pass which had just been attacked by planes, the truck in front had broken down, next to the crater of a delayed-action bomb which looked as if it would explode any moment, for the mountain was shaken every now and then by explosions. It was impossible to back up or to pass, and the Molotova in front skidded on the slope as soon as it tried to give the truck a tow. Finally, by pumping air through the tubes, the feed circuit of the

carburetor had been restored. When the bomb exploded, the convoy had just moved away. A little grimace appeared on Tha's childlike face at the thought, but sweat trickled down his back.[64]

The Failure of French Air Interdiction

Once the battle for Dien Bien Phu was joined, the Viet Minh lines of communication became relatively fixed and thus more vulnerable and more attractive as a target for French air forces. Viet Minh artillery, trucks, and porters clogged the roads leading to Dien Bien Phu, particularly the fifty-mile stretch of RP 41A from Tuan Giao to Dien Bien Phu. Despite an all-out effort, however, the French failed miserably in their attempt to shut down the flow of men, equipment, and supplies to the Viet Minh divisions around the beleaguered camp. The failure of French air interdiction was composed in equal parts of the inadequacy of their interdiction resources and the effectiveness of Viet Minh countermeasures.

Throughout the First Indochina War, French airmen, like their contemporary American counterparts in Korea, operated on the assumption that their enemy's lines of communication could be successfully interdicted by airpower. This unwarranted faith in the effectiveness of aerial interdiction, particularly the idea that around-the-clock bombardment of the enemy's lines of communication could prevent the movement of men and supplies to the front, had proven a notable failure during the massive Operation STRANGLE in Korea, although American airmen apparently neglected to inform their French comrades of that salient fact.[65] Be that as it may, an unwavering faith in the doctrine of air interdiction meant very little in the absence of a sufficient number of suitable aircraft to perform the air interdiction mission adequately.

The mission of interdicting the Viet Minh supply lines in Tonkin was assigned to the Northern Tactical Air Group (*Groupement Aérien Tactique d'Attaque et de Choc-Nord Viêt-Nam,* GATAC Nord), commanded by French Air Force brigadier general Jean Dechaux, but GATAC Nord lacked sufficient suitable aircraft to ensure the success of the effort. Until the beginning of April 1954, Brigadier General Dechaux had a maximum of 107 aircraft (32 fighters, 45 fighter-bombers, and 30 light bombers) at his disposal, or about three-quarters of all the combat aircraft in Indochina, but considering combat losses, damage, and scheduled maintenance, Dechaux had only about seventy-five aircraft available at any one time.[66] However, some relief was provided by an augmentation of six C-119s equipped for dropping napalm and eight French Navy Privateers of Squadron 28F used as strategic bombers.[67] Although designed for antisubmarine warfare, the Privateers could carry a bomb load of four tons and, equipped with a Norden bombsight, were ideal for interdiction of the Viet Minh supply lines and bombing of their rear area depots. Nevertheless, the overall lack of strategic bombers made it nearly impossible to fully interdict the Viet Minh supply lines near the Chinese border, which would have compelled the Viet Minh to portage their supplies for Dien Bien Phu over 372 miles rather than only the last ninety-three, and Dechaux's fighter-bombers and B-26s could not cover the last ninety-three miles adequately either.[68] Had all of the available aircraft been used to attack the Viet Minh supply installations and routes between the Chinese border and the region of Lang Son–Thai Nguyen, the French still would have needed another two hundred bombers to relieve Dien Bien Phu.[69]

Two air interdiction techniques were available: (1) the concentration on making one major cut on a route and attacking it repeatedly to ensure that it could not be repaired, or (2) the creation of multiple cuts along a line of communication that would cause the enemy to disperse his defensive and repair efforts. GATAC Nord tried both methods against the Viet Minh MSR along RP 13 and RP 41 without achieving notable success with either one.[70] The single cut method was obviously the potentially less effective of the two methods since the Viet Minh porters could simply create a bypass through the jungle or hordes of coolies protected by anti-aircraft batteries could quickly concentrate to repair a single cut. Consequently, the French elected to concentrate their interdiction efforts at a few key points (the crossings of the Red and Black Rivers, the junction of RP 13 and RP 41 at Co Noi, and the depot zone around Tuan Giao) while maintaining a number of smaller cuts all along the Viet Minh MSR to compel the Viet Minh to employ numerous repair teams and bypasses.[71] This effort also failed to achieve the desired results. For example, on December 25–26, 1953, twenty-three French fighter-bombers dropped twenty-three tons of bombs on cut-point MERCURE, but traffic through the cut-point was restored within twenty-four hours.[72] In the end, the French Air Force never succeeded in cutting the Viet Minh lines of communication to Dien Bien Phu, or even in slowing the traffic to the point at which the Viet Minh forces surrounding the entrenched camp felt themselves on the edge of the logistical precipice. In the words of General Giap: "The enemy bombers were very active . . . day and night they shelled our supply lines, dropped blockbusters on the roads, showered the roads with delayed action and 'butterfly' bombs, in an endeavour to cut our supply lines. These desperate efforts did not achieve the desired results. They could not check the flow of hundreds of thousands of voluntary workers, pack-horses and transport cars carrying food and ammunition to the front. They could not stop us from carrying out our plan of encirclement, the condition of their destruction."[73]

While the French Air Force attempted to cut the Viet Minh supply lines to Dien Bien Phu from the air, the French-led guerrillas of the GMCA/GMI crept through the jungles of northwestern Tonkin with the same objective in mind. They managed to tie down a considerable number of Viet Minh troops, perhaps three times their own number, but they were no more successful than the bombers and fighter-bombers in hampering the flow of supplies to the Viet Minh forces surrounding Dien Bien Phu.[74] Colonel Pierre Langlais attributed their failure to the lack of French knowledge of the region around Dien Bien Phu, the hostile population, and the decimation of the French-led T'ai partisan groups upon which the French special operations depended.[75]

The Viet Minh exerted every effort to keep their supply lines operating in the face of heavy rains and French interdiction attacks. The principal routes were well-protected with antiaircraft artillery, and the Viet Minh flak units, so deadly to the French transports over Dien Bien Phu, were equally dangerous to the French bomber and fighter pilots engaged in the air interdiction campaign. In 1953, the French identified 714 Viet Minh flak positions, 244 French aircraft were hit, and 10 were shot down. Determined to protect their supply lines to Dien Bien Phu, the Viet Minh created a virtual "flak corridor" along the MSR to Dien Bien Phu, and between November 24 and December 7 alone forty-five of the fifty-one French fighter-bombers working along RP 13A and RP 41 reported hits, and one fighter-bomber and two small reconnaissance planes were shot down. In December 1953, 367 combat sorties were flown and 49 aircraft were hit, with the result that on December 26 a greater number of bombers and fighter-bombers were diverted to flak suppression missions.[76] French Air Force and Navy losses continued to mount as the campaign progressed.

The Viet Minh also employed a range of passive measures, such as camouflage, air warning, and strict march discipline, as well as an efficient system for repairing the routes and facilities damaged by French bombs. They eventually identified some forty key points on which the French interdiction operations seemed to be concentrated, and a group of local civilian coolies (dân cong) was assigned to each point and given responsibility for maintaining a given segment of road.[77] The dân cong repair crews quickly appeared after every heavy rain or air attack to clear unexploded bombs, replace camouflage, fill bomb craters, repair landslides, or construct temporary bypasses. As a result, the main Viet Minh supply routes were seldom completely closed for more than twenty-four hours at a time.[78] Colonel Langlais noted the efficiency of the Viet Minh road repair crews and the efficacy of their camouflage efforts on his ride into captivity after the fall of Dien Bien Phu: "Two hours later the route was repaired, and the trucks started off again. A little before dawn, they left the road. An almost invisible detour penetrated into a tunnel in the jungle. There was the convoy stop: garages, water, silos of rice, multiple chimneys to disperse the revealing smoke. And these resting places had only their invisibility to protect them."[79]

Chinese Support to the Viet Minh at Dien Bien Phu

Most of the weapons, ammunition, and other supplies so laboriously moved forward to Dien Bien Phu by the thousands of Viet Minh porters and trucks were provided by the Chinese Communists. The French certainly recognized that it was essential to restrict the flow of supplies to the Viet Minh from Communist China, and the French government appealed to the British and American governments to put what pressure they could on the Communist Chinese to halt the flow of supplies to the Viet Minh, but to no avail. French estimates of Chinese Communist aid to the Viet Minh in the last months of 1953 were about eight hundred to one thousand tons per month.[80] Despite reports that the Chinese had increased the flow of supplies to the Viet Minh in the first days of 1954, as late as mid-February there had been no confirmation that that was the case.[81] However, French intelligence sources reported that between March 1 and March 26, an additional 2,500 tons of supplies, excluding food but including 640 tons of gasoline, were delivered to the Viet Minh by the Chinese at one border crossing alone.[82] The rather large tonnage was taken as substantiation of recent reports that the Chinese had increased their aid to the Viet Minh inasmuch as the largest tonnage reported for a similar earlier period was two thousand tons in June 1953. On April 3, Lieutenant General Navarre reported to Paris that among the military equipment and supplies recently provided by the Chinese to the Viet Minh were 40 37 mm anti-aircraft guns (each with a Chinese crew of twenty men), 1,000 trucks manned by Chinese drivers, 395 machine guns, 1,200 automatic rifles, 4,000 submachine guns, 4,000 rifles, 44,000 rounds of 37 mm ammunition, 15,000 105 mm howitzer shells, 10,000 75 mm rounds, 60,000 mortar rounds, 5 million cartridges (including 1.5 million 12.7 mm heavy machine gun rounds), over 1 million gallons of gasoline, and 4,300 tons of rice.[83]

In early April 1954, as the position of the French Union forces at Dien Bien Phu grew increasingly precarious, the U.S. ambassador to France, Douglas Dillon, met with members of the French cabinet to discuss the situation. In a cable to the Secretary of State on April 5, Ambassador Dillon relayed a report by the French on the degree to which the Chinese intervention in Indochina was already established:

> First. Fourteen technical advisers at Giap headquarters plus numerous others at division level. All under command of Chinese Communist General Ly Chenhou who is stationed at Giap headquarters.
>
> Second. Special telephone lines installed maintained and operated by Chinese personnel.
>
> Third. Forty 37 mm. anti-aircraft guns radar-controlled at Dien Bien Phu. These guns operated by Chinese and evidently are from Korea. These AA guns are now shooting through clouds to bring down French aircraft.
>
> Fourth. One thousand supply trucks of which 500 have arrived since 1 March, all driven by Chinese army personnel.
>
> Fifth. Substantial material help in guns, shells, etc., as is well known.[84]

In mid-April, French intelligence officers estimated that the shipment of supplies from Communist China to the Viet Minh forces around Dien Bien Phu in the previous few weeks had averaged ninety-five tons per day, of which seventy-five tons were being moved through Cao Bang and Lang Son and the remaining twenty tons, almost all foodstuffs, via Lai Chau.[85] The increased rate at which supplies were being received from China was taken as evidence that the Viet Minh were endeavoring to build up their reserves before the onset of the rainy season. At the end of the month, the French reported that the shipment of supplies from China directly to Dien Bien Phu was a divergence from the previous procedures, whereby the Chinese shipped supplies to the Viet Minh depots well in advance of planned operations.[86] The French intelligence officers, ever optimistic, took this as a sign that the Viet Minh logistical system was about to reach its breaking point, and American analysts added that "International Communism" attached great importance to a Viet Minh victory at Dien Bien Phu.

French intelligence services estimated that by the time the surviving defenders of Dien Bien Phu were marched into captivity by the victorious Viet Minh, the Chinese Communists had provided about 25 percent of the rice and at least two thousand tons of the artillery ammunition consumed by the Viet Minh in the battle (including 15,000 rounds of 105 mm howitzer ammunition, 10,000 rounds of 75 mm, and 44,000 rounds of 37 mm antiaircraft machine gun ammunition), plus 395 heavy machine guns, 4,000 submachine guns, 4,000 rifles, 5 million rounds of small arms ammunition, 4,000 cubic meters of fuel, and 4,300 tons of rice.[87]

Heavy shipments of materiel from China continued after the fall of Dien Bien Phu. In June 1954, the amount of weapons, ammunition, and other supplies received by the Viet Minh may have been as much as four thousand tons.[88] Under the Geneva agreements both sides were permitted to replace on a one-for-one basis war materiel "destroyed, damaged, worn out, or used up."[89] The Viet Minh took full advantage of their rights under the agreements, and French intelligence officers confirmed that between May 10 and July 23, 1954, the Chinese Communists provided the Viet Minh with the munitions shown in table 14.1.

The role played by Chinese Communist staff officers and troops in supporting the Viet Minh has long been debated. It appears that following approval of the attack on Dien Bien Phu by the Viet Minh political authorities on December 6, 1953, a Dien Bien Phu Campaign Command was established with Vo Nguyen Giap as commander in chief and the Chinese general Wei Guo Qing as chief military advisor.[90] Allegations that General Giap allowed the Chinese Communist advisors attached to his headquarters to dictate Viet Minh strategy and tactics are probably unfounded, and the idea that the Dien Bien Phu campaign was directed by China's General Ly Chen-hou is surely a canard.[91] As Jules Roy asserted:

There may have been a Chinese, General Li Chen Hou, at Giap's head-

Table 14.1. Munitions Provided by the Chinese Communists to the Viet Minh, May 10–July 23, 1954

Type	Quantity
Weapons (Items)	
Small Arms	2,027
Automatic Rifles	947
Machine Guns	405
Rocket Launchers	96
Mortars (61 mm to 120 mm)	322
Antiaircraft Guns, 37 mm	30
Artillery (including Recoilless Rifles)	282
Ammunition (Rounds)	
Small Arms Ammunition	293,000
Automatic Rifle Ammunition	1,651,000
Machine Gun Ammunition	1,418,000
Rockets for Rocket Launchers	14,470
Mortar Ammunition (61 mm to 120 mm)	179,300
Antiaircraft Gun Ammunition 37 mm	15,980
Artillery & Recoilless Rifle Ammunition	153,980
Hand Grenades	91,000
Mines	8,752
Explosive Charges	9,000
Detonators	10,700
Bangalore Torpedoes	1,000
Flares	40,000

Source: Indochina SITREP No. 47, July 30, 1954, paragraph 3.

quarters, but there were none at the divisional and regimental command posts, where the nationalist sensitivity of the Central Committee and the People's Army would have made them undesirable. The Vietminh waged its war as it saw fit, and waged it alone. If Navarre was to lose the battle of Dienbienphu, he would lose it to Giap and not because of the Chinese.

Every time I put this question to officers of the North Vietnam Army, indignation transformed every face, "It is inconceivable that we should ever take orders from foreign officers, even Chinese ones. We regard your question as deplorable. Nobody in the People's Army ever prepared baths for the Chinese; nobody ever walked beside their horses." Giap dismissed this allegation as a legend.[92]

However, reports that perhaps as many as twenty thousand Chinese troops were directly involved in the battle for Dien Bien Phu may have a basis in fact. French and American intelligence reports of the period frequently note the presence of Chinese Communist advisors and troops, particularly truck drivers and antiaircraft crewmen. For example, a Viet Minh prisoner reported on April 20 that the Chinese antiaircraft artillery advisors accounted for the accuracy of the 37 mm flak around Dien Bien Phu, and American intelligence sources reported at the end of April 1954 that there were Chinese observers and advisors with the higher Viet Minh staffs as well as one Chinese Communist technical advisor assigned to the Viet Minh crew of each 37 mm antiaircraft gun.[93] There is also good evidence that at least a dozen PLA engineers with recent experience in Korea were sent to Dien Bien Phu to assist the Viet Minh in the construction of the elaborate system of trenches that surrounded the besieged camp.[94]

The Viet Minh leaders were not eager to share the credit for the victory at Dien Bien Phu with their Chinese comrades, thus there is little mention of the tons of weapons, ammunition, and other materiel supplied by the Chinese Communists or of the advice, technical assistance, and planning work that they may have provided.[95] In his postwar book on the battle, General Giap, whom the Chinese general Chen Geng described as "slippery and not very upright and honest," made the obligatory bow toward the Chinese: "Generally speaking, relationships between us and friendly military experts ever since the Border Campaign had been excellent. Our friends had given us the benefit of their invaluable experience drawn from the revolutionary war in China and the anti-US war in Korea," but he never identifies or credits the Chinese advisors, including Wei Guo Qing or Ly Chen-hou, in any way.[96]

Sustaining the Battle Force at Dien Bien Phu

The Viet Minh combat forces eventually assembled in the immediate area of Dien Bien Phu included the 308th, 312th, and 316th Divisions, part of the 304th Division, and part of the 148th Independent Infantry Regiment (for a total of twelve infantry regiments), plus the 351st Heavy Division, which included two artillery regiments (the 45th and 675th), an engineer regiment (the 151st), a heavy weapons regiment (237th), a field rocket unit, and an antiaircraft artillery regiment (the 367th).[97] In addition, there were enormous numbers of porters, laborers, and other logistical support personnel. The task of sustaining such a large force around Dien Bien Phu was not easy, but the Viet Minh logistical services managed the feat that the French intelligence officers and staff planners had considered impossible. The trucks and porters delivered an enormous tonnage of weapons, ammunition, food, and other supplies to the Viet Minh fighters at Dien Bien Phu. Based on Vietnamese sources, Kevin M. Boylan prepared an elaborate table showing logis-

Table 14.2. Viet Minh Supply Data for the Battle of Dien Bien Phu

Item	Unit	Planned	Allocated	Consumed
Rice	tons		25,056	14,950
Salt	tons			268
Meat	tons		907	577
Dried Food	tons		917	565
Other Food	tons		469	469
Total Rations			**27,349**	**16,829**
Total Medical Supplies	**tons**	**45**	**55**	**55**
Total Military Gear	**tons**		**71**	**71**
Total Gasoline	**tons**		**1,783**	**1,783**[a]
Lubricating Oil[b]	liters	1,800	1,860	
Grease[b]	kilograms	280	280	
Pick[b]	each	5,200	4,950	4,700
Shovel[b]	each	8,000	8,700	7,800
Machete[b]	each	3,000	3,200	2,900
Total Miscellaneous	**tons**		**51**	**51**
Ammunition				
Machine Gun	rounds	1,388,500	1,285,000	950,000
Submachine Gun	rounds	885,000	907,000	840,000
57 mm Recoilless Rifle	rounds	4,300	4,150	4,000
75 mm Recoilless Rifle	rounds	4,000	4,000	530
90 mm Rkt Launcher (Bazooka)	rounds	1,720	1,820	1,800
60 mm Mortar	rounds	22,700	21,800	23,230
81/82 mm Mortar	rounds	34,934	34,993	37,300
120 mm Mortar	rounds	4,750	4,360	3,000
75 mm Howitzer	rounds	3,750	3,754	4,700
105 mm Howitzer	rounds	15,094	15,118	16,600
102 mm Rocket	rounds	4,000	4,000	836
37 mm AA Gun	rounds	46,000	40,600	31,750
12.7 mm AA Machine Gun	rounds	700,500	706,600	512,000
Hand Grenade	rounds	96,180	96,480	86,080
Explosive Charge Launcher	rounds	3,000	4,000	1,500
Bangalore Torpedo	meters	6,000	5,300	4,000
Explosives	tons	26	27.5	25
Total Ammunition	**tons**	**1,500**	**1,450**	**1,200**
Grand Total	**tons**		**30,759**	**19,989**

[a] Another 10 tons of gasoline were captured from the French.
[b] Tonnages included with Total Ammunition tonnage.
Source: Boylan, "No 'Technical Knockout,'" 1372, table 8 ("VPA Logistical Data for the Siege of Dien Bien Phu"), based on Gia Duc Pham et al., *Dien Bien Phu, Moc Vang Thoi Dai* [Dien Bien Phu: Landmark of the Golden Era], 401–2.

tical data for the Viet Minh forces at Dien Bien Phu.[98] Table 14.2 is a condensation of Boylan's table. It should be noted that the estimates of other authorities are much lower.[99]

The effort to keep the forces surrounding Dien Bien Phu supplied was exhausting. By early April, the French were again reporting that, based on information that the Viet Minh had begun to ration artillery ammunition, the enemy was experiencing logistical difficulties due to problems with the porters, heavy rains, and French air strikes.[100] The French hoped that these problems would hamper the movement of supplies to the frontline Viet Minh troops around Dien Bien Phu. A sure indication that the Viet Minh were indeed experiencing some difficulty in maintaining their forces in the encirclement of Dien Bien Phu came with the surrender of a soldier from the 209th Regiment of the Viet Minh 312th Division on April 20. Under interrogation he painted the picture of a unit composed of at least 50 percent raw recruits living uncomfortably in the rain under a hail of French artillery fire and of supply shortages caused by the French air interdiction of RP 41.[101]

One area in which the Viet Minh logistical system was definitely inadequate was medical support.[102] Despite the mobilization of thousands of doctors, nurses, medical students, pharmacists, and other medical personnel, the fifty thousand Viet Minh troops surrounding Dien Bien Phu were without sufficient medical support during the entire period of the siege, with only one surgeon and six assistant doctors in the immediate area of the battle.[103] It was only at the end of April that the Viet Minh began the organization of a three*thousand-bed hospital south of Son La and requested ten thousand mosquito nets for their troops around Dien Bien Phu.[104] In all, the Viet Minh medics treated some 10,130 wounded during the two-month battle.[105]

The important role that the Viet Minh artillery and antiaircraft batteries played in the defeat of the French makes the concentration of artillery at Dien Bien Phu and the supply of ammunition for that artillery an excellent reflection of the performance of the entire Viet Minh logistical system at Dien Bien Phu. The French miscalculation regarding the ability of the Viet Minh to concentrate a substantial battle force at Dien Bien Phu and sustain it there was often repeated by the French artillery commander at Dien Bien Phu, Colonel Charles Piroth, who, as Bernard Fall has noted, was fond of proclaiming: "Firstly, the Viet-Minh won't succeed in getting their artillery through to here. Secondly, if they do get here, we'll smash them. Thirdly, even if they manage to keep on shooting, they will be unable to supply their pieces with enough ammunition to do us any real harm."[106] Of course, Piroth was wrong on all three counts, and as a consequence the defenders of Dien Bien Phu found themselves outgunned. Thus, when the battle proper began, the Viet Minh quickly neutralized the French artillery and then began to destroy it systematically. Piroth subsequently killed himself in his bunker with a hand grenade.

The total number and types of guns that the Viet Minh concentrated around Dien Bien Phu are still uncertain after nearly sixty years. General Giap never revealed the secret, and the estimates made at the time by the French and later by a number of historians vary widely. Two experts on the battle, Bernard Fall and Jules Roy, put the total number of guns deployed by the Viet Minh at Dien Bien

Phu at over 200 and 218, respectively, and other authorities have suggested different numbers.[107] A more recent estimate is that of Martin Windrow, who puts the total number of heavy guns, mortars, and antiaircraft guns concentrated by the Viet Minh around Dien Bien Phu at:

45th Artillery Regiment	36 x 105 mm howitzers
675th Artillery Regiment	24 x 75 mm howitzers
	20 x 120 mm mortars
237th Heavy Weapons Regiment	30 x 120 mm mortars
367th Antiaircraft Artillery Regiment	100 x 12.7 mm antiaircraft machine guns
	37 x 37 mm antiaircraft guns
Field Rocket Unit[108]	12–16 multiple rocket launchers[109]

To date, the most definitive analysis of the Viet Minh artillery at Dien Bien Phu is that of Kevin M. Boylan, published in the *Journal of Military History* in October 2014.[110] Boylan's conclusions as to the number of Viet Minh artillery pieces by type at Dien Bien Phu are shown in table 14.3.

Table 14.3. Viet Minh Heavy Weapons at Dien Bien Phu

Weapon	Number
57 mm Recoilless Rifle	57
75 mm Recoilless Rifle	12
90 mm Rocket Launcher ("bazooka")	72
60 mm Mortar	179
81/82 mm Mortar	162
120 mm Mortar	16
75 mm Howitzer	18
105 mm Howitzer	24
102 mm Rocket	12
37 mm Antiaircraft Gun	33
12.7 mm Antiaircraft Machine Gun	85

Source: Boylan, "No 'Technical Knockout,'" 1372, table 8 ("VPA Logistical Data for the Siege of Dien Bien Phu"). There may also have been a few of the super-heavy Soviet 1943-model 160 mm mortars in the Dien Bien Phu area. See Fall, *Hell in a Very Small Place*, 105. By contrast, the French defenders had four 155 mm HM1 howitzers, twenty-four HM2 105 mm howitzers, ten 75 mm howitzers, twenty-eight 120 mm mortars, four .50-cal. four-barrel machine guns ("Quad 50s"), and ten tanks. See Boylan, "No 'Technical Knockout,'" 1372, table 7 ("Comparison"), and Windrow, *The Last Valley*, 702, appendix 2 ("French Order of Battle").

The number of Viet Minh guns at Dien Bien Phu is perhaps less important than the number of rounds they fired. Here again the French intelligence pre-battle estimates of the Viet Minh capability for bringing forward ammunition were seriously under the mark.[111] The French knew from intercepted and decoded Viet Minh radio transmissions that in the first week of March 1954 the Viet Minh already had in place in the area around Dien Bien Phu: 5,000 75 mm howitzer shells, 15,000 105 mm howitzer shells, 21,000 81 mm mortar shells, 3,000 120 mm mortar shells, and 44,000 37 mm antiaircraft shells.[112] After the battle, the same French intelligence officers estimated that at least 2,000 tons of artillery ammunition had been consumed by the Viet Minh in the battle for Dien Bien Phu, including 11,000 75 mm howitzer shells; 20,000 105 mm howitzer shells; 35,000 82 mm mortar rounds; 10,000 120 mm mortar shells; 4,200 75 mm recoilless rifle rounds; and 60,000 37 mm antiaircraft shells, for a total of 140,200 shells.[113]

Estimates of the total number of shells fired by the Viet Minh range as high as 350,000, most of which had to be carried to the battlefield from a distance.[114] After detailed analysis, Boylan puts the total number of rounds larger than 57 mm fired by the Viet Minh at Dien Bien Phu at about 92,000, probably the definitive number or close to it.[115] Of those 92,000 shells, a substantial proportion were probably French shells misdropped by parachute into the Viet Minh lines. Again, the estimates of the number of shells misdropped by the French into the Viet Minh lines vary widely, with the perhaps most accurate being that of John D. Plating, who states that the French transports misdropped 14,800 rounds of 105 mm howitzer ammunition alone into Viet Minh lines.[116] The large quantities of supplies of all types dropped by the French transports after March 13, 1954, that fell into their hands caused the Viet Minh soldiers, when they saw the C-47s come into view, to laugh and yell: "*Tân công trên troi!*" ("Here come the air porters!")[117]

At the end of April there was every indication that the Viet Minh were making logistical preparations to continue operations during the rainy season, probably in an attempt to influence the course of the negotiations at Geneva. But the rain falls on the just and the unjust alike, and at the end of April and beginning of May 1954 it fell heavily on both the defenders of Dien Bien Phu and its attackers. Even the sure-footed Viet Minh porters were hard put to stay on the slippery trails with their heavy loads. It was perhaps fortuitous that the siege ended on May 7; the Viet Minh, too, had nearly reached the end of their logistical endurance.

Aftermath

Around 1730 hours on May 7, 1954, Viet Minh soldiers entered Brigadier General de Castries's command bunker in the center of Dien Bien Phu, and the hard-fought fifty-six-day siege came to an end. The scene was horrendous and was described by Nguyen Thi Ngoc Toan, a Viet Minh medic: "The place stank, there was filth and garbage, they were stacked on top of one another, there was blood everywhere—it was like hell on earth."[118] The Viet Minh lines were not much better, the *Chu Luc* and their support troops forced to occupy squalid bunkers surrounded by the dead.[119] The Viet Minh were the victors and held the field of battle, but they had paid a heavy price. Viet Minh casualties have been estimated at seventy-nine hundred dead and more than fifteen thousand wounded.[120] Despite the sacrifices made by the Viet Minh soldiers and their civilian comrades, the battle for Dien Bien Phu tied down only 4–5 percent of the French Union combat forces in Indochina but required the commitment of 50–60 percent of the Viet Minh regular forces and most of the aid received from China.[121]

The Viet Minh victory was surely won by the bravery and determination of the *Chu Luc* infantry, the skill of the Viet Minh artillerists, and the accuracy of the Viet Minh antiaircraft gunners, but if the triumph can be attributed to any one group, the laurel must be awarded to the thousands of Vietnamese, military and civilian, who labored on the roads and paths leading to the encircled fortress to carry forward the weapons, ammunition, and rations that enabled the Viet Minh combatants to carry out their mission. General Giap himself provided their epitaph when he wrote:

> Throughout the long years of the Resistance War, our people never made so great a contribution as in the Winter 1953–Spring 1954 campaign, in supplying the army for the fight against the enemy. On the main Dien Bien Phu front, our people had to ensure the supply of food and munitions to a big army, operating 500 to 700 kilometers from the rear, and in very difficult conditions. The roads were bad, the means of transport insufficient and the supply lines relentlessly attacked by the enemy. There was, in addition, the menace of heavy rains that could create more obstacles than bombing.[122]

For the French, the most obvious cost of the battle of Dien Bien Phu was the loss of Indochina, but the battle also took an enormous toll in lives and suffering and a not inconsiderable amount of treasure. Between November 20, 1953, and May 5, 1954, the French Union forces at Dien Bien Phu lost some 7,184 casualties (about 47.6 percent), of whom 1,142 were killed in action, 4,436 were wounded (of whom 429 died of their wounds), and 1,606 were listed as missing in action. Perhaps more than 10,000 were marched into captivity.[123] The total French losses in the battle of Dien Bien Phu, including those taken prisoner by the Viet Minh, amounted to only about 6 percent of the total French Expeditionary Corps, but the impact of such losses was devastating, and the demoralization and radicalization of the French survivors of Dien Bien Phu contributed substantially to the subsequent problems in Algeria.[124]

The fate of the French Union troops taken prisoner at Dien Bien Phu was tragic, not so much because the victorious Viet Minh were inclined to treat them badly, but because they simply overwhelmed the Viet Minh logistical system. Already debilitated by fifty-six days of short rations and hard fighting, the survivors had to endure thirty-sixty days of marching at a rate of twelve miles per day carrying their rations, sick, and wounded. Water was limited in the area through which they marched, and the Viet Minh were able to provide only fourteen ounces of rice per day and ten peanuts every tenth day.[125] Of an estimated 10,863 French Union soldiers taken prisoner at Dien Bien Phu, including 3,578 wounded, only 3,290 were returned to French control four months later; 7,573 (about 70 percent) died in captivity.[126]

The disaster at Dien Bien Phu upset the entire French position in Tonkin and precipitated a decision for the immediate evacuation of the southern portion of the Red River delta that had been most heavily infiltrated by the Viet Minh guerrillas in order to concentrate the remaining forces on the defense of the vital Haiphong–Hanoi supply artery.[127] Given the code name AUVERGNE, the last major operation of the First Indochina War began on June 30, 1954. Four mobile groups (two armored and two motorized) sought to cover the withdrawal of all French Union forces in the southern delta to a shorter line along the vital Hanoi–Haiphong road (RC 5). The flight of loyal Vietnamese from the Catholic bishoprics in the southern delta began long before the formal evacuation of Operation AUVERGNE was ordered, but in the event the French abandoned some 1.5 million Vietnamese Catholics to the Viet Minh.[128] Operation AUVERGNE was itself a major logistical undertaking. In the last two weeks of June 1954 alone, some twelve thousand tons of materiel moved over RC 5 from Hanoi toward the port of Haiphong, a striking reversal of the flow only two months before.[129] The last French ship left Haiphong harbor on May 15, 1955.

The battle of Dien Bien Phu was costly for the French in monetary terms as well. Materiel losses alone included 13 field guns, 125 mortars, 950 machine guns, 1,200 submachine guns, 8,000 rifles, 1,300 tons of supplies and ammunition, and 450 vehicles.[130] One French estimate placed the cost of the battle for the army alone at 15.18 trillion francs, of which 12.9 trillion represented the costs of supplies and equipment consumed or lost during the battle and 2.28 trillion represented the cost of air transport for the establishment and maintenance of the base.[131] These figures do not include the considerable amount of materiel provided by U.S. aid, which amounted to about 60–70 percent of the total.

Meeting at Berlin in March 1954, France, Great Britain, the United States, and the Soviet Union agreed that a conference should be held to resolve the problems of Korea and the war in Indochina. The conference convened at Geneva on April 26, 1954, and two days later a Franco-Vietnamese declaration of Viet Nam as a sovereign and independent state was made public. The prospect of a negotiated settlement of the Indochina conflict in the talks at Geneva upped the ante for both sides at Dien Bien Phu by posing the possibility of a decisive advantage at the talks for the side that won. Initially, the conference focused on the Korean situation, but following the disastrous defeat of the French at Dien Bien Phu on May 7, attention turned to a solution that would end the war in Indochina. Meanwhile, the French and Viet Minh high commands concluded a cease-fire agreement for Viet Nam on July 20, as well as separate cease-fire agreements for Laos and Cambodia. The Viet Nam cease-fire provided for the withdrawal of all French and State of Viet Nam forces north of the 17th Parallel and a similar evacuation by the Viet Minh south of the demarcation line. A period of three hundred days was established during which free movement was to be allowed for all persons desiring to move from one area to the other. The introduction of any additional military forces into Viet Nam was prohibited except for the purpose of rotating existing forces, and the introduction of new weapons was also restricted to replacement of existing arms. Both sides agreed to restrictions on the establishment of foreign military bases on their territory. An International Control Commission consisting of personnel from India, Canada, and Poland was established to oversee implementation of the cease-fire agreements.

In their Final Declaration on July 21, 1954, the Geneva conferees also provided for the holding of general elections throughout both North and South Viet Nam in July 1956 under supervision of the International Control Commission. Ngo Dinh Diem, the prime minister of the State of Viet Nam, refused to sign either the cease-fire agreement or the Geneva Accords, protesting the manner in which the truce was arrived at as well as the partitioning of the country and the setting of a date for elections without consultation with his government. The United States also refused to concur with either the cease-fire or the Geneva agreements, but declared that it would not use force to overturn them. Instead, the United States stated its determination to seek unification of the two halves of Viet Nam in accordance with the will of the Vietnamese people expressed in free and fair elections to be held under U.N. supervision. In the end, of course, the United States found the risk of Communist success in such elections to be too great and worked to prevent their being held.

If, as Bernard Fall has written, the battle of Dien Bien Phu was lost between November 25 and December 7, 1953, in the air-conditioned map room of the French *commandant en chef,* it was won on the muddy, bomb-pocked roads stretching from the Chinese border to the gates of Dien Bien Phu. The commanders and staff officers on both sides understood from the start that Dien Bien Phu could very well be the decisive battle of the war and that it would be the ultimate battle of logistics, in which victory would go to the side that could best keep their own troops supplied while reducing the flow of supplies to the enemy. The logistical services of both sides nearly reached the end of their endurance during the 169 days from November 20, 1953, to May 7, 1954, but it was the Viet Minh that prevailed. They did so not because their cause was just, but because they believed in their cause; not because they placed their faith in machines, but because they placed their faith in men; not because they were superior, but because they were determined.

15

Logistics and the War in Indochina, 1945–1954

The First Indochina War ended on May 15, 1955, when the last French ship left Haiphong harbor loaded with the remnants of the once-powerful French colonial regime in Indochina. Nearly ten years of terrible war had concluded with the victory of the pro-Communist Viet Minh nationalists in Tonkin and the establishment of a faltering pro-Western government in the south. The costs of the war had been high. In monetary terms, the war cost the French about $11 billion, not counting the nearly $1 billion in United States aid delivered before the cease-fire in 1954.[1] The human costs were incalculable, but the French government estimated the number of French Union dead (killed in action and noncombat) and missing at 92,797, the number of wounded at 76,369, and the number evacuated for medical reasons at 48,673.[2] The number of Viet Minh soldiers and Indochinese civilians who lost their lives will never be known, but may have been between 450,000 and 1 million.[3]

The traditional elements of victory in war have always included good leadership, good intelligence, good planning, and the valor, endurance, and initiative of the individual soldier, but the outcomes of modern wars have been determined increasingly by the relative effectiveness of the logistical organization of the opposing sides. The stunning victory of the Viet Minh over the French colonial regime in Indochina exhibited all of the classic elements in full measure, but the key to Viet Minh victory was the superior performance of their logistical system, which, although greatly inferior to that of the French in size and technological sophistication, nevertheless proved altogether more flexible and thus more effective. The Viet Minh won the war of logistics fair and square, taking all the logistical campaigns of the war on points. The Viet Minh, not the French, developed effective combat forces and an efficient logistical system suited to the physical and operational environment of Indochina. The Viet Minh, not the French, emerged from the campaign for the base areas between 1950 and 1952 with their headquarters and depots intact and their rear areas relatively free of enemy infiltration and harassment. The Viet Minh, not the French, won the campaign for control of the lines of communication in 1953 and 1954. And the Viet Minh, not the French, triumphed in the war's ultimate battle of logistics around Dien Bien Phu between November 1953 and May 1954.

The logistical systems developed by both the French and the Viet Minh during the ten years of the First Indochina War were influenced by many common constraints and challenges. The physical realities of the Indochina theater of operations, particularly the great distances, the varied and difficult terrain, the harsh climate, and the limited transportation infrastructure, hampered the logistical performance of both the French Union forces and the Viet Minh. The impact on the French was perhaps more severe in that the French Union forces were highly mechanized and thus more sensitive to the lack of roads and other infrastructure and to local conditions of visibility and trafficability. Moreover, the French had to cover all of Indochina while the main focus of Viet Minh activity was in Tonkin.

Similarly, the efficiency and effectiveness of both logistical systems were adversely affected by limited resources. The French as well as the Viet Minh experienced chronic shortages of key items of materiel and of trained logistical personnel. Such shortages were perhaps less critical for the leaner and less technology-dependent Viet Minh forces. For both the French and the Viet Minh the solution to inadequate material resources was almost total dependence on outside suppliers for the arms, ammunition, vehicles, and other equipment that they needed to pursue the war. The French Union forces, as a matter of policy as well as a matter of necessity, relied on military supplies imported from metropolitan France, the countries of the French Union, and above all from the United States. For their part, the Viet Minh would not have been able to pursue the war at the level they did without purchases made in nearby countries and the large-scale logistical support provided by Communist China after 1949.

Against the background of challenges shared with the Viet Minh, the French Union forces in Indochina coped with a number of unique logistical problems. Chief among these were the necessity of converting the static territorial support system of pre–World War II colonial Indochina to a unit-oriented support system capable of supporting mobile operations, the magnitude and diversity of the forces supported, and the restrictions on mechanized ground transport imposed by both the environment and enemy action. French Union logisticians met the first challenge successfully, albeit with some difficulty. The second was more complex. The force structure of French Union forces in Indochina grew ten-fold over the course of the war without a corresponding increase in the proportion of logistical support personnel, and the support of the newly formed Vietnamese, Cambodian, and Laotian national armies after 1950 imposed additional burdens on the already overloaded French logistical services. The ethnic and technological diversity of the French Union forces only added to the difficulties of determining logistical requirements and planning and executing operations. On the whole, the French were reasonably successful in coping with the challenges of size and diversity, but the chronic shortages of logistical support forces served to reduce the overall efficiency and effectiveness of the support provided.

The third challenge was the most difficult to overcome. The highly mechanized French Union forces were generally restricted to the limited roads and waterways of Indochina and were thus vulnerable to both the effects of the weather and enemy action. As a result of insufficient manpower, the French were unable to fully protect their multiple lines of ground and water communication, and as a result they often were subject to Viet Minh sabotage and ambush. To solve the problem of inadequate and insecure ground transport, the French turned to air transport and aerial resupply, but this most striking French logistical advantage was largely negated by generally poor flying conditions in the main area of operations in Tonkin, limited numbers of airfields, aircraft, and aircrews, a scarcity of parachutes and other airdrop materials, technical limitations on aerial resupply practices, and a constantly improving Viet Minh antiaircraft capability. In the end, the French reliance on air transport and aerial resupply contributed to their failure in the decisive battle of the war at Dien Bien Phu.

The Viet Minh had their own set of unique logistical problems. The principal challenges faced by the Viet Minh were an initial lack of logistical expertise and experience in supporting large forces in extended campaigns, the vulnerability of their logistical facilities and lines of communication to French airpower, and the necessity of substituting manpower for technology. However, the Viet Minh had the unusual advantage of building a logistical system from scratch and focusing its development on the immediate requirements of the physical and military situation.

Although some time was required for them to gain the experience necessary to provide adequate logistical support for large forces engaged in complex, extended operations far from their fixed bases, the Viet Minh eventually overcame the problem with the adoption of Soviet and Chinese Communist support doctrines and the training of logistical staff officers and specialists in Communist China. Although they successfully met the challenge of an initial lack of logistical staff experience, they were less successful in developing the technical expertise required to support an army that grew and became more technologically sophisticated as the war went on. Thus, they remained largely dependent on the Chinese for technical expertise.

Possessing no air forces of their own, the Viet Minh had to overcome total French air superiority through flexibility, innovation, and sheer determination. Rear area logistical facilities were well-dispersed and well-camouflaged, and strict camouflage and march discipline were enforced on the lines of communication. As the war went on, the Viet Minh, with substantial Chinese assistance, developed a formidable antiaircraft artillery capability, as was conclusively demonstrated around Dien Bien Phu in 1954. In large part, the success achieved by the Viet Minh in avoiding the worst effects of French air superiority was due to their relatively low logistical requirements—only about one-third those of the French on a kilograms-per-man-per-day basis—and their heavy reliance on porters for the movement of food, ammunition, and other supplies. Viet Minh combat units operated effectively on comparatively small supply tonnages, and even large numbers of porters could be dispersed quickly under cover and concealment and were capable of operating off the established roads and trails if necessary.

Indeed, the most striking characteristic of the Viet Minh logistical system was the substitution of manpower for mechanization. Thousands of Viet Minh supporters labored in primitive cave factories to produce crude but usable arms and ammunition. Lines of communication were constructed and maintained using only hand tools and thousands of coolies. And, although Viet Minh motor transport capacity grew steadily throughout the war, the Viet Minh remained dependent on the extensive use of porters and animal transport. Albeit with great difficulty, the Viet Minh organized almost endless streams of porters to support their operations, and those porters had few technical limitations, being able to perform in all kinds of terrain and weather, day and night, while remaining relatively invulnerable to French interdiction. Often difficult to recruit and retain, porters nevertheless proved particularly well-suited to the climate and terrain of the Indochina theater of operations and played a major role in the Viet Minh victory.

For both the French and the Viet Minh, logistical considerations dominated the development of strategy and the operational conduct of the war in Indochina between 1945 and 1954. Logistical factors determined in large measure the objectives, timing, planned duration, and general nature of the operations conducted by both sides in the First Indochina War. The operational strategies of both sides were focused largely on destroying the enemy's forces and will to resist by the destruction of his logistical support facilities and the interdiction of his lines of communication. Thus, the infiltration and sabotage of the rear areas under nominal French control and the ambush of French road and river convoys were prominent parts of the Viet Minh strategy. Similarly, French strategy sought to eliminate the Viet Minh as a political and military force by denying them access to the rice production of the Mekong and Tonkin deltas, destroying their military base areas, depots, and workshops, and interdicting their lines of communication, particularly the routes leading from China to their base areas in northern Tonkin.

The effect of the seasonal monsoons on trafficability was a major factor in determining the limits of the active campaigning season and the types of operations that could be carried out at different times of the year. Both the French and the Viet Minh required lengthy periods to assemble supplies and organize transport prior to the beginning of an offensive operation, and to some degree both sides timed their offensive campaigns to coincide with the expected arrival of equipment and supplies provided by their outside supporters. In general, offensive operations were not initiated until these careful preparations were completed, and their duration was often determined by the ability to sustain the operation logistically with men and supplies. Until late 1953, otherwise successful Viet Minh offensive operations were often prematurely terminated by the exhaustion of available supplies or the evaporation of the manpower on which they relied for transportation support. The French, too, frequently found themselves overextended logistically and thus required to terminate operations that offered every promise of success because they had exhausted critical supplies or because the available air, water, or ground transport was more urgently required elsewhere. But while the French continued to overcommit themselves until the very end, the Viet Minh finally achieved in the last year of the war an effective balance between their logistical capabilities and their operational requirements.

Logistical factors also determined to an important degree the nature and outcome of every major campaign and engagement of the First Indochina War, notably the struggle for the base areas in 1950–1952, the campaign for the control of the lines of communication in 1953–1954, and the decisive battle for Dien Bien Phu in 1954. The dominant factor in this respect was without doubt the availability and the efficiency of the means of transporting men and materiel to the area of operations. The Viet Minh had the advantage of largely secure base areas, including after 1949 all of southern China, which was off limits to French counteraction. Although subject to periodic raids by the French Union forces, the Viet Minh base areas, located in remote and difficult terrain and heavily defended but often still capable of great mobility, were largely invulnerable. Moreover, the dispersion of their logistical facilities and their high degree of mobility allowed the Viet Minh to avoid crushing defensive battles for their protection. Instead, the raw materials, tools, and finished supplies as well as the workers and guards could be quickly removed from the path of advancing French raiders. On the other hand, the French were obliged to maintain a static defense of their many large fixed bases scattered throughout Indochina. Despite the dedication of a high proportion of their scarce manpower to that task, the French facilities remained all too vulnerable to Viet Minh infiltration, sabotage, and direct attack. Similarly, the campaign for control of the lines of communication clearly demonstrated the principle that strategic and tactical mobility are key factors in military operations. At the same time, the Viet Minh demonstrated that such mobility is a function of will and adaptation to the physical environment rather than strictly a function of mechanization. Indeed, they established the axiom that the more sophisticated and mechanized the transportation component of a logistical system is, the more vulnerable it may be to internal failures and interdiction by the enemy.

The critical error of the French, perhaps the single error that led to their defeat in Indochina, was their consistent underestimation of Viet Minh logistical capabilities. Far too often the French judged the Viet Minh by their own standards, standards derived from their experience in conflicts between evenly matched mechanized armies operating on European battlefields. By obstinately refusing to recognize the skill and capability of their enemy, the French delayed until it was too late the correction of faults in their own logistical support system, such as poor maintenance practices and poor supply discipline. The French disdain for the Viet Minh, fed by racial stereotypes and cultural hubris, is all the more striking in that it was contradicted by nearly a century of direct experience of Vietnamese military prowess, a fact that has been commented upon eloquently by one of the foremost experts on the war in Indochina, Bernard B. Fall, who wrote:

> The Vietnamese People's Army . . . which faced the French Expeditionary Corps in Indochina, was perhaps the least known and worst misunderstood adversary that France had faced in her history up to that time. Not that the elements of information were lacking—they had lived with the Vietnamese for eighty years; they had known them to be rather good soldiers whose ancestors had stopped the invasion of southeast Asia by the Mongols; they knew that they had a lively spirit and were good with their hands. They had furnished to France regiments of riflemen, hordes of "military workers," engineers . . . , and good aviators. . . . They knew that despite their frail appearance they were astonishingly robust, capable of covering enormous distances in a murderous climate balancing on their shoulders a load nearly equal to their own weight, all the while nourished by a ball of rice seasoned with a little fish sauce.[4]

The Viet Minh refused to recognize the theoretical limitations on their logistical capabilities and frequently surprised the French by their rapidity of movement, their ability to concentrate men and supplies undetected, and their logistical stamina. Thus, the First Indochina War demonstrated above all that an army with a large and sophisticated logistical system will not always triumph over an army with a smaller and less complex logistical system. The Viet Minh proved decisively that the effective application of combat power is neither precluded by simplicity of force structure nor a necessary result of technological sophistication. Indeed, they demonstrated clearly that even in the mid-twentieth century, a lack of superiority in materiel could still be overcome by the intelligent application of sheer manpower and a determined will.

By 1954, the Viet Minh, who began with fewer initial resources and a rather primitive logistical structure, had developed a relatively lean and manpower-intensive logistical system well-adapted to its physical and military environment and thus of substantial efficiency and effectiveness. On the other hand, the French, hampered by rigidity, inattention, and lack of will, failed to turn their initial advantage in modern equipment and advanced logistical techniques into a system fully attuned to the physical, strategic, and tactical environment in which they were required to operate. Thus, the outcome of the First Indochina War, seen from a logistical perspective, offers four general lessons for the future. First, in certain situations, particularly in a theater characterized by difficult terrain, a harsh climate, and undeveloped transportation facilities, the technological sophistication of a logistical system may be a negative rather than a positive factor. Second, it is possible for an army to conduct extended combat operations of sizable forces far from their bases of supply supported primarily by human labor rather than mechanized equipment. Third, air interdiction has only limited effectiveness when employed against an enemy with a relatively lean and flexible logistical system, particularly when that enemy is imbued with determination and resourcefulness. Last, human qualities, such as commitment, determination, resourcefulness, and flexibility, rather than material factors, still determined the outcome of battles and wars in the twentieth century—just as they always had in the past.

The architect of Viet Minh victory in the First Indochina War should be granted the last word on the ten years of terrible struggle. General Vo Nguyen Giap's words, written about the Dien Bien Phu campaign, summarize the principal reason for the Viet Minh triumph: "The supply of food and munitions was a factor as important as the problem of tactics; logistics constantly posed problems as urgent as those posed by the armed struggle. These were precisely the difficulties that the enemy thought insuperable for us. The imperialists and traitors could never appreciate the strength of a nation, of a people. This strength is immense. It can overcome any difficulty, defeat any enemy."[5]

Notes

Book epigraph: Quoted in Jules Roy, *The Battle of Dien Bien Phu* (New York: Harper and Row, 1965), 220.

1. A War of Logistics

1. Julian Thompson, *The Lifeblood of War: Logistics in Armed Conflict* (London: Brassey's, 1991), 135–36.

2. Useful contemporary descriptions of the geography and climate of Indochina include: The Joint Intelligence Study Publishing Board, *Joint Army-Navy Intelligence Study of Indochina (JANIS 70)*, 2 vols. (Washington, D.C.: JISPB, October 1945); Headquarters, Department of the Army, Assistant Chief of Staff, G-2, *Terrain Estimate of Indo-China*, IRP No. 6006 (Washington, D.C.: HQDA, OACS G-2, December 22, 1950); and Headquarters, U.S. Army Forces, Far East (Advance), Office of the Assistant Chief of Staff, G-2, Intelligence Division, Strategic Branch/Geographic Branch, *Special Report No. 127: Some Geographical Aspects of Indochina* (Tokyo: HQ, USAFFE, OACS G-2, March 12, 1953). Of particular interest is Memorandum, Secretary of the Army (Robert T. Stevens) to Secretary of Defense (Charles E. Wilson), Washington, May 19, 1954, subject: Indo-China, in *The Pentagon Papers: The Defense Department History of United States Decisionmaking in Vietnam*, vol. 1, ed. Mike Gravel (Boston: Beacon, 1971), document 48, 508–9, in which Secretary Stevens enumerates the many environmental factors making a U.S. military intervention in Indochina very difficult from a logistical point of view.

3. Commandement en Chef des Forces Terrestres Navales et Aériennes en Indochine, État-Major Interarmées et des Forces Terrestres, Bureau "Instruction," *Notes sur le combat en Indochine* [Combat Notes from the War in Indochina] (DA-G2-TR/G-4086, ID No. 1265063; Washington, D.C.: HQDA, OACS G-2, March 30, 1954), 5.

4. Lucien Bodard, *The Quicksand War: Prelude to Vietnam* (Boston: Little, Brown, 1967), 21.

5. Phillip B. Davidson, *Vietnam at War: The History, 1946–1975* (Novato, Calif.: Presidio, 1988), 38.

6. Thompson, *Lifeblood of War*, 140.

7. Harvey H. Smith and the other authors of the *Area Handbook for North Vietnam* (Department of the Army Pamphlet No. 550-57 [Washington, D.C.: U.S. Government Printing Office, 1968], 22) wrote that reptiles were seldom seen and that deaths from snakebite were rare. Soldiers who have humped the jungles and paddies of Indochina are somewhat less sanguine about the dangers of the native reptile population. The authors of *JANIS 70*, vol. 1, chapter 11 ("Health and Sanitation"), were perhaps more correct in their assessment that thirty-eight species of poisonous snakes plus twenty-three species of poisonous sea snakes were to be found in Indochina and its coastal waters and that "the state of Tonkin is considered one of the most snake-infested areas of the world" (23).

8. Fredrik Logevall, *Embers of War: The Fall of an Empire and the Making of America's Vietnam* (New York: Random House, 2012), 325.

9. Ibid., 172–75; Martin Windrow, *The Last Valley: Dien Bien Phu and the French Defeat in Vietnam* (New York: Da Capo, 2004), 97.

10. In general, the available airfields in Indochina were suitable only for light and medium transports and propeller-driven fighters and light bombers. See Headquarters, U.S. Military Assistance Advisory Group, Indo-China, *Indo-China Country Statement for Presentation of the 1955 MDA Program* (Saigon: HQ MAAG-Indo-China, January 26, 1954), 17.

11. "Airborne Operations in Indochina," *Intelligence Review* 197 (October 1952): 9.

12. Traditionally, the war in Indochina has been divided into three main periods, corresponding generally to those described by the Viet Minh commander-in-chief, General Vo Nguyen Giap, in his various writings. See, for example, *Inside the Viet Minh* (Washington, D.C.: Marine Corps Association, 1962); *La Guerre de libération et l'armée populaire* [The War of Liberation and the Popular Army] (Washington, D.C.: HQDA, OACS G-2, 1955); and *People's War, People's Army: The Viet Cong Insurrection Manual for Underdeveloped Countries* (New York: Praeger, 1962). General Giap divided the war into a period of purely guerrilla warfare from 1945 to the beginning of French operations against the Viet Minh bases in the Viet Bac in 1947; a transitional period from late 1947 into 1950 during which the Viet Minh gradually advanced from guerrilla warfare toward what he called the "general counteroffensive"; and the "general counteroffensive" itself, a period of large-scale conventional warfare extending from 1950 to the final victory of the Viet Minh in 1954.

13. Bernard B. Fall, *Le Viet-Minh: La République Démocratique du Viet-Nam, 1945–1960* (Paris: Librairie Armand Colin, 1960), 221.

14. Ronald H. Spector, *Advice and Support: The Early Years, 1941–1960* (Washington, D.C.: Center of Military History, U.S. Army, 1983), 169.

15. Jean Boucher de Crèvecoeur, "Le Problème Militaire Français en Indochine," mimeographed notes on a lecture at the École Superièure de Guerre, Paris, July 16, 1953, 28.

16. Bernard B. Fall, *Street without Joy: Insurgency in Indochina, 1946–63*, 3rd rev. ed. (Harrisburg, Pa.: Stackpole, 1963), 363.

2. French Union Combat Forces

1. Peter Drake Jackson, *French Ground Force Organizational Development for Counterrevolutionary Warfare between 1945 and 1962* (Master of Military Art and Science thesis, Fort Leavenworth, Kans., U.S. Army Command and General Staff College, 2005), 26–27. The two parachute companies were organized along American lines, the two commando units along British commando lines, and the *Commando Ponchardier* similarly to British Special Air Service units of the time.

2. Ibid., 27.

3. Gilbert Bodinier, ed., *La Guerre d'Indochine, 1945–1954: Texte et Documents,* vol. 1, *Le retour de la France en Indochine, 1945–1946* (Château de Vincennes: SHAT, 1987), 41–42; Gilbert Bodinier, ed., *La Guerre d'Indochine, 1945–1954: Texte et Documents,* vol. 2, *Indochine, 1947—Règlement politique ou solution militaire?* (Vincennes: SHAT, 1989), 21.

4. Headquarters, U.S. Military Assistance Advisory Group, Indochina, *Indo-China Country Statement for Presentation of the 1955 MDA Program* (Saigon: HQ MAAG-Indo-China, January 26, 1954), 2.

5. Jean Claude Devos and Jean Nicot Philippe Schillinger, *Inventaire des Archives de l'Indochine: Sous-serie 10H (1867–1956)*, 2 vols. (Château de Vincennes: SHAT, 1990), vol. 1, preface. Devos and Schillinger state that from October 4, 1948, both the office of high commissioner and that of the *commandant supérieur/commandant en chef* were held simultaneously by a military officer, but the evidence indicates that Lieutenant General de Lattre was the only person to serve formally in both positions simultaneously. See, for example, Henri Navarre, *Le Temps des Vérités* (Paris: Plon, 1957), 251.

6. Devos and Jean Nicot Philippe Schillinger, *Inventaire des Archives de l'Indochine*, vol. 1, preface. Despite its name, the joint General Staff was composed primarily of army officers. See Michel Dupouy, "Les rapports entre l'armée de l'Air et l'armée de Terre en Indochine: 1946–1954," *Revue Historique des Armées* 177 (December 1989): 110.

7. Although the actual title changed several times during the course of the war, the joint General Staff is referred to as the EMIFT throughout this work.

8. Although they received some logistical support from the ground forces (for example, petroleum and rations), the French naval and air forces in Indochina had essentially separate logistical systems. This study focuses on the logistical organization of French ground forces, and the intricacies of the logistical support of the French Navy and Air Force in Indochina are not discussed in detail.

9. Debriefing of Major General Thomas J. H. Trapnell (former chief, MAAG-Indochina), May 3, 1954, document 41, in *The Pentagon Papers: The Defense Department History of United States Decisionmaking in Vietnam*, vol. 1, ed. Mike Gravel (Boston: Beacon, 1971), 488.

10. Ibid., 1:489.

11. Jackson, *French Ground Force Organizational Development*, 29. The CEFEO continued to exist as the designation for the overall French ground forces in Indochina until it was officially disbanded in 1956.

12. Ibid., 31.

13. Merritt B. Booth (Mutual Defense Assistance Office, U.S. Department of State), Memorandum for Mr. Bell, Washington, April 12, 1950, subject: Military Information re Indochina, Thailand and Indonesia, 1, in folder "SE Asia 032. to 091.3, 1949–1950," box 61 ("SE Asia to Syria"), Project Decimal File, 1950–1952, Office of Military Assistance, Office of the Assistant Secretary of Defense (International Security Affairs), Record Group 330 (Records of the Office of the Secretary of Defense), National Archives II, College Park, Maryland.

14. Ibid.

15. The old Catalinas were replaced by PB4Y-2 Privateers (long-range naval surveillance/antisubmarine aircraft) in 1951–1952, and by 1954 there were two squadrons of Privateers, each with seven aircraft. See Michèle Battesti, "La Marine et la guerre d'Indochine," *Revue Historique des Armées* 177 (December 1989): 87.

16. National Intelligence Estimate 91 ("Probable Developments in Indochina through Mid-1954"), June 4, 1953 [NIE 91], document 15, annex D, in Gravel, ed., *The Pentagon Papers*, 1:404.

17. Charles W. Koburger Jr., *The French Navy in Indochina: Riverine and Coastal Forces, 1945–54* (New York: Praeger, 1991), appendix C and passim. The French carrier forces were

under the administrative command of the navy, but the embarked aircraft operated under the direction of the French Air Force area tactical commands. See Trapnell debriefing, May 3, 1954, document 41, in Gravel, ed., *The Pentagon Papers,* 1:494.

18. Lieutenant General John W. O'Daniel, USA (Chief, U.S. Joint Military Mission to Indochina), *Report of U. S. Special Mission to Indochina (23 January–5 February 1954)— Situation in French Indochina and FUF Materiel Requirements, February 1954,* Pearl Harbor, Hawaii, February 5, 1954, cover letter, 3, in box 10 ("092 Asia [6-25-48] [2] Section 22"), Geographical File, 1954–1956, RG 218 (Records of the U.S. Joint Chiefs of Staff), National Archives II, College Park, Maryland. O'Daniel noted dryly that Admiral Philippe Auboyneau, the commander of French naval forces in the Far East, chose to ignore requests from officers in Tonkin for additional personnel and equipment.

19. Headquarters, Department of the Army, Assistant Chief of Staff, G-2, *Implications and Effect upon Western Security of Voluntary French Withdrawal from Indochina during 1952* (Washington, D.C.: HQDA, OACS G-2, [1952]), appendix 2, tab A, 2.

20. Battesti, "La Marine et la guerre d'Indochine," 87–88.

21. Michel Dupouy, "Les rapports entre l'armée de l'Air et l'armée de Terre en Indochine: 1946–1954," *Revue Historique des Armées* 177 (December 1989): 112.

22. Ibid., 110–11.

23. Patrick Facon, "L'Armée de l'Air et la guerre d'Indochine (1945–1954)," *Revue Historique des Armées* 177 (December 1989): 101.

24. Ibid., 107 and passim.

25. Ibid., 95–99 passim.

26. Booth, Memorandum for Mr. Bell, 4–5.

27. Facon, "L'Armée de l'Air et la guerre d'Indochine," 104–5.

28. Lieutenant General John W. O'Daniel, USA (Chief, U.S. Joint Military Mission to Indochina), *Progress Report on Military Situation in Indochina as of 19 November 1953,* Pearl Harbor, Hawaii, November 19, 1953, annex E, 59, in box 10 ("092 Asia [6-25-48] [2] Section 22"), Geographical File, 1954–1956, RG 218. A (South) Vietnamese national air force was created on June 25, 1951, and gradually augmented the French Air Force in Indochina.

29. Trapnell debriefing, May 3, 1954, document 41, in Gravel, ed., *The Pentagon Papers,* 1:494. For the French air order of battle as of June 1953, see NIE 91, June 4, 1953, document 15, annex C, in Gravel, ed., *The Pentagon Papers,* 1:402–3.

30. Facon, "L'Armée de l'Air et la guerre d'Indochine," 107.

31. HQ MAAG-Indochina, *Indo-China Country Statement for Presentation of the 1955 MDA Program,* 6. The remaining 30 percent was composed of indigenous personnel enlisted as regulars in the French forces.

32. HQDA, OACS G-2, *Implications and Effect,* tab a, page 5, and tab a, appendix 2, page 1. See table 2.3. Martin Windrow gives slightly different figures in *The Last Valley: Dien Bien Phu and the French Defeat in Vietnam* (New York: Da Capo, 2004), 170.

33. Bernard B. Fall, *The Two Viet-Nams: A Political and Military Analysis,* 2nd rev. ed. (New York: Praeger, 1967), 109. Draftees could volunteer for service in Indochina. By May 1954, the normal tour of duty in Indochina was twenty-seven months, and French personnel received substantial pay increases for Indochina service. See Trapnell debriefing, May 3, 1954, document 41, in Gravel, ed., *The Pentagon Papers,* 1:491.

34. Major General Graves B. Erskine, USMC (Chief, Military Group, U.S. Joint Mutual Defense Assistance Program Survey Mission to Southeast Asia), *Summary Report No. 1—Situation in Indochina, August 1950,* Saigon, August 5, 1950, 4, in folder "SE Asia, 319.1–452, 1949–1950," box 61 ("Africa to Austria"), Project Decimal File, 1950–1952, Office of Military Assistance, Office of the Assistant Secretary of Defense (International Security Affairs), RG 330.

35. Ibid., 5–7.

36. For women in the French forces in Indochina, see, *inter alia,* Windrow, *The Last Valley,* 685–86, and the exposition brochure prepared by Michèle Bonnier, Soraya Djebbour, and Gilles Bonnier (*La guerre d'Indochine, 1946–1954* [Paris: Impression Copytop, May 2009], 16).

37. Trapnell debriefing, May 3, 1954, document 41, in Gravel, ed., *The Pentagon Papers,* 1:492.

38. Headquarters, Department of the Army, Office of the Assistant Chief of Staff for Intelligence, *Resistance and Regional Factors: Indochina* (Washington, D.C.: HQDA, OACSI, April 1959), 472. The Cambodian Surface Defense Force, a militia, was created in 1952.

39. Ibid., 359.

40. Ronald H. Spector, *Advice and Support: The Early Years, 1941–1960* (Washington, D.C.: Center of Military History, U.S. Army, 1983), 153.

41. Headquarters, Department of the Army, General Staff, Office of the Assistant Chief of Staff, G-2, *Data for Mutual Defense Assistance Program—1 May 1951* (Washington, D.C.: HQDA, OACS G-2, June 11, 1951), under "France—Ground Forces—1 May 1951." For an excellent summary of the evolution of the organization of French ground forces in Indochina from 1945 to 1954, see Jackson, *French Ground Force Organizational Development,* chapters 2 and 3 and passim.

42. O'Daniel, *Progress Report . . . 19 November 1953,* annex B, appendix 2 (Development of a Strong Striking Mobile Force in the Tonkin Delta), 23; Headquarters, Department of the Army, Office of the Assistant Chief of Staff, G-2, *Probable Viet Minh and/or Chinese Communist Courses of Action in Indo-China* (Washington, D.C.: HQDA, OACS G-2, [1952]), tab A, 4.

43. Bodinier, ed., *La Guerre d'Indochine,* 2:31.

44. Some 52.3 percent of the French forces in Indochina consisted of infantry troops, versus about 12 percent of the U.S. Army in World War II. See Jackson, *French Ground Force Organizational Development,* 49–50.

45. Jackson, *French Ground Force Organizational Development,* 51.

46. Bodinier, ed., *La Guerre d'Indochine,* 2:31; Jackson, *French Ground Force Organizational Development,* 51–52; Commander in Chief, French Forces in the Far East, *A Translation from the French: Lessons of the War in Indochina,* vol. 2 (Santa Monica, Calif.: RAND Corporation, May 1967), 221–23 (hereafter cited as *Lessons Learned in the Indochina War*). The static defense battalions retained the older infantry battalion organization.

47. *Lessons Learned in the Indochina War,* 2:222.

48. Jackson, *French Ground Force Organizational Development,* 52.

49. *Lessons Learned in the Indochina War,* 2:198.

50. Ibid., 2:222, 288.

51. Douglas Pike, *Viet Cong: The Organization and Techniques of the National Liberation Front of South Vietnam* (Cambridge, Mass.: M.I.T. Press, 1966), 49.

52. *Lessons Learned in the Indochina War,* 2:68.

53. Jackson, *French Ground Force Organizational Development,* 39.

54. O'Daniel, *Progress Report . . . 19 November 1953,* annex B, 23.

55. Jackson, *French Ground Force Organizational Development,* 47.

56. *Lessons Learned in the Indochina War,* 2:193. As Jackson points out, the CEFEO, which arrived in Indochina in late 1945, was a mobile organization but soon transitioned to a territorial force, leaving only a few parachute battalions, small riverine forces, and cavalry units to take on the highly mobile Viet Minh guerrillas. The appearance of Viet Minh division-size units in the early 1950s required more and heavier mobile French Union forces, but the formation of such units came too late. (*French Ground Force Organizational Development,* 57.)

57. *Lessons Learned in the Indochina War,* 2:151.

58. Ibid., 2:218.

59. Ibid.

60. Based on experience gained in North Africa, the French began to organize and employ a few mobile groups in Indochina in the late 1940s. See Jackson, *French Ground Force Organizational Development,* 59.

61. Commandement en Chef des Forces Terrestres Navales et Aériennes en Indochine, État-Major Interarmées et des Forces Terrestres, Bureau "Instruction," *Notes sur le combat en Indochine* [Combat Notes from the War in Indochina] (Washington, D.C.: HQDA, OACS G-2, March 30, 1954), 34; *Lessons Learned in the Indochina War,* 2:208.

62. *Lessons Learned in the Indochina War,* 2:210.

63. Ibid., 2:213–14.

64. Ibid., 2:212.

65. Commander in Chief, French Forces in the Far East, *Lessons from the Indo-China War,* vol. 3 ([Washington, D.C.]: DARPA, 1955), 77.

66. *Lessons Learned in the Indochina War,* 2:200.

67. Bernard B. Fall, *Street without Joy: Insurgency in Indochina, 1946–63,* 3rd rev. ed. (Harrisburg, Pa.: Stackpole, 1963), 12.

68. *Lessons Learned in the Indochina War,* 2:173–74.

69. For the *Dinassaut,* see *Lessons Learned in the Indochina War,* 2:348–54. By late 1946, the French riverine forces in Indochina consisted of some 110 landing craft and fourteen small amphibious ships. In all, seven *Dinassauts* were formed in the late 1940s. See Jackson, *French Ground Force Organizational Development,* 33, 57–58.

70. *Lessons Learned in the Indochina War,* 2:174–75.

71. Fall, *Street without Joy,* 41n. *Dinassaut* 3 was one of the larger formations and even had its own reconnaissance aircraft and an armor element transported aboard an LCT.

72. Victor J. Croizat, "Battle Honors of the Marine Amphibian: X. The French Indochina War (1946–1954)," *Marine Corps Gazette* (January 2000), 88.

73. Ibid., 88–89. The amphibious groups had substantial firepower: fifteen 75 mm howitzers mounted in the LVT(A)-4s plus five 57 mm recoilless guns and three 60 mm mortars per squadron. Each group carried three days' worth of supplies.

74. *Lessons Learned in the Indochina War,* 3:65.

75. The 5th Colonial Infantry Regiment, which arrived in Indochina in October 1945 as the vanguard of the CEFEO, included a small contingent of paratroops, and a demi-brigade of Special Air Service paratroops arrived in early 1946. These forces were used for company-size raids or to reinforce beleaguered outposts. See Jackson, *French Ground Force Organizational Development,* 30, 33–34.

76. *Lessons Learned in the Indochina War,* 2:244–45. The airborne surgical team, for example, consisted of a surgeon, three nurses, and four stretcher-bearers and had about thirty-three hundred pounds of equipment. See "Airborne Operations in Indochina," *Intelligence Review,* no. 197 (October 1952): 11.

77. *Lessons Learned in the Indochina War,* 2:253; Jackson, *French Ground Force Organizational Development,* 52. Each of the parachute battalions had a headquarters company much like that of the Far East–type infantry battalions and nine subunits called "commandos" (six French personnel and three indigenous personnel) grouped into three French companies and one indigenous company). Each "commando" had a small platoon headquarters and three fifteen-man "sticks." The "commandos" were authorized extra submachine guns to increase their firepower.

78. *Lessons Learned in the Indochina War,* 2:146.

79. Ibid., 2:252.

80. For example, French parachute units usually entered combat with only a limited supply of ammunition and were capable of a static defense only if reinforced with additional heavy weapons and ammunition. See Colonel Chavette, *Considérations sur les opérations aeroportées du theâtre d'opérations Indochinois* [Considerations on Airborne Operations in the Indochinese Theater of Operation] (Washington, D.C.: HQDA, OACS G-2, 1956), 8.

81. Jackson, *French Ground Force Organizational Development,* 60.

82. O'Daniel, *Progress Report . . . 19 November 1953,* annex B, appendix 5 (Progress in Guerrilla Warfare), page 36.

83. *Lessons Learned in the Indochina War,* 2:238.

84. Ibid., 2:253n1.

85. Commandement en Chef des Forces Terrestres Navales et Aériennes en Indochine, État-Major Interarmées et des Forces Terrestres, Bureau "Instruction," *Directive d'Application des Mésures Concernant l'Organisation, l'Instruction et l'Emploi des Commandos* (No. 887/EMIFT/B. INS., Saigon, March 11, 1954), 1.

86. Ibid., 6.

87. *Lessons Learned in the Indochina War,* 2:238–39.

88. O'Daniel, *Progress Report . . . 19 November 1953,* annex B, appendix 5, page 36.

89. *Lessons Learned in the Indochina War,* 2:159.

90. See Jackson, *French Ground Force Organizational Development,* 67.

3. Viet Minh Combat Forces

1. Headquarters, Department of the Army, Office of the Assistant Chief of Staff, G-2, *Order of Battle: Viet Minh Army* (Washington, D.C.: HQDA, OACS G-2, October 10, 1954), 3.

2. By 1945, the Viet Minh was already in existence. The first guerrilla forces had been created in September 1943, and the first elements of the regular Viet Minh army were

established on December 22, 1944. See Mike Gravel, ed., *The Pentagon Papers: The Defense Department History of United States Decisionmaking in Vietnam,* vol. 1 (Boston: Beacon, 1971), 45.

3. Giap was not promoted officially to four-star general until May 28, 1948.

4. Gilbert Bodinier, ed., *La Guerre d'Indochine, 1945–1954: Texte et Documents,* vol. 2, *Indochine, 1947—Règlement politique ou solution militaire?* (Vincennes: SHAT, 1989), 113.

5. George K. Tanham, *Communist Revolutionary Warfare: From the Vietminh to the Viet Cong,* rev. ed. (New York: Praeger, 1967), 38.

6. Ibid.; Phillip B. Davidson, *Vietnam at War: The History, 1946–1975* (Novato, Calif.: Presidio, 1988), 58.

7. Tanham, *Communist Revolutionary Warfare,* 39–41.

8. Qiang Zhai, *China and the Vietnam Wars, 1950–1975* (Chapel Hill: Univ. of North Carolina Press, 2000), 34.

9. Tanham, *Communist Revolutionary Warfare,* 40–41.

10. Ibid., 46–47; Bodinier, ed., *La Guerre d'Indochine,* 2:113; U.S. Far East Command, General Headquarters, Military Intelligence Section, Allied Translator and Interpreter Service, *Information on Viet Minh Forces, Indo-China* (Tokyo: GHQ, USFEC, MI Section, ATIS, August 11, 1951), 36.

11. Bernard B. Fall, *Le Viet-Minh: La République Démocratique du Viet-Nam, 1945–1960* (Paris: Librairie Armand Colin, 1960), 62; Tanham, *Communist Revolutionary Warfare,* 43–45.

12. Lieutenant Colonel Serieye, *Le Viêt-Minh: les origines et l'évolution des Forces Armées du Viêt-Minh* [The Viet Minh: The Origins and Evolution of the Viet Minh Armed Forces] (Washington, D.C.: HQDA, OACS G-2, February 1951), 3–4; Gilbert Bodinier, ed., *La Guerre d'Indochine, 1945–1954: Texte et Documents,* vol. 1, *Le retour de la France en Indochine, 1945–1946* (Château de Vincennes: SHAT, 1987), 94.

13. Fall, *Le Viet-Minh,* 62. "Interzone" is an abbreviation of "integrated zone," a term derived from the fact that their political and military structures were integrated.

14. Douglas Pike, *Viet Cong: The Organization and Techniques of the National Liberation Front of South Vietnam* (Cambridge, Mass.: M.I.T. Press, 1966), 46–47.

15. *Order of Battle: Viet Minh Army,* 2.

16. *Information on Viet Minh Forces, Indo-China,* 36.

17. Tanham, *Communist Revolutionary Warfare,* 44.

18. Ibid., 40.

19. *Order of Battle: Viet Minh Army,* 2.

20. The first engagements of the newly formed Armed Propaganda Team were attacks on two French mud forts at Phai Khat and Na Ngan on December 24–25, 1944, in which two French lieutenants were killed and a total of forty-six Vietnamese troops were captured with no Viet Minh casualties. For a very brief sketch of the early history of the Viet Minh, see Nowfel Leulliot and Danny O'Hara, eds., "Early Days: The Development of the Viet Minh Military Machine," http://indochine54.free.fr/vm/early.html (accessed December 2, 2012). See also: Fredrik Logevall, *Embers of War: The Fall of an Empire and the Making of America's Vietnam* (New York: Random House, 2012), 127, 149; Martin Windrow, *The Last Valley: Dien Bien Phu and the French Defeat in Vietnam* (New York: Da Capo, 2004), 80.

21. Edgar O'Ballance, *The Indo-China War, 1945–1954: A Study in Guerilla Warfare* (London: Faber and Faber, 1964), 43; Serieye, *Le Viêt-Minh*, 2.

22. Serieye, *Le Viêt-Minh*, 4.

23. Bodinier, ed., *La Guerre d'Indochine*, 1:96–97; O'Ballance, *The Indo-China War*, 56; Serieye, *Le Viêt-Minh*, 4. There were still five hundred to eight hundred Japanese deserters fighting with the Viet Minh in late 1950, and a number of European, North African, African, and Indochinese deserters from the French Union forces also joined the Viet Minh at various times. See *Information on Viet Minh Forces*, 40.

24. Joseph Jeremiah Zasloff, *The Role of Sanctuary in Insurgency: Communist China's Support to the Vietminh, 1946–1954* (Santa Monica, Calif.: RAND Corporation, May 1967), 31.

25. Tanham, *Communist Revolutionary Warfare*, 56.

26. Bodinier, ed., *La Guerre d'Indochine*, 1:96.

27. Ibid., 2:126.

28. Headquarters, Department of the Army, Office of the Assistant Chief of Staff for Intelligence, *Resistance and Regional Factors: Indochina* (Washington, D.C.: HQDA, OACSI, April 1959), 450, 453.

29. Fall, *Le Viet-Minh*, 191. See also Windrow, *The Last Valley*, 147–49.

30. Tanham, *Communist Revolutionary Warfare*, 60.

31. Lieutenant Colonel Boussarie, *La Situation des forces ennemies en Indochine (1945–janvier 1954)* [The Situation of the Enemy Forces in Indo-China (1945–January 1954)] (Washington, D.C.: HQDA, OACSI, 1954), 10. The typical regional force battalion consisted of a headquarters unit, three rifle companies of about 135 combatants each, and a support company that sometimes included an engineer platoon. See Leulliot and O'Hara, eds., "Early Days."

32. Serieye, *Le Viêt-Minh*, 10.

33. Tanham, *Communist Revolutionary Warfare*, 45. See also Leulliot and O'Hara, eds., "Early Days."

34. Tanham, *Communist Revolutionary Warfare*, 51.

35. Ibid., 46.

36. The first Viet Minh regiment, the 102nd "Capital" Regiment, was formed in January 1947 for operations around Hanoi. For the evolution of the Viet Minh divisions, see Wikipedia, "People's Army of Vietnam," http://en.wikipedia.org/wiki/Vietnam_People's_Army (accessed December 2, 2012).

37. *Order of Battle: Viet Minh Army*, 3; Tanham, *Communist Revolutionary Warfare*, 42.

38. Boussarie, *La Situation des forces ennemies en Indochine*, 11.

39. Ibid., 7–8; Tanham, *Communist Revolutionary Warfare*, 42.

40. Tanham, *Communist Revolutionary Warfare*, 42–43.

41. *Order of Battle: Viet Minh Army*, 4. In April 1953, Chairman Mao Tse-tung called for the formation within six months of two additional Viet Minh heavy divisions and two additional Viet Minh engineer regiments, to be formed from the existing Viet Minh infantry divisions. Apparently they were not created before the end of the First Indochina War. See Qiang Zhai, *China and the Vietnam Wars*, 45.

42. Tanham, *Communist Revolutionary Warfare*, 48.

43. *Order of Battle: Viet Minh Army*, 3.

44. *Information on Viet Minh Forces, Indo-China*, 50.

45. Serieye, *Le Viêt-Minh*, 9; *Order of Battle: Viet Minh Army*, 3.

46. *Order of Battle: Viet Minh Army*, 3.

47. *Information on Viet Minh Forces, Indo-China*, 50.

48. Boussarie, *La Situation des forces ennemies en Indochine*, 10.

49. Details on the organization of the Viet Minh infantry company, platoon (section), and squad are drawn from *Information on Viet Minh Forces, Indo-China*, 49.

4. French Logistical Doctrine and Organization

1. George A. Kelly, *Lost Soldiers: The French Army and Empire in Crisis, 1947–1962* (Cambridge, Mass.: M.I.T. Press, 1965), 59; Henri Navarre, *Le Temps des Vérités* (Paris: Plon, 1957), 279–80.

2. Bernard B. Fall, *Street without Joy: Insurgency in Indochina, 1946–63*, 3rd rev. ed. (Harrisburg, Pa.: Stackpole, 1963), 11.

3. The organization and functions of the French Union transport forces are discussed in greater detail in chapter 6.

4. Debriefing of Major General Thomas J. H. Trapnell, former chief, MAAG-Indochina, May 3, 1954, document 41, in *The Pentagon Papers: The Defense Department History of United States Decisionmaking in Vietnam*, vol. 1, ed. Mike Gravel (Boston: Beacon, 1971), 493.

5. Commander in Chief, French Forces in the Far East, *A Translation from the French: Lessons of the War in Indochina*, vol. 2 (Santa Monica, Calif.: RAND Corporation, May 1967), 54, 359–60.

6. Intendant Militaire de 1ère Classe Bunel, "L'Intendance militaire en opérations en Indochine," *Revue d'Histoire de l'Armée* 13, no. 4 (November 1957): 126; Commander in Chief, French Forces in the Far East, *Lessons from the Indo-China War*, vol. 3 (Washington, D.C.: DARPA, 1955), 137.

7. Bunel, "L'Intendance militaire en opérations en Indochine," 126; *Lessons Learned in the Indochina War*, 2:372.

8. Bunel, "L'Intendance militaire en opérations en Indochine," 126. In September 1951, there were four GEs in Tonkin located at Phu Ly, Hung Yen, Ning Giang, and Thai Binh. They were supported from SI depots at Hanoi, Haiphong, and Nam Dinh.

9. *Lessons Learned in the Indochina War*, 2:372n3.

10. 2e Section, 1er Bureau, EMIFT, "Note de Service: Service de l'Intendance de la Division d'Infanterie d'Extrême-Orient," T.E.D.-E.O.-INT-001 [No. 4.224/EMIFT/1, Saigon, October 19, 1954], in folder "1e Section, 4e Bureau, EMCEC—Archives (novembre 1954)—Organisation des Services—Organigrammes," box 10 H 1525, SHAT.

11. Cabinet, Direction Général d'Intendance, "Rapport sur les enseignements à tirer de la guerre d'Indochine, Annex I: Organismes du Service de l'Intendance des FTEO pour un Corps Expéditionnaire de 500.000 hommes," [Saigon, April 4, 1955], in folder "3e Bureau, EMIFT, *Enseignements à tirer de la campagne d'Indochine*, Fascicule III, p. 98: Documents Divers," box 10 H 983, Fonds Indochine, SHAT.

12. *Lessons Learned in the Indochina War*, 2:378–79.

13. 4e Bureau, EMIFT, "Note sur le service d'Intendance en Indochine," [Saigon, 1953], 5, in folder "1e Section, 4e Bureau, EMCEC, Archives 1953 (janvier), Directives Logistique," box 10 H 1536, Fonds Indochine, SHAT.

14. 1e Section, 4e Bureau, EMIFT, "Note: Taux d'Approvisionnements d'Indochine," 3–4 (tables 1 and 2), in folder "EMIFT, 3e Bureau, Enseignements à tirer de la campagne d'Indochine, Fasc. III, p. 98," box 10 H 983, Fonds Indochine, SHAT.

15. *Lessons from the Indo-China War,* 3:137.

16. Ibid.

17. L'Intendant Général Hornn (Directeur Général de l'Intendance), "Rapport sur les enseignements à tirer de la guerre d'Indochine," [No. 385/DI/Cabinet, Saigon, April 5, 1955], 11, in folder "3e Bureau, EMIFT, 'Enseignements à tirer de la campagne d'Indochine,' Fasc. III, p. 98: Documents Supplementaire," box 10 H 984, Fonds Indochine, SHAT; *Lessons Learned in the Indochina War,* 2:373.

18. "Note: Taux d'Approvisionnements d'Indochine," 13–14 (table 4).

19. *Lessons Learned in the Indochina War,* 2:374–76. The replacement of the steel helmet with the jungle hat and the development of the canvas and rubber jungle boot were notable successes.

20. "Note sur le service d'Intendance en Indochine," 2.

21. *Lessons Learned in the Indochina War,* 2:373.

22. "Les Rations Conditionnées," *Caravelle* 256 (November 12, 1950): 7.

23. *Lessons Learned in the Indochina War,* 2:373–74.

24. "La Chaine du Froid," *Caravelle* 256 (November 12, 1950): 7.

25. "Note sur le service d'Intendance en Indochine," 6.

26. *Lessons Learned in the Indochina War,* 2:374–75.

27. Quoted in *Lessons Learned in the Indochina War,* 2:203. Not all French troops were happy with their rations. See the telling anecdote in Martin Windrow, *The Last Valley: Dien Bien Phu and the French Defeat in Vietnam* (New York: Da Capo, 2004), 121.

28. "La Vie des TFEO: Les Économats des TFEO—'Vos' Économats," *Caravelle* 106 (December 28, 1947): 2.

29. "Un Aperçu de l'Action du Service de L'Intendance," *Caravelle* 256 (November 12, 1950): 6.

30. Trapnell debriefing, May 3, 1954, document 41, in Gravel, ed., *The Pentagon Papers,* 1:490.

31. Hornn, "Rapport sur les enseignements à tirer de la guerre d'Indochine," 11.

32. *Lessons Learned in the Indochina War,* 2:377–78.

33. Ibid., 2:372.

34. Ibid., 2:373.

35. Ibid., 2:378.

36. Ibid., 2:373.

37. Ibid., 3:139–40. A solid-fuel "camping stove" for individual use was recommended as a solution.

38. Ibid., 2:376–77.

39. Ibid., 3:140. Shrinkage was sometimes so severe that the original user of the item could no longer wear it.

40. Ibid., 2:374; Hornn, "Rapport sur les enseignements à tirer de la guerre d'Indochine," 9.

41. *Lessons Learned in the Indochina War,* 3:140–41.

42. Ibid., 2:374.

43. Ibid.

44. Ibid., 2:390; L'Ingenieur en Chef de 2ème Class Rigaudias (Directeur des Essences en Extrême-Orient), "Enseignements à tirer de la guerre d'Indochine," [No. 52/DEEO, Saigon, January 14, 1953], 3, in folder "EMIFT, 3e Bureau, Enseignements à tirer de la campagne d'Indochine, Fasc. III, p. 98: Documents Supplementaire," box 10 H 984, Fonds Indochine, SHAT.

45. Bodinier, ed., *La Guerre d'Indochine,* 1:53.

46. *Lessons Learned in the Indochina War,* 2:390.

47. Rigaudias, "Enseignements à tirer de la guerre d'Indochine," 5.

48. 4e Bureau, EMIFT, "Note sur le service des essences en Indochine," [Saigon, 1953], in folder "EMCEC, 4e Bureau, 1e Section, Archives 1953 (janvier), Directives Logistique," box 10 H 1536, Fonds Indochine, SHAT.

49. Rigaudias, "Enseignements à tirer de la guerre d'Indochine," 4.

50. "Note: Taux d'Approvisionnements d'Indochine," 3–4 (tables 1 and 2).

51. Rigaudias, "Enseignements à tirer de la guerre d'Indochine," annexe statistique, 3.

52. "Note: Taux d'Approvisionnements d'Indochine," table 6-2.

53. Rigaudias, "Enseignements à tirer de la guerre d'Indochine," 5, 9; "Note sur le service des essences en Indochine."

54. Rigaudias, "Enseignements à tirer de la guerre d'Indochine," 5.

55. *Lessons Learned in the Indochina War,* 2:390.

56. "Note sur le service des essences en Indochine."

57. Rigaudias, "Enseignements à tirer de la guerre d'Indochine," 6.

58. *Lessons Learned in the Indochina War,* 2:392–93.

59. Rigaudias, "Enseignements à tirer de la guerre d'Indochine," 5.

60. Ibid., 7.

61. *Lessons Learned in the Indochina War,* 2:391.

62. Rigaudias, "Enseignements à tirer de la guerre d'Indochine," 7.

63. *Lessons Learned in the Indochina War,* 2:391.

64. Ibid.; Rigaudias, "Enseignements à tirer de la guerre d'Indochine," 7.

65. "Note: Taux d'Approvisionnements d'Indochine," table 6-1.

66. Direction du Matériel des F. T. N. V., *Conference sur L'Organisation et le Fonctionnement du Service du Matériel en Indochine* ([Hanoi]: Direction du Matériel des FTNV, September 17, 1952), chapter 1, page 2 (cited hereafter as *Conference sur L'Organisation*). The same acronym, DIRMAT FTEO, is used to refer to both the Director and to the overall SM organization in Indochina.

67. Ibid., chapter 2, page 394n2.

68. Ibid., chapter 2, page 394; General Le Troadec, "Le Service du Matériel d'Indochine, 1949–1951," *Revue Historique de l'Armée* 12, no. 3 (August 1956): 111–13. Before 1949, combat units were entirely responsible for their own combat vehicle maintenance.

69. *Lessons Learned in the Indochina War,* 2:394.

70. DIRMAT FTEO, "Enseignements à tirer de la campagne d'Indochine," [No. 1734/ DM/Cabinet, Saigon, March 7, 1955], annex "Plan," chapter 1, page 7, in file "Matériel," in folder "EMIFT, 3e Bureau, *Enseignements à tirer de la campagne d'Indochine,* Fasc. III, page 98: Documents Supplementaire," box 10 H 984, Fonds Indochine, SHAT.

71. Le Troadec, "Le Service du Matériel d'Indochine," 112.

72. 2e Section, 1e Bureau, EMIFT, "Note de Service: Service du Matériel de la Division d'Infanterie," [No. 4,153/EMIFT/1/3331, Saigon, October 16, 1954], in folder "EMCEC, 4e Bureau, 1e Section—Archives (novembre 1954)—Organisation des Services—Organigrammes," box 10 H 1525, Fonds Indochine, SHAT.

73. *Lessons Learned in the Indochina War,* 2:397.

74. DIRMAT FTEO, "Enseignements à tirer de la campagne d'Indochine," annex "Plan," chapter 2, page 1; *Lessons Learned in the Indochina War,* 2:396.

75. Bodinier, ed., *La Guerre d'Indochine,* 2:49.

76. DIRMAT FTEO, "Enseignements à tirer de la campagne d'Indochine," annex "Plan," chapter 2, pages 2–3.

77. Commandement en Chef des Forces Terrestres Navales et Aériennes en Indochine, État-Major Interarmées et des Forces Terrestres, Chef d'État-Major, "La Situation en Indochine de Novembre 1951 à Mai 1953" [Saigon, 1953], 28, in folder "EMIFT, 3e Bureau, Enseignements à tirer de la campagne d'Indochine, Fasc. III, p. 98—Documents Supplementaire," box 10 H 984, Fonds Indochine, SHAT.

78. Bodinier, ed., *La Guerre d'Indochine,* 2:49.

79. Le Troadec, "Le Service du Matériel d'Indochine," 113.

80. *Lessons Learned in the Indochina War,* 2:402.

81. "La Situation en Indochine de Novembre 1951 à Mai 1953," 29.

82. Ibid., 62.

83. DIRMAT FTEO, "Enseignements à tirer de la campagne d'Indochine," annex "Plan," chapter 2, page 12.

84. *Lessons Learned in the Indochina War,* 2:362.

85. DIRMAT FTEO, "Enseignements à tirer de la campagne d'Indochine," annex "Plan," chapter 2, page 11. The theoretical requirement in 1954 was for only 471,288 square feet of covered storage.

86. *Lessons Learned in the Indochina War,* 3:44–45. The criticism of the MAS 36 was very similar to that directed at the U.S. M16 rifle some twenty years later. French infantrymen in Indochina frequently advocated a higher proportion of submachine guns and light automatic rifles, such as the U.S. M3 carbine.

87. Ibid., 2:404.

88. DIRMAT FTEO, "Enseignements à tirer de la campagne d'Indochine," annex "Plan," chapter 2, pages 4–5.

89. Ibid., tableau annexe 8.

90. DIRMAT FTEO, "Enseignements à tirer de la campagne d'Indochine," annex "Plan," chapter 2, pages 11–12.

91. Ibid., annex "Plan," chapter 2, page 13.

92. *Conférence sur l'Organisation,* 26.

93. *Lessons Learned in the Indochina War,* 3:144. The Morane 500, a French version of

the German Feisler Storch, required eight hours of daily maintenance for every hour of flight time, roughly eight times what was required for the L-19.

94. Ibid., 2:401; DIRMAT FTEO, "Enseignements à tirer de la campagne d'Indochine," annex "Plan," chapter 2, pages 15–16.

95. *Lessons Learned in the Indochina War,* 2:396–98.

96. DIRMAT FTEO, "Enseignements à tirer de la campagne d'Indochine," annex "Plan," chapter 2, page 24.

97. Commandant Lacour (DIRMAT, 4e Région Militaire), "Fiche relative aux enseigne-ments à tirer des combats d'Indochine," [Saigon, October 2, 1954], 1–2, in folder "EMIFT, 3e Bureau, Enseignements à tirer de la campagne d'Indochine, Fasc. III, 98: Documents Supplementaire," box 10 H 984, Fonds Indochine, SHAT. Commandant Lacour noted (on page 3) that damage to artillery pieces often was due not to the design of the gun but to lack of maintenance and lack of precautions during movement. He also recommended the creation of special units to perform first- and second-echelon maintenance, which would allow the drivers more rest. His proposal was tried by U.S. truck units in Viet Nam in 1968 with very little success.

98. Ronald H. Spector, *Advice and Support: The Early Years, 1941–1960* (Washington, D.C.: Center of Military History, U.S. Army, 1983), 258–59.

99. *Conférence sur l'Organisation,* 5–6.

100. 4e Bureau, EMIFT, *Instruction sur le Ravitaillement en Munitions en Indochine* [No. 111/EMIFT/4/1/4/S, Saigon, March 11, 1953], in file: "Documents Divers," in folder "EMIFT, 3e Bureau, Enseignements à tirer de la campagne d'Indochine, Fasc. III, p. 98," box 10 H 983, Fonds Indochine, SHAT; DIRMAT FTEO, "Enseignements à tirer de la cam-pagne d'Indochine," annex "Plan," chapter 2, page 19.

101. *Conférence sur l'Organisation,* 25, 32–33. The more important depots of the ERG-MU were served by several detachments, each of which had the theoretical capability during a twelve-hour day of supervising about eighty laborers, managing a depot of one thousand to twelve hundred tons, serving as a transshipment point, and establishing an ammunition workshop.

102. DIRMAT FTEO, "Enseignements à tirer de la campagne d'Indochine," annex "Plan," chapter 2, page 17.

103. *Lessons Learned in the Indochina War,* 2:275 (table 3).

104. ERG-MU management of French Union ammunition storage arrangements is dis-cussed in DIRMAT FTEO, "Enseignements à tirer de la campagne d'Indochine," annex "Plan," chapter 2, pages 19–21.

105. *Instruction . . . 1953,* chapter 1, paragraph 4, section 2, and annexes 5 and 6.

106. DIRMAT FTEO, "Enseignements à tirer de la campagne d'Indochine," annex "Plan," chapter 2, page 17.

107. Ibid., annex "Plan," chapter 2, page 18; *Instruction . . . 1953,* annex 8.

108. *Lessons Learned in the Indochina War,* 3:143.

109. Le Troadec, "Le Service du Matériel d'Indochine," 112, 116.

110. *Lessons Learned in the Indochina War,* 2:398–99.

111. Ibid., 2:399; DIRMAT FTEO, "Enseignements à tirer de la campagne d'Indochine," annex "Plan," chapter 2, page 5.

112. DIRMAT FTEO, "Enseignements à tirer de la campagne d'Indochine," annex "Plan," chapter 1, pages 7–8; *Lessons Learned in the Indochina War,* 2:395–96.

113. *Lessons Learned in the Indochina War,* 3:146.

114. Ibid., 2:362.

5. Viet Minh Logistical Doctrine and Organization

1. Phillip B. Davidson, *Vietnam at War: The History, 1946–1975* (Novato, Calif.: Presidio, 1988), 58.

2. Julian Thompson, *The Lifeblood of War: Logistics in Armed Conflict* (London: Brassey's, 1991), 162.

3. Bernard B. Fall, *Le Viet-Minh: La République Démocratique du Viet-Nam, 1945–1960* (Paris: Librairie Armand Colin, 1960), 192.

4. General Giap's military theories are laid out in Vo Nguyen Giap, *People's War, People's Army: The Viet Cong Insurrection Manual for Underdeveloped Countries* (New York: Praeger, 1962), and Vo Nguyen Giap, *Inside the Viet Minh* (Washington, D.C.: Marine Corps Association, 1962).

5. Giap, *Inside the Viet Minh,* I-4.

6. Edgar O'Ballance, *The Indo-China War 1945–1954: A Study in Guerrilla Warfare* (London: Faber and Faber, 1964), 261–63.

7. Giap, *People's War, People's Army,* 132–33.

8. Harvey H. Smith et al., *Area Handbook for North Vietnam,* Department of the Army Pamphlet No. 550-57 (Washington, D.C.: U.S. Government Printing Office, 1968), 192–93.

9. Giap, *People's War, People's Army,* 135.

10. Quoted in Fall, *Le Viet-Minh,* 197.

11. Commandement en Chef des Forces Terrestres Navales et Aériennes en Indochine, État-Major Interarmées et des Forces Terrestres, Bureau "Instruction," *Notes sur le combat en Indochine* [Combat Notes from the War in Indochina] (Washington, D.C.: HQDA, OACS G-2, March 30, 1954), 31.

12. Quoted in *Notes sur le combat en Indochine,* 31.

13. Ibid.

14. George K. Tanham, *Communist Revolutionary Warfare: From the Vietminh to the Viet Cong,* rev. ed. (New York: Praeger, 1967), 37.

15. Headquarters, Department of the Army, Office of the Assistant Chief of Staff, G-2, *Viet Minh Logistics* (Washington, D.C.: HQDA, OACS G-2, May 6, 1953), 1.

16. *Viet Minh Logistics,* 6. In current U.S. Army terminology the GSD would be considered an "operator" rather than a "staff" agency.

17. Headquarters, Department of the Army, Office of the Assistant Chief of Staff, G-2, *Order of Battle: Viet Minh Army* (Washington, D.C.: HQDA, OACS G-2, October 10, 1954), 6. Tran Dai Nghia was listed as chief of the General Supply Directorate as of October 1954. The functions of the various branches of the GSD are described by D. M. O. Miller, "'A Handful of Rice?': Logistics in the Viet Minh Campaign," *Army Quarterly and Defence Journal* 100, no. 1 (April 1970): 109–11.

18. Lieutenant Colonel Boussarie, *La Situation des forces ennemies en Indochine (1945–janvier 1954)* [The Situation of the Enemy Forces in Indo-China] (Washington, D.C.: HQDA, OACSI, 1954), 12–13.

19. For additional information on the Viet Minh medical services, see Christopher E. Goscha, "'Hell in a Very Small Place': Cold War and Decolonisation in the Assault on the Vietnamese Body at Dien Bien Phu," *European Journal of East Asian Studies* 9, no. 2 (December 2010): 201–23.

20. Giap, *People's War, People's Army,* 144–45.

21. O'Ballance, *The Indo-China War,* 66; Fredrik Logevall, *Embers of War: The Fall of an Empire and the Making of America's Vietnam* (New York: Random House, 2012), 150–51; Martin Windrow, *The Last Valley: Dien Bien Phu and the French Defeat in Vietnam* (New York: Da Capo, 2004), 89.

22. BDM Corporation, *A Study of Strategic Lessons Learned in Vietnam,* vol. 1, *The Enemy* (McLean, Va.: BDM Corporation, November 30, 1979), page 5-2.

23. O'Ballance, *The Indo-China War,* 81.

24. Ibid., 90.

25. Union Française, Section de Documentation Militaire, *Le Probleme militaire du Cambodge (1951)* [The Military Problem of Cambodia (1951)] (Washington, D.C.: HQDA, OACS G-2, [1955]), 8–9.

26. *Viet Minh Logistics,* 5 (table 1).

27. Commander in Chief, French Forces in the Far East, *Lessons from the Indo-China War,* vol. 3 (Washington, D.C.: DARPA, 1955), 36 and note 1.

28. U.S. Far East Command, General Headquarters, Military Intelligence Section, Allied Translator and Interpreter Service, *Information on Viet Minh Forces, Indo-China* (Tokyo: GHQ, USFEC, MI Section, ATIS, August 11, 1951), 50.

29. Claude Guigues, "Logistique Vietminh," *Indochine Sud-Est Asiatique* 16 (March 1953): 55.

30. *Lessons Learned in the Indochina War,* 1:5–24 (figure 5.5).

31. L. P. Holliday and R. M. Gurfield, *Viet Cong Logistics* (Santa Monica, Calif.: RAND Corporation, June 1968), 33 (table 4).

32. Ibid., 32–33.

33. *Information on Viet Minh Forces, Indo-China,* 50–51.

34. Ibid., 50.

35. Guigues, "Logistique Vietminh," 55; Howard R. Simpson, *Tiger in the Barbed Wire: An American in Vietnam, 1952–1991* (New York: Brassey's, 1992), 69.

36. *Lessons Learned in the Indochina War,* 1:5–24 (figure 5.5); Holliday and Gurfield, *Viet Cong Logistics,* 34.

37. *Lessons Learned in the Indochina War,* 1:5–24 (figure 5.5); Holliday and Gurfield, *Viet Cong Logistics,* 34. Viet Cong hospitals were required to maintain a sixty-day supply.

38. Fall, *Le Viet-Minh,* 191.

39. "Un chef de bataillon V. M. m'a dit," *Caravelle* 357 (October 19, 1952): 6–7.

40. Fall, *Le Viet-Minh,* 191.

41. *Information on Viet Minh Forces, Indo-China,* 50.

42. *Viet Minh Logistics,* 2.

43. Ibid.

44. *Lessons Learned in the Indochina War,* 1:5-2.

45. Gilbert Bodinier, ed., *La Guerre d'Indochine, 1945–1954: Texte et Documents,* vol. 2,

Indochine, 1947—Règlement politique ou solution militaire? (Château de Vincennes: SHAT, 1989), 127.

46. O'Ballance, *The Indo-China War,* 55–56. By late 1945, the Viet Minh may have had as many as one hundred thousand small arms and eight thousand light machine guns.

47. Boussarie, *La Situation des forces ennemies en Indochine,* 2; Bodinier, ed., *La Guerre d'Indochine,* 2:128.

48. Haut-Commissariat de France pour l'Indochine, État-Major Particulier, *Conditions offertes par le gouvernement français pour la cessation des hostilités entre d'une part, les forces françaises et les forces de police locales, d'autre part les forces armées se réclamant du gouvernement de fait présidé par M. Ho Chi Minh* (No. 1144/EMP, Saigon, August 4, 1947), from box 10 H 165, Fonds Indochine, SHAT (reproduced in Bodinier, ed., *La Guerre d'Indochine,* 2:280).

49. *Viet Minh Logistics,* 3. The estimates for machine guns and artillery weapons include a proportionate share of such weapons in the supporting Viet Minh artillery division.

50. Ibid., 4.

51. *Viet Cong Logistics,* 102 (table A-3-4).

52. Fall, *Le Viet-Minh,* 211.

53. Giap, *Inside the Viet Minh,* I-5. The same quotation appears in Giap, *People's War, People's Army,* 30.

54. Brigadier General Chapelle (Commandant du Train du FTEO), "Rapport sur les enseignements de la campagne d'Indochine," [Saigon, February 1, 1955], 5, in folder "EMIFT, 3e Bureau, Enseignements à Tirer de la Campagne d'Indochine, Fasc. III, p. 98," box 10 H 983, Fonds Indochine, SHAT. English translation by the author.

6. The Opposing Transport Systems

1. Commander in Chief, French Forces in the Far East, *A Translation from the French: Lessons of the War in Indochina,* vol. 2 (Santa Monica, Calif.: RAND Corporation, May 1967), 325.

2. "La Logistique dans la Guerre d'Indochine—Situation à la date du 1er octobre 1952," 8, in folder "EMCEC, 4e Bureau, 1e Section, Archives 1953 (janvier), Directives Logistique," box 10 H 1536, Fonds Indochine, SHAT.

3. Georges Couget, *Le Train en Indochine, 1945–1954* (Paris: Inspection du Train, 1973), 51. The official title was later changed to *Train* of Ground Forces in the Far East (*Train des Forces Terrestres en Extreme-Orient*).

4. *Lessons Learned in the Indochina War,* 2:319.

5. Brigadier General Chapelle (Commandant du Train du FTEO), "Rapport sur les enseignements de la campagne d'Indochine," [Saigon, February 1, 1955], 5, in folder "EMIFT, 3e Bureau, Enseignements à Tirer de la Campagne d'Indochine, Fasc. III, p. 98," box 10 H 983, Fonds Indochine, SHAT.

6. Ibid.

7. Couget, *Le Train en Indochine,* 31–33. The successive commandants of the *Train* of the CEFEO and the date on which they assumed command were as follows: Lieutenant Colonel Chabert (July 28, 1945); Colonel Chapelle (March 12, 1947); Colonel Montintin (January 1, 1949); Colonel Gallo (October 21, 1949); Colonel Derutin (June 16, 1950);

Brigadier General Lechaux (September 11, 1950); Colonel Martin (September 23, 1952); Colonel (later Brigadier General) Chapelle (May 1, 1954); and Colonel Ruffat (February 1955). See Couget, *Le Train en Indochine,* 40.

8. Ibid., 36.

9. Ibid., 39, 47–49 passim.

10. Commandement en Chef des Forces Terrestres Navales et Aériennes en Indochine, État-Major Interarmées et des Forces Terrestres, Chef d'État-Major, "La Situation en Indochine de Novembre 1951 à Mai 1953" [Saigon, 1953], 25 (table 1), in folder "EMIFT, 3e Bureau, Enseignements à tirer de la campagne d'Indochine, Fasc. III, p. 98—Documents Supplementaire," box 10 H 984, Fonds Indochine, SHAT; Couget, *Le Train en Indochine,* 52.

11. "La Logistique dans la Guerre d'Indochine—Situation à la date du 1er octobre 1952," 7. "Order-ship time" is the period from when an item is ordered until it is received.

12. Ibid., 8; *Lessons Learned in the Indochina War,* 2:369 (table 5).

13. *Lessons Learned in the Indochina War,* 2:370.

14. Lieutenant Colonel Blanchet (Chef du Bureau Transports, EMIFT), "Fiche: Enseignements de la guerre d'Indochine en matière de transports," [160/EMIFT/BT, Saigon, June 16, 1955], 2, in folder "EMIFT, 3e Bureau, Enseignements à tirer de la campagne d'Indochine, Fasc. III, p. 98," box 10 H 983, Fonds Indochine, SHAT.

15. DIRMAT FTEO, "Enseignements à tirer de la campagne d'Indochine," annex "Plan," chapter 2, page 23. The "chogie stick" was a device used throughout the Orient to aid in the carrying of loads. It was essentially a long pole or narrow board from which bundles of cargo were hung from each end. Carried across the shoulders, the "chogie stick" increased the carrying capacity of the porter. The term itself was probably coined by GIs in Korea and is closely related to the phrase "cut a chogie," meaning to move out smartly or to run away.

16. The estimate is based on Korean War data. See E. L. Atkins, H. P. Griggs, and Roy T. Sessums, *North Korean Logistics and Methods of Accomplishment* (Chevy Chase, Md.: Operations Research Office, Johns Hopkins University, 1951), 12.

17. *Lessons Learned in the Indochina War,* 2:320–21.

18. Ibid., 2:164. The French Army Veterinary Service, organized on a territorial basis, maintained the health of the mules, horses, war dogs, and other animals used by the French Union forces in Indochina.

19. Ibid., 2:321.

20. DIRMAT FTEO, "Enseignements à tirer de la campagne d'Indochine," annex "Plan," chapter 2, page 22.

21. For the organization of the CT, see *Lessons Learned in the Indochina War,* 2:319–20.

22. "A Statistical Comparison of the Mobility of the US and Communist-Bloc Infantry Divisions in the Far East," *USAFFE/EUSA Intelligence Digest* 6, no. 4 (April 1956): 10, chart 14, "Characteristics of Major US and USSR General Purpose Vehicles."

23. Couget, *Le Train en Indochine,* 52.

24. Ibid., 37.

25. Ibid., 182.

26. J. Delegorgue, "Les routiers des Plateaux," *Caravelle* 373 (February 8, 1953): 4–5.

27. "La Logistique dans la Guerre d'Indochine—Situation à la date du 1er octobre

1952," 9; Blanchet, "Fiche: Enseignements de la guerre d'Indochine en matière de transports," 1.

28. Note in *Caravelle* 100 (November 16, 1947): 3.

29. A. Mathieu, "La Rafale," *Caravelle* 376 (March 1, 1953): 4–5.

30. Couget, *Le Train en Indochine,* 26.

31. *Lessons Learned in the Indochina War,* 2:265.

32. Ibid., 2:321. The CFTT were habitually employed by platoon or smaller increment.

33. 3e Section, État-Major, Commandement du Train des Forces Terrestres en Indochine, *Mémento Provisoire sur l'Emploi des Pelotons Fluviaux en Indochine* (Saigon: Imprimerie S.P.I. des Forces Aériennes en Extrême-Orient, May 11, 1953), 45–46.

34. Commandement des Forces Terrestres du Sud-Viêtnam, *Marine Odyssée: Instruction sur l'Organisation et le Controle de la Navigation Fluviale* (Saigon: Imprimerie Française d'Outre-Mer, 1953), 66, passim. The *Marine Odyssée* contained the official French rules and regulations for river traffic in South Viet Nam and Cambodia, including information on the documents required as well as on the organization and execution of riverine convoys.

35. Couget, *Le Train en Indochine,* 182.

36. Lieutenant General John W. O'Daniel, USA (Chief, U.S. Joint Military Mission to Indochina), *Progress Report on Military Situation in Indochina as of 19 November 1953,* Pearl Harbor, Hawaii, November 19, 1953, 9–10, in box 10 ("092 Asia (6-25-48) (2) Section 22"), Geographical File, 1954–1956, Records Group 218 (Records of the U.S. Joint Chiefs of Staff), National Archives II, College Park, Maryland. John D. Plating ("Failure at the Margins: Aerial Resupply at Dien Bien Phu" [Master's thesis, Ohio State University, 2000], page 9) has noted that: "The French Expeditionary Force in Vietnam was perhaps the first force to consciously employ pre-planned aerial resupply as the sole means of support for a fixed garrison. . . . Conceptually, the French had keyed into the potential impact of airlift, but did not have an adequate airforce, nor an understanding of the doctrinal nuances to assure victory."

37. Lucien Bodard, *The Quicksand War: Prelude to Vietnam* (Boston: Little, Brown, 1967), 41–42.

38. *Lessons Learned in the Indochina War,* 2:166–67. Seno could normally be resupplied by land as well as by air, but it was designed to be supported entirely by air if necessary.

39. "Airborne Operations in Indochina," *Intelligence Review* 197 (October 1952): 11; Commander in Chief, French Forces in the Far East, *Lessons from the Indo-China War,* vol. 3 (Washington, D.C.: DARPA, 1955), 147.

40. *Lessons Learned in the Indochina War,* 2:370n2. In 1953, a total of 47,454 tons moved by air in Indochina.

41. Ibid., 3:148 and note 1.

42. Colonel Sauvagnac (Commandant des Troupes Aéroportées en Indochine), "Rapport du Colonel Commandant les T.A.P.I. sur les opérations de ravitaillement par Air pendant la bataille de DIEN BIEN PHU (novembre 1953–mai 1954)," [Hanoi, December 20, 1954], annex 5, in folder "EMIFT, 3e Bureau—Operations: Dien Bien Phu," box 10 H 1169, Fonds Indochine, SHAT.

43. Bodinier, ed., *La Guerre d'Indochine,* 2:61.

44. "La Situation en Indochine de Novembre 1951 à Mai 1953," 102–3.

45. Losses at Dien Bien Phu included forty-eight aircraft shot down, fourteen destroyed while landing, and 167 damaged. The Viet Minh commando raid on the airfield at Cat Bi near Haiphong resulted in a loss of eighteen transports, and a similar raid on Gia Lam airfield near Hanoi also succeeded. See Bernard B. Fall, *Street without Joy: Insurgency in Indochina, 1946–63*, 3rd rev. ed. (Harrisburg, Pa.: Stackpole, 1963), 258–59.

46. Fall, *Street without Joy,* 259n. The American aircraft and crews that for a time flew in support of Dien Bien Phu (including the famous pilot James B. McGovern, better known to his contemporaries as "Earthquake McGoon," who was killed in action on May 6, 1954) were ostensibly civilian and belonged to Civil Air Transport (CAT), a firm supported by the U.S. Central Intelligence Agency.

47. O'Daniel, *Progress Report . . . as of 19 November 1953,* annex E, "Air—Progress Report—French Air Force in Indochina," 68. Control of civilian contract aircraft was retained by EMIFT rather than being delegated to the air force.

48. "Airborne Operations in Indochina," 16.

49. *Lessons Learned in the Indochina War,* 3:150.

50. "Airborne Operations in Indochina," 11.

51. DIRMAT FTEO, Section Technique Aéroportée, "Rapport du chef de la Section Technique Aéroportée concernant les enseignements à tirer des opérations et relatifs aux matériels aéroportées," [Saigon, December 31, 1954], 4, in folder "EMIFT, 3e Bureau, Enseignements à Tirer de la campagne d'Indochine, Fasc. III, p. 98—Rapports Divers," box 10 H 983, Fonds Indochine, SHAT.

52. Valérie André, "The Helicopter Ambulance in Indochina," *L'Officier de Réserve* 2 (July 10, 1954): 2 (English translation in Major John H. Sidenberg, USAF [Air Attaché Paris], *Special Air Intelligence Information Report No. 1860-54,* Paris, December 9, 1954, subject: Translation of Two Articles from French Publication, *L'Officier de Réserve*). See also Martin Windrow, *The Last Valley: Dien Bien Phu and the French Defeat in Vietnam* (Cambridge, Mass.: Da Capo, 2004), 666.

53. *Lessons Learned in the Indochina War,* 2:299.

54. André, "The Helicopter Ambulance in Indochina," 2–3.

55. O'Daniel, *Progress Report . . . as of 19 November 1953,* annex E, 65.

56. Ibid., annex E, 64–65.

57. *Lessons Learned in the Indochina War,* 2:301 and note 1.

58. Ibid., 2:244–45.

59. George K. Tanham, *Communist Revolutionary Warfare: From the Vietminh to the Viet Cong,* rev. ed. (New York: Praeger, 1967), 109.

60. "Airborne Operations in Indochina," 9, 11.

61. *Lessons Learned in the Indochina War,* 2:247; Tanham, *Communist Revolutionary Warfare,* 109.

62. Colonel Chavette, *Considérations sur les opérations aéroportées du theâtre d'opérations Indochinois* [Considerations on Airborne Operations in the Indochinese Theater of Operations] (Washington, D.C.: HQDA, OACS G-2, 1956), 14.

63. Tanham, *Communist Revolutionary Warfare,* 110; *Lessons Learned in the Indochina War,* 2:249.

64. Chavette, *Considérations sur les opérations aéroportées,* 14.

65. "Rapport du chef de la Section Technique Aéroportée," 2.

66. *Lessons Learned in the Indochina War,* 3:151–53.

67. Fall, *Hell in a Very Small Place,* 349. The success rate was later increased to around 80 percent. See Plating, "Failure at the Margins," 110.

68. 2e Section, 1e Bureau, EMIFT, "Note de Service No. 292: Ravitaillement par Air," [Saigon, January 29, 1954], Piece No. 68 in folder "Organigrammes: Organisation et Soutien des TAPI," box 10 H 1525, Fonds Indochine, SHAT.

69. *Lessons Learned in the Indochina War,* 2:321 and note 5; ibid., 3:154–56.

70. R. Lesage, "La vie des FAEO: La C. R. A.," *Caravelle* 232 (May 28, 1950): 2.

71. Lieutenant Colonel Boussarie, *La Situation des forces ennemies en Indochine (1945–janvier 1954)* [The Situation of the Enemy Forces in Indo-China] (Washington, D.C.: HQDA, OACSI, 1954), 21. The Chinese also improved transportation routes on their side of the border leading to the Viet Minh supply enclaves in northern Tonkin.

72. Joseph Jeremiah Zasloff, *The Role of Sanctuary in Insurgency: Communist China's Support to the Vietminh, 1946–1954* (Santa Monica, Calif.: RAND Corporation, May 1967), 23.

73. Boussarie, *La Situation des forces ennemies en Indochine,* 28.

74. Headquarters, Department of the Army, Office of the Assistant Chief of Staff, G-2, *Viet Minh Logistics* (Washington, D.C.: HQDA, OACS G-2, May 6, 1953), 10.

75. Edgar O'Ballance, *The Indo-China War 1945–1954: A Study in Guerrilla Warfare* (London: Faber and Faber, 1964), 170.

76. Ibid.

77. Claude Guigues, "Logistique Vietminh," *Indochine Sud-Est Asiatique* 16 (March 1953): 55, 58.

78. Ibid., 56.

79. Ibid.

80. BDM Corporation, *A Study of Strategic Lessons Learned in Vietnam,* vol. 1, *The Enemy* (McLean, Va.: BDM Corporation, November 30, 1979), pages 5-7, 5-8, 5-12, and 5-53. The Ho Chi Minh Trail fell into disuse between 1954 and 1959.

81. Headquarters, Department of the Army, Office of the Assistant Chief of Staff for Intelligence, *Resistance and Regional Factors: Indochina* (Washington, D.C.: HQDA, OACSI, April 1959), 108–9.

82. *Viet Minh Logistics,* 11.

83. J. Wallace Higgins, *Porterage Parameters and Tables* (RM-5292-ISA/ARPA; Santa Monica, Calif.: RAND Corporation, August 1967), 205.

84. D. M. O. Miller, "'A Handful of Rice?': Logistics in the Viet Minh Campaign," *Army Quarterly and Defence Journal* 100, no. 1 (April 1970): 110.

85. Tanham, *Communist Revolutionary Warfare,* 69–70; *Lessons Learned in the Indochina War,* 1:5-4 and 5-5 (figure 5-1).

86. Union Française, Section de Documentation Militaire, *Le Probleme militaire du Cambodge (1951)* [The Military Problem of Cambodia (1951)] (Washington, D.C.: HQDA, OACS G-2, [1955]), 10. The methods used by the Viet Minh throughout Indochina were the same as those described for Cambodia.

87. Guigues, "Logistique Vietminh," 57; *Le Probleme militaire du Cambodge (1951),* 10.

88. Higgins, *Porterage Parameters and Tables,* 6 (table 1); Miller, "'A Handful of Rice?,'" 110. The typical North Korean or Chinese porter in Korea at the same time carried an average load of sixty pounds over a distance of fifteen miles in one working day/night. See E. L. Atkins, H. P. Griggs, and Roy T. Sessums, *North Korean Logistics and Methods of Accomplishment* (Chevy Chase, Md.: Operations Research Office, Johns Hopkins University, 1951), 7.

89. Roy, *The Battle of Dien Bien Phu,* 30, 105; Fredrik Logevall, *Embers of War: The Fall of an Empire and the Making of America's Vietnam* (New York: Random House, 2012), 415; Miller, "'A Handful of Rice?,'" 110.

90. Jacques Dalloz, *The War in Indochina, 1945–54* (New York: Barnes and Noble, 1990), 251.

91. Higgins, *Porterage Parameters and Tables,* 33 (table 15). The lower figure is based on the assumption that the porters do not carry their own food, and the higher figure on the assumption that they do. A staging operation over the same distance would require 5,630 porters.

92. Bernard B. Fall, *Le Viet-Minh: La République Démocratique du Viet-Nam, 1945–1960* (Paris: Librairie Armand Colin, 1960), 194. See also Logevall, *Embers of War,* 239.

93. O'Ballance, *The Indo-China War,* 167.

94. *Viet Minh Logistics,* 10. Phillip B. Davidson (*Vietnam at War: The History, 1946–1975* [Novato, Calif.: Presidio, 1988], 59) maintains that a ratio of two porters for every one combatant—or even four porters for each combatant—was necessary. See also Dalloz, *The War in Indochina,* 251.

95. Tanham, *Communist Revolutionary Warfare,* 71; Fall, *Le Viet-Minh,* 194.

96. Higgins, *Porterage Parameters and Tables,* 205, citing *Kinh te Viet Nam, 1945–54* (Hanoi: Nha Xuat Ban Khoa Hoc, 1966), 215.

97. Julian Thompson, *The Lifeblood of War: Logistics in Armed Conflict* (London: Brassey's, 1991), 145.

98. Fall, *Le Viet-Minh,* 194. On this topic, see also Higgins, *Porterage Parameters and Tables,* 5.

99. Thompson, *Lifeblood of War,* 145; Davidson, *Vietnam at War,* 60; and Tanham, *Communist Revolutionary Warfare,* 71.

100. Fall, *Le Viet-Minh,* 191–92.

101. Boussarie, *La Situation des forces ennemies en Indochine,* 23. English translation by the author.

102. *Lessons Learned in the Indochina War,* 1:5-5 (figure 5-1).

103. O'Ballance, *The Indo-China War,* 169–70.

104. Miller, "'A Handful of Rice?,'" 109; Tanham, *Communist Revolutionary Warfare,* 70.

105. Miller, "'A Handful of Rice?,'" 109.

106. Headquarters, Department of the Army, Office of the Assistant Chief of Staff, G-2, *Order of Battle: Viet Minh Army* (Washington, D.C.: HQDA, OACS G-2, October 10, 1954), 15; Tanham, *Communist Revolutionary Warfare,* 70.

107. Bac Kan was the main Viet Minh supply center, but important depots were located at Yen Bay, Phu Doan, and Hoa Binh. See O'Ballance, *The Indo-China War,* 171.

108. Fall, *Le Viet-Minh*, 194.

109. Tanham, *Communist Revolutionary Warfare*, 70; Fall, *Le Viet-Minh*, 194.

110. Boussarie, *La Situation des forces ennemies en Indochine*, 28; Thompson, *Lifeblood of War*, 172–73.

111. Tanham, *Communist Revolutionary Warfare*, 70–71.

112. Fall, *Le Viet-Minh*, 195.

113. "Enemy Motor Transport in North Korea," *USAFFE Intelligence Digest* 1, no. 9 (May 2, 1953): 35; Headquarters, U.S. I Corps, G-2 Section, *CCF Logistical Capabilities: A Study of the Enemy Vehicular Effort on I Corps Front* ([Korea]: HQ, U.S. I Corps, June 28, 1952), annex 2, 1. A later model, the GAZ-63, went into production in 1948, but most, if not all, of the trucks provided to the Viet Minh by the Chinese were the older GAZ-51 model.

114. Boussarie, *La Situation des forces ennemies en Indochine*, 22.

115. O'Ballance, *The Indo-China War*, 170; Zasloff, *The Role of Sanctuary in Insurgency*, 23.

116. Fall, *Le Viet-Minh*, 122.

117. *Lessons Learned in the Indochina War*, 3:35.

118. *Viet Minh Logistics*, 10.

7. French Sources of Supply

1. "La Logistique dans la Guerre d'Indochine—Situation à la date du 1er octobre 1952," 4, in folder "EMCEC, 4e Bureau, 1e Section, Archives 1953 (janvier), Directives Logistique," box 10 H 1536, Fonds Indochine, SHAT.

2. Julian Thompson, *The Lifeblood of War: Logistics in Armed Conflict* (London: Brassey's, 1991), 154.

3. Ronald H. Spector, *Advice and Support: The Early Years, 1941–1960* (Washington, D.C.: Center of Military History, U.S. Army, 1983), 146–48.

4. Gilbert Bodinier, ed., *La Guerre d'Indochine, 1945–1954: Texte et Documents*, vol. 2, *Indochine, 1947—Règlement politique ou solution militaire?* (Vincennes: SHAT, 1989), 49–51.

5. An excellent discussion of British aid to the French in the early days of the First Indochina War can be found in T. O. Smith, "Resurrecting the French Empire: British Military Aid to Vietnam September 1945—June 1947," *University of Sussex Journal of Contemporary History* 11 (2007): 1–12.

6. "La Logistique dans la Guerre d'Indochine—Situation à la date du 1er octobre 1952," 6–7.

7. Ibid., map ("Intendance") and "Organigramme du Service de l'Intendance."

8. General Le Troadec, "Le Service du Matériel d'Indochine, 1949–1951," *Revue Historique de l'Armée* 12, no. 3 (August 1956): 114.

9. Ibid.

10. "La Logistique dans la Guerre d'Indochine—Situation à la date du 1er octobre 1952," 5.

11. Ibid., 3.

12. Ibid., 2–3.

13. Ibid., 3–4.

14. Commander in Chief, French Forces in the Far East, *A Translation from the French: Lessons of the War in Indochina,* vol. 2 (Santa Monica, Calif.: RAND Corporation, May 1967), 366.

15. Ibid., 2:366.

16. Bernard B. Fall, *Street without Joy: Insurgency in Indochina, 1946–63,* 3rd rev. ed. (Harrisburg, Pa.: Stackpole, 1963), 253. Some cargo from the United States also showed signs of sabotage.

17. Debriefing of Major General Thomas J. H. Trapnell (former chief, MAAG-Indochina), May 3, 1954, document 41, in *The Pentagon Papers: The Defense Department History of United States Decisionmaking in Vietnam,* vol. 1, ed. Mike Gravel (Boston: Beacon, 1971), 492.

18. In addition to the works cited in the text, important sources for American support of the French in Indochina include U.S. Joint Chiefs of Staff, Office of Joint History, *The Joint Chiefs of Staff and the First Indochina War, 1947–1954,* History of the Joint Chiefs of Staff (Washington, D.C.: Office of Joint History, Office of the Chairman of the Joint Chiefs of Staff, 2004); Richard W. Stewart, *Deepening Involvement, 1945–1965,* CMH Publication 76-1 (Washington, D.C.: Center of Military History, U.S. Army, 2012); and Fredrik Logevall, *Embers of War: The Fall of an Empire and the Making of America's Vietnam* (New York: Random House, 2012).

19. He did so most notably in his *The Two Viet-Nams: A Political and Military Analysis,* 2nd rev. ed. (New York: Praeger, 1967) and in his posthumous *Last Reflections on a War* (Garden City, N.Y.: Doubleday, 1967).

20. Spector, *Advice and Support,* 34.

21. Fall, *The Two Viet-Nams,* 40.

22. Quoted by Fall in *The Two Viet-Nams,* 55.

23. Fall, *Last Reflections on a War,* 120; Fall, *The Two Viet-Nams,* 42.

24. Spector, *Advice and Support,* 23, 40.

25. Fall, *Last Reflections on a War,* 131–40 passim.

26. Spector, *Advice and Support,* 34.

27. Fall, *Last Reflections on a War,* 132; *The Two Viet-Nams,* 468–69n10 (quoting French Air Force general Lionel-Max Chassin). Fall (*The Two Viet-Nams,* 468n26) also states, "According to some sources, Chennault's dismissal on August 7, 1945, as 14th Air Force commander was due to his intervention on behalf of the French."

28. Claire L. Chennault, *Way of the Fighter* (New York: G. P. Putnam's Sons, 1949), 342.

29. But see Smith, "Resurrecting the French Empire," passim, for both British and U.S. support of the French in the early days of the First Indochina War.

30. Spector, *Advice and Support,* 23–24; Gravel, ed., *The Pentagon Papers,* 1:17–18.

31. Bodinier, ed., *La Guerre d'Indochine,* 2:49–51.

32. Gravel, ed., *The Pentagon Papers,* 1:18; Smith, "Resurrecting the French Empire," 4 and passim.

33. Fall, *The Two Viet-Nams,* 472n6.

34. "Memorandum du Général Leclerc pour le Colonel de Guillebon," Kandy [Ceylon], September 7, 1945, in Gilbert Bodinier, *La Guerre d'Indochine, 1945–1954: Texte et Documents,* vol. 1, *Le retour de la France en Indochine, 1945–1946* (Vincennes: SHAT, 1987), 162–63.

35. Spector, *Advice and Support,* 42–43.

36. Fall, *The Two Viet-Nams,* 68–69.

37. Henri Navarre, *Le Temps des Vérités* (Paris: Plon, 1957), 250. English translation by the author.

38. Spector, *Advice and Support,* 98–99.

39. Ibid., 105. See also Gravel, ed., *The Pentagon Papers,* vol. 1, chapter 4.

40. U.S. Joint Chiefs of Staff, *The Joint Chiefs of Staff and the First Indochina War,* 44.

41. Memorandum from General Omar Bradley (Chairman, JCS) to the Secretary of Defense, Washington, April 10, 1950, subject: Strategic Assessment of Southeast Asia, document 3, paragraph 6, in Gravel, ed., *The Pentagon Papers,* 1:364.

42. Ibid., paragraph 9 (page 365).

43. Ibid., paragraph 15 (page 366).

44. Ibid., paragraph 14 (pages 365–66).

45. U.S. Joint Chiefs of Staff, *The Joint Chiefs of Staff and the First Indochina War,* 54. As of July 31, 1950, the U.S. Army was scheduled to provide $11.9 million, the U.S. Navy $15.3 million, and the U.S. Air Force $4.9 million in military equipment to Indochina.

46. Press release by President Truman announcing military assistance to Indochina, June 27, 1950, document 8, in Gravel, ed., *The Pentagon Papers,* 1:372–73.

47. U.S. Joint Chiefs of Staff, *The Joint Chiefs of Staff and the First Indochina War,* 54. Formal military aid agreements between the United States, France, and the Associated States were not signed until December 23, 1950. Known as the Penta-Lateral Agreements, they provided the basis for U.S. economic and military aid to Indochina. See Major General George S. Eckhardt, *Command and Control, 1950–1969* (Washington, D.C.: Department of the Army, 1991), 7.

48. U.S. Joint Chiefs of Staff, *The Joint Chiefs of Staff and the First Indochina War,* 54; Lucien Bodard, *The Quicksand War: Prelude to Vietnam* (Boston: Little, Brown, 1967), 220.

49. U.S. Joint Chiefs of Staff, *The Joint Chiefs of Staff and the First Indochina War,* 59. The Hellcats arrived in Saigon in October. By the end of the year more than thirty B-26 light bombers were delivered, and ninety F8F fighters were scheduled for delivery in 1951. See Plating, "Failure at the Margins," 23n17.

50. U.S. Joint Chiefs of Staff, *The Joint Chiefs of Staff and the First Indochina War,* 55. The survey team completed their mission and left Saigon on August 7.

51. John F. Melby (Chairman, U.S. Joint State-Defense MDAP Survey Mission to Southeast Asia) and Major General Graves B. Erskine, USMC (Chief of Military Group, U.S. Joint State-Defense MDAP Survey Mission to Southeast Asia), Memorandum for the Foreign Military Assistance Coordinating Committee (FMACC), [Saigon], August 6, 1950, subject: Situation in French Indochina, August 1950, page 2, in folder "SE Asia 319.1–452, 1949–1950," box 43 ("Africa to Austria"), Project Decimal File, 1950–1952, Office of Military Assistance, Office of the Assistant Secretary of Defense (International Security Affairs), RG 330 (Records of the Office of the Secretary of Defense), National Archives II, College Park, Maryland.

52. U.S. Joint Chiefs of Staff, *The Joint Chiefs of Staff and the First Indochina War,* 55.

53. Melby and Erskine, Memorandum for the Foreign Military Assistance Coordinating Committee, 4.

54. Spector, *Advice and Support*, 145; Logevall, *Embers of War*, 284–85.

55. U.S. Joint Chiefs of Staff, *The Joint Chiefs of Staff and the First Indochina War*, 85–86.

56. Gravel, ed., *The Pentagon Papers*, 1:200.

57. U.S. Joint Chiefs of Staff, *The Joint Chiefs of Staff and the First Indochina War*, 118.

58. "La Logistique dans la Guerre d'Indochine—Situation à la date du 1er octobre 1952," 6. For example, on December 1, 1952, the FY 52 MDAP program for French forces in Indochina was nearly fulfilled (60 percent for French ground forces; 55 percent for Associated States ground forces; 75 percent for naval forces; and 80 percent for air forces), and some FY 1953 deliveries had already been made.

59. Spector, *Advice and Support*, 146.

60. "La Logistique dans la Guerre d'Indochine—Situation à la date du 1er octobre 1952," 4.

61. Spector, *Advice and Support*, 167–68.

62. Trapnell debriefing, May 3, 1953, document 41, in Gravel, ed., *The Pentagon Papers*, 1:498.

63. U.S. Joint Chiefs of Staff, *The Joint Chiefs of Staff and the First Indochina War*, 219. The measurement ton is a unit of volume in transportation by sea equal to forty cubic feet.

64. Ibid., 218.

65. Ibid., 218–19.

66. "Indochina," *Journal of Military Assistance* 14, no. 80 (December 1961): 125 (table "MA Ship & Harbor Craft Program"). The U.S. Joint Chiefs of Staff history (*The Joint Chiefs of Staff and the First Indochina War*, 219) and Gravel (*The Pentagon Papers*, 1:200) put the total number of vessels supplied by the United States at 438, plus seventy naval aircraft. In 1950, the French Navy in Indochina had only about forty major vessels and about two hundred landing craft. Subsequent MDAP deliveries by 1953 represented about one-third of the naval combatant craft in Indochina and included all the additions and replacements. See U.S. Military Assistance Advisory Group, Indo-China, *Indo-China Country Statement for Presentation of the 1955 MDA Program* (Saigon: HQ, USMAAG-Indo-China, 26 January 1954), 27. In the spring of 1954, the French Navy in Indochina had sixteen F8F fighters, twelve SB2C Helldivers, twenty-five Corsair fighters, eight Privateer long-range reconnaissance aircraft, and nine Grumman Goose scout planes, all supplied by the United States. See U.S. Joint Chiefs of Staff, *The Joint Chiefs of Staff and the First Indochina War*, 219.

67. "Indochina," 124 (table "MA Aircraft Program"). Again, the JCS historians (*The Joint Chiefs of Staff and the First Indochina War*, 219) put the number of aircraft provided to the French Air Force alone at 394 Hellcat fighters, B-26 light bombers, and C-47 cargo planes, and go on to state that in the spring of 1954 the French Air Force in Indochina had 140 F8F fighters, 55 B-26 bombers, 106 C-47 cargo planes, and 164 MO500 light liaison aircraft. In addition, there were 24 C-119 cargo planes, 25 B-26 bombers, and nearly 300 USAF maintenance personnel on loan from the United States. Gravel (*The Pentagon Papers*, 1:200) puts the number of aircraft supplied by the United States at about 500.

68. U.S. Joint Chiefs of Staff, *The Joint Chiefs of Staff and the First Indochina War*, 48.

69. Eckhardt, *Command and Control*, 7; Gravel, ed., *The Pentagon Papers*, 1:197. Brigadier General Francis Gerard Brink died on duty in Saigon on June 24, 1952, and was followed as chief, MAAG-Indochina, by Major General Thomas J. H. Trapnell (August 1,

1952–April 11, 1954), and Lieutenant General John W. "Iron Mike" O'Daniel (April 12, 1954–October 23, 1955).

70. Eckhardt, *Command and Control,* 7.

71. Gravel, ed., *The Pentagon Papers,* 1:78. French attitudes toward American aid grew out of a more profound concern with the decline of French power and influence and the rise of American prestige and leadership in the world. See Martin Windrow, *The Last Valley: Dien Bien Phu and the French Defeat in Vietnam* (Cambridge, Mass.: Da Capo, 2004), 178. For other views on French attitudes toward and impedance of MAAG-Indochina, see U.S. Joint Chiefs of Staff, *The Joint Chiefs of Staff and the First Indochina War,* 61; Logevall, *Embers of War,* 308–9; Stewart, *Deepening Involvement,* 11.

72. Gravel, ed., *The Pentagon Papers,* 1:200.

73. Ibid., 1:197.

74. Trapnell debriefing, May 3, 1954, document 41, in Gravel, ed., *The Pentagon Papers,* 1:493. Major General Trapnell noted at the same time, "Due to the stress of constant warfare, circumstances are such that strict control is impossible. For example, an MDAP rifle, abandoned in battle may be acquired by a Viet Minh soldier, who will forfeit the same weapon upon his death or capture by paramilitary forces."

75. Ibid., 1:490.

76. Eckhardt, *Command and Control,* 7; Gravel, ed., *The Pentagon Papers,* 1:200; Spector, *Advice and Support,* 115–17 passim.

77. Gravel, ed., *The Pentagon Papers,* 1:200; Eckhardt, *Command and Control,* 10. Of the total, only 128 were actually advisors. Another two hundred were U.S. Air Force aircraft mechanics who had accompanied the forty aircraft given to the French in early 1954.

78. Spector, *Advice and Support,* 118–19. One officer complained that the French never even provided the MAAG with an order of battle for their forces. See also Fredrik Logevall's account of the experiences of Howard Simpson, a press officer in the U.S. Information Service in Saigon in 1952, in *Embers of War,* 308–9.

79. Ibid., 119–20. The petty harassment of the MAAG by the French authorities cited by Spector depicts the all too common reaction of the French to outside assistance.

80. Gravel, ed., *The Pentagon Papers,* 1:78.

81. Spector, *Advice and Support,* 118–19, 148. For example, MAAG-Indochina officers were surprised to find that the French had no stock control system.

82. Ibid., 117.

83. Trapnell debriefing, May 3, 1954, document 41, in Gravel, ed., *The Pentagon Papers,* 1:496–97.

84. Ibid., 1:490. Emphasis in original.

85. Major General Graves B. Erskine, USMC (Chief, Military Group, U.S. Joint MDAP Survey Mission to Southeast Asia), *Summary Report No. 1,* Saigon, August 5, 1950, subject: Situation in Indochina, August 1950, tab A, part 1, pages 3–4, in folder "SE Asia, 319.1–452, 1949–1950," box 61 ("Africa to Austria"), Project Decimal File, 1950–1952, Office of Military Assistance, Office of the Assistant Secretary of Defense (International Security Affairs), RG 330.

86. Spector, *Advice and Support,* 107. Thomas J. H. "Trap" Trapnell (USMA 1927)

became chief of MAAG-Indochina on August 1, 1952, and served until replaced by Major General John W. "Iron Mike" O'Daniel on February 12, 1954.

87. U.S. Joint Chiefs of Staff, *The Joint Chiefs of Staff and the First Indochina War,* 47.

88. Ibid., 108, 120–21.

89. Gravel, ed., *The Pentagon Papers,* 1:67.

90. Spector, *Advice and Support,* 156.

91. Eckhardt, *Command and Control,* 11. Beginning in April 1952, Lieutenant General John Wilson O'Daniel, then commanding general of the U.S. Army, Pacific, was sent to Indochina three times by Admiral Arthur W. Radford, then commander in chief, Pacific, to report on the situation. He then became the third chief of MAAG-Indochina, serving from April 12, 1954, to October 23, 1955.

92. Gravel, ed., *The Pentagon Papers,* 1:215.

93. Eckhardt, *Command and Control,* 11–12.

94. Gravel, ed., *The Pentagon Papers,* 1:179.

95. Ibid., 1:54.

96. Ibid., 1:197.

97. Ibid., 1:179.

98. Such was the assessment of General Giap, the Viet Minh military commander. See Vo Nguyen Giap, *La Guerre de libération et l'armée populaire* (Washington, D.C.: HQDA, OACS G-2, 1955), 25.

99. Thompson, *Lifeblood of War,* 162.

100. Gravel, ed., *The Pentagon Papers,* 1:179–80.

101. Howard R. Simpson, *Tiger in the Barbed Wire: An American in Vietnam, 1952–1991* (New York: Brassey's, 1992), 32.

102. Ibid., 30.

103. Lieutenant General John W. O'Daniel, USA (Chief, U.S. Joint Military Mission to Indochina), *Report of U.S. Special Mission to Indochina (23 January–5 February 1954)—Situation in French Indochina and FUF Materiel Requirements, February 1954,* Pearl Harbor, Hawaii, February 5, 1954, 11, in box 10 ("092 Asia [6-25-48] [2] Section 22"), Geographical File, 1954–56, RG 218.

104. Navarre, *Le Temps des Vérités,* 250.

105. O'Daniel, *Report of U.S. Special Mission to Indochina (23 January–5 February 1954),* 3.

106. Fall, *Street without Joy,* 17, 50n.

107. U.S. Joint Chiefs of Staff, *The Joint Chiefs of Staff and the First Indochina War,* 217. Still, the combined expenditures in Indochina were only about half the amount expended by the United Nations in Korea in three years. See Fall, *Street without Joy,* 307–8.

108. U.S. Joint Chiefs of Staff, *The Joint Chiefs of Staff and the First Indochina War,* 217. In a memorandum for the Special Committee of the National Security Council, dated March 17, 1954, Major General Erskine, then a subcommittee chairman of the President's Special Committee, put the total French expenditure in Indochina from 1946 through 1953 at $5.4 billion. See Memorandum for the Special Committee, NSC, March 17, 1954, subject: Military Implications of the U.S. Position on Indochina in Geneva, document 24, in Gravel, ed., *The Pentagon Papers,* 1:452. The total given by George A. Kelly (*Lost Soldiers: The French Army and Empire in Crisis, 1947–1962* [Cambridge, Mass.: M.I.T. Press, 1965],

33) and Bernard Fall (*Street without Joy,* 308; *Two Vietnams,* 472n6) is around $11 billion, a sum that more closely represents the total expenditures by France, the Associated States, and the United States combined.

109. U.S. Joint Chiefs of Staff, *The Joint Chiefs of Staff and the First Indochina War,* 217. See also: Gravel, ed., *The Pentagon Papers,* 1:77; Fall, *Two Vietnams,* 472n6; Fall, *Street without Joy,* 308. Major General Erskine put the amount allocated by the United States as of March 17, 1954, at $2.4 billion. See Gravel, ed., *The Pentagon Papers,* 1:452, document 24. However, in *The Pentagon Papers* (1:200) Gravel put the amount provided by the United States by July 1954 at $2.6 billion.

110. U.S. Joint Chiefs of Staff, *The Joint Chiefs of Staff and the First Indochina War,* 217–18. The bulk of the funds were expended in FY 1954. For example, the MDAP funding for FY1950 through FY 1953 was $773 million, but the funding for FY 1954 alone was $535 million.

111. Joseph Jeremiah Zasloff, *The Role of Sanctuary in Insurgency: Communist China's Support to the Vietminh, 1946–1954* (Santa Monica, Calif.: RAND Corporation, May 1967), 56. General Giap also claimed that in 1952 the United States provided 35 percent of the total cost of the war to the French. See Edgar O'Ballance, *The Indo-China War 1945–1954: A Study in Guerrilla Warfare* (London: Faber and Faber, 1964), 173n1.

112. O'Ballance, *The Indo-China War,* 197.

113. Gravel, ed., *The Pentagon Papers,* 1:77. Congress appropriated $1.175 billion for 1954, including $400 million in direct payments to the CEFEO, $325 million for supplies, and $385 million for budgetary support of the Associated States. See Zasloff, *The Role of Sanctuary in Insurgency,* 56.

114. Newspaper quoted by Fall in *The Two Viet-Nams,* 473n15; Bodard, *The Quicksand War,* 221.

115. Memorandum from Admiral Arthur Radford (Chairman, JCS) for the President's Special Committee on Indochina, March 29, 1954, subject: Discussions with General Paul Ely, document 26, in Gravel, ed., *The Pentagon Papers,* 1:455–60.

116. Ibid., 1:456.

117. Ibid. General Ely also displayed little interest in Admiral Radford's offers of U.S. assistance in the conduct of "psychological, clandestine and guerrilla warfare."

118. Ibid., 1:457–58.

119. Ibid., 1:457.

120. Ibid., 1:457–58.

121. Gravel, ed., *The Pentagon Papers,* 1:202–3.

122. Radford memo, March 29, 1954, in Gravel, ed., *The Pentagon Papers,* 1:458.

123. U.S. Joint Chiefs of Staff, *The Joint Chiefs of Staff and the First Indochina War,* 220.

124. Ibid., 221.

125. Ibid., 220.

126. Gravel, ed., *The Pentagon Papers,* 1:201.

8. Viet Minh Sources of Supply

1. Bernard B. Fall, *Le Viet-Minh: La République Démocratique du Viet-Nam, 1945–1960* (Paris: Librairie Armand Colin, 1960), 187.

2. Allegedly, under the terms of the French–Viet Minh Anti-Japanese Accord of March 1944, the French supplied the Viet Minh with 165 Remington rifles and forty carbines on March 23, 1944, with another delivery made by a Colonel Reul on March 28. See Nowfel Leulliot and Danny O'Hara, eds., "Early Days: The Development of the Viet Minh Military Machine," http://indochine54.free.fr/vm/early.html (accessed December 2, 2012).

3. Leulliot and O'Hara, eds., "Early Days."

4. Hoang Van Chi, *From Colonialism to Communism* (New York: Praeger, 1964), 67, quoted in BDM Corporation, *A Study of Strategic Lessons Learned in Vietnam*, vol. 1, *The Enemy* (McLean, Va.: BDM Corporation, November 30, 1979), 5–51.

5. King C. Chen, *Vietnam and China, 1938–1954* (Princeton: Princeton Univ. Press, 1969), 11.

6. Leulliot and O'Hara, eds., "Early Days."

7. For example, Lieutenant Colonel Serieye (*Le Viêt-Minh: les origines et l'évolution des Forces Armées du Viêt-Minh* [The Viet Minh: The Origins and Evolution of the Viet Minh Armed Forces] [Washington, D.C.: HQDA, OACS G-2, February 1951], 6) wrote that the Japanese turned over thirty-five thousand rifles and about one thousand automatic weapons, and Joseph Jeremiah Zasloff (*The Role of Sanctuary in Insurgency: Communist China's Support to the Vietminh, 1946–1954* [Santa Monica, Calif.: RAND Corporation, May 1967], 18) wrote that the Japanese delivered to the Viet Minh thirty thousand rifles, one thousand automatic weapons, and several 75 mm guns that had been seized by the Japanese from the French after March 9, 1945.

8. Ronald H. Spector, *Advice and Support: The Early Years, 1941–1960* (Washington, D.C.: Center of Military History, U.S. Army, 1983), 39.

9. Mike Gravel, ed., *The Pentagon Papers: The Defense Department History of United States Decisionmaking in Vietnam*, vol. 1 (Boston: Beacon, 1971), 44. An OSS operative, Major Allison K. Thomas, parachuted into Tonkin near Thai Nguyen on July 16, 1945, and subsequently met Ho Chi Minh and supplied a few weapons to the Viet Minh. See U.S. Joint Chiefs of Staff, Office of Joint History, *The Joint Chiefs of Staff and the First Indochina War, 1947–1954*, History of the Joint Chiefs of Staff (Washington, D.C.: Office of Joint History, Office of the Chairman of the Joint Chiefs of Staff, 2004), 10–11. The Vietnamese story, perhaps a myth, is that in March 1944 the only modern weapons possessed by General Giap's troops were two Colt .45-caliber semiautomatic pistols and one .45-caliber Thompson submachine gun provided by the OSS. See Leulliot and Danny O'Hara, eds., "Early Days."

10. Gravel, ed., *The Pentagon Papers*, 1:51.

11. Ibid., 1:42.

12. Ibid., 1:43; Bernard B. Fall, *The Two Viet-Nams: A Political and Military Analysis*, 2nd rev. ed. (New York: Praeger, 1967), 100.

13. Bernard B. Fall, *Last Reflections on a War* (Garden City, N.Y.: Doubleday, 1967), 83.

14. U.S. Joint Chiefs of Staff, *The Joint Chiefs of Staff and the First Indochina War*, 11.

15. Martin Windrow, *The Last Valley: Dien Bien Phu and the French Defeat in Vietnam* (New York: Da Capo, 2004) 80.

16. Zasloff, *The Role of Sanctuary in Insurgency*, 6–7.

17. Fall, *The Two Viet-Nams*, 65; Chen, *Vietnam and China*, 127. It is apparently this

transaction that Serieye (*Le Viêt-Minh,* 6) and Zasloff (*The Role of Sanctuary in Insurgency,* 18) erroneously report as being a direct transfer from the Japanese to the Viet Minh. Fredrik Logevall (*Embers of War: The Fall of an Empire and the Making of America's Vietnam* [New York: Random House, 2012], 127) noted that Ho Chi Minh agreed to use the proceeds from the "Week of Gold" to buy thirty thousand rifles and two thousand machine guns from the Chinese. Perhaps the same transaction is cited by Fall, Chen, Serieye, Zasloff, and Logevall.

18. Bernard B. Fall, *Street without Joy: Insurgency in Indochina, 1946–63,* 3rd rev. ed. (Harrisburg, Pa.: Stackpole, 1963), 26.

19. George K. Tanham, *Communist Revolutionary Warfare: From the Vietminh to the Viet Cong,* rev. ed. (New York: Praeger, 1967), 67n.

20. Gilbert Bodinier, ed., *La Guerre d'Indochine, 1945–1954: Texte et Documents,* vol. 2, *Indochine, 1947—Règlement politique ou solution militaire?* (Vincennes: SHAT, 1989), 128, 130; Chen, *Vietnam and China,* 139.

21. Edgar O'Ballance, *The Indo-China War 1945–1954: A Study in Guerrilla Warfare* (London: Faber and Faber, 1964), 118.

22. Vo Nguyen Giap, *People's War, People's Army: The Viet Cong Insurrection Manual for Underdeveloped Countries* (New York: Praeger, 1962), 134.

23. Tanham, *Communist Revolutionary Warfare,* 67. Certain special items were worth up to three hectares of land.

24. Giap, *People's War, People's Army,* 52.

25. Headquarters, Department of the Army, Office of the Assistant Chief of Staff, G-2, *Viet Minh Logistics* (Washington, D.C.: HQDA, OACS G-2, May 6, 1953), 8–9; Chen, *Vietnam and China,* 160.

26. Joseph R. Starobin, *Eyewitness in Indo-China* (New York: Cameron and Kahn, 1954), 90.

27. Lucien Bodard, *The Quicksand War: Prelude to Vietnam* (Boston: Little, Brown, 1967), 219.

28. *Viet Minh Logistics,* 9.

29. U.S. Far East Command, General Headquarters, Military Intelligence Section, Allied Translator and Interpreter Service, *Information on Viet Minh Forces, Indo-China* (Tokyo: GHQ, USFEC, MI Section, ATIS, August 11, 1951), 30.

30. Douglas Porch, "Dien Bien Phu and the Opium Connection," *MHQ: The Quarterly Journal of Military History* 7, no. 4 (summer 1995): 102–4.

31. Chen, *Vietnam and China,* 189–90.

32. Starobin, *Eyewitness in Indo-China,* 100–106.

33. Chen, *Vietnam and China,* 262.

34. Bodinier, ed., *La Guerre d'Indochine,* 2:128.

35. The workshop at Quang Ngai was reported to have been under the management of one Major Saito, a former Japanese officer. See Windrow, *The Last Valley,* 89.

36. Tanham, *Communist Revolutionary Warfare,* 67–68.

37. Chen, *Vietnam and China,* 190.

38. Lieutenant Colonel Boussarie, *La Situation des forces ennemies en Indochine (1945–janvier 1954)* [The Situation of the Enemy Forces in Indo-China] (Washington, D.C.:

HQDA, OACSI, 1954), 3.

39. Tanham, *Communist Revolutionary Warfare,* 68.

40. Bodard, *The Quicksand War,* 245.

41. *Information on Viet Minh Forces, Indo-China,* 43.

42. Ibid., 46–47.

43. Giap, *People's War, People's Army,* 135.

44. The Viet Minh purchase of arms in Thailand is discussed in some detail by Bodinier (Bodinier, ed., *La Guerre d'Indochine,* 2:130–32), from which account the following description is derived.

45. Chen, *Vietnam and China,* 189.

46. Tanham, *Communist Revolutionary Warfare,* 67; Chen, *Vietnam and China,* 189; Fall, *The Two Viet-Nams,* 469n14. The office was moved to Rangoon, Burma, after the beginning of the Korean War.

47. *Viet Minh Logistics,* 9.

48. Bernard B. Fall, *Hell in a Very Small Place: The Siege of Dien Bien Phu* (New York: Vintage, 1966), 9.

49. Bodinier, ed., *La Guerre d'Indochine,* 2:94.

50. Logevall, *Embers of War,* 127.

51. Fall, *The Two Viet-Nams,* 70–71. Presumably, the French believed that the U.S. Central Intelligence Agency was behind such shipments.

52. Ibid., 119; Ronald J. Cima, ed., *Vietnam: A Country Study,* Department of the Army Pamphlet No. 550-32 (Washington, D.C.: U.S. Government Printing Office, 1989), 221. In the fall of 1945, Ho Chi Minh sent to Stalin two requests for military aid and Soviet advisors but received no reply. See Qiang Zhai, *China and the Vietnam Wars, 1950–1975* (Chapel Hill: Univ. of North Carolina Press, 2000), 13.

53. Fall, *Le Viet-Minh,* 119. However, Christopher E. Goscha ("'Hell in a Very Small Place': Cold War and Decolonisation in the Assault on the Vietnamese Body at Dien Bien Phu," *European Journal of East Asian Studies* 9, no. 2 [December 2010]: 204) has asserted that the Soviets did supply the Viet Minh with a number of the much-feared Katyusha truck-mounted multiple rocket launchers, which were used at Dien Bien Phu, as well as earlier deliveries of surgical equipment, medicines, and antibiotics.

54. American University, Special Operations Research Office, Foreign Area Studies Division, *U.S. Army Area Handbook for Vietnam,* Department of the Army Pamphlet No. 550-55 (Washington, D.C.: HQDA, September 1962), 457; Fall, *Le Viet-Minh,* 119.

55. Henry-Jean Loustau, *Les derniers combats d'Indochine, 1952–1954* (Paris: Éditions Albin Michel, 1984), 66.

56. Zasloff, *The Role of Sanctuary in Insurgency,* v.

57. Direct telegraphic communications between the two Party headquarters were not established until the spring of 1947. See Qiang Zhai, *China and the Vietnam Wars,* 12.

58. Qiang Zhai, *China and the Vietnam Wars,* 12.

59. Chen, *Vietnam and China,* 188.

60. Ibid., 260–61.

61. "Chinese Communist Assistance to the Viet Minh," *Intelligence Review* 190 (March 1952): 30.

62. Chen, *Vietnam and China,* 189.

63. Windrow, *The Last Valley,* 108. The Nationalists crossed into Tonkin east of Lang Son and were eventually passed on to Taiwan.

64. O'Ballance, *The Indo-China War,* 106; Chen, *Vietnam and China,* 261.

65. Chen, *Vietnam and China,* 261.

66. Qiang Zhai, *China and the Vietnam Wars,* 18.

67. Logevall, *Embers of War,* 242.

68. Chen, *Vietnam and China,* 269.

69. Ibid., 249, 251.

70. Ibid., 272.

71. Ibid., 272–73.

72. "Chinese Communist Assistance to the Viet Minh," 33.

73. Marina Berthier and Nicolas Chicheportiche, *Dossier Documentaire: L'année 1950 en Indochine—Le désastre de Cao Bang* ([Paris]: ECPAD, September 1, 2010), 12, http://www.ecpad.fr/wp-content/uploads/2010/08/indochine_1950.pdf (accessed December 6, 2012). King C. Chen (*Vietnam and China,* 262–63) estimates that between January and September 1950, the Viet Minh received from the Communist Chinese about 40,000 rifles, 125 machine guns, 75 mortars, 3,000 boxes of ammunition, and 870 tons of other military equipment. Qiang Zhai (*China and the Vietnam Wars,* 20) estimates that between April and September 1950, "China sent to the Viet Minh large quantities of military and nonmilitary supplies, including 14,000 rifles and pistols, 1,700 machine guns and recoilless rifles, 150 mortars, 60 artilleries [artillery pieces], and 300 bazookas, as well as munitions, medicine, communications materials, clothes, and 2,800 tons of food." See also Windrow, *The Last Valley,* 152–57.

74. "Chinese Communist Assistance to the Viet Minh," 33.

75. Chen, *Vietnam and China,* 271–72, citing a Radio Saigon broadcast of January 23, 1952.

76. Michael W. Clodfelter, *Vietnam in Military Statistics: A History of the Indochina Wars, 1772–1991* (Jefferson, N.C.: McFarland, 1995), 18–19. Yet another estimate of the monthly rate is provided by Martin Windrow (*The Last Valley,* 152), citing Pierre Recolle's *Pourquoi Dien Bien Phu?* (Paris: Flammarion, 1968, 67 et seq.): 250 tons per month in the first half of 1952; 450 tons in December 1952; 900 tons per month in early 1953; 2,000 tons per month by June 1953; and 4,000 tons per month in 1954. See also Chen, *Vietnam and China,* 275–76.

77. Fall, *Hell in a Very Small Place,* 294.

78. Headquarters, Department of the Army, Office of the Assistant Chief of Staff, G-2, *Indochina SITREP No. 9* (Washington, D.C.: HQDA, OACS G-2, October 30, 1953), paragraph 3, and Headquarters, Department of the Army, Office of the Assistant Chief of Staff, G-2, *Indochina SITREP No. 1* (Washington, D.C.: HQDA, OACS G-2, September 14, 1953), paragraph 3. To transport the additional supplies, the number of trucks available to the Viet Minh increased from about 450 in early 1953 to over 800 by September 1953. Nearly all of the additional trucks were provided by the Chinese.

79. Tanham, *Communist Revolutionary Warfare,* 68.

80. Boussarie, *La Situation des forces ennemies en Indochine,* 24–25.

81. *Viet Minh Logistics,* 12.

82. Qiang Zhai, "Transplanting the Chinese Model: Chinese Military Advisers and the First Vietnam War, 1950–1954," *Journal of Military History* 57, no. 4 (October 1993): 715.

83. Qiang Zhai, *China and the Vietnam Wars,* 19.

84. Boussarie, *La Situation des forces ennemies en Indochine,* 4; "Chinese Communist Assistance to the Viet Minh," 32.

85. "Chinese Communist Army Supply System," *USAFFE Intelligence Digest* 4, no. 4 (June 1954): 37; Boussarie, *La Situation des forces ennemies en Indochine,* 4; Serieye, *Le Viêt-Minh,* 9.

86. Fall, *Le Viet-Minh,* 196.

87. Chen, *Vietnam and China,* 276n196.

88. *Viet Minh Logistics,* 6; Chen, *Vietnam and China,* 261.

89. Qiang Zhai, "Transplanting the Chinese Model," 698; *Viet Minh Logistics,* 6.

90. Chen, *Vietnam and China,* 272.

91. Qiang Zhai, *China and the Vietnam Wars,* 35.

92. Ibid., 36.

93. Headquarters, Department of the Army, Assistant Chief of Staff, G-2, *Terrain Estimate of Indo-China* (Washington, D.C.: HQDA, OACS G-2, December 22, 1950), 4.

94. Chen, *Vietnam and China,* 276; Tanham, *Communist Revolutionary Warfare,* 69.

95. Bodard, *The Quicksand War,* 243; *Terrain Estimate of Indo-China,* 4; "Chinese Communist Assistance to the Viet Minh," 33.

96. *Terrain Estimate of Indo-China,* 4; *U.S. Army Area Handbook for Vietnam,* 438; Chen, *Vietnam and China,* 262–63, 269–70; "Chinese Communist Assistance to the Viet Minh," 33; *U.S. Army Area Handbook for Vietnam,* 438.

97. Chen, *Vietnam and China,* 262, 275; *Terrain Estimate of Indo-China,* 4.

98. Chen, *Vietnam and China,* 274.

99. *Information on Viet Minh Forces, Indo-China,* 40; Claude Guigues, "Les étrangers chez le Viêt Minh," *Indochine-Sud-Est Asiatique* 14 (January 1953): 48–49; Fall, *Last Reflections on a War,* 87.

100. Qiang Zhai, *China and the Vietnam Wars,* 11.

101. Ibid., 12.

102. Ibid.

103. Qiang Zhai, "Transplanting the Chinese Model," 693–94.

104. Qiang Zhai, *China and the Vietnam Wars,* 19. General Wei Guo Qing was the official chairman of the CMAG from April 1950 to September 1955, although he was outranked by General Chen Geng from July to November 1950. See also Logevall, *Embers of War,* 234–35.

105. Ibid., 29.

106. Arthur J. Dommen, *The Indochinese Experience of the French and the Americans: Nationalism and Communism in Cambodia, Laos, and Vietnam* (Bloomington: Indiana Univ. Press, 2001), 200, cited in Jeffrey Record, "External Assistance: Enabler of Insurgent Success," *Parameters* 26, no. 3 (autumn 2006): 44–45.

107. Qiang Zhai, *China and the Vietnam Wars,* 26. The PAVN designation was adopted in 1950.

108. Qiang Zhai, "Transplanting the Chinese Model," 708.

109. Boussarie, *La Situation des forces ennemies en Indochine,* 18; *Information on Viet Minh Forces, Indo-China,* 56, 59; Windrow, *The Last Valley,* 157–58; Zasloff, *The Role of Sanctuary in Insurgency,* 19; Nhu Phong, "Intellectuals, Writers, and Artists," *China Quarterly* 9 (January–March 1962): 51, cited in Zasloff, *The Role of Sanctuary in Insurgency,* 46.

110. Headquarters, Department of the Army, Office of the Assistant Chief of Staff, G-2, *Viet Minh Tactics and Techniques in Indo-China* (Washington, D.C.: HQDA, OACS G-2, November 17, 1950), 2–3.

111. Fall, *Le Viet-Minh,* 195; O'Ballance, *The Indo-China War,* 105–6; Chen, *Vietnam and China,* 262.

112. "Chinese Communist Assistance to the Viet Minh," 32; Zasloff, *The Role of Sanctuary in Insurgency,* 19; Chen, *Vietnam and China,* 263. The French were well aware of what was happening, but could do little about it.

113. *Viet Minh Tactics and Techniques in Indo-China,* 3.

114. "Chinese Communist Assistance to the Viet Minh," 33.

115. Ibid.

116. Fall, *Le Viet-Minh,* 196.

117. Chen, *Vietnam and China,* 274.

118. Ibid., 275.

119. Fall, *Le Viet-Minh,* 120, 196; Robert B. Rigg, *Red China's Fighting Hordes,* rev. ed. (Harrisburg, Pa.: Military Service Publishing Company, 1952), 320; Guigues, "Les étrangers chez le Viêt Minh," 52; Chen, *Vietnam and China,* 273; "Chinese Communist Assistance to the Viet Minh," 33.

120. Jules Roy, *The Battle of Dien Bien Phu* (New York: Harper and Row, 1965), 203.

121. Zasloff, *The Role of Sanctuary in Insurgency,* 20; *Viet Minh Logistics,* 11.

122. Boussarie, *La Situation des forces ennemies en Indochine,* 15–16.

123. Lieutenant General John W. O'Daniel (Chief, U.S. Joint Military Mission to Indochina), *Report of U. S. Special Mission to Indochina (23 January–5 February 1954)—Situation in French Indochina and FUF Materiel Requirements, February 1954,* Pearl Harbor, Hawaii, February 5, 1954, 4, in box 10 ("092 Asia [6-25-48] [2] Section 22"), Geographical File, 1954–1956, RG 218 (Records of the U.S. Joint Chiefs of Staff), National Archives II, College Park, Maryland.

124. Zasloff, *The Role of Sanctuary in Insurgency,* 20.

125. Qiang Zhai, "Transplanting the Chinese Model," 689–715. It should be pointed out that Qiang Zhai relies on Chinese sources, some of which were published during the Sino-Vietnamese conflict in the 1970s.

126. Douglas Porch, review of Howard R. Simpson, *Dien Bien Phu: The Epic Battle America Forgot,* in *Naval War College Review* 48, no. 2 (spring 1995): 157–58.

127. Porch, "Dien Bien Phu and the Opium Connection," 108.

128. Bodard, *The Quicksand War,* 246; *Viet Minh Tactics and Techniques in Indo-China,* 3; Zasloff, *The Role of Sanctuary in Insurgency,* viii.

129. Howard R. Simpson, *Tiger in the Barbed Wire: An American in Vietnam, 1952–1991* (New York: Brassey's, 1992), 219. Major General Tran Cong Man, a former Viet Minh engineer regiment commander, told Simpson this in Hanoi in 1991.

130. Roy, *The Battle of Dien Bien Phu,* 203.

131. Quoted in Gravel, ed., *The Pentagon Papers,* 1:49–50.

132. Qiang Zhai, *China and the Vietnam Wars,* 1.

133. For the passages quoted, see Qiang Zhai, *China and the Vietnam Wars,* 3–5.

134. "Report by National Security Council on the Position of the United States with Respect to Indochina," [NSC-64], February 27, 1950, document 1, in Gravel, ed., *The Pentagon Papers,* 1:362.

135. U.S. Central Intelligence Agency, *National Intelligence Estimate: Indochina: Current Situation and Probable Developments,* NIE-5 (Langley, Va.: USCIA, December 29, 1950), 2–3.

136. This and the following two quotations are from U.S. Central Intelligence Agency, *National Intelligence Estimate: Probable Developments in Indochina during the Remainder of 1951,* NIE-35 (Langley, Va.: USCIA, August 7, 1951), 2–4.

137. National Security Council Staff Study on United States Objectives and Courses of Actions with Respect to Communist Aggression in Southeast Asia, February 13, 1952, document 10, in Gravel, ed., *The Pentagon Papers,* 1:379.

138. U.S. Central Intelligence Agency, *National Intelligence Estimate: Probable Developments in Indochina through mid-1954,* NIE-91 (Langley, Va.: USCIA, June 4, 1953), document 15, paragraph 24, in Gravel, ed., *The Pentagon Papers,* 1:397.

139. Henri Navarre, *Le Temps des Vérités* (Paris: Plon, 1957), 244.

140. Starobin, *Eyewitness in Indo-China,* 176–77.

141. Zasloff, *The Role of Sanctuary in Insurgency,* v, 15, 77.

142. *Viet Minh Logistics,* 14.

143. Zasloff, *The Role of Sanctuary in Insurgency,* 53–54.

144. See, among others, Qiang Zhai, *China and the Vietnam Wars,* and Bob Seals, "Chinese Support for North Vietnam during the Vietnam War: The Decisive Edge," *Military History Online,* September 23, 2008, 1, http://www.militaryhistoryonline.com/20thcentury/articles/chinesesupport.aspx (accessed August 16, 2010).

145. Jung Chang and Jon Halliday, *Mao: The Unknown Story* (New York: Knopf, 2005), 357, quoted in Seals, "Chinese Support for North Vietnam," 6.

9. The Shape of Battles to Come

1. The history of Indochina in World War II and the immediate postwar period is relatively well-documented. For the brief outline that follows I have relied primarily on U.S. Joint Chiefs of Staff, Office of Joint History, *The Joint Chiefs of Staff and the First Indochina War, 1947–1954* (Washington, D.C.: Office of Joint History, Office of the Chairman of the Joint Chiefs of Staff, 2004); Bernard B. Fall, *The Two Viet-Nams: A Political and Military Analysis,* 2nd rev. ed. (New York: Praeger, 1967); Harvey H. Smith et al., *Area Handbook for North Vietnam,* Department of the Army Pamphlet No. 550-57 (Washington, D.C.: U.S. Government Printing Office, 1968); George K. Tanham, *Communist Revolutionary Warfare: From the Vietminh to the Viet Cong,* rev. ed. (New York: Praeger, 1967); and Commander in Chief, French Forces in the Far East, *A Translation from the French: Lessons of the War in Indochina,* vol. 2 (Santa Monica, Calif.: RAND Corporation, May 1967), 10. T. O. Smith, "Resurrecting the French Empire: British Military Aid to Vietnam September 1945–June 1947," *University of Sussex Journal of Con-*

temporary History 11 (2007): 1–12, provides an interesting British perspective.

2. American policy in the immediate postwar period was to avoid any appearance of supporting the reestablishment of the French and Dutch colonial regimes in Southeast Asia, but that policy soon softened. See U.S. Joint Chiefs of Staff, *The Joint Chiefs of Staff and the First Indochina War,* 15.

3. See Smith, "Resurrecting the French Empire," passim.

4. "Rapport du Général Leclerc à l'Amiral D'Argenlieu," August 28, 1945, in *La Guerre d'Indochine, 1945–1954: Texte et Documents,* vol. 1, *Le retour de la France en Indochine, 1945–1946,* ed. Gilbert Bodinier (Château de Vincennes: SHAT, 1987), 149–53. English translation by the author. Admiral Thierry d'Argenlieu did not arrive in Saigon until October 31, 1945.

5. Lord Louis Mountbatten, the commander of Southeast Asia Command, had hoped to turn over responsibility for Indochina to General Leclerc in October 1945. See Smith, "Resurrecting the French Empire," 3.

6. For Operation BEN TRÉ and the subsequent Franco–Viet Minh agreements, see Fredrik Logevall, *Embers of War: The Fall of an Empire and the Making of America's Vietnam* (New York: Random House, 2012), 132–33.

7. Headquarters, U.S. Army Forces, Far East (Advanced), Office of the Assistant Chief of Staff, G-2, Intelligence Division, Strategic Branch/Geographic Branch, *Special Report No. 127: Some Geographical Aspects of Indochina,* mimeograph (Tokyo: HQ, USAFFE, OACS G-2, March 12, 1953), 19 (cited hereafter as *Special Report No. 127*); American University, Special Operations Research Office, Foreign Area Studies Division, *U.S. Army Area Handbook for Vietnam,* Department of the Army Pamphlet No. 550-55 (Washington, D.C.: HQDA, September 1962), 293.

8. Of particular interest for the situation in Indochina from March 6 to November 19, 1946, is the series of reviews of Stein Tønnesen, *Vietnam 1946: How the War Began* (Berkeley: Univ. of California Press, 2010), in *H-Diplo Roundtable Review* 11, no. 19 (April 2010), http://www.h-net.org/~diplo/roundtable/PDF/Roundtable-XI-19.pdf (accessed May 9, 2014).

9. Edgar O'Ballance, *The Indo-China War, 1945–1954: A Study in Guerrilla Warfare* (London: Faber and Faber, 1964), 72–73.

10. George A. Kelly, *Lost Soldiers: The French Army and Empire in Crisis, 1947–1962* (Cambridge, Mass.: M.I.T. Press, 1965), 44; *Area Handbook for North Vietnam,* 58; Ronald J. Cima, ed., *Vietnam: A Country Study,* Department of the Army Pamphlet No. 550-32 (Washington, D.C.: U.S. Government Printing Office, 1989), 54. Estimates of the Vietnamese casualties, mostly civilian, range as high as twenty thousand.

11. Quoted in Kelly, *Lost Soldiers,* 44.

12. Ibid., 45.

13. Douglas Pike, *Viet Cong: The Organization and Techniques of the National Liberation Front of South Vietnam* (Cambridge, Mass.: M.I.T. Press, 1966), 49.

14. The process is described in detail in Fall, *The Two Viet-Nams,* 106–7.

15. Fall, *The Two Viet-Nams,* 108; Kelly, *Lost Soldiers,* 47.

16. Fall, *The Two Viet-Nams,* 108. The Catholic strongholds were secured in Operation ANTHRACITE.

17. *Lessons Learned in the Indochina War,* 2:16.

18. The following account of Lieutenant General Blaizot's activities is based primarily on *Lessons Learned in the Indochina War,* 2:16–18.

19. Viet Minh attacks along RC 4, which ran along the Chinese border for 150 miles from Tien Yen to Cao Bang, began to increase in frequency and severity in 1948. See Logevall, *Embers of War,* 207–8.

20. *Lessons Learned in the Indochina War,* 2:18.

21. Fall, *The Two Viet-Nams,* 108.

22. O'Ballance, *The Indo-China War,* 94.

23. Tanham, *Communist Revolutionary Warfare,* 101; Julian Thompson, *The Lifeblood of War: Logistics in Armed Conflict* (London: Brassey's, 1991), 145.

24. Thompson, *Lifeblood of War,* 146; Phillip B. Davidson, *Vietnam at War: The History, 1946–1975* (Novato, Calif.: Presidio, 1988), 70–71.

25. Tanham, *Communist Revolutionary Warfare,* 16–17.

26. Fall, *The Two Viet-Nams,* 112–13. On the three-stage concept in both its Maoist and Viet Minh forms, see Logevall, *Embers of War,* 150, 170–71, and Martin Windrow, *The Last Valley: Dien Bien Phu and the French Defeat in Vietnam* (New York: Da Capo, 2004), 146–47.

27. Lien-Hang T. Nguyen, *Hanoi's War: An International History of the War for Peace in Vietnam* (Chapel Hill: Univ. of North Carolina Press, 2012), 27.

28. Tanham, *Communist Revolutionary Warfare,* 23.

29. Bernard B. Fall, *Street without Joy: Insurgency in Indochina, 1946–63,* 3rd rev. ed. (Harrisburg, Pa.: Stackpole, 1963), 31–32.

30. Quoted in Fall, *Street without Joy,* 32.

31. Tanham, *Communist Revolutionary Warfare,* 73.

32. D. M. O. Miller, "'A Handful of Rice?': Logistics in the Viet Minh Campaign," *Army Quarterly and Defence Journal* 100, no. 1 (April 1970): 106.

33. Gilbert Bodinier, ed., *La Guerre d'Indochine, 1945–1954: Texte et Documents,* vol. 2, *Indochine, 1947—Règlement politique ou solution militaire?* (Château de Vincennes: SHAT, 1989), 328.

34. The concept for Operation LEA as it existed on July 9, 1947, is contained in Commandement des Troupes Françaises en Indochine du Nord, État-Major, 3e Bureau, "Étude sur la conduite d'une opération d'ensemble par le général commandant les T.F.I.N. pour disloquer le 'réduit national' viêt-minh," No. 15551/3.T 5, Hanoi, July 9, 1947, box 10 H 2516, Fonds Indochine, SHAT (reproduced in Bodinier, ed., *La Guerre d'Indochine,* 2:320–23). Additional details, including the listing of forces to be made available for the operation, were provided in Commandement Supérieur des Troupes Françaises en Extrême-Orient, État-Major, 3e Bureau, "Instruction personnelle et secrète pour le général commandant les T.F.I.N.," No. 1882/3/8, Saigon, August 4, 1947, boxes 10 H 165-1 and 10 H 950, Fonds Indochine, SHAT. Unless otherwise noted, the following account of the concept and execution of Operation LEA is based primarily on Bodinier, ed., *La Guerre d'Indochine,* 2:305–45 passim, with additional material from Thompson, *Lifeblood of War,* 141–44; Davidson, *Vietnam at War,* 48–50; Ronald H. Spector, *Advice and Support: The Early Years, 1941–1960* (Washington, D.C.: Center of Military History, U.S. Army, 1983), 89–90; Logevall, *Embers*

of War, 201–3.

35. Bodinier, ed., *La Guerre d'Indochine,* 2:331.

36. Fall, *Street without Joy,* 28; Davidson, *Vietnam at War,* 48–49.

37. Some commentators attribute the fact that the French did not achieve greater success in their autumn 1947 campaign at least in part to events five thousand miles away on the island of Madagascar. Reinforcements intended for the French forces in Indochina were diverted to suppress the nationalist rebellion on Madagascar that erupted in 1947. Consequently, their arrival in Indochina was delayed until after Operation LEA had reached its conclusion, thereby providing a convenient excuse for the lack of greater success in Operation LEA. See Fall, *Street without Joy,* 28.

38. Bodinier, ed., *La Guerre d'Indochine,* 2:341. The figures are for both Operation LEA and Operation CEINTURE, which followed. However, without indicating his sources Spector (*Advice and Support,* 90) puts the number of French casualties at over one thousand killed and three thousand wounded. It may be that Spector refers to total French Union casualties while Bodinier lists only the French (European) casualties.

39. Ibid., 2:341–42.

40. Ibid., 2:340.

41. *Lessons Learned in the Indochina War,* 2:170.

42. Bodinier, ed., *La Guerre d'Indochine,* 2:337–41 passim; Davidson, *Vietnam at War,* 50.

43. Tanham, *Communist Revolutionary Warfare,* 26.

44. Jean Boucher de Crèvecoeur, *La Bataille de la Frontière de Chine en Octobre 1950* [The Battle of the Chinese Frontier in October 1950] (Washington, D.C.: HQDA, OACS G-2, February 13–14, 1952), 2. The following narrative relies primarily on Boucher de Crèvecoeur's account, but see also Jacques Dalloz, *The War in Indochina, 1945–54* (New York: Barnes and Noble, 1990), 126–29; Davidson, *Vietnam at War,* 77; and Windrow, *The Last Valley,* 103–7.

45. For an excellent description of the terrain and the difficulties of conducting convoy operations in the area during this period, see Windrow, *The Last Valley,* 103–7.

46. Quoted in Lucien Bodard, *The Quicksand War: Prelude to Vietnam* (Boston: Little, Brown, 1967), 51.

47. Bodard, *The Quicksand War,* 240.

48. Tanham, *Communist Revolutionary Warfare,* 18–19.

49. Boucher de Crèvecoeur, *La Bataille de la Frontière de Chine,* 4.

50. Ibid., 5. The 308th Division, formed in late 1949 and armed and trained in China in early 1950, was the only full division to participate in the fall 1950 campaign, but the 304th, 312th, 316th, and 320th Divisions were all organized before the end of 1950. See Headquarters, Department of the Army, Office of the Assistant Chief of Staff, G-2, *Order of Battle: Viet Minh Army* (Washington, D.C.: HQDA, OACS G-2, October 10, 1954).

51. Tanham, *Communist Revolutionary Warfare,* 20.

52. Bodard, *The Quicksand War,* 136.

53. Fall, *The Two Viet-Nams,* 108.

54. Tanham, *Communist Revolutionary Warfare,* 20.

55. Ibid., 26.

56. Davidson, *Vietnam at War,* 76.

57. Ibid., 80–81.

58. The spring 1950 Viet Minh campaign is described in Davidson, *Vietnam at War,* 78–80.

59. Fall, *The Two Viet-Nams,* 108.

60. Davidson, *Vietnam at War,* 79.

61. Boucher de Crèvecoeur, *La Bataille de la Frontière de Chine,* 4. This was yet another manifestation of the French tendency to underestimate their enemy.

62. Kelly, *Lost Soldiers,* 48.

63. The reference is to the routes leading from Paris to the battle of the Marne in World War I. See Georges Couget, *Le Train en Indochine, 1945–1954* (Paris: Inspection du Train, 1973), 11.

64. Quoted in Bodard, *The Quicksand War,* 239.

65. Bodard, *The Quicksand War,* 239.

66. Spector, *Advice and Support,* 125.

67. Bodard, *The Quicksand War,* 188.

68. Fall, *The Two Viet-Nams,* 109; Boucher de Crèvecoeur, *La Bataille de la Frontière de Chine,* 5.

69. *Lessons Learned in the Indochina War,* 2:19.

70. The withdrawal from Cao Bang is described in Dalloz, *The War in Indochina,* 126–29; Fall, *The Two Viet-Nams,* 110; and Davidson, *Vietnam at War,* 90–91. Colonel Charton's account of the campaign has been published in his *RC4, Indochine 1950: La tragédie de l'évacuation de Cao Bang* (Paris: Éditions Albatros, 1975). Lieutenant Colonel Le Page's account is in his *Cao Bang: La tragique épopée de la colonne Le Page* (Le Vaumain: Nouvelles Éditions Latines, 1981).

71. Bodard, *The Quicksand War,* passim. The commanders of the frontier garrisons were instructed to not destroy the equipment and supplies to be abandoned lest the Viet Minh learn they intended to evacuate their post. Of course, the Viet Minh knew exactly what was happening.

72. Fall, *The Two Viet-Nams,* 110; Fall, *Street without Joy,* 29.

73. Tanham, *Communist Revolutionary Warfare,* 26–27.

74. Boucher de Crèvecoeur, *La Bataille de la Frontière de Chine,* 17–19.

75. Bodard, *The Quicksand War,* 323.

76. Fall, *Street without Joy,* 30. Some 60 percent of the French Union forces in the region were killed, wounded, or captured. See Stuart Pascoe, "A Critical Analysis of the Operational Performance of General Vo Nguyen Giap 1940–1954," in Australian Command and Staff College, *Geddes Papers 2005* ([Canberra]: Australian Defence College, 2010[?]): 21.

77. King C. Chen, *Vietnam and China, 1938–1954* (Princeton: Princeton Univ. Press, 1969), 264; Fall, *Street without Joy,* 30; O'Ballance, *The Indo-China War,* 118.

78. Bodard, *The Quicksand War,* 266.

79. Joseph Jeremiah Zasloff, *The Role of Sanctuary in Insurgency: Communist China's Support to the Vietminh, 1946–1954* (Santa Monica, Calif.: RAND Corporation, May 1967), 28.

80. For the impact of casualties and the inadequacies of the Viet Minh medical service at the time, see Christopher E. Goscha, "'Hell in a Very Small Place': Cold War and Decolonisation in the Assault on the Vietnamese Body at Dien Bien Phu," *European Journal of East Asian Studies* 9, no. 2 (December 2010): 211–14. The Viet Minh were barely able to deal with their own wounded, much less their many wounded French Union captives.

81. Tanham, *Communist Revolutionary Warfare*, 48.

82. Lieutenant Colonel Boussarie, *La Situation des forces ennemies en Indochine (1945–janvier 1954)* [The Situation of the Enemy Forces in Indo-China] (Washington, D.C.: HQDA, OACSI, 1954), 5.

10. The Campaign for the Base Areas

1. Bernard B. Fall, "Indochina—The Last Year of the War: Communist Organization and Tactics," *Military Review* 36, no. 7 (October 1956): 6; Fredrik Logevall, *Embers of War: The Fall of an Empire and the Making of America's Vietnam* (New York: Random House, 2012), 268–69.

2. King C. Chen, *Vietnam and China, 1938–1954* (Princeton: Princeton Univ. Press, 1969), 266; Logevall, *Embers of War*, 269.

3. De Lattre's successor, Lieutenant General Henri Navarre, writing after the war, lamented the priority of attention given to the delta, noting that it caused the French military leaders to lose sight of the Indochina theater of operations as a whole and that its defense tied down some 20 percent of the best French Union forces, who might have been used for offensive operations. See Henri Navarre, *Le Temps des Vérités* (Paris: Plon, 1957), 246–47.

4. Julian Thompson, *The Lifeblood of War: Logistics in Armed Conflict* (London: Brassey's, 1991), 363–64n13; Martin Windrow, *The Last Valley: Dien Bien Phu and the French Defeat in Vietnam* (New York: Da Capo, 2004), 116. Over 14 million cubic feet of crushed stone was used on the fortifications in the Red River delta alone. See Windrow, *The Last Valley*, 661.

5. Commander in Chief, French Forces in the Far East, *A Translation from the French: Lessons of the War in Indochina*, vol. 2 (Santa Monica, Calif.: RAND Corporation, May 1967), 20.

6. George A. Kelly, *Lost Soldiers: The French Army and Empire in Crisis, 1947–1962* (Cambridge, Mass.: M.I.T. Press, 1965), 48.

7. Edgar O'Ballance, *The Indo-China War 1945–1954: A Study in Guerrilla Warfare* (London: Faber and Faber, 1964), 120.

8. Kelly, *Lost Soldiers*, 48. It is interesting to compare General Jean de Lattre to General Matthew B. Ridgway, who played a similar role for U.N. forces in Korea at the same time.

9. George K. Tanham, *Communist Revolutionary Warfare: From the Vietminh to the Viet Cong*, rev. ed. (New York: Praeger, 1967), 27.

10. Phillip B. Davidson, *Vietnam at War: The History, 1946–1975* (Novato, Calif.: Presidio, 1988), 71–72.

11. Ibid., 105. In addition, Giap had at his disposal thirty-seven regional force battalions scattered across northern Indochina. See Stuart Pascoe, "A Critical Analysis of the Operational Performance of General Vo Nguyen Giap 1940–1954," in Australian Command and

Staff College, *Geddes Papers 2005* ([Canberra]: Australian Defence College, 2010[?]): 21.

12. Bernard B. Fall, *The Two Viet-Nams: A Political and Military Analysis,* 2nd rev. ed. (New York: Praeger, 1967), 116. The operation was named for Dê Tham, a Vietnamese patriot who led the guerrilla resistance in that area against the French between 1887 and 1913.

13. The events of the battle are described in O'Ballance, *The Indo-China War,* 125.

14. Ronald H. Spector (*Advice and Support: The Early Years, 1941–1960* [Washington, D.C.: Center of Military History, U.S. Army, 1983], 137) indicates that GM 1 lost "only" 540 men, or a little over one-fourth of its strength, in the battle.

15. Ibid., 136–37; D. M. O. Miller, "'A Handful of Rice?': Logistics in the Viet Minh Campaign," *Army Quarterly and Defence Journal* 100, no. 1 (April 1970): 111–12; Fall, *The Two Viet-Nams,* 116; Georges Couget, *Le Train en Indochine, 1945–1954* (Paris: Inspection du Train, 1973), 101. Other estimates put the number of Viet Minh casualties at six thousand to nine thousand killed, up to eight thousand wounded, and six hundred taken prisoner. See Pascoe, "A Critical Analysis of the Operational Performance of General Vo Nguyen Giap," 21n25. Christopher E. Goscha ("'Hell in a Very Small Place': Cold War and Decolonisation in the Assault on the Vietnamese Body at Dien Bien Phu," *European Journal of East Asian Studies* 9, no. 2 [December 2010]: 215) puts the Viet Minh death rate at Vinh Yen at 29 percent and notes that 63 percent of the Viet Minh killed and wounded were caused by artillery fire.

16. Headquarters, Department of the Army, Office of the Assistant Chief of Staff, G-2, *Probable Viet Minh and/or Chinese Communist Courses of Action in Indo-China* (Washington, D.C.: HQDA, OACS G-2, [1952]), tab A, 2–3.

17. Bernard B. Fall, *Street without Joy: Insurgency in Indochina, 1946–63,* 3rd rev. ed. (Harrisburg, Pa.: Stackpole, 1963), 37.

18. Ibid.; O'Ballance, *The Indo-China War,* 128n1; Miller, "'A Handful of Rice?,'" 111–12.

19. Fall, *Street without Joy,* 37.

20. Spector, *Advice and Support,* 118, 137. The first use of napalm in Indochina was near Tien Yen on December 22, 1950, but the Viet Minh were still not familiar with its effects. See Windrow, *The Last Valley,* 661.

21. Fall, *The Two Viet-Nams,* 116.

22. Thompson, *Lifeblood of War,* 149.

23. Spector, *Advice and Support,* 137.

24. Fall, *The Two Viet-Nams,* 116.

25. Spector, *Advice and Support,* 137.

26. Thompson, *Lifeblood of War,* 149.

27. For the battle of the Day River, see: *Lessons Learned in the Indochina War,* 2:20; O'Ballance, *The Indo-China War,* 134; Davidson, *Vietnam at War,* 119–21; Fall, *The Two Viet-Nams,* 116–17; Fall, *Street without Joy,* 41–43.

28. Davidson, *Vietnam at War,* 119.

29. Thompson, *Lifeblood of War,* 149.

30. Davidson, *Vietnam at War,* 119.

31. O'Ballance, *The Indo-China War,* 135.

32. Lieutenant Bernard de Lattre was killed on the first day of Operation HA NAM NINH when he and his platoon sacrificed themselves to delay the Viet Minh forces from a

rocky outcropping overlooking the town of Ninh Binh. See Fall, *The Two Viet-Nams,* 117.

33. O'Ballance, *The Indo-China War,* 138; Davidson, *Vietnam at War,* 120.

34. Davidson, *Vietnam at War,* 120.

35. Thompson, *Lifeblood of War,* 153.

36. Spector, *Advice and Support,* 118.

37. Davidson, *Vietnam at War,* 121.

38. Fall, *The Two Viet-Nams,* 117.

39. O'Ballance, *The Indo-China War,* 140.

40. Davidson, *Vietnam at War,* 125.

41. Ibid.

42. Thompson, *Lifeblood of War,* 150; Davidson, *Vietnam at War,* 124. The delay between the battle for RC 4 and the battle for Vinh Yen was two months, between Vinh Yen and Mao Khe two and a half months, and between Mao Khe and the Day River offensive two months.

43. O'Ballance, *The Indo-China War,* 141–42.

44. Fall, *Street without Joy,* 43–44; Spector, *Advice and Support,* 137.

45. *Lessons Learned in the Indochina War,* 2:20.

46. Ibid., 2:169 and note 1.

47. The following account of Operation LORRAINE is based primarily on Commandant, 1e Division de Marche du Tonkin et la Zone Ouest des Forces Terrestres du Nord Viet-Nam (Colonel Louis Dodelier, Commandant p.i.), *Rapport du Colonel Commandant la 1e D.M.T. and Z.O. sur l'Opération "LORRAINE,"* [No. 1,884/1 DMT/3, Hanoi, December 12, 1952], in folder "EMIFT, 3e Bureau, Operation LORRAINE, 29 octobre–26 novembre 1952," box 10 H 1208, Fonds Indochine, SHAT. Operation LORRAINE is also discussed in O'Ballance, *The Indo-China War,* 178–87; Davidson, *Vietnam at War,* 139–46, 156–57; Thompson, *Lifeblood of War,* 155–56; Fall, *Street without Joy,* passim. Davidson and Thompson appear to have followed O'Ballance in misunderstanding the first phase of the operation, which was not, as they describe, a simultaneous advance on two axes east of the Red River toward Phu Tho, but rather involved first an advance west of the Black River and the establishment of bridgeheads east of the Red River followed by a shift of forces onto an axis of advance north along RC 2 from Viet Tri to Phu Tho. Fall gets it nearly right.

48. Howard R. Simpson, *Tiger in the Barbed Wire: An American in Vietnam, 1952–1991* (New York: Brassey's, 1992), 4.

49. See Dodelier, *Rapport . . . sur l'Opération "LORRAINE,"* passim, for a complete listing.

50. Details of Operation MARION are given in Commandement des Troupes Aéroportées en Indochine, État-Major, 3e Bureau, *Opération Aéroportée MARION,* [Saigon, 1952], in folder "EMIFT, 3e Bureau, Operation MARS, 8–9 Mars 1951—Operation MARION, 9 Novembre 1952," box 10 H 1220, Fonds Indochine, SHAT.

51. According to Windrow (*The Last Valley,* 124), GM 1 and GM 4 suffered three hundred casualties.

52. This is apparently the same engagement described by Windrow (*The Last Valley,* 124) that resulted when the Viet Minh 176th Regiment cut RC 4 and heavy fighting ensued on the night of November 23–24.

53. Dodelier, *Rapport . . . sur l'Opération "LORRAINE,"* 28. O'Ballance (*The Indo-China War,* 184), Davidson (*Vietnam at War,* 146), and Windrow (*The Last Valley,* 124) all put the number of French Union casualties during Operation LORRAINE at twelve hundred without citing their source.

54. Ibid., 29.

55. Ibid., 29–30; Commandant, 1e Division de Marche du Tonkin et la Zone Ouest des Forces Terrestres du Nord Viet-Nam (Colonel Louis Dodelier, Commandant p.i.), *Bilan des armes et munitions capturées ou détruites à Tay Coc, 920 H 8, du 11 au 13 novembre 1952 au cours de l'Opération "LORRAINE,"* [No. 45/LORRAINE/2, Hanoi, November 13, 1952], in folder "EMIFT, 3e Bureau, Operation LORRAINE, 29 octobre–26 novembre 1952,—Phu Doan," box 10 H 1208, Fonds Indochine, SHAT. Various secondary sources (for example, Windrow, *The Last Valley,* 124) put the number of Molotova trucks captured at four, but the official count was three.

56. Fall, *Street without Joy,* 89–91.

57. Ibid., 92–93 and note.

58. Dodelier, *Rapport . . . sur l'Opération "LORRAINE,"* 31.

59. U.S. Far East Command, General Headquarters, Military Intelligence Section, "Order of Battle—Communist Ground Forces Far East (Indochina)," *FEC Intelligence Digest* 21 (April 17, 1952): 56.

60. Dodelier, *Rapport . . . sur l'Opération "LORRAINE,"* 31.

61. Ibid., 34.

62. Ibid., 35.

63. Fall, *Street without Joy,* 76.

64. Dodelier, *Rapport . . . sur l'Opération "LORRAINE,"* 37.

65. Ibid.

66. Spector, *Advice and Support,* 157–58, 161.

67. Thompson, *Lifeblood of War,* 156. Almost the entire French air transport fleet in Indochina (about one hundred C-47 Dakotas) was tied down by Operation LORRAINE.

68. The following account of Operation HIRONDELLE is based primarily on Commandement des Forces Terrestres du Nord-Viêt-Nam, État-Major, 3e Bureau, *Rapport sur l'Opération HIRONDELLE,* in five parts and two annexes as follows: "1e Partie—Instruction Personnelle et Secrete pour le Général GILLES" [No. 255/3.TS., Hanoi, 1953]; "2e Partie—Ordre Logistique No. 1" [EMFTNV Opérationnel No. 001/04/H1, Hanoi, July 13, 1953]; "3e Partie—" [Hanoi, 1953]; "4e Partie—Bilan Général" [Hanoi, 1953]; "5e Partie—Enseignements" [Hanoi, 1953]; "Annexe—Rapport du Chef du Bureau Transports de l'opération" [Hanoi, 1953]; "Annexe—Rapport du Chef du 2e Bureau sur l'opération HIRONDELLE" [Hanoi, 1953]. All are contained in folder "EMIFT, 3e Bureau—Operation HIRONDELLE," box 10 H 178, Fonds Indochine, SHAT.

69. For Operation MARS, see Commandement en Chef des Forces Terrestres Navales et Aériennes en Indochine, État-Major Interarmées et des Forces Terrestres, 3e Bureau, Section d'Instruction, *Operation "MARS," 8 au 9 mars 1951* [Saigon, 1951], in folder "EMIFT, 3e Bureau, Operation MARS, 8–9 mars 1951," box 10 H 1220, Fonds Indochine, SHAT; and Troupes Aéroportées d'Indochine-Sud, Operations Section, *Operation MARS [mars 1951]* (Washington, D.C.: HQDA, OACS G-2, [1951]). The latter is a translation of three French

documents, including the operations order, dealing with Operation MARS.

70. The French estimate of the enemy situation is outlined in *Rapport sur l'Opération HIRONDELLE*, 1e Partie, 1–2, and "Annexe: Rapport du Chef du 2e Bureau . . . ," passim.

71. *Rapport sur l'Opération HIRONDELLE*, 2e Partie, 1–2.

72. The concept of Operation HIRONDELLE is outlined in *Rapport sur l'Opération HIRONDELLE*, 1e Partie, 2–3, and the French Union forces assigned to the operation are listed in *Rapport sur l'Opération HIRONDELLE*, 1e Partie, 3–5.

73. An account of the Viet Minh reaction to Operation HIRONDELLE is given in *Rapport sur l'Opération HIRONDELLE*, "Annexe: Rapport du Chef du 2e Bureau . . . ," 3–4.

74. Details are provided in *Rapport sur l'Opération HIRONDELLE*, 2e Partie.

75. One unit of fire for a parachute infantry battalion amounted to about 12.4 tons and included, among other things, 37,350 rounds of rifle ammunition, 16,000 rounds of light machine gun ammunition, and 1,200 60 mm and 81 mm mortar rounds.

76. One unit of fire for a light tank squadron amounted to 13 tons and included 102,000 rounds of light machine gun ammunition, 4,000 heavy machine gun rounds, 1,700 rounds of 37 mm gun ammunition, and 400 rounds of 75 mm tank gun ammunition.

77. Details regarding BMT actions and transportation support of Operation HIRONDELLE are contained in *Rapport sur l'Opération HIRONDELLE*, "Annexe: Rapport de Chef du Bureau Mouvements Transports de l'Opération."

78. *Rapport sur l'Opération HIRONDELLE*, 4e Partie, 2.

79. Navarre, *Le Temps des Vérités*, 297.

80. *Rapport sur l'Opération HIRONDELLE*, 4e Partie, 1.

81. The lessons learned during the operation are summarized in *Rapport sur l'Opération HIRONDELLE*, 5e Partie.

82. *Lessons Learned in the Indochina War*, 2:168.

11. The Campaign for the Lines of Communication

1. George K. Tanham, *Communist Revolutionary Warfare: From the Vietminh to the Viet Cong*, rev. ed. (New York: Praeger, 1967), 89–90, gives a succinct description of Viet Minh ambush techniques.

2. Ronald H. Spector, *Advice and Support: The Early Years, 1941–1960* (Washington, D.C.: Center of Military History, U.S. Army, 1983), 113.

3. Commander in Chief, French Forces in the Far East, *A Translation from the French: Lessons of the War in Indochina*, vol. 2 (Santa Monica, Calif.: RAND Corporation, May 1967), 63.

4. Lieutenant General John W. O'Daniel, USA (Chief, U.S. Joint Military Mission to Indochina), *Report of U. S. Special Mission to Indochina (23 January–5 February 1954)—Situation in French Indochina and FUF Materiel Requirements, February 1954*, Pearl Harbor, Hawaii, February 5, 1954, annex A (Naval Situation), 28, in box 10 ("092 Asia [6-25-48] [2] Section 22"), Geographical File, 1954–1956, RG 218 (Records of the U.S. Joint Chiefs of Staff), National Archives II, College Park, Maryland.

5. Georges Couget, *Le Train en Indochine, 1945–1954* (Paris: Inspection du Train, 1973), 33.

6. The ambush of the Ban Me Thuot convoy is described in Couget, *Le Train en Indo-*

chine, 34. The drivers and other personnel of the *Train* were known as *trainglots*.

7. French route security and highway traffic control methods are described in *Lessons Learned in the Indochina War*, 2:63–65, and Couget, *Le Train en Indochine*, 52–55.

8. *Lessons Learned in the Indochina War*, 2:65. The watchtower system was the brain-child of Major General Pierre Boyer de la Tour du Moulin, the commander in southern Indochina.

9. Lucien Bodard, *The Quicksand War: Prelude to Vietnam* (Boston: Little, Brown, 1967), 1.

10. Howard R. Simpson, *Tiger in the Barbed Wire: An American in Vietnam, 1952–1991* (New York: Brassey's, 1992), 18.

11. *Lessons Learned in the Indochina War*, 2:76.

12. This is what a well-known French photojournalist, the late Henri Huey, who had served during the First Indochina War, told me in a conversation in 1967.

13. *Lessons Learned in the Indochina War*, 2:324n2.

14. Ibid., 2:323–24.

15. Ibid., 2:322.

16. Commandement en Chef des Forces Terrestres Navales et Aériennes en Indochine, État-Major Interarmées et des Forces Terrestres, Bureau "Instruction," *Notes sur le combat en Indochine* [Combat Notes from the War in Indochina] (Washington, D.C.: HQDA, OACS G-2, March 30, 1954), 130–31.

17. An interesting minute-by-minute account of a French convoy on the critical RC 5 between Haiphong and Hanoi late in the war can be found in Alfred Van Sprang, "L'opération 'route et rail,'" *Indochine-Sud-Est Asiatique* 30 (June 1954): 42–46.

18. Spector, *Advice and Support*, 90.

19. Couget, *Le Train en Indochine*, 82.

20. Ibid.; Merritt B. Booth (Mutual Defense Assistance Office, U.S. Department of State), Memorandum for Mr. Bell, Washington, April 12, 1950, subject: Military Information re Indochina, Thailand and Indonesia, 11, in folder "SE Asia 032. to 091.3, 1949–1950," box 61 ("SE Asia to Syria"), Project Decimal File, 1950–1952, Office of Military Assistance, Office of the Assistant Secretary of Defense (International Security Affairs), RG 330 (Records of the Office of the Secretary of Defense), National Archives II, College Park, Maryland.

21. Spector, *Advice and Support*, 113.

22. Couget, *Le Train en Indochine*, 82.

23. O'Daniel, *Report of U. S. Special Mission to Indochina (23 January–5 February 1954)*, annex A (Naval Situation), 29.

24. *Lessons Learned in the Indochina War*, 2:64, 325.

25. Riverine convoy procedures are described in *Lessons Learned in the Indochina War*, 2:175–79.

26. The organization and employment of the *Dinassaut* in Indochina are discussed in *Lessons Learned in the Indochina War*, 2:348–58.

27. O'Daniel, *Report of U.S. Special Mission to Indochina (23 January–5 February 1954)*, cover letter, 3.

28. Full designations for the various types of landing craft (LCM, LSSL, LSIL, etc.) can be found in the glossary.

29. *Lessons Learned in the Indochina War,* 2:61.

30. Spector, *Advice and Support,* 169.

31. *Lessons Learned in the Indochina War,* 2:61.

32. Ibid.

33. Spector, *Advice and Support,* 113.

34. *Lessons Learned in the Indochina War,* 2:80. The four routes studied were: RC 5 between Haiphong and Hanoi (forty miles); RI 39 between Ban Yen Nhan and Hung Yen (twenty-two miles); RP 17 Nord between Hai Duong and Sept Pagodes (seventeen miles), and RP 18 between Sept Pagodes and Dong Trieu (sixteen miles). Between one-fourth and one-half of the casualties were due to mines.

35. Ibid., 2:80–81. The calculation was based on the continuous requirement of one infantry battalion and one artillery battery to control a given section of road in an area which could be pacified by three infantry battalions in six months. Over a period of two years, the cost of pacifying the area would be only eighteen battalions (three battalions x six months), whereas the cost of simply controlling the road would be twenty-four battalions (one battalion x twenty-four months).

36. Ibid., 2:81.

37. Couget, *Le Train en Indochine,* 55.

38. Ibid., 82.

39. *Lessons Learned in the Indochina War,* 2:166n2; Bernard B. Fall, *The Two Viet-Nams: A Political and Military Analysis,* 2nd rev. ed. (New York: Praeger, 1967), 181.

40. Michèle Battesti, "La Marine et la guerre d'Indochine," *Revue Historique des Armées* 177 (December 1989): 84.

41. Bernard B. Fall, *Street without Joy: Insurgency in Indochina, 1946–63,* 3rd rev. ed. (Harrisburg, Pa.: Stackpole, 1963), 257.

42. Ibid.; Battesti, "La Marine et la guerre d'Indochine," 84.

43. O'Daniel, *Report of U.S. Special Mission to Indochina [23 January–5 February 1954],* annex A (Naval Situation), 31.

44. Bernard B. Fall in Roger Trinquier, *Modern Warfare: A French View of Insurgency* (London: Pall Mall Press, 1964; reprint, Fort Leavenworth, Kans.: Combat Studies Institute, January 1985), xiii.

45. A similar opinion of Special Forces, long-range reconnaissance patrols, and other unconventional units was held by most senior American commanders during the Second Indochina War, with a similar loss of a valuable tool that forced the enemy to face all of the problems of combating a guerrilla force that held the initiative.

46. Edgar O'Ballance, *The Indo-China War 1945–1954: A Study in Guerrilla Warfare* (London: Faber and Faber, 1964), 202.

47. Fall in Trinquier, *Modern Warfare,* xiv.

48. Tanham, *Communist Revolutionary Warfare,* 104; Fall in Trinquier, *Modern Warfare,* xvii.

49. Fall, *Street without Joy,* 271. Elsewhere (*Street without Joy,* 263) Fall states that the GMI consumed about three hundred tons per month.

50. Fall, *Street without Joy,* 270; Trinquier, *Modern Warfare,* 54; O'Ballance, *The Indo-China War,* 201–2; Bernard B. Fall, "Indochina—The Last Year of the War: The Navarre

Plan," *Military Review* 36, no. 9 (December 1956): 50.

51. Trinquier, *Modern Warfare,* 54.

52. Fall in Trinquier, *Modern Warfare,* xiv. The abandonment of the GCMA/GMI by the French government was perhaps the most shameful event of the war.

53. These handicaps are discussed in Tanham, *Communist Revolutionary Warfare,* 104–6. It should be noted that while air control (superiority) over the theater of operations was considered by the French air commanders as a necessary condition for success in Indochina, it was not a sufficient condition. See Commander in Chief, French Forces in the Far East, *Lessons from the Indo-China War,* vol. 3 (Washington, D.C.: DARPA, 1955), 32, 38. The French experience in Indochina only confirmed the experience of U.N. forces in Korea as to the inability of airpower alone to defeat a determined enemy.

54. Tanham, *Communist Revolutionary Warfare,* 106; *Lessons Learned in the Indochina War,* 2:340–41.

55. Fall, *Street without Joy,* 256.

56. Ibid., 257.

57. Spector, *Advice and Support,* 146, 167–68.

58. Battesti, "La Marine et la guerre d'Indochine," 86–87.

59. Julian Thompson, *The Lifeblood of War: Logistics in Armed Conflict* (London: Brassey's, 1991), 175.

60. Charles W. Koburger Jr., *The French Navy in Indochina: Riverine and Coastal Forces, 1945–54* (New York: Praeger, 1991), appendix C. The light carrier *Arromanches,* which took station for her second tour in September 1951 with forty-four aircraft (F6F fighters and SB2C dive-bombers), was the workhorse of the French carrier force.

61. Tanham, *Communist Revolutionary Warfare,* 107; BDM Corporation, *A Study of Strategic Lessons Learned in Vietnam,* vol. 1, *The Enemy* (McLean, Va.: BDM Corporation, November 30, 1979), 5-4.

62. Fall, *Street without Joy,* 257.

63. Tanham, *Communist Revolutionary Warfare,* 107.

64. Lieutenant Colonel Boussarie, *La Situation des forces ennemies en Indochine (1945–janvier 1954)* [The Situation of the Enemy Forces in Indo-China (1945–January 1954)] (Washington, D.C.: HQDA, OACSI, 1954), 24.

65. Fall, *Street without Joy,* 260–61.

66. Quoted in *Lessons Learned in the Indochina War,* 3:37–38.

67. Ibid., 3:32n2.

68. Ibid., 2:341.

69. Joseph R. Starobin, *Eyewitness in Indo-China* (New York: Cameron and Kahn, 1954), 49.

70. *Lessons Learned in the Indochina War,* 2:342.

71. Quoted in *Lessons Learned in the Indochina War,* 3:34.

72. *Lessons Learned in the Indochina War,* 2:20; Henri Navarre, *Le Temps des Vérités* (Paris: Plon, 1957), 247.

73. Phillip B. Davidson, *Vietnam at War: The History, 1946–1975* (Novato, Calif.: Presidio, 1988), 129. See also Fredrik Logevall, *Embers of War: The Fall of an Empire and the Making of America's Vietnam* (New York: Random House, 2012), 289.

74. Fall, *Street without Joy*, 45; Spector, *Advice and Support*, 149–50.

75. *Lessons Learned in the Indochina War*, 2:254; "Airborne Operations in Indochina," *Intelligence Review* 197 (October 1952): 11.

76. Operation LOTUS was the last operation in which the French used the old Ju 52 Toucan transports for parachute assault or aerial resupply missions.

77. Fall, *Street without Joy*, 48.

78. *Lessons Learned in the Indochina War*, 2:20–21; Davidson, *Vietnam at War*, 131; Fall, *The Two Viet-Nams*, 119.

79. Davidson, *Vietnam at War*, 131.

80. Fall, *Street without Joy*, 52; Davidson, *Vietnam at War*, 132; Thompson, *Lifeblood of War*, 151–52.

81. Operation AMARANTH is described in Fall, *Street without Joy*, 56–57; Davidson, *Vietnam at War*, 132–33; Spector, *Advice and Support*, 150.

82. Fall, *The Two Viet-Nams*, 118–19.

83. *Lessons Learned in the Indochina War*, 2:21. Other sources (for example, Thompson, *Lifeblood of War*, 152) put the losses at about five thousand for each side.

84. Spector, *Advice and Support*, 150.

85. Bodard, *The Quicksand War*, 329.

86. "Chinese Communist Assistance to the Viet Minh," *Intelligence Review* 190 (March 1952): 33; "Strategy and Tactics of the Viet Minh," *Intelligence Review* 192 (May 1952): 27–28.

87. Thompson, *Lifeblood of War*, 152.

88. O'Ballance, *The Indo-China War*, 167; Martin Windrow, *The Last Valley: Dien Bien Phu and the French Defeat in Vietnam* (New York: Da Capo, 2004), 119. At the beginning of 1952, the Viet Minh still had only about one hundred trucks.

89. Qiang Zhai, *China and the Vietnam Wars, 1950–1975* (Chapel Hill: Univ. of North Carolina Press, 2000), 36; Logevall, *Embers of War*, 321.

90. *Lessons Learned in the Indochina War*, 2:146.

91. Ibid., 2:147; Fall, *Street without Joy*, 44.

92. Davidson, *Vietnam at War*, 128; O'Ballance, *The Indo-China War*, 158.

93. For the dispositions and movements of the Viet Minh forces and the battle for Nghia Lo, see Logevall, *Embers of War*, 321–24; Davidson, *Vietnam at War*, 140–41; Fall, *The Two Viet-Nams*, 119, 181. Both the 308th and the 316th Divisions left behind one regiment to protect their rear areas east of the Red River.

94. The 6e BPC at Tu Le lost ninety-one killed and wounded. See "OP 'LORRAINE' 29th October–8th November 1952: Salan Strikes at Giap's Supply Lines," 1–2, http://indochine54.free.fr/ops/lorraine.html (accessed December 6, 2012); Logevall, *Embers of War*, 323.

95. The movements of the Viet Minh divisions are described in O'Ballance, *The Indo-China War*, 178, 184–86; Thompson, *Lifeblood of War*, 155; Davidson, *Vietnam at War*, 141.

96. For the French defenses of Na San prepared by Colonel Jean Gilles and his second-in-command, Major Vaudrey, see Windrow, *The Last Valley*, 159.

97. *Lessons Learned in the Indochina War*, 1:63. See also O'Ballance, *The Indo-China War*, 186.

98. Fall, *The Two Viet-Nams,* 119.

99. O'Ballance, *The Indo-China War,* 178.

100. Ibid., 186.

101. Davidson, *Vietnam at War,* 147–48; Thompson, *Lifeblood of War,* 156–57. The T'ai were reluctant to serve as porters and once conscripted threw down their loads and deserted at the first opportunity.

102. Jules Roy, *The Battle of Dien Bien Phu* (New York: Harper and Row, 1965), 61.

103. George A. Kelly, *Lost Soldiers: The French Army and Empire in Crisis, 1947–1962* (Cambridge, Mass.: M.I.T. Press, 1965), 49.

104. O'Ballance, *The Indo-China War,* 187.

105. Fall, *The Two Viet-Nams,* 121.

106. Ibid.

107. Davidson, *Vietnam at War,* 148.

108. D. M. O. Miller, "'A Handful of Rice?': Logistics in the Viet Minh Campaign," *Army Quarterly and Defence Journal* 100, no. 1 (April 1970): 112.

109. The movements of the Viet Minh divisions are described in Davidson, *Vietnam at War,* 150–53, 156; Thompson, *Lifeblood of War,* 160; O'Ballance, *The Indo-China War,* 190–91.

110. Fall, *The Two Viet-Nams,* 121; Miller, "'A Handful of Rice?,'" 112; Davidson, *Vietnam at War,* 152, 156.

111. Fall, *The Two Viet-Nams,* 181.

112. Ibid., 121; Qiang Zhai, *China and the Vietnam Wars,* 43.

113. Miller, "'A Handful of Rice?,'" 115.

114. Kelly, *Lost Soldiers,* 49.

115. Headquarters, Department of the Army, Office of the Assistant Chief of Staff for Intelligence, *Resistance and Regional Factors: Indochina* (Washington, D.C.: HQDA, OACSI, April 1959), 175–76.

12. Planning and Buildup for the Battle of Dien Bien Phu

1. Perhaps the most popular English-language account of the battle is Bernard B. Fall, *Hell in a Very Small Place: The Siege of Dien Bien Phu* (New York: Vintage, 1966). Also useful are Martin Windrow, *The Last Valley: Dien Bien Phu and the French Defeat in Vietnam* (New York: Da Capo, 2004); Howard R. Simpson, *Dien Bien Phu: The Epic Battle America Forgot,* paperback ed. (Washington, D.C.: Brassey's, 1996); Jules Roy, *The Battle of Dien Bien Phu* (New York: Harper and Row, 1965); Pierre Langlais, *Dien Bien Phu* (Paris: Éditions France-Empire, 1963); and Erwan Bergot, *Les 170 jours de Dien Bien Phu* (Paris: Presses de la Cité, 1979). The original French edition of Roy's book (*La bataille de Dien Bien Phu* [Paris: Julliard, 1963]) is more complete than the English translation. A detailed account of the French aerial resupply effort can be found in John D. Plating, "Failure at the Margins: Aerial Resupply at Dien Bien Phu" (Master's thesis, Ohio State Univ., 2000). The recently published analysis of the Viet Minh artillery at Dien Bien Phu by Kevin M. Boylan ("No 'Technical Knockout': Giap's Artillery at Dien Bien Phu," *Journal of Military History* 78, no. 4 [October 2014], 1349–1383) provides a careful—perhaps definitive—discussion of the critically important question of the quantity, employment,

and resupply of the Viet Minh artillery during the battle. Official documents concerning French logistical support of the battle are grouped in boxes 10 H 1169–1177 of the Fonds Indochine, SHAT.

2. Commandement des Forces Terrestres du Nord-Viêt-Nam, Le Chef d'État-Major (Commandant Baubeau, Sous-Chef Logistique, État-Major, Forces Terrestres du Nord-Viêt-Nam), "Aspects logistiques de la bataille de Dien Bien Phu" [No. 313/FTNV/CEM, Hanoi, July 6, 1954], 1, in folder "Dien Bien Phu 14—État-Major, Forces Terrestres du Nord-Viêt-Nam, 3e Bureau, Le Soutien logistique en Ravitaillement—4e Bureau Materials," box 10 H 1176, Fonds Indochine, SHAT. The first sustained Viet Minh assault on the main position began on March 13, and most accounts of the battle mark March 13 as the first day of a new period. However, when considering the battle from a logistical point of view, March 13 was the last day of an old period since the deliveries for March 13 were en route before the Viet Minh attack began. This is important for understanding how the statistical data are arranged.

3. Henri Navarre, *Le Temps des Vérités* (Paris: Plon, 1957), 284–85. English translation by the author.

4. Edgar O'Ballance, *The Indo-China War 1945–1954: A Study in Guerrilla Warfare* (London: Faber and Faber, 1964), 202.

5. George A. Kelly, *Lost Soldiers: The French Army and Empire in Crisis, 1947–1962* (Cambridge, Mass.: M.I.T. Press, 1965), 51.

6. Roy, *Battle of Dien Bien Phu*, 60–61.

7. The Navarre Plan is outlined by Phillip B. Davidson in *Vietnam at War: The History, 1946–1975* (Novato, Calif.: Presidio, 1988), 166–67. See also Peter Drake Jackson, *French Ground Force Organizational Development for Counterrevolutionary Warfare between 1945 and 1962* (Master of Military Art and Science thesis, Fort Leavenworth, Kans., U.S. Army Command and General Staff College, 2005), 43.

8. Navarre, *Le Temps des Vérités*, 284.

9. Bernard B. Fall, "Indochina—The Last Year of the War: The Navarre Plan," *Military Review* 36, no. 9 (December 1956): 49.

10. Navarre, *Le Temps des Vérités*, 297.

11. Bernard B. Fall, *The Two Viet-Nams: A Political and Military Analysis*, 2nd rev. ed. (New York: Praeger, 1967), 125.

12. O'Ballance, *The Indo-China War*, 200.

13. Fall, "Indochina—The Last Year of the War: The Navarre Plan," 50.

14. Commander in Chief, French Forces in the Far East, *A Translation from the French: Lessons of the War in Indochina*, vol. 2 (Santa Monica, Calif.: RAND Corporation, May 1967), 21; Ronald H. Spector, *Advice and Support: The Early Years, 1941–1960* (Washington, D.C.: Center of Military History, U.S. Army, 1983), 158.

15. Navarre, *Le Temps des Vérités*, 298.

16. Ibid.

17. Roy, *Battle of Dien Bien Phu*, 22.

18. O'Ballance, *The Indo-China War*, 201.

19. Davidson, *Vietnam at War*, 169, 171.

20. Fall, *Hell in a Very Small Place*, 34. Pierced steel planking was used to construct or improve forward airfields.

21. Windrow, *The Last Valley,* 216.

22. *Lessons Learned in the Indochina War,* 2:153–54; Navarre, *Le Temps des Vérités,* 319; Fall, *Hell in a Very Small Place,* 30–31.

23. Navarre, *Le Temps des Vérités,* 298.

24. Ibid., 318.

25. Ibid., 274–77 passim.

26. Fall, *The Two Viet-Nams,* 124.

27. Bernard Fall, *Street without Joy: Insurgency in Indochina, 1946–63,* 3rd rev. ed. (Harrisburg, Pa.: Stackpole, 1963), 310.

28. Kelly, *Lost Soldiers,* 58, 72–73.

29. Fall, *Hell in a Very Small Place,* 41–42.

30. O'Ballance, *The Indo-China War,* 207.

31. Navarre, *Le Temps des Vérités,* 318.

32. Fall, "Indochina—The Last Year of the War: The Navarre Plan," 52.

33. George K. Tanham, *Communist Revolutionary Warfare: From the Vietminh to the Viet Cong,* rev. ed. (New York: Praeger, 1967), 94. See also Pierre Asselin, "New Perspectives on Dien Bien Phu," *Explorations in Southeast Asian Studies* 1, no. 2 (fall 1997), www2 .hawaii.edu/~seassa/explorations/v1n2/art2/v1n2-frame2.html (accessed February 6, 2014). Asselin (page 3) stresses that the French high command in Hanoi "did not station a large garrison at Dien Bien Phu to provoke the enemy, draw him out of the jungle, and annihilate him with superior firepower in a 'pitched battle.' The *raison d'être* of the outpost at Dien Bien Phu was, in accordance with instructions received from Paris, to 'lock the door to Laos.'"

34. See, for example, Lucien Bodard, *The Quicksand War: Prelude to Vietnam* (Boston: Little, Brown, 1967), 21, 44, 46; Fall, *Hell in a Very Small Place,* 20; Howard R. Simpson, *Tiger in the Barbed Wire: An American in Vietnam, 1952–1991* (New York: Brassey's, 1992), 62–63.

35. Douglas Porch, "Dien Bien Phu and the Opium Connection," *MHQ: The Quarterly Journal of Military History* 7, no. 4 (summer 1995): 100–109.

36. Fredrik Logevall, *Embers of War: The Fall of an Empire and the Making of America's Vietnam* (New York: Random House, 2012), 385–86. Major General Cogny's chief of staff (Colonel Dominique Bastiani), deputy chief of staff for operations (Lieutenant Colonel Denef), and deputy chief of staff for logistics (Lieutenant Colonel Multrier) all concurred with their commander in resisting the Dien Bien Phu operation. See Windrow, *The Last Valley,* 224.

37. Ibid., 32.

38. Roy, *Battle of Dien Bien Phu,* 27, 32; Windrow, *The Last Valley,* 226, 417.

39. On November 18, the day after Lieutenant General Navarre announced his decision to proceed with Operation CASTOR, Rear Admiral Georges Cabanier arrived in Saigon from Paris bearing the word that funds were not available for extensive operations and that Navarre should leave matters to the politicians, who wished to find a negotiated settlement. See Logevall, *Embers of War,* 385.

40. Fall, *Hell in a Very Small Place,* 38, 44. It may be a question here of the complete operation plan or of "Personal and Secret Instructions for the Conduct of Operation No.

949," which contained Lieutenant General Navarre's concept of the operation and which was received by Major General Cogny on December 3. See Logevall, *Embers of War,* 392. Major General Cogny received instructions to begin planning in early November and would no doubt have been issued fragmentary orders before the parachute assault on November 20.

41. Navarre, *Le Temps des Vérités,* 319.

42. Vo Nguyen Giap, *Inside the Viet Minh* (Washington, D.C.: Marine Corps Association), 196.

43. See, for example, Logevall, *Embers of War,* 393.

44. Fall, *Hell in a Very Small Place,* 50; Roy, *Battle of Dien Bien Phu,* 30, 61.

45. Bernard B. Fall, *Le Viet-Minh: La République Démocratique du Viet-Nam, 1945–1960* (Paris: Librairie Armand Colin, 1960), 214; Julian Thompson, *The Lifeblood of War: Logistics in Armed Conflict* (London: Brassey's, 1991), 165.

46. Fall, *Hell in a Very Small Place,* 44.

47. Ibid., 50.

48. Commandement en Chef des Forces Terrestres Navales et Aériennes en Indochine, État-Major Interarmées et des Forces Terrestres, 4e Bureau, 1e Section, "Fiche: Volume de croisière de DIEN BIEN PHU" [Saigon, undated], 1, in folder "Dien Bien Phu 5—Transport, etc.—4e Bureau, BMT, decembre 1953–mai 1954," box 10 H 1177, Fonds Indochine, SHAT.

49. Ibid., 2.

50. Langlais, *Dien Bien Phu,* 38. Heavy casualties at Dien Bien Phu required the paradrop of entire battalions and thus additional aircraft.

51. Commandement en Chef des Forces Terrestres Navales et Aériennes en Indochine, État-Major Interarmées et des Forces Terrestres, 3e Bureau, "Fiche relative au trafic journalier d'un pont aérien en cas de vol I. F. R. et d'attérrissage Q. B. I." [No. 1803/EMIFT/3/SC, Saigon, December 17, 1953], in folder "Dien Bien Phu 5—Transport, etc.—4e Bureau, BMT, decembre 1953–mai 1954," box 10 H 1177, Fonds Indochine, SHAT.

52. Using the 3e Bureau's figure of ten thousand men and six fighter-bombers and the planning figures of the 4e Bureau, the daily maintenance requirement would be calculated correctly as 60 tons plus 24 tons, or 84 tons per day.

53. Commandant des Troupes Aéroportées en Indochine [Colonel Henri Sauvagnac], "Rapport du Colonel Sauvagnac, Commandant les T.A.P.I., sur la participation des Aéroportés à la Bataille de DIEN BIEN PHU et sur quelques enseignements à en tirer" [Hanoi, June 2, 1954], 32, in folder "EMIFT, 3e Bureau—Operations: Dien Bien Phu," box 10 H 1169, Fonds Indochine, SHAT (cited hereafter as Sauvagnac, *Report of June 2, 1954*).

54. Commandement en Chef des Forces Terrestres Navales et Aériennes en Indochine, État-Major Interarmées et des Forces Terrestres, Chef d'État-Major, "La Situation en Indochine de Novembre 1951 à Mai 1953" [Saigon, 1953], 102, in folder "EMIFT, 3e Bureau, Enseignements à tirer de la campagne d'Indochine, Fasc. III, p. 98—Documents Supplementaire," box 10 H 984, Fonds Indochine, SHAT. Windrow (*The Last Valley,* 704–6) provides a list of the air transport units that operated in support of Dien Bien Phu. The Amiot AAC 1 was a French-built version of the Junkers Ju 52.

55. Fall, *Street without Joy,* 259n. Fall notes that the same number of aircraft were in service at the time of the cease-fire, but elsewhere (*Hell in a Very Small Place,* 241) he indi-

428 *Notes to Pages 297–299*

cates that twenty-four of the twenty-nine C-119s flying in support of Dien Bien Phu were leased from the well-known Civil Air Transport Corporation (CAT). Lieutenant General Navarre (*Le Temps des Vérités*, 352) states that during the battle for Dien Bien Phu there were available about 100 C-47s and 16 C-119s and that the combat aircraft increased from 168 (48 B-26s, 8 Privateers, and 112 fighter-bombers [Hellcats, Bearcats, and Corsairs]) to 227, but that in reality there were never available in Indochina more than 90 transports and 175 fighter-bombers at any one time.

56. *Lessons Learned in the Indochina War*, 2:336. Among the civilian airlines that participated in the Dien Bien Phu operation were Aigle-Azur, Air Outre-Mer, CORSA, CLCT (Laos), Air Vietnam, and Civil Air Transport (CAT). The first CAT contingent arrived at Haiphong on March 9, 1954. See Plating, "Failure at the Margins," 58nn27, 79.

57. Thompson, *Lifeblood of War*, 175; Spector, *Advice and Support*, 117.

58. Commandement des Forces Terrestres du Nord Viet-Nam, État-Major, Bureau Mouvements Transports, "Fiche: Transports au Nord Viet-Nam—Améliorations à envisager" [No. 5/FTNV/F, Hanoi, February 18, 1954], in folder "Dien Bien Phu 5—Transport, etc.—4e Bureau, BMT, decembre 1953–mai 1954," box 10 H 1177, Fonds Indochine, SHAT.

59. Ibid., 1–2.

60. Commander in Chief, French Forces in the Far East, *Lessons from the Indo-China War*, vol. 3 (Washington, D.C.: DARPA, 1955), 149; Fall, *Street without Joy*, 259.

61. *Lessons Learned in the Indochina War*, 3:150.

62. Sauvagnac, *Report of June 2, 1954*, 33 (annex II). Most of the C-119 airlift was used for dropping barbed wire. See Debriefing of Major General Thomas J. H. Trapnell, former chief, MAAG-Indochina, May 3, 1954, document 41, in *The Pentagon Papers: The Defense Department History of United States Decisionmaking in Vietnam*, vol. 1, ed. Mike Gravel (Boston: Beacon, 1971), 496.

63. Fall, *Hell in a Very Small Place*, 2. See also Windrow, *The Last Valley*, 355.

64. Fall, *Street without Joy*, 260 and note. See also Windrow, *The Last Valley*, 543.

65. Fall, *Hell in a Very Small Place*, 327–28. The most famous of the thirty-seven American CAT pilots, Captain James B. McGovern, better known as "Earthquake McGoon" after a character in Al Capp's cartoon *L'il Abner*, his copilot Wallace A. Buford, and two French crewmen were killed when their C-119 was shot down over Dien Bien Phu on May 6, 1954. See Logevall, *Embers of War*, 529. In 2005, seven of the CAT pilots were awarded the *Légion d'honneur*, France's highest military decoration. See "U.S. Pilots Honored for Indochina Service," *News from France*, 05.02 (March 2, 2005), http://www.ambafrance-us.org/IMG/pdf/nff/NFF0502.pdf (accessed January 15, 2011). The CAT pilots were paid $65 per flight hour, with a minimum of sixty hours per month. See Windrow, *The Last Valley*, 687n74.

66. The activities of TAPI in support of Dien Bien Phu are reported in Sauvagnac, *Report of June 2, 1954*.

67. *Lessons Learned in the Indochina War*, 3:154; *Lessons Learned in the Indochina War*, 2:321 and note 5. The activities of the CRA are also detailed in Commandant des Troupes Aéroportées en Indochine [Colonel Henri Sauvagnac], "Rapport du Colonel Commandant les T.A.P.I. sur les opérations de ravitaillement par Air pendant la bataille de DIEN BIEN PHU (novembre 1953–mai 1954)" [Hanoi, December 20, 1954], in folder "EMIFT, 3e Bureau—Operations: Dien Bien Phu," box 10 H 1169, Fonds Indochine, SHAT (cited hereaf-

ter as Sauvagnac, *Report of December 20, 1954*). See also Windrow, *The Last Valley*, 433–36.

68. 1e Section, 4e Bureau, EMIFT, "Instruction relative à l'organisation générale au ravitaillement par Air des F. T. d'Indochine: Annexe No. II," [No. 441/4/1, Saigon, September 15, 1953], in folder "EMIFT, 3e Bureau, Operations: Dien Bien Phu, 4e Bureau Materials," box 10 H 1176, Fonds Indochine, SHAT. The *CRA du Nord* had a surge capability of 5,000 short tons per month. Normally, one CRA was capable of handling 150–200 short tons of air cargo per day. See *Lessons Learned in the Indochina War*, 3:155–56.

69. 2e Section, 1e Bureau, EMIFT, "Note de Service No. 292: Ravitaillement par Air," [Saigon, January 29, 1954], Piece No. 68, in folder "Organigrammes: Organisation et Soutien des TAPI," box 10 H 1525, Fonds Indochine, SHAT.

70. Georges Couget, *Le Train en Indochine, 1945–1954* (Paris: Inspection du Train, 1973), 60.

71. Langlais, *Dien Bien Phu*, 72–73.

72. Fall, *Hell in a Very Small Place*, 248. A bulldozer destroyed on a drop early in the operation was lost due to faulty parachute accessories rather than improper packing.

73. Colonel Chavette, *Considérations sur les opérations aeroportées du theâtre d'opérations Indochinois* [Considerations on Airborne Operations in the Indochinese Theater of Operations] (Washington, D.C.: HQDA, OACS G-2, 1956), 14.

74. Commandant en Chef des Forces Terrestres Navales et Aériennes en Indochine [Lieutenant General Henri Navarre], Letter to Chief of USMAAG, subject: "Parachutes à Matériel pour la Bataille de Dien Bien Phu" [No. 299/EMIFT/4/Section US, Saigon, April 18, 1954], in folder "Dien Bien Phu 5—Transport, etc.—5. BMT, 4e Bureau, decembre 1953–mai 1954," box 10 H 1177, Fonds Indochine, SHAT.

75. Fall, *Hell in a Very Small Place*, 11.

76. Logevall, *Embers of War*, 386.

77. Sauvagnac, *Report of December 20, 1954*, 5.

78. Baubeau, "Aspects logistiques," 4; Sauvagnac, *Report of December 20, 1954*, 7.

79. Note that the logisticians of the 4e Bureau estimated the number of troops to be supported much more accurately than the operations officers of the 3e Bureau.

80. Baubeau, "Aspects logistiques," 4. On November 21, a heavy drop of a pair of seven-short-ton bulldozers was made on Drop Zone OCTAVIE. The parachutes on the first bulldozer malfunctioned, and the bulldozer buried itself ten feet deep in a rice paddy. See Sauvagnac, *Report of June 2, 1954*, 28; Fall, *Hell in a Very Small Place*, 16.

81. Ibid.; Sauvagnac, *Report of December 20, 1954*, 5, 7.

82. For deliveries in the period from November 20, 1953, to January 26, 1954, see Sauvagnac, *Report of December 20, 1954*, 5 and annex 5; Baubeau, "Aspects logistiques," table ("Taux Moyens Journaliers d'Entretien à Dien Bien Phu [h/j]").

83. For deliveries during the period from January 27 to February 23, see Sauvagnac, *Report of December 20, 1954*, 8 and annex 5; Baubeau, "Aspects logistiques," table ("Taux Moyens Journaliers d'Entretien à Dien Bien Phu [h/j]").

84. For deliveries during the period February 24 to March 13, see Sauvagnac, *Report of December 20, 1954*, annex 5; Baubeau, "Aspects logistiques," table ("Taux Moyens Journaliers d'Entretien à Dien Bien Phu [h/j]").

85. *Lessons Learned in the Indochina War*, 2:370n2.

86. Ibid., 3:148; Sauvagnac, *Report of December 20, 1954,* 9.

87. Fall, *Hell in a Very Small Place,* 19.

88. Ibid., 62–72. See also Logevall, *Embers of War,* 404.

89. Details regarding the reinforcement of the Seno-Savannakhet base are contained in Commandement en Chef des Forces Terrestres Navales et Aériennes en Indochine, État-Major Interarmées et des Forces Terrestres, Bureau Transports, "Note concernant les transports exécutés pour le renforcement du Moyen-Laos au moment de l'offensive Viet-Minh vers le Mékong du 22 Décembre [1953]" [Saigon, February 3, 1954], in folder "EMIFT, 3e Bureau, Enseignements à tirer de la campagne d'Indochine, Fasc. III, p. 98—Documents Divers," box 10 H 983, Fonds Indochine, SHAT. See also *Lessons Learned in the Indochina War,* 2:326–27.

90. Headquarters, Department of the Army, Office of the Assistant Chief of Staff, G-2, *Indochina Military Situation Report (Indochina SITREP) No. 34* (Washington, D.C.: HQDA, OACS G-2, April 30, 1954), paragraph 1.

91. Fall, *The Two Viet-Nams,* 127; *Indochina SITREP No. 43,* July 2, 1954, paragraph 1.

92. Fall ("Indochina—The Last Year of the War: The Navarre Plan," 54; *Hell in a Very Small Place,* 64) inexplicably refers to the 316th Division as having "again marched upon Luang Prabang in four separate columns" and "the attack of the 316th Division upon northern Laos." Lai Chau was taken by the 316th Division on December 12, 1953, but it was certainly the 308th Division that made the January–February 1954 foray into Upper Laos, as Fall himself notes elsewhere (*Hell in a Very Small Place,* 133): "the enemy feint of January 25 and the return to Dien Bien Phu of the 308th Division from its stab into Laos." O'Ballance (*The Indo-China War,* 210), probably following Fall, also erroneously substitutes the 316th Division for the 308th.

93. Commandant, 3e Compagnie de Ravitaillement par Air, Base Aéroportée Nord [Captain Magnier], "État des Tonnages Posés, Droppés, et Parachutés sur DIEN BIEN PHU; de Novembre 1953 au 7 Mai 1954" [No. 1569/C/2, Hanoi], May 12, 1954, in folder "EMIFT, 3e Bureau, Operations—Dien Bien Phu, 4e Bureau Materials," box 10 H 1176, Fonds Indochine, SHAT.

94. Sauvagnac, *Report of December 20, 1954,* 7.

95. Fall, *The Two Viet-Nams,* 126.

96. *Indochina SITREP No. 27,* March 12, 1954, paragraph 1. There remains some uncertainty as to the exact number of aircraft destroyed or damaged in the Gia Lam and Cat Bi raids. Fall (*The Two Viet-Nams,* 126) states that thirty-eight aircraft were destroyed or damaged in the Cat Bi raid, but elsewhere (*Street without Joy,* 258–59) he states the losses as eighteen transports. Thompson (page 176, probably following Giap, *Inside the Viet Minh,* V-7) puts the toll for both raids at seventy-eight transports, an obviously incorrect figure since at the time the French had only about 110 transports in all of Indochina. See Fall, *Street without Joy,* 259n. U.S. intelligence sources (*Indochina SITREP No. 27,* March 12, 1954, paragraph 1) put the number of aircraft damaged or destroyed in the two raids at twenty, probably the correct figure.

97. Roy, *Battle of Dien Bien Phu,* 159.

98. For a discussion of the planning and execution of Operation CONDOR, see Fall, *Hell in a Very Small Place,* 314–23; Logevall, *Embers of War,* 513.

99. Fall, *Hell in a Very Small Place,* 318. The leader of the main infantry element was Lieutenant Colonel Yves Godard, and Colonel Jean Boucher de Crèvecoeur was the overall French commander in Laos.

100. Fall, "Indochina—The Last Year of the War: The Navarre Plan," 54–55; Fall, *Hell in a Very Small Place,* 45.

101. Roy, *Battle of Dien Bien Phu,* 179.

102. Ibid., 152–53.

103. Sauvagnac, *Report of December 20, 1954,* 8; Commandement des Forces Terrestres du Nord-Viêt-Nam, État-Major, 3e Bureau [Chef d'Escadron Henri Spangenberger, Chef du 3e Bureau], "Plan de stationnement du groupement operationnel Nord Ouest" [No. 10152/3/S, Hanoi, February 6, 1953 (should be 1954)], 2, in folder "EMIFT, 3e Bureau, Operations: Dien Bien Phu," box 10 H 1169, Fonds Indochine, SHAT. For the French order of battle at Dien Bien Phu on March 13, 1954, see also Fall, *Hell in a Very Small Place,* 479–81; Langlais, *Dien Bien Phu,* table ("Forces en presence le 13 mars"); Windrow, *The Last Valley,* appendix 2.

13. The Limits of Aerial Resupply

1. Commandement des Forces Terrestres du Nord-Viêt-Nam, Le Chef d'État-Major [Commandant Baubeau, Sous-Chef Logistique], "Aspects logistiques de la bataille de Dien Bien Phu" [No. 313/FTNV/CEM, Hanoi, July 6, 1954], 6, in folder "Dien Bien Phu 14—État-Major, Forces Terrestres du Nord-Viêt-Nam, 3e Bureau, Le Soutien logistique en Ravitaillement—4e Bureau Materials," box 10 H 1176, Fonds Indochine, SHAT (cited hereafter as Baubeau, "Aspects logistiques"); Commandant des Troupes Aéroportées en Indochine [Colonel Henri Sauvagnac], "Rapport du Colonel Commandant les T.A.P.I. sur les opérations de ravitaillement par Air pendant la bataille de DIEN BIEN PHU (novembre 1953–mai 1954)" [Hanoi, December 20, 1954], 8, in folder "EMIFT, 3e Bureau—Operations: Dien Bien Phu," box 10 H 1169, Fonds Indochine, SHAT (cited hereafter as Sauvagnac, *Report of December 20, 1954*).

2. Commandement en Chef des Forces Terrestres Navales et Aériennes en Indochine, État—Major Interarmées et des Forces Terrestres, Bureau Transports, "Étude sur les Aérotransports à Dien Bien Phu à partir du 13 mars 1954" [Saigon, May 21, 1954], 1, in folder "Dien Bien Phu 5—Transport, etc.—4e Bureau, BMT, decembre 1953–mai 1954," box 10 H 1177, Fonds Indochine, SHAT.

3. Ibid.

4. Pierre Langlais, *Dien Bien Phu* (Paris: Éditions France-Empire, 1963), 239, English translation by the author. Then–Lieutenant Colonel Pierre Charles Langlais, commander of GAP 2, was the de facto commander of French Union forces at Dien Bien Phu from the end of March onward. See Bernard B. Fall, *Hell in a Very Small Place: The Siege of Dien Bien Phu* (New York: Vintage, 1966), 176–77.

5. Langlais, *Dien Bien Phu,* 36–37.

6. Fall, *Hell in a Very Small Place,* 190.

7. Ibid., 185; Langlais, *Dien Bien Phu,* 37.

8. "Étude sur les Aérotransports à Dien Bien Phu," 1–2.

9. Paul Grauwin, *Doctor at Dienbienphu* (New York: John Day, 1955), 175.

10. "Étude sur les Aérotransports à Dien Bien Phu," 2.

11. Fall, *Hell in a Very Small Place*, 167.

12. Sauvagnac, *Report of December 20, 1954*, 8.

13. Bernard B. Fall, *Le Viet-Minh: La République Démocratique du Viet-Nam, 1945–1960* (Paris: Librairie Armand Colin, 1960), 213.

14. Commandant des Troupes Aéroportées en Indochine [Colonel Henri Sauvagnac], "Rapport du Colonel Sauvagnac, Commandant les T.A.P.I., sur la participation des Aéroportés à la Bataille de DIEN BIEN PHU et sur quelques enseignements à en tirer" [Hanoi, June 2, 1954], 28–29, in folder "EMIFT, 3e Bureau—Operations: Dien Bien Phu," box 10 H 1169, Fonds Indochine, SHAT (cited hereafter as Sauvagnac, *Report of June 2, 1954*); Sauvagnac, *Report of December 20, 1954*, 8.

15. Jules Roy, *The Battle of Dien Bien Phu* (New York: Harper and Row, 1965), 253–54.

16. Sauvagnac, *Report of June 2, 1954*, 30.

17. Fall, *Hell in a Very Small Place*, 454–55. For details on the Viet Minh antiaircraft artillery at Dien Bien Phu, see Boylan, "No 'Technical Knockout,'" passim.

18. Edgar O'Ballance, *The Indo-China War 1945–1954: A Study in Guerrilla Warfare* (London: Faber and Faber, 1964), 225.

19. Roy, *Battle of Dien Bien Phu*, 154; Julian Thompson, *The Lifeblood of War: Logistics in Armed Conflict* (London: Brassey's, 1991), 182. Boylan ("No 'Technical Knockout,'" 1366 [table 6], 1382), more accurately, I think, puts the numbers at twenty-four 37 mm antiaircraft guns and sixty 12.7 mm antiaircraft machine guns at the start of the battle on March 13, rising to thirty-six 37 mm guns and eighty-four 12.7 mm AA machine guns during the last phase from May 1 to May 7. The Soviet M1939 (61-K) 37 mm antiaircraft gun had a range of three kilometers and a maximum rate of fire of 160–170 rounds per minute.

20. Headquarters, Department of the Army, Office of the Assistant Chief of Staff, G-2, *Indochina Military Situation Report (Indochina SITREP) No. 29* (Washington, D.C.: HQDA, OACS G-2, March 26, 1954), paragraph 2b.

21. Fall, *Hell in a Very Small Place*, 223.

22. Ibid., 105.

23. Ibid., 337, citing a report prepared by the Fairchild Corporation (the maker of the C-119) in October 1955.

24. Ibid., 337.

25. Ibid. Martin Windrow (*The Last Valley: Dien Bien Phu and the French Defeat in Vietnam* [New York: Da Capo, 2004], 707) puts the transport losses from March 13 to May 7 as four C-47s and one C-119. In addition, four B-26s, two PB4Y-2 Privateers, two SB2C dive-bombers, and six fighters were lost.

26. Fall, *Hell in a Very Small Place*, 455; Bernard Fall, *Street without Joy: Insurgency in Indochina, 1946–63*, 3rd rev. ed. (Harrisburg, Pa.: Stackpole, 1963), 259. Lieutenant General Henri Navarre (*Le Temps des Vérités* [Paris: Plon, 1957], 354) stated that thirty-six aircraft were shot down and 150 damaged, with a loss of seventy personnel killed or wounded.

27. Michèle Battesti, "La Marine et la guerre d'Indochine," *Revue Historique des Armées* 177 (December 1989): 86–87. But see Windrow (*The Last Valley*, 707), who puts the total of navy losses between March 13 and May 7 at ten planes (two PB4Y-2 Privateers, two SB2C Helldivers, three F6F Bearcats, and three F8F Hellcats).

28. Baubeau, "Aspects logistiques," 7. Howard R. Simpson (*Tiger in the Barbed Wire: An American in Vietnam, 1952–1991* [New York: Brassey's, 1992], 96) states that Colonel Nicot made the decision to increase the drop altitude from two thousand feet to eight thousand feet on the evening of March 27. All altitude figures are distance above ground level. The camp itself was about sixteen hundred feet above sea level.

29. Baubeau, "Aspects logistiques," 7. Lieutenant General Navarre (*Le Temps des Verités*, 354) asserted that losses were less than 20 percent and that the Viet Minh recovered only a small part of the misdropped cargo. Langlais (*Dien Bien Phu*, 44) put the losses at around 30 percent from April 20. A drop at eight thousand feet subjected the parachute and its cargo to the effects of the wind for about six minutes, a comparatively long time.

30. Langlais, *Dien Bien Phu*, 43.

31. Baubeau, "Aspects logistiques," 11. Plating ("Failure at the Margins," 141) notes that the loss of HUGUETTE 6 on April 16 was critical in that the main drop zone was reduced "to the point where resupply was actually counterproductive," in that the French transports subsequently "supplied the Vietminh with nearly the same effectiveness as their own forces."

32. Fall, *Hell in a Very Small Place*, 285.

33. Quoted in Fall, *Hell in a Very Small Place*, 359.

34. Howard R. Simpson, *Dien Bien Phu: The Epic Battle America Forgot*, paperback ed. (Washington, D.C.: Brassey's, 1996), 116–17; Windrow, *The Last Valley*, 508. According to Simpson, one Viet Minh regiment alone obtained over fifty tons of supplies, including artillery shells and rations, from the misdropped cargo.

35. Windrow, *The Last Valley*, 508. Some of the airdropped and parachuted cargo also landed on structures, supplies, and personnel, causing serious losses. The camp was also subjected to friendly fire in the form of bombing errors by the supporting French aircraft. Two of the more serious incidents took place on April 12 and 14 and resulted in a number of casualties and a significant loss of materiel.

36. Baubeau, "Aspects logistiques," 7.

37. "Étude sur les Aérotransports à Dien Bien Phu," 2. At least ten tons of the daily one hundred tons were rations.

38. Baubeau, "Aspects logistiques," 8; Sauvagnac, *Report of December 20, 1954*, 9.

39. "Étude sur les Aérotransports à Dien Bien Phu," 2–3.

40. Ibid., 3. The paratroop bureaucracy strongly opposed the parachuting of personnel without proper training, but the desperate need for replacements in Dien Bien Phu overcame their objections. See Fall, *Hell in a Very Small Place*, 248. Colonel Pierre Langlais later argued forcefully for the award of the coveted French parachutist badge to those volunteers whose only jump was into the *cuvette* ("toilet bowl") of Dien Bien Phu. He lost. See Windrow, *The Last Valley*, 498.

41. Baubeau, "Aspects logistiques," 9.

42. Fall, *Hell in a Very Small Place*, 254–55.

43. Ibid., 328.

44. Baubeau, "Aspects logistiques," 9.

45. Ibid.

46. Sauvagnac, *Report of June 2, 1954*, 30–31.

47. Baubeau, "Aspects logistiques," 9 (*"le support logistique* possible *devenait*

insuffisant").

48. Ibid.

49. Quoted in Simpson, *Dien Bien Phu,* 151–52.

50. "Étude sur les Aérotransports à Dien Bien Phu," 3. During the last week before the garrison fell, some 396 men of the 1st Colonial Parachute Battalion (*1e Bataillon de Para-chutistes Coloniaux*; 1e BPC) parachuted into the doomed position.

51. Baubeau, "Aspects logistiques," 10. This was the largest drop in almost three weeks. See Fredrik Logevall, *Embers of War: The Fall of an Empire and the Making of America's Vietnam* (New York: Random House, 2012), 528.

52. "Étude sur les Aérotransports à Dien Bien Phu," table ("Aerotransport sur Dien Bien Phu"). Reinforcements between March 13 and May 5 included five parachute battalions (approximately 500 men each) and about 750 individual replacements. See Langlais, *Dien Bien Phu,* table ("Évolution des effectifs au cours de la bataille").

53. Sauvagnac, *Report of December 20, 1954,* annex 5; "Étude sur les Aérotransports à Dien Bien Phu," 4.

54. Baubeau, "Aspects logistiques," table ("Taux Moyens Journaliers d'Entretien à Dien Bien Phu [h/j]").

55. Fall, *Hell in a Very Small Place,* 176–78.

56. Ibid., 236–37.

57. Grauwin, *Doctor at Dienbienphu,* 180.

58. Fall, *Hell in a Very Small Place,* 268. Windrow (*The Last Valley,* 527) notes that "there were still a few jeeps running, but for the recovery gangs to gather up and transport 100 tons of supplies divided between 1,000 packages, with only a handful of ¾-ton [*sic*] jeeps to supplement human muscles was simply impossible." (The U.S. jeep used by the French was actually a ¼-ton vehicle.)

59. Sauvagnac, *Report of June 2, 1954,* 29–30.

60. Grauwin, *Doctor at Dienbienphu,* 259–60.

61. Ibid., 174; Fall, *Hell in a Very Small Place,* 255.

62. Fall, *Hell in a Very Small Place,* 252. Grauwin (*Doctor at Dienbienphu,* 174) noted that more than two hundred of the PIMs were killed or wounded by the end of their first week of collection duty.

63. Grauwin, *Doctor at Dienbienphu,* 175.

64. Langlais, *Dien Bien Phu,* 116, 199–200.

65. Ibid., 200.

66. Grauwin, *Doctor at Dienbienphu,* 160–61. Grauwin (pages 259–60) also tells the story of two Legionnaires of the 2e BEP on a difficult supply detail who collapsed in the mud with their loads and died on the spot from inanition, complete endocrine exhaustion brought on by the constant and extreme physical effort.

67. Fall, *Hell in a Very Small Place,* 252–53; Windrow, *The Last Valley,* 514.

68. Fall, *Hell in a Very Small Place,* 347. *Vinogel* was the French Army issue wine concentrate.

69. The failure was due in part to the traditional distaste of the French Army for serious digging in. See Windrow, *The Last Valley,* 316.

70. France, Ministére de l'Armée de Terre, École Superieure de Guerre et École d'État-

Major, *Aide-Mémoire pour les Travaux d'État-Major,* provisional ed. (Paris: École Superieure de Guerre et École d'État-Major, February 1952), part 2, section 461 (*"Emplacements de Combat"*) and section 462 (*"Tranchées et Communications En Terre [avec outils à main]"*). An automatic weapon position took one squad eight days to construct, and a squad bunker required the efforts of a platoon (*section*) for ten days.

71. Ibid., part 2, section 461 and section 462; Fall, *Hell in a Very Small Place,* 88.

72. Fall, *Hell in a Very Small Place,* 88; Windrow, *The Last Valley,* 316; Logevall, *Embers of War,* 406–7. Windrow (*The Last Valley,* 672n15) observes that each of the twelve battalions at Dien Bien Phu required five hundred tons of barbed wire, but that a total of only three thousand tons was provided for the entire camp, or less than half of each battalion's needs.

73. Baubeau, "Aspects logistiques," table ("Taux Moyens Journaliers d'Entretien à Dien Bien Phu [h/j]"); Fall, *Hell in a Very Small Place,* 89.

74. Fall, *Hell in a Very Small Place,* 89–90.

75. Letter, Commandant le Génie des Forces Terrestres du Nord-Viêt-Nam [Colonel Legendre] to Commandant des Forces Terrestres du Nord-Viêt-Nam [Major General Cogny], État-Major, 3e Bureau, concerning the tonnage of engineer materiel sent to Dien Bien Phu [No. 13,715/3, (Hanoi), undated (1954)], 1, in folder "EMIFT, 3e Bureau, Operations: Dien Bien Phu," box 10 H 1169, Fonds Indochine, SHAT.

76. Fall, *Hell in a Very Small Place,* 91.

77. Ibid., 95.

78. Ibid., 366.

79. Ibid., 256, 366–67.

80. Intendance operations in support of Dien Bien Phu are described in Direction de l'Intendance des Forces Terrestres du Nord-Viêt-Nam [Intendant Militaire de 1e Classe Faivre], "Compte rendu sur l'activité du service de l'Intendance au profit du G. O. N. O. entre le 20 novembre 1953 et le 8 mai 1954" [No. 23/Cabinet, Hanoi, June 12, 1954], in folder "EMIFT, 3e Bureau, Operations: Dien Bien Phu," box 10 H 1169, Fonds Indochine, SHAT (cited hereafter as *Faivre Report*). See also Windrow, *The Last Valley,* 326–27.

81. *Faivre Report,* table 1 ("Tableau faisant apparaître les volants théoriques et reéls").

82. Ibid., 7–8.

83. Ibid., 7.

84. Ibid., table 4 ("Articles d'habillement expédiés").

85. Fall, *Hell in a Very Small Place,* 249, 340.

86. Windrow, *The Last Valley,* 326.

87. *Faivre Report,* 4.

88. Ibid., 10; Fall, *Hell in a Very Small Place,* 402, 426.

89. *Faivre Report,* table 5 ("Situation detaillée des approvisionnements au C. R. de Dien-Bien-Phu le 13 mars à 17 H."). A total of eighteen rations per man were available for some Indochinese units. Details of the ration situation at Dien Bien Phu are drawn from the *Faivre Report* unless otherwise noted.

90. Fall, *Hell in a Very Small Place,* 247.

91. Ibid.

92. Ibid., quoting Colonel Langlais.

93. Ibid., 285.

94. Ibid., 247, 344.

95. Ibid., 344.

96. Baubeau, "Aspects logistiques," 9.

97. *Faivre Report,* table 6 ("Recapitulation").

98. Grauwin, *Doctor at Dienbienphu,* 259.

99. Direction du Matériel des Forces Terrestres du Nord-Viêt-Nam [Colonel Ferrer, Directeur], "Rapport du Colonel Ferrer, Directeur du Matériel des F.T.N.V., au profit de Dien Bien Phu, 20 novembre 1953–8 mai 1954" [No. 5270/FTNV/DIRMAT/Section Organisation, Hanoi, June 15, 1954], 1–2, in folder "EMIFT, 3e Bureau, Operations: Dien Bien Phu," box 10 H 1169, Fonds Indochine, SHAT (cited hereafter as *Ferrer Report*). Colonel Ferrer's report can be supplemented by Colonel Léonard, "Quelques aspects typiques du rôle du Matériel en Indochine," *Revue Historique de l'Armée* 12, no. 3 (August 1956): 117–27.

100. Léonard, "Quelques aspects typiques du rôle du Matériel en Indochine," 125.

101. Ibid.

102. *Ferrer Report,* 2.

103. Ibid.

104. Ibid., 1; Léonard, "Quelques aspects typiques du rôle du Matériel en Indochine," 125.

105. *Ferrer Report,* 1.

106. Ibid. Obviously, some vehicles were repaired more than once.

107. Ibid. Another platoon of five M24 tanks was flown to Luang Prabang and a company of M5 and M8 tanks to the Plain of Jars at about the same time. See *Lessons Learned in the Indochina War,* 2:270n4.

108. Fall, *Hell in a Very Small Place,* 97; Windrow, *The Last Valley,* 35, 307–8; Logevall, *Embers of War,* 408.

109. *Lessons Learned in the Indochina War,* 2:270.

110. Léonard, "Quelques aspects typiques du rôle du Matériel en Indochine," 125.

111. Ibid.

112. *Ferrer Report,* 10 (table). Another 475 tons were delivered to Luang Prabang and Muong Sai.

113. Baubeau, "Aspects logistiques," table ("Taux Moyens Journaliers d'Entretien à Dien Bien Phu [h/j]").

114. Forces Terrestres du Nord-Viêt-Nam, Commandant de l'Artillerie [Colonel Heeré], "Rapport Annuel 1954" [Hanoi, 1954], 3, in folder "EMIFT, 3e Bureau, Enseignements à tirer de la campagne d'Indochine, Fasc. III, p. 98—Artillerie du N. V.—Rapports Annuels, 1954," box 10 H 983, Fonds Indochine, SHAT; Fall, *Hell in a Very Small Place,* 350, 367.

115. Fall, *Hell in a Very Small Place,* 84.

116. Ibid., 471n10.

117. Ibid., 143.

118. Ibid., 226. See also Windrow, *The Last Valley,* 459–60, 679n12, 682n13.

119. Fall, *Hell in a Very Small Place,* 242; Fall, *Street without Joy,* 20.

120. Fall, *Hell in a Very Small Place,* 350.

121. Ibid., 458.

122. Commandement en Chef des Forces Terrestres Navales et Aériennes en Indochine, État-Major Interarmées et des Forces Terrestres, 4e Bureau, 1e Section, "Fiche: Aspect financier de l'opération de DIEN BIEN PHU" [Saigon, 1955], annex II, in folder "Dien Bien Phu 5—Transport, etc.—4e Bureau, Prix de Revient—Aspect financier de l'opération de DIEN BIEN PHU," box 10 H 1177, Fonds Indochine, SHAT.

123. Ibid., annex I; Sauvagnac, *Report of December 20, 1954,* annex 5.

124. Sauvagnac, *Report of December 20, 1954,* annex 5; *Lessons Learned in the Indochina War,* 3:148n1.

125. Plating, "Failure at the Margins," ii. Elsewhere Plating notes that "even outnumbered five to one, the French could probably have held had the airdrops reached them instead of their enemy—an enemy that was most likely on the verge of exhausting his ammunition had he not been supplied by French airlift" (125).

126. Baubeau, "Aspects logistiques," 12.

14. The Triumph of the Porters

1. Bernard B. Fall, *Hell in a Very Small Place: The Siege of Dien Bien Phu* (New York: Vintage, 1966), 384.

2. Vo Nguyen Giap, *Inside the Viet Minh* (Washington, D.C.: Marine Corps Association, 1962), 174–75.

3. Vo Nguyen Giap, *Dien Bien Phu,* 2nd ed. (Hanoi: Foreign Languages Publishing House, 1962), 32.

4. Martin Windrow (*The Last Valley: Dien Bien Phu and the French Defeat in Vietnam* [New York: Da Capo, 2004], 259) notes, "The People's Army had never successfully assaulted a fortified French position held by more than two companies."

5. Fall, *Hell in a Very Small Place,* 125.

6. Giap, *Inside the Viet Minh,* IV-19; Pierre Asselin, "New Perspectives on Dien Bien Phu," *Explorations in Southeast Asian Studies* 1, no. 2 (fall 1997): 3, www2.hawaii .edu/~seassa/explorations/v1n2/art2/v1n2-frame2.html (accessed February 6, 2014).

7. Fall, *Hell in a Very Small Place,* 50–51. For the essence of Giap's plan and the difficulties of carrying it out, see Fredrik Logevall, *Embers of War: The Fall of an Empire and the Making of America's Vietnam* (New York: Random House, 2012), 393–94.

8. Jules Roy, *The Battle of Dienbienphu,* trans. Robert Baldick (New York: Harper and Row, 1965), 68.

9. Ibid., xvii–xviii, 30.

10. Lieutenant General John W. O'Daniel, USA (Chief, U.S. Joint Military Mission to Indochina), *Report of U. S. Special Mission to Indochina (23 January–5 February 1954)—Situation in French Indochina and FUF Materiel Requirements, February 1954,* Pearl Harbor, Hawaii, February 5, 1954, 12, in box 10 ("092 Asia [6-25-48] [2] Section 22"), Geographical File, 1954–1956, RG 218 (Records of the U.S. Joint Chiefs of Staff), National Archives II, College Park, Maryland.

11. Roy, *The Battle of Dienbienphu,* xviii. As one junior officer on General Navarre's staff is quoted as having said: "In any case, Giap can't win the battle of Dien-Bien-Phu. He's never done a Staff College course." Plating, "Failure at the Margins," 80, citing French war correspondent Brigitte Friang, *Parachutes and Petticoats,* trans. James Cadell (London:

Quality Book Club, 1958), 223.

12. Quoted in Raoul Salan, *Indochine Rouge: Le Message d'Hô Chi Minh* (Paris: Presses de la Cité, 1975), 35.

13. Roy, *The Battle of Dienbienphu*, 58. One is reminded of the failure of U.S. intelligence officers to recognize the Chinese Communist intervention in Korea in the fall of 1950.

14. Headquarters, Department of the Army, Office of the Assistant Chief of Staff, G-2, *Indochina Military Situation Report (Indochina SITREP) No. 11* (Washington, D.C.: HQDA, OACS G-2, November 13, 1953), paragraph 3. Unless otherwise indicated, the following narrative of the lead-up to the Viet Minh assault on March 13, 1954, is based on the weekly *Indochina SITREP*s from November 13, 1953, to March 13, 1954.

15. Roy (*The Battle of Dienbienphu*, 32) notes that the rice stockpiled at Dien Bien Phu represented only a fraction of General Giap's requirements and thus did not constitute, by itself, a sufficient reason for him to undertake the difficult task of besieging the French in their entrenched camp.

16. *Indochina SITREP No. 20*, January 22, 1954, paragraph 3. A month of deliveries at the estimated rate were considered sufficient to supply three Viet Minh divisions, supported by field and antiaircraft artillery, for sixty days of combat.

17. Roy, *The Battle of Dienbienphu*, 138.

18. *Indochina SITREP No. 27*, March 12, 1954, paragraph 3.

19. Henri Navarre, *Le Temps des Vérités* (Paris: Plon, 1957), 332.

20. Roy, *The Battle of Dienbienphu*, 154.

21. Ibid.

22. *Indochina SITREP No. 28*, March 19, 1954, paragraph 3.

23. Giap, *Inside the Viet Minh*, IV-4–5.

24. Navarre, *Le Temps des Vérités*, 332; Pierre Langlais, *Dien Bien Phu* (Paris: Éditions France-Empire, 1963), table ("Forces en Presence le 13 Mars").

25. Navarre, *Le Temps des Vérités*, 332.

26. Fall, *Hell in a Very Small Place*, 133. Phillip B. Davidson (*Vietnam at War: The History, 1946–1975* [Novato, Calif.: Presidio, 1988], 223) puts the Viet Minh strength around Dien Bien Phu on March 13, 1954, at forty-nine thousand combatants and ten thousand to fifteen thousand logistical support personnel.

27. Windrow, *The Last Valley*, 292–93. Windrow gives a stirring description of the process.

28. Giap, *Inside the Viet Minh*, V-11. As historian Qiang Zhai points out (*China and the Vietnam Wars, 1950–1975* [Chapel Hill: Univ. of North Carolina Press, 2000], 42), the willingness of the Vietnamese peasants to serve as porters was enhanced by the 1953 land reforms carried out by the Viet Minh.

29. Roy, *The Battle of Dienbienphu*, 81; Fall, *Hell in a Very Small Place*, 59. For a general discussion of the Viet Minh supply routes and procedures, see Logevall, *Embers of War*, 414–17, and Windrow, *The Last Valley*, 259–65.

30. Navarre, *Le Temps des Vérités*, 326; Davidson, *Vietnam at War*, 214; Julian Thompson, *The Lifeblood of War: Logistics in Armed Conflict* (London: Brassey's, 1991), 172.

31. Navarre, *Le Temps des Vérités*, 326.

32. *Indochina SITREP No. 19,* January 15, 1954, paragraph 3.

33. Edgar O'Ballance, *The Indo-China War 1945–1954: A Study in Guerrilla Warfare* (London: Faber and Faber, 1964), 204.

34. *Indochina SITREP No. 18,* January 8, 1954, paragraph 3.

35. *Indochina SITREP No. 23,* February 12, 1954, paragraph 3.

36. Navarre, *Le Temps des Vérités,* 327; Davidson, *Vietnam at War,* 216; Thompson, *Lifeblood of War,* 171.

37. *Indochina SITREP No. 14,* December 4, 1953, paragraph 3. Elements of the 151st were also preparing ferry crossings on the Clear, Red, and Black Rivers. Earlier, during September and October 1953, the 151st was engaged in constructing a new road from Phu Tho west to the Black River. See *Indochina SITREP No. 3,* September 18, 1953, paragraph 3; *Indochina SITREP No. 5,* October 2, 1953, paragraph 3.

38. Commander in Chief, French Forces in the Far East, *Lessons from the Indo-China War,* vol. 3 (Washington, D.C.: DARPA, 1955), 34n2. See also Kevin M. Boylan, "No 'Technical Knockout': Giap's Artillery at Dien Bien Phu," *Journal of Military History* 78, no. 4 (October 2014), 1379.

39. Fall, *Hell in a Very Small Place,* 129.

40. Langlais, *Dien Bien Phu,* 45–46.

41. Quoted in Fall, *Hell in a Very Small Place,* 179.

42. Navarre, *Le Temps des Vérités,* 355n2. For Navarre's experiments in early April with using sacks of smoking charcoal impregnated with silver iodide dropped by parachute, see Roy, *The Battle of Dienbienphu,* 224–25.

43. See Windrow, *The Last Valley,* 265–67.

44. *Indochina SITREP No. 34,* April 30, 1954, paragraph 3.

45. *Indochina SITREP No. 35,* May 7, 1954, paragraph 3.

46. Asselin, "New Perspectives on Dien Bien Phu," 6 (33,500 *dân cong* mobilized); Windrow, *The Last Valley,* 265–67 (35,000 on March 13, 1954); Fall, *Hell in a Very Small Place,* 133 (54,500); Navarre, *Le Temps des Vérités,* 326 (75,000); Davidson, *Vietnam at War,* 216 (over 260,000); Thompson, *Lifeblood of War,* 171 (over 260,000). The first volume of the French official lessons learned from the war in Indochina, published in English translation by the BDM Corporation (*A Study of Strategic Lessons Learned in Vietnam,* vol. 1, *The Enemy* [McLean, Va.: BDM Corporation, November 30, 1979], 5-8) put the logistical forces supporting the four Viet Minh divisions at Dien Bien Phu at over seventy thousand coolies and at least twenty thousand Chinese military personnel. More recently, Christopher E. Goscha ("'Hell in a Very Small Place': Cold War and Decolonisation in the Assault on the Vietnamese Body at Dien Bien Phu," *European Journal of East Asian Studies* 9, no. 2 [December 2010]: 220) puts the total number of civilian porters, both men and women, mobilized by the Viet Minh for the Dien Bien Phu campaign at precisely 261,451. Such precision should perhaps be taken with more than a grain of salt. Logevall (*Embers of War,* 394) states that Giap's plan for the Dien Bien Phu operation called for 42,570 combat troops supported by only 14,500 civilian porters.

47. *Indochina SITREP No. 17,* December 30, 1953, paragraph 3.

48. Howard R. Simpson, *Dien Bien Phu: The Epic Battle America Forgot* (Washington, D.C.: Brassey's, 1994), 35.

49. On the use of modified bicycles for the movement of cargo by the Viet Minh, see Asselin, "New Perspectives on Dien Bien Phu," 6 (only 2,724 used); Logevall, *Embers of War*, 415; Goscha, "'Hell in a Very Small Place': Cold War and Decolonisation in the Assault on the Vietnamese Body at Dien Bien Phu," 205–6 (20,991 used).

50. Roy, *The Battle of Dienbienphu*, 105.

51. Ibid., 30, 105. Logevall (*Embers of War*, 415) notes that many of the bicycles were manufactured in France at St. Étienne or the Peugeot factories, that the bicycles were strengthened with wood struts on the frame and bamboo poles to extend the handlebars, and that such modified bicycles could carry up to three hundred kilograms.

52. Davidson, *Vietnam at War*, 216; Thompson, *Lifeblood of War*, 171.

53. *Indochina SITREP No. 29*, March 26, 1954, paragraph 3; *Indochina SITREP No. 27*, March 12, 1954, paragraph 3.

54. *Indochina SITREP No. 30*, April 2, 1954, paragraph 3.

55. Goscha, "'Hell in a Very Small Place': Cold War and Decolonisation in the Assault on the Vietnamese Body at Dien Bien Phu," 220. Windrow (*The Last Valley*, 261) cites the difficulties encountered by Viet Minh combat troops on long marches. Those difficulties applied to the porters as well. See also Windrow, *The Last Valley*, 267.

56. They also employed more than 11,000 sampans and other small boats and over 17,400 horses. See Goscha, "'Hell in a Very Small Place': Cold War and Decolonisation in the Assault on the Vietnamese Body at Dien Bien Phu," 205; Asselin, "New Perspectives on Dien Bien Phu," 6.

57. *Indochina SITREP No. 24*, February 19, 1954, paragraph 3; O'Ballance, *The Indo-China War*, 204; Simpson, *Dien Bien Phu*, 34; Logevall, *Embers of War*, 414; Windrow, *The Last Valley*, 262.

58. *Indochina SITREP No. 24*, February 19, 1954, paragraph 3; Davidson, *Vietnam at War*, 214.

59. *Indochina SITREP No. 24*, February 19, 1954, paragraph 3.

60. *Indochina SITREP No. 35*, May 7, 1954, paragraph 3.

61. Davidson, *Vietnam at War*, 214.

62. Simpson, *Dien Bien Phu*, 34.

63. *Indochina SITREP No. 34*, April 30, 1954, paragraph 3.

64. Roy, *The Battle of Dienbienphu*, 255.

65. Fall, *Hell in a Very Small Place*, 129.

66. Ibid., 130. As Fall notes, this was an extremely small force when matched against the two hundred U.S. combat aircraft regularly participating in a single raid against North Viet Nam in 1966.

67. Ibid., 131; Davidson, *Vietnam at War*, 217. One of the Privateers was shot down in the attempt to close RP 41. See Bernard B. Fall, *Street without Joy: Insurgency in Indochina, 1946–63*, 3rd rev. ed. (Harrisburg, Pa.: Stackpole, 1963), 261.

68. Fall, *Street without Joy*, 257.

69. *Lessons Learned in the Indochina War*, 3:33.

70. Fall, *Hell in a Very Small Place*, 131. Windrow (*The Last Valley*, 281) quotes General Fay, the chief of staff of the French Air Force, as having written after the war, "It would have brought better results if we had consistently concentrated the maximum of bombs on one or two points and ensured the almost permanent cutting of the route at these points by

harassing the repair work."

71. Ibid.

72. Roy, *The Battle of Dienbienphu,* 94–95.

73. Vo Nguyen Giap, *People's War, People's Army: The Viet Cong Insurrection Manual for Underdeveloped Countries* (New York: Praeger, 1962), 214.

74. Bernard B. Fall in Roger Trinquier, *Modern Warfare: A French View of Insurgency* (London and Dunmow: Pall Mall Press, 1964; reprint, Fort Leavenworth, Kans.: Combat Studies Institute, January 1985), xvii.

75. Langlais, *Dien Bien Phu,* 48–49.

76. Fall, *Hell in a Very Small Place,* 131, 133.

77. Roy, *The Battle of Dienbienphu,* 111.

78. Davidson, *Vietnam at War,* 215–16; Thompson, *Lifeblood of War,* 173.

79. Langlais, *Dien Bien Phu,* 47–48. English translation by the author. See also Windrow's *The Last Valley* (285), where he quotes Major Nicolas, the commander of the 1st Battalion, 4th Moroccan Rifle Regiment, regarding the Viet Minh ability to repair cuts in the roads quickly.

80. *Indochina SITREP No. 18,* January 8, 1954, paragraph 3.

81. *Indochina SITREP No. 25,* February 26, 1954, paragraph 3.

82. *Indochina SITREP No. 31,* April 9, 1954, paragraph 3.

83. Simpson, *Dien Bien Phu,* 117.

84. Cable no. 3710, Ambassador Douglas Dillon to Secretary of State John Foster Dulles, Paris, April 5, 1954, subject: Conversations with the French about Dien Bien Phu, document 29, in *The Pentagon Papers: The Defense Department History of United States Decisionmaking in Vietnam,* vol. 1, ed. Mike Gravel (Boston: Beacon, 1971), 461–62.

85. *Indochina SITREP No. 31,* April 9, 1954, paragraph 3.

86. *Indochina SITREP No. 35,* May 7, 1954, paragraph 3.

87. Davidson, *Vietnam at War,* 216; *Indochina SITREP No. 37,* May 24, 1954, paragraph 3; Plating, "Failure at the Margins," 126–27, citing Jean Pouget, *Nous étions à Dien Bien Phu* (Paris, 1964), 380. Pouget was General Navarre's aide-de-camp, but he jumped into Dien Bien Phu as a company commander with the 1er BPC. According to Qiang Zhai (*China and the Vietnam Wars,* 49), the Central Military Commission of the Chinese Communist Party instructed the CMAG "not to spare artillery shells" in order to achieve "a total victory."

88. Joseph Jeremiah Zasloff, *The Role of Sanctuary in Insurgency: Communist China's Support to the Vietminh, 1946–1954* (Santa Monica, Calif.: RAND Corporation, May 1967), 33.

89. *Indochina SITREP No. 48,* August 6, 1954, paragraph 3.

90. Qiang Zhai, *China and the Vietnam Wars,* 46. General Wei Guo Qing was the head of CMAG and was presumably the superior of General Ly Chen-hou, who was reportedly stationed at Giap's headquarters.

91. Qiang Zhai (*China and the Vietnam Wars,* passim) favors the view that the Chinese played a critical role, and Howard R. Simpson ("'Très Secret,'" *Army* 44, no. 4 [April 1994]: 47–49), for one, repeats the story of General Ly Chen-hou and the fourteen Chinese advisors at Viet Minh headquarters urging the early frontal attacks that resulted in heavy Viet Minh casualties and General Giap's subsequent independent decision to switch to a classic

siege warfare technique.

92. Roy, *The Battle of Dienbienphu*, 203.

93. *Indochina SITREP No. 34*, April 30, 1954, paragraph 3; Fall, *Hell in a Very Small Place*, 266.

94. Qiang Zhai, *China and the Vietnam Wars*, 45.

95. On this point, see Bob Seals, "Chinese Support for North Vietnam during the Vietnam War: The Decisive Edge," *Military History Online*, September 23, 2008, 4, http://www .militaryhistoryonline.com/20thcentury/articles/chinesesupport.aspx (accessed August 16, 2010).

96. Cheng Geng quoted in Qiang Zhai, *China and the Vietnam Wars*, 64. See also Giap, *Dien Bien Phu*, 23; Seals, "Chinese Support for North Vietnam during the Vietnam War," 4.

97. Windrow, *The Last Valley*, appendix 4 (pages 708–9); Fall, *Hell in a Very Small Place*, 451 and appendix D (page 486). Fall includes two additional artillery battalions and one additional heavy weapons company.

98. Boylan, "No 'Technical Knockout,'" 1372, table 8 ("VPA Logistical Data for the Siege of Dien Bien Phu"), based on Gia Duc Pham et al., *Dien Bien Phu, Moc Vang Thoi Dai* [Dien Bien Phu: Landmark of the Golden Era] (Hanoi: People's Army Publishing House, 2004), 401–2.

99. Windrow (*The Last Valley*, 452), for example, puts the total tonnage of Viet Minh supplies delivered to Dien Bien Phu at only 8,926 tons, or less than half the amount the French air transport services delivered to the defenders, whose numbers were only about one-fifth those of the Viet Minh. Windrow's 8,926 tons included 46 tons of weapons, 2,000 tons of ammunition, 4,620 tons of petroleum products, and 2,260 tons of consumable supplies, including 1,700 tons of rice.

100. *Indochina SITREP No. 31*, April 9, 1954, paragraph 3.

101. Fall, *Hell in a Very Small Place*, 266.

102. For the mobilization of the Viet Minh medical services for Dien Bien Phu, see Goscha, "'Hell in a Very Small Place': Cold War and Decolonisation in the Assault on the Vietnamese Body at Dien Bien Phu," 216–21 and passim.

103. Thompson, *Lifeblood of War*, 183.

104. *Indochina SITREP No. 35*, May 7, 1954, paragraph 3. The Viet Minh had three hospitals supporting the battle that were capable of dealing with the most serious casualties: one at Tuan Giao, one at Son La, and one near the battlefield itself. See Goscha, "'Hell in a Very Small Place': Cold War and Decolonisation in the Assault on the Vietnamese Body at Dien Bien Phu," 216–17.

105. Goscha, "'Hell in a Very Small Place': Cold War and Decolonisation in the Assault on the Vietnamese Body at Dien Bien Phu," 218. See also Asselin, "New Perspectives on Dien Bien Phu," 5.

106. Fall, *Hell in a Very Small Place*, 101.

107. Fall (*Hell in a Very Small Place*, 127) puts the total at forty-eight 75 mm howitzers, forty-eight 105 mm howitzers, forty-eight 120 mm mortars, thirty-six 37 mm antiaircraft guns, fifty 12.7 mm antiaircraft machine guns, and twelve to sixteen Katyusha rocket launchers, as well as at least forty-eight 75 mm recoilless rifles. But on page 451 and in appendix D (page 486) Fall gives the number of 75 mm howitzers as fifteen and the number of 37 mm antiaircraft guns as twenty. Roy (*The Battle of Dienbienphu*, 154) gives the total

as eighteen 75 mm howitzers, twenty 105 mm howitzers, an unknown number of 120 mm mortars, eighty 37 mm antiaircraft guns, and one hundred 12.7 mm antiaircraft machine guns. See also Davidson (*Vietnam at War,* 224) and Zasloff (*The Role of Sanctuary in Insurgency,* 35–36), the latter of whom cites a December 1964 interview with a former French intelligence officer stationed in Hanoi at the time. The officer argued that the Viet Minh had at Dien Bien Phu only *twelve* 105 mm howitzers, eight of which had been supplied by the Chinese and four of which had been captured from the French.

108. Boylan, "No 'Technical Knockout,'" 1356, more correctly notes that two companies of the 224th Rocket Artillery Battalion, each equipped with six H6 six-barrel rocket launchers (similar to the Russian Katyusha), along with a 75 mm recoilless rifle battalion joined the 237th Artillery Regiment in the last weeks of the battle. See also *Indochina SITREP No. 36,* May 14, 1954, paragraph 3; *Indochina SITREP No. 41,* June 18, 1954, paragraph 3; Qiang Zhai, *China and the Vietnam Wars,* 49; Goscha, "'Hell in a Very Small Place': Cold War and Decolonisation in the Assault on the Vietnamese Body at Dien Bien Phu," 213–14.

109. Windrow, *The Last Valley,* 294–95 and appendix 4 (pages 709–10). Unaccounted for are the mortars and recoilless rifles of the divisional artillery battalions and heavy weapons companies. There were perhaps sixty 75 mm recoilless rifles with the infantry heavy weapons companies. The following divisional artillery battalions were present at Dien Bien Phu: 345th (304th Division), 159th (312th Division), and 980th (316th Division). It is unclear whether or not the artillery battalion of the 308th Division was present. Heavy weapons companies present included the 812th (316th Division) and 121st (148th Independent Infantry Regiment).

110. Boylan, "No 'Technical Knockout,'" 1349–83.

111. Fall (*Hell in a Very Small Place,* 451) states that the French intelligence estimated that the Viet Minh were capable of amassing only about twenty-five thousand rounds of artillery ammunition in the Dien Bien Phu area.

112. Fall, *Hell in a Very Small Place,* 105. See also Navarre, *Le Temps des Vérités,* 332; Windrow, *The Last Valley,* appendix 4B (pages 710–11).

113. *Indochina SITREP No. 37,* May 24, 1954, paragraph 3.

114. Bernard B. Fall, "Indochina—The Last Year of the War: The Navarre Plan," *Military Review* 36, no. 9 (December 1956): 52. Fall later revised his figures (*Hell in a Very Small Place,* 451) and reported that after the battle French artillerymen who had been at Dien Bien Phu estimated that the Viet Minh had fired only about 103,000 shells of 75 mm or larger. For the other estimates, see Boylan "No 'Technical Knockout,'" 1369–73 passim.

115. Boylan "No 'Technical Knockout,'" 1371. By contrast, the French defenders fired about 131,500 shells at the Viet Minh.

116. Plating, "Failure at the Margins," 140. Fall (*Hell in a Very Small Place,* 473n2) argued that the Viet Minh would have run out of 105 mm ammunition in the last days of the battle had it not been for the shells misdropped by the French. See also Boylan, "No 'Technical Knockout,'" 1371; Windrow, *The Last Valley,* appendix 4B (page 711); and *Indochina SITREP No. 37,* May 24, 1954, paragraph 3.

117. Roy, *The Battle of Dienbienphu,* 220.

118. Quoted in Goscha, "'Hell in a Very Small Place': Cold War and Decolonisation in the Assault on the Vietnamese Body at Dien Bien Phu," 201.

119. See the testimony of Nguyen Nhu Thien, who led teams of Viet Minh porters recovering the dead and wounded. Quoted by Goscha ("'Hell in a Very Small Place': Cold War and Decolonisation in the Assault on the Vietnamese Body at Dien Bien Phu," 221) from Nguyen Nhu Thien, *Dien Bien Phu vu d'en face, paroles de bo doi* (Paris: Nouveau Monde Editions, 2010), 179–80.

120. Asselin, "New Perspectives on Dien Bien Phu," 6. The French estimated Viet Minh casualties to be as high as 20,000. Fall (*Hell in a Very Small Place,* 487) puts the Viet Minh casualties at 22,900 men, of whom some 7,900 were killed. The official Viet Minh figures at the time were 13,930 casualties, including 4,020 dead, and no updated figures have since been issued. See Goscha, "'Hell in a Very Small Place': Cold War and Decolonisation in the Assault on the Vietnamese Body at Dien Bien Phu," 224. See also "Breakdown of losses suffered at Dien Bien Phu," http://www.dienbienphu.org/english/html/bataille/losses.htm (accessed February 22, 2014).

121. Windrow, *The Last Valley,* 540; Logevall, *Embers of War,* 518.

122. Giap, *Dien Bien Phu,* 40.

123. Windrow, *The Last Valley,* 623–24. To the totals given should be added an estimated 400 KIA and 400 WIA on May 6–7. See also Windrow, *The Last Valley,* 692; Fall, *Hell in a Very Small Place,* 484 (2,242 KIA, 6,463 WIA, 3,711 MIA, and 6,500 made POW); "Breakdown of losses suffered at Dien Bien Phu" (1,726 KIA, 5,234 WIA, 1,694 MIA plus Air Force [15 KIA, 6 WIA, 33 MIA, 43 made POW], Navy [approximately 26 KIA], and American pilots [2 KIA, 1 seriously WIA]). Of the 2,440 PIMs (Viet Minh prisoners of war) held in the Dien Bien Phu camp and used as laborers, about half became casualties.

124. George K. Tanham, *Communist Revolutionary Warfare: From the Vietminh to the Viet Cong,* rev. ed. (New York: Praeger, 1967), 97.

125. Fall, *Hell in a Very Small Place,* 432.

126. Windrow, *The Last Valley,* 694; "Breakdown of losses suffered at Dien Bien Phu." Logevall (*Embers of War,* 774n47) puts the number taken prisoner by the Viet Minh at 10,061, of whom 2,257 were French, 932 were Moroccan, 804 were Algerian, 221 were African, 2,262 were Legionnaires, and 3,585 were Vietnamese and others.

127. George A. Kelly, *Lost Soldiers: The French Army and Empire in Crisis, 1947–1962* (Cambridge, Mass.: M.I.T. Press, 1965), 52.

128. Kelly, *Lost Soldiers,* 52; Bernard B. Fall, *The Two Viet-Nams: A Political and Military Analysis,* 2nd rev. ed. (New York: Praeger, 1967), 129.

129. *Indochina SITREP No. 43,* July 2, 1954, paragraph 1.

130. Windrow, *The Last Valley,* 661n18.

131. Commandement en Chef des Forces Terrestres Navales et Aériennes en Indochine, État-Major Interarmées et des Forces Terrestres, 4e Bureau, 1e Section, "Fiche: Aspect financier de l'opération de DIEN BIEN PHU" [Saigon, 1955], 1, in folder "Dien Bien Phu 5—Transport, etc.—4e Bureau, Prix de Revient—Aspect financier de l'opération de DIEN BIEN PHU," box 10 H 1177, Fonds Indochine, SHAT.

15. Logistics and the War in Indochina, 1945–1954

1. Bernard B. Fall, *The Two Viet-Nams: A Political and Military Analysis,* 2nd rev. ed. (New York: Praeger, 1967), 472n6. The amounts given are in 1954 dollars. The equivalents

today would be nearly $96 billion and $9 billion, respectively.

2. Douglas Pike, *Viet Cong: The Organization and Techniques of the National Liberation Front of South Vietnam* (Cambridge, Mass.: M.I.T. Press, 1966), 49 and note 7. Pike's figures are taken from a press briefing paper released by the French embassy in Saigon in 1960 that also distributed the total French Union casualties as follows: French (74,068); Foreign Legion (24,096); Africans (54,020); Indochinese serving in the French Army (48,331); and Indochinese serving in native armies (29,642). See also Martin Windrow, *The Last Valley: Dien Bien Phu and the French Defeat in Vietnam* (New York: Da Capo, 2004), 604n61; Jacques Dalloz, *The War in Indochina, 1945–54* (New York: Barnes and Noble, 1990), 185; Fredrik Logevall, *Embers of War: The Fall of an Empire and the Making of America's Vietnam* (New York: Random House, 2012), 607; Michèle Bonnier, Soraya Djebbour, and Gilles Bonnier, *La guerre d'Indochine, 1946–1954* (Paris: Impression Copytop, May 2009), 18–19, 26.

3. Fall (*The Two Viet-Nams,* 129) estimated the Viet Minh losses at three times those of the French Union forces (in other words, about 300,000) and the number of civilian dead at around 250,000.

4. Bernard B. Fall, *Le Viet-Minh: La République Démocratique du Viet-Nam, 1945–1960* (Paris: Librairie Armand Colin, 1960), 181. English translation by the author.

5. Vo Nguyen Giap, *Dien Bien Phu,* 2nd ed. (Hanoi: Foreign Languages Publishing House, 1962), 41.

Glossary of Abbreviations, Acronyms, and Terms

1e Bureau, 2e Bureau, etc.   General Staff sections corresponding to the U.S. G-1, G-2, etc.

AA; AAA	antiaircraft; antiaircraft artillery
airdrop	aerial resupply by free fall drop
Alligator	tracked amphibious vehicle (LVT-4)
ARK	*Armée Royale Khmère* (Royal Cambodian Army)
BAPN/S	*Base Aéroporté Nord/Sud* (Airborne Base-North/South)
basic load	amount of rations, POL, ammunition, etc. normally carried by a using unit; usually consists of one or more days of supply/fire
BCCP	*Bataillon Colonial de Chasseurs Parachutistes* (Colonial Light Infantry Parachute Battalion)
Bde	brigade
BEP	*Bataillon Étrangère Parachutistes* (Foreign Legion Parachute Battalion)
BM	*Brigade* or *Bataillon de Marche* (Provisional Light Infantry Brigade or Battalion or Task Force); *Base Militaire*
BMEO	*Brigade* or *Bataillon de Marche d'Extrême-Orient*; *Brigade de Marine d'Extrême-Orient* (Provisional Far East Light Infantry Brigade/Battalion; Far East Marine Brigade)
BMT	*Bureau Mouvement Transport* (General Staff transportation section)
Bn	*bataillon* (battalion)
BOTK	*Base Opérationnelle du Tonkin* (Tonkin Operational Base)
BPC	*Bataillon de Parachutistes Coloniaux* (Colonial Parachute Battalion); *Bataillon de Parachutistes de Choc* (Assault Parachute Battalion)
BRM	*Bataillon de Réparation du Matériel* (Maintenance Battalion)
BRMRG	*Bataillon de Réparation du Matériel du Réserve Générale* (General Reserve Ordnance Battalion)

CA	*Corps d'Armée* (Army Corps); *Compagnie d'Automobile* (Car Company)
CAB	*Compagnie Automobile de Base* (Base Car Company)
CAEO	Commandant de l'Air en Extrême-Orient (Commander, Air Forces, Far East)
CAQG	*Compagnie d'Automobile de Quartier Général* (Headquarters Car Company)
CASM	*Compagnie d'Approvisionnement du Service du Matériel* (Ordnance Supply Company)
CCMRM	*Compagnie Coloniale Moyenne de Réparation du Matériel* (Colonial Medium Maintenance Company)
CCQGT	*Compagnie Coloniale de Quartier-Générale et Transport* (Colonial HQ and Transport Company)
CCR	*Compagnie de Circulation Routière* (Highway Traffic Regulation Company)
CEFEO	*Corps Expéditionnaire Français d'Extrême-Orient* (French Expeditionary Corps, Far East)
CFTT	*Compagnie Fluviale de Transport du Train* (River Transport Company)
Chu Luc	Viet Minh Regular Army
Cie	*compagnie* (company)
Cie MU	*Compagnie des Munitions* (Ammunition Company)
Cie MURG	*Compagnie des Munitions du Réserve Général* (General Reserve Ammunition Company)
CINC	*commandant en chef* (French); commander in chief (U.S.)
CLI	*Corps Léger d'Intervention* (Light Intervention Corps)
CLR	*Compagnie Lourde de Réparation* (Heavy Maintenance Company)
CLRA	*Compagnie Lourde de Réparation Auto* (Heavy Automobile Maintenance Company)
CM	*Compagnie Muletière* (Pack Mule Company)
Cmdt	*commandant* (commander, or rank equivalent to U.S. major)
CMR	*Compagnie Moyenne de Réparation* (Medium Maintenance Company)
CMRA	*Compagnie Moyenne de Réparation Auto* (Medium Automobile Maintenance Company)
CMRG	*Compagnie Moyenne de Réserve Générale* (General Reserve Medium Ordnance Company)
CMRLE	*Compagnie Moyenne de Réparation de la Légion Étrangère* (Foreign Legion Medium Maintenance Company)

CMRM	*Compagnie Moyenne de Réparation du Matériel* (Medium Maintenance Company)
CRA	*Compagnie de Ravitaillement par Air* (Aerial Resupply Company)
Crab	tracked amphibious vehicle
CRE	*Compagnie de Ravitaillement de Essence* (Petroleum Resupply Company)
CREBLE	*Compagnie de Réparation d'Engins Blindés de la Légion Étrangère* (Foreign Legion Armored Engine Maintenance Company)
CRI	*Compagnie Ravitaillement d'Intendance* (Quartermaster Resupply Company)
CT	*Compagnie de Transport* (Transport Company)
CTQG	*Compagnie de Transport et de Quartier-Générale* (HQ and Transport Company)
Dai-Doan	Viet Minh division (originally brigade)
Dai-Doi	Viet Minh company
Dân Cong	Viet Minh porters and laborers
Dan-Quan	unarmed Viet Minh supporters in village areas
Dan-Quan Du-kich	Viet Minh armed village militia; Viet Minh guerrillas
DB	*Division Blindée* (Armored Division)
DBLE	*Demi-Brigade de la Légion Étrangère* (Foreign Legion Half-Brigade)
DCR	*Detachement de Circulation Routière* (Highway Traffic Regulation Detachment)
DE	*depot des essences* (petroleum depot)
DEEO	*Direction des Essences en Extrême-Orient* (Directorate for Petroleum Products, Far East)
Det.	*Detachement* (detachment)
DI	*Direction de l'Intendance* (supply service responsible for food and clothing)
Dinassaut	*Division Navale d'Assaut* (Naval Assault Division); French Navy tactical unit for river warfare
DIRMAT	*Directeur/Direction du Materièl* (Ordnance command element)
DMT	*Division de Marche du Tonkin* (Provisional Tonkin Infantry Division)
DMZ	Demilitarized Zone
DOS/DOF	days of supply/days of fire; the amount of supplies/ ammunition sufficient for one day's operations; may vary according to local conditions and the desires

	of the commander; usually applied to unit quantities rather than individual quantities
DRV	Democratic Republic of Viet Nam (*Viet-Nam Dan Chu Cong-Hoa*)
DS	direct support; providing support directly to customers
DZ	drop zone
Economat	French military commissary/post exchange
EM	*État-Major* (General Staff); enlisted men (U.S.)
EMIFT	*État-Major Interarmées et des Forces Terrestres* (French GHQ in Indochina, December 1950–December 1954)
ERG	*Établissement du Réserve Générale* (General Reserve Depot)
ERGM	*Établissement des Réserves Générales des Munitions* (General Reserve Ammunition Depot)
FFEO	*Forces Françaises d'Extrême-Orient* (French Forces, Far East)
FNEO	*Forces Navales d'Extrême-Orient* (French Naval Forces, Far East)
FOM	*France d'Outre-Mer* (French Overseas Territories, 1945–1958)
franc	French currency unit; from September 1949 to August 1957, 350 francs = $1 U.S.
FTC	*Forces Terrestres du Cambodge* (Ground Forces, Cambodia)
FTCV	*Forces Terrestres du Centre-Viet-Nam* (Ground Forces, Central Viet Nam)
FTCVP	*Forces Terrestres du Centre-Viet-Nam et des Plateaux* (Ground Forces, Central Viet Nam and the Central Highlands)
FTEO	*Forces Terrestres d'Extrême-Orient* (Ground Forces, Far East)
FTL	*Forces Terrestres du Laos* (Ground Forces, Laos)
FTNV	*Forces Terrestres du Nord-Viet-Nam* (Ground Forces, North Viet Nam)
FTPM	*Forces Terrestres des Plateaux Montagneux* (Ground Forces, Central Highlands)
FTSV	*Forces Terrestres du Sud-Viet-Nam* (Ground Forces, South Viet Nam)
FY	Fiscal Year
GAP	*Groupement Aéroporté* (Airborne Task Force)
GATAC	*Groupement Aérien Tactique d'Attaque et de Choc* (Air

	Force Tactical Air Support and Pursuit Group); French Air Force HQ responsible for one of five air commands in Indochina
GCMA	*Groupement de Commandos Mixtes Aéroportés* (Composite Airborne Commando Group); converted to GMI in December 1953
GE or GEO	*Groupement Opérationnelle d'Exploitation* (Intendance Operational Exploitation Group)
Gestion	Intendance Service unit
GHQ	General Headquarters (U.S.). See QG.
GM	*Groupement Mobile* (Mobile Task Force/Regimental Combat Team)
GMC	General Motors Corporation
GMI	*Groupement Mixte d'Intervention* (Composite Intervention Group); HQ for French guerrilla groups
GONO	*Groupement Opérationnelle Nord-Ouest* (Northwest Operational Group; overall HQ at Dien Bien Phu)
GS	General Staff; General Support; providing support to other support units
GT	*Groupement de Transport* (Transport Battalion)
GTA	*Groupement de Transport Aérien* (Air Transport Group)
INTSUM	Intelligence Summary
JCS	Joint Chiefs of Staff (U.S.)
KPH	kilometers per hour
LCM	Landing Craft, Mechanized
LCT	Landing Craft, Tank
LCVP	Landing Craft, Vehicle, Personnel
LOC	line of communication
LSSL	Landing Ship, Support, Large
LST	Landing Ship, Tank
LVT	Landing Vehicle, Tracked
LZ	landing zone
MAAG	Military Assistance Advisory Group (U.S.)
MDAP	Mutual Defense Assistance Program (U.S.)
MND	Ministry of National Defense
MSR	main supply route
Nam-Bo	Cochinchina (South Viet Nam)
para	parachutist
paradrop	aerial resupply by parachute
PCI	*Parti Communiste Indochinois* (Indochinese Communist Party)

PFTT	*Peloton Fluvial de Transport du Train* (River Transport Platoon)
piastre	currency unit used in French Indochina; 17 *piastres* = 1 *franc*
PIM	*Prisonniers-Internés Militaires* (military prisoners of war and civilian detainees of the French forces in Indochina)
PLA	People's Liberation Army (Communist Chinese)
Pltn	*peloton*; platoon (U.S.)
POL	petroleum, oils, and lubricants; may be either in bulk or packaged (in drums)
POW/PW	prisoner of war
PRC	People's Republic of China
PTA	*Peloton de Transport Amphibie* (Amphibious Transport Platoon)
QG	*Quartier général*; headquarters or general headquarters
QM	quartermaster
RACM	*Régiment d'Artillerie Coloniale du Maroc* (Moroccan Colonial Artillery Regiment)
ration	an amount of food, etc., sufficient for one man for one day
RC	*Route Coloniale* (Colonial Route; main highway)
Regt.	régiment; regiment (U.S.)
REI	*Régiment Étrangère d'Infanterie* (Foreign Legion Infantry Regiment)
RIC	*Régiment d'Infanterie Coloniale* (Colonial Infantry Regiment)
RICM	*Régiment d'Infanterie Coloniale du Maroc* (Moroccan Colonial Infantry Regiment)
RL	rocket launcher
RP	*Route Provinciale* (Provincial Route; secondary highway)
RTA	*Régiment de Tirailleurs Algériens* (Algerian Rifle Regiment)
RTM	*Régiment de Tirailleurs Marocains* (Moroccan Rifle Regiment)
SDECE	*Service d'Espionage et Countre-Espionage* (French secret security service)
serial	small group of ten to twelve vehicles serving as a subgroup in a motor convoy for better control
SITREP	Situation Report

SM	*Service du Matériel* (French ordnance service responsible for the supply and maintenance of weapons, vehicles, ammunition, and other major items of equipment)
SRA	*Section de Ravitaillement Aérien* (Aerial Resupply Section)
tabor	Moroccan infantry regiment
TAPI	*Troupes Aéroportés d'Indochine* (French Airborne Troops, Indochina)
Tay-Bac	Northwestern Viet Nam
TF	task force
TFEO	*Troupes françaises d'Extrême-Orient*; French Troops in the Far East
Tieu-Doan	Viet Minh battalion
TOE	Table of Organization and Equipment; a listing of authorized numbers of personnel and amounts of equipment by type
Train	transport service responsible for motor and water transport, especially that of tactical units
Trung-Doan	Viet Minh regiment/brigade
Trung-Bo	Annam; Central Viet Nam
unit of fire	concept used to forecast ammunition resupply requirements; an arbitrary quantity of ammunition, the amount of which is determined by the commander based on the tactical situation
USAFFE	U.S. Army Forces, Far East
USFEC	U.S. Far East Command
Viet Bac	Viet Minh stronghold area in northwestern Tonkin
Viet Minh; VM	*Viet-Nam Doc-lap Dong Minh Hoi* (Vietnamese People's Army)
VNA	Vietnamese National Army
VPA	Vietnamese People's Army; official designation of the Viet Minh

Selected Bibliography

Primary Sources

This study is based principally on contemporary French official military documents that now form part of the Sub-Series 10 H: *Fonds Indochine*, preserved by the Service Historique de la Defense, Centre Historique des Archives, Département de Armée de Terre, at the Château de Vincennes outside Paris. The individual items are cited in full in the text by carton (box) number. The Service Historique also preserves a number of published official studies and documents bearing on the war in Indochina. These, too, are cited in full in the text.

Of special importance are the official French "lessons learned" from the First Indochina War published in Commandement en Chef des Forces Terrestres Navales et Aériennes en Indochine, *Enseignements de la guerre d'Indochine*, 3 fascicules (Saigon, 1955). All three fascicules have been translated into English as follows:

Fascicule I: BDM Corporation. *A Study of Strategic Lessons Learned in Vietnam*, vol. 1, *The Enemy*. BDM/W-78-128-TR-VOL-I. McLean, Va.: BDM Corporation, November 30, 1979.

Fascicule II: RAND Corporation. *A Translation from the French: Lessons of the War in Indochina*, vol. 2. RM-5271-PR. Santa Monica, Calif.: RAND Corporation, May 1967.

Fascicule III: U.S. Department of Defense Advanced Research Projects Agency. *Lessons from the Indo-China War*, vol. 3. Washington, D.C.: U.S. Department of Defense Advanced Research Projects Agency, 1955.

U.S. official documents bearing on the First Indochina War are to be found in the U.S. National Archives, Archives II, in College Park, Maryland. The documents used to support this study can be found principally in Record Group 218 (Records of the U.S. Joint Chiefs of Staff); Record Group 319 (Records of the Army Staff); and Record Group 330 (Records of the Office of the Secretary of Defense). Other official documents concerning U.S. support for the French in Indochina are contained in Senator Mike Gravel, ed., *The Pentagon Papers: The Defense Department History of United States Decisionmaking in Vietnam*, 4 vols. (Boston: Beacon Press, 1971).

In the 1950s, the Office of the Assistant Chief of Staff, G-2, Headquarters, Department of the Army, translated many French primary documents bearing on the First Indochina War. The same office also prepared a number of Intelligence

Research Projects bearing on events in Indochina. Other U.S. forces headquarters published similar documents and studies. All such materials used in this study are cited in full in the text.

Secondary Works

Only the most frequently cited works are listed here. All works used in this study are cited fully in the text. Many of them are from contemporary magazines and historical journals, such as *Caravelle, Indochine-Sud-Est Asiatique, Revue Historique des Armées, Intelligence Review, FEC Intelligence Digest, USAFFE Intelligence Digest,* and the *Journal of Military Assistance.*

Asselin, Pierre. "New Perspectives on Dien Bien Phu." *Explorations in Southeast Asian Studies* 1, no. 2 (fall 1997). www2.hawaii.edu/~seassa/explorations/v1n2/art2/v1n2-frame2.html. Accessed February 6, 2014.

Bodard, Lucien. *The Quicksand War: Prelude to Vietnam.* Boston: Little, Brown, 1967.

Bodinier, Gilbert, ed. *La Guerre d'Indochine, 1945–1954: Texte et Documents.* Vol. 1, *Le retour de la France en Indochine, 1945–1946.* Château de Vincennes: Service Historique de l'Armée de Terre, 1987.

———. *La Guerre d'Indochine, 1945–1954: Texte et Documents.* Vol. 2, *Indochine, 1947—Règlement politique ou solution militaire?* Château de Vincennes: Service Historique de l'Armée de Terre, 1989.

Bonnier, Michèle, Soraya Djebbour, and Gilles Bonnier. *La guerre d'Indochine, 1946–1954.* Paris: Impression Copytop, May 2009. Brochure for an exposition held at the Maison des Associations 4, Paris, May 22–25, 2009.

Boylan, Kevin M. "No 'Technical Knockout': Giap's Artillery at Dien Bien Phu." *Journal of Military History* 78, no. 4 (October 2014): 1349–1383.

Chen, King C. *Vietnam and China, 1938–1954.* Princeton: Princeton Univ. Press, 1969.

Couget, Georges. *Le Train en Indochine, 1945–1954.* Paris: Inspection du Train, 1973.

Dalloz, Jacques. *The War in Indochina, 1945–54.* New York: Barnes and Noble, 1990.

Davidson, Phillip B. *Vietnam at War: The History, 1946–1975.* Novato, Calif.: Presidio, 1988.

Devillers, Philippe, and Jean Lacouture. *La fin d'une guerre.* Paris: Éditions du Seuil, 1960.

Fall, Bernard B. *Hell in a Very Small Place: The Siege of Dien Bien Phu.* New York: Vintage Books, 1966.

———. "Indochina—The Last Year of the War: Communist Organization and Tactics." *Military Review* 36, no. 7 (October 1956): 3–11.

———. "Indochina—The Last Year of the War: The Navarre Plan." *Military Review* 36, no. 9 (December 1956): 48–56.

———. *Last Reflections on a War.* Garden City, N.Y.: Doubleday, 1967.

———. *Street without Joy: Insurgency in Indochina, 1946–63,* 3rd rev. ed. Harrisburg, Pa.: Stackpole, 1963.

———. *The Two Viet-Nams: A Political and Military Analysis,* 2nd rev. ed. New York: Praeger, 1967.

———. *Le Viet-Minh: La République Démocratique du Viet-Nam, 1945–1960.* Cahiers de la Fondation Nationale Des Sciences Politiques No. 106. Paris: Librairie Armand Colin, 1960. Augmented version of *The Viet-Minh Regime* (New York: Institute of Pacific Relations, 1956) containing updated chapters on the Viet Minh.

Foreign Area Studies Division, Special Operations Research Office, The American University. *U. S. Army Area Handbook for Vietnam.* Department of the Army Pamphlet No. 550-55. Washington, D.C.: Headquarters, Department of the Army, September 1962.

Giap, Vo Nguyen. *Dien Bien Phu,* 2nd ed. Hanoi: Foreign Languages Publishing House, 1962.

———. *La Guerre de libération et l'armée populaire* [*The War of Liberation and the Popular Army*]. G-2 Doc Lib No. 1277386/G-2 Translation No. G-4864. Mimeograph. Washington, D.C.: Headquarters, Department of the Army, Office of the Assistant Chief of Staff, G-2, 1955. 34-page English translation of the work of Vo Nguyen Giap formally entitled *The War of Liberation and the Popular Army: The Three Strategic Phases* (Hanoi: Editions "Ve-Quoc Quan" National Army Publishing House, 1950).

———. *Inside the Viet Minh.* Washington, D.C.: Marine Corps Association, 1962. 92-page typescript in an English translation.

———. *People's War, People's Army: The Viet Cong Insurrection Manual for Underdeveloped Countries.* Praeger Publications in Russian History and World Communism No. 119. New York: Praeger, 1962. Facsimile reprint of the 1961 Hanoi (Foreign Languages Publishing House) edition with a preface by Roger Hilsman and a profile of Giap by Bernard B. Fall.

Goscha, Christopher E. "'Hell in a Very Small Place': Cold War and Decolonisation in the Assault on the Vietnamese Body at Dien Bien Phu." *European Journal of East Asian Studies* 9, no. 2 (December 2010): 201–23.

Grauwin, Paul. *Doctor at Dienbienphu.* New York: John Day Company, 1955.

Hammer, Ellen J. *The Struggle for Indochina, 1940–1955: Viet Nam and the French Experience,* 2nd ed. Stanford, Calif.: Stanford Univ. Press, 1966.

Higgins, J. Wallace. *Porterage Parameters and Tables.* RM-5292-ISA-ARPA. Santa Monica, Calif.: RAND Corporation, August 1967.

Holliday, L. P., and R. M. Gurfield. *Viet Cong Logistics.* RM-5423-1-ISA/ARPA. Santa Monica, Calif.: RAND Corporation, June 1968.

Jackson, Peter Drake. *French Ground Force Organizational Development for Counterrevolutionary Warfare between 1945 and 1962.* Master of Military Art and Science thesis. Fort Leavenworth, Kans.: U.S. Army Command and General Staff College, 2005.

Kelly, George A. *Lost Soldiers: The French Army and Empire in Crisis, 1947–1962.* Cambridge, Mass.: M.I.T. Press, 1965.

Koburger, Charles W., Jr. *The French Navy in Indochina: Riverine and Coastal Forces, 1945–54.* New York: Praeger, 1991.

Langlais, Pierre. *Dien Bien Phu.* Paris: Éditions France-Empire, 1963.

Lawrence, Mark Atwood, and Fredrik Logevall, eds. *The First Vietnam War: Colonial Conflict and Cold War Crisis.* Cambridge, Mass.: Harvard Univ. Press, 2007.

Logevall, Fredrik. *Embers of War: The Fall of an Empire and the Making of America's Vietnam.* New York: Random House, 2012.

Loustau, Henry-Jean. *Les derniers combats d'Indochine, 1952–1954.* Paris: Éditions Albin Michel, 1984.

Miller, D. M. O. "'A Handful of Rice?': Logistics in the Viet Minh Campaign." *Army Quarterly and Defence Journal* 100, no. 1 (April 1970): 105–15.

Navarre, Henri. *Le Temps des Vérités.* Paris: Plon, 1957.

Nguyen, Lien-Hang T. *Hanoi's War: An International History of the War for Peace in Vietnam.* Chapel Hill: Univ. of North Carolina Press, 2012.

O'Ballance, Edgar. *The Indo-China War, 1945–1954: A Study in Guerilla Warfare.* London: Faber and Faber, 1964.

Pascoe, Stuart. "A Critical Analysis of the Operational Performance of General Vo Nguyen Giap 1940–1954." In Australian Command and Staff College, *Geddes Papers 2005* ([Canberra]: Australian Defence College, 2010[?]): 19–29.

Plating, John D. "Failure in the Margins: Aerial Resupply at Dien Bien Phu." Master's thesis, Ohio State University, 2000.

Qiang Zhai. *China and the Vietnam Wars, 1950–1975.* Chapel Hill: Univ. of North Carolina Press, 2000.

———. "Transplanting the Chinese Model: Chinese Military Advisers and the First Vietnam War, 1950–1954." *Journal of Military History* 57, no. 4 (October 1993): 689–715.

Roy, Jules. *The Battle of Dienbienphu.* New York: Harper and Row, 1965. The original French edition (*La bataille de Dienbienphu* [Paris: Julliard, 1963]) is more complete.

Salan, Raoul. *Indochine Rouge: Le Message d'Hô Chi Minh.* Paris: Presses de la Cité, 1975.

Seals, Bob. "Chinese Support for North Vietnam during the Vietnam War: The Decisive Edge." *Military History Online* (September 23, 2008). http: // www.militaryhistoryonline.com/20thcentury/articles/chinesesupport.aspx. Accessed August 16, 2010.

Simpson, Howard R. *Dien Bien Phu: The Epic Battle America Forgot.* Washington, D.C.: Brassey's, 1994.

———. *Tiger in the Barbed Wire: An American in Vietnam, 1952–1991.* New York: Brassey's, 1992.

Smith, Harvey H., et al. *Area Handbook for North Vietnam.* Department of the Army Pamphlet No. 550-57. Washington, D.C.: U.S. Government Printing Office, 1968.

Smith, T. O. "Resurrecting the French Empire: British Military Aid to Vietnam September 1945–June 1947." *University of Sussex Journal of Contemporary History* 11 (2007): 1–12.

Spector, Ronald H. *Advice and Support: The Early Years, 1941–1960.* U.S. Army in Vietnam Series. Washington, D.C.: Center of Military History, U.S. Army, 1983.

Starobin, Joseph R. *Eyewitness in Indo-China.* New York: Cameron and Kahn, 1954.

Stewart, Richard W. *Deepening Involvement, 1945–1965.* CMH Publication 76-1. Washington, D.C.: Center of Military History, U.S. Army, 2012.

Tanham, George K. *Communist Revolutionary Warfare: From the Vietminh to the Viet Cong,* rev. ed. New York: Praeger, 1967.

Thompson, Julian. *The Lifeblood of War: Logistics in Armed Conflict.* London: Brassey's, 1991.

Trinquier, Roger. *Modern Warfare: A French View of Insurgency.* London: Pall Mall Press, 1964; reprint, Fort Leavenworth, Kans.: Combat Studies Institute, January 1985.

U.S. Joint Chiefs of Staff, Office of Joint History. *The Joint Chiefs of Staff and the First Indochina War, 1947–1954.* History of the Joint Chiefs of Staff. Washington, D.C.: Office of Joint History, Office of the Chairman of the Joint Chiefs of Staff, 2004.

U.S. Military Assistance Advisory Group, Indo-China. *Indo-China Country Statement for Presentation of the 1955 MDA Program.* Saigon: HQ, USMAAG-Indo-China, January 26, 1954.

Windrow, Martin. *The Last Valley: Dien Bien Phu and the French Defeat in Vietnam.* New York: Da Capo, 2004.

Zasloff, Joseph Jeremiah. *The Role of Sanctuary in Insurgency: Communist China's Support to the Vietminh, 1946–1954.* RM-4618-PR. Santa Monica, Calif.: RAND Corporation, May 1967.

Index

disadvantages of, 290; concept of, 116; establishment at Dien Bien Phu, 285, 286; Na San and, 289–90. *See also* Dien Bien Phu

base areas, campaign for: aftermath of the 1951 Viet Minh offensives, 223–26; aftermath of the fight for the Red River Delta, 223–26; attack and defense of the Viet Minh base areas, 226–47; attacks on and defense of Viet Minh base areas, 226–47; fight for the Red River Delta, 215–23, 247–48; overview and significance of, 7–8, 215, 247–48; Viet Minh commando raids on French bases, 225–26

base areas (French): absence of rear supply bases, 135–36; Viet Minh commando raids on, 225–26

base areas (Viet Minh): attacks on and defense of, 226–47; Operation LEA against, 197–204, 226; Operation LORRAINE against, 226–38; return to in 1947, 189, 195; in Viet Minh logistical and military strategy, 93–96, 196. *See also* Viet Bac base area

Base Opérationnelle du Tonkin. See Tonkin Operational Base

base-type river craft platoons, 114

battalions (French), 26

battalions (Viet Minh), 49–50

Béarn (French cruiser), 185

"Béarn." See GT 1/64 "Bearn" air transport group

BEATRICE stronghold, 315

Beaufre, Col. André, 199, 201

Berteil, Col. Louis, 293, 294

bicycles: used by Viet Minh to move cargo, 126; *xe thô*, 349–50

Bigeard, Lt. Col. Marcel, 323

Binh, Nguyen, 207, 223–24

black markets, 162

Black River: 1952 Viet Minh offensive, 227–28, 235, 237, 276, 278; battle for Hoa Binh and, 270–71, 272, 273

Blaizot, Lt. Gen. Roger Charles André Henri, *14*, 192–93

Blaizot plan, 192–93

BMT. See *Bureau Mouvements Transports*

Bodard, Lucien, 2, 115–16, 206, 274

Bo Doi Chu Luc. See Viet Minh

Bo Doi Dia Phuong Quan. See Regional Forces

Bois Belleau (French aircraft carrier), 266

Bollaert, Émile, *12*, 188

bomber aircraft. *See* B-26 bombers; Junkers Ju 52 Toucan transport aircraft

Bordeaux, France, 135

BOTK. *See* Tonkin Operational Base

Boylan, Kevin M., 358–59, 362

Brink, Brig. Gen. Francis G., 142, 146, 219, 223

Bristol 170 Freighter transport aircraft. *See* transport aircraft

Bureau Mouvements Transports (BMT), 55, 105, 244, 298

Bureau of National Defense (French), 13

Bureau of Organization (French), 13

Bureau Transport, 105–6

C-47 Dakota transport aircraft. *See* transport aircraft

C-119 Flying Boxcar transport aircraft. *See* transport aircraft

CAEO. See *Commandant de l'Air en Extrême-Orient*

Cambodia: in the Associated States, 14–15; Elysée Agreements, 189; independence from France, 139; U.S. military aid and, 149–50; Viet Minh tactical units in, 44

camouflage, 267–68

Cao Bang: battle of Route Coloniale 4 and, 205, 207, 209, 210; French materiel abandoned in retreat from, 160; Operation LEA and, 198, 202; Viet Minh supply route to Dien Bien Phu, 347, 349, 356

www.ingramcontent.com/pod-product-compliance
Lightning Source LLC
Chambersburg PA
CBHW030311100426
42812CB00002B/665